# The Algonquian Peoples of Long Island From Earliest Times to 1700

## John A. Strong

Prepared under the auspices of
Hofstra University

**Empire State Books**
Interlaken, New York
**1997**

Copyright © 1997
Long Island Studies Institute
Hofstra University
Hempstead, New York 11550
All rights reserved

The author has donated his honorarium for this book to the following:

The Friends of the Pharaoh Museum
PO Box 2566
Sag Harbor, NY 11963

The Shinnecock National Cultural Center and Museum
PO Box 5059
Southampton, NY 11968

Unkechaug Nation Cultural School
c/o Margo Thunder Bird
207 Poospatuck Lane
Mastic, NY 11950

A description of the jacket illustration is found on page 16

ISBN: 1-55787-148-5
Library of Congress Catalogue Number: 96-80102

*Quality* book production by
Heart of the Lakes Publishing
Interlaken, New York 14847

# Dedication

To my father, Ashley W. Strong, who inspired my interest in Native American culture and to my mother, Marie, who encouraged my intellectual growth.

# Contents

|   |   |   |
|---|---|---|
|   | Illustrations, Documents, and Tables | 8 |
|   | Foreword | 11 |
|   | Preface | 13 |
| 1. | **Introduction** | 17 |
|   | What is a Tribe? | 19 |
|   | From Place Name to Tribal Name | 25 |
|   | The Myth of Extinction | 28 |
|   | Summary | 33 |
| 2. | **Earliest Times to 3,000 B.P.** | 35 |
|   | The Paleo-Indian Period, 12,500–8,000 B.P. | 35 |
|   | The Archaic Period, 8,000–3,000 B.P. | 38 |
|   |     Village Locations | 39 |
|   |     Food Supply | 41 |
|   |     Social Organization | 42 |
|   |     Tool Technology | 43 |
|   |     Mortuary Rituals | 48 |
|   | Summary | 53 |
| 3. | **The Early and Middle Woodland Periods, 3,000–1,000 B.P.** | 55 |
|   | The Pottery Revolution | 55 |
|   | New Styles and Innovations in Ceramics and Stone Tools | 58 |
|   | Forest Efficiency | 59 |
|   | Religious Ceremonialism | 69 |
|   | Trading Networks | 76 |
|   | Summary | 77 |
| 4. | **The Late Woodland Period, 1,000 B.P.–1600** | 79 |
|   | Village Settlements | 79 |
|   | Native Architecture: Wigwams and Longhouses | 84 |
|   | The Gift of *Conconchus*: Origins of Plant Domestication | 91 |
|   | Native Gardens | 95 |
|   | Food Processing and Storage | 100 |
|   | Native Hearths | 102 |
|   | Summary | 107 |
| 5. | **The Algonquian Belief Systems** | 109 |
|   | Manitou: The Mana of the Algonquian People | 110 |
|   | *Powwaws:* The Voices of the Manitos | 116 |
|   | Seasonal Ceremonies | 118 |
|   | Rites of Passage | 122 |

|  | Curing Rituals . . . . . . . . . . . . . . . . . . 125 |
|  | Dreams, Star Gazing, and Vision Quests . . . . . . . . . 130 |
|  | Sacred Carvings . . . . . . . . . . . . . . . . . 132 |
|  | Tobacco Ceremonialism . . . . . . . . . . . . . . . 139 |
|  | Summary . . . . . . . . . . . . . . . . . . . 139 |

6. **The Early Contact Period, 1524–1638** . . . . . . . . . 143
   First Contact, 1524–1609 . . . . . . . . . . . . . . . 144
   Equal Status Trade: Lenape-Dutch Relations, 1609–1636 . . . . 148
   The Impact of the Pequot War (1636–1638) on Long Island . . . 154
   Summary . . . . . . . . . . . . . . . . . . . 161

7. **The Long Island Frontier: Patents, Purchases, and Warfare, 1636–1645** . . . . . . . . . . . . . . . . . . 163
   The Dutch Purchase of Western Long Island, 1636–1639 . . . . 163
   Interlopers, Vagabonds, and Fool's Faces: The Scramble
      for Long Island Begins . . . . . . . . . . . . . . 166
   "With Fire and Sword": Kieft's Campaigns Against the
      Raritans and the Wiechquaesgecks, 1640–1642 . . . . . . 171
   Miantonomi's "Conspiracy," 1642 . . . . . . . . . . . . 173
   "God Hath Delivered Them into Our Hands": Massacres at
      Pavonia and Corlaer's Hook, 1643 . . . . . . . . . . 176
   War and Peace on the Long Island Frontier, 1643–1645 . . . . 178
   Summary . . . . . . . . . . . . . . . . . . . 188

8. **Accommodation to Conquest: The Long Island Frontier, 1645–1654** . . . . . . . . . . . . . . . . . . 191
   More Rumors of Conspiracy . . . . . . . . . . . . . 191
   Governor Theophilus Eaton and the Scramble for
      Eastern Long Island . . . . . . . . . . . . . . 193
   Wyandanch's Alliance with the English Towns on the
      South Fork . . . . . . . . . . . . . . . . . 196
   "To augment their own kingdoms": Ninigret and the
      Anglo-Dutch Rivalry . . . . . . . . . . . . . . 201
   Ninigret's Raid on the Montauketts . . . . . . . . . . . 206
   Summary . . . . . . . . . . . . . . . . . . . 210

9. **Wyandanch and Tackapousha: Alliance Sachems on the Long Island Frontier, 1655–1660** . . . . . . . . . . 213
   Wyandanch: "Chiefe Sachem of Long Island" . . . . . . . . 213
   Tackapousha: "Chiefe Sachem" over the Massapequas,
      Matinecocks, Secatogues, Merricks, Rockaways,
      and Canarsies . . . . . . . . . . . . . . . . 215
   Wyandanch Faces Challenges at Home and Abroad . . . . . . 218
   "Deed Diplomacy" on the Long Island Frontier . . . . . . . 221

|     | "Melted down by this disease": The Smallpox Epidemics of | |
|     | 1659–1664 on Long Island | 233 |
|     | Summary | 235 |
| 10. | **Dispossession and Survival, 1660–1703** | 237 |
|     | Tackapousha and the Dutch, 1660–1664 | 237 |
|     | Governor Nicolls and the Long Island Sachems | 240 |
|     | "They take our land away every day, a little and a little" | 246 |
|     | The Impact of King Philip's War on Long Island, 1675–1678 | 252 |
|     | Struggling to Survive: Suscaneman Plays the Deed Game | 254 |
|     | "To Have and to Hold": The Matinecock Reservations | 257 |
|     | Holding on to the Land: The Unkechaugs, Montauketts, and | |
|     | Shinnecocks on Eastern Long Island | 260 |
|     | Summary | 265 |
| 11. | **Algonquian Labor Patterns in the Seventeenth Century** | 267 |
|     | "Ye Whale Designe" | 269 |
|     | Indentured Servitude | 276 |
|     | Indian Slavery | 279 |
|     | Indian Free Labor | 282 |
|     | Summary | 287 |
| 12. | **Epilogue: Continuity and Reaffirmation** | 289 |
|     | Appendix: Maps | 294 |
|     | A. Archaeological Sites | 294 |
|     | B. New Netherland Deeds, Treaties, and | |
|     |    Algonquian Place Names, 1636–1650 | 296 |
|     | C. Locations of Algonquian-English Deeds, 1643–1675 | 298 |
|     | D. Locations of Deeds to Land on the North and South | |
|     |    Forks of Long Island, 1640–1859 | 300 |
|     | Notes | 303 |
|     | Credits and Sources for Illustrations | 326 |
|     | References | 327 |
|     | Identification of Individuals Cited in Text | 354 |
|     | Index | 356 |
|     | About the Author | 366 |
|     | Long Island Studies Institute | 367 |

# Illustrations, Documents, and Tables

**Figures**

|  |  |  |
|---|---|---|
|  | Allard map of New York, 1673 | 10 |
|  | David Bunn Martine, Shinnecock artist | 12 |
| 1.1 | Seventeenth-century Algonquian man | 16 |
| 1.2 | Robert and Olive Pharaoh | 24 |
| 1.3 | Matinecock memorial | 30 |
| 2.1 | Lenape creation story | 34 |
| 2.2 | Projectile point chronology for Long Island | 37 |
| 2.3 | Making a dugout canoe | 44 |
| 2.4 | Drill, stone mortar and pestle, scrapers | 45 |
| 2.5 | Atlatl | 45 |
| 2.6 | Shinnecock baskets and bags | 46 |
| 2.7 | Algonquian man and woman in traditional dress | 47 |
| 2.8 | Steatite bowl | 47 |
| 3.1 | Eliza Fowler Beaman and Anthony Beaman | 54 |
| 3.2 | North Beach cord-marked pottery | 56 |
| 3.3 | Abbott-style zoned pottery | 58 |
| 3.4 | Women gathering wild plants | 59 |
| 3.5 | Women shelling and smoking clams | 61 |
| 3.6 | Wild plant foods | 63 |
| 3.7 | Wampum manufacture | 70 |
| 3.8 | Tubular smoking pipes | 72 |
| 4.1 | "Manatus" map, with Algonquian villages, 1639 | 78 |
| 4.2 | Longhouses, wigwams, fort, and corn fields | 82 |
| 4.3 | Fort Massapeag site | 83 |
| 4.4 | Bark longhouse construction | 85 |
| 4.5 | Wigwam construction | 87 |
| 4.6 | Wigwam interior | 90 |
| 4.7 | Corn | 91 |
| 4.8 | Women planting corn | 96 |
| 4.9 | Women storing food in storage pit | 101 |
| 4.10 | Cross-section of underground storage pit | 101 |
| 4.11 | Late Woodland pottery | 102 |
| 5.1 | Mesingw faces | 112 |
| 5.2 | Stone effigy pipes | 114 |
| 5.3 | Shaman and Mesingw dancer | 114 |
| 5.4 | Sebonac thunderbird symbol | 115 |
| 5.5 | Sweat lodges | 128 |
| 5.6 | Engraved shell pendant | 132 |

| | | |
|---|---|---|
| 5.7 | Orient tablet | 133 |
| 5.8 | Dosoris tablet | 134 |
| 5.9 | Great Neck tablet | 135 |
| 5.10 | Montauk tablets | 136 |
| 5.11 | Jericho petroglyph | 136 |
| 5.12 | Jericho glyph, 1955 | 137 |
| 6.1 | Algonquian couple in traditional dress | 142 |
| 7.1 | Algonquian man with war club | 181 |
| 7.2 | Hempstead purchase, 1643 | 183 |
| 8.1 | Algonquian couple | 190 |
| 9.1 | Tackapousha treaty with the Dutch, 1656 | 212 |
| 9.2 | Wyandanch "stick figure" signatures | 226 |
| 10.1 | Drawing on January 21, 1660 deed | 237 |
| 10.2 | Tackapousha's map of the Matinecock lands, 1668 | 247 |
| 10.3 | Transcription of Tackapousha's 1668 Testimony | 248 |
| 10.4. | Map of John West property with longhouse and wigwams | 256 |
| 10.5 | Tackapousha's Matinecock reservation patent | 258 |
| 10.6 | Suscaneman's Matinecock reservation patent | 259 |
| | James Kellis with scrub brushes | 266 |
| 11.1 | Alice Martinez holding a basket she made | 268 |
| 11.2 | Charles Bunn, with his duck decoys | 268 |
| 11.3 | Indian whalers | 271 |
| 11.4 | Whaling contract | 273 |
| 11.5 | Indian indenture | 277 |
| 11.6 | Sale of Beck, an Indian slave girl | 280 |
| 11.7 | Indian men constructing a fence | 285 |
| 12.1 | Powwow at Shinnecock, 1954 | 288 |
| 12.2 | Flag of Unkechaug Nation | 289 |
| 12.3 | Shinnecock Community Center | 290 |
| 12.4 | Chief Thunder Bird and his daughter, Chee Chee | 291 |
| 12.5 | St. David's Church | 292 |
| 12.6 | Shinnecock Nation Museum Seal | 293 |

**Tables**

| | | |
|---|---|---|
| 3.1 | Sources of Nutrients in Indian Diet | 60 |
| 3.2 | Medicinal Properties of Local Wild Plants | 66 |
| 3.3 | Plant Dyes | 68 |

Detail from Carolus Allard "Totius Neobelgir Nova et Accuratissima Tabula," Amsterdam, c. 1673. This map of New York is an amplifed version of the Jansson-Visscher prototype (see Allen 1991:49-51).

# Foreword

Native Americans are an intriguing topic to those interested in Long Island history and culture, from Daniel Denton in the seventeenth century to today's visitors at the annual Shinnecock Powwow. Recent studies by archaeologists and historians have enhanced our knowledge of the original inhabitants, but this information has not always reached teachers and the general public. The Suffolk County Archaeological Association has made valuable contributions in its "Readings in Long Island Archaeology and Ethnohistory" series by reprinting older primary sources and earlier articles and presenting new research. What has been lacking until now is a comprehensive narrative overview.

Professor John A. Strong of Southampton College, Long Island University, spoke at the Long Island Studies Institute's first conference in 1986. His paper, "From Hunter to Servant: Patterns of Accommodation to Colonial Authority in Eastern Long Island Indian Communities," appeared in our first publication, *To Know the Place* (1986). He has continued his research on the Algonquian peoples of Long Island, and the Institute is honored to publish his monograph.

Dr. Strong provides an important synthesis and careful analysis of archaeological evidence and historical records for the precontact period and the first two centuries of contact. This book which presents current scholarship in a readable narrative will be valuable to teachers, scholars, and the general public. Those interested in exploring topics further can pursue citations in the extensive references. The brief epilogue, "Continuity and Reaffirmation," discusses the situation today of Shinnecock, Unkechaug, and other Algonquian peoples on Long Island. Readers seeking additional information on the contemporary period should consult Dr. Strong's companion book, *"We Are Still Here!" The Algonquian Peoples of Long Island Today.*

This work has been in process for much longer than any of us expected when we undertook the project. John Strong provided the manuscript on disk and patiently responded to innumerable queries. Shinnecock artist David Martine prepared the cover illustration and many drawings especially for this book; they add an important visual dimension. Irene McQuillan, former Institute secretary, and Victoria Aspinwall, current secretary, carefully and diligently entered many additions and revisions in the manuscript. Eileen Hessman assiduously copyedited and indexed the volume; she maintained her good humor dealing with all the variations in Algonquian spellings. Dorothy B. Ruettgers and Ms. Aspinwall proofread and aided copyediting at later stages. Walt Steesy, publisher of more than a dozen Institute books, has provided his usual good advice and assistance. Our sincere thanks and appreciation to all involved for their contributions to this work.

Natalie A. Naylor, Director
Long Island Studies Institute

David Bunn Martine, Shinnecock artist painting a mural for the Shinnecock Museum

# Preface

This book grew out of a discussion I had several years ago with Dr. Natalie A. Naylor, director of the Long Island Studies Institute at Hofstra University, about the need for a comprehensive volume on the Algonquian peoples of Long Island, which could serve as a basic resource for educators and for the general public. Almost before I realized what I was getting into, I had embarked on an exciting and challenging project which kept me occupied, along with my teaching and other faculty responsibilities at Southampton College, for the next five years.

The cultural development of the Algonquian peoples of Long Island is traced from earliest times to the end of the seventeenth century. A brief epilogue discussing contemporary Algonquian life was added to inform readers about the modern descendants of these ancient peoples, who remain an important part of our Long Island community today.

The sources of information for this book include archaeological reports, observations written by European visitors in the seventeenth century, state, county, and town records and archives, published materials about Native American peoples on Long Island and adjacent areas, and interviews with Shinnecock, Unkechaug, Montaukett, and Matinecock informants. David Bunn Martine, the Shinnecock artist who did most of the illustrations for the book, was an important source of information about the history and culture of his people. His illustrations are based on his research in the archaeological reports and his familiarity with his own cultural traditions.

Some material in this book has appeared in the following previous publications by the author: "Wyandanch, Sachem of the Montauk," in *Northeastern Indian Lives,* edited by Robert S. Grumet (Amherst, MA: University of Massachusetts Press, 1996), 48-73; "Indian Land and Labor During the Post-Contact Period on Long Island," in *To Know the Place: Exploring Long Island History,* edited by Joann P. Krieg and Natalie A. Naylor, 2d ed. (Interlaken, NY: Heart of the Lakes Publishing, 1995), 13-39; and "The Thirteen Tribes of Long Island: The History of a Myth," *Hudson Valley Regional Review* 9, no. 2 (Spring 1992):39-73.

I am indebted to many people for their help and encouragement. First and foremost, to Dr. Gaynell Stone for urging me to begin researching the history of the Algonquian peoples of Long Island. She recruited me to write articles for the Suffolk County Archaeological Association volumes on the Shinnecocks and Montauketts. Her command of the data base for eastern Long Island history and her high standards of scholarship and professional integrity were an inspiration for me.

I am also deeply indebted to my editor, Dr. Naylor, who initially proposed the book and then worked so patiently with me over the years. I came to depend on her critical judgment and her knowledge of western Long Island history. Her eagle-eyed copyeditors, Eileen Hessman and Victoria Aspinwall, deserve a great deal of credit for fine tuning the manuscript. Dr. Mildred DeRiggi of the Nassau County Museum, Long Island Studies Institute, and David Christman, Dean of New College, Hofstra University, provided very helpful comments on several chapters.

I owe a special debt to the following scholars who gave generously of their time to read and critique the manuscript: Herbert Kraft, Professor of Anthropology and Director of the Archaeological Research Center, Seton Hall University (South Orange, New Jersey); Dr. Helen Rountree, Professor of Anthropology, Old Dominion University (Norfolk, Virginia); Dr. David Bernstein, Director of the Institute for Long Island Archaeology at the State University of New York at Stony Brook; and Robert S. Grumet, anthropologist, National Park Service, Philadelphia, Pennsylvania.

The following colleagues at Southampton College have, over the years, answered my questions about technical matters related to themes in the book: Susan Habib, archaeology; Keith Serafy, field biology; Daniel Duberman, zoology; Howard Riesman, ichthyology; Sandra Shumway, marine biology; and Maureen Krause, marine biology. I am also indebted to Philip Rabito-Wyppensenwah, who shared with me his comprehensive knowledge of Montaukett history and culture.

Over the past decade many Algonquian people from Long Island have encouraged, informed and critiqued my research, but the following deserve a special word of thanks: Roberta Hunter, Marguerite Smith, Lamont Smith, Gerrod and Josephine Smith, Sherry Blakey-Smith, Eugene Cuffee, Harriett Crippen Gumbs, Chee Chee (Elizabeth Haile), the Reverend Holly Haile-Davis, Margo Thunder Bird, Michelle Johnson, Jonathan Smith, Norman Smith, Ella Smith, Lanette Cooke, and the Reverend Michael Smith from Shinnecock; the late Donald Treadwell, Chief Harry Wallace, and Karla Miller from Poospatuck; Robert Cooper, Ralph Bunn, Robert, Caroline, and Olive Pharaoh from the Montaukett; Osceola Townsend, Cheryl Brady, and Asiba Tupahache of the Matinecock; and Wati Wampatoques (James Waters), John Kenney, and the Reverend Sharon Jackson, who have kinship ties with several of the Long Island Algonquian communities. Many other scholars and local Algonquian people who have provided information about various themes in the book are identified after the references. They are cited by name in the text with "pers. com." signifying a personal communication.

Most of the original documents consulted for the book are located in local libraries and in town archives. My research would not have been possible without the full cooperation and professional skill of the research librarians and town historians. In particular, Dorothy King, the knowledgeable director of the Long Island collection in the East Hampton Public Library, deserves a special acknowledgment for her help over the years. The following reference librarians, archivists, and town historians also provided indispensable service: Robert Battenfeld and Elizabeth Herbert, Southampton College Library; David Y. Allen, State University of New York at Stony Brook; Steve Czarniecki, William Floyd Estate, Fire Island National Seashore Archives; Evelyn Hanson, Southampton Colonial Society; Emily Oster, Southampton Town Archivist; James D. Folts, New York State Archives, Albany; Ronald Wyatt, Nassau County Museum; Robert Keene, Southampton Town Historian; the late Rufus B. Langhans, Huntington Town Historian; Joan Cohn, Indian and Colonial Research Center, Old Mystic, Connecticut; Walter Smith and Ellen Barcel, Southold Indian Museum; Joanne Brooks and David Kerkhof, former Suffolk County Historical Society librarians; and Lois Trippoleo, Administrative aide, Oyster Bay Town Clerk's Office.

I also thank the students in my 1995 and 1996 summer session classes who read the draft manuscript of this book. Gwen Bronson, Cathleen Curran, Bryan Bruno, Nicholas Coleman, Hilary Leyden, Mary Graves, and Gordell Wright (Shinnecock) served as editors and brought to my attention any portions of the book which they felt were unclear. Two Southampton Fine Arts majors also contributed to the book. Fred Kossen drew some illustrations and Christina Grupico did the graphics for three of the maps.

The deepest debt is to my wife, Jane, and to my daughters, Lisa and Lara, for their understanding, comfort, encouragement, and for their informed critique of parts of the manuscript.

## Technical Notes

Spelling and punctuation in some of the colonial documents have been modernized to facilitate readability. Maps in the appendices indicate the locations of archaeological sites (Appendix A) and Algonquian deeds (Appendices B-D). Additional information on each site or deed is provided in each map key.

The English documents in the seventeenth century were dated according to the "old style" Julian calendar, which began the new year on March 25. The Dutch had converted to the "new style" Gregorian calendar much earlier, but the English dates for the seventeenth century can cause some confusion. Dates from January 1 to March 25, refer to the end of a given year. March 10, 1640, for example, marked an event at the end of 1640 and should be adjusted to March 10, 1641. Frequently, but not always, the dates from January 1 to March 25 were recorded with a slash to indicate the Gregorian date. March 10, 1640, for example, might be recorded on a deed as March 10, 1640/41. If there is only a single date, the historian must find some way of corroborating the year. Specialists in colonial documents have indicated that there is no set rule for determining the year of seventeenth and early eighteenth-century documents dated from January to March (James Folts, Nov. 1995: pers. com., and Peter R. Christoph, Nov. 1995: pers. com.). The dates cited in this text, therefore, may differ from the "unadjusted" dates in the primary records.

Fig. 1.1. Seventeenth-century Algonquian man. This painting by Shinnecock artist David Bunn Martine, is based on insights and information in the Smithsonian's National Museum of the American Indian collections in New York City. The shirt is a seventeenth-century colonial garment. The wampum bandoleer across his shoulder is a replica of those worn by the Lenape who lived in New Jersey and on western Long Island. The arm bands are leather decorated with porcupine quill. The headdress is made of deer hair, hawk feathers, and porcupine quills. The ceremonial war club with a shell inlay and birdhead design is a copy of the ones commonly found in the Northeast. The tobacco pouch of squirrel skin, decorated with tin cones and deer hair is also based on artifacts in the museum collections.

# 1

# Introduction

The history of the prehistoric inhabitants of Long Island and their descendants presents many problems to the historian. One of the first and more challenging of these concerns is the choice of a generic reference for the original inhabitants. Columbus, believing he was in the East Indies, called the Arawak people he met "Indians." The term was soon in use throughout Europe to describe the several thousand distinct cultures and societies inhabiting the Western Hemisphere in 1492. The arbitrary conceptual reference, imposed collectively upon all native peoples, must have puzzled them. In Massachusetts, missionary John Eliot was asked: "Why do you call us Indians?" Roger Williams was asked the same question by a Narragansett. The questioners did not identify with a "generic" label lumping together all of the original inhabitants of the Western Hemisphere. They referred to themselves in their own languages in terms of geographic location, lineage systems, totem ancestors, or simply as "human beings." The name of the Lenapes, who are closely related to the original inhabitants of western Long Island, means "the ordinary people" (Kraft 1986:xvii).

There were, of course, many pejorative terms used by Europeans. The Dutch referred to the Lenapes as *Wilden* (wild men); the French used the term *sauvage*, derived from *silvaticus*, a Latin word for a forest dweller. The more common appellations used by all of the European settlers were "barbarians," "heathens," "infidels," or simply "red men." Although the term "Indian" is certainly more neutral than these, Robert Berkhofer, Jr. argues that the word has become a stereotype invested with ethnocentric value judgments. In his analysis of the problem, Berkhofer defines the "Indian" as a diffuse collection of positive "noble savage" and negative "brutal and/or lazy savage" images beclouding the perceptions of far too many whites. He suggests that the term "Native American" would be a more appropriate generic label (1979).

The problem is viewed by some whites as merely an annoying petulance on the part of some "Indians" and an overreaction by a few liberals. This response, of course, tells us more about the respondent than it does about the issue. When a conquering group or a dominant majority imposes a label on a minority, there is generally some resentment expressed to whatever term is chosen by the "outsiders." The label is resented because the imposition of such references symbolizes the dominance of the whites. Resistance to the label can become a compelling force uniting and strengthening a minority group. African American rejection of the term "Negro" during the civil rights struggles of the sixties was an attempt to replace an imposed label with one of their own choosing. For some native people, the term "Indian" is viewed in the same way as "Negro" is today by many African Americans.

There is, however, no clear consensus among native peoples about these labels. A spokesperson from the American Indian Community House in New York, who was asked about the terms "Indians" and "Native Americans," replied that they were both flawed. Identifying themselves as "Native Americans" is questioned by many because the continent itself was named by a German map maker who mistakenly believed that the Italian navigator Amerigo Vespucci was the first European to encounter this land. Vespucci is a particularly insulting choice because his published reports were rife with denigrating characterizations of native peoples. These reports were among the first to be read throughout Europe, and they undoubtedly contributed to the emergence of negative stereotypes which continue to burden the descendants of the original inhabitants.

One of the inherent dangers in all collective labels is the tendency to fix a list of specific characteristics or behavior patterns to them. Lazy-minded assumptions lump the rich diversity of native cultures and individuals into one blurred category. This is expressed in such references as "Indian religion," Indian food," and "Indian houses," which ignore not only the enormous variety of cultures at the time of conquest, but also the many historical changes these diverse cultures experienced before and after the Europeans arrived. Such imagery locks native peoples into an idealized time warp.

Many tourists drive by the Shinnecock Reservation on eastern Long Island and complain that they did not see many "real Indians." These tourists had apparently come looking for a static image and were disappointed to see the Shinnecocks wearing shoes and driving cars. For these casual visitors, there are no "authentic Indians" left. One reason for this perception, suggests Berkhofer, is that most history textbooks do not mention native peoples after the colonial period except for a brief account of the Plains wars in the nineteenth century. For the troops on the frontier, the only good "Indian" was a dead one. For many whites today, the only "real Indian" is one that died before the frontier closed. It is this narrow perception which played such a tragic role in the long bitter court battle for the ancient Montaukett homeland that began in 1893, and ended in a crushing defeat for the Indians in 1918 (see Strong 1993).

Whenever appropriate, one can use specific group names such as the Shinnecocks, Pequots, or Matinecocks, or a common linguistic affiliation such as Algonquian, Siouan, or Athapascan rather than a generic label. All of the original inhabitants in what is now Long Island, New Jersey, Pennsylvania, and southern New England, for example, shared a common language root called "Algonquian," which distinguished them from their Iroquoian-speaking neighbors to the north.[1]

It is the generic reference to all of the original inhabitants of the Western Hemisphere which causes the real problem. Perhaps the only unencumbered generic references are "original inhabitants" or "native peoples." The absence of a clear consensus among the descendants of the original inhabitants of the Western Hemisphere poses a problem for writers, particularly historians, classroom teachers, and all those who are sensitive to the concerns of minority groups. An ethnic group should determine how they are to be addressed, but it would be nearly as arrogant for outsiders to demand that they come forth with a convenient label as it was to impose an arbitrary one in the first place. The discussion about the issue, albeit frustrating for outsiders, can serve a useful purpose because it forces a fuller consideration to the diversity and complexity of native cultures. In the absence of any consensus, the terms "Indian," "Native American," "original inhabitant," and "native people" are used interchangeably in the text whenever a generic reference is unavoidable.

## What is a Tribe?

Another label which has caused no end of confusion for the general public and no small amount of controversy among scholars is "tribe." What exactly is a "tribe?" People use the word without giving it much thought. If you ask most any Long Islander about the local Indians, you will likely hear that there were thirteen tribes joined in a loose confederacy led by Wyandanch, a Montaukett chief who befriended Lion Gardiner, the first English settler on eastern Long Island. Your informant might even produce a map of the "thirteen tribes" of Long Island from a local newspaper, such as the one which appeared in the "Big Apple Almanac" series in the Long Island *Newsday* (November 10, 1991). Variations of this map have appeared through the years in newspapers and school texts. One elementary school textbook, for example, reprints one such map showing the island neatly divided into thirteen tribal units, beginning with the Canarsie who lived in what later became Brooklyn, followed by the Rockaway, Matinecock, Merrick, Nissaquogue, Massapequa, Secatoag, Setauket, Unkechaug or Patchoag, Corchaug, Shinnecock, Manhasset, and ending with the Montauk (Montaukett) on the far eastern end of the Island (Sesso and White 1990:21). A popular seventh grade textbook has the same map and recitation of "tribal" names (Mannello 1984:15). Many of the texts will even have each tribal name translated into English. Your informant might also add, with a note of pathos, that all of these tribes became extinct. The few remnants who remain, you might be told, have lost their "Indianness" as a result of miscegenation with African Americans.

Yet any contemporary scholar will point out that there were probably no native peoples living in tribal systems on Long Island until after the Europeans arrived (C. Smith 1950:103; Salwen 1978:168; Brasser 1978:85; Hawk 1984:12-16). The tribal systems which developed later did so in response to the pressures from the expanding European communities. Where, then, did the popular notion of the thirteen tribes come from? In order to trace the history of this myth we must begin with a discussion of the conceptual problems posed by the term "tribe."

Although the term "tribe" has been replaced by such ambiguous references as "groups," "families," and "communities" in local histories, beginning with Benjamin Thompson's classic three-volume *History of Long Island* (1918, 1:123), the press and popular literature continue to perpetuate the myth of the thirteen tribes of Long Island. Robert Coles wrote in the introduction to his 1954 booklet, *The Long Island Indian*, that his goal was to "correct some of the popular misconceptions that are so widespread concerning the Long Island Indians" (8). On the previous page he had informed his readers that "The Long Island Indians have practically disappeared." He then proceeded to tell his readers that the groups were not tribes, they were "chieftaincies," which governed a number of small communities, and that there were probably more than thirteen. In spite of this qualification, the statement was followed by the traditional list of thirteen names (27-30).

Part of the problem is that local historians have been unwilling or uninterested in mastering the relevant anthropological data necessary to present a more accurate description of Long Island's original inhabitants. They provide the reader with little more than a brief disclaimer about the term "tribe" and then proceed to discuss the thirteen "groups" of Long Island. There is apparently something infectious about the number thirteen which makes it difficult for authors and readers to abandon. Perhaps it calls to mind the thirteen colonies, evoking a romantic nostalgia for the past. Even when local historian Paul Bailey correctly noted that the "generally accepted term of tribe in dealing with local Indians is a misnomer," and that "they might better be called communities," he entitled his booklet *The Thirteen Tribes of Long Island* (1959:6). This booklet was reprinted in 1982 with no significant changes and remains in print today.

John Morice, who wrote an article on "The Indians of Long Island" for Bailey's two-volume history of Long Island (1949, 1:107), noted that, although inappropriate, the term "tribe" was too convenient to be abandoned. William Wallace Tooker, Long Island's pioneer ethnographer, whose encyclopedic *Indian Place Names on Long Island* (1911, reprinted 1962) remains the primary source for English translations of local Algonquian names, made it clear that a "place name" should not be confused with a "tribal" name. Tooker quoted Roger Williams's observations of the Rhode Island Indians' social structure, "They had no name to difference themselves from strangers, except the names they took from the place of residence." Although Tooker concluded that this description was also true for the Long Island Indians, his place name translations are generally cited on the "tribal" maps misleading the reader to conclude that a particular tribal group occupied each shaded or colored area.

Most Long Island children learn about the thirteen "tribes" from their fourth and seventh grade teachers who follow the state curriculum guidelines requiring that they teach students about local Native Americans. The best intentioned teachers are often forced by time constraints and a crowded curriculum to rely on the most accessible sources. The Gloria Sesso and Regina White fourth grade textbook, *The Long Island Story,* published in 1990, repeats Bailey's approach. The authors use the term "family" rather than "tribe," but they reproduce the conventional map showing Long Island divided into thirteen "family" groups. George Mannello's seventh grade textbook, *Our Long Island,* subtitles his chapter on the Long Island Indians, "The Thirteen Tribes"; yet in the 1984 "corrected edition," he inserts a fourteenth "tribe," the Unkechaugs. In spite of this, one of the student exercises at the end of the chapter is to draw a map of the thirteen tribes and then locate the areas where they lived. More importantly, neither of these widely used textbooks attempts to confront the complexity of the Native American extended family and kinship systems. The readers are left with no meaningful alternative to a term they have been told is inappropriate.

The reluctance of these local authors to discuss the subject in more depth is understandable. Professional anthropologists themselves are divided on the usefulness of the label. Human social systems have been classified by anthropologists into categories based on levels of social complexity. The simplest groups, called "bands," are nomadic, egalitarian, hunting and gathering societies. Leadership is based on personal influence rather than inheritance and is generally shared by several adults. A "tribe" is a more complex, sedentary, social system composed of scattered villages. These villages generally practice some form of rudimentary horticulture and are governed by a hereditary leader who has very limited power.

Tribes are much larger than bands and are unified by age and gender associations which cross lineage and clan affiliations. One crucial difference between a band and a tribe is that tribal societies are ideological groups which have a distinctive name that is usually invested with deeply felt emotional symbolism, while bands have an informal collective identity rooted in clan or kinship relations (Sturtevant 1983:6). The next level of complexity is the "chiefdom," a much more populous society with an economic system which produces a significant surplus of goods. The highest level of complexity is the "state," with a market economy and a hierarchy of specific social roles.

The problem here is that human societies seldom fit neatly into these classifications, nor do they progress through evolution from the simplest to the most complex. Although there are some scholars who feel that these ideal types are so imprecise that they hesitate using them at all, others find them useful as general reference points. William Sturtevant, while agreeing that "these ideal types have a rather ambiguous relation to the real world," argues that they are still useful "as guides for investigation and understanding of the real world" (1983:3). The term "tribe" is particularly troublesome, however, even to some of the scholars who agree with Sturtevant about the general usefulness of ideal types. There is general agreement about such conceptual models as band and chiefdom, but there is no such consensus about "tribe." Some scholars ignore the term, arguing that a more accurate model of group organizational complexity posits the band as the simplest social system and the chiefdom as the next level

(Harris 1993: ch. 16, 17; Barnouw 1982: ch. 12). In this model, "chiefdoms" are defined as amalgamations of bands which have fused.

Some of the scholars who include "tribe" in their analytical models are cautious and define the category broadly. Aceves and King (1979:301-3) define a tribe as "not much more than an extension of a band," and Michael Howard (1989:315) describes a tribe as a "loose alliance" of small, "stateless societies" which occasionally join together. Morton Fried (1975) has argued persuasively that, in many cases, bands came together to resist conquest by Europeans or were coerced into an administrative structure to facilitate colonial control over them. Tribal systems emerged within Native American societies, concludes Fried, as a response to pressures from expanding European settlements. Alfred L. Kroeber, one of the founders of modern anthropology, noted that European conquerors arbitrarily imposed the term on Native American societies, by simply rolling small bands and village systems into neatly packaged units, which they labeled "tribes" (Weatherhead 1980:6).

Lynn Ceci, in her analysis of coastal Long Island and Southern New England Native American societies, argues that horticulture and sedentary settlement patterns, two crucial criteria for tribal level systems, did not emerge on Long Island until after the arrival of the European settlers (1990:2-3). Although some scholars have challenged Ceci's conclusions, most acknowledge that the shrinking of hunting and gathering territory as more and more land was taken over by whites, forced the small Native American communities to become more sedentary and to increase their dependence on horticulture.

Another model, more appropriate for prehistoric Long Island, was used by Robert Grumet in his study of the Delaware (1979:23-28). Grumet suggests a more fluid, atomistic model of fissioning and fusing social structures, wherein villages come together temporarily in a loose confederation for a specific purpose and then return to a village centered system again. These fusions would not always include the same village or clan groupings each time. An ethnographic map of Long Island would show continually moving concentrations of dots rather than the conventional tribal boundaries (Grumet, 1992: pers. com.; Aceves and King 1979:246). This pattern was widespread in North America. Plains Indians, such as the Cheyenne, fissioned off into small extended families in the winter when food was scarce and then fused together again in the summer for the buffalo hunt (Hoebel 1960).

Naming or identifying Native American groups on Long Island illustrates some of the difficulties inherent in these rubrics. The first-hand accounts by the seventeenth-century Dutch and English observers and the small number of archaeological excavations suggest the following idea. The indigenous groups here were organized into village level systems with varying levels of social complexity. They lived in village communities which were connected in an intricate web of kinship relations (Salwen 1978:164-70; Brasser 1978:78). The communities appear to have been divided into two general culture areas which overlapped in the area known today as the Hempstead plains. The western groups probably spoke the Delaware-Munsee dialect of Algonquian and shared many cultural characteristics with their Lenape brethren in what is now New Jersey and Pennsylvania (Kraft 1986:xiii).

The linguistic affiliation of the eastern groups is less well understood. Ives Goddard, who has studied this problem, concluded that the languages here are related to the southern New England Algonquian dialects. However, he could only speculate on the nature of these relationships (1978:72). Working with a few brief vocabulary lists of Montaukett and Unkechaug, he suggested that the Montauketts might be related to Mohegan Pequots. The Unkechaugs, who live on the Poospatuck Reservation, he thought might possibly be grouped with the Quiripi of western Connecticut.

Little permanent social structure existed beyond these linguistic and kinship systems. On occasion, several villages might form temporary alliances to accomplish a limited goal, such as a military alliance against a common enemy or a large hunting expedition. Once the goal was reached or hopelessly frustrated, the groups went off on their own again. Fears of "Indian conspiracies" frequently resulted in widespread hysteria during the latter half of the seventeenth century. Nevertheless, few of these alliances ever posed a threat to the colonists. Shared religious ceremonies, which drew groups from some distance to a host village, were often viewed with great fear by some whites who suspected that a "confederacy" was being formed. The reality of indigenous life on Long Island prior to the intervention of the whites, was the autonomous village linked by kinship to its neighbors.

The Montauketts (under the leadership of Wyandanch in the mid-seventeenth century), the Shinnecocks (under the sachems Mandush, Chice, and Pongumo), and the Matinecocks (under the sachems Suscaneman and Tackapousha) developed tribal systems as a result of their contact with the English settlers. Lion Gardiner promoted Wyandanch, enabling him to assert control over his people and influence Native American affairs in other parts of the Island. The distinction between the place "Montauk" and the tribe "Montaukett" first appears in a 1687 deed when the "sachems of Meantauk with the consent of the Meantauket Indians" sold their land to the English (RTEH, 2:213-14).[2] Most of the documents in the seventeenth, eighteenth, and nineteenth centuries, however, used the term "Montauk" for both the tribe and the place. The distinction was revived in the twentieth century by the Montaukett descendants when they began to reorganize. Montaukett is used in this book to refer to the people and Montauk for the geographical place.

Although the Montauketts and Matinecocks later lost their land base and are now scattered across Long Island in small enclaves, they have managed to retain their identity and have revived a loose system of tribal communication. William Hawk, a descendent of an indigenous community which once lived along the

Nissequogue River, studied the revival of the Matinecock people in his doctoral dissertation (1984).

Osceola Townsend, the Matinecock chief, and Cheryl Brady, chairperson of the Matinecock Council of Elders, are currently leading the tribal struggle to reclaim their lands. There are informal longhouse communities in Flushing, Manhasset, and Amityville. Asiba Tupahache, a Matinecock spokesperson, is a strong advocate of the cultural revival. Robert Cooper, a Montaukett who served on the East Hampton Town board from 1992 to 1995, the Reverend Sharon Jackson, Terry Caldwell, and Ralph Bunn from the Montaukett enclaves in central Long Island from Bay Shore to Sayville, and the Pharaoh family, Olive, Peggy, Carolyn, and Olive's son Robert from the Eastville clan in Sag Harbor, are currently involved in reviving the Montaukett tribal structure. Robert Pharaoh began the lengthy process of petitioning the Bureau of Indian Affairs in Washington for Montaukett tribal recognition in the fall of 1995 (Sept. 19, 1995: pers. com.). The Shinnecocks and the Unkechaugs (Poospatucks) have a land base and a system of tribal governance which serve as a common bond uniting the people and sustaining their Indian identity.

Fig. 1.2. Robert Pharaoh and his mother Olive Pharaoh (1927–1996), 1988

The other indigenous communities on Long Island, however, were dispersed by the pressures of European settlements and never adopted more complex political structures. Many of the remnants who had lived in the villages of Rockaway, Canarsie, Keshaechqueseren, Techkonis, Nayack, Marechkawieck, Maspeth, Secatogue, Merrick, Wichquawanck, and Nissequogue settled quietly in nearby English or Dutch settlements. Azariah Horton, the missionary who preached to the Indians of Long Island in the mid-eighteenth century, traveled from Rockaway to Montauk visiting small enclaves of surviving groups (1993:195-220).

## From Place Name to Tribal Name

Where, then, did the list of thirteen "tribes" come from? How did the prevailing "conventional wisdom" about the "thirteen tribes" of Long Island become entrenched in the historical literature? Most of the "tribal" names with which we are now familiar do not appear to have been recognized by either the first European observers or by the original inhabitants until the process of land purchases began after the first settlements were established. We simply do not know what these people called themselves. All the ethnographic data on North American Indian cultures, however, suggest that they identified themselves in terms of lineage and clan membership. These village communities did not have clearly defined, hierarchical political structures, with rulers who could command absolute obedience from their followers. The borders of their hunting territories were very loosely drawn and must have overlapped those of their neighbors on all sides. The English and Dutch were frustrated by this lack of structure because it made land purchase so difficult. Deeds, according to the European concept of property, had to be signed by identifiable owners with authority to sell and have specific boundaries on a map.

The relatively amorphous leadership structure of the Long Island communities, the imprecise delineation of hunting ground boundaries between these groups, and their view of the land as a living entity to be used made conventional European real estate deals nearly impossible to negotiate. The surviving primary records suggest that the Dutch and English remedied this situation by pressing cooperative local sachems to establish a more structured political base in their communities and to define their communities as "tribes" with specific boundaries.

The first list of names for "tribes" on Long Island appears in the journal of the Reverend Charles Wolley (1968), who served as chaplain to the administration of Governor Andros from 1678 to 1680. By this time, many of the villages in western Long Island had been destroyed in the Dutch Wars (1640–1645) or were displaced by the growing European settlements. The Reverend Mr. Wolley relied on an English-speaking Native American named "Nicolas" as his primary informant for about twenty-six pages of ethnographic information in his journal.

Wolley refers to the surviving groups as "Nations which may more properly be called Tribes of Indians" (1968:54). Wolley's list (with his spellings and locations) includes seven "tribes": the *Rockoway* (south of Jamaica), *Sea-qua-ta-eg* (south of Huntington), *Unckah-chau-ge* (near Brookhaven), *Se-tauck* (north of Setauket), *Ocqua-baug* (north of Southold), *Shin-na-cock* (which he described as the "greatest" tribe, near Southampton), and the *Mun-tauck* (east of East Hampton). Surprisingly, Wolley does not mention the Matinecocks who had sold so much land to the English settlers. We do not know what Wolley's criteria for "tribe" were, but he probably lumped together villages that had developed some trade connections with the English.

Silas Wood, Long Island's pioneer historian, writing in 1824, was probably not aware of Wolley's journal when he identified thirteen "tribes" in his oft-quoted roster (Wood 1826:50-51). According to nineteenth-century historian and archivist Edmund B. O'Callaghan, there were only three copies of Wolley's journal in the United States in 1850 (Jaray 1968:9). Wood's list, with a few minor alterations made by local historians from time to time, has, unfortunately, become the standard reference for Native Americans of Long Island and has been repeated by historians and classroom teachers to the present day. Wood located, from west to east along the north shore of Long Island, the Matinicoc, the Nissaquague, the Setauket, and the Corchaug. On the south shore were the Canarse, the Rockaway, the Merrikoke, the Marsapeague, the Secatauge, the Patchogue, the Shinecoc, the Manhanset (Shelter Island), and the Montauk (Wood's spellings for the "tribal" names are used here). Wood examined the Dutch and English records carefully, but he appears to have relied primarily on the deeds for his conclusions about tribal names and boundaries.

Benjamin Thompson (1918), Nathaniel Prime (1845), Edmund B. O'Callaghan (1845), Gabriel Furman (1874), and Richard Bayles (1874), regarded by many as the first professional historians to write about Long Island, merely repeated Wood's list of thirteen "tribes" with the above mentioned disclaimer about the term. Martha Flint (1896), one of the few who actually used the word "tribe" without apology, listed twelve "chief tribes" omitting the "Secatagues" without comment.

Nearly all of these "tribal" lists include an English "translation" which gives the names an added appearance of authenticity. Most of the "translations" come from William Wallace Tooker's 1911 book, *Indian Place Names on Long Island*. Tooker attempted to translate the Algonquian place names on Long Island by looking through the scattered word lists in the colonial records for words which appeared to be similar. His interpretations are highly speculative and, in the absence of a complete Algonquian vocabulary, must be treated with considerable caution. When Tooker wrote to the Bureau of American Ethnography (BAE) in Washington about his research on Algonquian names in 1887, he received a very cool response from John Wesley Powell's special assistant, James Pilling. The BAE was established in 1879, under the direction of John Wesley Powell who wanted to set disciplined scientific standards to ethnographic research. Pilling, a meticulous researcher who had compiled a linguistic classification and bibliography file begun in 1877, was characteristically abrupt with Tooker. Powell and his staff were anxious to discourage such amateur ethnographers as Tooker from publishing works that did not meet professional standards. Tooker was told that one could

> ... reach no satisfactory results in tracing etymologies unless you have good vocabularies of the Algonkin dialects spoken on or about Long Island, and unless you possess as well an extensive knowledge of Algonkin languages generally. Algonkin roots which "appear in English" and other languages are mere coincidences and are scarcely worth the trouble noting, much less of serious study. The origin and signification of Algonkin place names is to be found by searching Algonkin languages and in no other way (Levine and Bonvillain 1980:192).

Robert Schur, a local historian who published several articles in the *Long Island Forum*, a popular, widely-read history magazine, noted that, "there were, in fact, no distinct tribes on Long Island, and the names frequently assigned to the Indians, such as the Montauks and the Shinnecocks, in reality indicate only their place of settlement and not any distinct tribal cleavage" (1942:105). Schur, however, accepted Tooker's translations without comment. Another frequent contributor to the *Forum* was John Morice, who, as we have seen, recognized the fallacy of the tribal designation. Morice also acknowledged the existence of the two linguistic groups identified later by Goddard, but his reference to these groups as "races" indicates that he was out of touch with the larger body of modern anthropological scholarship. Morice made some minor changes in Wood's list. He believed that Wood's "Patchogue" was actually a subgroup of the Unkechaug, but he did not refer to any new documentation which would support his argument. In addition to the thirteen "tribes," Morice listed five small "remnant" groups: Maspeths, the Marechkewicks (Marechkawiecks), the Nayacks, the Jamecos, and the Yennecocks (1949:107-46). Morice squeezed four of these into the existing list as subgroups: Maspeths (Rockaways), Marechkewicks (Merricks), Jamecos (Canarsies), and Yennecocks (Corchaugs). The Nayacks, who lived near Fort Hamilton just south of the Maspeths were said to have left the island shortly after the Dutch settlers arrived.

Paul Bailey (1959) and Jacqueline Overton (1969), two of the most widely used sources on Long Island Native Americans, repeated the conventional list and Tooker's translations. Bailey, as we have seen, acknowledged that the term "tribe" was inappropriate; nevertheless he went on in the next paragraph to say, "The 13 tribes living here at the beginning of the white era were as follows," and he repeated Wood's list with Tooker's translations (Bailey 1959:7).

George Weeks (1965:22) broke with the Wood's model and described seventeen "principal communities," adding the "Maskutchoung," a village community near Hempstead and listing the "Maerckaawicks" (Weeks' spelling) as a separate community from the Merricks. The disagreement between Morice and Wood over the Patchogues and Unkechaugs was resolved here by including both. The Unkechaug appeared twice in Weeks' list, once as "Unkachogues" and a second time as "Poosepatucks." If we add the Yennecocks, the Nayacks, the Jamecos, and the Maspeths, we now have a total of twenty-one groups. More could easily be added by a thorough search through the local town archives. Weeks' publication complicated the tidy picture of the thirteen "tribes" and, perhaps for that reason, has seldom been mentioned in the popular literature.

In fairness to the local authors cited above, it should be noted that most of them were not attempting to write a comprehensive survey of Native American history on Long Island. Their primary goal was to celebrate the colonial achievement of their European ancestors. The simplistic account of the thirteen tribes was a convenient vehicle. These writers embroidered their stories with a cardboard presence which would not distract the reader. The Native American descendants today are burdened by these shallow images of their ancestors. The more serious issue here is not the artificial creation of "tribes" which never existed; it is the assertion that there are no "real tribes" or "Indians" left on Long Island.

## The Myth of Extinction

In order to discuss this popular myth, we must attempt to define "race," a term even more controversial than "tribe." Many anthropologists and geneticists have concluded that the attempts in the nineteenth and early twentieth centuries to divide people into distinct "racial" categories failed because physical characteristics in human societies—such as pigmentation, hair texture, and nasal index—are in constant flux and do not fall into neat identifiable units such as "negroid," "caucasoid," and "mongoloid" (Hicks and Gwynne 1994:58–59). Native Americans, for example, were identified as a subgroup of the "mongoloid" race, in spite of the fact that there are as many distinct physical differences within this category as there were differences distinguishing them from other "mongoloids." Geneticists agree that "pure" Native American genotypes, if, indeed, they ever existed at all, disappeared very soon after the European conquest (Driver 1969:5–6; Snipp 1991:30–31).

These racial classifications are, at best, general groupings which have very limited usefulness in dealing with real human beings. Most anthropologists agree that identifiable physical types or "phenotypes" are found in certain population groups, but that the more important reality is a constant fluidity of genes throughout all human societies. This fluidity of genes across cultural lines was evident here on Long Island even before the Dutch settlements were established. The sachem from Rockaway reminded his Dutch visitor in 1643 that his people had given the Dutch traders "their daughters to sleep with, by whom they had begotten children and there roved many an Indian who was begotten by a Swanneken [Dutchman]" (De Vries 1909:231). The parish records in colonial

Hempstead include many references to petitions from Native American women who claimed that the English fathers of their children had abandoned them (Marshall 1962:50). The exploitive relationship between European men and Native American women was seldom mentioned by local historians, who tended to focus on Native American relations with people of African descent.

"Race," like "tribe," is also imbued with negative stereotypes and racist perceptions. Social and mental attributes are arbitrarily fused onto the biological criteria (Aceves and King 1979:152–57). Native Americans, for example, have been idealized in the minds of many non-Indians into two compelling cardboard images: the "noble savage" and the "brutal savage" (Berkhofer 1979; Huddleston 1967). There is also a historical dimension to the stereotyped image. The idealized "true Indian" is pictured dressed in buckskin and feathers, on horseback or in the woods, staring stoically at the horizon. The "Indianness" of Native Americans dressed in contemporary clothes and driving cars is questioned. This view, frozen in time, assumes that social change and cultural adaptation discredit "authentic Indianness." The more important assumption here is that the dominant white group has the right to certify the cultural identity of non-whites.

The "disappearance" of the Indian "race" on Long Island is a recurring theme in local history books. Daniel Denton, the son of the Hempstead minister, wrote in 1670, that the Indians had "decreast by the Hand of God . . . a Divine Hand makes way for them [the English], by removing or cutting off the Indians either by wars one with the other, or by some raging mortal disease" (1968:7). Denton set the tone for the extinction myth by asserting that the native people were nearly gone and that it was God's will rather than any action by the whites which was responsible. Warfare between Native American groups was characterized by sporadic raiding which seldom took many lives, whereas the wars waged against them by the English and the Dutch were brutal and devastating. The epidemics of smallpox, cholera, and measles were introduced by the Europeans, and not by "a Divine Hand." In spite of these injuries inflicted by the white settlers, the Native Americans did not dwindle as Denton claimed.

Native Americans were still around in the mid-nineteenth century when Gabriel Furman announced their virtual extinction in his *Antiquities of Long Island*. He pressed the same theme introduced by Denton, announcing that nature itself, in the form of disease, was wiping out the Indians to make way for the more dynamic white race. Furman added a new twist, which appealed to intellectuals in the latter half of the nineteenth century following the publication of Darwin's work on evolution. He argued that there had never been any significant miscegenation between whites and Indians because mixed blood "scarcely ever lasts beyond the second generation . . . but gradually wastes away" (1874:52). Furman's conclusions about mixtures of "Indian" and "African" blood are not recorded. Culture and "blood" were blended into one concept by the nineteenth-century writers in spite of the fact that blood has nothing to do with either physical appearance or culture.

Local newspapers usually announced the death of an elderly Indian as the passing of the "last pureblood." When Mary Walkus died at the age of 100 in 1867, a town official solemnly noted in the town death records that she was "the last full-blooded squaw and oldest of the Shinnecocks" (SHTA: Death Records). This biological inaccuracy, with its false ring of finality, implied that the "real Indians" had died out. When Wickham Cuffee died in 1915, he was anointed "last of the Shinnecocks" by historian John Morice, who later wrote an epitaph lamenting that the "Indians of Long Island have gone with the forests and little now remains to remind us of the virile life of the people who roamed the woods and fields of our island three centuries ago" (1943:137). In 1936, when Mary Rebecca Kellis died at the age of 102, she was duly heralded as "the last full-blooded Indian living on Long Island" (*Long Island Press,* April 22, 1936). And so it goes.

The popular fourth grade textbook by Sesso and White has a photograph of Stephen Pharaoh under the conventional map of the thirteen tribes. The caption reads, "Stephen Pharaoh, the last full-blooded Montauk, lived until 1879" (1990:21). The authors perpetuate both of the myths on the same page. George Mannello's seventh grade textbook leaves a similar impression. Near the end of his chapter on the Long Island Indians, a section is subtitled, "The Disappearance of the Indians" (1984:22). Three years before Paul Bailey wrote *The Thirteen Tribes of Long Island* (1959), he published an article in the *Long Island Forum*

Fig. 1.3. "Here Rest the Last of the Matinecoc." The remains of several Indians unearthed when Queens Boulevard was widened in 1929 were reburied in the cemetery of Zion Episcopal Church in Douglaston, Queens. The misleading words on the memorial suggest that the Matinecocks no longer exist. When the memorial was unveiled in 1936, however, Susan and Oney Waters were present in their Indian regalia to represent the Matinecock descendents who were still living in the area.

(1956) entitled "Decline and Fall of Tribal Life." In the article he ignores the development of tribal systems at Poospatuck and Shinnecock because he accepts the nineteenth century concept of an absolute relationship between genetic phenotype and social behavior. Bailey assumes that miscegenation and tribal systems are incompatible. This article was reprinted in the 1982 edition of *The Thirteen Tribes of Long Island* under the title, "The Indians' Decline." Ironically, many of the people of African descent who were marrying into the local Native American communities during the seventeenth century had been born and raised in tribal systems in Africa. It is certainly possible that this mixture actually enriched and strengthened tribal systems and traditional belief systems.

The obvious problems with "blood quantums" and genetic "ideal types" have led Congress to define an "Indian" as anyone who identifies as an Indian and is accepted by an Indian community as a member. Although many federal agencies in the western states continue to limit access to services to one-fourth "bloods," and many Indian reservations still use the blood quantum criterion because it is an arbitrary solution to controversies over membership, the general tendency now is to move towards a more objective, value free classification system based on self-identification and ethnicity (Snipp 1991:59-61). This enlightened approach has a considerable impact on the "myth of extinction" here on Long Island. An ethnic group is defined as a human population group which shares a significant number of the following attributes: geographic location, race, language, religion, kinship, traditions, values, symbols, folklore, unique political institutions, a sense of distinctiveness, and a defined criterion for membership which is enforced by the group itself. "Ethnicity" is, therefore, a broad category which includes race as one factor among many others. Native Americans are an ethnic group which includes a variety of diverse cultural communities. Few of these communities share all of the attributes in the list, and there will always be controversy over where the line is drawn which determines a legitimate membership in the larger group. The most recent federal administrative ruling on the definition of tribal status follows this model. Groups who apply for recognition as Indian tribes must provide evidence that they have had a continuous history since 1900; have a genealogical connection with a precontact tribe; have evidence of political organization; maintain community rituals or ceremonies; and have a membership list based on established criteria for members (*Federal Register,* February 25, 1994, sec. 83.7).

Although the myth of Native American extinction on Long Island, which focused on the outdated and misleading concept of "pure blood," has been rejected by contemporary scholars, it is still a widely held perspective among local non-Indians (Stone 1989:167). Deeply rooted racial prejudices are virtually impossible to dispel with scholarly argument, but ignorance and misinformation can be addressed. Let us first examine the case for the Shinnecocks and Unkechaugs today. These communities each have their own common geographic land base on state-recognized reservations, and they have documented genealogical connections to well-known precontact Indian groups. They also have an extended family kinship system which unites clan groups (Hayes 1983:336-43; Cuffee and Stone 1983:311-29). At Shinnecock there are eight clans, each including an average of about forty members and several smaller family groupings (Harriett Crippen Gumbs, January 13, 1996: pers. com.). The Shinnecocks join together for seasonal celebrations which intensify a sense of community and mark them as distinct from their non-Indian neighbors (Strong 1983:44-45). Both reservations have well-established procedures for electing their leaders and determining tribal membership (Strong and Holmberg 1983:226-30; Papageorge 1983:141-225; Gonzales 1986:132-33).

Many of the precontact customs have survived in Shinnecock culture to the present day. Anthropologist Rose Oldfield Hayes, who did her Ph.D. dissertation (1976) on the Shinnecocks, noted that there were "highly critical and effective remnants" of prehistoric culture which remained in practice. She concludes that, "the contemporary Shinnecock . . . have selectively adopted, adapted, and organized enduring cultural themes of the ancient Shinnecock; the pervasive American high technology and its organization washes against these themes with little effect" (1983a:334).

Some traditions, of course, have disappeared or have been significantly altered, but this is also the case among nearly every Native American community in North America. All of the Long Island Native Americans, along with a large number of Indian tribes, have lost their original language. Only thirty-one percent of the Native American communities still speak their own languages (Snipp 1991:56). Many of these groups, however, are now in the process of reconstructing their languages from the fragmented vocabulary lists and missionary records. Both the Shinnecocks and Unkechaugs are working actively on language recovery projects.

Some of the ancient religious rituals and beliefs are also being restored. Sweat Lodge ceremonies, for example, are now observed regularly at Shinnecock. Many of the aboriginal ceremonies and beliefs, however, were never completely lost; they have been incorporated into Christian observances. An example of this tradition of adaptive incorporation was documented in the eighteenth century when the Reverend Paul Cuffee, a Shinnecock minister, adapted the traditional June Meeting to include a Christian service. This tradition of incorporation continues today. Funerals and weddings often include the drum, chants, processionals, and a community meal.

The Matinecock and Montaukett descendants have had a much more difficult time maintaining their tribal identities because they have no land base. They are now scattered across Long Island, but they maintain loose community networks which have enabled them to survive against considerable odds. Many of the Montauketts left the Island to join an expatriate community in Wisconsin, where they live today. The Montauketts are presently undergoing a tribal revival led by a small group of dedicated Montaukett descendants. The process of registration

*Introduction* 33

on a tribal roll has begun, and there is talk of another attempt to reclaim the ancestral lands at Montauk (Pharaoh, 1995: pers. com.).

The Matinecock Longhouse organizations in Nassau and western Suffolk counties continue to carry on many of the traditional ceremonies which revitalize their sense of community. It is, of course, a very difficult struggle to maintain cultural integrity in the absence of a land base. Under the leadership of Chief Osceola Townsend and Cheryl Brady, they have moved to reclaim their land and to reestablish such ancient traditions as *Nunnowa,* a community celebration in the fall thanking the earth for the harvest (Townsend, 1994: pers. com.).[3]

## Summary

The myth of the thirteen tribes actually incorporates two related myths: the tribal myth and the myth of extinction. The first reduces Native American culture and history to a shallow cardboard backdrop for the drama of European "discovery," "settlement," and "progress." The second myth conveniently discredits the identity of the Native American descendants and assuages any feelings of guilt or remorse. These myths continue to be perpetuated in the popular media and in the classrooms, often by people who are genuinely sympathetic to the contemporary Native American peoples on Long Island.

A large part of the problem is the understandable tendency to rely on secondary sources for information about the Algonquian experience on Long Island. The primary documents make it quite clear that there were no tribal systems on Long Island prior to the sporadic series of raids known as Governor Kieft's War (1640–1645), which resulted in the deaths of more than one thousand Native Americans and a few dozen whites. After 1650, tribal systems emerged among the Montauketts, Shinnecocks, and Matinecocks. A similar structure developed at Poospatuck after the reservation was established in 1700 for the Unkechaugs and the remnants of several western Long Island groups. These social adaptations, imposed to manipulate and control, were later turned into mechanisms for group survival by the Algonquians themselves.

The four communities did not die out as alleged in the white folk traditions. There was considerable miscegenation with whites and African Americans, but there is no relationship between genetic phenotypes and cultural attitudes. The basic sense of belonging to a distinct Native American community remains strong, particularly among the Shinnecocks and Unkechaugs where a land base has been preserved. The Matinecocks and the Montauketts have had a much more difficult time of preserving their identity. Their struggle has been burdened by the need to defend themselves against the continual reinforcement of the myths about their past and their premature obituaries in the media.

Fig. 2.1. Lenape creation story. The first man and woman grow from the sacred tree on the back of the turtle.

# 2

# Earliest Times to 3,000 B.P.

Archaeologists have provided us with a general chronological outline which is a convenient guide for understanding the evolution of Native American cultures in North America prior to the arrival of the Europeans. These dates are very general reference points marking gradual shifts in the lifeways of the people which have been interpreted from the excavations by professional archaeologists. These changes are often very difficult to date with any precision. William Ritchie, in his classic *The Archaeology of New York State* (1969), proposed a chronology which has since been refined by several scholars (Kraft 1986; Snow 1980; McBride 1984). The technical rubrics listed below, based on discussions with Dr. David Bernstein, director of the Institute for Long Island Archaeology at the State University of New York (SUNY) at Stony Brook, provide the most accurate chronology for Long Island:

| | |
|---|---|
| Paleo-Indian Period | 12,500 – 8,000 B.P. (Before Present) |
| Archaic Period | 8,000 – 3,000 B.P. |
| Woodland Period | 3,000 – 1,000 B.P. |
|   Early Woodland | 3,000 – 2,000 B.P. |
|   Middle Woodland | 2,000 – 1,000 B.P. |
| Late Woodland | 1,000 B.P. – 1600 |

### The Paleo-Indian Period, 12,500–8,000 B.P.

Our story begins with the land. When Jasper Danckaerts, a Dutch minister, visited New Netherland in 1679, he asked Tantaque, an elderly Lenape man, about the origin of the land. The old man picked up a piece of coal from the fire and drew the form of a turtle on the cabin floor. There was only water at first, he explained, and then a turtle surfaced and when his back dried, a tree grew in the middle. "The root of this tree," he continued, "sent forth a sprout beside it and there grew upon it a man, who was the first male. This man was then alone . . . but the tree bent over until its top touched the earth, and there shot another root, from which came forth another sprout, and there grew upon it the woman."[1] (See fig. 2.1.) The following spring, Danckaerts met another Lenape who told him that the turtle had been created by a great god named Kickeron, who gave it the power to produce the earth, the trees, and all living things (Danckaerts 77–78, 174–75).

Modern science, of course, has a different explanation for these events. About forty thousand years ago, a giant glacier formed this land we now call Long Island as it pushed before it huge amounts of earth scraped off the mainland. The huge wall of ice, nearly two miles thick, came to a halt on Long Island, where the warming air currents from the ocean turned the destructive force into life-sustaining water. As the edge of the Pleistocene ice sheet gradually melted, the Ronkonkoma Moraine, a line of low hills averaging about 350 feet in altitude, emerged forming the spine of the new island (Murphy 1991:4). Large chunks of ice which had been pressed into the earth melted, forming "kettle" holes which often filled with water. These depressions ranged in size from Lake Ronkonkoma, nearly one hundred feet deep, to the small ponds and dry holes scattered all across the island. About ten thousand years ago, as the warming winds and ocean currents continued to erode the glacier, the Sound was formed and the outline of the Island began to take shape.

The rising waters from the "great melt" formed two peninsulas extending out from the eastern end of the island giving it a "fishtail" appearance. Nestled between the "fishtail" are three small islands: Robins Island, Shelter Island, and Gardiners Island. The southern peninsula stretches out for about forty miles to Montauk Point where the waters of the Sound meet the Atlantic Ocean. The warming waters from the Gulf Stream flowing from the south meet the cold Labrador current off the Long Island shore and create a unique climatic pattern slightly warmer than the normal temperate climate. Although the growing season on eastern Long Island begins two weeks later than on the west end, it lasts nearly three weeks longer (Murphy 1991:9).

As the land was forming during the following millennia, equally dramatic changes were occurring on the surface. Several habitats established themselves. Along the south shore, the Atlantic barrier beaches protected salt meadows and shallow bays where water fowl and shellfish flourished. Streams flowing into the bays created freshwater wetlands rich in plant and animal resources for the first human inhabitants. Hemlock, white pine, maple, and chestnut trees gradually established themselves on the barren ground left by the glacier. After several millennia, mixed pine-oak forests, meadows, and wetlands characterized the landscape. These features provided a habitat for a rich variety of edible plants such as blueberry, strawberry, huckleberry, chenopodium, amaranth, ground nuts *(Apios americanus),* wild grapes, and beach plums. The forests now included oak, hickory, spruce, and tulip trees. An abundance of deer, turkey, squirrel, water fowl, sea mammals, and shellfish also flourished in this environment.

The evolution of this new ecosystem gradually attracted the first human explorers to Long Island. Some of the early Paleo-Indians may have arrived even before this transition was completed. These nomadic hunters left behind their "calling card," a distinctive stone projectile point with flutes chipped from the base on both sides where the shaft was attached (see fig. 2.2a). Fluted points are a very reliable time marker because they were found embedded in the bones of a mammoth killed by hunters over 10,000 years ago near what is now Clovis, New Mexico. The point style, named "Clovis" for the site where they were first discovered, was used for about 2,000 years by hunting and gathering bands across

*Earliest Times to 3,000 B.P.*

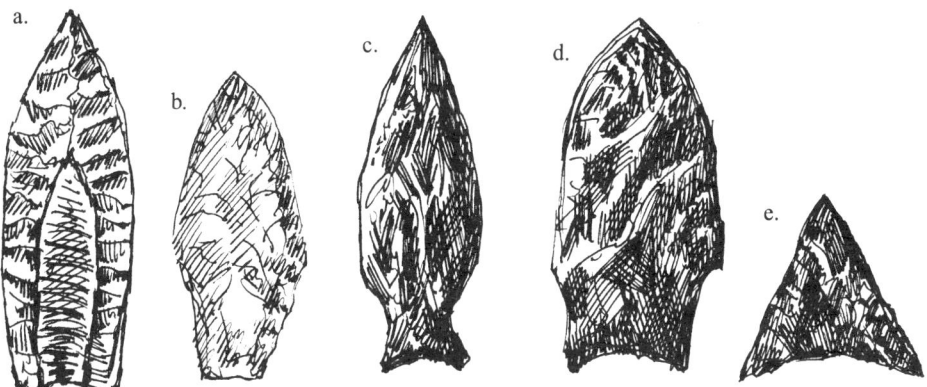

Fig. 2.2. Projectile point chronology for Long Island. *a*. Clovis projectile point: Paleo-Indian Period; *b*. Wading River point: Archaic Period; *c*. Orient "Fishtail" point: Late Archaic Period; *d*. Fox Creek point: Middle Woodland Period; *e*. Levanna point: Late Woodland Period. Appendix A has location of sites.

North America. The preferred material in North America for these points was "chert," a subvitrious variety of quartz with a slightly lower percentage of silicon than flint. Although the term "flint" is often used to describe chert artifacts, geologists argue that there are few, if any deposits of pure flint in North America. Chert may be somewhat inferior to "Old World" flint for tool making, but it is far superior to any other local lithic material because it fractures in a fairly predictable pattern when worked by a skilled craftsman.

Unfortunately for the native peoples of Long Island, there are no deposits of chert here. Local craftsmen were forced to work with a very poor quality quartz which is extremely difficult to flake down to a thin cutting edge (Rutsch 1978:187–91). These quartz nodules, found in such abundance along Long Island's beaches, tend to crumble and shatter rather than flake when fractured.

A small number of fluted points have been found on Long Island from Brooklyn to Riverhead (Saxon 1978:251–61). Three of these points were made from local quartz indicating that they were probably made here on Long Island. The others, made from non-local materials such as chert, chalcedony, and jasper, were probably carried here by the nomadic hunters. In 1988 a Clovis point was found by a team from Stony Brook University who were working on a site just east of Riverhead (Turano and Donahue 1988). Unfortunately all of the points were found on the surface, so we have no record of the archaeological context.[2]

The three points manufactured from local materials are significant, however, because their presence indicates that the Paleo-Indians were spending some time here rather than simply passing through on a hunting expedition (Saxon 1978:259). Having exhausted their supply of imported chert points, they turned, probably with some reluctance, to the local materials. Undoubtedly, there were many other points and artifacts from this period which were destroyed or simply paved over as Long Island was developed.

When we try to understand the lifeways of the first people on Long Island, we find that most of the pieces of the puzzle are missing. Our information must be teased from the points themselves, and supplemented, with some caution, from excavations of Paleo-Indian sites in other parts of North America and from ethnographic studies of nomadic hunting communities in Australia, Africa, and the Pacific. These Native American explorers were the first to locate the sources of fresh water, shellfish habitats, sheltered places for winter camps, and open spaces near the tidal wetlands for summer camps. It was these adventurous explorers who "mapped" Long Island for the generations to follow. When the Europeans arrived, their map makers were guided by native people who passed along to them knowledge accumulated over thousands of years.

Although we know very little about the everyday life of the Paleo-Indians who scattered across North America after the last ice age, some clues have emerged from a small number of archaeological excavations. Their lives were probably centered around the animals they hunted. The size of the community may have been determined by the number of young men necessary for an effective hunting team. These communities of forty to fifty people were composed of extended families connected by kinship and renewed through exogamous marriages to members of neighboring groups. Exogamous marriage systems also provided avenues of communication for trade, shared religious ceremonies, and seasonal hunting and fishing expeditions. The dog was probably domesticated during this period providing an alarm system, an effective scavenger to clean the camp, a companion, and an emergency food supply in mid-winter if needed.

As the climate continued to warm and the mixed deciduous forest established itself, the lifeways of the people undoubtedly went through some significant changes, but we know very little about these Long Island lifeways prior to about 5,000 B.P. Many of the earlier occupation areas were probably inundated as the warming climate melted the glacial ice and raised the sea level.

## The Archaic Period, 8,000–3,000 B.P.

Our understanding of the Archaic settlers on Long Island has been evolving over the past half-century. Many of the early Archaic sites which were settled prior to 5,000 years ago have been covered by the rising sea. Many others, particularly on western Long Island, were built on or paved over before much modern, scientific research could be conducted. Carlyle Smith, in his 1950 survey of Long Island archaeology, identified only one Archaic site on the Island (173–76). He found evidence of a "pre-ceramic" occupation on the Grantville site near College Point on Flushing Bay, but he did not attempt to interpret the data because he lacked a context for comparison.

In the decade following the publication of Smith's research, William Ritchie, the New York State Archeologist, excavated several Archaic sites in Suffolk County, and in 1970 Ronald Wyatt completed his excavation of an important

Archaic site near Wading River. Since 1970 many Archaic sites have been located by archaeologists under contract to developers, who are required by law to survey sites in areas determined to be "archaeologically sensitive." These surveys are often limited to shovel probes and an occasional test pit, but they have revealed a surprising number of Archaic campsites and "work shops" where stone tools were crafted. As a result of this increased data base, we can now reconstruct a very general outline of the Archaic Period lifeways.

**Village Locations**

One of the major contributions of the recent archaeological investigations is an upward revision of previous population estimates. William Ritchie, writing in 1969, and Lynn Ceci in 1977, both concluded that the Archaic population was very small on Long Island (Ritchie 1969:124; Ceci 1977:3, 86). Ceci thought that the estimate of 6,000 made by Smithsonian anthropologist James Mooney in 1928 was much too high. David Bernstein has concluded from the more recent research that the population during the late Archaic Period may have been much larger than Mooney believed. Unfortunately, there is not enough data to make even a general population estimate, but we know much more about where these people located their villages.

Ronald Wyatt, writing in 1977 following his excavation of a late Archaic site on the western bank of Wading River (where it flows into Long Island Sound), characterized the communities of this period as small villages located "on the banks of streams, inland ponds or kettle lakes, and marshes . . . covering an acre or two" (Wyatt 1982:76). The small band living here, concluded Wyatt, probably moved on a seasonal round from this summer camp, where a fresh water stream flowed into the tidal bay, to a winter camp in the more protected wooded sites away from the wetland shores. Wyatt suggested that the food procuring activities at the inland sites focused on hunting deer and fowl, fishing, and gathering.

This model of "seasonal round" settlement patterns has recently been challenged by archaeologists working for the past several years on sites around Mount Sinai harbor on the north shore of Long Island. These excavations have produced increasing evidence that late Archaic coastal village sites were occupied year-round (Lightfoot and Cerrato 1988; Gwynne 1982; Bernstein 1990, 1990a, 1995). This pattern undoubtedly included inland sites along fresh water streams and by kettle ponds as well. There were also many small inland sites used by men on hunting expeditions and, perhaps, by women collecting wild plants. Excavations on one of these inland sites in the Pine Barrens, for example, found large amounts of tiny flakes and chips, but very little evidence of any domestic activity (Bernstein 1995). These data suggest that projectile points, broken during the hunt, were being reshaped or sharpened here in a temporary campsite. The movement of small groups to these special purpose sites may have been the source of the references in the colonial documents to a "seasonal round" settlement pattern.

Similar patterns have been noted by archaeologists studying the riverine settlements along the lower Connecticut River Valley (McBride 1984:369–73). Although Wyatt's model for settlement patterns has been modified, he was correct in his description of typical locations for Archaic villages. Excavations at Pipestave Hollow near Mount Sinai Harbor (Gramley 1982:161–72), and work by David Bernstein and Linda Barber in the Town of Southampton (1992: pers. com.) support Wyatt's conclusions that the banks of small streams near tidal bays and marshes or on ponds were the favored locations for Archaic villages.

William Ritchie, with a team of professional archaeologists, excavated two sites from the Archaic Period. The most productive of the two was located near the present-day village of Stony Brook where Aunt Amy's Creek flows into Smithtown Bay (Ritchie 1965:10–49). The site was well chosen because it is protected by a high ridge which blocks the cold winter winds from the north. To the south, the land slopes gradually into a marshland free of trees, exposing the village to the welcome rays of the winter sun. It was also ideally situated to harvest shellfish and waterfowl from the marshes and tidal bays. Ritchie found several hearths, but no sign of house structures. He looked carefully for small, uniform, circular stains in the earth which formed a pattern. These stains, called "post molds" by archaeologists, are left long after the wooden post rots away and provide evidence of structures such as circular wigwams, rectangular longhouses, or stockade walls. The absence of such data led Ritchie to conclude that the villagers lived in very simple structures consisting of light wooden poles and woven mats. It is also possible that the housing was located in a nearby area which Ritchie missed.

Although we have no data at all about the nature of the shelters used by these early settlers on Long Island, the excavations at the Wapanucket site in Massachusetts and the Lamoka site in upstate New York provide some clues. The Wapanucket people, who were probably closely related to the bands on eastern Long Island, lived in circular structures framed in saplings and covered with bark (Robbins 1959:24–32). The structures at Lamoka Lake (near present-day Geneva, New York) were rectangular, perhaps an early variation on the longhouse design which was used by the Lenapes and the Iroquois during the Woodland Period (Ritchie 1969:36–79; Kraft 1986:79).

The second site was found by Ritchie on the sheltered western bank of Wading River, a few hundred feet from the Archaic site excavated a decade later by Ronald Wyatt. This small site produced only a few shallow "refuse" pits and a scattering of artifacts, which included fire-cracked rock, seventy projectile points, a grooved ax, an abundance of deer bone, and some pottery sherds. The sparseness of features and materials led Ritchie to describe it as a temporary hunting camp. Ritchie's excavation, however, took about three weeks and was, by his own account, incomplete (1965:81). Wyatt found three more sites within a few hundred yards of the camp (Wyatt 1982:73). The stream banks near the confluence with the tidal marsh were rich in archaeological data, but, unfortunately, this whole area has since been bulldozed and developed by the Long Island Lighting Company.

Another site from this period was discovered about forty miles east of Stony Brook on the North Fork of Long Island near the small village of New Suffolk (Salwen 1982:39–43). Located on the west bank of Downs Creek where the stream flows into Peconic Bay, the Baxter site closely resembles the Stony Brook settlement. The ancient villagers here also took full advantage of the terrain. The warming rays of the winter sun in the southeast fell unobstructed on the site and the dense woods in back blocked the cold northern winds.

**Food Supply**

The people living in the small village on Wading River were harvesting shellfish from the tidal bays and fishing for sea sturgeon, rockfish, bluefish, flounder, shad, and striped bass. The smaller fish in the bays and streams were taken in nets, probably cast by hand. Wyatt found many grooved stones which appear to have been used as net sinkers. The villagers' diet also included a rich variety of shellfish. Wyatt found an abundance of clam, scallop, and oyster shells in his excavations.

The recent work at Mount Sinai, Shelter Island, and in southern New England has demonstrated that shellfish were being harvested year-round, further supporting the argument for permanent village habitation rather than seasonal movement (Gwynne 1982; Lightfoot and Cerrato 1988:147; Bernstein 1990, 1990a). Although deer and wild turkey were also a part of the basic food supply, the chief source of protein came from the sea. Two deer-bone harpoons which appear to have been used on sea sturgeon and seals were also discovered at Mount Sinai (Johannemann, 1993: pers. com.). Large fish and, perhaps, even small whales, were probably taken when they became disoriented and trapped themselves in the shallow tidal bays. This may have been the beginning of a practice which later developed into the more sophisticated whale hunting technology involving teams of men in canoes who ventured out into the coastal waters for their prey.

It is likely that fish weirs were also a part of the fishing complex. Although no evidence of this practice has survived on Long Island, archaeologists working on a site in the Charles River near Boylston Street in Boston found thousands of wooden stakes preserved in the silt which appear to have been a series of small fish traps (F. Johnson 1942; Dincauze 1973:31). Brush was woven in between the stakes rather than a net to prevent the fish from going through. The fishermen made ingenious use of the tide as a part of the trapping mechanism. The wall of stakes and brush was stretched across the mouth of a tidal pond at low tide level. The incoming tide rose over the barrier carrying the fish into the trap and the outgoing tide left them helpless in the shallow water where the women scooped them into baskets.

Game animals and fowl were also plentiful. Deer, raccoon, squirrel, woodchuck, duck, and wild turkey bones and box turtle remains have been found in abundance on most Long Island Archaic sites. Unfortunately, we know very little about the plants which were gathered by these early settlers. We can assume that they were harvesting the berries, nuts, greens, and roots which flourished here. Pollen samples from Archaic sites in eastern North America indicate that such plants as chenopodium, commonly called goosefoot *(Chenopodium berlandieri)*, sunflower *(Helianthus annus)*, maygrass *(Phalaris caroliniana)*, ground nut *(Apios americana)*, and knotweed *(Polygonum erectum)* were a regular part of the diet (B. Smith 1985:51; Cowan 1985:211–17). Women from the villages undoubtedly knew where stands of these plants were located and probably watched them carefully to determine the best time for harvesting. The basic concepts of plant domestication probably emerged out of this early relationship between village women and the wild plants.

**Social Organization**

Hunting and gathering societies do not produce enough surplus to sustain an elite class. The food which is produced is shared with the whole community according to need. The leadership in these village communities was generally based on persuasion rather than coercion. The elderly and those with specific skills were often deferred to for advice and direction. Sachems or village headmen had limited responsibilities and very little authority over their fellow villagers. This form of political organization characterized nearly all human societies prior to the development of agriculture.

The eastern coastal Algonquian social structure prior to the eighteenth century is poorly documented, but it appears to have been based on a kinship system which probably linked families to a wide ranging network of relations all across Long Island, and what is now eastern New Jersey and southern New England (Salwen 1978:167). In such kinship systems, families generally share responsibilities for food production, protection, and religious ceremonialism. The kinship networks, which trace their ancestry back to a common founder through the father or mother or both, are called "lineages." If the genealogy is not well understood or the particular founder is a mythical being or a totem animal, the kinship system is called a "clan" by anthropologists. These lineages and clans were usually exogamous, marrying outside their own group.

The patterns of postmarital residence of the northeastern Algonquian are poorly understood, but there appears to have been a great deal of movement from one village to another, suggesting that a couple could choose to live in the village of either spouse (Salwen 1978:167). This pattern linked the eastern Long Island and southern New England communities together into a constantly intermeshing network. A similar pattern of lineages probably connected the Munsee-speaking villages on western Long Island and eastern New Jersey. Very likely, these lineages and clans renewed their relationships with regular communal feasts and religious ceremonies.

*Earliest Times to 3,000 B.P.*

**Tool Technology**

Although the recent studies of settlement patterns on Long Island have made significant contributions to our understanding of the Archaic Period, we still know very little about the origin and early development of village life. We can, however, gain some significant insights from the artifacts they left behind. The settlers improved their tool technology to exploit the environment more efficiently. Stone axes and adzes, combined with the ingenious use of fire, enabled them to fell the trees for their dug-out canoes. The tall tulip trees (now nearly extinct on Long Island) and the sycamore were preferred for canoes. The Indians in what is now New Jersey referred to sycamore as "canoe wood" (Cross 1986:25), and the Indians on western Long Island told Adriaen van der Donck, a Dutch land owner and author of *Description of New Netherland* (1655), that the tulip tree was called "canoe wood" in their language (1968:23). Although sycamore and tulip wood was apparently preferred, chestnut, cedar, and oak were also used.

First the trees were girdled by a fire around the base and the charred wood was then hacked away with stone axes. This process was continued until the tree was felled. Next a fire was built along the length of the trunk to soften the wood for the adzes which gouged out the burned areas (see fig. 2.3). These vessels, along with fishing nets and deer bone harpoons, were part of a steadily expanding maritime economy. The canoes were also used to carry trade goods to neighboring communities (Kevitt 1968:1–5). John Winthrop reported that the large canoes could carry as many as eighty men (Hosmer 1946 1:109), but such large canoes were probably quite rare. Captain John Smith, whose ethnographic observations of the Powhatan Indians are generally applicable to most other Atlantic coastal Algonquian peoples, noted that whereas some canoes he saw in Virginia were forty to fifty feet long and carried forty men, most were smaller, carrying from ten to thirty men (Barbour 1986, 1:163).

Other simple hand tools were developed to aid in the preparation of the daily diet. Mortars and pestles and grinding stones were used to process the forest harvest of nuts and seeds (see fig. 2.4). Women gathering roots and tubers dug them out with clam shells and hand-held choppers. Scrapers and drills, which can be traced back to the Paleo-Indian Period, were now being used to work with wood and bone to produce a variety of eating and cooking utensils.

The fluted point style used so successfully to bring down the large game animals such as the mammoth was abandoned by the Archaic settlers who added a variety of small point forms to their hunting technology (see figs. 2.2b, 2.2c). The points were hafted to spears and launched by hand or with the aid of an ingenious invention called the *atlatl,* an Aztec word meaning "water spear," because it was apparently used first as a fishing spear. The atlatl is a wooden shaft about two feet long with a hand grip on one end and a carved hook on the other (see fig. 2.5). A dart about four or five feet long was buttressed against the hook and held in place with one or two fingers of the hand on the grip. The

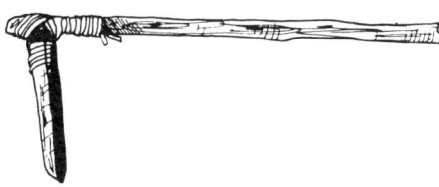

Fig. 2.3. Use of fire and tools to make a canoe. Felling a tree (*left*); using fire to make dugout canoe and using tools to dig out charred wood from log (*below*); Tools: *a*. ax and *b*. adze (*above*).

*Earliest Times to 3,000 B.P.*

Fig. 2.4. Drill, stone mortar and pestle, scrapers

combined implements were then raised aloft and carried several running strides to gather momentum and leverage for a forceful launch. The upraised arm was then thrust forward and downward with a snap as the dart was released. The wooden "spear thrower" acted as an extra length of forearm, providing increased leverage as it whips downward, giving the dart the striking power of an arrow fired from a sixty pound bow. The bow and arrow was not used in North America until much later.

The Archaic craftsmen had to work with lithic materials indigenous to Long Island. High quality chert, as we have noted, is not found on the island. The loose structure of most local white quartz makes it very difficult to thin into an effective blade. In spite of this challenge, resourceful craftsmen managed to locate relatively workable nodules and produced an impressive variety of stone tools. Research on local lithic assembleges indicates that the Indians carefully selected the milky, translucent cobblestones to make their tools (Leonardi and Bernstein 1995). The tool makers began by chipping the stones down to form a "blank" core on the beach and carrying the blanks back to the village or some other more convenient place where they further reduced them to form knives, scrapers and projectile points. The tool complex, however, was much richer than the surviving stone implements suggest. Archaic settlers used a wide variety of bone and

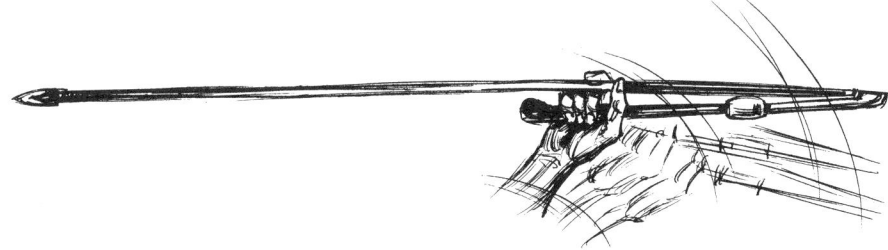

Fig. 2.5. Atlatl (spear thrower)

Fig. 2.6. Shinnecock baskets made in the late nineteenth and early twentieth centuries and woven shoulder bags

wooden implements. Unfortunately, the baskets, awls, textiles, rope, wooden bowls and utensils, needles, and fish hooks did not survive long in the acid soils of Long Island. Nevertheless, we know that Archaic peoples in other parts of North America made extensive use of these materials (Kraft 1986:62-68).

In spite of the meager data base, anthropologist Kathryn Browning-Hoffman has provided some important insights into the prehistoric basket and textile technology by examining the colonial records and studying the relations between incised pottery designs and basket weave patterns (1982:276-80; 1982a:268-75). The English colonists observed local Indians making rope, bags and clothing from dogbane *(Apocynum androsaemfolium)*, false nettle *(Boehmeria cylindrica)*, and milkweed *(Asclepias syriaca)*. Pottery designs were sometimes made by pressing textile fabrics into the wet clay before firing. Browning-Hoffman's (1982:277) close examination of fabric marked pottery indicated that "the basic technique was hand twining—that is, twisting two woof threads (horizontal) around each warp thread (vertical) in turn. This horizontal line was then usually pressed down tightly, completely concealing the warp threads." The beautiful turkey feather capes worn by prominent Algonquian elders were probably made by sewing feathers into a variation of this pattern. John Smith noted that these turkey mantles were "so prettily wrought and woven with threads that nothing could be discerned but the feathers" (Barbour 1986, 1:161). Browning-Hoffman (1982a: 268) concluded that the designs on pottery were copied from basket weaves. She noted that the herringbone pattern, so common on Woodland

Fig. 2.7. Algonquian man and woman in traditional dress. The woman is wearing a turkey feather mantle

pottery, was "identical in intention to the plaiting pattern" in some Indian baskets from the colonial period.

Surprising as it may seem, bark vessels were actually used for cooking. This innovative process involved the use of hot stones to boil water for cooking. The stones were heated and then removed from the fire with wooden implements and dropped into bark containers containing water or stew. Archaeologists who experimented with this process were surprised with the effectiveness and speed of "stone boiling."

During the last centuries of the Archaic Period, vessels fashioned from steatite, a soft soapstone, may have been used by the Long Island villagers. Stone bowls and cooking kettles have been found in village sites along the Atlantic coast from New England to the Carolinas. On the mainland, steatite was used for a variety of goods including gorgets (pendants), pipes, plummets, carved effigies, and atlatl weights (Fowler 1975:1, 5–6). The absence of steatite quarries on Long Island indicates that the material was imported, probably from southern New England where there are several abundant sources (1968:6–16). Steatite vessels on Long Island were used primarily in ceremonial sites or mortuaries. An explanation for this has been suggested by recent studies in California, the Southeast, and in the Mid-Atlantic areas (Klein 1995:5). In these areas, steatite vessels were part of an exchange system which gave them a value beyond their util-

Fig. 2.8. Steatite bowl

ity as cooking pots. The bowls were used during ritual gatherings and as indicators of social status. The bowls were scarce items involving a great deal of time and labor to produce. Ownership, therefore, demonstrated power and status for an individual or for a group.

**Mortuary Rituals**

The last centuries of the Archaic Period and the early centuries of the Early Woodland Period in what is now New York State (from 3,300 to about 2,700 B.P.) were marked by the use of steatite vessels in mortuary sites, a distinctive "fishtail" projectile point style (see fig. 2.2c), and the emergence of a religious cult on eastern Long Island (Ritchie 1969:150–79; 1965:74–78, 88–93; Boyd 1982:64). Chunks of steatite were fashioned into rectangular or oval bowls with a lug on each end. These bowls all have charcoal stains on the bottoms, indicating that they were used over a fire. Nearly all of them were found in burial sites, leading archaeologists to conclude that they may have been used to prepare a funeral feast in an elaborate mortuary ritual. The vessels were purposely broken or "killed" prior to burial, perhaps in accordance with a belief that this will release the spirits of the vessels to accompany the deceased in the next world.

Four of these mortuary sites have been excavated on the eastern forks of Long Island, two on the eastern-most end of the North Fork in Brown's Hills on Orient Point (Orient One and Orient Two), one on a hill in Jamesport, about twenty miles west of the Orient sites, and the fourth on the Sugar Loaf Hill in the Shinnecock Hills on the southern fork of Long Island, west of Southampton village (near the Shinnecock Reservation).[3] All of these sites were located near the crest of the hills on the southeastern slope.

Orient One, the first to be excavated, was a complex of twenty-five circular pits ranging from three to five feet in depth and about three feet in diameter. This discovery was made serendipitously in 1935 by some Boy Scouts who were building a cabin on Orient Point. They were digging for sand at a depth of five feet when they began to uncover celts (ungrooved axes) and quartz fishtail points. Roy Latham, an amateur archaeologist who lived near the site, was notified and he immediately recognized the importance of the discovery. Latham organized an excavation of what was to become one of the most significant archaeological discoveries in New York State.

On the floors of the pits were caches of grave goods which included fragments of steatite vessels, quartz fishtail projectile points, perforators, gorgets, and fire making kits (Latham 1935:4–5). The number of items in each cache ranged from four or five to more than thirty.[4] One of the pits contained the fragments of six steatite vessels, five of which had been placed in the pit upside down and then broken with a blow from a celt or some heavy tool. The sixth vessel, shaped differently from the others, was upright but had also been broken. This vessel had a handle on one end and a scoop opening on the other. Latham noted that the "scoop" was highly polished from long use, perhaps from moving sand. Most of the projectile points were fashioned from local quartz in the characteristic fishtail form which soon became a "diagnostic" trait for the last centuries of the Archaic period. Some of the artifacts in the pits, like the steatite vessels, had been ceremonially "killed," but large numbers of projectile points were undamaged (1978b:66).

After Latham completed his work on Orient One, he searched the surrounding area and soon made a much more dramatic discovery. A short distance from the cluster of pits, he located the second of the four ceremonial sites which came to be identified in the literature as expressions of an "Orient Burial Cult." Latham's excavation, which he designated "Orient Two," revealed a huge, oval-shaped pit about thirty feet long, twenty feet wide and five feet deep (1935a:1). Convinced that the eastern slopes of high hills were purposely selected for religious ceremonies, perhaps related to the rising sun, Latham searched eastern Long Island for more sites. Within a few years he found the sites at Jamesport and Sugar Loaf Hill. The excavations at these sites revealed large pit features similar to those at Orient Two. All three sites had oval-shaped pits about the same size which contained from twenty-eight to forty-one caches of artifacts, large deposits of red ocher, "sacred circles" of red ocher, stones, and mixtures of charcoal and cremated animal, bird, and human bone fragments, and extensive scatterings of charcoal and bone fragments sprinkled over the caches (1941:8).

One of the more striking aspects of these sites is that the cremated human remains were not concentrated in units indicating that they were from a single individual. Only one feature contained complete skeletal remains. This was an uncremated "bundle burial" of two adults which had been buried beneath the floor of the pit on the Orient Two site. The two skeletons had been compressed together into a bundle about eleven by sixteen inches and buried with a grooved ax stained with red ocher, a white quartz fishtail point, half of a pestle, and a steatite fragment from one of the largest pots in the pit (Latham 1935a:2).

The cremated human remains were often mixed with charcoal and cremated animal and bird bones. Apparently, the cremation "mixtures" were sprinkled over the caches, perhaps as some sort of consecration for the artifacts. The cremations appear to have taken place in another location and the remains carried to the sites for this purpose (Ritchie 1965:55). Although the mixtures were concentrated in a small area resembling a hearth, they were not true hearths because the sand underneath the features showed no signs of fire stains. Archaeologists have reported similar patterns of Late Archaic mortuary rituals in Massachusetts (Robbins 1963; Sautter 1966).

There was, however, at least one *in situ* fire at the Orient Two site. The hearth, located in the center of the pit floor, was oval-shaped, three and one-half feet wide by five feet in length. In association were three fire-stained stones seven to ten inches in diameter. There was an area of fire reddened sand underneath and a layer of charcoal over the bone material, suggesting to Latham that a fire had been rekindled over the bones (1935a:1). The other eighteen similar concentrations at Orient Two, Jamesport, and Sugar Loaf Hill which Latham also described as "hearths" or "crematories," however, were not associated with any evidence of fire (1935:2–3). It is possible that some fires were built in the sites but, once again, we are confronted with the difficulties inherent in such a meager data base.

Another intriguing theme is the presence of so much red ocher. Red ocher is generally believed to represent "life blood" and resurrection. Upper Paleolithic burials throughout Europe were often sprinkled with red ocher. Some of the burial rituals in both Europe and North America involved a complex process in which the body was exposed on a platform until the flesh decayed. Then the bones were cleaned, painted with red ocher, and buried in a leather bundle. The Choctaw in the Southeast were observed practicing this ceremony in the eighteenth century and some of the Late Archaic burials in the Midwest were stained with red ocher and graphite paints. Red paint was also used by the living as body decoration for ceremonial purposes. Several Late Archaic burial sites in Massachusetts contain red ochre deposits in association with human cremations (Mellgrin 1959:47). Red ocher is such a powerful symbol that it continued to be used in Indian burials as late as the nineteenth century (Robbins 1956:18–22).

There was a total of twenty-four deposits of red ocher in the large pits at Orient Two, Jamesport, and Sugar Loaf Hill. Eighteen of the red ocher deposits were in clumps which ranged in size from small concentrations to large masses containing more than a bushel of red ocher. There were three of these large masses, one in each of the pits.[5] Red ocher stains were found on an ax and on two hammerstones, which had apparently been used to powder the small hematite nodules. These nodules, or "paint pots," are found in abundance on Long Island. Latham believed, however, that the small nodules were not the source of the "earthy" red ocher in the large deposits. That material, he said, was not found locally and had, therefore, to have been imported from the mainland (1935).

Clearly, these large red ocher deposits had some unique ceremonial function. Latham suggested that they may have been communal offerings to all of the honored dead in the site (ibid.). The presence of a single large deposit of such a highly valued ceremonial item at each site does indicate that there was some very important religious purpose intended, but the nature of that purpose remains a mystery.

Six of the red ocher deposits were in the form of "sacred circles" around caches. One of the circles in the Sugar Loaf Hill site was about fifteen inches in diameter and three inches wide (Latham 1936:4). Unfortunately, Latham's notes give no data which would help to explain why these particular graves were so honored. Cache seven at Sugar Loaf Hill, for example, was enclosed in a red ocher circle about a foot in diameter and included three nodules of hematite, a flint chip, three projectile points, and a small round pebble (C. Goddard 1936). The number and nature of the artifacts in the caches does not distinguish them from the other caches in the four sites. Ritchie found a "streak" of red ocher twenty inches long, three inches wide and one inch thick at the Jamesport site which may have been part of a similar feature. There were also three circular features made from stones: one at Orient Two made from cobblestones enclosing a cache of crushed hematite, an adze, and some fishtail points; and two at Jamesport. One of the Jamesport circles, made from small red sandstone slabs and about a yard in diameter, enclosed three steatite pot sherds, an assortment of stone tools, and a concentration of charcoal and bone fragments. Latham concluded that the red sandstone may have been chosen to express the same ceremonial concept as the red ocher (1940:3).

Roy Latham's work on the burial sites soon came to the attention of New York State Archaeologist William Ritchie, who studied the artifacts and features described in Latham's field notes. Ritchie, a meticulous professional, was appalled at Latham's crude techniques and unsystematic records, but he recognized the importance of the sites and was able to provide scientific dates. It was not until two decades later, however, that Ritchie was able to place them in the larger context of Archaic mortuary traditions in the Northeast.

In 1951, Ritchie found pit graves containing red ocher, mixtures of charcoal and cremated human remains, fire kits, projectile points, and other tools on a ridge above Lake Muskalonge near the Saint Lawrence River (1955:61–65). The following year, he excavated a similar site a few miles away on Red Lake. During the fall of 1953, Ritchie came to Long Island and re-excavated the Jamesport site. He found two more caches of grave offering and the charred remains of deer and fowl. These, he suggested, may have been part of a funeral feast or food sacrifice (1965:76–77).

By the end of 1953, Ritchie felt confident enough to define the general outline of a religious system shared by Indian peoples from the Great Lakes to Long Island and south to the Potomac River (1955:61–65, 80–84). He continued to work on Long Island for three more years, excavating the Stony Brook site mentioned above and re-excavating Sugar Loaf Hill. Ritchie was now able to provide a chronology for the mortuary cult based on radiocarbon tests. The burials had been placed in these Long Island hills over a three hundred year period from 3,000 B.P. until 2,700 B.P. (1969:75). These dates suggest that the mortuary cult may have been part of a cultural transition from the Archaic Period to the Early Woodland Period.

In 1965, when he published his classic study of New York state archaeology, he described the Orient burials as a "burial cult" and listed several shared traits (Ritchie 1969:175–78). These characteristics, revealed in the excavations by Latham and Ritchie, include: burials on the eastern slopes of high ground overlooking bodies of water; cremation burials, both individual and large; communal pit burials; an inhumation ceremony, which often included a communal feast or the sacrifice of animals; a belief in the sacredness of red ocher, perhaps as a symbol of life blood; small "sacred circles" of stones or bands of red ocher enclosing burials; and a belief that fire was a vital sacrament for the deceased. This list certainly does not do justice to the beliefs and rituals it describes.

The circle is a powerful, universal symbol in human culture. It is most commonly related to the sun and the moon. The ancient Greeks saw the circle as the one pure form. In Native America, most traditional people believed in the magical potency of the circle symbol. According to anthropologist Robert Hall, "The very geometry of the circle contributes to the magical effect." The Prairie Potowatomi and the Cherokee both believed that a circle made with ashes or sand around an area would protect it from harmful spirits. A circle of bright red sand enclosed one of the Wisconsin burial mounds, and the Early Woodland mounds in Ohio were frequently enclosed in a circular earthen embankment (1976:360–64).

Although no more Archaic burial sites have been found on Long Island since 1956, several were excavated in southern New England between 1960 and 1975. These excavations revealed similar patterns, artifacts, and features on sites which were several centuries older than the Orient burials. The Bear Swamp site near Berkeley, Massachusetts, for example, is about 4,640 years old (Dincauze 1975:28). Dena Dincauze, an anthropologist from the University of Massachusetts who has studied these sites, concluded that the Orient burial cult may represent the later stages of a burial cult which had originated in what is now eastern Massachusetts (1968:83; 1975:30).

Dincauze also offered a hypotheses about the social function of the burial rituals. She began by noting that a distinction should be made between burials and graves in these Archaic sites. A burial might not include human remains at all, whereas a grave was primarily a repository for a deceased human being. A grave, therefore, would include the complete or nearly complete remains of at least one individual. Most of the cremated remains in the burials are scattered among other artifacts, indicating that they may have been a sacrament blessing the offering rather than the grave of a specific individual. The cremated remains with the caches of artifacts, noted Dincauze, " rarely appear to be more significant than any other inclusions, and we may be going too far in suggesting that the deposition of the human remains was the primary purpose of the features" (1975:31–32).

What, then, was the purpose of these burials? Dincauze suggests that they may have been part of a seasonal ritual related to the solstice (1975:31). Such periodic ceremonies serve in all human societies as *rites of intensification,* validating group membership and renewing communal ties. She cautiously notes, however, that this is only a speculation. James Tuck, an archaeologist who has done extensive work on mortuary sites in eastern Canada, also suggested that these rituals were validation rites which served to solidify a community facing the stress of social disorder or a natural disaster that depleted food resources (1975:76). The burials, he suggested, may have been a group effort to placate the spiritual powers and ask for their help. William Ritchie also noted the "pervading aura of high religious drama" he sensed about the sites. "There is also," he continued, "a good deal of lost symbolism, some of it of a more universal nature, in which high places, the east, the sun, fire, and red ocher figure as elements of a vigorous religious movement" (1969:178).

## Summary

The archaeological record has provided us with a dim outline of the Native American lifeways which evolved from the time of arrival on Long Island until about 2,700 B.P. The Paleo-Indians came to hunt here and left very little trace of their passing. Only a few of their characteristic fluted projectile points have been found to indicate the presence of these small bands of intrepid hunters. The dog had become a part of camp life, serving as a scavenger, an alarm system, and, if the hunt failed, an emergency food supply.

During the Archaic period, permanent village communities established themselves along the banks of freshwater streams where they flowed into tide water bays rich in shellfish. The men hunted and fished as the women gathered an abundance of nuts, fruits, and tubers from the woodlands. Their tool kits included axes, adzes, drills, hammerstones, quartz blades and points, fire making implements, and atlatls (spearthrowers). The tools were used to make their wigwams, canoes, baskets, mats, and a variety of bone and wood utensils.

The excavations of the hilltop cemeteries on the eastern end of Long Island have provided rich insights into the development of religious ceremonialism. Although we cannot learn much about the specific content of the belief system, we can see clear evidence of an elaborate ritual which undoubtedly served important social functions. More research is needed, however, before any further interpretations can be made.

Fig. 3.1. Eliza Fowler Beaman, Montaukett herbalist, who informed ethnographers about ancient remedies (see p. 65). She is shown with her husband Anthony Beaman (Shinnecock) at a Shinnecock Powwow, c. 1950.

# 3

# The Early and Middle Woodland Periods, 3,000–1,000 B.P.

The lifeways of the people on Long Island did not change dramatically after 3,000 B.P., but there were some innovations which mark a shift from the Archaic Period. The more important and best documented of these was the widespread use of pottery which had been introduced during the last centuries of the Archaic Period (Kraft 1978:154). During the centuries referred to by some archaeologists as the "Early Woodland Period" (3,000–2,000 B.P.), the Indians in eastern North America perfected a ceramic technology which greatly facilitated the storage and preparation of food. Evidence of other innovations and changes which increased the "forest efficiency" of peoples throughout eastern North America is limited for Long Island, but we do know that sometime around 2,000 years ago, new styles in pottery and projectile points emerged which mark a transition to the Middle Woodland Period.

## The Pottery Revolution

The origin of pottery in North America remains a mystery. The earliest ceramics were found along the Gulf Coast from what is now Florida to Mississippi (Muller 1978:290-91). It is possible that the invention of ceramics occurred here around 3,700 B.P. and spread north, but it is just as likely that many villagers throughout North America discovered the process on their own. These inventors probably experimented with different methods over an extended period of time.[1] The innovation which made the development of a ceramic technology possible was a discovery. The addition of small amounts of sand, "grit" (crushed igneous, sedimentary, and metamorphic stone), crushed shells, or plant fiber temper would bond with the clay to strengthen the vessel walls and prevent the clay from cracking or crumbling when fired (Shepard 1968:26–27).

The walls of the vessels were thick, cord-marked inside and out, and the bottoms were pointed (cone-shaped) rather than flat. As the ceramic artisans became more experienced and sophisticated, they produced vessels with thinner walls, which were decorated with geometric designs.

Thick-walled, grit-tempered pottery has been found on sites along the north shore of Long Island from Flushing Bay to Shoreham, and at Hands Creek on Three Mile Harbor near East Hampton. The pottery from sites at North Beach on the west side of Flushing Bay, at Matinecock Point near Glen Cove, and at Pelham Boulder in Pelham Bay Park were studied by Carlyle Smith, the first professional archaeologist to develop a chronology for prehistoric Long Island

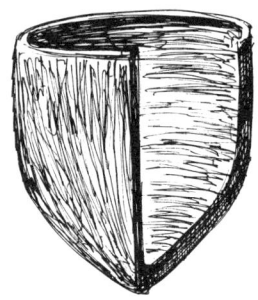 

Fig. 3.2. North Beach interior cord-marked pottery (*left*) and cord-wrapped paddle marking technique (*right*)

(1950:107,135; 1982a:238–39). Smith identified a "North Beach" style characterized by thick, elongate, straight walls; grit temper; pointed bottoms; and straight or slightly flared, unmarked rims (see fig. 3.2). The interior and exterior walls were marked with impressions which appear to have been made by a cord-wrapped stick. Small amounts of this pottery have been found at many sites on Long Island, mixed in with materials from a later period. Archaeologists have concluded that some artisans continued to produce "old style" vessels long after they had gone out of fashion (Smith 1950:181; Lopez 1982:241).

We can never be certain about the techniques used by the villagers to produce the pottery found at North Beach and the other Early Woodland sites on Long Island, but we can draw from a considerable body of data compiled by archaeologists, anthropologists, and ethnographers to reconstruct a general description of the process (Wilbur 1978:39-42; 1990:84-86; Parker 1927:84-89; Russell 1980:62-64; Howes 1954:82-86; Shepard 1968:50-94). The inventors and ceramic artisans were probably women who experimented with clay in the routine of storing and cooking food.

We have some interesting insights into the pottery process from a site report by Mark Harrington who excavated a Shinnecock village at the Sebonac site near the present-day reservation in 1902. Harrington, who was sponsored by the American Museum of Natural History, found the remains of a potter's workshop and was able to reconstruct the stages of pottery manufacture:

> In one pit, we were lucky enough to find the greater part of a potter's outfit, which shed considerable light on the Shinnecock method of making earthenware. The first stage was illustrated by a lump of raw clay and some clay thoroughly mixed with the crushed shells . . . used as a tempering material; the second, by pieces of clay coils and part of a small unfinished vessel, all preserved by accidental burning, which showed that the clay had been worked out into long rolls with which the vessel was then built up, coil on coil, the coils being smoothed and blended as the work proceeded. The pit even yielded some tools with which the blending was done, in the shape of two beach pebbles showing wear and still daubed with clay. In other parts of the site were

found clay-covered shells of the "hen clam," the worn edges of which showed long use for such purposes (1977a:55).

A few years later, Harrington observed some Cawtaba Indians in North Carolina who were still making pottery by the same method (1977a:57). He noted that the Catawba rolled out the coils, shaped them into vessels, and blended the walls with wet pebbles and fresh water clam shells. The potters dried the vessels for a few days in the shade and then placed them around a fire with their mouths to the flames. When the pots darkened, indicating that they were hot enough, they removed the burning wood and carefully set the vessels, mouth down, into the hot coals. Then they pushed the coals up around the pots and piled dry pine bark over them. The bark quickly ignited into an extemely hot flash fire. After the fire ebbed, they pulled the pots out to the edge of the hearth where they could cool slowly.

Arthur C. Parker (Gawaso Wanneh), the Iroquois ethnographer, described the process as an incorporation of four sacred elements: earth, water, air, and fire (1927:84). The first stage of the process involved earth and water and the final stages of drying and firing required air and fire. For the Indian, therefore, the process was more than a mechanical operation, it was a reverent manipulation of the four elements.

Parker also contributed to our understanding of the grit tempering process. The grit, which could be composed of one or more of the following materials—granite, quartz, steatite, mica, iron pyrite, or sand—was pulverized and mixed with the clay. "In mixing the tempering material," wrote Parker, "some workers spread out the clay in flat sheets, sprinkled it thoroughly with temper, folded the clay, repeated the process, and then kneaded it with stone pounders or wooden billets" (1927:86).

The unusual cone-shaped bottom on some prehistoric vessels always draws comments from people who see these pots for the first time. Predictably they ask, "why make a vessel that you can't stand up?" Actually we are not sure why. Several theories have been offered. The pots were well designed for use as storage vessels which were often buried about halfway into the ground to keep them cooler. It is also possible that the cone shape allowed the heat from the fire to cook the ingredients of the pot more effectively. Herbert Kraft noted that the rounded bottoms were stronger than the flat bottoms and were less likely to separate from the vessel (September 1995: pers. com.). They must have had some form of support when in use for cooking. John White, the artist who lived briefly in the ill-fated colony of Roanoke, drew a picture of a cone-shaped pot supported in the cooking fire with logs (Hariot 1972: plate 15). Another possibility is that stones, in the form of a tripod, supported the vessel (Kraft, April 1995: pers. com.).

## New Styles and Innovations in Ceramics and Stone Tools

About 2,000 years ago, new pottery styles, which mark a transition from Early Woodland to Middle Woodland, began to appear in the Northeastern woodlands. The changes in ceramic technology and style were first documented by Carlyle Smith when he excavated the Clearview site on the north shore of Long Island near Whitestone in Queens (1950:134-35). The site is located directly across the East River from the Schurz and Pelham Bay sites in the Bronx and a few miles east of the North Beach site. The pottery here tended to have more shell temper than the earlier pottery, and there were some changes in style.[2] Some of the vessels at Clearview were marked with "dentate" (indented) stamping on both the interior and exterior walls, made, perhaps, by a wooden comb. The dentate marks on the interior walls were set horizontally in contrast to the vertical lines on the outside. Other vessels were decorated with brush marks or fabric impressions. The artisans living in the villages along the north shore were departing from the conservative styles of the past.

The most striking innovations were found on pottery from the Oakland Lake site near Little Neck Bay (Kaeser 1978:263-68). Influenced by ceramic styles from the Delaware River area, the Oakland Lake potters began decorating vessels with incised geometric designs, dentated patterns, cord markings, and net impressions on an unmarked background. The designs were separated and highlighted by blank spaces or "zones," a style first identified at the Abbott Farm site on the Delaware River near present-day Trenton, New Jersey, by Dorothy Cross (Lopez 1982a:253; Cross 1956, vol. 2). "Abbott-style" pottery has been found on sites from the Delaware River in the west to Suffolk County in the east (Lopez 1982a:254).

There were some minor changes in projectile point styles, but the stemmed, corner, and side notched points continued to be used. One significant variation was a stemmed lance-shaped point style identified as "Fox Creek" after a site on Fox Creek in Schoharie County, New York (see fig. 2.2d). These points have become recognized as a reliable chronological marker for the Middle Woodland period in New Jersey and on Long Island (Silver 1991:263; Kraft 1986:105-13). Many of these Fox Creek-style points were made of gray and purple argillite (sandstone with a high percentage of clay) imported from what is now western New Jersey and eastern Pennsylvania (Venuto 1982a:140). Excavations at the

Fig. 3.3. Abbott-style "zoned" pottery

Oakland Lake site uncovered a cache of argillite "blanks" which had been brought here for local craftsmen to work down into points or other small tools (1982:131). Long Island artisans were always eager to find any alternative to the local quartz for their tools and points. The larger significance here is the clear evidence that the Oakland Lake villagers were part of an extensive trade network that included communities in present-day New Jersey and Pennsylvania.

## Forest Efficiency

The Long Island villagers lived in the middle of a natural "shopping mall" complete with bountiful supermarket, pharmacy, clothing, hardware, and jewelry outlets. The term, "forest efficiency," was first used by Joseph Caldwell to describe his theoretical model for pre-horticultural settlements in North America (1958). Caldwell, whose contributions to anthropological theory are widely recognized, developed this analytical approach to study the groups who lived in year-round villages prior to the emergence of horticulture.

Horticulture is distinguished from agriculture on the basis of technology. Agriculture involves more complex forms of tools, irrigation systems, and extensive acreage. Horticulturists, in contrast, use simple digging sticks to cultivate small village plots. Scholars writing during the early decades of the twentieth century had presumed that there was a direct cause and effect relationship between year-round settlement patterns and dependence upon horticulture. The reason people settled down, it was argued, was because the crops needed to be tended on a regular basis. When Caldwell and others studying the elaborate earthworks and ceremonial centers of the Adena and Hopewell in the midwestern United States could find no trace of maize horticulture at these sites, they abandoned the old model and came to appreciate the highly efficient methods used by these ancient settlers to harvest food, extract medicine, and make tools from the forests, streams, and meadows.

Let us consider first the "supermarket" which provided the food. In order to have a balanced diet, five classes of nutrients —carbohydrates, proteins, fats, vitamins, and minerals—in addition to water are required. Many wild plants and fauna in the Long Island ecosystem contain nutrients from several classes. Table 3.1 lists the categories and natural sources of the nutrients which have been documented in the

Fig. 3.4. Women gathering wild plants

## Table 3.1
### Sources of Nutrients in Indian Diet

| Carbohydrates | Proteins and Fats | Vitamins | Minerals |
|---|---|---|---|
| ground nut (*Apios Americana*) | black walnut (*Juglans nigra*) butternut (*Juglans cinerea*) | lambs quarters (*Chenopodium album*) A, B, and E | oysters, shrimp, clams (calcium, iodine) |
| pond lily (*Nymphaea*) | hickory (*Carya glabra*) | pokeweed (*Phytolacca americana*) A, B, and D | green leaf plants (calcium) |
| Jerusalem artichoke (root) (*Helianthus tuberosus*) | white oak acorn (*Quercus alba*) | berries, beach plum, grape, cranberry, strawberrry Vitamin C | hickory nuts (Phosphorus) |
| arrowhead (*Sagittaria latifolia*) | game animals fish, fowl | animal and fish liver Vitamin A, D | game animals, fish, fowl (copper and phosphorus) |

archaeological and ethnographic records (Silver 1991:58-60; Gwynne 1982; Denton 1968:2-7; Tantaquidgeon 1977; Carr and Westez 1980; Harrington 1977:5; Kavasch 1994:5-12). This list is only a representative sample of the foods available to the native peoples on Long Island.

The primary hunting and trapping season was in the fall and winter when the game was fat and their fur was thick. The deer were vulnerable during this season because of their preoccupation with mating and their preference for white oak acorns. The deer could easily be located near the white oak stands feeding on the thin-shelled, sweet acorns, which begin to drop in early September. About a month later, the mating season begins and reaches a peak in late October.

Indians in the Northeast employed several strategies for hunting deer (Kraft 1986:157; Rountree 1989:39-42; Russell 1980:178-79). The best known, and most romantic strategy, was to stalk the deer, pitting the hunter's knowledge and skill against the deer's instinct for survival. Hunters often covered themselves with deer skins and crawled close enough to get an easy shot at the unsuspecting prey. A successful hunter was accorded high status within his community.

A much more productive strategy was to form a large hunting party and either encircle the deer or drive them into a pond or tidal bay where they could easily be killed from canoes. David De Vries, a Dutch merchant who lived in New Netherland from 1633 to 1643, described this strategy by a hunting party:

> They stand a hundred paces more or less from each other, and holding flat thigh-bones in the hand, beat then with a stick, and so drive the creatures before them into the river . . . When the animals swim into

the river, the savages lie in their canoes with lassos, which they throw around their necks (1909:220).[3]

Although there are no accounts of the use of fire by the Long Island Indians to surround or drive the deer, it is well documented in adjacent areas (Kraft 1986:156; Rountree 1989:40; Ewan 1970:385). Hunters formed a circle about five miles in radius and slowly collapsed the circle trapping the deer and disorienting them with smoke and loud noise. A wall of fire could be used effectively to drive the deer into the water as well. Fires were also set routinely in the fall after the wild plants were harvested to clear the forest undergrowth for the hunters. These fires had a positive ecological effect which has been recognized recently by environmentalists (Mitchell 1978:26). The burning process stimulates the spring growth of wild plants and kills the ticks.

Smaller game animals such as raccoon, rabbit, and squirrel, were also a regular part of the diet. These smaller animals were caught in snares or trapped. In addition to their flesh, raccoons provided grease for cooking and fur for winter clothing. The raccoon grease was also rubbed on the skin for warmth in the winter and to protect against mosquitoes and sunburn in the summer (Kraft 1986:129, 157).

Water fowl was another important source of protein and minerals in the diet. From August until October great flocks of southbound geese and ducks stopped to rest and feed in the coastal wetlands. In the spring they returned north, stopping once again in the salt marshes and tidal bays of Long Island. Daniel Denton, writing in 1670, reported that there was a "great store of . . . cranes, geese of several sorts, brants, ducks, widgeon, teal, and diverse others" (1968:5). Hunters used nets and snares to capture these game birds in great numbers. When the English arrived with their guns they were astounded at the amount they could kill with relative ease. A colonial account from southern New England in 1648

Fig. 3.5. Women shelling and smoking clams

reported that, "It is incredible what multitudes of them are killed daily. It was ordinary for one man to kill eight or ten dozen in half a day" (quoted by Russell 1980:91).

Although game birds and animals were a primary source of protein in the Indians' diet, large quantities of fish and shellfish were also consumed. The coastal waters provide a steady, year-round, predictable supply of food. Oysters and clams are relatively easy to harvest, even during the winter. The Atlantic blue crab is available until late November when it digs down in the mud and hibernates for the winter. In the fall and winter, bay scallops, bluefish, stripers, blackfish, and flounder are plentiful (Gwynne 1982:94). Some remains of Atlantic sturgeon *(Acipenser oxyrhyshus)* have also been found in archaeological sites on Long Island (Lopez and Wisniewski 1978a:240), but these large fish much prefer the waters of the lower Hudson where they come to spawn in the spring. Although the commercial fishermen go out offshore for flounder in the early spring, these fish can be taken all winter long from the shallow waters of the bays on the south shore of Long Island (Mades, January 17, 1995: pers. com.). The flounder, unlike most fish, prefers to spawn in the cold winter months. In the spring the Indians harvested the alewives, shad, striped bass, and other fish which came into the freshwater streams to spawn (Kraft 1986:76-78; Rountree 1989:34-38; Denton 1968:5-6).

Beached whales, dolphins, seals and other small sea mammals, were also plentiful. Denton reported in 1670 that "an innumerable multitude of seals, which make an excellent oyle," were vulnerable during the winter when they "haul out" onto sand bars in the tidal bays to sun themselves (1968:6). Kevin McBride reported finding significant amounts of seal bone in his excavation of a site on Block Island (McBride, 1994: pers. com.).

Another important source of protein and minerals are the nuts from hickory, white oak, walnut, butternut, and chestnut trees (Cassedy 1995; George 1995; Wiegand 1995). The white oak acorn, in particular, is a very easy nut to process. It resembles the pecan in size and has a paper-thin shell. This acorn is much sweeter than the red and black oak acorns, which must be boiled several times to remove the bitter taste of the tannic acid. The white oak acorns can be parched and ground into a flour, mixed with blueberries and baked or boiled in a stew with other ingredients (Rountree 1989:41, 44, 53; Russell 1980:83; Kraft 1986:80). According to Captain John Smith of Virginia, the Powhatan Indians relied on acorns, chestnuts, and walnuts to sustain them through the winter (Barbour 1986, 1:151; 2:116).

Daniel Denton described an abundance of fruits and berries in 1670, including grapes, mulberries, huckleberries, cranberries, plums and raspberries. He wrote, "In June the fields and woods are died red" with the fruits of the strawberry (1968:3-4). Such wild foods as nuts, berries, meat, and fish are familiar to most readers, but the tubers and greens are probably not as recognizable because they were never adopted by the European colonists. Even though these plants still

*The Early and Middle Woodland Periods, 3,000-1,000 B.P.*  63

Fig. 3.6. Wild plant foods. *a.* Strawberry; *b.* Blackberry; *c.* White Oak; *d.* Butternut; *e.* Hickory; *f.* Jerusalem Artichoke Roots; *g.* Gound Nut Roots

thrive on Long Island, they are generally ignored or destroyed as "weeds." The ground nut, for example, is an all but forgotten tuber, yet it continued to be a major food source among the Shinnecocks long after the arrival of the Europeans. The small, thin, twining vine thrives in damp soil and produces a string of tubers on its root system about the size of hen's eggs (Beardsley, 1940:507). The plant is similar in taste, texture, and carbohydrate content to the potato but has three times the protein. Some Shinnecocks still gather and eat this ancient food source today. Lamont Smith, a Shinnecock, adds them to his succotash, which he sells along with clams and sassafrass tea at the annual Shinnecock Powwow.

The Southampton and East Hampton town records mention problems with Indians who were constantly digging holes for ground nuts in the area near the white settlements. In 1654 the Town of Southampton passed a law prohibiting Indians from digging up the tubers on lands ceded to whites. The penalty was a public humiliation in the stocks for the first offense and a whipping for the second (Thompson 1918, 2:152). These were rather extreme measures for such an offense. The harvesting of the tubers, which grow about three inches under the soil, would certainly not have done much damage to the land. A likely explanation is that the collection of tubers might have been regarded by the English as a challenge to the boundaries of their land claims. The views of the Shinnecocks are not documented, but it may be that they were simply reluctant to give up the ground nut in their daily diet.

Ground nuts were a favorite among Native American communities throughout the Northeast and were eaten by the Pilgrims during the first year at Plymouth. The Lenapes served ground nuts dipped in raccoon fat to a European captive who reported that they tasted like sweet potatoes. They were also eaten raw, boiled, roasted in coals, and dried. The Menomini put the dried tubers in maple syrup and stored them for the winter. The English, however, found the ground nut to be too slow in maturing and too difficult to harvest (Beardsley 1940:513).

The Jerusalem artichoke is better known than the ground nut, but it is generally regarded as a nuisance to be weeded out. This plant grows in disturbed soil, a characteristic which may account for its early discovery by the Indian villagers. The women probably noticed them near the wigwams and began to experiment with them. For the Native Americans, the tuber roots, which can be harvested in the late fall and even during the winter thaws, were a highly valued source of carbohydrates. The plant could be left in a natural storage for the winter months when other food supplies might run low. Some Shinnecocks still gather Jerusalem artichokes today. Josephine Smith from the Shinnecock Reservation prepares Jerusalem artichokes in a salad with diced scallions, nut oil, cider vinegar, honey, mint leaves, and greens. Other tubers, pond lilies, arrowhead (duck potato), cattails, and solomon's seals, can all be prepared by boiling or roasting, just as one would prepare a potato. Readers who are interested in experimenting with recipes for wild plants should consult Barrie Kavasch's *Native Harvests Recipes* (1979) and David Hunt's *Native Indian Wild Game, Fish and Wild Foods Cookbook* (1992).

The green leafed plants are an extremely important source of nutrients. Most of the plants listed are rich in vitamins C, E, K, B complex, and in minerals such as iron, magnesium, copper, and calcium. They require very little preparation; in fact, they are most nutritious when eaten raw. Chenopodium (also called lamb's quarters and goosefoot) has been documented on prehistoric sites throughout the Northeast. Early Woodland peoples in the Connecticut Valley regarded chenopodium so highly that they placed seeds in a grave as a final gift to the deceased for the trip to the spirit world (McBride and Dewar 1987:308).

Chenopodium flourishes in disturbed soil, as any gardener in the Northeast can tell you, but it gets little respect today. This nutritious relative of domestic spinach is usually pulled up and tossed away. The Indians, however, knew that chenopodium provided them with tasty leaves and seeds. In the spring and summer the green leaves and stems could be eaten as a salad or cooked in water and in the late fall the tiny seeds could be gathered and ground into a flour paste or a cereal gruel. The plant contains rich amounts of Vitamin A, calcium, B1(thiamine), B2 (riboflavin), and niacin (Angier 1974:126).

Pokeweed was another important green, but it required very careful processing. The plant had to be gathered in the spring before it matured because the mature plant is toxic. If the small, tender shoots and leaves are harvested before the plant reaches a height of eight inches, they make safe salad greens. This variety of greens enabled the village women to organize their harvest strategies and ensure a regular supply from April to November. The milkweed and pokeweed are best suited for an early spring harvest, sorrel in mid-summer, amaranth in the fall, and the basic staple, chenopodium, all season long.

Nature's pharmacy was also very well stocked with medicinal supplies as Table 3.2 indicates. When the Europeans arrived, they were quick to adopt Native American herbal medicines, although they made little mention of the debt in their records. Recent studies by contemporary scientists have documented over 800 species of plants growing in the eastern United States as having some medicinal value (Foster and Duke 1990:1). We will limit our discussion here, as we did with the food sources, to a few well documented native remedies for common health problems (Angier 1978; Tantaquidgeon 1977; Vogel 1973; Foster and Duke 1990; Moerman 1986; Duke 1986).

The medicinal qualities of these plants were discovered through centuries of experimentation and the information was stored in oral traditions. These traditions were probably kept by women because they were more familiar with the plants in the ecosystem (Hoffman 1885-86:159). As they foraged for the daily meals, the women studied the characteristics of all the plants in the area and passed this information along to their daughters. The women who mastered this body of knowledge and could accurately identify the sources of important cures must have gained considerable status in their communities. They were also respected because they knew which plants could kill or bring a painful illness to an enemy. The women knew what worked, but probably assumed that the particular plant was effective because it had a spiritual power of its own which could overcome the disease causing spiritual force. Daniel Denton said the Indians told him that, "there is no disease common to the country, but may be cured without materials from other nations" (1968:4).

Shinnecock and Montaukett women were still using herbal remedies in the early twentieth century. Eliza Beamon (see fig. 3.1, p. 54 above), whose mother was a Montaukett, and Ada Bunn, a Shinnecock, described their herbal remedies for coughs, fever, diarrhea, headaches, and sore muscles to ethnographers J. D. Carr and Carlos Westez (1980:279). Two Montaukett women, Olive and Carolyn Pharaoh, remember the herbal lore passed along to them from their great-grandmother, Maria Pharaoh (Rabito-Wyppensenwah and Abiuso 1993:586).

Plants were also used to deal with annoying insects. Extracts of bloodroot *(Sanguinaria canadensis)* and gold seal *(Hydrastis canadensis)* mixed with bear grease were excellent insect repellants. Lice and other similar parasites were doused with a solution made by boiling the roots of American hellebore *(Veratrum viride)*; (Vogel 1973:301-2; 340-41).

### Table 3.2
### Medicinal Properties of Local Wild Plants

| Problem | Plant | Application | Source |
|---|---|---|---|
| bleeding | yarrow (*Achillea milleforum*) | leaves steeped in water | Angier 1978:316 |
| burns | bracken fern (*Pteridium aquilinum*) | root poultice | Foster and Duke 1990:308 |
| cardiovascular | hawthorne (*Crataegus*) | tonic dilates blood vessels | Angier 1978:134 |
| childbirth | sawbrier (*Smilax glauca*) | root tea taken to expel afterbirth | Foster and Duke 1990:296 |
| diarrhea | dogwood (*Cornus florida*) blackberry root (*Rubus hispidis*) | root bark tea root tea | Foster and Duke 1990:270 Carr and Westez 1980:280 |
| fever | boneset (*Eupatorium perfoliatum*) | Leaf and root tea | Tantaquidgeon 1977:33 |
| headache | willow (*Salix*) | bark tea (salix = aspirin) | Vogel 1973:379-80 |
| infection | white oak (*Quercus alba*) | inner bark tea; mold on acorns is an antibiotic | Angier 1978:185-86; Foster and Duke 1990:278 |
| rash | yellow jewelweed. (*Impatiens pallida*) | juice from the leaves and stem | Foster and Duke 1990:106 |
| pain | pokeweed (*Phytolacca Americana*) | root poultice | Angier 1978:199 |
| cough | sweetgrass (*Hierchole odorata*) white pine (*Pinus strobus*) | leaves boiled into tea chew pitch from tree | Foster and Duke 1990:314 Carr and Westez 1980:281 |

The forest also provided the materials necessary for tools, utensils, dyes, and housing (Silver 1991:71). Bluestem grass *(Andropogon gerardi)* was used to line their storage pits and mats were woven from cattails. The manufacture of clothing and the construction of housing and other structures required tough, durable material for binding. Thread and twine from hemp, milkweed, and false nettle fibers or strips of elm, cedar, and hickory bark, as well as grape vines served this purpose very well. The first European settlers often purchased hemp *(Apocynum cannabinum)* ropes from the Indians because they believed them to be superior to those made from European plant fibers (Hostek 1976:62). Hickory, white oak, and red cedar woods were used for tools and construction. Hickory and red cedar staves and posts formed the frames for the wigwams which were then covered with bark and mats. Wood from the white oak was used for canoes, paddles, and splints for baskets (Tantaquidgeon 1977:80).

The baskets and mats were probably decorated with dyes made from plants and earth pigments. The first English settlers in New England praised the Indian basket makers for their skillful use of colors and their artful designs (Russell 1980:60). Adriaen van der Donck described the use of dyes and paints by Indians in New Netherland (1968:37-39). The Dutch observer reported that the Indians made their colors from both plants and minerals. They carried these paints in small bags, keeping separate the red, blue, green, brown, white, black and yellow colors. They made the brightest of these colors from minerals, "which they know how to prepare by pounding, rubbing and grinding." All of the paints were apparently mixed with animal fat, because they felt quite greasy. Red and yellow ocher, of course, were important sources of pigment. The red ocher color could be intensified by heating or burning the ore.

Although Van der Donck did not observe the production of pigment from minerals, he did witness the process used to make the color purple from a plant. Unfortunately, his description of the plant is not precise enough for an identification. He said it resembled orache or "golden herb," which he had seen in Europe, but that the plant was larger than the orache and produced clusters of brown and red berries. Orache *(Atriplex patula)* in North America more closely resembles lambs quarters *(Chenopodium album)* and does not produce berries; the only plant sources of dark blue or purple listed by Douglas Leechman in his study of North American plant dyes are blueberry, elderberry, grape, and currants (1969:26-27).

In spite of Van der Donck's failure to identify the plant, he did document the process in some detail:

> The Indians bruise, and press out the juice, and pour the same on flat pieces of bark, about six feet long and three broad, prepared for the purpose; these are placed in the sun to dry out the moisture. If it does not dry out fast enough, or if they intend to remove, which they frequently do in the summer, then they heat smooth stones, and place the same into the juice of the berries on the bark, and thus they dry out the moisture speedily. The dry substance which remains on the bark is then scraped out, and put into small bags for use. This produces the finest purple color I have ever seen (1968:38).

The dried scrapings are then added to water and the paint can be applied to the mats, baskets, and hides, or used as body paint.

Two Shinnecock baskets in the National Museum of the American Indian, which were collected in 1902 by the Heye Foundation, have colored designs made from plant dyes (Stone and Smith, et al. 1983:291-93). The technology and craft involved is undoubtedly very ancient. The universal human fascination with color for decoration and symbolism suggests that experimentation with the production of paints and dyes may even predate the Archaic Period. It is very likely, therefore, that these early basket makers on Long Island understood how to make colors and dye textiles.

The dyeing process is divided into three stages, beginning with the production of the dye. The northeastern environment may have limited the number and intensity of the colors used by prehistoric artisans. Most of the shades, according to Arthur Parker, were soft variations of six or seven colors. This may explain why the Indians were so struck by the brightly colored textiles brought here by the Europeans (Parker 1927:67). Van der Donck, however, noted an exception to the soft colors described by Parker. He described a brilliant scarlet dye used to color woven strands of hair which, "excites our astonishment and curiosity." It was, he continued, "so well fixed that rain, sun, and wind not change it . . . such beautiful red was never dyed in the Netherlands with materials known to us" (1968:39). Unfortunately, Van der Donck and the other colonial observers did not identify the specific plants used by the Indians, but the sources shown in Table 3.3 would have been available to them (Parker 1927:66; Leechman 1969).

The brief list in Table 3.3 may not do justice to the Archaic basket makers, who might have developed many other natural sources of dyes and pigments which were never documented. The red color, so admired by Van der Donck, was particularly difficult to make and the process was often kept secret. Black was made from a mixture of charcoal and graphite. Craftsmen from the Lenapes, who lived along the Mid-Atlantic coast and on western Long Island, dyed a deerskin so skillfully that the black color lasted for over a century (Parker 1927:68).

The second task of the artisan was to prepare the mordant which would bond the dye to the textile. Although a few dyes, such as those made from wild grape and bloodroot, will hold fast without the action of an acidic or metallic oxide substance, most require a bonding agent. Tannic acid, boiled from black and red

## Table 3.3
## Plant Dyes

| Plant | Latin Name | Process | Color |
|---|---|---|---|
| goldenrod | *Solidago canadensis* | boil berries | yellow |
| bloodroot | *Sanguinaria canadensis* | crush roots, mix with red ocher | red |
| staghorn sumac | *Rhus typhina* | boil berries | brown |
| wild grape | *Vitus spp.* | boil berries | purple |
| blueberry | *Vaccinium spp.* | boil berries | blue |
| bearberry | *Uva ursi* | boil leaves | gray |

oak acorns, was readily available on Long Island, whereas such metallic oxides as alum and iron oxide might have been imported. There were several alternative methods for applying the mordant, but the more common one was to rinse the material in warm water and place it in a mordanting bath overnight (Leechman 1969:15-16). The last step was completed after the textiles had dried. The material was rinsed once again, squeezed dry and carefully placed into a dye bath. The bath was brought to a simmering boil for about a half hour and then the material was taken out and rinsed until the water ran clear.

Personal ornaments and sacred strings of shell ornaments were made from the quahog *(Mercenaria mercenaria)* and whelk *(Busycotypus aruanum* and *B. canaliculatum)* which are found in such great abundance on the beaches of eastern Long Island (Beauchamp 1901:327-36; Ceci 1978:306-12; Wilcox 1982:295-305; Burggraft 1982:285-89; Speck 1919:56-66). Colonial records suggest that the wampum from Long Island was of superior quality (Hosmer 1946, 1:109; NYCD, 1:129). The Pequots and Narragansetts from southern New England came here to collect shells for wampum (Beauchamp 1901:330; RCNP, 10:199). Unfortunately, we do not know what the specific characteristics of the shells were which made them so highly valued by the Indian craftsmen. Marine biologists agree that shellfish do have regionally specific attributes caused by genetic and environmental factors, but there is no consensus about what those might have been in the seventeenth century on Long Island (Shumway and Krause, November 1995: pers. com.).

The quahog was highly valued because it has a striking dark purple rim, which runs along the outer lip of the shell. The purple beads enhanced the value of a necklace and any item they decorated. The white beads were made by breaking the center stem or columela of the whelk shell and cutting it into sections (Burggraf 1982:286-87; Solecki 1950:28-29). Strings of the white and purple disk-shaped beads were probably traded to the Iroquois and other inland communities, but there is no evidence that the more elaborate strings and belts of cylindric shell beads called "wampum," which were used as a medium of exchange in the latter half of the seventeenth century, were produced during the Early and Middle Woodland Periods. The wampum industry appears to have developed after Indian craftsmen obtained metal drills from the Europeans (Ceci 1982:307).

The villagers made such efficient use of the environment that there was no rush to change from the old ways when an innovation such as plant domestication was introduced. Corn, beans, and squash, the three sisters so important to the Iroquois, never made much of an impact on Long Island until after the European settlements destroyed the rich sources of natural foods, medicines, and supplies.

## Religious Ceremonialism

Mortuary ritualism appears to have changed from the elaborate Orient ceremonialism, but the data base is too limited to support any meaningful

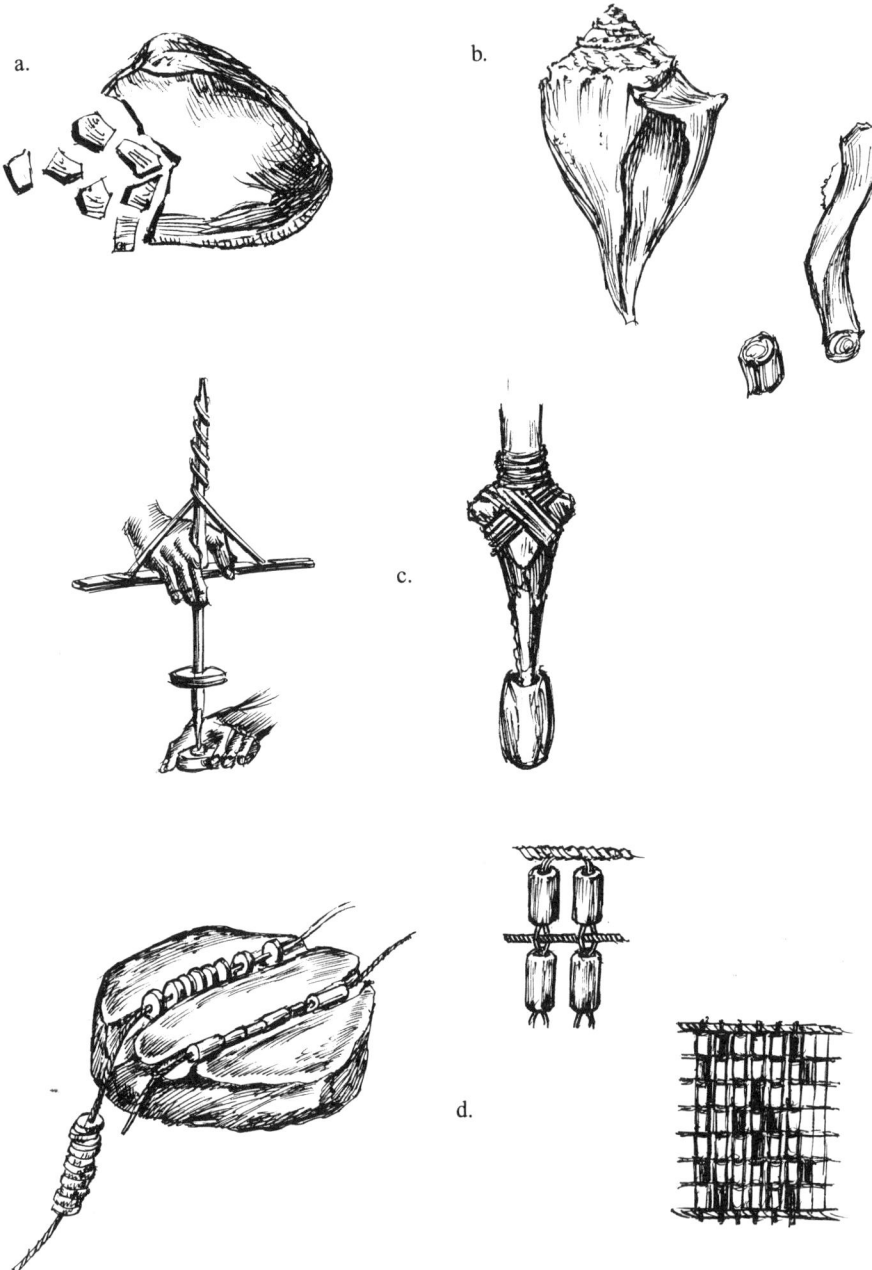

Fig. 3.7. Wampum manufacture. *a.* Blanks for discordal beads were removed from the purple rim of the quahog; *b.* The columnae was removed from the whelk shell and cut into small tubular sections; *c.* Pump drills or bow drills to make holes in the beads for stringing; *d.* The beads were strung or woven into belts.

conclusions. The only Early Woodland burial on Long Island was excavated at the Matinecock Point site by Mark Harrington, one of the pioneer archaeologists who worked on Long Island during the first decades of this century. The burial was described by Carlyle Smith as "a group of disarticulated human bones . . . that may have been a secondary inhumation" (1950:135). Such secondary burial practices are not uncommon in the Eastern Woodlands. The deceased were exposed on a platform until the flesh decayed and the bones were dry. The remains were then cleaned and placed in a bundle for burial in the ground.

An Early Woodland burial in southern New England, found at a campsite near the Connecticut River, consisted of a single cremation placed in a small, shallow pit without any grave goods (McBride 1984:132). Although the Orient burial complex included both secondary inhumations and cremations, the contrast between the Orient and the Woodland mortuary systems is striking. The two Early Woodland burials were located near campsites rather than on isolated hilltops, and there is no evidence of elaborate ceremonialism or status distinctions.

It is possible, of course, that more complex Early Woodland mortuary sites on Long Island have been destroyed by suburban growth or remain undiscovered. Groups who lived along the banks of Lake Champlain and on the Delaware River during this time period left behind evidence of a rich mortuary tradition, including cremations, high status burials with grave offerings and red ocher (Kraft 1986:101-4; Ritchie 1969:201-4). It is likely, therefore, that the villagers at Matinecock Point, North Beach, and Pelham Point participated in a much richer religious ceremonialism than is revealed in the excavations.

Our understanding of Middle Woodland (2,000–1,000 B.P.) religious ceremonialism also rests on a very slim data base, but we do have some intriguing clues. Three tubular smoking pipes were found on sites in what is now Pelham Bay Park and Throgs Neck peninsula. A highly polished stone tubular pipe was excavated in a shell midden along with Abbott-style pottery sherds at the Pelham Boulder site (Lopez 1982a:250). A second stone pipe was found on the surface near the Schurz site (Lopez 1982c:104). The third, made of fine grained brown limestone, was found on the Morris Estate Club site. The latter two sites are so close together that they should be regarded as one settlement (Kaeser 1978c:43-44).

Although no pipes have been excavated from Middle Woodland sites by professional archaeologists, a few have been discovered by amateurs. A tubular pipe was found by an amatuer on a site near Little Neck Bay which probably dates to this period (*Newsday*, Sept. 27, 1977). Annette Silver, whose Ph.D. dissertation on this period is the most authoritative and comprehensive source available, suggests that smoking rituals were probably introduced from the Ohio Valley where tubular pipes were in widespread use by this time (1991:274). The sparsity of pipes in the archaeological record on Long Island may be because of the small number of Middle Woodland sites which have been scientifically

 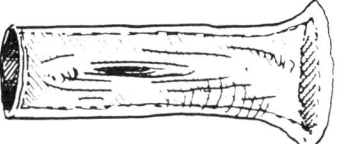

Fig. 3.8. Tubular smoking pipes

excavated. Pipes are certainly well documented in both Early and Middle Woodland sites in what is now upstate New York (Ritchie 1969:182, 232).

Pipes were undoubtedly used in some form of religious ceremony. The tubular form may have evolved from two closely related curing rituals. The "sucking tube" was used to draw the evil spirit, which was believed to be the cause of the sickness, out of the patient (Kraft 1986:97-98; Harner 1982:148-73; Grim 1987:140-44; Aceves and King 1979:447). The source of the pain would be sucked up through the tube and spit out. Another curing technique involved inhaling smoke from an open fire. Medicinal herbs were carefully prepared and burned for the patient to inhale. Maladies including insomnia, headaches, arthritis, and even respiratory problems were treated in this manner (Vogel 1973:176). The Comanches believed in the purifying effect of inhaling smoke from burning juniper leaves, and the Creeks attempted to cure neck cramps with the fumes from red cedar. Possibly the smoking rituals evolved out of a combination of these related ideological concepts.

The smoking of herbal mixtures was also a part of deer hunting and other, less well understood, shamanic rituals. Native peoples in the Great Lakes area combined such plants as the musquash root *(Circutamaculata)*, blue wood aster *(Aster cordifolius)*, and hawthorne *(Cratnegus)* in a smoking mixture that was believed to attract deer (Yarnell 1964:85-86, 145). Some mildly narcotic plants such as the sumac and the flowering dogwood, which may have been smoked as a part of the sacred vision quest, were probably used long before the introduction of tobacco.

People are often surprised to learn that the tobacco smoked by the native peoples in the Northeast, *Nicotiana rustica,* is not native to this area. The arrival of tobacco in North America is not well documented, but scholars estimate that the plant was imported here from Central America during the Middle Woodland Period (Asch and Asch 1985:195-96). Ironically, pipes are generally not found in prehistoric sites in South and Central America where tobacco was first used. Tobacco was chewed, steeped in water, and consumed as a drink, or rolled and smoked as a cigar. The pipe smoking tradition appears to have a northern origin which may have preceded the arrival of tobacco. This was probably true for the Long Island area during the Middle Woodland Period because no clear evidence of tobacco has been found here (Silver 1991:275). When tobacco arrived in the Northeast, it may simply have been added to the smoking mixtures already in use. The smoking rituals, which have a central role in Native American ceremonialism, were certainly well established throughout North America by 1,000 B.P.

The settlement on the north shore of the East River, along what is now Schurz Avenue in the Bronx, where two of the pipes were found, may have served as a center for seasonal religious ceremonies. We can only speculate about this because the data base is so slim, but there are some intriguing aspects of the site which lend support to this conjecture. The size and location of the site suggest that it was a settlement of some importance for trade as well as for ceremonial purposes. In what appears to have been the center of the settlement, there was a large ash pit, which was interpreted by archaeologist Alanson Skinner to be a "community fire-pit," which served "as a general source of fire and heat" (Lopez 1982c:103-4). Skinner, who along with Mark Harrington and Foster H. Sayville were among the first professional archaeologists to study the Long Island and coastal New York sites, regarded the central fire pit as a feature which distinguished a permanent village settlement from a campsite (Skinner 1919).

The Shurz site is located on the shore within easy reach of the major documented sites on western Long Island and the Bronx. Most of these sites are located within a five mile radius of the Schurz settlement. The villagers living on the southern extreme of the radius at Oakland Lake (near Little Neck Bay) could easily paddle north to the Schurz site shore in two hours if the wind and tides were right. The villagers at Pelham Bay and North Beach could also make the trip in two hours or less by canoe. Those living at closer locations such as Clearview, Weir Creek, and Clasons Point, could arrive in less than an hour.

In addition to size and convenience of access, the Schurz site had features and artifacts which suggest ceremonial functions. In the eastern section of the site on the Morris Estate Club, archaeologist Edward Kaeser discovered a stone circle about eight feet in diameter. The stones were water worn cobbles and averaged ten inches in diameter (1978c:40). Kaeser suggested that the circle might have anchored wigwam matting, but there is no evidence of this building technique anywhere in the prehistoric northeast.

The artifacts which Kaesar found inside the circle suggest that the feature is an expression of the sacred circle. Kaeser reported finding a cache of 150 mica plates about two inches in diameter (1978c:42). This unusual cache must have had considerable cultural significance. Mica is rarely found on Middle Woodland sites on the Mid-Atlantic coast, but the Ohio Hopewell imported enormous amounts of the material from the rich deposits in the southern Appalachians to make ceremonial effigies, mirrors, and ornaments (Seeman 1979:333-35). The Hopewell trade routes, which spanned the Northeast during this time period, may have brought some ideas about the ritual use of mica to the east coast.

The direct connection for the mica at the Schurz site (Morris Estate Club section), however, appears to be the communities along the Delaware River. Large amounts of mica were found on the Abbott Farm site in association with the zoned, shell-tempered pottery (Cross 1956, 2:161-62; Silver, 1991:222-23).

Mica has also been found in several other sites around Trenton, New Jersey (Abbott 1876:246-380). There was, undoubtedly, some ceremonial significance to the use of mica in at least three instances. Two of the Abbott Farm burials contained mica; in pit number 2, mica bits were scattered over the burial, and in pit number 58, the burial was laid on mica sheets (Cross 1956, 2:65).

In the third instance, at another site near Trenton, a foot square piece of cut mica, about one-half inch thick, was found serving as a cover on a small pot filled with black powder from burned animal bones (Abbott 1876:345). The pot, less than four inches high and about the same dimension at the mouth, held a little over a pint of the powder. Two more miniature vessels were excavated from the site by Dorothy Cross, but no mention was made of any possible ritual context (1956, 2:125, 133; Silver 1991:165). Similar vessels were found at Henry Lloyd Manor, on the Archery range site in Pelham Park, and on the Westheimer site near Schoharie, New York. The ritual importance of such vessels has been discussed by several scholars, but their specific function remains a mystery (Silver 1991:265, 267-68). They are often found in Hopewell graves, but there is no consensus about their function (Struever and Houart 1972:76-77). The black substance in the Abbott Farm vessel, which, unfortunately, was never analyzed, may have been a dye or a medicine.

Mica was also a fairly common Hopewell grave item but there is no apparent relationship between the vessels and the mica. Thousands of mica plates have been excavated from the Ohio Hopewell ceremonial sites. Archaeologists who have studied the Ohio sites have concluded that the Hopewell settlements along the Scioto River processed the trimmed mica plates and exported them all over the Northeast (Seeman 1979:333). The specific function of the plates is not clearly understood. Mica was used in burials and probably played some role in divination rituals. One of the more spectacular Hopewell tombs was completely lined with mica sheets, and another was partially paved with small circular mica disks (Mills 1922:448, 492-94). The extent of Hopewell influence, however, has been questioned by some scholars who remain unconvinced about any significant connection between the two areas (Thulman 1978:72-78; Stewart 1994:85-87).

The communities on the Atlantic coast who never achieved this level of social complexity and material wealth could not be expected to build similar mortuary structures, but the concept is expressed, albeit modestly, in the two Abbott Farm burials described above, and in a mica-lined grave of a one-year-old child on the Archery Range site in Pelham Bay Park (Kaeser 1978d:22), and in an elaborate child's grave at the Burial Ridge site on Staten Island (Jacobson 1980:33-36, 66). The body at the Archery site had been defleshed, perhaps after exposure on a funeral platform, and bundled together for burial. This aspect of the burial is similar to the double inhumation under the floor of the Orient Two mortuary pit. There were no grave goods in the small tomb, but the elaborate mica enclosure suggests that the child was either from an important family or had been part of a ceremonial ritual. The burial form presents us with a tantalizing clue to Middle Woodland ceremonialism, but, unfortunately, the data base is far too limited to support any further speculation.

Another intriguing child burial in association with mica was discovered on the Burial Ridge site near Tottenville on the southern tip of Staten Island. The burial was one of sixty excavated in a three and one-half acre area, but none of the others contained comparable grave goods or evidences of elaborate ceremony (Jacobson 1980:28-31). The child was placed on a bed of yellow sand with a block of white sandstone at its head and a slab of gray slate at its feet. A small stone pipe rested on the sandstone. There was a string of shell beads around the child's neck, evidence of a copper plate of some sort over the face and a four inch plate of worked mica under the head.

The mica graves and caches at Schurz might also be related to other forms of religious expression. The Maya and other Central American cultures used mica, obsidian, and iron pyrite mirrors in their divination ceremonies (Seeman 1979:381). Unfortunately, there is very little information in the archaeological record about the specific nature of these ceremonies. The absence of mica caches or mica ornaments on other related sites in the Long Island area is puzzling, but it may simply be because most of the Middle Woodland sites have been destroyed by development or remain undiscovered.[4]

The concentration of mica, the sacred circle, and the smoking pipes at Schurz and the absence of all these on the nearby sites does suggest that this was a special place where people may have gathered to participate in ceremonies. Unfortunately, little more can be said about this until more research is completed.

The mortuary ritualism during the Early and Middle Woodland Periods in the Long Island area is not well documented either. The Abbott Farm site, however, revealed eighty-eight burials in shallow pits. The Middle Woodland burials here were flexed into a fetal position and placed in pits which may have formerly been used for food storage (Cross 1956:182). The burial positions of the two individuals in the Abbott site mica graves described above were impossible to determine because the skeletons were incomplete. Apparently, the elaborate Late Archaic mortuary rituals in isolated hilltop cemeteries had been abandoned. Pit burials similar to the ones at Abbott Farm were excavated by Alanson Skinner at the Weir Creek site near Throgs Neck (Skinner 1919:54-58). In pit number 17, Skinner found the skeleton of a small child, in a flexed position lying under a twenty pound stone slab. A stemmed quartz projectile point had been placed below the knees as a grave gift.

The smoking pipes, burials, mica caches, and grave goods provide us with a frustratingly dim outline of the ceremonial practices. It is impossible to reconstruct the religious system of the Early and Middle Woodland villagers on such limited data, but the information we do have certainly suggests that a rich complex of theological beliefs played a very important part in their lives.

## Trading Networks

The "mica" connection between the Schurz site and the Abbott Farm site on the lower Delaware Valley, which was developed by Annette Silver in her dissertation on the Henry Lloyd Manor site, brings us to an important insight about the Middle Woodland period on Long Island. Silver's study is the first, and so far the only, comprehensive analysis of the Middle Woodland on Long Island. Working with a concept which has served as a theoretical focus for archaeologists studying the Hopewell sites in the Midwest, Silver has developed a regional context for the sites here (1991:206-46). The regional "interaction sphere" model set forth by Joseph Caldwell and other scholars working with Hopewell materials is defined by trade networks and shared ideological values which connect a group of sites. The evidence of participation in the sphere is demonstrated by the flow of trade items back and forth within the region and/or shared ceremonialism and religious paraphernalia (Caldwell 1970; Seeman 1979:240-48).

Silver has identified a trade network connecting the Long Island sites with the Abbott Farm site in the lower Delaware Valley (1991:214-70). This "Abbott Interaction Sphere" includes sites which share three aspects: Fox Creek projectile points made from Delaware Valley argillite, Abbott-style pottery, and caches of mica (1991:215-16). Fox Creek points make up nearly two-thirds of the points in the Middle Woodland component at Abbott Farm. Most of the argillite used by artisans in the Mid-Atlantic coastal areas can be traced to the outcrops along the central Delaware River. The excavations at Lloyd Manor, for example, indicate that the Long Island villagers were importing finished or nearly finished argillite implements from the Delaware area (Silver 1991:218, 282).

Unlike the Hopewell Interaction Sphere, there does not appear to be significant evidence of shared religious ceremonialism in the Abbott sphere (Silver 1991:149). The mica, for example, might have been imported from Abbott Farm, but the only evidence of any religious use of the material is limited to the mica graves at Pelham and Abbott Farm. The presence of mica in these few burials, however suggestive, is not sufficient evidence to demonstrate that a common pattern of rituals existed. The trade in argillite and pottery decorated by Abbott Farm potters carries no discernible evidence of any ideological content.

Silver has concluded that the settlements at Oakland Lake, Schurz (Morris Estate Club), Pelham Bay, Henry Lloyd Manor, Sebonac (Southampton), and Hands Creek (East Hampton) all participated in an interaction sphere based primarily on trade. The sphere extended southward along the Delaware River Valley into what is now Salem County, New Jersey, eastward to the end of Long Island, and northward into the southern Connecticut Valley (1991:225-28). Argillite blades and projectile points and Abbott-styled pottery were found on all of these sites, but the mica trade apparently did not reach the eastern Long Island sites at Sebonac, Henry Lloyd Manor, and Hands Creek.

The flow of trade back and forth between the western Long Island villages and the Delaware Valley communities parallels the linguistic and cultural affinities identified in the early historic period by Ives Goddard (see Chapter 1 above). Villagers living in what is now the Bronx, Brooklyn, Queens, and western Nassau counties probably shared a common linguistic and cultural base with the ancestors of the Lenapes in New Jersey and Pennsylvania.

The trade network appears to have collapsed sometime around a thousand years ago as many significant changes began to occur in the lifeways of the Long Island villagers. People began to experiment with the domestication of plants, although they never became dependent on cultigens for subsistence. New pottery and projectile point styles were introduced, and new forms of religious expression emerged. These new developments define a cultural period labeled by archaeologists as the "Late Woodland Period." Our understanding of this cultural period is greatly enhanced by the records of the first Europeans who visited and then settled among the original inhabitants.

## Summary

The small number of Long Island sites from this period makes it impossible to reconstruct a detailed description of daily village life. Some additional data from a scattering of related sites in the Lower Connecticut Valley and New Jersey have expanded our understanding somewhat, but the picture remains incomplete (Kraft 1986:94-105; Snow 1980:279-80). The sites in the Lower Connecticut Valley where thick walled, grit tempered pottery have been found, closely resemble the North Beach sites (McBride 1984:294-95; Lavin 1987:26-30). The only information about house structures comes from a site in New Jersey where excavators found evidence of circular and oval-shaped dwellings as large as twenty feet by thirty feet (Kraft 1986:104-5).

The major changes from the Archaic Period included the development of new pottery technology and design, new projectile point styles, new forms of religious rituals, the establishment of more permanent year-round settlements, and expanded trade networks. These resourceful early settlers also developed a "forest efficient" economic system which skillfully used the resources in the natural environment. The cultural innovations helped to spark a cultural transition to the Middle Woodland Period about a thousand years ago.

The settlers on Long Island had established a comfortable lifeway based on a productive relationship with the environment, an enriched religious system, a trade network which brought them a regular supply of goods from the mainland, and an improved tool technology. Although we can only reconstruct the dim outlines of this lifeway, we can appreciate the genius and adaptive ingenuity of these ancient people. They passed along to their descendants a rich heritage and a beautiful landscape little scarred by their passing.

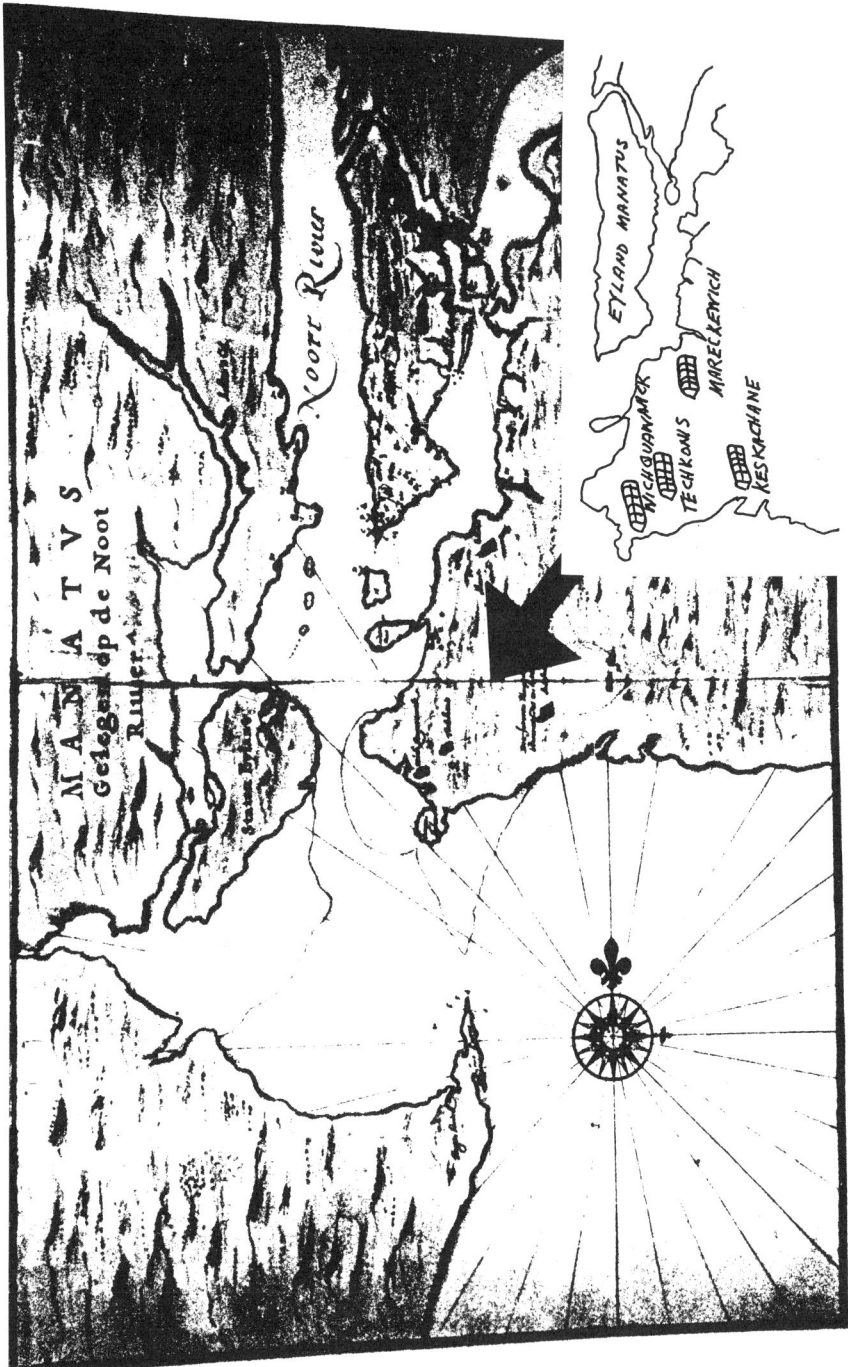

Fig. 4.1. "Manatus" map with detail showing Algonquian settlements on western Long Island (1639)

# 4

# The Late Woodland Period, 1,000 B.P.–1600

Our understanding of Late Woodland village life has been enhanced by the eyewitness accounts of the first European visitors to North America. These sources must be consulted with some caution because the authors had little understanding of Native American culture. Many of these observers also had their own agendas, which may have distorted their reports. Some wanted to show how much the work of a missionary was needed, others were concerned with justifying the acquisition of Native American land, and a few merely wished to gain profit or public attention by exaggerating the more "exotic" behavior of the native peoples. In spite of these hidden agendas, the eyewitness reports are an invaluable source of information. Even those observations which reveal more about the reporter than about the Native Americans can still provide rich insights to the skilled ethnographer. Of course we also have the reports of archaeologists and ethnographers whose continuing studies enlarge our understanding of this period.

Most of the sites described in the two previous chapters were also occupied during the Late Woodland Period (see Appendix map A). Although this continuity in settlement patterns on Long Island underscores the limited significance of prehistoric period designations established for eastern North America, there are some significant chronological horizon markers which identify the gradual transition from Middle Woodland to Late Woodland. These cultural shifts include the introduction of plant domestication, increased sedentism, new patterns of religious ceremonialism, expanded trade networks, and new styles of pottery and projectile points. The bow and arrow, which had been introduced earlier, had gradually displaced the atlatl for hunting and warfare throughout North America.[1] This chapter focuses on plant domestication, sedentism, and shifts in technology, while the new patterns in religion, the nature of trade and warfare, and the complexities of kinship and lineage systems will be discussed in later chapters.

## Village Settlements

The limited archaeological and ethnographic data from Long Island and adjacent areas suggest that the native people of Long Island may have lived in settlements with populations which ranged from less than twenty to as many as five hundred inhabitants. Two very general settlement "types" have been identified, based on population and the presence of features indicating levels of social complexity. The smallest and least complex are the campsites which served as hunting or fishing stations or workshops located near the sources of shell or clay. These sites may have consisted of only one or two structures where ten to twenty people resided.[2] The larger settlements may have been occupied by one hundred to five hundred or more people, with a communal building large enough to hold twenty or thirty people, a burial place, planting grounds, menstrual houses, a small palisaded enclosure, sweat houses, and winter storage areas for surplus food (Ceci 1990:19; Sears 1956; Callahan 1981:136-37).[3]

The European observers were struck by the differences between their own villages back home and the organization of structures and activity areas in the Native American settlements. An Englishman who visited a coastal Powhatan settlement in Virginia in 1612 said that the wigwams were arranged "without forme of a street, far and wyde asunder," and interspersed among small stands of trees (Rountree 1989:58). This informal, random selection of wigwam sites in a dispersed settlement pattern has also been documented in the archaeological excavations of longhouse structures in the northern sections of the Delaware River (Kraft 1986:122).

Unfortunately, we have only a few scattered descriptions of Long Island Indian settlements in the colonial records. Dutch reports of their attacks on Native American villages during Governor Kieft's War (1640–1645) state that they killed one hundred and twenty people in the village of Matsepe and attacked another settlement so small that only fourteen soldiers were sent out. The location of this village is uncertain; some scholars believe that it was Maspeth near Newtown Creek, while others argue that it was at Fort Neck in Massapequa (Trelease 1971:79). Matsepe may have had a population of two hundred or more and the smaller settlement may have been a campsite with one or two longhouses and twenty or thirty people. These two general settlement patterns can be found along the Atlantic coast from southern New England to Virginia during the Late Woodland Period.

John Smith estimated that the number of structures in a Powhatan settlement could range from two to fifty with six to twenty people living in each one, but other observers said that "the largest towns did not have more than twenty or thirty houses" (Barbour 1986, 2:116; Rountree 1989:60). The settlement at Nayack (near present-day Fort Hamilton in Brooklyn), visited in 1679 by Jasper Danckaerts, a Labadist minister, had a population of about twenty people living in one longhouse (1969:55). Henry Hudson visited a settlement on the west bank of the Hudson north of Manhattan in which forty men and seventeen women lived (De Laet 1909:49). Although settlements with as many as six to seven hundred people have been reported by European observers in what is now New Jersey and Pennsylvania and in southern New England (Kraft 1986:121; Russell 1980:24; Mason 1897:31), there is no evidence of such population concentrations on Long Island.[4] It appears that the Late Woodland settlements here on

Long Island ranged in size from a campsite of about twenty people to a village of more than two hundred inhabitants.[5]

What did these settlements look like? Seventeenth-century European artists drew several illustrations of villages, but most were idealized and misleading.[6] Few of those artists had ever seen any of these villages themselves. With the exception of a few such as John White, who came with the first settlers to the ill-fated colony of Roanoke in what is now North Carolina, and Samuel de Champlain, who traveled along the north Atlantic coast in 1604, the artists relied on written reports or interviews with people who had visited America. Two maps, one of the Delaware River settlements and one of Manhattan and western Long Island, attributed to a Dutch mapmaker Johannes Vingboons in 1639, do have fairly accurate drawings of longhouses, but they do not show the village layout (see fig. 4.1).

The only illustrations of villages along the Atlantic coast north of Virginia were drawn by the French explorer, Samuel de Champlain, in 1604. His maps of a village on the Saco River in what is now Maine and the villages around Plymouth Harbor show corn fields, longhouses, and wigwams. The village on the Saco had, in addition, a stockade around one of the longhouses where the villagers could find refuge from an attack. Although the drawings by Champlain (see fig. 4.2), may not have been intended to portray an actual village, they undoubtedly illustrate different types of structures and activities which had been observed in one village or another along the Atlantic coast.

There is no evidence of any fortified villages on Long Island such as the Pequot fort near Mystic or Fort Shantok near Norwich, Connecticut. The Pequot settlement was enclosed by a stockade wall made from poles, about fifteen feet long and three to six inches in diameter, which were set about three feet into the ground and braced with an earthen wall at the base (McBride 1990:98-99). Although there are no fortified villages, there were some small stockade enclosures which were probably associated with settlements. Two of these small enclosures, Fort Massapeag near Massapequa on western Long Island, and Fort Corchaug at the far east end of the Island, were examined by Ralph Solecki, who wrote his M.A. thesis at Columbia University on the Fort Corchaug site (1950). The more extensive excavation of the two was done on the Fort Corchaug site. Solecki reported that the earthen embankment was rectangular, about 160 feet by 210 feet. He did not find enough evidence of a palisade wall in association with the embankments to determine a pattern or to estimate the average diameter of the wooden poles (1950:15-16).

The Fort Massapeag site was purchased from the Indians in 1693, but English farmers had used the meadow in 1687. A 1687 map of the neck in the Lloyd family papers shows a row of seven wigwams along the upland border of the neck (Lloyd 1926, 1:92-93). There are reports of two quadrangular forts on the neck, one was an earthen enclosure surrounded by a ditch and the second, located on the southern end of the neck, was a palisaded structure with posts which were

Fig. 4.2. Longhouses, wigwams, fort, and cornfields (based on Champlain's map of Saco and Plymouth Bay)

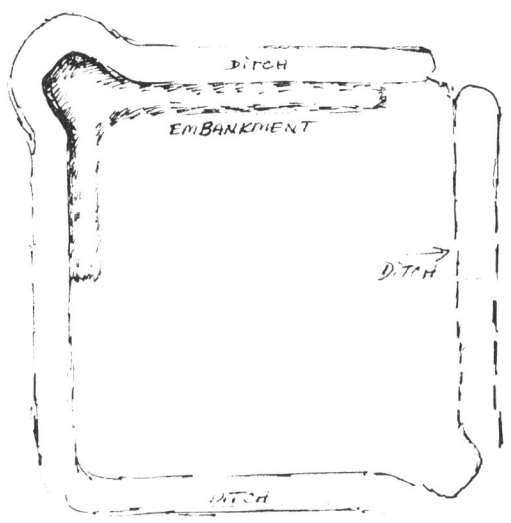

Fig. 4.3. Fort Massapeag site

still visible at the end of the eighteenth century (Jones 1821:328). Carlyle Smith and Ralph Solecki excavated several test pits, and a sixteen foot trench on the southern portion of the earthen enclosure. Solecki also made two shovel probes in the center (Solecki and Grumet 1994:22-25; C. Smith 1954:67-68). The enclosure, which was about one hundred feet square, was still visible when Smith first visited the site in 1950.

All of these structures enclose less than one-quarter the area of the Pequot fort at Mystic and appear to be similar in size and function to the small stockades depicted at Saco on Champlain's map. Fort Corchaug and the Massapequa fort, for example, appear to have been a temporary refuge adjacent to the living areas of the village, whereas the Fort Shantok settlement was a much more densely populated village enclosed in a palisade wall (Williams 1972: ch. 2). Kevin McBride, who excavated a fortification on Block Island very similar to the Long Island forts, concluded that these structures were built during the early post-contact period in response to the conflicts and tensions provoked by the European presence (1994:43-45).

Five other stockade sites have been reported in the literature: two near the Shinnecock Reservation; one overlooking Napeague Harbor west of Montauk; one on Fort Hill near the village of Montauk; and one on Shelter Island. William Wallace Tooker, who visited the Montauk stockade site at the end of the nineteenth century, said that the outline of a walled enclosure about 180 feet square was still visible (1962:143). The fort at Napeague is mentioned in a 1662 deed, but no trace of it has ever been found (R. Smith 1926:25-29). Tooker is also the source of information about a stockade which may have existed on Shelter Island. A neck of land on the south side of the island was called Mashomuck, an Algonquian word which Tooker believed means "great stockade place" (1962:108). No trace of a stockade, however, has ever been found nor is there any mention of a fort there in the historical record. According to Tooker (*Brooklyn Daily Eagle,* November 22, 1892), there were two forts near Shinnecock, one on the north shore of the South Fork (near Sebonac), and a second one some distance to the south. The second fort may be the one discovered by Miller in 1990. His excavation in the Shinnecock Hills near the Sugar Loaf burial site uncovered evidence of a structure which may have been similar to the enclosure at Fort Corchaug (Miller 1990). Suffolk County purchased the site to preserve it, but no further excavations have been done there.

Most villages, however, apparently did not have a stockade structure. The arrangement of wigwams and longhouses may have changed with the seasons and for specific functions such as hunting, fishing, and planting. According to William Wood, who lived in Massachusetts Bay from 1629 to 1634 and wrote his observations of the Indians in *New England's Prospect,* the summer wigwams were smaller and more dispersed. During the winter, dwellings may have been enlarged and moved closer together near the common food storage areas. Wood's journal suggests that the Indians in Massachusetts often expanded their summer wigwams into longhouses for the winter. During the cold months, he wrote, they made a house sixty feet long which could sleep forty or fifty men (Wood 1968:94). Herbert Kraft, an archaeologist from Seton Hall University, reported that his excavation of a longhouse site on the upper Delaware also indicated that wigwams were expanded into longhouses when needed. One of the dwellings on the site, he reported, "began as a round house twenty-two feet in diameter, and it was extended into a longhouse thirty-two feet long and twenty-two feet wide" (1970:6).

Wigwams were also moved when necessary to facilitate access to fish, game, wild plants, and planting fields. It appears from Wood's description that the houses were often in motion throughout the year.[7] Although villages appeared chaotic and disorderly to the European accustomed to more densely concentrated villages and towns, the Native American settlements were practical and well suited to a lifestyle which depended on limited horticulture and foraging over an extended territory.

We have very limited archaeological information about village settlement patterns, therefore, we can make only a few guarded generalizations. There appear to have been two types of settlements here on Long Island: the small campsite, where about ten to twenty people resided, and the village or hamlet, populated by as many as two or three hundred. Unlike the European concept of a village, these settlements were often dispersed over a wide area and some of the houses were moved seasonally. The community bond was reinforced by the sharing of such public areas as a sweat lodge, a large communal building or a plaza, menstrual houses, planting grounds, food storage areas, and craft stations for tool making, weaving, tanning, shell working, and food processing.

## Native Architecture: Wigwams and Longhouses

Today we are accustomed to thinking of our house as a year-round "living place" where we spend much of our time engaged in domestic and leisure activities. The Native American villagers, in contrast, thought of the wigwam or longhouse only as a place to sleep and find shelter. Their "living place" was outdoors. Much of their daily activity, even in the winter, took place outside in the public spaces. Social and religious gatherings, for example, were probably held in a communal house or in the main plaza. Although we have no information about communal houses in the villages on Long Island, we do know that most Native American communities had a structure near the center of the village where people gathered for social, political, or religious activities. Frequently, European visitors mistakenly described these buildings as "chief's houses."

The two building forms most commonly found on Long Island are the circular or oval dome-shaped wigwam from ten to fifteen feet in diameter, made of saplings and bark or woven mats; and the longhouse structure, an ovate shape about sixty feet long by twenty feet wide made from the same materials. Both circular and oval structures have been excavated on a Woodland site along the upper Delaware in New Jersey (Kraft 1986:105, 124, 126), and longhouses sixty feet long and twenty feet wide have been found in southern New England (Russell 1980:53; Willoughby 1906:115-20). According to Roger Williams, the Narragansett word *Neesquttow* meant a longer house with two fires, and *Shwish-cuttow*, a house with three fires (1973:117).

The Dutch described longhouses in what is now Brooklyn and evidences of similar structures have recently been discovered in what are now the towns of Huntington and Smithtown (Miller 1990a; Miller, July 20, 1995: pers. com.). A few smaller, oval and circular-shaped structures have been excavated on eastern Long Island (Harrington 1977a; Werner 1982). Henry Hudson described a circular house in a village he visited in 1609, but, unfortunately, he does not

Fig. 4.4. Bark longhouse construction

mention any other structures (De Laet 1909:49). Our most definitive account of the longhouses comes from the Dutch minister Jasper Danckaerts, after his visit to the village at Nayack mentioned above. About twenty people, according to Danckaerts, lived in a longhouse about sixty feet long and fourteen or fifteen feet wide. The frame was made from saplings, which had been stuck into the ground and bent over in an arch to form a roof (1969:54-56).

Danckaerts does not describe the size of the saplings but we can get a general idea from a longhouse excavated by Herbert Kraft at the Miller Field site in New Jersey. This structure, sixty feet long by twenty feet wide, was formed by 220 saplings with fire-hardened tips about two and one-half to three and one-half inches in diameter. The saplings had been driven a foot and one-half into the ground at nine inch intervals and tied together at the top to form a series of arches (Kraft 1970:5-7; 1986:122-27). John Smith described similar construction techniques that he observed in Virginia. "Their houses are built like our arbors of small young springs [saplings] bowed and tyed, and so close covered with mats or barkes of trees very handsomely" (Barbour 1986, 1:161).

The process sounds simple enough until we try to figure out how the saplings were sunk so deeply into the ground. There was no evidence of trenching or holes dug to set in the pole. Herbert Kraft, who has researched longhouse structures, suggested that the builders may have driven holes into the ground with small hardwood stakes which could be pounded in with stone tools. The short stakes were then removed and fire hardened saplings were forced into the openings (Kraft 1986:124-25). Kraft's theory is supported by the findings in Errett Callahan's experimental archaeology research project on the Pamunkey Reservation in Virginia (Callahan 1981:359) and by Gerrod Smith, a Shinnecock, who has used this method to reconstruct replica wigwams for the American Indian Archaeological Institute in Washington, Connecticut (February 20, 1993: pers. com.). The next step was to tie thin sapling poles horizontally around the arches to frame the wall (see fig. 4.6). Another important source of information about the details of bark house construction comes from the experiments of Errett Callahan's Pamunkey Reservation project. Callahan experimented with the inner bark of the locust, which worked well, but he preferred cordage from the root of the yellow pine *(Pinus virginiania)*. The inner bark of the linden tree was also used for this purpose (Kraft, April 1995: pers. com.). Callahan also found that saplings from red maple *(Acer rubum)* worked best for the horizontal braces and black locust *(Robina pseudoacacia)* and red cedar *(Juniperus virginiana)* made the best vertical posts (Callahan 1981:321-24, 378-92; Rountree 1989:60-61).

Once the frame was completed, the next challenge was to prepare the mats or bark sheets for the walls. Danckaerts tells us that the villagers at Nayack used reed mats and sheets of chestnut bark to cover the frame, but he says nothing about the techniques used to procure the bark or to secure it on the frame. We must turn once again to the research of Herbert Kraft and Errett Callahan for some insights. Kraft notes that, in addition to chestnut, the bark from oak and

Fig. 4.5. Wigwam construction

elm were used in house construction. Strips of bark six feet long were stripped off the trees in a process which began by slitting the desired section on the tree around the top and the bottom. Next, a vertical slit was made in the section. Kraft (1986:125) believes that this was probably done in June when the sap was flowing because the bark would peel more easily. The bark was then pried off with sharpened wooden staves in a slow, arduous operation which required a great deal of skill and patience. Once freed from the tree, the bark strips were spread on the ground and pressed with a layer of stones to hold them in position as the bark dried. Callahan experimented with chestnut *(Castanea dentata)*, black walnut *(Juglans nigra)*, and tulip poplar *(Liriodendron tulipifera)*, and concluded that chestnut worked the best (Callahan 1981:333-38; Rountree 1989:61).

Overlapping rows of these bark sheets were lashed to the frame by drilling small holes in the sheets for the lashings. The holes were then sealed with pine resin. When this was completed, an outer frame of saplings was sometimes placed over the whole structure tightly clamping the bark sheets against the inner frame. The inner wall was insulated with woven mats which were lashed to the frame. Danckaerts reported that the roof had a narrow opening running along the center from end to end, which allowed the smoke from the hearths to escape. The longhouse had entrances at each end which, he said, were "so small and low that they had to stoop down and squeeze themselves to get through them. The doors were made of reed or flat bark" (1969:55). There were undoubtedly many architectural variations in longhouse construction. The longhouse excavated by Herbert Kraft on the Miller Field site, for example, had only one door located on the side of the structure (Kraft 1970:5).

According to Danckaerts, there were several hearths inside the longhouse he visited. There was one for each family unit: "by each fire are the cooking utensils, consisting of a pot, a bowl, or calabash, and a spoon also made of a calabash" (1969:57). Post mold patterns in some longhouse excavations demonstrate that partitions inside the structure may have marked off family areas (Kraft 1970: fig. 1, plates 2, 3).

The longhouse was also a convenient place to store food. Baskets, ceramic pots, leather bags, and gourd vessels filled with corn, herbs, and tobacco could be hung from the rafters within easy reach (Kraft 1986:126). Most of the food, however, was kept in large storage pits under the floor of the longhouse. Kraft excavated several of these pits at either end of the Miller Field longhouse (1970: fig. 1; 1986:123, fig. 32).

The smaller, dome-shaped wigwams were constructed in a similar fashion and with many of the same materials used for the longhouse. Seventeenth-century accounts of wigwam construction in southern New England indicate that a "typical" wigwam was a circular structure, framed with sapling poles, and covered with mats or bark sheets, which were so artfully stitched together that they "deny entrance to any drop of rain, though it come fierce and long, neither can the piercing North winde finde a cranny" (Wood 1968:94).[8] The outer layer of mats was reinforced with a second layer on the inside of the wigwam frame which helped to keep in the warmth from the central fire (Mourt 1841:144-45). Daniel Gookin, who served the colony of Massachusetts as Indian commissioner from 1652 until his death in 1686, said that he had often stayed overnight in wigwams and had always found them to be as warm as any English house (Gookin 1972:10). The "chimney" hole in the center of the roof could be covered during a rain storm by pulling a mat cover over the hole.

Very few archaeological excavations on eastern Long Island have uncovered wigwam or longhouse features in Late Woodland sites. Mark Harrington's excavation of a Shinnecock village on the west bank of Sebonac Creek, about a mile from the present-day Shinnecock Reservation in the town of Southampton, revealed the floors of two wigwams. The first was an oval-shaped structure fifteen feet wide by twenty feet long, and the second, also oval-shaped, was ten feet wide by fifteen feet long (1977a:36-37). Dr. Harrington, who excavated the site in the summer of 1902 for the American Museum of Natural History in New York, located fireplaces in the center of both wigwam features. He also recovered pieces of pottery, deer bones, two large pieces of a whale's jaw, some shell, and several bone fragments in the "floor" areas.

Harrington then turned to the Shinnecocks to help him interpret the data. Wickham Cuffee, an elderly member of the tribe, made Harrington a small model of a wigwam he remembered seeing as a young child. Cuffee had been born in 1826 and is said to have been one of the first of his tribe to be born in a house rather than a wigwam (Cuffee and Stone 1983:317). According to Cuffee and several other Shinnecocks, the process began by setting saplings vertically into the ground and then bending them together at the top to form an arch. The next step was to lash smaller saplings horizontally around the frame and then to cover it with mats woven from tall grass or reeds (Harrington 1977a:41).[9] The Shinnecock wigwams apparently did not have an outer frame to clamp the mat wall in place as did the longhouses on the west end of Long Island.

The simple construction design made it easy to remove the mats, pull up the saplings, and move quickly to another spot. Roger Williams wrote that he slept as a guest in a wigwam while he was traveling. When he returned the next evening, the wigwam was gone. The women, said Williams, rolled up the mats and removed them to a new location and built a new structure. Another English observer reported, "I have seen half a hundred of their wigwams together in a piece of ground and they shew prettily, within a day or two, or a week they have all been dispersed" (Josselyn 1988:91).

The interior of the wigwam was designed for comfort and practicality. Benches constructed of small saplings lashed together, were placed around the walls. Unfortunately, Harrington did not press for more details about the Shinnecock structures. We do have some data from an excavation on Long Island by Ben Werner (1982), but the site had been partially destroyed by bulldozers. Werner excavated a circular pattern of post molds around a hard packed "floor" about twelve feet in diameter. The nearly perfect circular form was unusual. Most of the post mold features excavated on Long Island and in New England tend to be oval-shaped. Interpretation of this site is difficult because it had been partially destroyed by bulldozers before Werner arrived and was vandalized before he could finish.

The descriptions of wigwams in New England help us understand how the interior might have looked. Ezra Stiles drew diagrams of the wigwams described to him by representatives from the Niantic and Mohegan tribes. The benches, about eighteen inches high, ran around three of the walls, stopping at the two entrances on opposite sides of the southern end of the oval (Sturtevant 1975:438). Thomas Morton, writing in 1637, reported that he observed a wigwam in New England furnished with mats and robes of deer, bear, otter, raccoon, and beaver skin which were spread on the benches. The space underneath the benches served as storage areas (Morton 1967:136-37).

There were probably benches around the walls and shelves near the ceiling for storage. Danckaerts tells us that the people he visited preferred to sit on mats rather than on benches, but another observer says that the Lenapes used the benches as seats, beds, and tables (Kraft 1986:126). John Smith reported that the

Fig. 4.6. Wigwam interior

wigwams in Virginia were furnished with beds about a foot high which were covered with mats (Barbour 1986, 1:162).

Europeans who stayed as guests or as captives in wigwams provide us with conflicting accounts of the level of comfort in these structures. Stephen Hopkins and Edward Winslow could not adjust to the lack of privacy and space when they stayed overnight with sachem Massasoit. "He laid us on the bed with himself and his wife, they at one end and we at the other. Two more of his chief men, for want of room, pressed by and upon us" (Mourt 1841:210). They also complained about lice and fleas and the custom among the Indians of singing themselves to sleep. During the winter of 1633-34, a French guest in a northern Algonquian wigwam with about thirteen square feet of space, slept with nineteen Indians and several dogs. "The dogs," he said, "were not an unmixed evil, for by sleeping on and around him they kept him warm at night; but, as an offset to this good service, they walked, ran, and jumped over him as he lay" (Morton 1967:137-38).

Although some Europeans had difficulty in adjusting to the style of life in a wigwam, other visitors found them quite comfortable. English visitors who spent a week in a Powhatan village in what is now Virginia reported that "wee were never more merrie, nor fed on more plenyie of good oysters, fish, wild fowl, and good bread; nor never had better fires in England than in the drie warm smokie houses of Kecoughtan" (quoted in Callahan 1981:63-64). Roger Williams complained about the smoke, but conceded that the structures were warm and comfortable. He reported that in the Narragansett villages, "two families will live comfortably and lovingly in a little round house of some fourteen or sixteen foot over" (Williams 1973:118).

### The Gift of *Conconchus:* Origins of Plant Domestication

In modern industrial society food production is a highly specialized activity which engages a relatively small proportion of our population. Most of us spend only an hour or two each week shopping for the family food supply. By contrast, the prehistoric Long Islanders spent a major part of each day in communal or individual tasks related to food production, preparation, and storage. The primary change in this process, which took place very gradually sometime after 1,000 B.P., was the integration of a few cultivated plants into the food supply.[10]

Although the origins of plant domestication are fairly well documented for the midwestern areas of North America, the archaeological data base for Long Island is very sparse.[11] Our information about Native American food production, therefore, comes primarily from the reports of the seventeenth-century European observers. We do not have a clear understanding about the chronology of plant domestication here, but it was well established on western Long Island by the time the Dutch arrived. Corn is mentioned by several Dutch observers in the seventeenth century.[12]

We have no way of knowing how the process of crop domestication was introduced to the native peoples on Long Island, but the ideas probably spread along with the trade items imported from the Midwest where cultigens were well established by 2,000 years B.P. (Asch and Asch 1985:202). These new ideas did not spark any dramatic changes in the process of food production here because the native peoples saw no pressing need to change. They were doing fine with the food they hunted and gathered from the woodlands and adjacent waters. There was undoubtedly a long period of experimentation with cultigens on a relatively small scale as they were gradually intro-

Fig. 4.7. Corn

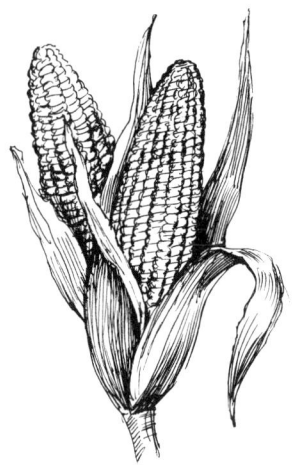

duced into the diet. One of the last things people change is their accustomed diet. Native Americans, like any other ethnic group, were probably reluctant to experiment with new foods and methods of production (Binford and Binford 1986). In fact, the concept of plant domestication may have been understood by people in eastern North America long before such cultigens as tobacco, corn, beans, and squash were introduced from the Midwest. Plants which were used for medicines, dyes, tools, and utensils may have been cultivated first (Cohen 1977:26).

An example of a utilitarian plant is the bottle gourd *(Lagenaria siceraria)*, one of the most widespread cultigens in the western hemisphere. Bottle gourd remains have been found in Mexican sites dating back 9,000 years before the present (King 1985:76; Whitaker and Cutler 1965:344). Although no *Lagenaria* remains have been found in excavations on Long Island, Dutch observers reported seeing gourd vessels being used in native households (Danckaerts 1969:55; Russell 1980:153), and the Unkechaug vocabulary recorded in 1791 by Thomas Jefferson lists the word *whorammok* for gourd (Jefferson 1980:17). Although this data does not tell us much about the origins of gourd cultivation on Long Island, we do know that gourds were grown in the Midwest more than 4,000 years ago (B. Smith 1987:8; Ford 1985:10; King 1985:76) and may have been introduced here by traders.

We cannot be sure whether the gourd was cultivated on Long Island or imported from the Midwest or the South, nor do we have any clear evidence that the pre-maize horticultural complex, which developed in the Midwest, was a part of the food base here. Evidence from archaeological excavations in Ohio and Illinois provide some insight, however, into what might have happened here as well. Scholars noted that certain plants such as chenopodium, marsh elder, maygrass, knotweed, and sunflowers colonized the disturbed soil around the villages long before corn was introduced (B. Smith 1985:52). These plants flourished in areas where their competitors had been removed by human intervention.[13]

Women probably tended these convenient edibles for many centuries before any attempt was made to manipulate them. Plants such as Jerusalem artichoke, ground nut, sunflower, marsh elder, and chenopodium may have been pruned and weeded to encourage their growth long before they were cultivated. The Pueblo people in the Southwest still tend patches of medicinal herbs in this manner today (Ford 1985:4). The use of digging sticks to harvest such wild tubers as the Jerusalem artichoke and the ground nut would have resulted in an expanding crop the following year. Gardeners today complain about the prolific growth of these "weeds" in their tilled soil. The tilling process detaches the bublets of the tuber plants and encourages the rapid expansion of the plant community.

The next stage of this slow process towards horticulture probably involved the transplanting of selected seeds or roots to a more convenient location for harvesting or to a place where the conditions for growth were better. Sometime around 2,000 years ago, Native Americans living along the Ohio and Illinois river systems began to select the larger seeds from these "village" plants and sowed them. Smithsonian archaeologist Bruce Smith studied caches of chenopodium seeds that were found in storage pits in two midwestern caves and discovered that they were larger than the wild chenopodium seeds. The size indicated that the inhabitants of the cave site had, over the years, carefully selected and planted the largest seeds (B. Smith 1995:186-87). This process, which eventually resulted in the increased size of the grain, was the first stage of plant domestication. Although no such evidence of a pre-maize complex has yet been found on Long Island, it is quite possible that a similar scenario took place here.

Corn, the most important of the plant complex called the three sisters by the Iroquois, was first domesticated in Mexico about 7,000 years ago, but the plant was not fully established north of the Rio Grande until about 2,300 B.P. (Galinat 1985:259, 263; B. Smith 1995:178; Ford 1985:350-51). Several centuries later, Native Americans living along the Ohio and Illinois rivers had begun to grow corn, beans, gourds, and squash (Asch and Asch 1985:197-203). The adoption of these new crops was a very slow process. We know, for example, that corn was present east of the Mississippi for over a thousand years before it became a significant part of the food base (Ford 1981:15). By 1,000 B.P. corn horticulture had spread to the northeast and become a permanent part of the Iroquois economic system (Ritchie and Funk 1973:330).

The prehistoric corn found on Long Island was *Maiz de Ocho,* an eight-row variety of northern flint corn, which was common throughout the Northeast.[14] The earliest documented evidence of corn on or near Long Island comes from excavations at Bowmans Brook on Staten Island, Pleasant Hill near Shoreham on the north shore of Long Island, and at Sebonac on the east end of the island near the Shinnecock Reservation.[15] Corn remains were also reported at three other Long Island sites: Matinecock Point near Oyster Bay; Old Field, near Southold on the North Fork; and Throgs Neck. None of these specimens could be found when Dr. Lynn Ceci did her study of Long Island corn remains for her dissertation in 1977 (1977:102-3).

The corn from the three documented sites was planted about 600 years ago (Ceci 1990:6-7; Silver 1980:124). It is certainly possible that corn was introduced earlier because Kevin McBride reports finding evidence of it in southern Connecticut and on Martha's Vineyard by 900 B.P. (McBride and Dewar 1987:309; see also Ritchie, 1969a:25,187; Cassedy 1993). The sparse remains found on Long Island may be due, in part, to errors and oversights made by the excavators who worked here prior to 1950, but the negative data suggest that the prehistoric communities here grew only small amounts of cultigens which supplemented the wild food sources. The degree of dependence on cultigens remains unclear, but it is likely that individual families may have cultivated small gardens near their villages. European observers reported that small gardens of twenty to two hundred square feet were scattered around adjacent to the settlements (Barbour 1986, 1:162; Rountree 1989:46).

The domestication and migration of the bean *(Phaseolus vulgaris)* follow the pattern of her corn sister. The wild ancestor of the bean, which grows in Mexico and Central America, was domesticated there about 7,000 years ago and introduced into North America between 2,300 and 1,500 B.P. (Gentry 1969:55; Ford 1985:352). The plant has two major variations. The "bush" beans grow in low shrubs and are best suited to more arid habitats whereas the "pole" variety do well in temperate and humid habitats. This latter form adapted easily to the northeastern climate and was established east of the Appalachians by 1,000 B.P. (Ford 1985:352).

Tobacco *(Nicotiana rustica)* probably traveled along with the other cultivated crops from Mexico to North America and was adopted in similar fashion into an existing cultural niche. The earliest archaeological evidence for tobacco places the plant in the Northeast about 1,000 years ago (Ford 1981:19). Just as the three sisters were gradually integrated into the existing food base, so tobacco was added to the mixtures which had been used in the smoking rituals for centuries. Although the plant evolved from ancestors in warmer southern climates, it adapted remarkably well to regions as far north as Canada.

Squash *(Cucurbita)*, the oldest of the three sisters, was domesticated in Mexico nearly 10,000 years ago (King 1985:73). The plant has many subspecies and the two most important edible groups of *Cucurbita*, which were established in eastern North America in prehistoric times, come in several variations. The first group is *Cucurbita pepo*, the "summer squashes": pattypan or scallop, yellow crookneck, zucchini, and acorn. Recent discoveries by C. Wesley Cowan of the Cincinnati Museum of Natural History and Bruce Smith of the Smithsonian indicate that these plants were actually domesticated here in North America (B. Smith 1995:192-94). Cowan and Smith examined some 7,000 year old *Cucurbita pepo ozarkana* seeds recovered from a site in the Ozark highlands along the banks of the Ozark River. They found that the seeds showed no signs of cultivation and must, therefore, have been the wild ancestor of the domesticated squashes grown by the Native Americans in the Midwest about 3,000 years ago. The second major subspecies, *Curcurbita moschata,* the "winter squashes," include the pumpkin and the butternut. These squashes appear to have originated in Mexico along with corn, beans, and tobacco and migrated north. Another member of the cucurbitaceae family, the watermelon *(Citrullus vulgaris)* is less well documented, but seventeenth-century English and Dutch observers mentioned it (De Vries 1909:219; Russell 1980:154).

The Algonquian peoples of Long Island have their own stories about the origins of these plants. According to their ancestors, corn came to them from a crow, who flew over the village and dropped planting seeds from his beak (Wooley 1968:36). Samson Occom recorded a Montaukett tradition about *Cauwonnuntoh,* the god of the west, who brought them corn, beans, and squash, but he made no mention of a crow (1993:151-52). A Narragansett from Rhode Island told Roger Williams that *Conconchus,* the crow, brought both corn and beans to them (Butler 1948:6). Conconchus, the Narragansett believed, brought these gifts from the garden of the god Cautantouwit who dwelled far away to the southwest. The crow, said Williams was revered by the native peoples for this gift and was seldom killed even though it often "took back" the corn at harvest. Crows were driven from the corn fields but were not harmed.

## Native Gardens

The importance of spring planting is expressed in the calendars kept by Algonquian peoples of New England and Long Island (Butler 1948:10-11; Thomas 1976:5-11; Van Wassenaer 1909:73). The last weeks of the English month of April and all of May were called *Suquanni kesos* by the Massachusett Indians, *Nskekehigai kesos* by the Abenaki, and *Oneratack* by the Munsee speakers on western Long Island. These Algonquian words mean "when the corn is set" or "the planting month" in all three languages. Some evidence suggests that the Iroquoian and eastern Algonquian Indians marked the beginning of the planting season when the Pleiades, a bright cluster of stars, completed its winter trek across the sky and disappeared in the west during the first week in May (Ceci 1978:304-12). The cluster reappears in October, coinciding with harvest time. Astronomical observation by native peoples on Long Island may actually have its roots in the Late Archaic Period, because shell and bone artifacts with markings which appear to be a crude lunar calendar were excavated in a site at Mount Sinai Harbor (Gwynne 1982a:14-19).

Verrazano and Van Wassenaer both mention that native people were familiar with the Pleiades and associated them with the planting season. According to Roger Williams, the Narragansett called this star cluster *chippapuok,* the "brood hen." The Munsee people of western Long Island called them *asi'seke-*

*wataya'sak,* the "bunched up ones," and believed that they represented seven pine trees which later became seven holy prophets. There were other signs which nature gave to the women telling them that it was time to plant. When the alewives came up the fresh water streams from the oceans and bays in March and April, and the dogwood leaves grew to the size of a squirrel's ear in early May, the community knew that the winter was over and it was time to go to the planting grounds (Ceci 1978:304-6).

Although we have no detailed descriptions of the native gardens, random, anecdotal accounts from Dutch and English observers suggest that crops were grown in small plots ranging from one-half to two acres.[16] European observers in seventeenth-century Virginia reported seeing small gardens of two hundred square feet scattered around adjacent to Indian settlements (Barbour 1986, 1:162; Rountree 1989:46). The plots were prepared by burning off the desired area in late March or early April, a custom which was followed by the Shinnecocks and Montauketts into the twentieth century. If any trees blocked the sunlight, the trunks were girdled with an ax. The offending trees soon became standing supplies of fire wood for the next winter (Butler 1948:13). Smith described a

Fig. 4.8. Women planting corn

similar technique used by the Powhatan in Virginia. "To prepare the ground," wrote Smith, "they bruise the bark of the trees neare the root, then do they scortch the roots with fire" (Barbour 1986, 1:157).

Once the field was cleared, the whole community began the process of breaking up the top soil with digging sticks and hoes made of stone, clam shell, horse shoe crab shell, and deer scapula.[17] According to Roger Williams, "All the neighbors men and women, forty, fifty, a hundred, joyne, and come in to help freely. With friendly joyning they break up their fields" (Butler 1948:13). The planting was probably done right after the last frost, between the last week in April and the first week in May. Rather than breaking up the whole surface of the field as the Europeans did, the women dug up small mounds of earth, creating raised beds about a yard in diameter. The Dutch observer, Isaack de Rasieres, describing the planting process on western Long Island, said, "They make heaps like molehills, each about two and a half feet from the others, which they sow or plant in April with maize, in each heap five or six grains" (1909:107).[18]

The Narragansett fertilized the seed corn, which they called *Scannemeneash*,[19] with fish remains. According to the English accounts, the Indian women buried the fish in the corn mounds just below the seed. Bradford stated in his journal that a Wampanaog named Squanto told the English that their corn would not do well unless it was fertilized in this manner (Butler 1948:16). Winthrop reported that the "Indians used to put two or three . . . fishes under or adjacent to each corn hill, whereby they have many times a crop double to what the ground would otherwise produced" (1937:128).[20] Winslow, writing from Plymouth in 1621, said that "according to the manner of the Indians we manuered our ground with Herrings or rather Shadds, which we have in great abundance, and rake with great ease at our doors" (quoted by Ceci 1975:26).

These reports and the subsequent references to the Native American origins of the practice in history textbooks have been challenged by some scholars who argue that the idea was given to Squanto when he was living in England prior to 1620 (Ceci 1975:27; Rostlund 1957:227). Squanto had been taken to England in 1618 by a merchant named Thomas Dermer and may have seen English farmers fertilizing their fields with fish, but there is no evidence to support this speculation. There is evidence that some English farmers, apparently not the Pilgrims' ancestors, did use fish remains as fertilizer, but Lynn Ceci's speculation that Squanto merely carried the idea of fish fertilization from one group of Englishmen to another remains unproved. Until such evidence is discovered there is no reason to doubt the words of such competent observers as Bradford, Winslow, and Winthrop (Silver 1980:120-21).

New evidence and insights into this issue were reported by Stephen Mrozowski, who excavated a seventeenth-century Native American corn field on Cape Cod (1994). Mrozowski, an archaeologist at the University of Massachusetts, found the bones of silver hake *(Merluccius bilinearis)*, cod *(Gadidae sps.)*, and a close relative of the alewife in the corn hills. Although the five radiocarbon dates from the site are not precise enough to determine the exact decade in the seventeenth century when the fish were placed in the corn hills, it is possible that the fields were being worked prior to the arrival of the English settlers.

Was fish used as a fertilizer on Long Island? We cannot say for sure. Ceci is correct in noting that too often people assumed that the process was a common trait found in all Native American communities. The soil and climatic conditions and the availability of fish were determining factors. Inland communities did not have access to an abundance of fish and the coastal groups south of the Delaware did not need fertilizer because of the warm, humid climate and fertile soils. On Long Island, particularly on the east end, the conditions were similar to those in southern New England. Here too, the alewives crowded the fresh water streams and ponds every spring, offering themselves for fertilizer. If fish were used, the fields would have to be guarded all the time against dogs and raccoons.

When the corn shoots are about five or six inches high in mid-May, three or four bean seeds were planted in each hill around the base of the corn stalks (De Rasieres 1909:107; De Vries 1909:219). The beans, called *mais-cusseet* in Unkechaug, *maugueseets* in Montaukett, and *manusqussedash* in Narragansett, came in a variety of colors and served as an excellent nutritional companion to corn. The two plants formed a reciprocal relationship. Corn stalks provided support for the bean vines and the bean roots support colonies of nitrogen-fixing bacteria. Corn must consume a considerable amount of nitrogen in order to produce a healthy harvest. Squash, melon, and pumpkin were planted in between the corn hills, providing a ground cover with their large leaves which discouraged the growth of weeds (Winthrop 1937:128).

The first serious weeding was done in June. This process was so crucial that it was ritualized and became a seasonal marker in the calendar of many Algonquian groups. June was called *Moonesquanimock,* or "the weeding month" by the Nipmuk, and *Monaskunnemun,* meaning "to weed," by the Narragansetts, who called the broad hoe used for this task *Monaskunnummautawwin* (Butler 1948:17). William Wood voiced admiration for the horticultural skills of the Indian women, "they exceede our English husband-men, keeping it so clear with their clam shell hoes, . . . not suffering a choaking weede to advance his audacious head above their infant corn, or an undermining worme to spoil [it]" (1968:94). A month after the weeding was completed, the women hilled the corn by pulling earth up around the base of the stalks to encourage the growth of prop roots which would strengthen the base of the stalks and prevent them from being blown over by a heavy wind. In our experimental garden on the Southampton campus, we found that the hilling process was difficult because the young bean shoots around the base of the corn stalks were so vulnerable. We had to scoop up dirt by hand and pile it carefully around the beans.

The gardens needed constant tending from planting to harvest. Small, temporary wigwams were often built near the fields where the young boys who were not old enough to go hunting with their fathers could stay to watch the field day and night (Rountree, April 1995: pers. com.). They had to be ever vigilant against a variety of predators. The most voracious of these were the crows, blackbirds, and cranes. De Rasieres tells us that the Indians of western Long Island called them "maize thieves" because they could descend on a corn field in huge numbers and strip a whole crop (1909:114). One means of combating these thieves was to plant the seeds deeper in the ground, taking care not to place them so deep that they could not push up to the surface. The process protected the newly sown seeds and enabled them to form a stronger root system so that the new shoots could not be easily plucked up (Butler 1948:19). Roger Williams reported that the Narragansetts domesticated hawks to protect their corn fields.

Four-legged creatures and tiny insects were also a threat to the corn. Raccoons could do considerable damage during their frequent raids. Deer were an even greater threat because a small herd could destroy several acres of corn in a single foray. A close watch had to be kept on the field day and night. The invasion of insects required a different remedy. John Winthrop, Jr. reported that in the summer of 1632 worms had eaten the corn down to the ground (Butler 1948:21-22). The worms were described by John Josselyn as "a dark dunnish worm or bug . . . an inch long, that lye at the root of the corn and garden plants all day, and in the night creep out and devour them." The native peoples of southern New England dug the worms out of the soil covering the roots of the corn and collected them in a birch bark basket. The baskets were then carried to the shore and launched on the ebb tide in a ceremony led by the *powwaw*. Although the English observers did not believe in the spiritual powers of the *powwaws*, as the Algonquian shamans were called, they acknowledged the effectiveness of the procedure. John Josselyn remarked that "within a day or two if you go into your field you may look your eyes out sooner than find any of them" (quoted in Butler 1948:22).

Another threat, the weather, was beyond human control. Drought, unseasonable cold, or dampness could destroy a winter supply and endanger the whole community. There is no evidence that any form of irrigation was used in the coastal Algonquian gardens. The people turned to the *powwaws* to lead them in prayers and ceremonial dancing to persuade the gods to change the weather. If the weather was good and the birds were kept away, the harvest could be bountiful, providing enough surplus for the winter and, perhaps, even some for trade. The corn ears were about nine inches long and had eight rows of kernels with about thirty in each row. According to John Smith, "Every stalke of their corn commonly beareth two eares, some 3, seldom 4. . . . Every eare ordinarily hath betwixt 200 and 500 grains" (Barbour 1986,1:157). Roger Williams estimated that a Narragansett woman and her family working on an acre of land could produce around forty bushels of corn each year. If corn were a basic staple in the diet, those forty bushels would have fed about five people for a year (Thomas 1976:12-13). However, as we have seen, corn, beans, and squash were probably "luxury crops" which supplemented the harvest of wild plants, fish, and game.

Although the women were in charge of the village gardens, tobacco or *ottomoak,* as it was called by the Narragansetts, was in the male domain (Williams 1973:103).[21] The men planted, tended, and harvested the sacred plant, which was generally grown in a separate area some distance away from the other crops.[22] John Josselyn (1988:54) described the procedures for cultivating tobacco as follows:

> It is sown in April upon a bed of rich mold . . . . they make a bed about three yards long , . . . . this they tread down hard, then they sow their seed upon it as thick as may be and sift fine earth upon it, then tread it down again . . . . when it hath gotten four or six leaves, they remove it into the planting ground; and when it begins to bud towards flowering, they crop off the top, for the flower draws away the strength of the leaf.

Lamont Smith follows a procedure similar to this for the Shinnecock ceremonial tobacco he raises in his reservation garden today.

## Food Processing and Storage

The villagers harvested their crops in late August or early September and set aside the best seeds for the next year's crop (Wood 1968:70). As the food came into the village, the women began immediately to process it for winter storage. They used several different procedures for drying corn. If they wanted to preserve the sweetness of the fresh corn they boiled it on the cob first and then shelled it with clam shells. The women laid out the kernels to dry in the sun and then placed them in storage or in small leather bags called *denotas* for the men to carry when they went away from the village for any length of time to hunt or to embark on trading expeditions (Butler 1948:22-23). Another method of drying corn was to parch it in hot ashes (Barbour 1986, 1:157). This corn will retain its sweetness for several months and can be eaten dry or boiled in water. When the water is added the kernels will swell back up and taste just as sweet as the day the cob was picked.

Another procedure for drying the corn required the construction of drying racks from saplings. The women stripped back the husks, tied them together in small bunches, and left them to dry slowly in the open air. They prepared the squash by slicing them into rings and sliding a pole through the center of each slice like a barbecue skewer which they mounted on a rack where the squash could dry in the open air. To prevent the squash from being damaged by rain and mold during the initial stages of the drying process, the women either built a thatched roof over the rack or brought the squash poles into the wigwam on damp days. Beans were thrashed out of their pods and left to dry on open mats. Jasper Danckaerts reported seeing an elderly woman in the Munsee village at Nayack using a stick to thrash beans "with astonishing force and dexterity" (1969:54-55).

The Late Woodland Period, 1,000 B.P. - 1600                    101

Fig. 4.9. Women storing food in a storage pit

After the drying was complete, the women placed the food in baskets or woven bags in preparation for winter storage.

The storage areas, called *Auqunnash* by the Narragansetts (Butler 1948:22) and "Indian barns" by the English were actually pits from three to six feet deep with openings ranging from three to four feet in diameter. Archaeologists have found remains of such pits in New England, New Jersey, upstate New York, and on Long Island (Butler 1948:23-24; Ritchie 1969:280; Kraft 1986:139-41; Russell 1980:175-78; Johannemann 1993:643-55). The shape, size, and manner of construction varied. The Munsee-speaking peoples along the Delaware shaped their pits in the form of silos, about five feet deep and three to five feet wide, lined them with clay and placed layers of bark or mold resistant big bluestem grass *(Andropogon gerardi)* over the floor and walls (Kraft 1986:139). The ancestors of the Iroquois, in what is now central New York State, lined their storage pits with hemlock bark and bluestem grass (Ritchie 1969:280). On Cape Cod, the Wampanaog dug trenches in the sand, put in baskets and hemp bags filled with food, and covered the storage area with a small mound of sand (Russell 1980:176; Wood 1968:95).

The pits excavated on the Pharaoh (Pharoah) site at Montauk on the eastern end of Long Island were much shallower

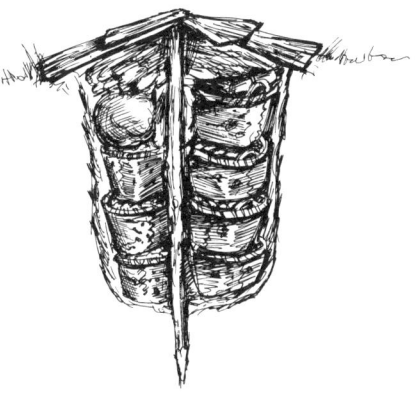

Fig. 4.10. Cross-section of underground storage pit.

and may have been the foundations for above ground storage structures (Johannemann 1993:643-54). Mark Harrington photographed one such structure which was still in use on the Shinnecock Reservation at the turn of this century. A Shinnecock named John Henry Thompson constructed the "barn" by digging a cellar about five feet deep and framing a roof over the cellar with saplings. He then covered the frame with chunks of sod, which were held in place by poles laid over the top (Johannemann 1993).[23]

## Native Hearths

The Native American diet included a rich and varied mix of wild and domesticated foods prepared by the village women. Iroquois women could prepare up to forty different corn dishes, and a woman from a western tribe was able to recite, from memory, more than one hundred fifty detailed recipes to Arthur Parker (Russell 1980:76). Unfortunately, few of the recipes used by the Algonquian women on Long Island were ever recorded. We do have some general observations about Native American meals from the Dutch on western Long Island, however, and a few detailed accounts from southern New England.

The Algonquian kitchens were equipped with utensils for storing, processing, and cooking food. The women stored their food in woven and bark baskets, wooden bowls, ceramic pots, gourds, and textile bags of various sizes. The basic food processing utensil was the mortar and pestle, which came in two basic sizes: the small one-to-two quart form, and the large two-to-three gallon mortar (De Rasieres 1909:107). This implement was so important to the women that it was sometimes placed in their graves just as hunting tools were buried with the men (Butler 1948:33).

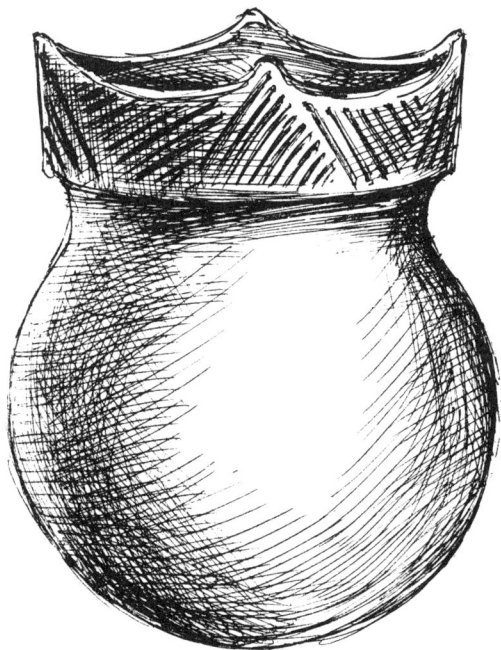

The pottery found on the eastern Long Island sites tends to be shell tempered with a cone-shaped bottom and decorated around the rims (Ritchie 1969:268; Smith 1950: plates 8-10, 12-14). Some of the pots excavated near East Hampton have human faces staring out in the four cardinal directions (Lopez and Latham

Fig. 4.11. Late Woodland pottery. "Bowmans Brook" style, "castellated" rim vessel.

1982:258-62). The possible religious significance of these heads will be discussed in Chapter 5. One of these pots was eighteen inches deep and fifteen inches wide at the mouth, a size which could easily hold enough food for the seven to ten people who shared the average size wigwam or hearth area in a longhouse. Pottery found on sites in western Long Island where the Munsee-speaking peoples lived is more likely to be tempered with grit or a mix of grit and shell and have a "castellated" rim (see fig. 4.11; Kaeser 1978a:74-75).

The women also used a variety of small tools such as flint knives to slice and skin the flesh of plants, game, fowl, and fish, and wooden spoons to stir and ladle out the food from the cooking pot. They sifted the flour in artfully woven hemp baskets designed to allow the fine particles to flow through (De Rasieres 1909:107; De Vries 1909:218). Wooden trays, called *wunnauganash* by the Narragansetts, were used when mixing dough and serving food (Butler 1948:32-33). Most of the cooking was done in large ceramic pots which could hold several gallons.

A great majority of the recipes reported by Dutch and English observers called for corn in some form. The women prepared corn cakes, one of the most common foods, by boiling the shelled corn, grinding it into a flour, and then sifting it to separate the fine grains. These grains were sprinkled with water and kneaded into small flat cakes about an inch thick. Dried strawberries, blueberries, raspberries, cherries, and currents were often added to the mix. The women wrapped the cakes in corn or grape leaves and baked them in the ashes of the open fire (De Vries 1909:218-19).

The coarser grains, which remained in the sieve, were parched and stored in small bags to be used as rations on long trips. A small handful of the grain, called *yokeg (yokeag)* by the Pequots, was enough for a meal on the trail. Three such portions, washed down with long drinks of water, were sufficient for a full day if there was no time to stop to prepare a more complete meal (Wood 1968:98). In fact, one had to be careful not to "over eat" because the corn swells in the stomach when it mixes with the water. Daniel Gookin, a Massachusetts Bay colony official responsible for Indian affairs, reported that, "an Indian will travel for many days with no other food but this meal, which he eateth as he needs, and after it, drinketh water" (Gookin 1972:11).

John Winthrop, Jr. described another form of yokeg which is known to the modern reader as "popcorn." This corn, reported Winthrop, is "tender and turned almost quite the inside outward, which will be almost white and flowery" when it is parched in the embers (Winthrop 1937:129). Yokeg was also a regular staple of the village diet. The women boiled it until a thick porridge called *sappaen* was formed. Isaack de Rasieres (1909:107-8) said that the sappaen was good eating, even better with Dutch butter, and easily digested. Another Dutch observer, Adriaen van der Donck (1968:75-76), noted that sappaen was a basic part of the Indian's daily diet: "It is the common food of all; young and old eat it; and they are so well accustomed to it, and fond of it, that when they visit our people, or each other, they consider themselves neglected unless they are treated with *sappaen.*" The Narragansett called this corn mixture *nausamp.* The English shortened it to "samp" (Butler 1948:27) and the Long Island settlers adopted it into their regular diet.

When beans were added to the porridge it became "succotash," one of the more familiar Native American meals. The many variations of succotash recorded in different Native American communities suggest that the women used the basic corn and bean mixture as a stock to which they added whatever was available in the village at the time. Fish or clams, ground nuts, leeks, and Jerusalem artichokes, for example, turned the succotash into a tasty and nutritious chowder. After a successful whale hunt, the native peoples living on what is now the south coast of Maine prepared a whale stew by boiling whale meat, skimming off the oil and then adding corn and beans (Rosier 1907:392). Van der Donck described similar meals of boiled corn and beans combined with fish or meat in his account of the native peoples on western Long Island (1968:75). This combination is very nutritious because the beans provide vitamins A, C, and riboflavin as well as albumin and amino acids, and the corn contributes vitamins A and C and adds niacin. The meat and fish are rich in vitamin D, protein, and such minerals as calcium, iron, copper, phosphorus, and iodine.

The squash and pumpkin were not often mixed in with the corn stews. Algonquian women baked them in the ashes or boiled them whole and served them. The flesh would be scooped out with wooden spoons and clam shells. A group of four Native American men from the upper Delaware valley were observed sitting around a boiled pumpkin eating it in this fashion by Francis Pastorius, a German schoolmaster in Pennsylvania (1910:384). If Pastorius had looked more carefully, he probably would have found that the men were steaming, not boiling, the pumpkin. The Indian women advised other English visitors that squash should be cooked in as little water as possible. The squash or pumpkin would be placed in a large pot with a small amount of water and covered over with pumpkin leaves to control the steaming process (Russell 1980:81).

Steamed squash was enjoyed in the fall after the harvest and the surplus was dried for winter and spring. The women would soak the dried slices, add some corn flour, and bake them into bread or boil them into a thick pudding. The seeds, removed and parched in the ashes, were a great delicacy any time of the year. Squash not only supplemented the nutrients in corn and beans by adding fiber, complex carbohydrates, potassium, and thiamin to the diet, but it also provided additional sources of vitamin A and C, niacin, riboflavin, iron, and calcium. Recent studies of butternut squash indicate that it is also a source of beta carotene, an important antioxidant nutrient, which some scientists believe reduces the risk of cancer and heart disease (Bittman 1993:67)

Although corn, beans, and squash were playing an increasingly important role in the daily diet after 1,000 B.P., wild foods such as berries, nuts, tubers, and a variety of green leaf plants, fish, fowl, sea mammals, and game animals were still basic staples (Kraft 1986:142). The primary hunting weapon was the bow, made from hardwood, which shot arrows tipped with small, stemmed, triangular projectile points fashioned from chert, quartz, and bone (Kraft 1986:154; C. Smith 1950:126; Ritchie 1969:266-72). The bows described by John White in 1585 and Martin Pring in 1603 were made from maple or witch hazel and stood between five and six feet high, about as tall as the hunter himself. These long bows fired arrows of wood or reed, which were over a yard long and fletched with three feathers (Kraft 1986:154). A party of hunters left the village in October for the hunt and did not return until December, according to a Dutch observer, but it is likely that the men returned frequently carrying both fresh and smoked meat to the village (De Rasieres 1909:108). A colorful account of the use of the bow and arrow in a whale hunt was written by James Rosier, who accompanied Captain George Waymouth on a voyage along the eastern shore of North America in 1605:

> One especial thing is their manner of killing the whale which they call Powdawe; and will describe its form; how bloweth up in the water; and that he is twelve fathoms long; and that they go in company of their king with a multitude of their boats, and strike him with a bone made in the fashion of a harping iron fastened to a rope, which they make strong from the bark of trees, which they veer out after him; then all boats come about him, as he riseth above the water, with their arrows they shoot him to death; when they have killed him and dragged him to shore, they call all their chief lords together, and sing a song of joy (Rosier 1907:392).

European observers who emphasize Native American horticulture often tend to underestimate the resources available to the Algonquian villagers through their traditional practices of hunting, gathering, and fishing. In time of war, the English destroyed the Indian's corn fields expecting that this would starve them into surrender. They found, to their dismay, that the Indians were able to feed themselves from the forests, just as their ancestors had done (Russell 1980:94).

Not all of the European observers understated the role of wild plants in the Native American diet. Daniel Gookin reported that Jerusalem artichokes, ground nuts, chestnuts, acorns, and walnuts were still basic staples in the Native American diet as late as 1674 (Gookin 1972:10-11). The women boiled, shelled, and ground the nuts into flour, which they used to bake nut bread or to mix with corn into a thick pudding (Russell 1980:82). Although the European observers seldom mentioned the use of green leaf plants, it is likely that they continued to be a part of the Algonquian diet as well. Perhaps these common plants were simply not considered worthy of comment. A variety of berries, as we have seen, supplemented the corn bread recipes, and Van der Donck mentions that the Lenapes in western Long Island made a drink out of grapes (Russell 1980:85).

Fish, fowl, and game were undoubtedly consumed at the same rate per capita throughout the prehistoric periods on Long Island. The introduction of cultivated foods supplemented and greatly enriched the diet, but probably did not cause any significant decline in fish and meat consumption. The European colonists reported numerous Native American recipes for preparing fish, fowl, and meat. Although the most convenient communal meal was stew prepared in a large pot, the women also baked fish, fowl, and small game in clay molds. The first step in this ingenious process was to encase the body in a clay coat "two fingers thick" (Parker 1927:189). Fowl and such small game animals as rabbits were often stuffed with pot herbs before they were encased.

The clay baking dishes were then placed in the embers and covered over with hot coals. This process cooks the flesh in its own juices and preserves the natural flavor and vitamins. When the mold is removed from the fire and broken open, the fish scales and outer skin stick to the clay surface. The mold, if it is properly cracked open along the outer edges, forms a convenient serving dish. The success of this recipe has been verified by the members of the Suffolk County Archaeological Association. The organization's annual June meeting includes a traditional Native American dinner prepared on an open hearth. The baked fish entree is always a great favorite with the members.

Another ingenious method of preparing food, perhaps the only Native American meal better known than succotash, is the clam bake. The women dug a pit, placed stones in the bottom, and built a fire on top of them. When the stones were red hot they covered them with a layer of moist eelgrass *(Zostera marina)* which produced the steam heat. Next, they laid in the clams and, perhaps, some corn and pieces of fish as well, covered them with more damp eelgrass and sealed the pit with sand (Russell 1980:75). The Shinnecock today still use this procedure when they steam clams and corn for large family dinners, although Gerrod Smith, director of the Shinnecock Nation Museum, says with a sly smile, "sometimes we cheat a little and put plastic over the top instead of sand." He also pointed out, however, that neither sand nor plastic is necessary for the process to work, because the top layer of eelgrass will do the job, it just takes a bit longer with the eelgrass cover. David De Vries, a Dutch colonist, was fed oysters and fish when he visited the villagers at Rockaway, but he did not mention how they were prepared (De Vries 1909:231).

Ten cooking pits which may have been used for ancient clam bakes were excavated on a Late Woodland site at Strongs Neck near Setauket (Werner 1982:205, 212). The pit walls were fire stained and there were fire cracked quartz cobblestones on the bottoms. The excavators found shells from scallops, oysters, whelk, snail, and hard and soft shelled clams, as well as fragments of unidentified animal bones and some broken pottery. Although some small pieces of meat were steamed in the pits, most of the game animals were roasted on a spit over an open fire or boiled in the stew. The roasting meat was turned slowly and basted regularly (Russell 1980:75). The women prepared the surplus fish and meat for winter storage by placing it on wooden racks to dry. If they wanted to smoke the flesh, they simply built a fire under the rack. This food could be eaten without cooking or it could be pulverized and added to the winter stew pot.

In summary, the Native Americans had a balanced, nutritious diet of meat, nuts, vegetables, leafy greens, and fruit. All of the European observers commented on the good health of the native peoples prior to the arrival of European diseases, although there is archaeological evidence that some Native Americans did suffer from viral infections, arthritis, and tuberculosis. Their endurance during long distance travel over difficult terrain made a great impression on the Europeans. Two very popular ingredients in modern cooking, which the native peoples of this area did not have or used sparingly may also have been a factor in their good health. There is no mention of sugar or salt in any of the recipes used in southern New England and Long Island (Russell 1980:86-91).

## Summary

Our understanding of the Late Woodland horticulturists is enriched by the reports of archaeologists, ethnographers, and the journals of the seventeenth-century European visitors to New England, Long Island, and the mid-Atlantic coastal area. The early European visitors often reported descriptions of material culture as well as stories and lore from native informants, preserving them for the ethnographers in the twentieth century and for Native Americans today who wish to revive their own heritage. The data from these sources help us to understand the primary changes in lifeways which mark the transition from Middle Woodland "forest efficient" settlers to Late Woodland horticulturists. These gradual shifts include the introduction of plant domestication, increased sedentism, new patterns of religious ceremonialism, expanded trade networks, and new styles of pottery and projectile points. Increased sedentism was further encouraged when domesticated plants such as corn, beans, and squash were integrated into the food base.

The structures in the villages were made of saplings, bark, mats, and fiber lashings. There were two dominant architectural styles: the wigwam, a circular or oval-shaped building about ten by fifteen feet; and an ovate-shaped longhouse, sixty feet or longer by twenty feet wide. The wigwam is more common in southern New England and on eastern Long Island, whereas the longhouse appears on most of the Lenape sites in New Jersey and on western Long Island. It is important to note, however, that both forms do appear in all of these areas. In some New England villages, for example, wigwams were extended into longhouses for the winter months.

The corn, beans, squash, and tobacco were planted after the last frost, usually in late April or early May. The women tended the food crops while the men had the responsibility for the tobacco plots. The women processed the food and prepared a rich variety of nutritional dishes for their families. Wild plants, game, and fish continued to be very important parts of their daily cuisine. The surplus food was dried and placed in storage pits where it would be available during the winter. Some of these pits were inside family houses, but the larger ones were located on common ground near the residences.

All of the evidence from the various sources clearly indicates that the native peoples here had developed a very successful lifeway in harmony with the environment. They established a balance between domesticated and wild food sources which sustained them through the seasonal round. Their warm, dry dwellings were ingeniously designed to make efficient use of limited space. The people conveniently organized their settlements around open spaces and public activity areas. The rich heritage and landscape the Woodland horticulturists had received from their ancestors remained intact, but their own descendants would not be so fortunate.

# 5

# The Algonquian Belief Systems

Excavation of the Archaic and Middle Woodlands sites described in the previous chapters revealed a vague, albeit intriguing, glimpse into the belief systems of the Native American peoples on Long Island. Although the artifacts provide a limited basis for interpretation, we can be fairly certain that the religious system included a belief in an afterlife, in the importance of honoring the deceased with grave gifts for use in the spirit world, in the power of smoking rituals, and in the symbolic importance of red ocher and the circle form.

Our understanding of the Late Woodland Period is enriched by the written observations of the Europeans who arrived early enough to have witnessed Indian religious ceremonies and to have interviewed some of the participants. Unfortunately these religious beliefs were dismissed by many of the European observers as composites of exotic, unstructured superstitions, which could not be studied in a systematic fashion. These attitudes prevailed until the emergence of anthropology in the last two decades of the nineteenth century (Fogelson 1989:150-54). Modern scholars now approach the study of Native American religions as they would any other belief system. Religion, at all levels of social complexity, answers basic human needs in the following ways: it calms anxieties about death, the afterlife, and the risks of accidental injury; it serves to reinforce a social bond, to establish rules of conduct, to present models of proper behavior, and to celebrate such rites of passage as birth, puberty, marriage, and death; it offers an explanation about human origins, about the origin of the universe, and about the destructive and beneficial forces of nature; and it offers hope of a cure to those sick in body and in spirit (Lehmann and Myers 1993:2-3; Wallace 1966:3-29).

Modern scholars have revisited the Dutch and English accounts written down in the first few decades after the first Europeans arrived and the ethnographic data collected by missionaries in the eighteenth century. Another important source of information comes from anthropological studies of tribal peoples who are still practicing their ancient traditions. The material collected by missionaries, of course, cannot be taken at face value because they framed their descriptions of Native American beliefs in a Christian context. It may never be possible to reconstruct an objective description which fully comprehends the rich texture and deeper meaning of the ancient belief systems from these sources. We can, however, with the proper humility and a critical eye to the sources, present an anthropological anatomy of the beliefs, rituals, and ceremonies which were at the vital center of aboriginal lifeways when the Europeans arrived on Long Island.

The basic premise of all religions is that supernatural forces exist which influence people and events (Wallace 1966:52). Beginning with this premise, human groups have constructed an infinite variety of beliefs, rituals, and social institutions which play a central role in most societies. It is important that we approach the study of Native American religion in this context, rather than view it as a "primitive curiosity" (see Axtell 1985:13-19). All too often simplistic accounts of happy hunting grounds and a "great spirit" are presented as the basic elements of traditional belief systems. This approach reflects a common tendency to force Native American beliefs into a "Christian" format rather than view both religions as expressions of a universal human quest for meaning (Rountree 1989:139).

## *Manitou:* The Mana of the Algonquian People

The concept of *mana,* a belief in "impersonal power" which permeates the universe, is shared by most traditional peoples in all parts of the globe (R. Underhill 1965:20-21; Lehmann and Myers 1993:7, 12). Mana, a Melanesian term used by anthropologists as a generic reference for unseen, mysterious forces, is called *wakan* by the Sioux, *orenda* by the Iroquois, and *manitou (manitu, manetu, manito)* by the Algonquian people (E. Tooker 1979:16-17; Grim 1987:6; Axtell 1986:16). This powerful and highly unpredictable force can do harm as well as good and must, therefore, be invoked in the proper context. Some anthropologists have compared this spirit power to electricity, an invisible force which can be very useful, but can kill if used improperly by untrained people (R. Underhill 1965:21-22; Wallace 1966:7).

The word *Manitou* was often used by Algonquian people in reference to an event which was surprising, remarkable, miraculous, or simply mysterious. Anything which evoked a sense of awe was believed to be an indication that Manitou was present. The Lenapes in western Long Island told a Dutchman that Manitou was "whatever is wonderful and strange that surpasses human understanding" (De Laet 1909:49-50). William Jones, an Indian who had studied anthropology, described Manitou as "a cosmic, mysterious property which is believed to be existing everywhere in nature" (Jones 1905:190; Tooker 1979:13-19).

The Lenapes believed this spirit force was the "active, hidden spirit of the universe . . . the abstract conception behind all life, light, energy, and action" (Brinton 1884:133). When Samuel Bownas, a Quaker missionary, asked a Lenape sachem from Jamaica, Long Island, to define "Manitou," the sachem replied by drawing a circle with a piece of charcoal and said Manitou was "all eye, that he saw everything at once; and all ear, that he heard everything in like manner; and all mind, that he knew all things, and that nothing could be hid from his sight, hearing or knowledge" (quoted by Densmore 1992:439). This description personalizes Manitou more than the other accounts, perhaps because the sachem was hoping that this frame of reference would be more understandable to a Christian.

A reference to Manitou in the Long Island folklore comes from historian Gabriel Furman, who recounted a legend associated with Manetto Hill near Plainview, Long Island (1874:62-63). The "hill" is actually a ridge, running from Manetto Hill Road along Washington Boulevard, rising to a height of about 240 feet. During a great drought Manitou instructed a sachem, perhaps in a dream or through an intermediary, to stand on Manetto Hill and fire an arrow into the air. On the spot where the arrow landed, said the spirit message, the people should dig until they found water. The sachem did as he was told and the arrow landed at the foot of the hill in a hollow. The Indians dug there and found a spring which soon formed a pond in the hollow. There was a pond at the foot of the hill called "Mascopas," according to local historians Iris and Alonzo Gibbs, which is now under the athletic field of John F. Kennedy High School (1981:10-11). Although we cannot be certain, it seems likely that the high ridge was a sacred place, so named because the Indians living in the area believed that the Manitou spirit force was present there.[1]

The Algonquian peoples believed that Manitou was expressed in deities called *manitos,* which took the form of men, women, children, and animals, as well as inanimate objects such as fire, water, sea, colors, the sun, the moon, the four directions, the seasons, and plants (Simmons 1986:38-41). All of nature was alive with spirit power. Most prominent among these manitos were the gods of the directions: *Wompanand,* god of the east; *Chekesuwand,* god of the west; *Wunnanameant,* god of the north; *Sowwanand,* god of the south; and *Cautantowwit,* the god of the southwest (Williams 1973:190).[2] The manitos of the four cardinal directions control the winds and the weather. Samson Occom reported similar beliefs held by the Montauketts, and so did the Lenape sachem interviewed by Samuel Bownas. The sachem added four small circles around the edges of the large circle he had drawn to explain Manitou, saying that they were the "four quarters of the world" (quoted in Densmore 1992:439).

The more powerful deity, however, was Cautantowwit, who created the first human beings from wood and later sent them corn and beans by his messenger, *conconchus,* the crow. After death, all souls return to Cautantowwit's house in the southwest where the days are warm and the food is plentiful. He was generally considered to be an aloof, impersonal, benevolent force, who ensured the harvest each year, but he could send disease and misfortune if he was angered (Simmons 1986:49).

Another closely related deity was a more personal mysterious force, which took many forms and was known by several different names. This manito was called *Hobbamock (Abbomacho)* or *Cheepi (Chepi, Chepian)* in southern New England (Simmons 1986:219-20). According to Samson Occom, the Montaukett called it *Mutcheshesunnetooh* (Occom 1993:152). Hobbamock had a powerful hold on the imagination of the people because it was directly involved in an individual's daily routine in this world and represented the souls of the dead in the afterworld. Hobbamock might appear in any form, often in dreams or visions, and bring a person good fortune or disaster. This spirit force could also bestow supernatural powers on a person.

The Europeans, imposing their concept of Christian dualism on the Algonquian deities, tended to interpret Hobbamock as the devil and Cautantowwitt as god (Young 1841:357; Josselyn 1988:95-96). This oversimplification was often used by missionaries as a bridge to bring converts across the theological divide from their traditional beliefs to Christianity. Samson Occom, for example, identified Cauhluntoowut (Cautantowwitt) as "the supreme being" and Mutcheshesunnetooh (Hobbamock) as the "evil power" (Occom 1993:152). The importance of Hobbamock in the Indian's pantheon convinced the Europeans that their religion was nothing more than devil worship. The subtleties of Hobbamock's nature was of no interest to the colonists.

The Lenapes did believe that some spirits were harmful, but there was no supreme evil manito equivalent to the Christian devil in the Algonquian pantheon (Harrington 1921:194). When Samuel Bownas asked the Lenape sachem from Jamaica what his people thought of the devil, the man told him that they did not think about evil forces as separate from Manitou. There was, apparently, no independent evil power in the Indian cosmology. All power was in Manitou.

A deity of great importance to the Lenapes of western Long Island was *Mesingw*, the Master of Animals (see fig. 5.1). Mesingw, "the mask being," appeared in human form, but his face was a large mask, painted on the left in solid black and on the right in solid red, and his body was completely in a coat

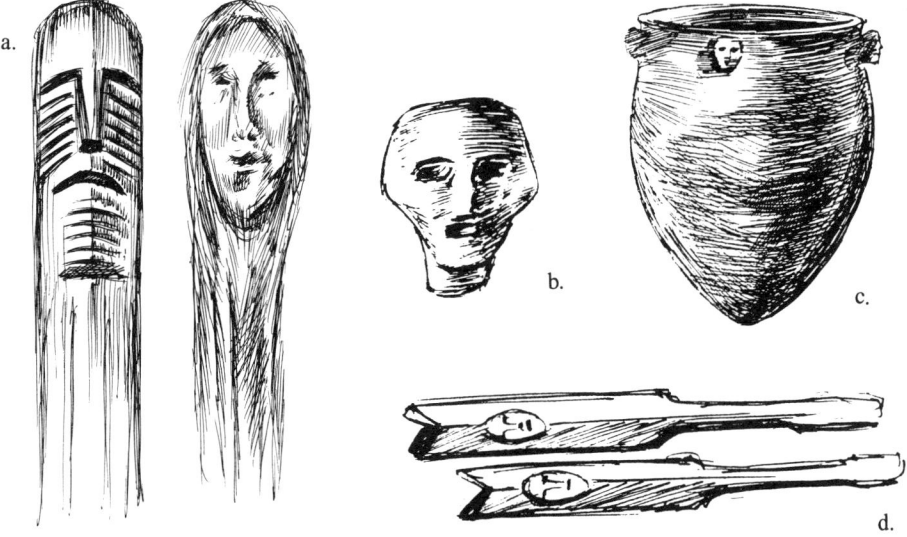

Fig. 5.1. Mesingw faces. *a*. Mesingw posts; *b*. Sebonac vessel; *c*. Pipe bowl; *d*. Mesingw drumsticks

of thick black hair (Kraft 1986:169-73, 1991:5-7; Harrington 1921:32-33). The Lenapes said Mesingw was often seen riding through the woods on the back of a male deer as he watched over both hunter and prey. He had to make sure that the game was plentiful and that the hunters appeased the manitos of the animals they killed. If the hunters killed indiscriminately or did not ask forgiveness of the manito after a kill, Mesingw would take the animals away where they could not be found by the hunters.

According to the Lenapes, Mesingw appeared to them and told them that they must "take wood and carve a face just like mine, painted half black and half red, as mine is and I will put power in it, so that it will do what you ask. When the man who takes my part puts the face on, I will be there, and this is how I will live among you" (Harrington 1921:150). The Lenapes followed Mesingw's instructions and added a bearskin coat and leggings to complete the costume. A missionary to the Lenapes in the eighteenth century described the costume as "a coat of bear skins dressed with hair on, hanging down to their toes; a pair of bear skin stockings; a great wooden mask painted, one half black, the other half tawny, about the color of the Indian's skin, with an extravagant mouth, cut very much awry; the face fastened to a bear skin cap, which was drawn over his head" (quoted by Kraft 1991:6). A designated family would store the costume, honoring it frequently with tobacco rituals. The costume was used by an impersonator in an annual ritual attended by the whole community. The Lenapes believed that once the costume was in place, Mesingw became one with the impersonator.

Although there is no way to determine with certainty that the Mesingw ceremonies were a part of the prehistoric Lenape belief system, archaeologists have found convincing circumstantial evidence of continuity. Human face images carved on the posts of longhouses have been reported by seventeenth-century observers, and archaeologists have unearthed similar images on the rims of pottery, on tobacco pipes, on small pendants, and on small stone carvings in excavations from New Jersey to the eastern end of Long Island (Kraft 1986:170, fig. 37; Kraft 1991:1-3; Smith 1980:311; Levine and Bonvillain 1980:319; Lopez and Latham 1982:258-61).

The Southold Indian Museum has two unique stone effigies found near Mattituck which may be related to Mesingw ceremonies (see fig. 5.2). One is an argillite elbow pipe six centimeters high, with a human face carved on the front of the bowl. The other, a carved sandstone human head about the same size as the pipe bowl, may be an unfinished pipe. Unfortunately the museum records only report the general area where they were found. (Barcel, October 16, 1994: pers. com.). The effigies which have been dated indicate that the veneration of Mesingw may have begun as early as 4,000 B.P. and continued long after the Europeans arrived (Kraft 1986:172). The Lenapes believed that the Meswingw faces which were carved on pipes and wooden posts had a special power. The images were "fed" in a ceremony every year and were given a sacred burial if they became damaged (Kraft 1991:8).

Fig. 5.2. Stone effigy pipes

There is also some ethnographic evidence from the seventeenth century which suggests that the Mesingw rituals were practiced among the Lenapes on western Long Island. According to Daniel Denton, the Indians held dances *(canticas)* in which the participants' faces were painted "black and red, or some all black, some all red, with some streaks of white under the eyes" (1968:11).

Fig. 5.3. Shaman in bearskin costume (*left*) and Mesingw dancer (*right*)

Although Denton did not describe the ceremony in any more detail, it is possible that this was a Big House ceremony honoring Mesingw.

The next category of deities included those who were associated with more specific aspects of nature and daily village life. The most important of these beings was the sun god, called *Gickokwita* by the Lenapes and *Keesuckquand* by the Narragansetts. The Lenapes believed that Gickokwita dressed in the finest buckskin and wore a headdress of red feathers as he traveled every day across the sky. Next in order of importance were the *Pethakoweyuks,* or thunder-beings, who made the rain come and guarded the people from monsters such as the great horned water serpent. The thunder-being, armed with a bow that shot lightning arrows across the sky, was a composite of human and bird attributes.

According to Lenape legends, the thunder-beings captured the great horned serpent who lives in the great sea and held it prisoner (Skinner 1914:71). They scraped some of the scales off the back of their captive and gave them to the Lenapes. Whenever there is a drought, the Lenape lay out one of these scales on some open ground and it attracts the lightening arrows of the thunder-beings and brings rain. The thunderers also gave strength to the warriors who protected the village from human enemies. They brought sacred objects wrapped in bundles from Gickokwita, the sun, to the Lenapes. The warriors believed that the talismans in the war bundles would deflect enemy arrows and blows during the battle.

Although no similar legends from the eastern Long Island peoples have survived, we do have some evidence that they shared this belief with the Lenapes. A splayed bird image found on a pottery fragment excavated at the Sebonac site near the Shinnecock Reservation (see fig. 5.4) has been identified as a thunder-being symbol (Skinner 1914:72; Harrington 1977a:56). Similar forms of man-bird symbolism can be found in nearly every religion around the globe, from the Egyptian horus and Christian angels to the Maya bird deity and the Navajo Thunderers (Strong 1989:216-19).

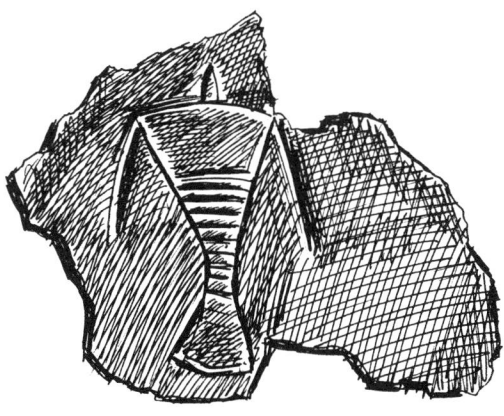

Fig. 5.4. Sebonac thunderbird symbol

One group of manitos was associated with the family hearth. The Lenapes believed that each plant had its own manito (McCartlin and Rementer 1986:15). Mother Corn, however, was the dominant manito over all of her sister plants. The feminine form undoubtedly reflects the role of the woman as gatherer and cultivator of the domestic crops. Mother Corn appeared in the form of an elderly woman and was given sacrificial offerings of bear's flesh (Harrington 1921:43-44). These plant deities were related to *Wetuomanit,* who protected the wigwam, *Squauanit,* the woman's manito, and *Muckquachuckquand,* who guarded the children (Williams, 1973:190). Unfortunately very little has been recorded about the rituals and stories associated with these manitos.

Each species of animals, birds, and reptiles was represented by a manito, who often established a close relationship with an individual human. The Algonquian peoples believed that these manitos would serve as a guardian to the honored person (Harrington 1921:77-78). Some of the manitos, however, were honored by the whole community in sacred ceremonies. The deer, who provided a basic part of the diet, the bear, whose courage and ferocity were admired, the eagle and falcon, who commanded the skies, the snakes, who lived in the mysterious underworld and below the water, the whales, who sacrificed themselves on the beaches, and the turtle, who represented long life and carried the world on its back, were all addressed with a special reverence in communal rituals. The turtle, in particular, was a very powerful presence in the Algonquian cosmology (see fig. 2.1). It represents that from which all else arises, the first cause, the earth mother (Brinton 1884:133).

The Lenapes, for example, honored the deer at seasonal ceremonies by placing a deerskin with the head and horns on a post near the center of the longhouse (Harrington 1921:129-30). The Montauketts, according to an account in the Gardiner family records, held a communal ritual and feast whenever a great whale trapped itself in the bays or washed up on the beach. The ceremony probably honored the manito called *Moshup (Mosup)* by the Algonquian peoples on Martha's Vineyard and Nantucket. Moshup, they believed, sent the whales to cast themselves on the beach as a gift to the people (Little and Andrews 1982). When a whale beached itself, the villagers prepared a great powwow, lasting several days, to give thanks to Moshup. They prepared a great fire and sacrificed the tail or a fin and then danced and sang their thanks (D. Gardiner 1871:3).

### *Powwaws:* **The Voices of the Manitos**

In all cultures there are holy men and women who supervise religious rituals and ceremonies and serve as a liaison between their community and the spirit world. These religious practitioners were probably the first to develop specialized roles in the egalitarian social systems of this period. The colonial settlers described these religious specialists pejoratively as "medicine men or "witch doctors," who worshipped the devil (Simmons 1986:37-38; Rountree 1989:135). Modern anthropologists have adopted the term "shaman" from the Tungu, a hunting and gathering culture in Siberia (Grim 1987; Laufer 1917). In the Tungu language, the word "shaman" was the title given to the religious specialist who served as healer, dream interpreter, and intermediary with the spirit world. The word for such holy men in the southern New England and eastern Long Island Algonquian societies is *powwaw* (Williams 1973:192; Simmons 1975:222-23).

The more familiar term *powwow* refers to the ceremony which was supervised by the *powwaw*.[3]

The *powwaw* gave shape and substance to the religious life of the small community (Aceves and King 1979:447-48; Simmons 1986:41-45). The Montauketts believed that a spirit appeared to a person in a dream or a vision, generally in the form of an animal or a serpent, and bestowed upon him or her the supernatural powers of the *powwaw* (Occom 1993:152). This visitation could come at a very early age. According to the report by Nicolaes van Wassenaer, a child was "selected" at the age of twelve and elevated to office when he or she "came of age" (1909:68). The Massachusetts Indians, for example, told John Eliot that Hobbamock appeared as a serpent and gave powers to their *powwaws* (Simmons 1986:41).

There are many reports of the unusual powers of the *powwaws*. These were probably exaggerated by the Indians themselves to impress the Europeans, who undoubtedly embellished the stories even more when they wrote them down. William Wood, for example, told his readers that *powwaws* could "bring to pass strange things." The Indians told him that a *powwaw* named Pisscannawa could "make water burn, the rocks move, the trees dance, metamorphose himself into a flaming man." These were not simply deceptive tricks, Wood believed, because the *powwaw* could also burn old leaves to ashes in the middle of winter, put the ashes in water, and produce new green leaves when there were none to be found. Wood also reported that this same *powwaw* could turn a snake skin into a living snake, as Moses did with the wooden rod (Wood 1968:82-83).

Wood and most of the English settlers never doubted that the *powwaws* could actually do such things because they believed the *powwaws* to be in league with the devil (Gookin 1972:14). Samson Occom also reported stories about the unusual powers of the *powwaws* and found no reason to disbelieve these accounts. The *powwaws* "would run into fire; and at other times run to the tops of trees and tumble down headlong to the ground, yet receive no hurt by all these." Occom continued, "and I don't see for my part, why it is not as true as the English and the other nation's witchcraft, but is a great mystery of darkness" (1993:152).

The *powwaws* played many important roles in the life of their community. They supervised the seasonal ceremonies and the rites of passage, cured the sick, interpreted dreams and visions, invoked spells and countered curses from witches, influenced the weather, aided hunters and warriors, and advised their sachems on all important matters. All of these duties, of course, presumed that the *powwaw* was on very good terms with the appropriate manitos. A *powwaw*'s status and influence was measured by his degree of success in performing these duties.

There was a darker side as well. Some *powwaws* were believed to have the power to bewitch and kill people. It was widely believed by whites as well as by Indians, that these particular *powwaws* could bring death to an unfortunate victim within twenty-four hours. Some *powwaws* were reputed to have the power to cause death in villages at great distances from them (Weslager 1973:12). Cases of death from unknown causes were attributed to such *powwaws,* thus exaggerating their power and influence. Often the *powwaws* made use of their herbal knowledge to administer poisons to their victims. Samson Occom noted that some *powwaws* could administer poison and provide the antidote as well (1993:152). *Powwaws* who were reputed to have these powers were often recruited by sachems to assassinate their rivals, particularly during the period after the arrival of the Europeans when the tribal rivalries intensified.

## Seasonal Ceremonies

The important seasonal rituals, supervised by the *powwaws,* were held in the spring to celebrate the rebirth of plants, in midsummer, in the fall when the crops were harvested, and in midwinter. Van Wassenaer reported that the Lenape midwinter powwow was celebrated when the first full moon appeared after the end of February. "They watch it with great devotion, and when it comes, they complement it with a festival; then they collect together from all quarters and revel on their way, with wild game or fish, and drink clear river water to their fill. They have nothing with which they can become intoxicated" (1909:69). Van Wassenaer also mentioned a midsummer festival which he said took place at the time of the August full moon. This celebration may have been a ceremony of thanks for the first corn crop.

The Narragansetts called these events *Nickommo,* "a feast or dance" (Williams 1973:191; Simmons 1975:226-27). These were major undertakings because the host village could expect hundreds of guests and could last for several days and sometimes weeks. These gatherings, called *kintecoy* (meaning "great dance") by the Lenapes, brought together Indians from all over Long Island (Harrington 1921:115-16). Van der Donck described the kintecoy he witnessed in New Netherland as a time when everyone ate lustily, the middle-aged men smoked, and the young sang all night (1968:89). Preparations were extensive. The Narragansetts, for example, built a longhouse about two hundred feet long near the sachem's court for a fall harvest ceremony which, according to Roger Williams, attracted thousands of men and women (Simmons 1986:45).

These numbers so frightened the whites that they made several attempts to prohibit "powwowing." In 1665, the colony of New York forbid all powwows, but the order was apparently difficult to enforce (Lincoln 1894, 1:42). Ten years later a kintecoy at a Secatogue village on the south shore of Long Island was broken up by the governor, who feared that the Indians might join King Philip in his war against the English in New England (NYCD, 14:709; see Chapter 10 below). The Indians apparently complied because there is no further mention of the kintecoy and no evidence of a plan to aid Philip. Although there certainly was plenty of opportunity for the participants at such gatherings to organize military campaigns, the primary focus was usually on religious ceremonies.

Roger Williams briefly described the role of the *powwaw* in these ceremonies, "These doe begin and order their service, and invocation of their gods, and all the people follow, and join interchangeably in a laborious bodily service, of unto sweating, especially of the priest, who spends himselfe in strange antick gestures, and actions even unto fainting." The *powwaw* had opened the ceremony with a prayer and then led the people in an exhaustive dance, which Williams dismissed as "strange antick gestures" (1973:192). His description is typical of the reports in the colonial records about Native American dances. The *powwaw* probably did not simply faint; he probably used the physical exertion, and perhaps fasting as well, to put himself into a trance or "dream state" where he could communicate with the spirit world (Grim 1987:138-67).

Alice Kehoe, an anthropologist who has studied the nineteenth-century Ghost Dance movement, provides us with a more objective interpretation of Native American ceremonial dances that helps us understand what Williams witnessed. The ceremonial dance, says Kehoe, builds rhythm and sounds in increasing intensity to excite the participants.

> Gestures may focus listeners' attention on the speaker to the point where the audience is almost hypnotized. Changing the pitch of voice, now high, now deep, induces subconscious mood changes in the listeners. Frenzied dancing tends to induce hyperventilation and causes that mental dissociation we term trance (1989:101).

Williams, unfortunately, never attempted to find out the religious significance of these rituals because he believed that the Narragansetts were under the influence of the devil. He feared that his own soul would be at risk if he attended the Nickommos after he saw his first one. "I must confess," he wrote, "I durst never to be an eyewitness, spectator, or looker on, least I should have been partaker of Satan's inventions and worships" (1973:192). Perhaps what frightened Williams was the hypnotic attraction he felt the first time he witnessed a ceremony.

Although most of the colonial references are no more detailed than Williams' account, we can get a general sense of the seasonal celebrations. We have a brief mention of a June Powwow held in 1669 by Ninigret, the Narragansett sachem, with invited guests from southern New England and eastern Long Island (RCNP, 2:277). The powwow was a time for Indian people to gather and share ideas and news as well as to honor sacred rituals. An elderly Wampanaog was sent by King Philip to teach the Niantics a new dance, and some Indians from Connecticut came to advise Ninigret's men about the process of removing cedar bark from trees for their wigwams (RCRI 1968, 2:273, 275).

The Shinnecocks and Unkechaugs still follow this tradition today, although the nature of the gathering has changed over the centuries. During the colonial period all powwowing was prohibited by law, forcing the Indians to go "underground." They continued to honor the fall and spring ceremonies on a smaller scale in family gatherings. The June Meeting today is a time for Long Island

Indian families to reunite for a weekend on the reservations and to observe formal services in church and informal meetings and meals in their homes (Strong 1996a).

The Lenapes also held seasonal celebrations, but there is only a brief mention of them in the colonial records (Myers 1912:73).[4] The twentieth-century accounts of the Lenape fall ceremony, however, drawn from the descendants of the Lenapes by anthropologists Frank Speck and Mark Harrington, provide us with much more information. This ceremony was held in *Watekan,* the "Big House." This sacred longhouse was constructed on an east-west axis with a door on each end. In the center was a large pole standing between two hearths. According to Lenape tradition, the instructions for the building were sent to the shamans in a dream (Speck 1931:85). They were told to carve two large face masks of Mesingw on the sides of the pole facing the east and the west doors. Smaller images of Mesingw were generally carved on the door posts as well. The Lenapes, according to Speck, believed that the Big House represented the universe and that the pole stood at the vital center (1931:22). William Jones described the Big House as "a holy symbol . . . a place where one can enter into communication with higher powers, where with sacrifice and offering, with music and dance one obtains audience and can ask for things beyond human control" (1905:189).

One of the Big House Ceremonies, held at harvest time, lasted for twelve days (Kraft 1986:174; Harrington 1921:81). Although there are some scattered references to this ceremony in the seventeenth-century records, most of our information comes from the modern descendants of the Lenapes who now live in Oklahoma. Mark Harrington (1921) and Frank Speck (1931) interviewed many of these Lenapes who were still holding Big House rituals in the early twentieth century. Although many changes have been made over the centuries, the studies by Harrington and Speck do provide significant insights into the nature and function of the prehistoric Big House ceremony.

The floor of the Big House was swept clean with a turkey wing brush; the sacred fires were lit, and the people assembled to hear the sachem's opening prayer. He asked Mesingw, whose spirit was present in the mask on the center post, to take his prayers of thanks to Gickowita, the sun, and ask for a plentiful harvest and good weather. Next he thanked the spirits of the four directions, the thunder-beings, and mother earth (Harrington 1921:87-92). Then people representing each clan entered and took designated seats on the north, west, and south areas of the Big House. After they were seated, the people who had had visions or dreams which they believed to be messages from Manitou got up in turn and danced with a turtle shell rattle as they recited the message. This first day of the ceremony ended with a feast of boiled corn *(sappaen).*

These rituals were repeated each day beginning with the relighting of the sacred fire. The old ashes were carried out through the west door and a new fire, symbolizing purification and spiritual renewal, was lighted with the sacred pump fire drill called *tudai wahenji,* "fire maker of the manitos" (Harrington 1921:10; Speck 1931:47-51). On the fourth morning, the most skilled hunters were called forth, blessed by Mesingw, and sent out to bring in game for a communal feast. After they departed, the Mesingw impersonator, who in the minds of the Lenape had now become possessed by Mesingw, entered the Big House and danced (Speck 1931:141). The dances, prayers, and communal feasting continued until the seventh night when the hunters returned.[5] The deer were skinned and the meat was prepared for a feast. The deer heads and skins were then mounted on posts to honor the deer manito.

On the ninth day the Big House was cleaned again with turkey wing brushes. Painted prayer sticks were distributed, and a woman carried a bowl of paint to the participants, who anointed their faces. The twelfth night was reserved for the women to relate their visions and dreams (Harrington 1921:105-7; Speck 1931:155-57). Cedar needles were burned in the fire and everyone inhaled the smoke to purify themselves for the recitations. In preparation, two women attendants carried bark vessels containing grease and paint around to all the women, marking their left cheeks with red paint and their foreheads with the grease. Then two men took the vessels and painted the masks, drumsticks, drum, and rattles. Each woman in turn took the turtle rattle and danced as she recited her vision. The next day the ceremony was completed with a prayer ritual in which the people danced around the center post and the appointed singers prayed twelve times to Manitou.

These ancient seasonal ceremonies served many important functions. The gatherings were a forum for communication about Indian affairs. The sachems and *powwaws* addressed the people in lengthy speeches about a variety of religious, political, social, and economic topics (Williams 1973:192). The pow-wow also provided for the strengthening of social and economic networks. A village or clan could invest in their future security by giving gifts which put others in social and economic debt to them. Williams noted that great quantities of wampum and goods were exchanged at the powwows. These gifts established the status of the giver and set a challenge to the recipient to match or increase the gift when the time came for the debt to be paid. In times of drought or after a defeat in battle, a village could call in the debt to help them survive. The gift exchange, therefore, was a form of disaster insurance. These large gatherings also provided an opportunity for courtship and marriages which served to expand and strengthen kinship networks. Clans frequently required their members to marry spouses from other clans.

The powwow is a *rite of intensification* which continues to reaffirm community values and group solidarity. The act of meeting together and participating in ritual behavior reinforces the group bond, provides a feeling of security, and reminds everyone of the values they share. Although many of the forms have changed over the centuries, the powwow remains an important part of Indian life on Long Island (see Strong 1996a).

## Rites of Passage

All societies mark life's important transitions such as birth, puberty, marriage, and death with ritual celebrations.[6] As people go through their age cycles, they abandon one set of relationships and behavior patterns and adopt a new one. The first of these transitions, birth, was marked by the ritual burying of the umbilical cord. According to the Lenapes now living in Oklahoma, the umbilical cord of the male child was taken into the woods and buried there to establish a spiritual bond with the forest. This bond would be important later when he became a hunter. The female umbilicals were buried in the village near the wigwam to symbolize the female bond to home and hearth (Kraft 1986:136).

The Lenapes had no formal rituals devoted to the infants because they believed that the newly formed soul might easily be reclaimed to the spirit world. This belief was probably related to the high rate of infant mortality. The children, therefore, were not given a formal name until they had survived infancy (Weslager 1973:52). When the appropriate time came, a Name-giver was called upon to supervise a naming ceremony. Samson Occom described a similar custom among the Montauketts (1993:151-52). He reported that several families often gathered together to hold a naming ceremony, which included dancing, feasting, and exchanges of gifts. There were two different ways of announcing the names. Some families had each recipient of a gift stand and shout the name of the child three times; others called upon a few elders to speak the name. This name was only the first of several the child would have during his or her lifetime. It was common practice to take on a new name in response to a dream or an unusual personal experience or accomplishment. Adults, for example, might take on a new name at the same ceremony where the children's names were announced.

The child's first new name was given during the puberty rites which marked the transition from childhood to membership in the adult community. When young girls had their first menstruation, their hair was cut off, and they were sent to a special wigwam where they remained away from all males for several weeks (Rainey 1936:36). The girls were visited by the older women, who stayed with them during the last few days of their isolation. Puberty rites for the boys generally involved isolation from the village, fasting, and other arduous initiation rituals designed to prepare them for the hardships of hunting expeditions and warfare and to open a communication with the spirit world. This communication, usually in the form of a vision or a dream, would be interpreted by the *powwaw*. The vision was often the source of the boy's adult name and might also play a role in determining his status in the community.

After puberty, the next major transition was marriage. Samson Occom described the ancient marriage customs of the Montauketts in some detail (1993:151). According to Occom, the first and probably the most common form of wedding began soon after the prospective bride and groom were born. The father of a male child went to the parents of a new born female with a gift of animal skins. The father asked the parents if they would engage their daughter to marry his son when the children came of age. If the parents of the girl agreed, they accepted the gifts; if not, they returned the skins and sent the father away. If there was an agreement, a great wedding feast was prepared by both sets of parents and their families for all of the friends and relatives.

At the appointed time the girl's parents brought their daughter to the home of the boy and presented her to the boy's mother, who took the girl and suckled her to one breast and her son to the other. The girl's mother then suckled them both in the same manner. This ceremony symbolized the merger of the two families and established a strong psychological personal bond, uniting the two children and the mothers. At the completion of this ritual, the communal feast began. When all had finished eating, more presents were distributed, further solidifying the bonds between the two families. The girl was then taken back home to remain with her family until she reached puberty. At that time the engaged couple made their own decision about marriage. They were not forced to honor the arranged marriage, but it seems likely that they were under a great deal of pressure to conform if larger family or village interests were involved.

In the case of adult marriages, there was a much simpler ceremony. The father of the bride brought his daughter to the prospective husband's wigwam and they shared a ceremonial wedding meal. Sometimes a couple might decide to live together and make no fuss about it. The woman would come by herself to the man's wigwam carrying food she had prepared herself, and they would quietly share the food. These adult marriages may have been less stable than the ones sanctified with a public ceremony, because, as Occom noted, "on small provocation," they would part and marry others (1993:151).

We have very little information about the Lenape marriage customs. There is no mention of betrothal at birth in the scattered accounts by early European observers, but that may only mean that the custom was not noticed (De Rasieres 1909:106-7; Heckewelder 1876:161, see also Kraft 1986:131-32). The Dutch merchant, Isaack De Rasieres, did make a brief reference to wedding practices. He noted that it was the custom among the Lenapes for a young man to negotiate a bride-price in wampum with the bride's family. Daniel Denton (1968:10-11) also reported this custom on western Long Island. The wampum gift did not mean that the man simply "bought" his bride as the early missionaries reported, but rather that it demonstrated his seriousness of purpose and his ability to support his new bride.

The last rite of passage, of course, is the funerary ritual. Anxiety over death is one of the universal concerns found in all cultures and is addressed, in some form, by most religions. The trauma experienced by the family of the deceased undoubtedly evoked a curiosity and a concern about the life force which had departed, leaving behind a lifeless body. All religions, therefore, seek to conquer death by providing a meaningful explanation about the future state of the life force or spirit of the deceased, and by dictating the proper rituals to assure that the spirit will find a peaceful rest for eternity. The evolution of funerary rituals from the Orient burial complex through the Early and Middle Woodland Periods has been described in previous chapters.

The Late Woodland peoples continued to honor many of the burial practices of their Middle Woodland ancestors. Although few burials from this period have been excavated, the geographic distribution of the sites provides representative sampling from eastern and western Long Island. Excavations in the Lenape area at Port Washington (Harrington 1982), Aqueduct (Solecki 1982), and Beach Haven (Orchard 1977), and at the Sebonac site (Harrington 1977a) on eastern Long Island near the Shinnecock Reservation, indicate that the burial customs were quite similar in the two culture areas.

Although most of these excavations were inadequately reported by modern standards, some general patterns can be discerned nevertheless. The data from the Late Woodland sites suggest that infants and children were buried in pit graves near their villages. Few of the burials were accompanied with grave goods for use in the after life. A small number of adults were found buried in similar conditions. The sex of these adults could not be determined in most cases, but those which could be identified were all female.

What appears to have been an intriguing pattern of dog sacrifices was first discovered in 1900 by Mark Harrington, who excavated sites in both culture areas on Long Island. Harrington worked on a site near Port Washington on the north shore where he discovered eighty pit features, sixteen of which contained human skeletal remains. (1982:83). Four of these burials, three infants and an adult female, were buried with dogs. The dogs were buried intact, clearly indicating that they had not been killed for food. If the dog had been butchered and eaten, the bones would have been scattered in amongst the debris associated with a hearth. Rituals involving dog sacrifices are well documented practices in many Eastern Woodland tribes, such as the Iroquois, the Huron, and the Fox (Wallace 1972:207-8; Underhill 1965:74).

One infant grave in the Port Washington site included three small dogs. The dogs had been placed in the pits first, at depths ranging from 29 to 42 inches. Next, a layer of soil was added; the human burials were laid on top of this and then covered over. Three different methods of dispatching the dogs were suggested by the data. The dog with the adult had a projectile point, probably from an arrow, among the ribs; one appeared to have been buried alive because the animal lay in a contorted position; a third dog, which lay on its back, may have been strangled in a manner similar to that used by the Iroquois and Huron to sacrifice dogs.

Similar patterns were discovered several years later at the Beach Haven site, a short distance north of Port Washington. F. P. Orchard working under the sponsorship of the Heye Foundation in New York, which had also sponsored Harrington, found five pits containing human remains (Orchard 1977). Two of the five pits included dogs. In one, a small dog had been "carefully buried" near the bottom and covered with a layer of soil about twelve inches thick. On top of the layer Orchard found a "sacred circle" of oyster shells, each carefully placed on edge about five inches apart. Another layer of soil covered the circle and then an adult in a flexed position was laid in the pit. The second dog burial also had a dog in the bottom of the pit covered with a layer of earth, but there was no shell feature and the grave included the remains of two individuals, a child and an adult.

Late Woodland burials on the eastern end of Long Island also include some dog sacrifices (Booth 1982:56). Roy Latham excavated the skeleton of a puppy which had been placed in a shallow grave on the Noyac site, four miles west of present-day Sag Harbor. The puppy had a long bone pin in its ribs. Latham speculated that the pin had been used to kill the dog or, perhaps, to hold together a wrapping around the burial (1978c:17). One of the more fascinating graves excavated on Long Island was discovered at Lake Montauk by Roy Latham in 1927-1928. A construction crew broke through a wooden coffin containing the skeleton of an adult female and a small dog. The woman was buried with a rich assortment of grave goods including copper pots, glass beads, pewter, and clay pipestems, indicating that she held high status in her community (Strong 1993a:609).

The significance of these dog-human burials is unclear, but it is possible that the dogs were intended to serve as guide and protector as the soul passed into the spirit world. The Iroquois and the Fox Indians believed that the dog served in this capacity (Strong 1985:33). This belief is understandable because the dog is at home in the wilderness world of Manitou as well as in the domestic world of humans. Dogs, therefore, embody a duality which can easily be appreciated by peoples living close to nature.

The only other indication of Late Woodland mortuary practices was found associated with a female and infant burial excavated by Ralph Solecki on the Aqueduct site on Jamaica Bay. Solecki found evidence of a wooden structure around the pit where the burials were located, but he noted in his conclusion that there was no evidence of such funerary structures in any other Late Woodland sites (1982). He pointed out that such structures were often placed over storage pits, and suggested that the burial may have been placed in one of these abandoned pits. The Late Woodland burials in southern New England are very similar to those excavated on Long Island (Brenner 1984:185-88). It is possible that the adults, particularly the males, were buried some distance from the villages in mortuary areas which have yet to be located.[7]

## Curing Rituals

One of the primary duties of the *powwaw* was to cure all forms of physical and mental illness which could not be cured with herbal medicine. Physical ailments such as wounds, fevers, stomach disorders, arthritis pain, menstrual discomfort, and tooth aches were treated with herbal remedies, poultices, teas, and ointments (see Chapter 2). "There is scarcely an ailment they have not a remedy for," reported Van Wassenaer (1909:72). A similar account of their effective treatment of wounds comes from an English observer in Virginia (Berkeley and Berkeley 1965:23-27). Although most women in the village were knowledgeable about medicinal plants, the diagnosis and administration of these remedies was probably the duty of a herbalist or *nentpike,* who worked closely with the *powwaw* (McCartlin and Rementer 1986:15).

The Lenape herbalists were described by John Heckewelder as "good and honest practitioners who are in the habit of curing and healing diseases and wounds, by the simple application of natural remedies" (quoted by Kraft 1986:180-81; see also Weslager 1973:13-14). The tradition of female nentpikes continues among the Lenape descendants who now live in Oklahoma. Two Lenape nentpikes, Wemeehelexkwe (Minnie Fouts) and Nora Thomas Dean, have preserved a significant body of herbal lore which has been recorded by modern anthropologists (McCartlin and Rementer 1986:15-20; Weslager 1973; Hill 1971).[8]

The more serious infections and diseases, however, were believed to have been caused by *spirit intrusion* into the patient's body (Vogel 1973:15). Angry manitos or curses conjured by an enemy *powwaw* could place an evil spirit into a victim's body. *Powwaws* each had their own style and individual paraphernalia for the curing ritual. John Heckewelder described a very dramatic persona adopted by a *powwaw* to frighten away the offending spirit. The healer wore a garment made "of one or more bear skins, as black as jet, so well fitted and sewn together, that the man was not in any place to be perceived. The whole head of the bear, including the mouth, nose, teeth, ears, etc., appeared the same as when the animal was living; so did the legs with long claws; to this were added a huge pair of horns on the head, and behind a large bushy tail, moving as he walked . . . the man, walking on all fours might be taken for a bear of an extraordinary size" (Heckewelder 1876:235-36). Heckewelder admitted that he was unsettled by the sudden appearance of the frightening figure and asked one of the Lenapes if it would have an adverse effect on the patient. The man said no, because the patient knows that strong measures must be taken to drive out the evil spirit (Weslager 1973:14).

Although the *powwaw* is responsible for casting out the evil infusion with chants, dances, and amulets, the relatives and the village community all join in the healing process because they fear that the same evil spirit might find its way into others if it is not defeated and driven out. The *powwaw* is the leader, but it is understood that it is the combined efforts of the whole village which will cure the patient. Perhaps the most important aspect of the ceremonies is the drawing together of the family and members of the local community in a bedside vigil. The psychological effect of this support generally proves beneficial to the patient.

The closeness and support of friends and family during the healing process is becoming more fully appreciated by some physicians who have worked on

Indian reservations. They have acknowledged that the traditional ceremonies not only help patients get through psychosomatic illness, but they also serve to reduce the patient's shock and anxiety and allow the body to mend itself. Dr. Morgan Martin, writing in the *Journal of the American Medical Association,* noted that "The American Indian medicine man uses traditional ways of healing that are curiously modern, and from which his post-traditional medical brethren can learn" (1981:141). "The task of the healer," continued Martin, "is to help the patient mobilize psychological and spiritual, as well as bodily, resources. The hope and faith of the patient in his healer, coupled with the healer's use of meaningful symbols and group forces, may contribute more to therapeutic results than is ordinarily recognized" (Martin 1981:143; see also Kiev 1964:13; Lehmann and Myers 1993:134-85; and Underhill 1965:84).

Several reports of aboriginal healing rituals were published by English and Dutch observers who did not fully appreciate what they were seeing. Nevertheless, these reports provide scholars with many important insights about the nature of the rituals and the role of the *powwaw*. The earliest report of a healing ceremony in New England, written by Edward Winslow in 1624, demonstrates the important role of the friends and relatives in the ceremony. Winslow visited Massasoit, the Wampanaog sachem, when he was ill and wrote the following account: "When we came hither, we found the house so full of men, as we could scarce get in. . . . There were they in the midst of their charms for him, making such a hellish noise. . . . About him were six or eight women, who chafed his arms, legs and thighs, to keep heat in him" (quoted in Simmons 1986:56).

The role of the *powwaw* as a leader in a communal rite was described by William Wood in *New England's Prospect*. Although the terms used by Wood reflect his biases about the process, he does provide us with the basic outlines of the ritual:

> the parties that are sick or lame being brought before them, the *powwaw* sitting down. The rest of the Indians giving attentive audience to his imprecations and invocations, and after the violent expression of many a hideous bellowing and groaning, he makes a stop, and then all the auditors with one voice utter a short canto. Which done, the powwaw still proceeds in his invocations, sometimes roaring like a bear . . . foaming at the mouth . . . smiting his naked breast and thighs . . . Thus he will continue sometimes half a day (Wood 1968:83).

Another first hand account comes from eastern Long Island where Samuel Taylor, a Quaker minister, witnessed a ceremony in the summer of 1659. Several men carrying drumsticks about two feet long and very thick came to the wigwam of the patient and sat down.

> So they began to pow-wow, as they called it; and it was thus: the sick man sitting up as well as he could, and having a dish or calabash of water in his hand, he supped a little of it, sat the dish down and spirted it with his mouth into his hands, and threw it over his head and naked

body . . . and beating himself with his arms and clapping his hands till he was all of such a foam with sweat and did speak something in his own tongue very loud; and as he spoke they all spoke very loud, as with one voice, and knocked on the ground with their truncheons, so that it made the very woods ring and the ground shake (quoted in Levine and Bonvillain 1980:285-86).

Here again, as in all of the cases cited above, the community involvement assures the patient that he is loved and supported by his family and his village.

Another important curing ritual took place in the sweat lodge. The belief that sweating purged the body of evil spirits was common, though not universal, in Native American cultures. Colonial observers identified five different types of sweat lodge construction, but there were undoubtedly other variations as well (Butler 1945:14). The first, described by Roger Williams, was a small cave about eight feet in diameter, dug into a hillside. The second, located in western Long Island, was described by David De Vries as a small oven-like structure made of small branches and covered with clay. A third form was a pit lodge with an excavated floor and a domed mat or bark roof. The fourth form was actually a conventional wigwam which had been converted to a sweat lodge by adding an extra layer of bark, matting, or skins for added insulation. A fifth form, described by a Dutch observer, was "made of earth and lined with clay. A small door serves as an entrance. The patient creeps in, seats himself down" (quoted in Levine and Bonvillain 1980:267; see also van der Donck 1968:95).

The sweat lodges were heated with hot stones, usually piled in the center. The stones were either carried in from a large fire outside or were heated in a fire inside the lodge. In the latter case, the smoking embers had to be removed before the ceremony began. Water was then sprinkled on the stones releasing clouds of steam. Often the participants drank a brew of herbal diaphoretics to

Fig. 5.5. Sweat lodges

induce even more profuse sweating (Heckewelder 1876:225). Many such plants have been identified by ethnobotanists. Tea brewed from the leafy twigs of the eastern hemlock *Tsuga canadensis* (Vogel 1973:303) and the root of the spotted coralroot *Corallorhiza maculata* (Foster and Duke 1990:94) induce very heavy sweating. At least thirty other plants, all available on Long Island, can be used to increase the flow of sweat. Some of the more common ones include sweet goldenrod *(Solidago odora),* boneset *(Eupatorium perfoliatum),* marsh-marigold *(Caltha palustris),* milkweed *(Asclepias syriaca),* yarrow *(Achillea millefolium),* catnip *(Nepetic cataria),* and horsemint *(Monad punctata).* Many Algonquian groups also sprinkled the leaves or powdered inner bark of these plants on the hot stones to send off a strong diaphoretic vapor which the participants would inhale (Ewan and Ewan 1970:379; Vogel 1973:241-44).

In addition to their diaphoretic powers, most of these plants contained medicinal ingredients which were released in the teas or in the vapor. The clouds of steam also had symbolic meaning. According to William Jones, the Algonquian peoples who lived in the Great Lakes area believed that the spirit force residing in the stones "becomes roused by the heat of the fire, and proceeds out of the stone when the water is sprinkled on it. It comes out in the steam and it enters the body wherever it finds entrance, it moves up and down and all over inside the body, driving out everything that inflicts pain. Before the Manitou returns to the stone it imparts some of its nature to the body. That is why one feels so well after having been in the sweat lodge" (1905:184).

The nature of the ceremonies conducted in the sweat lodge is not as well documented for southern New England and Long Island, but we do have several reports by seventeenth-century European observers. Some reports indicate that the Lenapes on western Long Island used the sweat lodge for routine bathing and relaxing as well as for curing. According to the account written by Heckewelder (1876:226), the Lenape men went into the sweat lodge weekly, and the women also used it regularly, but less often than the men. When the sweat lodge was heated, said Heckewelder, "a public cryer going his rounds, calls out *Pimok!* go to sweat." David De Vries wrote, "When they wish to cleanse themselves of their foulness, they go into the sweat lodge until they sweat profusely and then they rush out and jump into a cold stream, they then become entirely clean and are more attractive than ever" (1909:217-18). The sweat lodge was also used simply to relax and relieve minor aches and pains (Weslager 1973:96-97). A Dutch observer reported that the Lenapes were "remarkably addicted to the use of sweating baths" (quoted in Levine and Bonvillain, 1980:267).

The other references, however, indicate that the primary function of the sweating experience was to restore mental and physical health. The curing sweats were distinguished from the other uses of the lodge by formal ceremonies involving a *powwaw*, who gave a lengthy prayer, and a singer, who sang the sacred chants and songs (E. Tooker 1979:224-26; Ewan 1970:379; Wati, Jan. 1992: pers. com.). Charles Wolley reported that the Indians around New York used the sweat lodge as a general remedy for all diseases. "When they find themselves in any ways indisposed, they make a small wigwam or house, nigh a riverside, out of which in the extremity of the sweat they plunge themselves into the water" (1968:45). A similar practice was observed in the Algonquian communities of Virginia in the seventeenth century (Ewan and Ewen 1970:379). William Penn, writing in the winter of 1684, witnessed a sachem using the sweating process to cure a fever and pain in his head and limbs (1970:49-51). While he was in the lodge, his wife went out to the river and cut a hole in the ice. The sachem came out after a half an hour and jumped into the icy water.

Although the practice of rushing from the sweat bath to plunge into a stream is mentioned in most accounts, John Heckewelder (1876:225-26) reported that the Lenapes in western Pennsylvania did not finish their baths in this manner. Roger Williams also described a Narragansett sweat ceremony which apparently did not end with a bath in a stream. The Narragansetts called their ceremony *Npesuppaumen,* "I go to sweat." According to Williams, "ten, twelve, twenty more or less enter at once starke naked . . . here do they sit around their hot stones an hour or more, taking tobacco, discoursing and sweating together . . . to purge their bodies . . . and recovering them from diseases, especially from the French disease" (1973:244). There were undoubtedly many variations of sweating procedures from area to area, but the basic concept was similar. The healing, cleansing and relaxing all came after the bad spirits were expelled through the pores.

The sweating rituals gradually died out in the eastern United States, but the Canadian and western Indian communities preserved these ancient traditions and still practice them today. The sweat lodge ceremony has been revived on the Shinnecock Reservation by several men and women who visited these western communities and participated in the ceremonies.[9] The larger significance of the revivalist movement among the Long Island Indians is discussed in the companion volume, *"We Are Still Here!" The Algonquian Peoples of Long Island Today* (Strong 1996a).

## Dreams, Star Gazing, and Vision Quests

The *powwaws,* said Occom, "get their art from dreams" (1993:152). The Lenapes also believed that the manitos spoke to the *powwaws* when they were in a dream state or in a vision trance (Kraft 1986:178). These communications with the spirit forces, it was believed, enabled the *powwaw* to predict the future, diagnose the cause of illness, influence the weather, control game, and put a curse on an enemy. Dreams and visions, of course, could come to anyone in the community. People were very concerned about their dreams or visions because they believed that their personal guardian manito would appear and explain what they wanted in exchange for their protection.

Young men sought such visions as a part of their puberty rites. The Lenape youths were taken into the woods by the older men and left alone to fast and meditate. They would often be given a bitter drink which induced vomiting in order to purify themselves. As their bodies responded to these stressful conditions, their mental states altered and the visions came. John Heckewelder reported the following Lenape puberty rite: "When a boy is to be thus initiated, he is put under an alternate course of physic and fasting . . . so that he sees, or fancies he sees visions and has extraordinary dreams. Then he has interviews with the manito . . . who inform him of what he was before he was born and what he will be after his death" (quoted in Harrington 1921:79). Dreams, of course, came to people at any time and were taken very seriously as omens which must be understood. The dream might predict the future and require a change in behavior or the performance of a specific ritual (1921:77).

The use of hallucinogenic plants by the eastern Algonquian peoples to induce trances is not well documented. There are some references to an intoxicating tea made from datura *(Datura stramonium),* also called "jimson weed," and other plants which have not been identified. Datura may have been introduced to the Northeast from South America, along with tobacco. The drink was reportedly given to young men during puberty rituals (Schultes 1976:9, 143). Datura was used by the Powatan Indians in what is now Virginia, but little is known about its specific role in religious rituals (Rountree 1989:127; Vogel 1973:312-14). Although the plant can be found all over Long Island, there are no documented references to its use here by the Indians.

The Lenapes were careful observers of the heavens because they believed that the stars were living beings (Speck 1931:48). The celestial beings, who were not worshipped in any formal sense, were respected because they provided some very practical information about planting and harvesting to the Algonquian people (Van der Donck 1968:102). The most skilled star gazers were the women, probably because they were responsible for gathering wild plants and tending the domestic crops (see Chapter 3 above; Ceci 1978:304-12). "The women there," reported Van Wassenaer, "are the most skillful star-gazers; there is scarcely one of them but can name all the stars; their rising, setting" (1909:69). A Lenape man told Frank Speck that his people "recognize the morning star, the evening star, and a constellation known as beast chasing the bear." The constellation represented a myth about the change from summer to fall. "At a certain season of the year you will find the leaves of the forest lying on the ground, appearing greasy and covered with spots of water . . . the beast has caught the bear, the greasiness of the leaves is believed due to the bear grease" (1931:48).

The Lenapes also studied the position of the stars and the phases of the moon to learn when the best time came for harvesting specific parts of various herbs for medicines. They believed that the active properties of the leaves, stems, and roots of some plants were strongest at different times. The celestial bodies also provided important information about the appropriate times for procuring their basic food supplies. The star gazers informed the hunters when it was time for the game animals to breed and for the fish to go upstream and spawn. They told

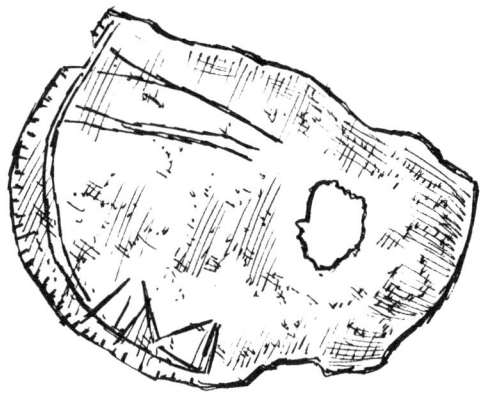

Fig. 5.6. Engraved shell pendant

the women when to plant and when each variety of plant should be harvested to produce the best fruit (Speck 1931:49; Van Wassenaer 1909:72; Ceci 1978:304-12). An engraved whelk shell pendant was recovered during an excavation of a Late Archaic site on Mount Sinai Harbor (see fig. 5.6). It may have served as a lunar calendar (Gramley and Gwynne 1982:172; Gwynne 1982a).

In making the connection between the movement of the constellations and planets and the frost-free planting season, these women passed from the sacred to the secular. Anthropologist Claude Levi-Strauss noted that traditional people became scientists as they studied the skies, making systematic calculations and producing valid scientific results (1966:10-11; Ceci 1978:310). The scientific information, however, was clothed in myth to remain in harmony with the spiritual orientation of their belief system.

## Sacred Carvings

There are several references to small idols kept by individuals among the Indians of eastern Long Island, but, unfortunately, we have no explanation about their religious significance. Samson Occom said that the Montauketts kept "images as oracles," which the *powwaws* consulted. The Montauketts believed that the idols spoke to the *powwaws* giving them wisdom and power. The *powwaws* were told when to hold feasts, dances and other ceremonies (1993:152). The *powwaws* then informed their people what the manitos said. Similar idols were apparently consulted by the Indians long after the whites had established their towns here. Azariah Horton, a missionary who preached to the Long Island Indians from 1741 to 1744, reported that an Indian woman owned two "wooden gods" (1993:197). The woman assured Horton that she did not worship them, she kept them only because they were a gift from her father. Unfortunately we have no further accounts of these intriguing objects.

It is possible that the idols were similar in nature to the doll deities of the Lenapes. The Doll Beings, called *nanitis (nahneetis)*, were small wooden carvings in human form, usually female. The dolls were dressed in full costumes which were changed each year in a special ceremony. The family regarded the doll as a sacred presence in the household. Unlike the carved faces of Mesingw, which only had power when they were worn, the nanitis actually possessed a power of their own. The Lenapes believed that the nanitis understood what was said to them and could speak to humans who were under their protection (Harrington 1921:45-46,162-71).

According to the Lenapes, the nanitis came to them when a *powwaw* ordered a patient's family to make a small human female effigy as a part of the curing ritual.[10] The patient got well and the family decided that the nanitis' power might continue to protect all of them. They kept the effigy, placed it carefully in a box, and made clothes and moccasins for it. Every year at harvest time the nanitis was removed from the box and honored with a yearly feast and dance. The Lenapes believed that the effigy had the power to travel around on its own because it was said that when the nanitis was removed from the box at the end of the year its clothing and moccasins were worn and dirty (ibid.).

One of these nanitis idols, collected in the nineteenth century, is in the collection of the American Museum of Natural History (Harrington 1921:168). The wooden effigy is a female figure, eight inches tall and elaborately dressed in a wrap around skirt and jacket, and wampum beads. A Lenape woman, named Eunice Hanks, gave it to a missionary when she converted to Christianity. She called it her "health guardian," and said that she and her friends worshipped it with a feast, a deer sacrifice, and a dance every year. At the feast many presents would be exchanged.

Another nanitis was given to a missionary in Wisconsin under similar circumstances. This time it was a fifty year old man, named Big Deer, who came to the Reverend Cutting Marsh in 1839 to present him with the effigy. Big Deer told the missionary that it was one hundred years old and had been given to him by his mother. The nanitis, which had been in the family for four generations, was covered with expensive silver brooches, wrapped in broad cloth, and tied with a red ribbon. This nanitis was also a female and was addressed as "mother"

Fig. 5.7. The Orient tablet

by Big Deer's family. The nanitis was worshipped every fall at harvest time to insure good health for the next year (Harrington 1921:29).

Although none of the idols mentioned by Occom and Horton has survived, a few carved artifacts have been recorded by scholars. Daniel Brinton, one of the pioneer anthropologists in the nineteenth century, described a tablet found "towards the east end of Long Island" (1980: 304). The tablet is made of slate, about six inches long, and inscribed on both sides. Unfortunately, only one side is legible (see fig. 5.7). Brinton described the carvings as follows:

> We see, beginning at the top of the diagram, the figure of a man; below it that of a canoe; then a line beginning on the left with a rude outline of a quadruped, perhaps a deer; a bow and arrow; the footprint probably of a bear; sign of a fire; an unknown figure; and in the line below, a fish, an eel, some vague lines, ending with the symbol of a wigwam (1980:306).

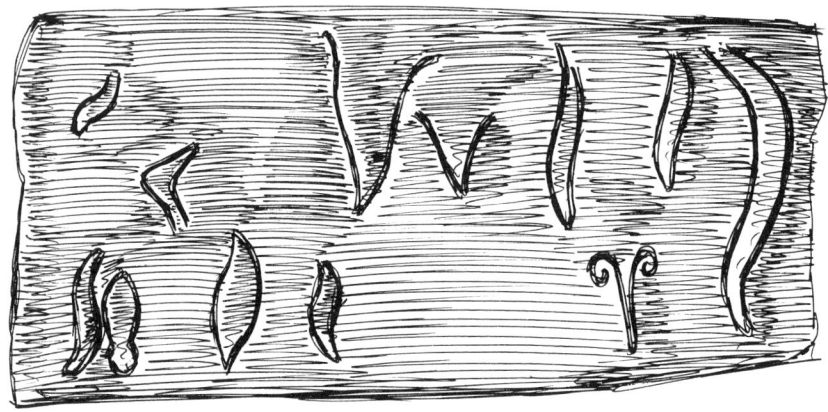

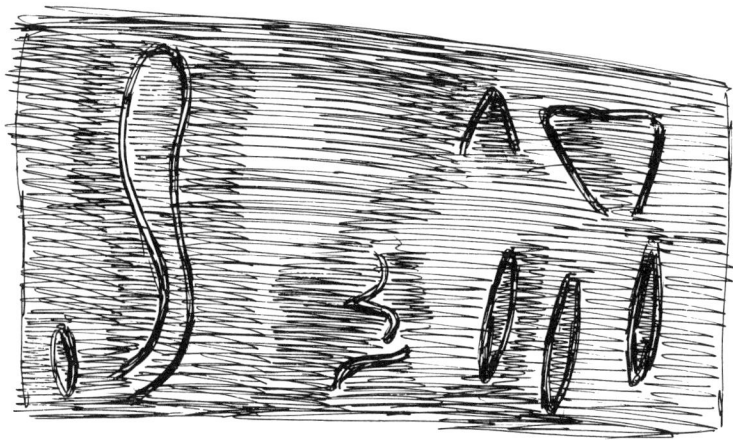

Fig. 5.8. The Dosoris tablet

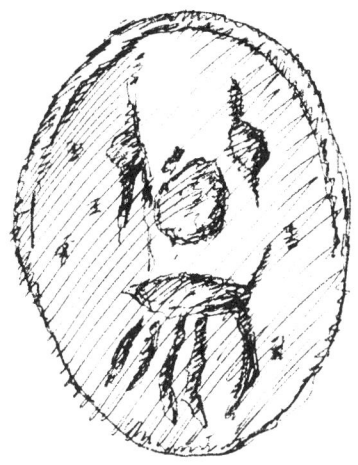

Fig. 5.9. The Great Neck tablet

He suggested that the symbols may have been a mnemonic aid for a hunting song or a shaman's chant evoking the spirits to grant a successful hunt. Unfortunately we have no ethnographic context on Long Island in which to place this intriguing object.

A second stone tablet was found by archaeologist Mark Harrington at a site near Glen Cove (Levine 1980:301; C. Smith 1980:311). This tablet is also inscribed on both sides, but the symbols do not appear to represent human or animal forms (see fig. 5.8). Harrington did not speculate on the meaning of the curious markings. Some of the symbols appear to be similar to markings on a stone effigy face, carved on an oval-shaped cobblestone found at Great Neck in 1940 and reported by Carlyle Smith (1980:311); see fig. 5.9. Among the twenty-one symbols on the two faces of the tablet are fifteen tear-shaped symbols, twelve on one surface and three on the reverse side. The effigy face appears to have five similar "tear drop" shapes descending from the mouth. Unfortunately there is not enough data here to justify an attempt to interpret the meaning of these interesting artifacts. The face on the cobblestone represents another category of sacred carvings, discussed above, which appear to be Mesingw images.

Roy Latham also found a small engraved tablet on the Noyac site near Sag Harbor. The claystone tablet, about three inches square, had etchings which Latham believed represented a spider's web (1978c:16). It is possible that the markings on the tablet were associated with a spider manitou. The Arapaho, for example, believed that the spider's web, which the spider spins out of its own body, was the foundation of the earth. Like the creator Manitou, the spider creates something out of nothing (Hultkrantz 1980:31). Two more small slate tablets were given to the East Hampton Library's Long Island collection by Morton Penneypacker, a local historian and collector. One tablet is an oval-shaped slate with notches around the edge, about four inches long with a cross-hatched pattern on one side and an uneven rectagular-shaped design inside a circle on the reverse side. A similar cross-hatched design appears on a red slate gorget found in present-day Summit, New Jersey (Kraft 1975:14). This motif, usually associated with the rattlesnake, is found throughout North and South America. The second tablet is a three-by-five inch rectangular slate with symbols which do not appear to be of Native American origin; see fig. 5.10.[11]

Another intriguing set of carved images was discovered on the face of a boulder located near the intersection of the Jericho Turnpike and the Long Island

Fig. 5.10. Montauk tablets

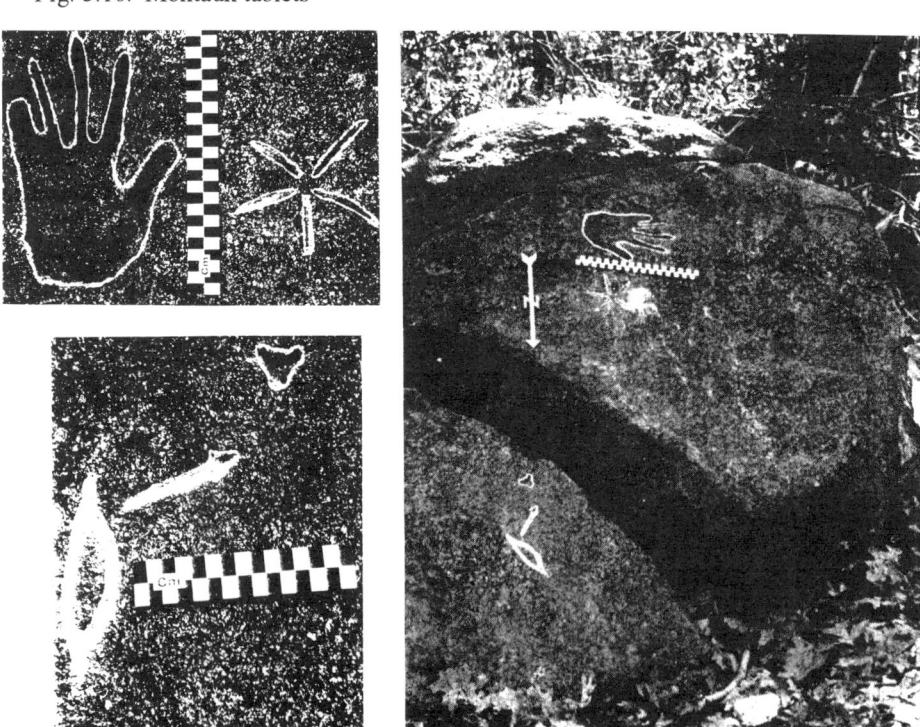

Fig. 5.11. The Jericho petroglyph

## The Algonquian Belief Systems

Fig. 5.12. The surviving Jericho glyph, photographed December 1995

Expressway. The Jericho Petroglyph consists of five images pecked into the surface of the stone: a human hand, a star-shaped figure, a shallow triangular hole, and what appears to be a bow and arrow; see fig. 5.11. The petroglyph was examined by archaeologist Edward Lenik, who concluded that, with the exception of the triangular hole, the images were authentic Indian artifacts dating back to the Late Woodland Period. Lenik reported that a patina had formed on the carved areas, indicating considerable age. He also noted that the point of the arrow appeared to have been retouched with what he thought might have been a metal tool and that the triangular hole was of recent origin (1978:349-53).[12]

A note of caution about the petroglyph was sounded by Ronald Wyatt, who also studied the glyph and its surroundings. Wyatt, an archaeologist with Nassau

County at the time, agreed with Lenik that the glyph motifs were legitimate Native American symbols, but indicated that there were three factors which gave him concern. He pointed out that there were no other glyphs like this found anywhere on Long Island. If glyph carvings were a cultural pattern here, one would expect to find more of them. Another question concerned the choice of a granite boulder. Indians, he argued, generally selected softer materials, such as limestone, for their glyphs because these stones were so much easier to work with stone tools. His third concern was the evidence of the metal tool marks, which Lenik also reported. Although Wyatt was cautious, he felt that as long as there was a possibility that the glyph was authentic, it should be preserved for further analysis (Wyatt, Jan. 24, 1996: pers. com.).

Lenik responded to Wyatt's critique by noting that he had observed glyphs in the Northeast on a variety of surfaces including granite, sandstone, and greywacke, and that the Indians' stone tools were capable of cutting shallow designs on granite. He also said that although few glyphs on Long Island have been recorded, they are not unique to the coastal area around the Island (Lenik, February 8, 1996: pers. com.).

We can only speculate about the interpretation of these symbols. Lenik, who researched the literature on northeastern rock carvings, looking for similarities with the Jericho glyphs, found similar hand symbols on petroglyphs in New Jersey and in the upper Ohio Valley. The human hand symbol is a universal image found in many chronological contexts. Lenik found no parallels with the triangular design, and he was uncertain about the "bow" glyph, suggesting that it might be a symbol for a hill rather than a bow. This symbol also resembles one of the images on the inscribed tablet found at the Dosoris Site on Glen Cove. The bow and arrow glyph may be related to a legend recorded by Gabriel Furman (see above) about the sachem who fired an arrow into the air to locate a fresh water spring. The triangular hole may represent the spring. One has to be cautious about such interpretations, however, because they are speculations based on a very limited data base.

These intriguing tablets and glyphs remain a fascinating mystery. Some of them may not even be authentic Indian artifacts. Until more of them are found in scientific excavations, we can come to no valid conclusions about their meaning. Unfortunately, this does not prevent some people from inventing connections with the Vikings, Libyans, or Carthaginians. An article in *Newsday* (March 22, 1981), for example, entitled "New Theory on Ancient Long Island Visits," reported a controversy over the symbols on the Orient Tablet between Barry Fell, an amateur linguist and author of *America B.C.,* and James Smith, curator at the National Museum of the American Indian in New York. Fell asserted in his book that the tablet described by Brinton was engraved by Libyan visitors nearly three thousand years ago. Smith sharply retorted that this was absolute nonsense and that no professional scholar accepted Fell's interpretations. Anthropologists at the Smithsonian Institute in Washington, D.C. issued a position paper rejecting Fell's conclusions as unscientific and fanciful. Fell rejected these criticisms, stating that he had no intention of withdrawing what he said about the Long Island inscription. Fell, however, has never responded to the specific questions raised about his conclusions by the professional scientists.

## Tobacco Ceremonialism

Although the colonial records are full of references to tobacco, there is very little information about the religious significance of the plant. This is most unfortunate because the archaeological data (see Chapter 2) clearly suggests that tobacco smoking was a very important aspect of Woodland religious expression. Anthropologist Eva Butler did an extensive study of references to tobacco in the New England colonial records and found little information about the paraphernalia or specific ritual procedures (Butler nd:17-30, 39-40).[13] The best documented use was for peace ceremonies and other agreements. Tobacco pipes were lit and passed around to all participants as a symbol of respect. When the ceremonies were completed, the pipe would again be shared to seal the agreement. Another common use was the more casual offering of the pipe as a sign of welcome to any guest who entered the host's wigwam.

This limited data base has been enriched by ethnographic data from related Algonquian areas. The Ojibwa shaman, for example, invoked Manitou with the smoke from the sacred pipe to begin the healing ceremony (Grim 1987:127). The smoke was believed to serve as a vehicle carrying the prayers and messages from the shaman to the spirit world. Anthropologist Ralph Linton commented on the importance of tobacco among the Central Algonquian communities:

> [N]o ceremony could take place without it. As a sacrifice it might be burned as incense, cast into the air or on the ground, or buried. There were sacred places at which every visitor left a tobacco offering. . . . Smoking was indulged in on all solemn occasions, such as councils, and was a necessary part of most religious ceremonies (1924:23).

To the Abenaki, tobacco smoke symbolized the life force, the essence of being. The pipe was also used for social occasions. In Algonquian villages throughout what is now New England, guests were usually offered a pipe upon their arrival in the host's wigwam (Russell 1980:45, 160).

Some of the Shinnecocks today have revived the ritual uses of tobacco. Lamont Smith grows native tobacco *(Nicotiana rustica)* and processes it for ceremonial purposes. The Shinnecocks have had to adopt many of these rituals from the same Indian groups who have helped them with the sweat lodge customs. These exchanges are part of a pan-Indian movement which has spread throughout North America as tribes seek to reclaim their ancient heritage.

## Summary

Native American religious systems differ significantly from those which are based on a written document such as the Bible or the Koran. As anthropologist

Sturtevant noted in his preface to Elizabeth Tooker's *Native North American Spirituality of the Eastern Woodlands,* the Indians are not "People of the Book." They saw no need to explain their beliefs to others as the missionary religions do. Non-Indians, therefore, often find it difficult to relate to the more open, unstructured nature of aboriginal religion. Often the result of this frustration is the imposition of such superficial artifices as "the great spirit" and the "happy hunting grounds" to force Native American religion into a European frame of reference. In order to help bridge this cultural gap without distorting traditional beliefs, we have used an anthropological structure to provide the reader with a rudimentary understanding of this complex subject.[13] The primary focus here is on the functions of religion in the Indian social system, rather than on the deeper spiritual aspects.

The concept of "Manitou," the impersonal power which is at the center of the Algonquian cosmology and its expression in the form of manitos, provides the believer with an explanation for all that is unknown about the universe. The *powwaws,* who play a role very similar to priests, ministers, and rabbis, served as the liaison between their people and the spirit world of the manitos. These holy men and women supervised seasonal religious ceremonies and rites of passage, interpreted dreams, advised sachems, invoked spells, and cured illness.

The most important seasonal ceremonies were held at harvest time, in midwinter and in the late spring when the corn had sprouted. These rites of intensification solidified communal bonds and reinforced traditional values. Although we do not have much specific information about the Lenape "big house" ceremonies in the Northeast prior to the arrival of the Europeans, we can gain many important insights from the studies of the Lenapes in Oklahoma and Canada. In Oklahoma the "big house" was a longhouse constructed for sacred ceremonies, such as those honoring Mesingw, which lasted twelve days. The fall powwows held on eastern Long Island are related to ancient seasonal gatherings which were probably intended to be a similar expression of gratitude for the harvest. These ceremonies have been revived at Shinnecock and now draw thousands of people to the Reservation each Labor Day weekend.

The rites of passage marked transitions in the life cycle from birth to death. These rites also served to reinforce a sense of community, but their primary purpose was to help an individual establish his or her personal identity within the context of the community. In these rituals the community honored individual members and reminded them that they were now expected to take on new roles and responsibilities. The initiation period usually involved some kind of training or preparation for the new role.

The *powwaw* was responsible for the health of his community. The first line of defense against disease and injury was herbal medicine. The village women inherited a vast knowledge of the healing powers in local plants from their mothers. If these medicines did not work, the *powwaw* would usually supervise a sweat ceremony and a sucking ritual to draw out the evil spirit which was causing the disharmony in the patient's body. Modern medicine has now acknowledged the efficacy of many herbal remedies and some physicians who have spent time working on Indian reservations are convinced that the ancient rituals which involve family and community support for the patient are very beneficial.[14]

Fig. 6.1. Algonquian couple in traditional dress

# 6

# The Early Contact Period, 1524–1638

In 1801, John Heckewelder, the Moravian missionary, asked several "aged and respected" Delaware, Munsee, and Mohican men what their ancestors had told them about the arrival of Henry Hudson in 1609. "Many years ago," said the elders, "when men with a white skin had never yet been seen in this land, some Indians who were out fishing at a place where the sea widens . . . espied at a great distance something remarkably large floating on the water . . . some believed it to be an uncommonly large fish or animal, while others. . . [thought it was] a very big house floating on the sea" (1876:71). Runners spread the news to all of the neighboring villages. The people prepared food, brought out the religious masks and effigies, held a great dance, and asked the *powwaws* for guidance.

As the floating house drew closer, word came back that it was a house of bright colors and crowded with people. The leader, who they thought at first must be a manito, was dressed in red pants and a red coat covered with glittering gold lace. The brilliant coloring of the European flags and clothing delighted the Indians. The deep hues made a dramatic impact on the aesthetic imagination of the Indians and created a nearly insatiable demand for richly colored cloth, beads, and blankets. Within a relatively short period, Indian artisans were using these materials to produce their own decorative art.

An entourage, led by the man in the red suit, came on shore and accepted the greetings of the sachems and elders. The red-suited man then poured a glass of an "unknown substance," drank it, refilled the glass, and passed it to the nearest sachem. The sachem smelled it and passed it to one of the elders who did the same. When all of the greeting party had received the offering and smelled the contents, they handed the full glass back to the man in the red suit. Then one man, a great warrior, stood up and said that they had made a mistake and may have offended the visitor by giving him back the full glass. He volunteered to drink it himself and drained the glass. He fell down into a stupor for a time and then jumped up shouting that he was happy and wanted more. Soon the whole greeting party became intoxicated. The elder's account suggests that the Indians regarded the introduction of alcohol, with its destructive attraction, as one of the most significant aspects of the first encounter.[1] The Iroquois told a similar "first encounter" story about a ship's captain who introduced them to alcohol (O'Callaghan 1966, 1:39).

After the Indians recovered from the effects of the alcohol, the man in the red suit gave them gifts of axes, hoes, and stockings and promised to return in a year with more gifts. Before they left, the visitors said that they would need a small piece of land for their crops when they returned. The next year the visitors came back and asked again about the planting ground. They spread an ox hide on the ground and asked the Lenapes for the land covered by the skin. The Indians readily agreed to the small grant of planting space. Then the white men took out a knife and cut the hide into thin strips, tied them together to form a long rope and laid it out in a large circle encompassing a much larger planting ground. The old men who told the story to Heckewelder undoubtedly intended the account to be a foreshadowing of the tragedy which later befell their people.

## First Contact, 1524–1609

Heckewelder did not appreciate the subtle wit and irony of this apocryphal account. The story is an engaging mixture of fact and imagination. The almost childlike awe expressed by the Indians, a common theme in European folklore about the first encounters with aboriginal peoples, may have been exaggerated in Heckewelder's retelling of the old men's words. In fact, Henry Hudson was a late comer. The Indians who greeted Hudson probably saw their first European ship nearly a hundred years before Hudson's *Half Moon* sailed into the mouth of the Cohotatea. Giovanni da Verrazano, sailing for the King of France, dropped anchor in New York harbor on April 17, 1524 and reported that he was greeted by friendly Indians in dugout canoes who invited him ashore. Unfortunately, a sharp shift in the wind forced him to hoist anchor and sail north along the coast of Long Island and into Narragansett Bay. Even before Verrazano's brief visit, stories about white strangers on great ships had undoubtedly reached the Indians here through the trade networks which linked them with Algonquian communities all along the shores of the Atlantic Ocean.

In 1497, three years after the Pope had given his blessing to Spain's claim to Long Island and the rest of North America, John Cabot, an Italian navigator sailing for King Henry VII of England, made a landfall on Newfoundland. He came ashore and claimed all of North America for England (Morison 1971:170-77). Both the English and the Spanish presumed that the Indians were a part of the natural landscape and had no more claim to the place where they lived than did the deer and the moose to their feeding grounds. When the Spanish ambassador complained to Henry, the English monarch casually waved his concerns aside and replied that discovery was necessary but not sufficient to determine title. The key to ownership, he said, was occupation. Thus the scramble for land began.

Portuguese sailors made the next landfall on the north Atlantic coast in 1500. This incident foreshadowed an unpleasant theme in the historical relations between Europeans and Native Americans. The Portuguese kidnapped fifty-seven Beothunk Indians and took them back to Portugal where they sold them into slavery. In 1502 English sailors landed again on Newfoundland and this time kidnapped three Indian men as evidence that they had successfully made a landfall. When the Portuguese fishermen attempted to establish a permanent fishing station on Cape Bretton in 1524, they were driven off by the Indians, who were certainly no longer in awe of the white men. In July 1525, a Spanish expedition kidnapped fifty-eight Indian men and women in Narragansett Bay near Newport, Rhode Island, and took them back to Spain as slaves (Morison 1971:331).

The Basque fishermen, however, appear to have established more positive relations with the Indians along the Labrador coast. While Portuguese and English fisherman began to exploit the rich cod fishing grounds on the Grand Bank off Newfoundland, it was the Basques who established the first extensive contacts with the Indians. They specialized in whale hunting, sending as many as 1,000 men to the Labrador shores each season. By the middle of the sixteenth century, a five month whaling season could produce nearly one-half million gallons of whale oil. Dutch whalers were also hunting along the coast further south and may have located base camps on the Long Island coast before 1600 (Stokes 1967, 2:63, 64). These fishermen set up temporary fishing camps all along the coast, established trading contacts with the Indians, and undoubtedly exchanged information about fishing and whaling techniques (Barkham 1984:515-19; Strong 1989a:29-30). Archival studies and underwater excavations by archaeologist James Tuck indicate that about 900 Basques spent the summer at Red Hook, Labrador, one of ten seasonal whaling ports along the coast (Barkham 1984; Tuck and Grenier 1981). This is significant because they pioneered the development of shore whaling, which was later to become so important to the settlements on eastern Long Island.

The English combined Basque technology and Native American skill and experience hunting in the shore waters (see Chapter 4 above). The twenty-six foot long Basque whaling boats, called *chulpas,* were adapted by the New England and Long Island whalers in the seventeenth century. The relations between the Basque and the Beothunk Indians were not well documented, but there must have been a considerable amount of interaction. The Basque undoubtedly relied on the Beothunk fishermen for information about the seasonal habits of the sea mammals in the coastal waters. Unfortunately, we know very little about the interaction between the Indian whale hunters and the Basque fishermen. We do know that Captain George Waymouth kidnapped five Indians and took them back with him to England. Some of them later returned as guides and interpreters with expeditions (Brasser 1978:81).

The European fishermen began to bring back furs, with their cargoes of fish, for supplemental income. As the demand for beaver fur increased, the trade in pelts soon became a major enterprise. By the time Jacques Cartier explored the St. Lawrence River system (1534–1536), the Indians along the coast were familiar with the European demand for furs (Brasser 1978:79). The Indians asked for such items as red cloth, metal hatchets, knives, colored glass beads, kettles, liquor, and guns in exchange for the furs.

Trade and the scramble to establish territorial land claims soon resulted in the search for suitable locations for permanent settlement. The English explorer Martin Frobisher made three voyages (1576–1578) along the north Atlantic coast. These explorations led to the first attempts to establish permanent settlements at Roanoke (1585–1587) in what is now the state of North Carolina, and at Sagadahoc (1607) in what is now the state of Maine. Although both failed to survive, the experience provided settlers who came in the following years with information which enabled them to succeed. The French established settlements on Sable Island (1598), at Tadoussac (1601), and St. Croix (1604) in Canada. When Samuel de Champlain explored the Atlantic coast from Nova Scotia to Cape Cod, he found Indians wearing English clothing and speaking some French and Basque (Brasser 1978:81). Captain John Smith reported finding Susquehannock Indians in the Chesapeake Bay with hatchets, cloth, and other European goods which had been traded from tribe to tribe along the aboriginal inland trade routes from Canada.

By the time the first successful English settlement was established at Jamestown in 1607, the European influence had already begun to make a significant impact on Native American culture. Historians writing before 1960 tended to view the initial contacts as a unilateral European experience (Burton 1976:19-59). Little attention was paid to the Native American response beyond a few patronizing references to alcohol and accounts of Indian raids. The Indians had at first been friendly and quite curious about the new arrivals, but the incidents of violence and kidnapping soon made them wary. This wariness is reflected in a pattern which emerged during the early decades of coastal trade—the Indians, reluctant to expose the locations of their villages, came out to meet the ships in their canoes (Burton 1976:30-31).

In spite of their fears and suspicions, the demand for European goods, which had grown dramatically in a relatively short period of time, drew more and more of the Algonquian communities into the coastal trade. Europeans were often identified in native languages as the "Coat men," "Iron men," or "Knife men," after the highly valued trade items they brought with them (Brasser 1978:86; Axtell 1992:135-51). The speed with which metal tools were adapted by the Indians is a testament to both their pragmatic resourcefulness and the efficiency of their extensive trade networks. The networks had emerged over the centuries as groups gathered for religious ceremonies and feasts (see Chapter 3 above). Before the first English settlements had been established, the traditional stone industry had been nearly abandoned by the coastal Indian communities. Most arrowheads, knives, and hatchets were now made from European metal.

Control over access to European trade networks became a major factor in the relationships between Indian communities. Sachems began to negotiate alliances which would enable them to monopolize the European trade (Brasser 1978:84-85). These alliances often resulted in violent conflicts between rivals, upsetting the traditional kinship and clan systems that had been the basis for stable relations between Indian communities (Trigger 1991:1213-15; see also Jennings 1990:80, 81).

The focus on European trade also prompted changes in settlement patterns and social structure. Coastal groups began to concentrate near the ports where the European traders set up their camps. The establishment of intergroup alliances resulted in the formation of larger population groups under the control of politically astute sachems, who had cultivated close associations with the Europeans. This process gradually transformed loose alliances of small groups into tribal systems and confederacies (Brasser 1978:84).[2] Massachusett and Narragansett sachems, for example, took advantage of their locations on the coast to serve as intermediaries between the Europeans and the inland communities (Burton 1976:54; see also Jennings 1990:80-81). These sachems used their economic power and their access to European firearms to expand and strengthen their political influence. The demand for these manufactured goods gradually increased European influence over internal affairs in Indian communities (Trigger 1991:1213-15; see also Jennings 1990:80-81). However, as ethnohistorian James Axtell has pointed out, the increased presence of European manufactured goods does not indicate significant changes in Indian culture (1981:256). Although the forms had changed, the functions remained constant. Metal knives, kettles, and guns, for example, were used for the same functions as flint tools, ceramic pots, and bows had been .

There were two particularly devastating consequences of the European trade. The first was the introduction of the diseases which were later to decimate the population of Algonquian peoples in the Northeast. Smallpox, typhus, influenza, and measles took a heavy toll as the newly introduced pathogenic microorganisms raged through populations which had virtually no immunity to them (Cronon and White 1978:421-22; Axtell 1981:250-53). The Indian communities in southern New England and perhaps eastern Long Island as well, suffered dramatic reductions in population in 1617 when an epidemic swept through the area. The groups which were hardest hit often joined neighboring groups and formed new political units or merged with larger tribal systems (Cronon and White 1978:422). The second disaster was the introduction of alcohol, which quickly became a major part of every trader's store of goods. Alcohol and disease wrecked havoc on the Indian communities, depleting populations, disrupting family life, and debilitating many (Axtell 1992:142-43).

Some changes in the Native American communities have been documented by archaeologists who have studied seventeenth-century burial grounds. The mortuary customs appear to have changed dramatically by the end of the sixteenth century, soon after the Europeans began visiting the Atlantic coast in increasing numbers. The graves were much more elaborate and contained a rich store of grave goods. They were no longer located in village areas. Archaeologists have classified these as "Presettlement Period" burials (c.1580–c.1640) and suggest that the unusually rapid shift in burial tradition was a response to

European contact. The consolidation of the Algonquian communities into larger, confederated political units is reflected in more complex burial rituals (Brenner 1984:189, 1988:175-76; Crosby 1988:202).[3] These changes in burial forms, however, should not be interpreted as evidence of radical shifts in basic cultural values. The new burial forms were very similar to the adaptations of European manufactured goods. They were simply using new forms for old functions (Axtell 1981:110-28).

## Equal Status Trade: Lenape-Dutch Relations, 1609–1636

Henry Hudson's brief encounter with the Lenapes in 1609 has to be seen in the larger context of the sixteenth and early seventeenth-century coastal contacts. Robert Juet, one of Hudson's officers, described the encounter in his journal. Hudson had been sent by the Dutch to find a passage through North America to the Orient where his sponsors hoped to establish a lucrative trade in spices. He made his landfall on Newfoundland in July, took on a supply of codfish, and sailed south to Penobscot Bay where he spent a week repairing his ship from the battering it had taken during the crossing. At that time, he and his crew were hosted by friendly Indians. He sailed south, stopping to trade with Indians at Cape Cod, and continued past Long Island to Chesapeake Bay and then back north to Delaware Bay.

On August 28, 1609, Hudson anchored in the bay and "officially" claimed all the land between Delaware Bay and Nova Scotia for the Dutch. Spain, England, and now the Netherlands held overlapping claims to extensive areas, all of which included Long Island. Not one of the claimants, however, had made a landfall on Long Island, nor had they spoken a word to the Algonquian inhabitants. The European assumption that the land was theirs to take may have been satirized in the Indian elders' account of the deer-hide circle.

Hudson sailed north and anchored off what is now the New Jersey coast, by Sandy Hook, to continue his search for a northwest passage. It was here, on September 4, 1609, that the first contact between the Algonquian villagers and the Dutch took place. Several men from the highlands called "Navasink," wearing turkey feather mantles and fur robes, came to the ship with tobacco to trade for knives, clothing, and glass beads. "They desire clothes and are very civil," wrote Juet (1909:18). Juet, of course, could not appreciate or understand the delight the Navasink villagers took in the bright colors of the Europeans' beads and clothing, but he certainly understood the trade value of such items.

When the sailors came on shore the next day, they were greeted in a friendly manner and were given more tobacco by a large number of men, women and children. The Indians took them on a guided tour of the woods nearby, but apparently did not show the visitors their village. They may have led the Dutch away from the village because they feared the possibility of a raid. After the Dutch returned to their ship, some Indians dressed in feather mantles and furs brought them dried currents which, Juet noted, were sweet and good (Juet

1909:18). In spite of this friendly exchange, he wrote in his journal that he "durst not trust them." This curious entry may have been added later by Juet to impress his readers with his foresight.

The harmonious relations were abruptly interrupted on the following day when a crew of sailors, exploring through the Narrows into what is now New York Bay, was attacked by a party of twenty-six Indians in two large canoes. These Indians may have come from one of the villages on the western end of Long Island, such as Wichquawanck, near what is now Fort Hamilton (see Chapter 4 above). The people from Navasink, who returned the next day with more goods to trade, were surprised to hear about the attack. They were probably telling the truth because the two communities were virtually autonomous. Although they both spoke the same Munsee dialect of the Algonquian language root and shared many cultural characteristics and kinship links, they were not under a unified political system with a common leadership.

Juet apparently did not distinguish one group from another and assumed that all of the Indians were conspiring against the Dutch. He claimed in his journal that the attack was unprovoked, but this is most unlikely. The sailors may have done something which they did not want to report to Juet. One sailor, John Coleman, was killed in the encounter, but the rest escaped under cover of darkness and made it back to the *Half Moon*. Coleman, who was buried on a small point of land which still bears his name, has the dubious honor of being the first European to be killed on Long Island (Brodhead 1853, 1:29).

The following day, two large canoes full of men came alongside the ship and wanted to trade for knives and coats. Hudson allowed two of them to come on board, gave them both red coats to distract them, and then took them captive apparently as hostages to guarantee safety from another attack. The old men who spoke to Heckewelder said that Hudson wore a red coat and never mentioned the kidnapping incident. This is a significant alteration of the historical account, but it is clear that the Indians valued the brightly colored coats. A short time later the Dutch kidnapped a third man, but he managed to escape. We can only speculate on the feelings of the Navasink people toward the Dutch as Hudson sailed away with his prisoners.

Hudson proceeded north through the Narrows into what is now New York harbor. Several Indians came out to greet his party and offered them tobacco, oysters, and corn in trade. The Dutch remained distrustful even though these Indians made a great show of friendliness. When a canoe of women and children approached the ship, the Dutch assumed it was a plot to put them off their guard. Even though no such attack occurred, Juet again noted in his journal that, although they make a show of love, "we durst not trust them" (1909:20). They left the harbor and sailed for forty miles up the Cohoatea and anchored north of what is now West Point. Here the two captives managed to crawl out of a port hole and escape, shouting back words of anger and scorn at the Dutch.

The Dutch pressed on north into the country of the Mohicans, just south of what is now Albany where the incident with the alcohol, described by Heckewelder, actually occurred. The Mohicans greeted them as friends and brought beaver and otter skins to trade. Juet reported that Hudson became suspicious of the Mohicans in spite of the friendly reception he had received from every group of Indians before and after the attack on the boat crew. According to Juet, Hudson took several sachems into his cabin and gave them brandy, claiming that he wanted to see if the alcohol would loosen their tongues about any threat to the Dutch (Brodhead 1853, 1:31).

There was no plot to be revealed. The Indians all became intoxicated except for the wife of one of the sachems, who, according to Juet, "sat so modestly, as any of our country women would do in a strange place" (Brodhead 1853, 1:31). One man passed out and was left behind on the ship, but when the others returned for him the next day, he asked for more brandy and refused to leave. Juet's explanation for encouraging the Indians to drink seems a bit strained, in spite of Hudson's fears and suspicions. Possibly the alcohol was introduced to facilitate the sale of the beaver and otter pelts (ibid.).

Hudson now returned south, stopping several times to trade for more furs. When he anchored near what is now Haverstraw Bay, about twenty miles north of Manhattan, a party of Indians, described by Juet as "mountain Indians," came out to trade. One of them climbed onto the ship undetected and began to explore Juet's cabin. He took a pillow, two shirts, and two bandoleers from the cabin, and was leaving the ship when he was seen by the ship's mate. This petty theft was punished with tragic severity by the mate. Apparently without any warning or questions, the mate opened fire, killing the man. The Dutch then lowered a boat into the water to retrieve Juet's possessions. One of the Indians, incensed at the brutal slaying of an unarmed man, swam to the Dutch boat, grabbed the gunnel, and tried to overturn it. One of the sailors promptly hacked off the man's hand. As soon as the boat was safely hauled onto the *Half Moon,* Hudson weighed anchor and sailed south.

The next day, over a hundred men, including one of the Navasink men who had been kidnapped by Hudson, attacked the *Half Moon,* killing three sailors. Hudson retaliated by firing a cannon at them, killing two men and driving away the others. The Indians regrouped and attacked again, but once more the Dutch cannon and musket fire prevailed. Hudson anchored the next night near what is now Hoboken and then sailed for the Netherlands, leaving behind a legacy of sharp contrasts. The incidents of violence left both sides angry, distrustful, and suspicious, yet both wanted to continue the trade connection. The Indians wanted more clothing, metal tools, guns, beads, and, unfortunately, alcohol, and the Dutch wanted furs.

When Hudson showed his cargo of furs to his Dutch sponsors, they began to reconsider their emphasis on establishing trade with the Far East. Dutch merchants had been purchasing furs at relatively high prices from Russia to meet the steady demand in northern Europe. Now they learned from Hudson that they could buy high quality beaver and otter pelts very cheaply from the Indians in North America. The Dutch sent several more ships to obtain more information about the economic potential of the beaver trade. The optimistic response from these expeditions led to the establishment of trade relations with the Indians in 1613. A small settlement of four crude buildings was located in lower Manhattan just north of where the National Museum of the American Indian stands today. Hendrick Cortiaensen, the supervisor, who was successful in overcoming the hostility engendered by Hudson's visit, traveled to Algonquian villages, encouraging the Indians to change their hunting priorities and specialize in the production of beaver pelts.

The English, who had never recognized the legitimacy of the Dutch land claims, soon noticed Cortiaensen's presence on Manhattan. In a foreshadowing of future conflicts, an English ship, commanded by Captain Samuel Argall, stopped at the Dutch post in the fall of 1613 and demanded that Cortiaensen acknowledge the sovereignty of the English king (O'Callaghan 1966, 1:69). Cortiaensen, who had no choice, submitted to the authority of the governor of Virginia, the closest English settlement at the time. The Dutch responded by ignoring Argall's order and sending out more expeditions to explore and map the area in their claim.

One of these expeditions was led by Adriaen Block, who made the first accurate map of Long Island (Allen 1991:46). This map, dated 1616, has the first mention of an Algonquian name for the inhabitants of Long Island. Block identified the people living on the eastern half of Long Island as "Nahicans," perhaps because of their close kinship ties with the Mohegan-Pequots in southern New England.[4] The Dutch navigator undoubtedly visited many Algonquian villages on Long Island, but, unfortunately, he left no written record about them. Block, who spent the winters of 1614 and 1616 on Manhattan, may have been a guest in the Lenape village of Keshaechquereren on western Long Island. Based on his information, the Dutch government issued a four year license in 1614 to a company of merchants incorporated as the United New Netherland Company. The company immediately constructed a fort near where Albany is today and expanded Cortiaensen's post.

Trade flourished, enriching the Dutch investors and bringing more Algonquian villages into contact with European goods. In 1621, a year after Plymouth was founded, the Dutch West India Company took over the trading operation from the United New Netherland Company and made plans to expand the enterprise. The English again protested the presence of the Dutch on "their land." They sent a delegate to Holland with a written protest, but the Dutch simply ignored them and developed the trading posts into an official province of Holland.

When the Dutch traders learned that the Indians in the interior valued wampum made from the quahog and whelk shells, so plentiful in the Long Island coastal waters, they began to purchase large quantities for trade (Salisbury 1984:147-49; McBride 1994:32-33; Ceci 1990a:48-63). Isaack de Rasieres, the colony's secretary, noted that the Indians "consider it as valuable as we do money here, one can buy with it everything they have" (Hagerty 1985:104). The Algonquian villagers, who had probably trapped the beaver on Long Island to near extinction fairly quickly, began to specialize in the manufacture of wampum. The Dutch encouraged this manufacture and provided the fine metal drills called "muxes" to make the tiny holes in the shells for the string (Ceci 1982:307). The importance of these two commodities was reflected in the seal for the new province, which depicted a beaver surrounded by wampum. For the next forty years, the wampum and fur trade played a central role in the economy of New Netherland (Hagerty 1985:111)

The return on the Dutch investments came quickly. One Dutch ship alone carried 7,246 beaver skins to merchants in Amsterdam in 1624 (Janiver 1967:85-87). Profits were enormous by any standard. In 1635, the New Amsterdam merchants shipped out pelts worth 135,000 guilders or about six million 1990 dollars. The success of the enterprise prompted the Dutch to expand across the East River into what is now Brooklyn. In 1624 a small number of Walloons (French-speaking Protestants from an area that is now in Belgium), settled on what is now Wallabout Bay, where the Brooklyn Navy Yard was located. The following year, more Walloon families arrived with cows, pigs, and sheep. The former trading post was being transformed into a thriving, self-sufficient settlement. Unfortunately, we have no record of the relations between this small Walloon community and the Indians from the neighboring village of Marechkawieck on Wallabout Bay. Concerned about the reaction of the Indians to the growth of the colony, and, perhaps, recalling Hudson's disastrous actions, the company directors set down fairly specific guidelines for relations with them. The colonists were advised not to cheat them, not to "give them any offense without cause as regards their persons, wives or property" (DRNN 1924:17). The same instructions, however, set wages for Indian labor at half the earning of a Dutch worker for the same labor.

The fundamental expression of sovereignty is the power to inflict punishment for the violation of an official edict or law. The Dutch guidelines made it clear that they assumed full sovereignty over the Indians even before a deed or a treaty was negotiated. Dutch people who harmed an Indian would be tried in Dutch courts and, if found guilty, punished by the Dutch authorities. The Indians were also to punish any one of their people who injured Dutch persons or property, but if the Dutch were not satisfied, they claimed the authority to arrest and try the accused Indian in their own court. The Indians, of course, rejected this assertion of European authority until they were defeated in two bloody conflicts, first in New England and then in New Netherland.

The Dutch West India Company also had a clause in their 1621 charter requiring them to purchase all lands in their grant from the Indians. No action was taken until 1626, when the Dutch purchased Manhattan from the Indians for sixty Dutch guilders (NYCD 1:37; Bolton 1975). The purchase gave more weight to their territorial claim which had already been challenged by the English. Much has been written about the conflicting concepts of land ownership which often resulted in misunderstandings and occasionally in some violence (Grumet 1979:155-63; Snyderman 1951:16-29; Kraft 1986:220-22). The Europeans viewed land as a commodity which could be bought and sold, often by parties who never set foot on the property in question. Sales were final and absolute. The Indians, by contrast, saw the land as a part of nature which could be used by an entire community. It made no sense to the Indians for land to be divided up into privately owned parcels. Could one divide up any part of nature in such a manner? Could one "own" the deer or the water? The Indians did understand the concept of sovereignty over their hunting grounds and would go to war to defend access to them. For the Indians, therefore, the important concern was access and use, not abstract "ownership."

For three decades after Cortiaensen established the first post on Manhattan, the Indians and the Dutch traded peacefully. Both parties enjoyed benefits from the exchange. There was, unfortunately, one incident in 1626 which threatened to disrupt the trade. Three of Peter Minuit's farm hands robbed and murdered an Indian from one of the Wiechquaesgeck (Wechquaeskeck) villages, who was bringing furs to Fort Amsterdam. The villages were located in what is now northern Manhattan, the Bronx, and Westchester County (Appendix B). The murder was witnessed by the victim's young nephew, who vowed to seek revenge when he became a man. In Algonquian society the vow would have been rescinded if the Dutch had compensated the victim's family or punished those responsible. The Dutch did neither and were to pay a tragic price in the future.

The Algonquian communities on Long Island were now producing a steady supply of wampum. Isaack de Rasieres wrote in 1626 that the Shinnecocks on eastern Long Island supported themselves by producing wampum and maize (1909:103). He also described the development of the trade patterns. One of the items which was particularly valued by the Indians was the coarse textile called "duffel" cloth produced by the Dutch. The New Amsterdam merchants brought large quantities of this material along with the other standard trade items and purchased wampum from the Long Island Indians. The wampum could be easily carried into the interior where it was traded to the inland communities at greatly inflated prices (Ceci 1982:308). Wampum worked so well as legal tender that it soon became an acceptable currency in both the English and Dutch colonies. Wages were often paid and debts settled in wampum. The English became interested in the wampum from eastern Long Island after an expedition, sent out by John Winthrop, Sr., reported that the Indians here produced a high quality wampum from the local quahog shells. "They had a store," he reported, "of the best wampampeak, both white and blue" (Hosmer 1946, 1:109).

## The Impact of the Pequot War (1636–1638) on Long Island

The Dutch expanded their trade into the Connecticut Valley with the purchase of a plot of land near the site of present-day Hartford from Tatobem, a Pequot sachem (Jennings 1976:188; Salisbury 1984:207). In 1633 they built a small fort and established a settlement called "Good Hope." The treaty with the Pequot established a "free trade zone" around the fort which allowed any Indian with furs to enter. The Pequot were so eager to bring the Dutch into the Connecticut Valley that they signed away their previous monopoly over trade in this area.

The Dutch presence alarmed Governor John Winthrop, Sr. of Massachusetts Bay, who reported to the other English colonies that the Dutch were taking thousands of beaver skins a year out of the Hudson and Connecticut River systems. The English and Dutch both claimed sovereignty over the Connecticut Valley, but the Dutch had strengthened their claims with a deed from the local Indians. In the fall of 1633, Plymouth Colony challenged the Dutch by establishing Windsor, the first English settlement in the Connecticut Valley, a few miles north of Good Hope. When the Dutch troops arrived to chase them out, the English held their ground. The failure of the Dutch to enforce their exclusive rights to the Connecticut Valley marked the beginning of their decline in North America.

The Pequot sachems were also concerned with the developments at Good Hope. The intrusion of the two European powers into the Connecticut Valley had disrupted the traditional relationships between the various Algonquian lineage systems. The Pequots had been expanding their network of tributary groups in Connecticut and on eastern Long Island. The Algonquian communities living at Shinnecock, Montauk, Corchaug, and Manhanset (Shelter Island) were closely connected by language and kinship to the Pequots (Williams 1972:5; Smith 1950:106-107). Exogamous marriage customs created a network of family ties connecting communities on both sides of the Sound. The small Long Island groups paid tribute to their Pequot relatives in exchange for protection. The Pequots employed a strategy which was being adopted by several rival sachems in southern New England. They began to use the traditional rituals of gift exchange, intermarriage, and communal feasts to expand and solidify their spheres of influence.

The loosely knit structure of the Algonquian societies made it difficult for the Pequots to forge a political unity which would hold for long. Among their tributaries were many who followed the Pequot leadership only when it served their interests. The Mohegan band led by Uncas frequently challenged the Pequot sachems. Uncas was banished on at least five different occasions, but each time the rebellious young sachem humbled himself and was allowed to rejoin the Pequot alliance. Undoubtedly, one of the factors which enabled the Pequots to turn back Uncas' challenges was their alliance with the Dutch. Although we have very sparse information about the developments on eastern Long Island prior to

1640, it seems clear that a young sachem from Montauk named Wyandanch was ready to abandon the Pequot alliance at the first opportunity.

In 1635 an English company, led by John Winthrop, Jr., engaged Lion Gardiner, a young military engineer, to build a fort at the mouth of the Connecticut River as the first step in the planting of a new English colony. The Dutch had already marked out this same area for their own fort. They had placed a marker there with the official Dutch coat of arms naming the projected settlement "Kievet's Hook." The English arrived shortly before the Dutch construction crew, tore down the Dutch marker, dragged two cannons ashore, and refused to allow the Dutch to land (Brodhead 1853, 1:260-61; O'Callaghan 1966, 1:169-70). The Dutch protested this intrusion into their sovereign territory and once again the English ignored them. When the Dutch declined to defend their claim with military force, they left the English free to continue their plans to establish the colony of Connecticut.

Winthrop now turned to confront the Pequots, demanding that they acknowledge English sovereignty by turning over the men responsible for the murders of two English traders, John Stone and John Oldham, and paying a fine of 400 fathoms of wampum, forty beaver, and thirty otter pelts. Sassacus, the Pequot sachem, replied that they were innocent of both murders and refused to comply. The Pequots reported that Stone, an unscrupulous Virginia trader, who had been banished from Massachusetts Bay, was killed when he attempted to kidnap two Niantic Indians and that Oldham had been killed by men from a different Niantic group.[5] Although the Pequots were not directly involved with either murder, they did give refuge to some of the Niantics who were involved. The English seized upon this rather flimsy issue and prepared for war.

In July 1636, the English sent out a punitive expedition, which attacked Sassacus's village (near present-day Mystic, Connecticut) and burned it. Sassacus was on Long Island at the time, perhaps attempting to shore up his alliances with the sachems. Several of the villages on Long Island tended crops of corn for the Pequots as a form of tribute. When Sassacus returned and witnessed the destruction, he led his men in an attack on Fort Saybrook. When they failed to storm the fort, the Pequots laid siege throughout the winter and into the spring of 1637. Relying primarily on bows and arrows, they were unable to inflict much damage on the English soldiers. The failure of the attack encouraged many of the Pequots' allies and tributaries to reconsider their position.

Uncas saw an opportunity to defeat his rival, Sassacus, and placed himself and seventy of his men under the command of John Mason, who was raising a troop of soldiers for Connecticut. Wyandanch undoubtedly kept in close contact with these events but did not become involved in the conflict. John Underhill, who led the Massachusett Bay troops, joined Mason at Fort Saybrook where the English officers planned their campaign against the Pequots. They learned from captives released by the Pequots that the Indians had about sixteen guns and a very limited amount of powder. Mason and Underhill decided to launch a surprise attack on the Pequot village near present-day Mystic. Rather than sailing up the Mystic River to attack from the front, the English sailed to Narragansett Bay and marched overland back west to hit the fort from behind. Miantonomi, the Narragansett sachem, gave them permission to cross his territory and sent some men to join in the attack.

Early in the morning of May 26, 1637, the English attacked the fort, breaking through the two entrances before the Pequots could recover from the surprise. Once inside they set fire to the wigwams and retreated outside where they regrouped and formed two rings around the fort. The English with their guns, stood in the first circle and the Mohegan and Narragansett allies stationed themselves in the outer ring.[6] The English soldiers shot down the men, women, and children as they fled in panic from the fire. Those who got through the English line were cut down by the Mohegans and Narragansetts. When the slaughter ended, only six or seven villagers remained alive. Estimates of the dead ranged as high as eight hundred.

When the Pequots held council the next day, Sassacus urged his people to regroup and attack the English, but his elders rejected the idea. Instead, the small villages who had coalesced to form Sassacus' confederation now split off on their own seeking refuge wherever they could. The Pequot response to the disastrous defeat illustrates the nature of Native American social and political structure. The temporary fusion, which had formed around Sassacus's leadership quickly dissolved as a response to the crisis. As news of the massacre spread, former tributaries of the Pequots sought out new alliances. Three days after the massacre, Wyandanch came to Gardiner at Fort Saybrook and asked for an alliance with the English (Gardiner 1980:137).

Wyandanch was particularly interested in establishing a trade connection which would give him control over the access to European goods on eastern Long Island. Gardiner told the Montaukett sachem that there could be no trade until all the Pequots who had fled to Long Island for refuge were destroyed. Gardiner, of course, did not understand the nature of the kinship network shared by the Pequots and the communities on eastern Long Island. A purge of the Pequots would have turned close relatives in the same village against each other. Wyandanch may have resolved his dilemma by joining with Uncas and the English troops in pursuit of Sassacus. He brought Gardiner twelve severed heads that he may have taken in this campaign (Gardiner 1980:138).

During the two months following the massacre, as the English troops with their Indian allies pursued the half-starved Pequot remnants across southern Connecticut, more Long Island sachems made overtures to the English. Captain Israel Stoughton, one of the officers from Massachusetts Bay who had accompanied Mason in pursuit of the Pequots, wrote to Governor Winthrop that a *sunksquaw* from Long Island wanted to establish alliances with both the Narragansetts and the English (Forbes 1929–1947, 3:442). This is the first reference to a female Algonquian leader on Long Island. Although they were not uncommon in Algonquian society, the role and status of sunksquaws is not well documented and, apparently, varied from one group to another (Strong 1995; Strong and Karabag 1991:189; Grumet, 1980:50-51; Lamb 1981:1-3). Roger Williams characterized them as "Queens" with the power to make policy decisions for their communities (Williams 1973:201).[7]

The Long Island sunksquaw told Stoughton that she had two hundred men and that her people had never shed any English blood. She said that her people had paid tribute to the Pequots in the past, but only because they had been forced to do so. She also promised to help the English find Sassacus, who was rumored to have fled to Long Island. Unfortunately, Stoughton never mentioned the name of the sunksquaw, nor the location of her village on Long Island. The English term "tributary" does not adequately describe the complex relations which allied small groups such as the one led by the sunksquaw to a larger, more powerful one such as the Narragansetts. Among the Iroquois, for example, such subordinate groups were referred to as "brethren," "cousins," or "nephews" (Jennings 1990:8-9). Although the sunksquaw claimed that she was forced by the Pequots into a tributary relationship, perhaps to convince Stoughton of her new loyalty, her people undoubtedly had benefitted from the Pequot alliance. There was a great deal of variety in such reciprocal relationships but they generally included trading privileges and military protection (Thomas 1979:50-51).

After he confirmed her story with Mohegan, Pequot, and Narragansett informants, Stoughton told the woman that if she submitted to English authority she would not be harmed. Stoughton was very pleased with this alliance because he hoped that it would encourage other sachems to accept English sovereignty. He soon discovered, however, that the political upheaval caused by the defeat of the Pequots and the emergence of the English as the dominant power in the Connecticut Valley had disrupted previous alliances and loosened forces over which the English had very limited control. As Stoughton himself noted in the same letter, the Algonquian sachems now sought to advance their own interests and to "augment their own kingdoms and that upon that matter they use us as their stalking horse: and if God do not help us . . . I fear our being here will not be to that purpose as was desired" (Forbes 1929–1947, 3:442). Algonquian sachems, in other words, were very adept at the same strategies of manipulation and intrigue which characterized English relations with the Dutch and even among their own colonies. Similar patterns of resourceful diplomatic maneuvers by sachems in seventeenth-century Virginia have been documented by historian, Helen Rountree (1993:190-92; see also Metcalf 1974:651-52).

Stoughton learned that the Long Island sunksquaw had sent thirty fathoms of wampum to Miantonomi and asked him to give ten to his uncle, Canonicus (another Narragansett sachem), ten to the English, and keep ten for himself. Miantonomi, unaware that she had reported this to the English, kept it all for himself and told her that he would deal directly with the English on her behalf. When Miantonomi learned that the English knew what he had done, he came to them and attempted to discredit her. Miantonomi was concerned about her because she had arranged a marriage with a rival Narragansett sachem which would increase the sachem's power and influence. Unfortunately, there is no other reference to the sunksquaw or to her intended husband, who also is not mentioned by name in Stoughton's letter.

Miantonomi, intent on extending his political power and influence in southern New England, pressed Stoughton for his share of the Pequot captives, territory, and corn supplies.[8] Miantonomi's independence in pursuit of his own interests annoyed Stoughton and prompted an arrogant response. Stoughton told him that these issues would be addressed after Sassacus's followers were captured, "Let us first subdue him, and talk of that afterwards." He went on to tell the Narragansett sachem it was English firepower that defeated the Pequots and that the Pequot captives said that they had no fear of any Narragansetts who did not have English support. We have no record of Miantonomi's response, but he was politically astute enough not to allow his anger at the insult to push him into renouncing his alliance with the English.

Sassacus's small band was finally trapped in a swamp near the Housatanic River in western Connecticut. Two hundred captives were taken, but Sassacus escaped and fled west to seek refuge with the Mohawk. Fearing to jeopardize their fur trade with the Europeans, the Mohawks executed Sassacus and sent his head back to the English. As news of this final defeat spread throughout New England and Long Island, more sachems sought alliances with the English. Yovawan (Youghco), a sachem from "Mowhaset" (Manhansett, present-day Shelter Island), and another sachem, who was probably Wyandanch, came to Stoughton asking for an alliance (RCNP, 9:102-3; Forbes 1929–1947, 3:457; Hosmer 1946, 1:231). The sachems brought forty fathoms of wampum to be distributed to officials in Massachusetts Bay and Connecticut. Stoughton also made them promise not to permit any Pequots to take refuge on Long Island.

The Long Island sachems believed that they would receive the same protection that they had as tributaries to the Pequots. Although the Connecticut leaders, such as Roger Ludlow and John Mason, were eager to use one Indian sachem against another, Massachusetts Bay was very reluctant to intervene in disputes between Algonquian sachems unless some clear interest of their own colony was at stake. Massachusetts Bay, the more populous and secure of the English colonies, much preferred to serve as a mediator. The role of mediator was less costly, and it reaffirmed English dominance over both sachems in the dispute.[9]

The colonies were often involved in their own disputes as well. Frequently the sachems were able to gain some small advantage by playing one colony against another. The complex political affairs in southern New England, therefore, were not simply conflicts between the English and the Algonquian communities. When Connecticut urged the colonies to unite in a common front against the Dutch and the Indians, the matter was debated for six years before an agreement was reached to form the United Colonies, and even then, Rhode Island was excluded.

The tangle of conflicting interests became evident in the late spring of 1638 when Ninigret, the Niantic sachem, led a war party of eighty men across the Sound to convince Wyandanch that he should ally himself with the Niantics, a southern branch of the Narragansetts, instead of Massachusetts Bay or Connecticut (Forbes 1929-1947, 4:43-5). Ninigret was attempting to take advantage of what he believed was a power vacuum on Long Island. He hoped to break the newly formed alliance between the Montauketts and two English colonies and draw the former Pequots tributaries into an alliance with his Niantics. It was a daring plan which would strengthen his position against his rivals, Uncas and Miantonomi.[10]

The Niantics lived east of the Pagawtuck River in between the former lands of the Pequots to the west and Miantonomi's Narragansett territory to the east and north. All three sachems were maneuvering to absorb as many of the remaining Pequot remnants and former tributaries of the defeated tribe as they could (Sainsbury 1971:115). Ninigret's position was further complicated by the fact that both Connecticut and Rhode Island claimed his lands in a border dispute that lasted several decades.

Shortly after he landed on Long Island, Ninigret sent a delegation to Wyandanch and urged him to abandon the English and accept a tributary status with the Niantics (Forbes 1929-1947, 4:43-44). Wyandanch refused and went into hiding to avoid capture, perhaps hoping the English would intervene on his behalf. Ninigret finally did catch the Montaukett sachem and pressed him to reconsider, arguing that Connecticut and Massachusetts Bay would take the Montauketts' wampum, but would not protect them as well as the Niantics could. The Englishmen, said Ninigret, "are liars they do it but only to get your wampum." The English of Connecticut, he continued, "will speak much but do little."

The report of this incident and the quotes attributed to Ninigret were written by Roger Ludlow, one of the founders of Connecticut, to John Winthrop, Sr., of Massachusetts Bay. The letter was heavily biased towards Wyandanch and was, no doubt, intended to provoke an angry response from the leaders of the two colonies. There was more at stake here than the question of Wyandanch's security. Ludlow realized that if the Long Island sachems became tributaries of the Niantics, who allied with Roger Williams of Rhode Island, Connecticut would lose an important advantage in future attempts to gain jurisdiction over the area. In spite of Ludlow's own agenda, his report of the raid itself is probably accurate, however much he embellished Ninigret's words.

When Wyandanch refused to abrogate his alliance to the English, Ninigret humiliated him by stripping him in front of his people, seizing thirty fathoms of wampum and other goods, and burning several wigwams. The Niantics then attacked several neighboring villages, finally convincing some of the Montaukett elders to accept his terms. Ninigret demanded future payments in corn and wampum as terms of the alliance. Although Ludlow portrays this as a coerced agreement, it is possible that there was some genuine support among the Long Island communities for Ninigret because his agents made several overtures to sachems there over the next three decades. In 1669, for example, a Montaukett faction traveled to Ninigret's village and freely offered to accept him as their sachem (RCRI 1968, 2:269–73).

Ninigret's raid was a strategy commonly used by Indians to establish authority over tributaries (Johnson 1996). The purpose was not to seize territory or to kill people; Ninigret wanted to assert his dominance over Wyandanch in a dramatic gesture. Another example of this strategy has been described by Eric Johnson in his study of the rise to prominence of Uncas, who had been a very minor Mohegan sachem prior to the Pequot War. Uncas used a number of traditional Algonquian strategies as well as some cleverly adapted European diplomatic tactics to help him become one of the most powerful sachems in New England. Uncas' raid on the Pequot community at Naumeag in 1647, was very similar to Ninigret's actions on Long Island. The intent of the raid, says Johnson, was to humiliate the Naumeags. The people were stripped of their clothing, their wigwams were destroyed, and their goods were stolen. The Naumeags were tributaries of the English at the time.

Uncas, Ninigret, and Miantonomi were attempting to establish themselves as the primary intermediaries between the English and the smaller Algonquian communities in each of their areas. They wanted to control the flow of information, trade, and tribute between the English and the smaller groups such as the Naumeags and the Montauketts. Each sachem also seized any opportunity to gain control of one of their rivals' tributaries.

Wyandanch went immediately to Roger Ludlow and demanded that his wampum be recovered by the English. According to Ludlow, the Montaukett sachem made a compelling argument. "How can I pay tribute to the English," asked Wyandanch, "if they allow Ninigret to come and steal it from me at will?" Ludlow agreed and so did John Mason, the commander of the troops who massacred the Pequots. Mason took an armed guard of eight men to confront Ninigret, telling him that unless he made restitution to Wyandanch, the English would send an army against him (Forbes 1929–1947, 4:45). The Niantic sachem, whose village was only a few miles from the site of the Pequot massacre, reached a peaceful accommodation with Mason.

Wyandanch must have been pleased with the success of his diplomatic efforts, but he also realized how vulnerable he was to such raids in the future. These fears undoubtedly prompted the eastern Long Island sachems to invite Lion Gardiner to establish the first English presence on Long Island the following year. The sachems decided that they would be safer from attack if an English military man took up residence nearby. The English were very receptive because they wanted to obtain a foothold on Long Island before the Dutch expanded eastward from New Amsterdam. Once again the English and Dutch were to clash over land claims.

## Summary

The Indians of Long Island had contact with European explorers and traders for a hundred years before the Dutch established a small trading post on the southern tip of Manhattan. Many of these first contacts involved incidents of cruelty, violence and kidnapping by the Europeans. The Portuguese and Basque fishermen, came to the coast of Newfoundland for codfish and whales early in the sixteenth century. The whalers, who lived in fishing stations along the coast during the spring and fall hunting seasons, undoubtedly had many contacts with the local Indian communities. The Basque were followed by Dutch whalers, who hunted farther south and may have located temporary base camps on Long Island. These European whalers undoubtedly had contact with the Indian whalers, such as those described by Captain George Waymouth in 1605.

By 1540 the emphasis had shifted from fishing to the fur trade. The profits from this trade soon led to a scramble by the French, Dutch, and English for permanent trading posts along the coast and on the major inland waterways. The Indians were receptive to the proposals for these posts because they wanted access to European manufactured goods. Competition for control over the trade networks led to significant changes in Indian political systems. Sachems used their new economic power and access to European firearms to increase their political influence and transform loose alliances of small communities into tribal systems and confederacies. Two devastating results of this contact for the Indians were the introduction of European diseases and alcohol. These forces disrupted Indian communities and depleted populations.

In spite of the violent confrontations with Henry Hudson's crew in 1609, the Lenapes allowed the Dutch to establish a trading post on Manhattan in 1613. Trade flourished and soon the Dutch began to expand their small post into a more extensive network. The Dutch soon learned that wampum, manufactured from the shells so abundant on the coasts of Long Island, was in great demand among the inland tribes who trapped beavers. Wampum was easy to transport and soon became a form of legal tender in the British and Dutch economies. The Dutch, therefore, began to purchase large quantities of the beads from the Long Island Indians, drawing them into the new economic network.

The Pequot War of 1637 had a very significant impact on the Indians of Long Island, particularly those on the eastern end who had established tributary relations with the Pequots. The devastating defeat of the Pequot left a power vacuum on eastern Long Island. Several Long Island sachems, including Wyandanch, a Montaukett, believed that their peoples' interests would best be served by allying themselves with the English. Wyandanch approached Lion Gardiner and asked to establish trade with the English.

Ninigret, the Niantic sachem, sought to block any alliance between the English and the Long Island Indians, because he wanted to fill the power vacuum left by the Pequots, himself. He came to Long Island with a band of armed men to force the communities there to accept a tributary status with him. Although Ninigret succeeded in capturing and humiliating Wyandanch, the Montaukett sachem appealed to the English, who forced Ninigret to abandon his plans for Long Island, at least for the time being. It was the English, therefore, who now replaced the Pequots as the primary military authority on Long Island.

The complex political affairs in southern New England and Long Island cannot be simplified into "European" and "Algonquian" interests because both groups were divided into sharply contending factions who frequently formed alliances across racial lines in pursuit of their goals. The Dutch and English were imperial enemies and the English colonies frequently clashed with each other over their boundaries. The Europeans wanted to acquire and possess as much land as possible and they frequently turned their guns on each other in the scramble. The Algonquian sachems, Uncas, Ninigret, Miantonomi, and Wyandanch, engaged in intricate schemes to strengthen their power and influence at the expense of their rivals. Contrary to stereotyped images of Indians as childlike folk who were easily manipulated by whites, the Algonquian sachems proved to be just as adept at diplomacy and intrigue as the Europeans.

# 7

# The Long Island Frontier: Patents, Purchases, and Warfare, 1636–1645

The procedures followed by the European countries for establishing a colony were fairly similar. The claims based on discovery became royal property. The ruler then gave a charter to a court favorite or an important political supporter, or sold it to a company of private stockholders. The charter was a legal document which gave the owner the right to govern a specific territory in the name of the sovereign. The holder of the charter, whether it was the colonial court of Massachusetts Bay or the Dutch West India Company in New Netherland, had the authority to make and enforce laws and settle all disputes, subject only to the will of the home government (Barnes 1966:22-23).

In 1635 Charles I granted William Alexander, the Earl of Stirling, one of his primary supporters in Scotland, a patent which included all of Long Island, Martha's Vineyard, Nantucket, and parts of New England (Calder 1966:77). Lord Stirling intended to establish a colony on Long Island, but was unable to find any recruits in Scotland. Although little progress was made in the English plans for Long Island over the next five years, their interest in colonization may have been one of the factors, along with the decline of the New Netherland's fur trade, which prompted a shift in Dutch policy from an emphasis on commerce to a concern for increasing the permanent settler population in the colony (Trelease 1971:44; O'Callaghan 1966, 1:214). The Dutch began to encourage the immigration of farm families to the colony and to negotiate treaties with the Indians for more land.

### The Dutch Purchase of Western Long Island, 1636–1639

In the summer of 1636 the first land on Long Island was purchased from the Algonquian people by Europeans. Although the Walloon families had been living since 1626 at Wallabout near the Algonquian villages at Marechkawieck (where Brooklyn Borough Hall is located today), there is no record of any land purchase. Now the Dutch wanted to establish an official presence which would thwart any legal challenge from the English. The Dutch West India Company had ordered Director Wouter Van Twiller and the Council of New Netherland to take great care to negotiate a written deed, acceptable to the local Indians, which could be used to counter English claims to Long Island (Van Lear 1924:51-52; Jennings 1976:132).

The Dutch officials negotiated with two sachems, Penhawis and Cakapeteyno, and seven others who may have been village headmen, for the sale of three sections of meadowland called Castuteeuw (kes-asketu), "where the grass is cut or mowed" (Grumet 1981:7-8; Tooker 1962:36). These tracts of land, located in what is now southeastern Brooklyn (see Appendix B-1 map), were purchased with trade goods which, unfortunately, are not described in the deeds (NYCD 14:2-4). The company officials acted on behalf of private citizens who paid for the trade goods and became the owners of the land. This arrangement enabled the company to supervise all land transactions between Dutch citizens and the Algonquian villagers.[1] The Dutch policy prevented the chaos which plagued the English officials on eastern Long Island where, with the exception of the early purchases by Governor Eaton of New Haven, private citizens were allowed to negotiate directly with the Indians for land. Frequently these deeds overlapped, causing lengthy and expensive court battles.

The wording in the Dutch deeds presumed that the Algonquian political structure was similar to that of the Dutch. Penhawis and Cakapeteyno are identified in three deeds as the "chiefs over the district," who were negotiating the sale for seven men, Tenkirauw, Ketamu, Ararijkan, Awachkouw, Suarinkchink, Wappittawachkenis, and Ehetyl, who were identified as the "owners" of the meadowland (NYCD 14:2-4; Gehring 1980:5-6). Although the sachems did not have the same authority over their people as the Dutch officials exercised over the colonists, the fact that the Dutch recognized them as men of authority and made the payments to them enhanced the sachems' status and power. The deeds reflect a pattern in the relationships between the two cultures which resulted in the strengthening of the sachems' powers over their followers. Penhawis and Cakapeteyno were undoubtedly men of high status in their communities and the seven "owners" were probably local village headmen who had acknowledged the temporary authority of the sachems.

The following year, about a month after the massacre of the Pequots by the English, the Dutch negotiated another deed with Penhawis and Cakapeteyno, who are identified this time as "owners" rather than chiefs. The two men said that they had the consent of the community of Keshaechquereren to sell for trade goods the island called Pagganack (Governors Island) and a tract of land called "Rinnegaconck," on the southwest side of Wallabout Bay (Appendix B-2 and B-3; NYCD 14:4). Rinnegaconck was purchased for George Rapalje, the Walloon settler, perhaps to clear up any question about his land title. Keshaechquereren (Keskachane), as noted in the previous chapter, may have been an important central village where influential sachems and shamans lived. The two sachems had undoubtedly gained considerable influence from these transactions. They were able to distribute the highly valued European goods to their most loyal supporters and they had proved that they could deal effectively with the Dutch, or so it seemed at the time.

One month later Director Van Twiller met with two other sachems named Seyseys and Numers, who are identified as "chiefs of Marychkenwikingh" (Marechkawieck). The sachems sold Tenkenas (Wards Island) and Minnahanonck (Randalls Island) in the East River for trade goods, which again were not itemized (Appendix B-4). No local headmen were identified by name, but the two sachems said that they had a "special order" from the rulers and the "consent of the community" (NYCD 14:5; Grumet 1981: 34).

In the summer of 1638, a month after Ninigret's raid, the Dutch met with Cakapeteyno again, but this time Penhawis was not present. Cakapeteyno was accompanied by Menquew and Suwirau who were identified as the chiefs of Keshaechquereren. Once again the importance of this village center is underscored. Sachems residing here had the authority to sell land in neighboring areas. The Dutch purchased a parcel of land where the Bushwick section of Brooklyn is located today (Appendix B-5; NYCD 14:14). This deed does list the trade goods given for the land, providing an insight into the trade goods which were sought by the Indians. The sachems asked for forty-eight feet of "duffel" cloth, eight strings of wampum, twelve kettles, eight axes, eight hatchets, and an unspecified number of knives, beads, and awls. The cloth, metal tools, and kettles were rapidly displacing animal skins, stone tools, and ceramic ware. These valued items, which could not be produced by the Indians themselves, had to be purchased with commodities, services, or real estate desired by the whites.

The Dutch purchased the remaining portions of western Long Island, what is now Queens and part of Nassau county, from Mechowodt (Mechoswodt), "chief sachem" of Marossepinck (Massapequa), Sint Sinck (Schout's Bay, Manhasset Bay, Cow Bay) and its dependencies, his cousin, Pisacome, and three others named Wattewochkeouw, Kachpoher, Ketchquawars, who are identified as the "co-owners" of the lands (NYCD 14:15). Wattewochkeouw may be the man identified as "Awachkouw," who had accompanied Penhawis (MacCleod 1941). There is some confusion about the identity of Mechowodt. MacCleod argues that he is the former Penhawis, who simply changed his name (1941:13-16). MacCleod, however, admits that this is speculation because he could find no confirming document (see note 10 in Chapter 6). This deed, signed on January 15, 1639, lists vaguely defined boundaries as reaching in length along the south side of the island from Rockaway to "Sicketeuwhacky," somewhere east of present-day West Islip and then back north to "Martin Garritsen's Bay" (Appendix B-6). David Allen, the map librarian at SUNY Stony Brook, believes that Sicketeuwhacky may have been as far east as the Carmans River in the town of Brookhaven (Allen 1991:51-54).

None of this land had been mapped at the time and scholars are still uncertain about the locations of such places as Martin Garritsen's Bay and Sicketeuwhacky (Allen 1991:51-54). Although historians have variously located Martin Garritsen's Bay at present-day Little Neck Bay, Huntington Bay, Manhasset Bay, Hempstead Bay, and Oyster Bay (Flint 1967:71, 128-31; Smits 1994:26; O'Callaghan 1966, 1:210), John Cocks, a local historian, wrote, "there is no doubt that Oyster Bay, West harbor was called Martin Garritsen's Bay" (RTOB, 1:624). He argued that Martin Garritsen's Bay was renamed "Oyster Bay" by William

Leverich, one of the first English settlers in that area. Cocks cited a 1655 Dutch document which stated that Leverich had settled on "Martin Garritsen's Bay, by him called Oyster Bay" (RTOB, 1:624, 671).

Questions about the boundary lines to these unsurveyed lands led to title controversies which lasted for decades. The most serious dispute, which involved conflicting English and Dutch claims, erupted six months after the deed was signed. The Dutch, now under the administration of William Kieft who had arrived in the spring of 1638 to replace Van Twiller, had two goals in mind when they purchased Indian land. The first, as we have mentioned, was to strengthen their original title, based on the right of discovery, against conflicting English claims. The second goal was to make a diplomatic gesture to the Indians which would placate them and prevent hostilities. Although the English and the Dutch described the deeds as simple exchanges of real estate for the trade goods, it is quite clear that they did not view these transactions as they would sales between European parties.

These early deeds, as noted in Chapter 6, reflect a cultural misunderstanding about the nature of property, tenancy, and ownership. The deeds often included clauses allowing the Algonquian villagers to remain living on the land that they had "sold" (Bolton 1975:7-10). The Dutch included a provision in the 1639 deed which guaranteed Mechowodt and his people the right to continue living on the land, "to plant corn, fish, and hunt, and make a living there as well as they can," under the protection of the Dutch (NYCD 14:15). This was, therefore, more than a simple real estate transaction. Mechowodt and the "co-owners" had, in the Dutch view, accepted a tenant status under Dutch jurisdiction.

The Indians had a different view. They often interpreted such transactions as leases rather than as permanent transfers of land. The Europeans, who understood that in traditional Indian culture valued goods were often exchanged to confirm an alliance or an agreement between two or more parties, used what became a "working misunderstanding" to their advantage. They were usually willing to renew the deeds and give them more trade goods whenever the Indians returned to renegotiate or confirm the transaction. This policy suggests that the Europeans saw these payments as a means of buying time until the Indian communities declined in population and gradually disappeared as the impact of warfare and disease began to take its toll during the latter half of the seventeenth century.

### Interlopers, Vagabonds, and Fool's Faces:
### The Scramble for Long Island Begins

The Dutch had now extended their boundary eastwards to a vaguely defined area east of what is now Little Neck Bay on the north shore to West Islip on the Atlantic shore. While the Dutch were consolidating their claim to western Long Island the English were also at work. In May 1639, Lion Gardiner negotiated the purchase of an uninhabited island at the mouth of Peconic Bay on the far eastern end of Long Island, from Yovawam, who is identified in the deed as the "sachem of Pomanocc" (C. Gardiner 1890:58-59; Appendix D-1).[2] Yovawan may have been one of the sachems who approached Israel Stoughton after the Pequot War seeking an alliance with the English (see Chapter 6). The sachem may have wanted Gardiner to locate near his village hoping that this would lead to a closer relationship between his people and the English. Gardiner paid Yovawam and his wife, Aswaw, ten cloth coats for the property. The island was called Manchonat, "the place where they all died," perhaps because of an epidemic which wiped out the population. Gardiner renamed the island after himself and moved his family there later that year.

Wyandanch's role in the transactions is not recorded, but he undoubtedly was the one who brought the two parties together. He saw the advantages for trade and military security if the English established a presence near his villages. Common interests shared by Wyandanch and Gardiner, therefore, served as a primary basis for a close relationship between the two men, which later became celebrated in local folklore.

Gardiner's purchase, of course, was not valid under English law because the title to Long Island was owned by Lord Stirling. Under English law, only Stirling, through his appointed agent in New England, James Farrett (also spelled Forrett in some documents), had the right to sell land. Yovawam had little interest in the finer points of English procedure, but Gardiner must have known that he should have purchased a patent from Stirling before he made a purchase from Yovawam. The patent became, in effect, the legal right from the English authorities to negotiate with the Indians for a deed. Farrett, therefore, was selling "rights to purchase," not the land itself. For the English, however, the "real" purchase was the patent. The purchase from the Indians, of course, protected their title from challenge by the Dutch or fellow Englishmen and was necessary to keep peace with the local sachems. What James Farrett thought of Gardiner's purchase is not recorded, but it illustrates the arbitrary nature of the European land claims. In this case the issue was resolved the following March, when Gardiner agreed to pay Farrett an annual rent of £5 for an official patent (Wunderlich 1989:7)

James Farrett had arrived from England in the spring of 1639 with instructions to consult with John Winthrop, Sr. and, with his guidance, to recruit settlers from Massachusetts Bay for settlements on Long Island (Calder 1966:81-82). Farrett received a £100 stipend from the Earl of Stirling on June 7, 1639 and set up a temporary residence on Shelter Island, the largest island in Peconic Bay (Calder 1966:81; Brodhead 1853, 1:297). Farrett traveled around the waters of eastern Long Island and southern New England in a small sloop exploring the area in the patent and soon became Long Island's first real estate developer. Farrett, following Winthrop's instructions, sold a patent to a small group of investors from Lynn, Massachusetts, led by Daniel Howe and Edward Howell, and encouraged them to locate as close to the Dutch as possible.

Winthrop was employing the same strategy used by both the Dutch and the English in the struggle over the Connecticut Valley. Both nations pressed their claims by attempting to establish permanent settlements in contested areas. If the settlement could not be dislodged they won the ground and fixed their claim. The group from Lynn appears to have been a pawn in the imperial game.

The Dutch may have learned about the English designs on the north shore of Long Island because they moved quickly to strengthen their title to the lands east of Little Neck Bay which were so vaguely defined in the Mechowodt purchase. On May 10, 1640 they purchased from Penhawis "all the lands left as an inherence to him by his ancestors, situate on Long Island within the limits of New Netherland" (NYCD 14:28).[3] There was some question, however, about Penhawis' authority over land on the north shore. He had previously sold land on the south shore and was identified as a sachem from the Canarsie area in what is now Brooklyn.

James Farrett had the temerity to take his patent to New Amsterdam early in 1640, and inform the Dutch that all Long Island belonged to the English. He was summarily dismissed by Governor Kieft and "jeered" out of town by a mob (NYCD, 1:285-86; O'Callaghan 1966, 1:215). Undaunted, Farrett continued to sell off parcels and made plans with Winthrop to give the Dutch a direct challenge. Although there is a great deal of uncertainty about this event, it appears that Howe and his associates negotiated with some local Indians, perhaps those from the Matinecock villages, for permission to settle on land which the Dutch had purchased from Penhawis a few days earlier (RTOB, 2:687). This was to become a recurring pattern with these early deeds as cultural differences and the uncertainty about boundary lines resulted in one conflict after another.

Rival sachems, who had never viewed the land as a commodity which could be exchanged for goods, found themselves drawn into conflicts over "ownership." Indian communities now began to think in terms of boundary lines and land title for what had previously been vaguely determined hunting grounds. This led to a great deal of confusion and conflict as sachems laid claim to overlapping areas which had never been conceived of as "property" in the European sense.

Unfortunately, the only reference to Howe's purchase is in a statement by Thomas Terry, one of Howe's associates, asserting that Matinecock sachems had sold land to Farrett and Howe (RTOB, 2:687). No other details of the negotiation have survived. We do not even know the Matinecock sachem's name. We do know what Penhawis' reaction was. The sale of this land to the English immediately challenged the authority of both Penhawis and the Dutch. Howe and Farrett never fully informed the Lynn investors about the risks involved in their venture, because they later complained that they had been deceived by Farrett (NYCD, 2:144-50; NYCD, 14:31). The two men led a small party of eight men, a woman, and her young child, across the Sound in the spring of 1640 and landed somewhere on the north shore of present-day Nassau County. The men had been sent ahead to construct some houses for the families who would follow. Farrett and Winthrop had a second agenda in mind, as well. They wanted to test the resolve of the Dutch. If the de facto seizure of this territory were allowed to stand, the English would have gained all of Long Island east of the settlement and would have blocked further Dutch expansion.

When the party encountered a Dutch coat of arms on a tree indicating that this was Dutch territory, Farrett and Howe tore it down and replaced it with a "fool's head" (NYCD, 14:29). In so doing, the English repeated an action that had worked for them at Kievet's Hook (now Saybrook) at the mouth of the Connecticut River (see Chapter 6 above).

Soon after Howe and Farrett's building crew was at work on the houses, Penhawis came to New Amsterdam and reported the presence of foreign "interlopers and vagabonds" on the land that he had just sold to the Dutch (NYCD 2:145). His major concern, however, was that a local sachem had flaunted his authority and had taken an independent course of action. The Dutch, therefore had two concerns. They wanted to prevent the English from gaining a foothold which would block their expansion eastwards, and they needed to prevent their ally Penhawis from losing his base of power. The Dutch realized the importance of having an alliance with an Indian leader strong enough to help them further their interests in trade and territorial expansion.

On May 14, 1640, the Dutch sent out a troop of twenty-five men under the command of Cornelis Van Tienhoven, an influential member of the director-general's council, who served as the chief military officer under the Kieft administration. Van Tienhoven arrested all of the party except Farrett and Howe, who had returned to New Haven, and two of the men who were left with the woman and child. The men confessed that Farrett had torn down the sign, but defended themselves by blaming Farrett for deceiving them (NYCD, 2:150). The Dutch accepted the rather lame excuse because their primary concern was to evict the settlers without provoking a military confrontation with the English. The settlers were released after they made a public confession of their trespass and agreed not to return.

The English returned to Connecticut undoubtedly upset at being used as pawns in the colonial scramble for territory. Farrett issued them a new patent, endorsed by Winthrop, which specified an eight mile square area of land in what is now the eastern portion of the town of Southampton (RTSH, 1:9-11). The sachem who defied Penhawis' authority did not get off so easily. Later that summer, the Dutch sent a sloop with a troop of soldiers to capture the man and "to bring said Indians under our obedience" (NYCD, 14:32). The sachem, who is not named, refused to be humbled and openly admitted his actions in what must have been considered a direct insult to both Penhawis and the Dutch. According to a report of the incident written by an English official in 1663, the unfortunate man was "staked out," a particularly cruel form of execution in which the victim is seated on a wooden stake and left to die, slowly, in excruciating pain (CSP, 1661-1668:178).[4]

The Lynn group established the settlement of Southampton in the late spring of 1640 and put in a crop, but no effort was made to negotiate a deed with the Indians until the following December. About this same time another group of English settlers arrived on the North Fork to establish the town of Southold (Appendix D-2). Unfortunately, all the early records, including their deed, have been lost. Later Indian deeds for land on the North Fork indicate that the Southold patent was also an eight mile square area (see Chapter 8). The English viewed the Indian title to the land as casually as did the Dutch. The patent from James Farrett instructed the settlers to "make purchase in their own name and at their own leisure from any Indian that inhabit or have lawful right to any of the aforesaid land" (RTSH, 1:11). John Winthrop, Sr., who wrote his endorsement on the back, treated the Indians' claim even more lightly. "The land," he said, "being a mere wilderness and ye natives of ye place pretending some interest which ye planters must purchase" (RTSH, 1:11-12).

A delegation of Englishmen, led by John Gosmer, Edward Howell, Daniel Howe, and the Reverend Abraham Pierson, negotiated a deed with Pomatuck, Mandush, Mocomanto, Pathemanto, and eight other Indians who are identified as the "true owners of the eastern part of Long Island" (RTSH, 1:12-14). The Indians received sixteen coats, sixty bushels of corn to be paid the following year, and a promise of military protection in exchange for all of the land on the South Fork of Long Island "lying eastward" from what is now the Shinnecock Canal.

This description of the eastern boundary raises some serious questions about the deed. Farrett's patent specifically limited their purchase to a parcel of land eight miles square and the local Indians certainly did not have the authority to sell the lands of their eastern neighbors at Montauk. The Southampton settlers may have been attempting to extend their claim well beyond the boundaries of the patent. This extravagant claim was simply ignored when Theophilus Eaton and Edward Hopkins purchased what is now East Hampton from the Montauketts in 1648. The two towns quarreled over the location of the boundary line for decades, but the Southampton settlers did eventually double the land in their original patent by establishing their border with East Hampton some sixteen miles east of Canoe Place.

The promise of military protection indicates that the Indians viewed the agreement as an arrangement similar to the one that they had with the Pequots. Pomatuck, Mandush, and their people would provide certain goods and services in exchange for a guarantee of peace. In a memorandum on the bottom of the deed the Indians were granted the right to plant crops in the fields lying to the west of the Southampton settlement, adjacent to where the Shinnecock Reservation is located today.

The fact that the Indians were to continue living on the land they had just sold gave rise to confusion on both sides about the nature of the agreement. This confusion later turned to anger as the English population grew and began to take over more and more of the planting fields and to reduce the available hunting territory. Over the next decade, however, the English settlement grew in peace as the flames of war nearly destroyed the Dutch.

In spite of the English success in establishing a permanent presence at Southampton, the Dutch believed that they had thwarted the English imperial threat to western Long Island. They strengthened their alliance with Penhawis, and were now confident that they had secured the whole of western Long Island for Dutch settlement. How wrong they were.

## "With Fire and Sword": Kieft's Campaigns Against the Raritans and the Wiechquaesgecks, 1640–1642

As the numbers of settlers increased, so did the potential for conflicts with their Indian neighbors. The establishment of European farms disrupted a delicately balanced ecosystem. The introduction of domestic livestock brought many far-reaching changes in the landscape. The farmers cleared meadowland and fenced in large areas of former Indian hunting grounds; their livestock, particularly pigs, frequently destroyed Indian crops (Williams 1995:253). The Indians often responded by killing and eating the stray animals (NYCD, 1:273; Trelease 1971:64). Dogs from Indian villages often attacked sheep and calves in their pens.

The number of grievances from Indians led Governor Kieft to issue an ordinance in 1640 fining farmers who did not keep their livestock confined. Kieft appealed to the settlers on the basis of self-interest, arguing that the crop damage by stray cattle might provoke attacks on the Dutch homesteads (Trelease 1971:64). Unfortunately, Kieft's attempt to prevent ill feelings against the Dutch was undermined by some of his other policies. In the fall of 1639, Kieft made an ill-advised attempt to tax Indians for the maintenance of the Dutch militia on the grounds that the Dutch troops were protecting the Indians around New Amsterdam from their enemies. Those who do not pay, warned Kieft, "we shall endeavor to induce . . . by the most suitable means." One sachem sent back a sharp reply warning the Dutch not to attempt to take away any of his corn (NYCD, 13:6; O'Callaghan 1966, 1:223). In spite of the ominous Dutch threat, there is no evidence that Kieft ever made any attempt to collect the taxes, but the conceit and the tone of the tax law characterized Kieft's attitude towards the Indians, which proved to be as bad as his judgement.

The following spring, a group of Indians from the Raritan villages west of Staten Island insulted the crew of a trading sloop by bringing squirrel pelts on board instead of beaver, and slapping a crew member in the face with them. These actions may have been a response to Kieft's tax, but, unfortunately, we have no record of their intent. The crew reported to Kieft that they had been threatened and had barely escaped with their lives (NYCD, 13:22-3). A short time later, some Dutch servants stole a few pigs from the farm of David De Vries, a prominent landowner on Staten Island, and blamed the Raritan Indians. Kieft believed the servants and, without investigating further, sent out a troop of sixty soldiers and twenty sailors in a sloop against the Raritan village to demand restitution.

Cornelis Van Tienhoven, one of the few Europeans to become fluent in the local Algonquian languages, commanded the troops. He had apparently become so fascinated with Indian culture that he spent a considerable amount of time in their villages. His enemies, and there were many in New Amsterdam, suggested that his primary interest was not intellectual curiosity, but rather a lecherous desire for Indian women.[5] He was reported to have frequently "run about as an Indian, with a little covering and a small patch in front, from lust," after Indian women, "to whom he has always been mightily inclined" (quoted in Kammen 1975:64; Kessler and Rachlis 1959:80-81).

Van Tienhoven's familiarity with Indian culture did not, however, incline him to be sympathetic to the Indians as a people. He urged Kieft to take a very hard line and to rely primarily upon military force rather than diplomacy. Van Tienhoven marched into the Raritan village and demanded immediate payment for the pigs. The Raritans were not given a chance to protest their innocence, because the Dutch soldiers set upon them killing several and burning their crops (O'Callaghan 1966, 1:226-67). The sachem's brother was captured and tortured to death by Govert Lockermans, the captain of the Dutch sloop who, according to David De Vries, "misused the chief's brother in his private parts with a piece of split wood" (1909:208-9).

The attack on the Raritans turned many of the neighboring Indian communities against the Dutch and led to a political division within the New Netherland community. One faction, led by David De Vries, called for a policy based on negotiation and diplomacy, and the other, represented by Van Tienhoven and Kieft, favored the use of military force. The following year, two incidents brought the factions into sharp contention. The first was a raid by the Raritans on De Vries' Staten Island plantation in retaliation for Van Tienhoven's attack the previous spring. The Dutch, said the Raritans, "shall have dead men instead of dead hogs to fight for," as they descended on the plantation, killing four men and burning buildings (O'Callaghan 1966, 1:239). Kieft, rejecting the advice of the council members who called for diplomatic overtures to the Raritan, called for their extermination and issued an ordinance offering ten fathoms of wampum for every head of a Raritan Indian delivered to him in New Amsterdam (NYCD, 13:7-8; Grumet 1979:34-36). The Raritans, however, had satisfied their honor and made peace with the Dutch.

Kieft and Van Tienhoven viewed the Raritan peace settlement as a vindication for their hard line policy. This encouraged them to take a similar position a short time later when a Wiechquaesgeck Indian killed a Dutch trader. The Indian said that he had acted out of revenge for the murder of his uncle by Peter Minuit's servants in 1626 (see Chapter 6). Kieft called a meeting of council and all of the heads of families in the colony on August 28, 1641, and, supported by Van Tienhoven, advocated the immediate destruction of the man's village unless he was turned over to the Dutch authorities.

The Wiechquaesgeck sachem responded in anger that the nephew of the man killed by Minuit's men in 1626 had now regained his honor and there was no more to be said. Both the Raritans and the Wiechquaesgecks held views of justice in common with most of the native peoples of North America. For them, the murder of a clan member was a matter for that clan only, not the whole community. To restore honor, a killing must be answered with some form of compensation to the victim's family. If no agreement was reached about this, the victim's clan might decide to exact a blood sacrifice. There was no particular interest in finding out which member of that clan committed the act; all that mattered was that a member of that clan must die or that restitution be paid to the victim's family. If outsiders believed that they could injure or kill a clan member without fear of retribution, no member of the clan could feel safe (White 1991:76-80). The Europeans, in contrast, believed that the particular individual who committed a crime must be tried and punished by the authorities who governed the community.

The council and assembly, learning of the sachem's refusal to surrender the man, agreed that force should be used, but advocated delay until the crops were harvested in the fall. When Kieft came back to them in November, they again called for patience and delayed action. Kieft was angry over the delays, but he could not act without the support of the council. In January 1642, he again called for a military campaign against the Wiechquaesgecks, and the council agreed.

A troop of eighty men under the command of Hendrick van Dyck marched north under orders to execute vengeance on the tribe "with fire and sword" (O'Callaghan 1966, 1:249). Van Dyck planned to attack the unsuspecting village by night, but he got lost in the darkness and couldn't find it. Frustrated and fearing an open engagement in enemy territory, he returned in humiliation to New Amsterdam. The Wiechquaesgecks, aware of their close call, agreed to surrender the man responsible for the death of the trader and negotiated a peace settlement. Once again Kieft's policy appeared to have been vindicated.

## Miantonomi's "Conspiracy," 1642

Shortly after the peace was concluded, Miantonomi, the Narragansett sachem, mounted a campaign to expand his power base by gaining tributaries on Long Island. He arrived on western Long Island early in the spring of 1642 with a retinue of about one hundred men to consult with local sachems (NYCD, 3:183). Panic swept the Dutch frontier on Long Island as rumors of conspiracies fed on one another. Reports spread that some Indians attempted to set fire to the building where the Dutch stored their powder and that the Indians planned "to poison the Director or enchant him by their deviltry" (NYCD, 3:183). Accounts of Indian cruelty and a belief that their shamans were in league with the devil fueled the wild fears of the Europeans. Director Kieft became convinced that the Indians were going to curse him with a "diabolical incantation" (O'Callaghan 1966, 1:263). Such curses were not taken lightly by Indians or Europeans, not only because each believed that witches existed, but also because shamans frequently administered a dose of deadly poison to make sure the curse took effect (Butler 1979:322; see Chapter 5 above).

There is no indication that any of the sachems in the Dutch territories responded to the Narragansett sachem. Penhawis apparently remained content in his alliance with the Dutch, at least for the time being. Miantonomi's overtures to the Montauketts, however, are better documented, but the source is Lion Gardiner, who was cultivating a close alliance with Miantonomi's rival, Wyandanch (L. Gardiner 1980:140-43).

Gardiner reported that Miantonomi visited Wyandanch and a council of Montaukett elders and told them to stop sending wampum to the English in Connecticut. Wyandanch replied that he did not want his people to suffer the same fate as the Pequots at Mystic. The Pequots were destroyed, said Miantonomi, because they had killed an Englishman, but since the Montauketts had no English blood on their hands they need not fear. This line of argument clearly indicated that Miantonomi had no intention of organizing a conspiracy against the English and raises serious questions about the credibility of other aspects of Gardiner's account.

Wyandanch reported this to Gardiner, who told him to stall the Narragansetts by telling them he needed a month to discuss their proposal with the other Long Island sachems. As soon as Miantonomi left, Gardiner sent Wyandanch with a letter explaining the matter to John Haynes, a wealthy Connecticut settler, who was elected governor of the colony the following year. Haynes advised Wyandanch not to pay any tribute to Miantonomi and informed Gardiner of this in a letter. When a Narragansett delegation returned to Montauk, Gardiner met them and sent them away with a copy of Haynes' letter, telling them to have their ally Roger Williams read it to Miantonomi. Haynes and Gardiner believed that Williams, who had considerable influence over the Narragansett sachem, would dissuade him from interfering with the English alliances on Long Island.

Unfortunately, there is very little documentation about these events other than Gardiner's account. If Williams attempted to intervene, he was not successful because, according to Gardiner, Miantonomi came back to Montauk when Wyandanch was away, and delivered an address in secret to the Montaukett elders telling them that the Mohawks had joined in an alliance with the Narragansetts to destroy all of the English settlements. Miantonomi laid out a very specific plan calling for the Montauketts to raise one hundred men from the Shinnecocks and another hundred of their own warriors and to prepare for an attack forty days later. The signal for the action would be three fires, apparently on Block Island, on the given night. The elders, again, according to Gardiner, enthusiastically endorsed the plan.

When Wyandanch returned, the elders would not reveal the contents of Miantonomi's message. For three days they rebuffed his efforts to learn about the Narragansett sachem's negotiations with the Montaukett leaders. This affront to Wyandanch suggests that the loss of honor he suffered during Ninigret's raid had not been fully restored by his alliance with the English. Some of the Montaukett elders apparently remained skeptical about him and about his policy of accommodation with the English. Frustrated, Wyandanch turned to Gardiner for advice. Gardiner now realized that Wyandanch would need more military and economic support from the English in order to strengthen his position within the Montaukett community.

Gardiner said that he then gave Wyandanch a plan to "beguile" the elders into revealing the purpose of Miantonomi's visit. The plan, which Gardiner never revealed, worked and Gardiner sent word to New Haven about the alleged plot. Gardiner's account of the plot is suspect because there is little evidence to suggest that Miantonomi actually intended to make war on the whites, nor is there any evidence that the Mohawks, who had executed Sassacus the Pequot sachem when he sought refuge among them, had any such interest.

A more likely explanation of Miantonomi's expedition to Long Island was that he was attempting to form alliances with Long Island sachems which would strengthen him against his rivals in southern New England. His primary goal was probably the same as that of Ninigret four years earlier. The inflammatory rhetoric put in the sachems' mouths by Ludlow and Gardiner may have been exaggerations of bravado speeches designed to impress the sachems' audiences.

The only corroboration of a plot comes from an account by Roger Ludlow, who reported that a sachem near Fairfield came to him with a similar story (MHSC, 3rd Series, 3:161-64; Sainsbury 1971:117). Ludlow, however, had also reported that Ninigret had made threats against the English in his report of the Niantic raid on Long Island in 1638. Both Ludlow and Gardiner feared that Rhode Island and Massachusetts Bay might gain a foothold on Long Island if sachems allied to them held the Long Island sachems in a tributary status. They may have used the threat of an "Indian Conspiracy" to make sure that the Long Island sachems remained under the influence of Connecticut. The struggle for Long Island was, therefore, not merely a matter of Dutch-English rivalry; there were many other agendas at work in both European and Native American camps.

Possibly another incident about that time in Southampton may have contributed to the concerns about Miantonomi's alleged conspiracy. Daniel Howe and several armed men surrounded the wigwam of a man at Shinnecock who had been accused of killing an Englishman and called on him to surrender. When the man came out wielding a knife in a desperate attempt to break free, Howe and his men shot him. Unfortunately, the only information we have about the incident is a brief paragraph in William Hubbard's *General History of New England*, written about 1682. He cited Howe's action as an example of the proper way to handle Indian affairs: "If they had been always so handled, they would not have dared to have rebelled, as they did afterwards" (1848:449) Hubbard's belief that violence would deter violence belies a profound ignorance of both human nature and Algonquian codes of honor. Several years later, Howe's act was avenged, causing more unrest.

Connecticut responded to the reports of Miantonomi's conspiracy with an immediate call to arms, but John Winthrop, Sr. wanted to talk directly with Miantonomi before he took any precipitous action. He called the Narragansett sachem to Boston where he could question him face to face. Miantonomi denied that he was involved in any plot against the English, and asked to confront his accusers. Winthrop acknowledged that all of the reports were from secondhand sources and was satisfied with Miantonomi's explanation (Hosmer 1946, 2:76; Sainsbury 1971:117).

## "God Hath Delivered Them into Our Hands": Massacres at Pavonia and Corlaer's Hook, 1643

Just as the tensions eased somewhat on eastern Long Island, they increased sharply in the west. Some Dutch traders plied an Indian from one of the Hackingsack villages with alcohol and stole his beaver fur robe. The victim took revenge by killing two white men shortly thereafter (O'Callaghan 1966, 1:263-64). Several elders from Hackingsack came to New Netherland to offer a restitution payment of wampum to the relatives of the two men. In Algonquian culture such restitution would restore the victim's honor and remove the obligation of blood revenge.

Governor Kieft would not listen, demanding that the murderer be turned over to Dutch authorities. The man responsible, said the elders, was the son of an influential sachem and had fled the area. Kieft remained adamant, repeating his demand that the man be surrendered. The elders protested, admonishing the Dutch, "You ought not to sell brandy to the Indians to make them crazy, for they are not accustomed to your liquors . . . we wish you, so as to prevent all mischief, to sell no more fire-water to our braves" (O'Callaghan 1966 1:264). The elders left and the issue remained unresolved.

The following February, a troop of Mohawks attacked the Wiechquaesgeck villages killing seventeen, taking many women and children prisoner, and demanding tributary payments (NYCD, 3:184). Unlike Miantonomi and Ninigret, the Mohawks took a very aggressive approach to the process of bringing smaller groups into a tributary status. Wiechquaesgeck refugees fled in terror, seeking protection from the Dutch in New Netherland. The hapless survivors were given refuge in an Indian village near Corlaer's Hook on Manhattan and at Pavonia, across the Hudson (Appendix B). The Mohawk war parties did not pursue them into Dutch territory, nor did they take any hostile action against the Dutch. The Mohawk actions provide further evidence that, contrary to the reports by Gardiner and Ludlow, they had no interest in waging war against either the Dutch or the English.

The Wiechquaesgecks were soon to discover that the Dutch could be as cruel as the Mohawks. No sooner were the refugees settled in than some of Kieft's supporters, led by Cornelis Van Tienhoven, began to call for an attack on them in retribution for the traders killed by the Wiechquaesgecks and the Hackingsacks. "God hath delivered them into our hands," they said in a petition to the governor's council asking for permission to launch an attack on the refugee encampment at Corlaer's Hook, while the regular militia troops attacked the camp at Pavonia (NYCD, 1:193).

The petition, welcomed by Kieft, sparked a debate among the council members. David De Vries led a faction opposed to such drastic and brutal action, calling for patience and restraint. The Indians, argued De Vries, would do no harm if harm were not done to them (O'Callaghan 1966,1:265). Other members of De Vries' faction warned that such action might plunge the colony into a major conflict with other Indians around New Netherland. De Vries emphasized this point saying, "You go to break the heads of Indians; it is our own nation you are about to destroy" (O'Callaghan 1966, 1:266). Maryn Andriaensen, one of the more strident of the petitioners, rejected these arguments, proclaiming that Dutch honor required severe reprisals against the Indians.

Kieft agreed with Andriaensen and granted his petition, authorizing him and his associates "to attack a party of Indians lying behind Corlaer's plantation, and to act with them as they think proper" (NYCD, 13:10). Kieft gave a blank check to an untrained and undisciplined mob of armed men to fall upon the helpless Indian villagers. Maryn Andriaensen and Govert Lockermans, who had tortured the Raritan prisoner, led the attack on the village by Corlaer's Hook. No effort was made to distinguish between the Wiechquaesgeck refugees and their hosts, who were closely allied to Numers, the sachem from Marechkawieck, directly across the river on Long Island.

The militia, commanded by Van Tienhoven, was given orders to drive away the Indians camped at Pavonia and to spare, as much as possible, the women and children. On the cold winter night of February 25th, 1643, after three days of careful planning, the two parties of armed men went out of the fort on their grim missions. Neither the militia nor the citizen's party exercised any discipline or restraint. The following account of Van Tienhoven's attack at Pavonia was written by an eyewitness.

> Young children, some of them snatched from their mothers, were cut in pieces before the eyes of their parents, and the pieces were thrown into the fire or into the water; other babes were bound on planks and then cut through, stabbed and miserably massacred, so that it would break a heart of stone; some were thrown into the river and when the fathers and mothers sought to save them, the soldiers would not suffer them to come ashore but caused both old and young to be drowned. Some children of from 5 to 6 years of age, as also some old infirm

> persons, who had managed to hide themselves in the bushes and reeds, came out in the morning to beg for a piece of bread and for permission to warm themselves, but were all murdered in cold blood and thrown into the fire or the water. A few escaped to our settlers, some with the loss of a hand, others of a leg, others again holding in their bowels with their hands, and all so cut, hacked and maimed, that worse could not be imagined (NYDH, 4:103-4).

The Dutch killed at least eighty men, women, and children at Pavonia and another thirty at Corlaer's Hook. Andriaensen's attack on Corlaer's Hook was not described in the Dutch records, but it was undoubtedly as brutal. The troops returned to New Amsterdam with thirty prisoners and several severed heads taken as trophies by the Dutch soldiers (O'Callaghan 1966, 1:269). De Vries called the two massacres a disgrace to the Dutch nation.

Kieft, however, applauded the success of the attacks and so did many of the settlers on Long Island. Van Tienhoven's mother-in-law was said to have taken great delight in kicking around the severed heads which had been put on public display (O'Callaghan, 1:169). The news of the massacre encouraged some of the settlers in Brooklyn, led by Gerritt Wolfersten, to request permission for an attack on Marechkawieck, one of the more prominent Indian towns on western Long Island. Kieft, perhaps sobered by the atrocities committed at Pavonia and Corlaer's Hook, and fearful that he might lose control of his administration to Adriaensen, Wolfersten, and their followers, refused to sanction a raid. He did, however, give them permission to defend themselves against any hostile action by the Indians. His response left the settlers free to decide what constituted "hostile action" (O'Callaghan 1966, 1:270). A few days later in what may have been an attempt to provoke the Indians, some of the Long Island settlers stole two wagon loads of corn from Marechkawieck, killing two of the villagers in the process.

## War and Peace on the Long Island Frontier, 1643–1645

De Vries' prediction about the destruction of New Netherland nearly came true as the western Long Island frontier plunged into chaos. As word spread through the Indian villages about the massacres at Pavonia and Corlaer's Hook, preparations were made for war. Penhawis and the Long Island sachems had now turned against the Dutch. By mid-March the Dutch found themselves besieged by a coalition of Indians from Long Island, New Jersey, and Westchester. The Long Island farmsteads were vulnerable because they were scattered and could easily be cut off from help. The Indian war parties swept across what is now Brooklyn and Queens, killing settlers and burning down homes and barns. Settlers fled across the East River to the relative safety of New Amsterdam.

Roger Williams, who had come to New Amsterdam to get a ship to London, reported that he saw the flames from burning buildings dot the skyline. "Mine eyes saw the flames of their towns, the frights and hurries of men, women, children, and the present removal of all that could to Holland" (RCNP, 10:440). Two of the Dutch farmers reported that "our people were killed and murdered within a few weeks, at diverse places around the fort, by the Indians . . . we continued in the greatest terror, with the cattle which still remained." They described the piles of ashes from burnt houses, barns, barracks and other buildings, and the bones of the cattle left after the raids and lamented the loss of nearly fifty "first class farms and plantations abandoned in the war by our Dutch" (NYCD, 1:205).

The attacks continued for several weeks and then abated as the Indians turned themselves to preparations for spring planting. In late March 1643, Penhawis sent three messengers to the fort in New Amsterdam seeking peace talks. The Indians arrived at a time when many of the Dutch officials were shifting their support away from Kieft to De Vries' peace faction. Kieft himself now claimed that he had been pressured into the attacks on Pavonia and Corlaer's Hook by Maryn Adriaensen and his supporters (Trelease 1971:75). The bloodshed unleashed by Kieft's policies convinced many of the Dutch leaders that they should now take a more conciliatory approach.

Maryn Andriaensen, furious at Kieft for accusing him of provoking the Indians to violence, approached him with a pistol and tried to shoot him. The angry planter was overpowered and thrown in prison. The incident further divided the Dutch community. Andriaensen's son Marynsen, hearing of his father's arrest, rushed into town with a friend and chased Kieft to his house, firing his pistol as he ran. Before the young Andriaesen could do any real damage, he was killed by one of the guards. In an attempt to intimidate Andriaensen's supporters, Marynsen's head was mounted on a gibbet in public view (O'Callaghan 1966, 1:273). Facing these divisive internal tensions, Kieft wisely sought to end the Indian war as quickly as possible.

The governor sent David De Vries and one of his supporters, Jacob Olfertzsen, to meet with Penhawis and the other Long Island sachems. We have a brief report of this meeting from De Vries himself (1909:230-32). The Dutch emissaries crossed the East River to Long Island and marched about sixteen miles eastward, reaching a village near present-day Rockaway in the evening. There were about thirty dwellings and from two to three hundred people in the village. Penhawis, who was described as having only one eye, welcomed the Dutchmen and brought them to his wigwam where they were served a meal of fish and oysters.

The next day they met with sixteen sachems from Long Island and Staten Island. The sachems, who, unfortunately, were not named by De Vries, sat in a circle around the two Dutchmen. The group probably included such sachems as Numers, Seyseys, Cakapeteyno, Gauwarowe, Witaneywen, Pugnipan, and Penhawis' son, Witaneywen, who later took the name Tackapousha (Grumet 1995:33). The names of these men appear on documents during this decade. The meeting began with a speech by their best orator. He held a bundle of small sticks in his hand which apparently served as memory aids as he spoke. The sachem carefully laid down one stick and then he spoke, reminding the Dutchmen that when the Europeans first came to this land, they were often in need of food. The Indians gave them food and taught them how to fish and find oysters. After he laid down the next stick he spoke again, pointing out that the Indians had taken in the traders to live with them until the ships returned for them. Indian women gave them comfort and bore their children. Their reward for this help, he continued, as he laid down another stick, was to suffer the Dutch fire and sword. Some of the dead had Dutch fathers. The Dutch, he said, "had become so villainous as to kill their own blood," and he laid down another stick (De Vries 1909:231; O'Callaghan 1966, 1:275-78).

De Vries told the speaker that he knew all of this, but that it had been done "unwittingly," and invited the sachems to accompany him to New Amsterdam where restitution payment in gifts would be presented to them. The return trip by canoe was about three hours shorter than the march overland. Kieft received the sachems and negotiated a peace treaty with Penhawis. Both sides acknowledged that "blood has been shed, houses destroyed." Kieft gave them gifts and asked them to send word to the sachems of Hackingsack and Tappan about the Dutch peace offers (NYCD, 14:44-45).

Oratamin, the sachem from Hackingsack, came to New Amsterdam on April 22, 1643, in response to Kieft's offer. He represented the Tappan, Rechgawawanck, Sint Sinck, and Kichtawack villages along the Hudson River north of Manhattan (NYCD, 13:14; Grumet 1979:110-12, 1981:66). Oratamin offered the Dutch the following terms: all injuries done to each other in the past would be forgiven and forgotten, neither side would molest the other in the future, and if any other tribe would plot against the Christians, Oratamin and his allied sachems would give warning and would not give them any support. The terms were accepted and the peace treaty was endorsed by both parties. Gifts were exchanged, although, according to De Vries, the Dutch insulted the Indians by not giving enough to adequately compensate for the massacres at Pavonia and Corlaer's Hook (De Vries 1909:232).

The peace, unfortunately, was short-lived. In September a second phase of the war began in the north when Pachem, the Tankiteke sachem who had a large following in what is now Westchester County (Appendix B), urged the sachems under his influence to resume attacks on the Dutch following the summer harvest. His appeal met an enthusiastic response because many of the villagers there had relatives among the dead at Corlaer's Hook and Pavonia. The tensions began to build as the Indians finished storing away the crops for the winter. By the end of August fighting had resumed along the northern border of New Amsterdam. Pachem's men burned several farms and attacked trading vessels on the Hudson. The Wiechquaesgecks soon joined Pachem and the war began to spread.

The fragile peace with the Long Island Indians was also eroding. In July one of the sachems came to De Vries to report that the young men were pressing their elders to renew hostilities against the Dutch (De Vries 1909:232). The sachem may have been Penhawis, but De Vries does not mention his name. One of the young men, said the sachem, remained angry at the Dutch because they had killed his father and there were many other men who had lost close friends and relatives in the Dutch attacks. This was inevitable because the custom of exogamous marriage had established an expanding kinship network connecting villages on all sides of New Amsterdam. There were, therefore, hundreds of Long Island families who had similar grievances against the Dutch. The sachem warned De Vries that he must not venture too far from the Dutch fort because of the growing danger.

Fig. 7.1. Algonquian man with war club

De Vries took the sachem to Governor Kieft where the grim warning was repeated. Kieft's response indicated how little he understood the Algonquian political system. He told the sachem that he must execute all of the young men who threaten to upset the peace. Many of the contemporary Dutch observers had noted that the Algonquian sachems had no such power over their followers. There was, therefore, no excuse for Kieft's ignorance in this matter. Kieft then insulted the sachem by offering to pay him two hundred fathoms of wampum as a reward for the executions. Had Kieft offered to give wampum as compensation to the relatives of the people killed by the Dutch, he might have saved the peace.

The failure of Kieft to negotiate with the Long Island sachems, the increasing pressure from the younger men for war, and the success of Pachem in the north, encouraged the Long Island Indians to renew the fighting against the Dutch. Some of the Dutch officials suspected that Penhawis had begun planning for this campaign back in February when the sachems met with De Vries. "He had given dangerous council to his people," they reported, and had told them "that they should wait and not attack the Dutch until all suspicions had been lulled and then divide themselves equally through the houses of the Christians and slaughter all of them in one night" (NYCD, 1:186). Unfortunately, the records of the war from the Indian side are so sparse that we do not know if Penhawis ever made such plans nor is there any information about his involvement in the attacks on the white settlements.

War parties attacked the settlement at Gravesend, which had been established by Lady Deborah Moody the previous fall. Moody, a Baptist driven out of New England because of her religious beliefs, had been granted permission by the

Dutch to settle at Gravesend in Brooklyn (O'Callaghan 1966, 1:258, 287). A group of forty settlers from nearby farmsteads gathered at her home to repel several attacks (Trelease 1971:77). The attack on Newtown, a few miles north of Gravesend, was more successful, leaving the town in ruins. By the late fall no farmstead on Long Island was safe from attack. David De Vries finally gave up all hope for a peaceful settlement and returned to Holland.

The New Amsterdam council wrote to Holland describing the conditions in New Netherland. "Long Island is destitute also of inhabitants and stock, except a few insignificant places over against the main, which are about to be abandoned. The English who have settled among us have not escaped. They too, except in one place, are all murdered and burnt" (O'Callaghan 1966, 1:290). There were less than three hundred settlers in New Amsterdam and their supply of ammunition was running low.

In desperation, the Dutch appealed to the English in New Haven for aid, but found them distracted with their own problems. The English colonies, Connecticut, New Haven, Plymouth, and Massachusetts, concerned that the civil war between Cromwell's Puritan forces and the royalist supporters of King Charles would leave them defenseless against a potential threat from the French, the Dutch, or the Indians, had formed a confederation the previous May (Ward 1961:37-38). Rhode Island, of course, was not included because Roger Williams was viewed as a dangerous heretic by the Puritans. The confederation, called the United Colonies, refused the Dutch request for 150 men and financial aid, but allowed New Haven to send some supplies of corn.

Although the conditions on Long Island were certainly not very inviting for new colonists, a group of dissenters from the Puritan regimes in New England decided to emigrate in the late fall of 1643. Following the example of Lady Moody, they sought to establish a colony under the more tolerant Dutch authorities. Led by the Reverend Richard Denton, the small community made plans to move from their homes in Stamford, Connecticut, across the Sound to an area east of the existing Dutch settlements. The Dutch, desperate to expand the white population of New Netherland even if it meant taking in English settlers, welcomed these new colonists.

Denton sent John Carman and Robert Fordham to Long Island seeking permission from the Indians to establish the settlement of Hempstead (Smits 1994:16-17; Marshall 1962:10-11). Fordham and Carman met with Tackapousha, "the sagamore of Massapeage," and six others named Aarane, Pamaman, Remoj, Waines, Whanage, and Yarafus, to negotiate a deed to Hempstead (Appendix B-8 map; NYCD, 14:530; RTNSH, 1:312-13).[6] The sagamore was probably the young Tackapousha, who was still known as Witaneywen at that time. Apparently, his father, Penhawis, was attempting to gain some advantage against the Dutch by establishing friendly relations with the English.

The Dutch, who remained convinced that Penhawis was involved in a secret plot to attack them when they least expected (NYCD, 1:186-87), were unable to obtain military aid from the English colonies, but they were able to recruit Captain John Underhill, one of the officers who led the troops in the Pequot massacre at Mystic, to direct campaigns against the Indians (O'Callaghan 1966, 1:289). In February 1644, Underhill and a Dutch officer, Johannes La Montagne, led a troop of 120 men against Penhawis. Three boats carrying the soldiers sailed east from Manhattan along the north shore to Schout's Bay where they disembarked and marched south to the tiny community of Hempstead.

The campaign is not well documented, but it appears that at least two raids were launched from Hempstead (NYCD, 1:186-87).[7] Underhill led a small group of fourteen Englishmen to attack a small village near Hempstead and La Montagne took the others to raid a large village identified as "Matsepe." There is some debate among historians about the location of this battle. O'Callaghan and Brodhead believed that Matsepe was the village of Maspeth on the Newtown Creek in western Queens, across the river from Manhattan (O'Callaghan 1966, 1:299-300; Brodhead 1853-71, 1:388-89). Marshall (1962:39-41) and Trelease (1971:79) argue that the conflict took place near the present-day community of Massapequa on Fort Neck.

It is possible that the fort embankments mapped by Ralph Solecki and Carlyle Smith (see Chapter 4) were part of Penhawis' village complex. A grave, which was excavated near the fort site in 1935, containing the remains of twenty-four people, may have been related to this incident. All of this data must be considered

Fig. 7.2. Purchase of Hempstead in 1643. This mural was painted in Hempstead Village Hall in 1947 by Robert Gaston Herbert.

with some caution, because it has not been corroborated by colonial documents or by a professional archaeological excavation.[8]

Although the site is uncertain, the battle is well documented and it took a heavy toll on the Indians in the area. The Dutch reported killing 120 Indians while suffering only one casualty. Penhawis may have been killed in the battle because he disappears from the colonial records thereafter (MacCleod 1941:15-16).

Underhill now turned to his campaign against Pachem's forces in the north. He led a troop against a Wiechquaesgeck village, which was probably located near the present-day town of Pound Ridge in Westchester County (see Appendix B map; NYCD, 1:187; Trelease 1971:80). Underhill repeated the strategy which had been so devastatingly effective against the Pequot fort at Mystic. His men surrounded the unsuspecting village during the night and opened fire into the village. Within a short time, over 180 Indians lay dead. The rest took refuge inside their wigwams, firing arrows through small openings; apparently, none of the men had guns. At that point, Underhill, as he had done at Mystic, set fire to the wigwams. Forced out into the open, the villagers were cut down by musket and sword. Some, in desperation, ran back into the fire to avoid being cut to pieces by the swords. Only eight men survived and five of them were badly wounded. The final death toll is not known, but estimates range from five to seven hundred (O'Callaghan 1966, 1:301).

Underhill returned in triumph to New Amsterdam where a public feast was held in his honor (Brodhead 1853, 1:391). The devastating defeats prompted sachems from both areas to sue for peace. Kieft signed a treaty on April 9, 1644, with four of the northern sachems and a few days later he negotiated a similar agreement with Guawarowe, a Matinecock sachem (NYCD, 14:56). This is the first mention of Matinecock (Matinnekonck) in the colonial records (Grumet 1981:32). The sachem said that he spoke for villages on the south shore at Marospinc (Massapequa) and Sicketeuwhacky (east of Massapequa). Guawarowe promised that he would not aid or give refuge to Indians from Reckonhacky (Rockaway), the Bay (Canarsie), and Marechkawieck, who were still at war against the Dutch.

A ship carrying 130 Dutch soldiers arrived in July 1644 to reinforce the Dutch troops, but they saw little action because the Indian resistance was gradually fading. The sachems on eastern Long Island followed Gauwarowe's example and went to the second annual meeting of the United Colonies, held in Hartford, to reaffirm their status as tributaries of the English (RCNP, 9:18-19). The men were identified as Youghco, the sachem of Munhauset, Wiantause (Wyandanch), Moughmaitow (Momoweta), and Weenagaminin. Only Youghco, who is probably the sachem who sold Gardiner his island in 1639, was associated with a place name. Related documents identify Wyandanch with the communities at Montauk and Momoweta as a sachem from Corchaug on the North Fork of eastern Long Island. Tooker believed that Weenagaminin may have been from Shinnecock, but his identity is uncertain. Tooker's speculation is based on later documents which will be discussed below.

The commissioners of the United Colonies, who included Governor Theophilus Eaton of New Haven and Governor Edward Hopkins of Connecticut, saw an opportunity to reinforce their land claims on Long Island. After the Earl of Stirling's death in 1640, his family cut off Farrett's funds, leaving him stranded in New England. Farrett sold his small boat and his title to Robin's Island, and mortgaged the remaining Long Island land in the Stirling Patent to a group of entrepreneurs including Edward Hopkins and Theophilus Eaton, for £110 sterling. If Farrett did not pay off the debt in three years he forfeited the patent to Eaton, Hopkins, and the other investors.

It may have been at this time that Stephen Goodyear, a wealthy merchant and close associate of Governor Eaton, purchased Shelter Island from Farrett (Appendix D-8). Unfortunately no deed or record of the transaction has survived (RTEH 1:96-97). The local Indians were never consulted and they challenged Goodyear's title several years later claiming that neither Farrett nor Goodyear had ever paid them anything. Farrett left for England in 1642 and never returned. The three-year period for the mortgage ended on July 24, 1644, just two months prior to the arrival of the four sachems in Hartford. When, as expected, no word came from Farrett nor from any other representative of the Stirling family, Hopkins and Eaton assumed possession of the Stirling patent lands on Long Island (Calder 1966:87-92). It is quite possible that the Stirling family was never informed of Farrett's transactions at all.[9]

The commissioners responded to the request of the Long Island sachems by issuing a certificate of agreement describing the tributary status of the people represented by the four sachems. The document begins, however, by asserting the legitimacy of the Stirling Patent, validating the transfer of the Long Island land title to the group led by Eaton and Hopkins, and establishing exclusive purchase rights from the Indians (RCNP, 9:18-19). The sachems agreed not to harm any English or Dutch nor to injure or kill any of their livestock. If any member of the sachems' communities were to commit such acts against the whites, the sachems were to turn them over to the English for punishment. In return, the English agreed only to leave them alone to dwell in peace. No promise was made, as the Southampton settlers did in their treaty with the Shinnecocks in 1640, to provide military aid in case of attack by other Indians.

The agreement amounted to an erosion of political sovereignty. The sachems acknowledged the right of the English to punish Indians who committed crimes against their citizens, but no such right was recognized for Indians to punish Englishmen who harmed Indians or their property. The commissioners, anticipating their acquisition of the Stirling Patent for Long Island, had also taken away the Indians' sovereign right to sell their land to the highest bidder. This later became an issue when Dutch and Rhode Island entrepreneurs attempted to purchase land on eastern Long Island. It was a one-sided contract which reflected the growing military and demographic strength of the Europeans. Although sporadic fighting continued in western Long Island, the overwhelming defeats inflicted by Dutch and English troops must have convinced the sachems that their options were very limited.

The increasing number of complaints from Dutch citizens about Governor Kieft's administration led to an inquiry by the States General in Holland. The complaints stressed that Kieft, who advocated the extermination of the Indians and called for an additional force of 150 soldiers, based his policy on the belief that there were only about three hundred Indians allied against him. The critics argued that there were at least a thousand Indians engaging in a protracted conflict characterized by hit and run tactics which made Kieft's policy impractical, as well as unchristian. Kieft's critics also believed that he was so hated and distrusted by the Indians that he could not negotiate a peace settlement (Trelease 1971:82).

One of the more controversial charges against Kieft was an accusation that he had personally supervised the barbarous torture of an Indian prisoner. In April 1644, about the time that the peace agreement with Guawarowe was signed, Robert Fordham imprisoned seven Indians in his cellar in Hempstead, believing that they had stolen some of his pigs. This is one of the earliest accounts of conflicts arising from the introduction of European domestic animals into the Long Island ecosystem. The settlers allowed their pigs to range freely in the woods until early fall when they were brought in to be fattened for slaughter. The Indians often treated the pigs like wild game and killed them when they came upon them in the woods or found them in their planting grounds or rooting up their shellfish beds.

Fordham sent word to Governor Kieft about the captives and Kieft ordered Underhill to go to Hempstead and bring the Indians to New Amsterdam (NYDH, 4:67; Marshall 1962:37-38). According to the testimony presented later to the Dutch authorities who investigated the charges against Kieft, three of the Indians were killed in the struggle to tie them up for the trip to New Amsterdam. The four survivors were taken to Underhill's boat, but when they were being loaded aboard, Underhill decided that the boat would be too crowded. Two of the captives were callously tied behind the boat and dragged along until they drowned (NYDH, 4:67-68).

The two surviving captives were placed in the guardhouse for several days and then brought out in the presence of Van Tienhoven and Kieft. One of the men was stabbed by a guard and seriously wounded. Instead of begging for mercy, he defiantly asked to be allowed to dance the *Kinte Kaeye* or "Dance of Death." Before he could begin, he was brutally cut to pieces by the guards (NYDH, 4:67-68; Brodhead 1853-71, 1:387-88). The second man was cruelly tortured. Strips of flesh were cut from his body and his genitals were sliced off. Finally his agony ended when the guards decapitated him.

The charges against Kieft included a bitter note of tragic irony. It was later discovered that the pigs had been taken by another Englishman. The Dutch authorities investigating the charges asked Cornelis Van Tienhoven about the incidents involving his mother-in-law and the severed heads of the Pavonia Indians and the torture of the Indian captives in front of himself and Governor Kieft (NYCD, 1:412-13). The questions were included in a list of fifty-nine inquiries presented to Van Tienhoven for "categorical answers," but there is no record of his response (NYCD, 1:409). The authorities asked a second time for a complete account, but again, he apparently did not respond to the charges (NYCD, 1:433-34).

Some scholars are skeptical of the accusations because they were made by Kieft's enemies (Grumet, 1995: pers. com.; Trelease 1971:79), but others have accepted them as a part of the historical record for the Kieft administration (Brodhead 1853-71, 1:387-88; Marshall 1962:37-39; O'Callaghan 1966, 1:300-301). The fact that Van Tienhoven did not take the opportunity to refute the accusations when asked specific questions about the incidents and his prior involvement with the Pavonia massacre, suggests that the charges may have been true.

Kieft was removed in the spring of 1645, but financial problems within the Dutch West India Company delayed his replacement by Peter Stuyvesant for nearly two years. The censure of Kieft encouraged several members of the Council of New Netherland to open negotiations with some of the Long Island sachems in the spring of 1645. Penhawis may have been killed in the fighting because the Dutch recruited his son, Witaneywen, to lead a troop of forty-seven men against an enemy, who, unfortunately, is not identified in the document (NYCD, 14:60.) Underhill's victories may have convinced Witaneywen that it was in the interests of his people to seek a rapprochement with the Dutch. The sachem returned six days later with a head and an unspecified number of hands as proof that he had accomplished his mission.

The Dutch then negotiated a peace settlement with Witaneywen, who claimed that he represented Youghco, the "greatest sachem" of "Cotsjewaminck" (probably Shelter Island); Momoweto, sachem of Corchaug; and Wyandanch, "sachem of Montauk"; and that this alliance now controlled the villages of Ouheywichkinch (an Unkechaug village near Mastic), Sichteyhacky (near Setauket), Sicketauwhacky (east of Islip), Nisinckqueghacky (on the Nissequogue River), and Reckonhacky (Rockaway) (NYCD, 14:60). These villages, pledged Witaneywen, would not make war on the Dutch.[10] This expanded the peace settlement negotiated with Guawarowe and opened the way for a final end to the fighting a few months later.

The three eastern sachems apparently wanted to form alliances with both of their European neighbors for purposes of trade and military protection. They may have joined with Witaneywen, who had influence over the western villages of Reckonhacky, Nisinckqueghacky, and Sicketauwhacky, to help them make contact with the Dutch. The three eastern sachems spoke for the villages of Sichteyhacky and Ouheywichkinch. These villages may have formed a temporary relationship with them in hopes of obtaining economic and military advantages.

The long and bloody five-year conflict was finally brought to an end on August 30, 1645, when sachems representing ten confederated groups of Indians from Long Island and the areas adjacent to New Amsterdam, ambassadors from the Mohawks and Mohicans, met with the Council of New Netherland in an outdoor ceremony, "under the blue canopy of heaven," witnessed by the whole Dutch community (NYCD, 13:18; O'Callaghan 1966, 1:356-57). Witaneywen (spelled Magauwetinnemin in this document) who later took the name Tackapousha, represented the Long Island Indians in the negotiations.

The two parties agreed that they would submit all future grievances to peaceful negotiations between the Dutch leaders and the sachems. The Indians agreed not to come to Manhattan carrying weapons and the Dutch agreed that they would not approach the Indian villages with weapons except on occasions when they were escorted there by Indians. The treaty marked the end of warfare between the Europeans and the Indians on Long Island, but tensions, rumors of war, and sporadic outbreaks of violence were to continue for another decade.

## Summary

The European purchase of Algonquian land on Long Island was a three step process which began with an arrogant assertion of ownership by the governments of England and Holland. These claims were based on the "voyages of discovery," discussed in Chapter 6. Next, the governments granted or sold patents or charters to companies or individuals, who brought settlers to the island. The English king had granted all of Long Island to Lord Stirling and the Dutch government granted most of the same area to the Dutch West India Company. The last step, almost an afterthought, was to negotiate a purchase with the Algonquian occupants of the land.

The Dutch began the last stage of the process in 1636 with the purchase of land in western Long Island from sachem Penhawis and his associates. They were soon challenged by the English who attempted to establish a settlement within the eastern boundary of territory claimed by the Dutch in 1640. The English were forced to move and finally settled at Southampton on the South Fork of eastern Long Island.

The growth of Dutch settlements on western Long Island and Governor Kieft's arrogant attitude towards the Algonquian people led to a five-year conflict which nearly destroyed the Dutch settlements on Long Island. These settlements were soon restored as new immigrants arrived, but the losses sustained by the Indians were more devastating. An estimated one thousand Indians lost their lives in the conflict and the stage was now set for a steady erosion of their hunting grounds.

The war was finally ended in 1645 with a treaty which called for all grievances to be settled through negotiation between the sachems and the Dutch officials. The Algonquian sachems promised that they would not allow their people to enter Manhattan with their weapons and the Dutch agreed not to approach Indian villages unless they came escorted by Indians. Although the war had ended, tensions and minor conflicts continued for another decade.

Fig. 8.1. Algonquian couple

# 8

# Accommodation to Conquest: The Long Island Frontier, 1645–1654

Although the fighting had ended in 1645 with a day of thanksgiving in New Amsterdam celebrating "the long desired peace with the savages," the Algonquian and the white communities continued to view each other warily. The settlers in Gravesend on western Long Island passed a resolution calling for mutual support against the Indians because "the peace with the Indians being new and rawe, there was still feares of their uprising to warre" (O'Callaghan 1966, 1:358n).

These fears did not halt the growth and expansion of the English and Dutch settlements. The peace now freed the European powers to continue their scramble for Indian land. A month after the treaty was signed, the Dutch purchased Coney Island and some adjacent lands from Seyseys, Sepinto, and Ponitaranchgyne, who are identified as the "owners of the lands" (Gehring 1980:16). The following year, Governor Eaton of New Haven purchased a neck of land on the east side of Huntington Bay (Appendix C-2) from Asharoken (Raseoken), a Matinecock sachem. The neck was later named after the governor and the narrow strip of land connecting it with the north shore was named after the sachem. Unfortunately, the deed has not survived, but there is a reference to it in an affidavit signed by several Matinecock men years later (Street 1882:9–10; RTH, 1:7n, 49–51). Eaton never made an effort to challenge the Dutch by establishing a settlement there at the time. He was apparently more concerned with establishing a paper claim to land as far west on Long Island as possible.

## More Rumors of Conspiracy

This competition for Algonquian land may have been behind a report in the summer of 1647, that Indians were planning to renew the war against the whites on Long Island. Fears of such conspiracies so terrified the white settlers that rumors were sometimes used unscrupulously to gain support for covert plans. Soon after the arrival of the new governor, Peter Stuyvesant, the English settlers at Hempstead reported to him that Witaneywen, who had taken the name "Antinome" (which he later changed to Tackapousha), had sent wampum to several sachems inviting them to join him in a war against both the English and the Dutch (NYCD, 14:79; Trelease 1971:86; O'Callaghan 1966, 2:45). The "wicked plot," they said, called for an attack on Hempstead in the early fall when the settlers were in the fields harvesting their crops. The Hempstead settlers claimed that the plot had been revealed to them by two Indians, one named

"Adam" and another who was not identified. Adam, one of the first Indians to assume an English name, spoke fluent English and may have had an English father. His Indian name, mentioned in a later document, was "Achitteronose" (DSBD, 2:161). People of mixed parentage frequently played important roles as intermediaries between Indian and white communities on the frontier.

The Dutch authorities were very suspicious of the Hempstead report because they knew that the Hempstead settlers wanted to expand their boundaries into the Massapequa lands. Stuyvesant suspected that the English were trying to provoke a conflict with Witaneywen in the hope that it would provide an opportunity to seize Indian land. The sachems accused in the report appear to be the same ones who signed the peace treaty with the Dutch in 1645 (see above).

Stuyvesant sent Cornelis Van Tienhoven, whom he had retained from Kieft's administration, to investigage. Van Tienhoven was apparently able to understand enough of the Algonquian languages to communicate with the Indians throughout Long Island. He went by ship to eastern Long Island where he met with "the chief of the Corchaug and his brethren" (probably Momoweta, Wyandanch, and Youghco) to ask why they had broken their alliance with the Dutch. Unfortunately, no details of the discussions were recorded, but the matter was resolved peacefully. Van Tienhoven reported that he had given the sachems three coats and other gifts and that the peace agreement was still in effect.

Relations between the English and the Dutch, however, began to deteriorate. The English viewed the Dutch expedition into their territory with alarm, suspecting that a secret alliance involving the distribution of guns had been negotiated under the guise of the peace mission. Governor Eaton of New Haven sent a sharply worded letter to Stuyvesant accusing him of selling arms to the Indians and encouraging them to attack the English (RCNH, 2:514–16). Stuyvesant denied the charges and assured Eaton that he would punish any of his subjects who sold guns to the Indians (RCNH, 2:522–23). The sale of contraband arms to Indians, as Stuyvesant soon discovered, was impossible to control because the demand for weapons was so great (Hagerty 1985:123–34). Governor Bradford of Plymouth noted that the Indians were "mad for the guns," and would pay any price for flintlocks in good condition (Malone 1971:179). This demand was eagerly met by private traders who were "mad for furs."

Near the end of 1647, the English fears deepened when the Southampton officials learned that private Dutch entrepreneurs were meeting with eastern Long Island sachems to purchase land and sell weapons. David Provost, who had served as an officer at Fort Good Hope, the Dutch trading post on the Connecticut River, came to the Indians living near the Southampton settlement with an offer to purchase some of their land (RCNH, 1:524). Provost was a very effective diplomat because he could speak English and he understood some of the Algonquian languages spoken on Long Island (O'Callaghan 1966, 2:222). The English moved quickly to block what they considered to be an intrusion into their sphere of interest and a violation of the Stirling Patent. The English were not going to allow the Dutch to do the same thing that Governor Eaton had done to them when he bought Eaton's Neck. The right of the Indians to negotiate with whom they pleased was simply ignored. Unfortunately, we do not know what means the English used to force an abrogation of the sale.

About that same time, Govert Lockermans, who had become one of the wealthiest men in New Netherland since his arrival in 1633, visited Youghco on Shelter Island purportedly to buy some game fowl and venison (NYCD, 14:94, Tooker 1980:179). Lockermans, who had tortured the sachem captured in the raid on the Raritans in 1641, had now become involved in the lucrative contraband weapons market. Lockermans, like Provost, understood English and some Algonquian. The following year, when one of Lockermans' ships was seized and found to be full of contraband goods, the Dutch authorities investigated charges that his visit to Youghco was part of a gun running operation. Lockermans and his crew denied the accusations of gun smuggling and said that they had only traded one pound of powder with Youghco for the meat (O'Callaghan 1966, 2:62–63). The English remained convinced that Lockermans' visit with Youghco concerned more than the purchase of geese.

## Governor Theophilus Eaton and the Scramble for Eastern Long Island

Led by Governor Theophilus Eaton of New Haven and Governor Edward Hopkins of Connecticut, the English entrepreneurs, who now owned the Stirling Patent rights to land on Long Island, took immediate notice of the Dutch threat and increased their efforts, begun in 1646, to purchase more land on Long Island. In the spring of 1648, Eaton and Hopkins provided Thomas Stanton with trade goods valued at £30, four shillings, and eight pence, and authorized him to purchase thirty thousand acres of land lying to the east of Southampton. Stanton, who was reputed to be one of the most skilled interpreters in the colonies, Robert Bond, and Job Sayre, met with four sachems: Momoweta, Wyandanch, Nowedonah from Shinnecock, and Poggatacut from Munhansett, and made the purchase (see Appendix D-4 map). These were probably the same four sachems who had negotiated the alliance at Hartford in 1644.

Weenagamin and Youghco, Tooker believed, had assumed new names and were now called Nowedonah and Poggatacut (Tooker 1980:179). Although Tooker's conclusions are plausible, there is no corroboration of this in the records. There is no doubt, however, about another important person involved in the negotiation. His name was Cockenoe (Chectanoo, Cheekanoo, Chekkonnow) and he is identified as "the interpreter" (RTEH, 1:2–4). This is the first appearance of his name in the colonial documents, but he was soon to become widely known for his ability as an interpreter and as a shrewd diplomat and one of Wyandanch's closest advisors (Tooker 1980:176-89). Although nothing is known about him prior to 1648, William Wallace Tooker believed that Cockenoe may have been the Long Island Indian trained by John Eliot to help him preach to the Indians. Eliot mentions that he taught a young Long Island Indian to read and write English, but never identified him. Eliot said that the young man left him around 1648 and he never heard from him again. Possibly Cockenoe was that person, but a document dated in 1652 identifies him as an Indian from "Menhansick" (Shelter Island).

One of the patterns described above in Chapter 7 appears in this deed. The Montauketts were granted the right to hunt, fish, and gather shells on the land they had just sold. They also retained a claim to the fins and tails of beached whales. The Montauketts may not have realized the consequences of the distinction made in English law between tenancy and ownership until the East Hampton officials began to impose restrictions on them.

The English purchasers gave the sachems twenty coats, twenty-four looking glasses, twenty-four hoes, twenty-four knives, and one hundred small iron drills called muxes, which were used primarily to drill holes in the shell wampum beads. One interesting aspect of this deed is that the Montauketts wanted hoes. In 1640, the settlers at Southampton gave the Indians corn, but now the Montauketts wanted metal tools in order to increase their own corn production.

Having secured the English title to most of the South Fork, Eaton and his deputy governor, Stephen Goodyear, sent their agents to Southold, on the North Fork, and purchased all the rest of the land on both sides of the town. Prior to this, a tract of land near Hashamomuck Pond on the eastern border of Southold had been purchased by William Salmon, a Southhold settler, from a sachem named Paucump in 1645 (STR, 2:276). A week after the East Hampton transaction, Eaton and Goodyear bought a tract of land lying to the east of Southold from Momoweta (Appendix D-5). The boundary began at a stream named Pautuckatux near Hashamomuck (Hashamomuk) Pond just east of the Southold settlement and extended eastwards to the end of the island. The deed also included title to Plumb (Plum) Island, a small piece of land located a few hundred yards off the eastern end of the North Fork (DSBD, 2:214; Tooker 1980:180).

According to the deed, Momoweta gave the land to Eaton because of the "love and affection he beareth unto Theophilus Eaton," and a payment of six cloth coats. Taken literally, it would seem that Momoweta held a naive, childlike affection for Eaton. This most certainly was not the case. The flowery term more likely described a tributary relationship similar to the one that the Long Island sachems had with the Pequots. Momoweta may have been attempting to establish an alliance with the English which would give him military protection and access to European trade goods.

Whatever Momoweta's intent was, his agreement with Eaton was immediately challenged by a sachem named Uxroupasson (Uxsquepassem), who claimed "an ancient right to and in the said land" (NHCHS). The sachem claimed that Momoweta had no right to sell Plumb Island without his consent. Unlike Penhawis, who had his rival executed, Momoweta resolved the conflict by reaching an agreement with Uxroupasson. The cultural differences in perceptions of property and "ownership" are clearly illustrated here. The two sachems had no papers to present. They spoke of "ancient rights," which may have been based on inheritance or conquest, to land which had never been surveyed.

The English, as we have seen, viewed all such questions of aboriginal title as mere "pretended interests." Their primary concern was to reach a settlement which would strengthen English title against Dutch claims and keep the local Indians content for the moment. The English were quite willing to establish trade ties with the sachems, but they were often reluctant to promise military protection unless their own interests were threatened.

In the late spring of 1648, about the same time that Eaton's agents were at work on the east end of Long Island, a small group of Englishmen led by Robert Williams and Richard Willets purchased a parcel of land from a Matinecock sachem named Pugnipan and four of his men. This area called "Ciscascata or Cantiag" included present-day Jericho, Woodbury, Plainview, and Hicksville (RTOB, 1:625–26). The nine square mile tract of land in what is now Oyster Bay (Appendix C-3), was southwest of Eaton's 1646 purchase from Asharoken and northeast of the settlement of Hempstead. Asharoken signed this deed as a witness along with several of his men. The Matinecocks were paid with an undisclosed amount of duffel cloth.

We do not know whether or not Williams and his party actually established a settlement at that time, but it is unlikely because the Dutch claimed the area and they would certainly not have allowed Williams to proceed without their permission. Williams, apparently, was using the same strategy as Eaton. He wanted to establish a claim that could be pressed at a later time. The English now held paper claims to an area of land which ran from Eaton's Neck on the north shore, southwest through what is now Hicksville, to the Atlantic Ocean. These purchases were to play a major role in the negotiations which led to the Treaty of Hartford in 1650.

Eaton and Goodyear sent their agents back to the North Fork early the following spring and purchased two more parcels of land. The first, on March 14, 1649, was a tract of land called Aquebanck (Aquebogue), bounded on the east by a creek called "Uncawaamuck" (near the present-day boundary between the towns of Riverhead and Southold), and on the west by a creek called Pauquacumsuk (Wading River); see Appendix D-6 (DSBD, 2:210–11; Tooker 1962:16–17; 183–84, 263–64). The tract also included meadowland south of the Peconic in what is now Flanders. The Indians were paid three coats, two fathoms of wampum, four hatchets, four knives, and four tobacco pipes. The market value of wampum depended on its quality. A string of wampum one fathom long had 360 white beads and 180 purple beads and was valued at four Dutch guilders (Hagerty 1985:114). The land south of the Peconic later became the center of a dispute between the English settlements of Southold and Southampton which was finally settled in favor of Southampton by the Court of Assizes in 1667 (NYCD, 14:600–2).

The purchase is significant because the English agents negotiated the sale with an Indian named Occomboomaquus and a woman identified as the wife of Mahahamuck, who were the "true Indian owners" of the land. This is the first reference in any of the land transactions on Long Island to an Indian woman who held title to land. Unfortunately her name is not entered on the deed, perhaps because the English did not accord their own women any legal status in such matters. When a confirmation of the deed was negotiated in 1660, Mahahamuck's wife was identified this time as the "daughter of Ockemnugan" (DSBD, 2:212–13).

In both documents, the woman was identified only in terms of her relationship with a male. These documents, however, offer early evidence that women played an important role in decisions about the ownership and transfer of land. Although the English never mentioned the woman by name, they did acknowledge that she was "of the sachem's blood," and "sole heir and legal proprietor of Accabogue" (DSBD, 2:212). Ockenmnugan had only two children, a daughter and a son who died in infancy. Upon the sachem's death, the daughter inherited the property and retained control after her marriage to Mahahamuck. Under English law a woman's property became her husband's after she married.

The second purchase made by Eaton and Goodyear a week later was negotiated with Uxroupasson (now called Paummis) and his three brothers, Weewacup, Nowconneey, and Neesantquaggus (Craven 1906:14–15). The tract was a relatively small piece of land which began at the border of the Aquebogue purchase and extended eastward to the present-day village of Cutchogue (Appendix D-7). The Indians were paid two fathoms of wampum, one iron pot, six coats, ten knives, four hooks, and forty needles—a far greater sum than either Momoweta or Occomboomaquus and Mahahamuck's wife received for much larger tracts of land. There appears to be no direct relationship between the value of goods and the amount of land involved in any of these early deeds. This suggests, once again, that the Indians viewed the exchanges as diplomatic gestures rather than as permanent instruments of dispossession.

## Wyandanch's Alliance with the English Towns on the South Fork

Governor Eaton had accomplished his purpose. Now that eastern Long Island was reserved exclusively for the expansion of the English, a group of nine families moved east from Southampton and established the settlement of East Hampton. From the outset Wyandanch sought to strengthen his alliance with the English. According to a local legend, recorded in the *East Hampton Trustee's Journal,* a Montaukett hunting party discovered the settlers and were invited in for a meal. The hunters, apparently unaware of Wyandanch's sale and unmoved by the gesture of hospitality, returned to their village and made plans to drive the English out. The men then consulted with their sachem, presumably Wyandanch, about the attack. The sachem asked them "Did they invite you into their houses?—they did.—Did they give you [food] to eat?—they did.—Did you experience any harm from what you ate; did it poison you?—It did not.—The reply of the sachem, turning to his warrior, was, You shall not cut them off" (EHTJ, 1:158–59). The account may be apocryphal, but as later events clearly indicate, Wyandanch was eager to establish good relations with the English, and there was some opposition among the Montauketts to this policy of accommodation.

Although Wyandanch and a few other sachems welcomed the English, the expansion of their settlements increased the potential for conflict and confrontation with the Algonquian communities. As the number of domestic livestock grew, the settlers began to fence off grazing lands encroaching on aboriginal hunting grounds. Pigs rooted out shellfish beds and broke into Indian planting fields with increasing frequency. In 1648 the Southampton settlers moved the center of their village to its present location and constructed several new buildings. The following February, the town proprietors granted John Ogden the right to locate six families on a tract of land lying to the north of the village near an Indian settlement. Howes (Homes, Homeboy), one of the sachems who had signed the 1640 land transaction, may have lived there (Adams 1918:74–75; RTEH, 1:260). The establishment of this small settlement, known today as North Sea, may have contributed to the tensions between Indians and the English settlers.

In the spring of 1649, following the expansion of the Southampton settlement, a white woman, the wife of Thomas Halsey, was murdered in her home by Indians. Lion Gardiner believed that the murder was in retaliation for the death of an Indian killed at Shinnecock several years earlier. Gardiner may have been referring to Daniel Howe's execution of an Indian man which was described in Hubbard's *General History of New England* (see Chapter 7 above).

The Shinnecock sachems apparently felt that the woman's death had restored their honor and that the matter should not be pursued any further. The two cultures held very different views of justice in homicide cases. Both were concerned with deterring murder, but, for the Indians, as noted earlier, the murder of a clan member was a matter for that clan only, not the whole community.

When the English demanded that the Indians turn over the person or persons responsible for the murder of the English woman, their sachem refused to cooperate. The impasse led to an armed standoff between the two communities which lasted for several days (RCNP, 9:143). John Gosmer and Edward Howell, the Southampton magistrates, attempted to resolve the crisis by calling upon Wyandanch to honor the clause in the 1644 treaty requiring that Indians accused of crimes against English people be turned over to the English authorities. Wyandanch consulted with Gardiner, who urged him to go to Southampton and capture those responsible for the murder. Gardiner, who saw an opportunity to enhance Wyandanch's status as a sachem, gave the Montaukett sachem a paper which asked the English settlers to grant Wyandanch safe conduct and to provide him and his men with food while they were on this mission for the English (L.

Gardiner 1980:145). Gardiner's charge to Wyandanch was very similar to the one he had given the Montaukett sachem at Fort Saybrook after the Pequot War. Wyandanch was again asked to prove his loyalty to the English and once again he used the opportunity to strengthen his alliance with the English.

One man had already been apprehended when Wyandanch and his men arrived. He soon captured two more men, one of whom was described as "a great man among them, commonly called the Blue Sachem" (L. Gardiner 1980:145).[1] Unfortunately, no record of the discussions which must have taken place within the Indian community has survived, nor is there any clue as to the identity of the "Blue Sachem." If the sachem was an influential leader, as Gardiner states, he must have had supporters who would have sought to protect him from Wyandanch and the English. There is no record, however, of any resistance to the arrests of the Indian men accused of the murder.

Wyandanch brought the accused men to Southampton where the Indians were "gathered together in an hostile posture," and called for a conference (RCNP, 9:143). Mandush, one of the sachems who had signed the 1640 deed for Southampton came forward as a spokesperson. He broke the impasse by publicly acknowledging that the Montaukett sachem was now sovereign over him and his people (RTSH, 1:158). Mandush cut up a piece of turf, gave it to Wyandanch and stroked the Montaukett sachem on his back, symbolizing his acceptance of a tributary status. The elders in the local villages gave their consent to Montaukett sovereignty, perhaps because they decided that it would be better than risking a war with the English.

Wyandanch took the accused men to Hartford where they were all hanged. Wyandanch's status and influence increased steadily after this. He now held the power to sell land belonging to his new tributaries, but he also had the responsibility to assure their good behavior. The following December when another dispute broke out over the planting grounds at Sebonac, about two miles west of Southampton, Wyandanch was again called upon to help negotiate a settlement.

The villagers at Sebonac, who were identified as the "Seaponack Indians," lived on the banks of Sebonac Creek where it flows into Peconic Bay. This is the first "tribal" reference in the Southampton town records. It appears to be derived from a place name. The Indian villages around Southampton were apparently not lumped together as "Shinnecock" until nearly a decade later when tribal structures began to appear as a response to English intrusions into their lifeways. There are sixteen references to "Indians" in the Southampton town records between 1640 and 1657, but no mention of Shinnecock as a tribal entity. The English encouraged the emergence of tribal structures and clearly defined tribal boundaries so that they could purchase land and control the village systems more effectively (see Chapter 1). Ironically, the tribal systems also served to protect and preserve the identity and culture of the Indians who became known as the Shinnecocks.

The problems inherent in the "working misunderstanding" between the two cultures about the nature of property and the purchase agreement had now surfaced. The Seaponack villagers continued to plant in the meadows near their village, unaware that the English now viewed them as tenants subject to English sovereignty. The growing English settlement, requiring more grazing land for their livestock, demanded that the Seaponack villagers move their planting ground to accommodate them. A meeting attended by large delegations from both groups was held to discuss the issues. Thomas Stanton again served as interpreter for the English, but there is no mention of an interpreter such as Cockenoe for the Seaponack villagers.

The arrogant and patronizing tone of the 1649 agreement with the Seaponacks indicates the English frustration with the cultural differences separating the two communities. "Notwithstanding plaine written covenants between the said Indians, and the said town of Southampton, concerning the land which they bought of them, there hath been some trouble with the said Indians in regard to their planting on ground that belonged not to them but to said town" (Strong 1983a:69). The Indians were forced to shift their planting grounds to the west, into the area now known as Shinnecock Hills where the ground is less productive and more difficult to cultivate.

A related complaint raised by the English concerned the Indian practice of storing their food in underground pits. In the spring, when the covered pits were nearly empty, they undoubtedly became a trap for wandering cattle and horses. The grazing animals frequently fell into the pits and suffered serious injury. Abandoned pits were also a hazard. When a wigwam was moved to a new location, the pits were emptied and abandoned. The English insisted that these now be filled in.

The Indians were also told that they were responsible for building and maintaining fences to protect their crops from wandering English livestock. The introduction of domestic animals was beginning to have a significant impact on the ecosystem which had sustained the Indians. The settlers had apparently brushed aside Indian complaints and told the Indians that the English were not liable for damage done by English livestock. Fences, of course, were an alien concept to the Indians, but they were taken for granted by the English. In English custom, however, wandering cattle were the responsibility of the owner, who was liable for any damage they did to his neighbor's property. It was the responsibility of the owner to keep his livestock fenced in. If his cattle or hogs broke loose and damaged someone's crops, they would be impounded and the owner fined.

Placing the burden of fencing on the Indians was also unfair because fence construction required skills, knowledge, and tools which few Indians had at that time. The fencing used on Long Island was undoubtedly the "New England" style, constructed with six foot long cedar posts and eleven foot long oak rails (Hawke 1988:35). A good fence was described as being "horse high, bull strong, and pig tight." Such a fence was so expensive to build and maintain that farmers often complained that their fences cost nearly as much as the land they enclosed. Small wonder that the issues of fencing and wandering livestock were to be a major source of contention between the two communities for the remainder of the seventeenth century (Williams 1995: 259–64).

The 1649 agreement also introduced practices which soon became widely employed on Long Island. The Indians agreed to allow the English livestock, except hogs, into their fields ten days after the harvest to graze for the winter. The cattle were turned out in the early spring before planting time. The English also claimed the right to make roads through Indian land wherever they wished.

The one-sided agreement reflects the intrusive impact of the English on the Indians and on the ecosystem which had sustained their traditional way of life. Mandush and his followers, however, had little choice at the time. Wyandanch's alliance with the English discouraged any resistance at that time. The fragile peace held for another decade.

Wyandanch's growing influence on eastern Long Island concerned Ninigret, who saw his hopes for gaining tributaries there diminishing. The Niantic sachem sent one of his agents to live at Montauk, gain Wyandanch's trust, and wait for an opportunity to assassinate him (RCNP, 10:97–98). The man lived at Montauk for a year and was successful at gaining Wyandanch's confidence, but when the opportunity came he botched it badly. Ninigret's agent was given the responsibility of accompanying Wyandanch on a trip, and assigned to carry the sachem's pistol. When the two men were some distance from the village, Ninigret's agent pulled the pistol and fired at Wyandanch. The firing was delayed allowing Wyandanch time to step aside and the bullet went through his coat. The man was immediately taken prisoner and returned to Montauk.

The Montaukett sachem decided not to take action independently of the English. Instead, he took the prisoner to Hartford for trial. Wyandanch may have hoped that by turning to the English courts and acknowledging their sovereignty over him, he would draw them into a closer alliance which would force them to provide him with military protection from Ninigret.

A precedent for this had been set in 1643 when Uncas captured his rival, Miantonomi, and brought him to Hartford for trial by the United Colonies commissioners. The commissioners found Miantonomi guilty and authorized Uncas to execute him outside the jurisdiction of Connecticut. The English sent a court officer to serve as a witness, but sought to avoid direct involvement with the killing lest they be drawn into a conflict between Uncas' Mohegans and the Narragansetts (Jennings 1976:266–68; Salisbury 1984:234–35; Ward 1961: 120–22).

Wyandanch apparently sought to have his revenge on Ninigret's agent under the shield of English authority. The man confessed and the Connecticut court found him guilty. The court followed the same policy established by the United Colonies and authorized Wyandanch to execute the prisoner just outside of

Hartford. An officer of the court went out with Wyandanch to serve as a witness to the execution. Following the execution, Wyandanch and his men added a final insult to the victim by burning his body. Ninigret, however, was not intimidated by Wyandanch nor by the English. He waited patiently for the next opportunity to advance his interests. It would not be a long wait.

## "To augment their own kingdoms": Ninigret and the Anglo-Dutch Rivalry

The tensions and fears aroused by the events in Southampton and by Ninigret's threat to the Montaukett leadership were exacerbated by new reports that Govert Lockermans and other Dutchmen were actively trading guns to Indians on Long Island, in spite of Governor Stuyvesant's efforts to curtail this activity (RCNP, 9:143). The Southampton officials complained to the United Colonies commissioners that the Dutch had sold guns and so much powder and lead to the local Indians that they were holding target practice and improving their marksmanship. They had grown insolent, reported the officials, and had driven English cattle into the water to be drowned (RCNP, 9:209–11). The commissioners asked for proof that the Indians had willfully drowned the cattle, but they acknowledged the complaints about the weapons trade and sent an angry letter to Stuyvesant. The Southampton officials apparently could not produce the necessary proof about the drowning of the cattle because no further action was taken in the matter.

In an attempt to resolve the tensions between the two European powers, Stuyvesant met with the English leaders at Hartford in 1650. They reached an agreement which drew a boundary line from "the westernmost part of Oyster Bay" on the north shore directly south to the Atlantic (Appendix B). The Hartford Treaty, however, was sharply criticized by Stuyvesant's constituents back in New Amsterdam who deplored the abandonment of the Dutch claims on eastern Long Island. Van Tienhoven, for example, advised Stuyvesant to purchase lands on the eastern boundaries of Southold and East Hampton from the Indians and then squeeze the English towns from both directions. "The whole of Long Island," he argued, "would be thereby secured to New Netherland" (NYCD 1:360–61). The controversy in the Dutch community continued until after the Anglo-Dutch war of 1652. Although the Dutch authorities in Holland finally ratified the treaty in 1656, the English home government refused. They would not acknowledge that the Dutch had any right at all to any land in North America and reminded the United Colonies that they had no business meddling in foreign policy (O'Callaghan 1966, 2:151–55, 313; Hawke 1966:174).

Soon after his return to New Amsterdam, Stuyvesant was faced with angry petitions from the settlers at Gravesend and Hempstead. In the five years since the end of the devastating war, the white settlements had recovered and expanded taking more and more of the Indians' former hunting grounds. In November, for example, the settlers in Gravesend confirmed an earlier deed and purchased a new tract of land called "Maseebackhun" (Massebackhun, Massabarkem; see Appendix B) from Indians named Tahasurtum, Arree, Mackhans, Chippahicke, and Sawwosson (RTG, 1:15; Grumet 1981:31). The Indians received fifteen rolls of cloth, three fathoms of wampum, one kettle, two hatchets, two hoes, three knives, one long coat, one pair of scissors, two combs, one sword, and thirty awls. The Indians continued to live in villages located in this tract along Sheepshead Bay long after the land was sold (Bolton 1975:50).[2]

The same problems which created the troubles in Southampton plagued the relations between the Indian and white communities on western Long Island. Livestock from the colonial towns frequently invaded Indian corn fields destroying vital food supplies needed for the winter. Often, the Indians responded by killing the animals and eating them, or, in some cases, selling the beef back to settlers telling them it was venison (Trelease 1971:90).

When the naval war between Holland and England broke out in the spring of 1652, the colonies kept a wary eye on each other. The tensions between the two European powers were seen by many Algonquian sachems as an opportunity to advance their interests. Youghco, the sachem from Manhanset (Shelter Island), complained to the United Colonies commissioners that Captain Thomas Middleton, a New Haven citizen, was trying to evict him from his island.

Youghco sent Cockenoe, the interpreter who had helped negotiate the 1648 deed for East Hampton, to represent him before the commissioners at Plymouth on September 2, 1652 (RCNP, 9:377). Cockenoe demonstrated that some Indians were quick to understand the workings of the English political system and quite adept at using it to protect their own interests. Appearing before the commissioners at a time when they were concerned about the Dutch attempts to recruit Indians in case of war, Cockenoe knew that the commissioners could not easily dismiss the complaints of one of the more influential sachems on eastern Long Island. Both Cockenoe and the English were well aware of Govert Lockermans' visit with Youghco in 1647.

Cockenoe argued that Middleton's deed was based on a fraudulent title. Middleton had purchased the island from Stephen Goodyear on June 9, 1651, but, said Cockenoe, Goodyear's claim came from James Farrett, who never paid the Indians for the land (Appendix D-8). This, of course was quite true, because Farrett always left the task of negotiating with the Indians to his customers. The commissioners promised to review the case and take action on their findings.

There is no record of their response, but they must have supported Cockenoe because, three months, later on December 27, Middleton met with Youghco and three of his elders, Actoncocween, Captain Yowoconogus, and Sorrquoquoequahesick, to pay them for the island. Unfortunately, none of the original deeds to Shelter Island have survived. Our only source of information about this is an account of the transactions which was entered into the East Hampton Town records in 1656 (RTEH, 1:96–97). Ironically, a year later Youghco died and many of his people did begin to migrate from the island.

Youghco and Cockenoe were not the only Indians to decide that now was the time to make demands on the two European adversaries. The tensions between the English United Colonies and Dutch New Netherland intensified when Uncas reported to the English that his old enemy, Ninigret, had spent the winter of 1652–53 as a guest of Peter Stuyvesant in New Amsterdam. Ninigret, said Uncas, gave the Dutch some wampum in exchange for guns, powder, and shot. Uncas also charged that the Dutch had encouraged Ninigret to attack the English (RCNP, 10:4, 11–12; O'Callaghan 1966, 2:217).[3] Uncas, of course, had his own agenda. He feared that a Dutch alliance with Ninigret would enable the Niantic sachem to increase his power and influence among the Indian communities in southern New England.

Uncas frequently attempted to undermine alliances between his Algonquian enemies and the English with a variety of accusations. In 1647, he had charged that Ninigret and some Narragansett sachems were conspiring with the Mohawks to attack him, and, failing that, to kill him by witchcraft (RCNP, 9:143–44). In September 1652, Ninigret had, himself, brought a charge of witchcraft against Uncas to the United Colonies commissioners (RCNP, 10:376). As noted above, curses from highly reputed shamans were taken quite seriously, even by Europeans such as Governor Kieft. Three years later, Uncas accused Wyandanch of bewitching him and killing some of his men (RCNP, 9:167). These charges were investigated by the commissioners and dismissed. Although the commissioners may have had their doubts about these new charges, they had to investigate them because of the war.

The commissioners of the United Colonies called an emergency meeting in April 1653 and questioned Ninigret about the charges. Ninigret denied them, assuring the English that he had visited New Amsterdam to see a French doctor recommended by Peter Stuyvesant (RCNP, 10:10). The doctor charged him ten fathoms of wampum, said Ninigret, and with the rest he bought some coats from Stuyvesant, but no guns.

As might be expected, Ninigret's answer was greeted with considerable skepticism by the English. The Connecticut and New Haven colonies began to prepare for war. The Southold settlers confiscated guns from the Algonquian villagers in response to one Indian who, they claimed, carried his gun in a threatening manner. The Indians protested this action to the colonial authorities in New Haven, who investigated the matter and decided that Southold had acted unwisely. Fearing that the seizure of guns had actually increased the tensions in the area, the New Haven court ordered that the "guns so taken be restored to the Indians againe, that no publique quarrell may be begun with the Indians by us upon any such account" (RCNH, 1:16). This incident reflected the undercurrent of fear which pervaded the English settlements, but it also demonstrated that the Indians were becoming adept at using the English political system to protect their interests. They took their complaint over the heads of the local settlers to appeal to a higher authority in New Haven.

The rumors of war and conspiracy did not slow the pace of land acquisition by either the Dutch or the English. On November 22, 1652, about the time Ninigret arrived for his doctor's appointment, Dutch settlers had purchased what is now the Bay Ridge area of Brooklyn from sachems Seuseu (Seyseys) and Mattana for "six shirts, two pairs of shoes, six pairs of stockings, six chisels, six axes, six hatchets, six knives, two pairs of scissors, and six cans" (buckets?). The deed included a most revealing clause which obligated the Indians to vacate the boundaries of the deed immediately "and never to return to live in the limits of the district as described in the foregoing nor ever make any claim on it" (NYCD, 14:190; O'Callaghan 1966, 2:186). This provision suggests that the settlers were now aware that the Indians viewed these deeds as temporary grants of occupation which were open to renegotiation in the future.

In spite of such language in the deeds, the Algonquian villagers either ignored or simply refused to acknowledge the concept of absentee ownership. They considered any land which was not occupied to be open and free territory. We have no record of the effectiveness of this clause, but it clearly reveals the nature of the continuing cultural misunderstandings which resulted in tension and conflict for the remainder of the century. Asharoken, for example, saw no problem with his grant of occupation to different groups of Englishmen as long as the land in question was not occupied at the time.

On April 2, 1653, a group of English settlers led by Richard Holbrook, Daniel Whitehead, and Robert Williams, purchased from Asharoken, the Matinecock sachem, a six mile tract of land in what is now the town of Huntington between Cold Spring Harbor and Northport Bay on the north shore of Long Island (Appendix C-5). The boundaries of the tract, known as the "First Purchase," included two large necks of land which extend into Long Island Sound—Eaton's Neck and Horse Neck (Lloyd Neck). The fact that Asharoken had sold Eaton's Neck to Governor Eaton in 1646, did not appear to deter either party to the sale at the time, but it did lead to a boundary dispute which was not settled until 1664. Holbrook and his party paid Asharoken six coats, six kettles, six hoes, six hatchets, six shirts, ten knives, six fathoms of wampum, thirty muxes, and thirty needles (RTH, 1:1–3; Street 1882:9).

Asharoken's view of the transaction suggests that he believed he was granting a lease to use the land because he "sold" the same land to two different parties. The sachem may have concluded that since Eaton had never made an effort to occupy the tract, he had forfeited his lease. The following year, Asharoken sold the other large neck, Horse Neck (Lloyd Neck; Appendix C-7), to Samuel Mayo and the founders of Oyster Bay, for three coats, three shirts, three hatchets, three hoes, two fathom of wampum, six knives, two pairs of stockings, and two pairs of shoes (RTH, 1:4–5; Street 1882:12). These transactions suggest, again, that many of the Algonquian sachems understood the "deeds" to be temporary grants rather than absolute transfers of ownership.

In 1653 the "First Purchase" of land in what was to become the town of Oyster Bay was negotiated with Asharoken by Peter Wright, Samuel Mayo, and the Reverend William Leverich (see Appendix C-6; RTOB, 1:334, 355–56, 628–29). Actually, it was the second purchase if you count Robert Williams' 1648 deed with Pugnipan, which had been witnessed by Asharoken. The Oyster Bay settlers agreed to pay Asharoken six coats, six kettles, six hatchets, six hoes, three shirts, twenty knives, three pairs of stockings, thirty eel spears, six fathoms of wampum, £4 sterling worth of purple wampum beads, thirty muxes, and thirty needles. According to testimony given thirty years later, however, the payment was delayed until Asharoken protested angrily and demanded his goods (RTOB, 1:692; RTOB, 2:690).

The tract of land was bounded on the north by Oyster Bay, but did not include Oak Neck, Pine Island, and Hog Island, and extended south to the northern boundary of the tract purchased by Robert Williams from Pugnipan in 1648 (Appendix C-14). The boundary, however, remained in dispute for nearly two decades. Such disagreements were common because so few of the areas had ever been properly surveyed.

In late April 1653, the attention of the English again focused on Ninigret. Although the Niantic sachem's actions are not well documented, it appears that he may have used Dutch influence and funds to gain allies among the Montauketts. He hoped to finally establish a tributary relationship over the Montauketts, a goal he had set for himself after the Pequot War. Apparently, he very nearly succeeded because the East Hampton Trustees reported, in April 26, 1653, that the Dutch had hired Indians against them and that the Montauketts "hath cast off their sachem" (JTEH, 2:313). There is, however, no other reference to a change in leadership at Montauk. It is possible that this was only a rumor, but there may have been some move among the Montaukett elders to challenge Wyandanch's authority. This challenge may have come from Montauketts who favored an alliance with Ninigret.

Curiously, Lion Gardiner is not mentioned in the reports of this incident. His familiarity and influence with the Montauketts would certainly have been crucial in this crisis. The East Hampton officials apparently had no regular communication with any of the Montaukett leaders. They passed a resolution ordering that no Indians be allowed into the town at night. If the Indians did not halt after the third warning, or tried to run away, they were to be shot (RTEH, 1:31). This was necessary, they said, because "we not knowing Indians by face cannot distinguish friends from enemies" (JTEH, 2:313).

In May 1653, Adam, the Indian who had accused Witaneywen of plotting against the English at Hempstead in 1647, came to the English on Long Island with more reports of the alliance between Ninigret and Stuyvesant. Adam told the English that a young sachem living at Canarsie named Ronnessoke, who later took the name "Suscaneman" (Grumet 1994:86), said that Ninigret had summoned him to New Amsterdam for a meeting. When Ronnessoke refused to come, Ninigret came to him in Canarsie and offered him a bag of wampum to recruit as many men as he could to join the Dutch in an attack on the English settlement at Stamford, Connecticut. Ronnessoke said that he rejected the proposal and decided to report the plot to the English.

Adam also reported that Witaneywen had been approached by Govert Lockermans and was asked to aid the Dutch as he had in 1645. The Massapequa sachem refused this time saying that the English had never harmed him and that he could not be of much help anyway because he had only twenty men at his command (RCNP, 10:45). Lockermans then gave him a copper kettle and asked him not to reveal the Dutch plans. The western Long Island sachems who had vivid memories of the recent long and bloody war were apparently not interested in getting caught up in a European conflict. Witaneywen, who certainly had more power and influence than he acknowledged to Lockermans, wisely avoided involvement in a European conflict.

Although Stuyvesant had made no plans for attacking the English, his attempts to form military alliances with Algonquian sachems as a defensive measure alarmed the English colonies on his borders (O'Callaghan 1966, 2:229–30). Stuyvesant had been ordered in 1652 to negotiate alliances with Indian sachems as a defensive measure in case New England decided to attack New Netherland (NYCD, 14:186). It was not an unwise precaution because there were some firebrands in New England who were eager to do just that. Connecticut and New Haven began to press the United Colonies for a preemptive strike against the Dutch. Massachusetts Bay, however, was not eager to wage a costly war on the evidence brought forward by the Algonquian sachems. They were particularly suspicious of Uncas, but they were also skeptical of Connecticut's motives. The Massachusetts officials knew that Connecticut wanted to extend its western border towards the Hudson at the expense of New Netherland.

The commissioners reached a compromise whereby a troop of five hundred men was to be raised, but no declaration of war was to be voted on until the reports of the conspiracy were fully investigated (Ward 1961:179). Massachusetts Bay continued to stall until the following year when the English and Dutch ended their hostilities.

## Ninigret's Raid on the Montauketts

Ninigret may have considered an alliance with the Dutch, but it is unlikely that he would have risked going to war against the English. His primary interest appears to have been in establishing a tributary relationship over the Algonquian communities on eastern Long Island. It is quite possible that Ninigret was in close contact with the Montaukett elders who had challenged Wyandanch's authority in April of 1653.

In a letter to the Massachusetts Bay Council, Roger Williams reported that Ninigret had come to Governor Endicott of Massachusetts Bay and told him that a Long Island sachem named Acassasotic had killed some of his men. Acassasotic was identified by Williams as "proud and foolish, a very inferior sachem," friendly to the English (RCNP, 10:441). It seems most likely that the incident referred to was Wyandanch's execution of Ninigret's agent. Ninigret, according to Williams, asked the governor if he had any serious objection to a retaliatory raid.

The governor, said Williams, gave Ninigret "implicit" approval for the raid. Endicott probably told Ninigret that Massachusetts Bay would not interfere in Algonquian matters, leaving the Niantic sachem free to pursue whatever policy he wished. Ninigret's request for Endicott's endorsement followed the pattern set by Uncas before he attacked Sequassen, a Narragansett sachem, who had killed one of Uncas' men. Uncas asked the English authorities at Hartford if he could avenge the murder of some of his people by attacking Sequassen. The Hartford magistrates gave their approval and Uncas launched a raid killing or wounding about twenty of Sequassen's men (De Forest 1852:187–88).

Ninigret may have chosen to go to Endicott because he knew that he could not get a similar pledge from Connecticut or New Haven. These colonies both had settlements on Long Island and would not tolerate an attack on their Indian tributaries there. Ninigret cleverly set one English settlement against the other in this matter. Once Massachusetts Bay was pledged to neutrality, Ninigret promptly launched a series of raids against the Montauketts. The most dramatic attack came late in the spring of 1653. Ninigret attacked Wyandanch's village at Montauk and trapped the Montaukett warriors in a narrow valley which became known as "massacre valley," and killed at least thirty of them. The victorious war party took fourteen prisoners, including two sachems and Wyandanch's daughter. One of the captives was killed and his body was burned in response to Wyandanch's similar treatment of Ninigret's agent.

John Mason and Governor John Haynes of Connecticut were outraged and sent word of Ninigret's raid to the September meeting of the United Colonies in Boston (RCNP, 10:88–89). The United Colonies sent for Ninigret to come to Boston and answer the charges that he had attacked a loyal ally of the English. The messengers were met with taunts and threats and were not even allowed to see the prisoners. Ninigret refused to return with them to Boston, arguing that the English had no right to interfere in his conflict with Wyandanch. The raid, he said, was a justifiable act of retaliation against Wyandanch. "Why doe they inquire the ground of my war against the Long Islanders, did they not heare that the Long Islanders murdered mee a man?" (RCNP, 10:96). Ninigret did not mention that he had consulted with Endicott about the raid. He wisely left it to Simon Bradstreet, the representative from Massachusetts Bay, to block any military action against the Niantics.

When the messengers reported Ninigret's response, the commissioners were outraged. Connecticut, New Haven, and Plymouth noted Wyandanch's loyal support of the English and said that they had been "called by God to make a present war against Ninigret" (RCNP, 10:98). Following this impressive endorsement, the three colonies voted to send a troop of two hundred and fifty men to punish Ninigret for his attack on a loyal English ally and for his alleged alliance with the Dutch (RCNP, 10:98–99, 101–3).

Simon Bradstreet, as Ninigret hoped, vetoed the action, arguing that the English were under no treaty obligation to aid the Montauketts. It was bad policy, he said, to intervene in an argument between two Algonquian sachems. The Massachusetts Bay leaders were also concerned about being drawn into a conflict which might escalate into a war with New Netherland. They suspected that Connecticut and New Haven might be hearing the voice of territorial expansion rather than the voice of God.

Apparently, Massachusetts Bay felt that Ninigret's gesture of submission in seeking permission from Governor Endicott satisfied the crucial aspect of their relations with the Niantic. The proper policy now was to let the two sachems resolve the issue themselves. The incident demonstrates the way some of the more astute Algonquian sachems such as Ninigret, used diplomatic strategy to manipulate the English. The Niantic sachem had cleverly divided the English colonies, preventing them from responding to his campaign against the Montaukett.

He soon followed up the first attack with another in which several more Montauketts were killed and a few more captives were taken. Following this attack, according to an account given two years later by Newcom, one of Ninigret's agents, Ninigret sent a Niantic woman to Montauk to open up peace negotiations with Wyandanch (RCNP, 10:170–71). The next phase of the negotiations, Newcom said, was completed when a Montaukett delegation went to the village of Pessacus, Miantonomi's brother, and reached a settlement which was witnessed by two Englishmen. According to Ninigret, Wyandanch agreed to become a tributary to the Niantic sachem and to give him control over the sale of Montaukett lands in exchange for the release of his daughter and the other captives. These terms had serious implications for Southampton and East Hampton because all of the unpurchased lands on their boundaries would be under the control of Ninigret. The Niantic sachem might sell the property to purchasers in Rhode Island or Massachusetts Bay, a fear that was to concern the towns on eastern Long Island for the rest of the century.

Wyandanch denied Ninigret's account of the settlement. He said that when the Niantic emissary came to him with these proposals, he rejected them and sent the woman back with a counter proposal to pay a ransom for the prisoners (RCNP, 10:170). He acknowledged that he had sent a delegation to Pessacus' village, but denied that he ever gave them the authority to accept tributary status under the Niantics. The final settlement involved only a ransom, nothing more. The ransom, he said, had been paid for him by Lion Gardiner, who "as a father . . . giving us money and goods . . . ransomed my daughter and friends" (DSBD, 2:118–19). Given the clear implications of Ninigret's demands, Gardiner's "generosity" is easy to understand.

Ninigret's agent said that Robert Wescott, one of the English witnesses to the agreement made in Pessacus' village, would testify for Ninigret. Newcom went to get Wescott, but for some unexplained reason Wescott never appeared to testify in support of Ninigret. The United Colonies commissioners assumed that Wescott did not appear because Ninigret's account was false and did not pursue the investigation (RCNP, 10:170).

Neither of the accounts has been corroborated and the sequence of events following the kidnapping is also uncertain. In the spring of 1654, according to a letter from the Reverend Thomas James of East Hampton to John Winthrop, Wyandanch agreed to accept an offer from Uncas to "avenge him upon the Narraganset, for the blood they shed last year" (EHPLC, doc. no. JJ, 102). Wyandanch sent seven hundred fathoms of wampum to Uncas, with a promise of more to follow, if he would attack Ninigret. There is, unfortunately, no further mention of this conspiracy, but we do know that Uncas never carried out Wyandanch's request. What happened to the wampum is unknown.

The following September, the issue was still unresolved. Wyandanch had, apparently in desperation, sent wampum to Ninigret to ransom the captives, but Thomas Stanton intercepted it for reasons which remain unclear. On September 6, 1654, the Reverend James wrote again to Winthrop on Wyandanch's behalf, asking that the wampum he sent to Ninigret be delivered to him as soon as possible. Wyandanch feared that harm would come to the prisoners if there was more delay (WP, 7:482–83). The letter appears to have helped resolve the impasse because Roger Williams reported in October, that the captives had been released "upon ye mediation and desire of ye English," but no other details are mentioned (RCNP, 10:442).[4]

The kidnapping of Wyandanch's daughter was later celebrated in local folklore. The story was told and retold, and, of course, embellished over the centuries. One of the earliest accounts was written by Lion Gardiner's descendent, David Gardiner in 1840. "Tradition has it," said Gardiner, that the raid took place during the festivities celebrating the wedding of the daughter. The tragic drama was further embellished by adding that her intended husband had been killed by the cruel Niantic warriors. Although none of these details is documented, the story of the wedding feast has been repeated many times (1871:23; Strong and Karabag 1991:192; Strong 1991:253–59).[5]

The United Colonies commissioners endorsed Wyandanch's assertion that he was not a Niantic tributary, but there remained some uncertainty about the Montaukett status. This may have been a factor in a surprise attack launched by the Montauketts against a party of Niantics who were visiting the Indians on Block Island. The raid must have taken place soon after the captives were released because Ninigret reported it to the United Colonies on September 18, 1654, claiming that his nephew, two Niantic sachems, and sixty of his men were killed by Wyandanch's men (RCNP, 10:125).[6]

The raid may have been encouraged by the English towns on eastern Long Island because it would dramatically demonstrate Wyandanch's independence from Ninigret and the defeat of his opposition among the Montauketts. The New Haven court voted on August 23, 1654, to send twelve pounds of gunpowder and thirty pounds of shot to Wyandanch (RCNH, 1:117–18). This aid may have played a significant role in Ninigret's defeat. The military victory also increased Wyandanch's influence with the English and among his own people. This new status, however, was soon to bring the Montaukett sachem serious troubles and new challenges at home.

## Summary

Following the defeat of the Algonquian resistance on western Long Island in 1645, the Dutch and English began a scramble for Indian land. The competition gave rise to rumors of conspiracy and encouraged a flourishing trade in arms to the Indians on Long Island and in southern New England. Governor Theophilus Eaton of New Haven led a campaign to purchase as much land as he could from the Indians east of the Dutch boundaries, in order to secure it for the English.

The deeds reflect the patterns described in Chapter 7 wherein the Indians tended to view the agreements as temporary leases rather than absolute dispossessions. The Montauketts, for example, were allowed to remain on the land and to continue hunting and fishing there as they had always done. In their minds, little had changed. The English were granted permission to cultivate the land around their villages, but they did not appear, at first, to need very much space. This soon changed as the English settlements grew and began to intrude into the Algonquian hunting and planting grounds.

These intrusions soon led to minor conflicts which were to continue for several more decades. The most dramatic encounter was the murder of Thomas Halsey's wife in Southampton, in 1649. The dangerous impasse which followed was resolved when Wyandanch, with the help of the English, assumed control of Shinnecock affairs.

When the English and Dutch back in Europe went to war in 1652, the Long Island frontier became a volatile arena for rumor and intrigue. Ninigret sought to take advantage of the animosity between the Europeans to advance his own interests. The Niantic sachem negotiated with the Dutch, who needed help from the Indians because they were so far outnumbered by the English; but, with the exception of a few minor skirmishes, the European war never spread to the North American colonies.

Ninigret then turned his attention to his old rival, Wyandanch. The Niantics launched a raid on the Montauketts, took several captives, including Wyandanch's daughter, and declared the Montauketts to be his tributaries. With the help of Lion Gardiner, who put up the money and goods, Wyandanch paid a ransom and got back the captives. Shortly thereafter, Wyandanch attacked

*Accommodation to Conquest, 1645-1654*

Ninigret's men when they were visiting on Block Island and re-established his independence from Ninigret.

Another important pattern which emerged during this period was the growing sophistication of the Algonquian sachems and elders with the European political and economic institutions. Ninigret and Wyandanch cleverly manipulated the English and Dutch to gain advantages for themselves and for their people and Cockenoe was successful in using the English court system to protect the rights of the Indians on Shelter Island. Although these advantages were temporary and did not prevent the gradual erosion of sovereignty which eventually left the Algonquian people with only two small reservations, it is important to record that the Indians were not childlike and easily manipulated by the Europeans. Today, their descendants are again making effective use of American political and economic institutions to protect and strengthen their sovereignty.

Articles of Agreement Betwixt the Governor of ye
New Netherlands And Tackpousha, March ye 12th, 1656. As followeth:

*First* That All Injuries formerly past in the time of the Governors predecessors shall be forgiven And forgotten sence ye yeare 45 and never be remembred.

*Secondly* That Tackpausha being chosen ye chiefe Sachem by All ye Indian Sachems from Marssapege Maskinekang Seacutang Meracock Rockaway and Conarisie wth ye names of ye rest both Sachems and Natives, Doth take the Governor of ye Newnetherlands to his and his Peoples protector, And in concideration of that to put under the said protection All theire lands and territories upon Longe Iland, soe farr As the Dutch line doth runn, According to the Agreement made at Hartforde.

*3dly* The Governor of ye New-netherlands doth promise to make noe peace with the Indians that did the spoile at ye Manhatans the 15th of September last, but likewise to Include ye Sachem in it.

*4thly* That Tackpausha shall make noe Peace wth ye said Indians wthout ye Consent and knowledge of the Governor.

*5thly* The Sachem doth promise, for himselfe and his people, to give noe dwelling-place, Entertainment nor Lodgeing to any of the Governors or their owne Enemies.

*6thly* The Governor doth promise Betwixt this date and Six monthes to build A howse or A forte upon such place as they shall show upon the north-side, And the fort or howse shall be furnished with Indian trade or Comodities. And the Sachem doth promise, that in this place Such people as shall thereon be placed by the Governor shall live in safety from him or any of his Indians.

*7thly* That the Inhabitants of Hemsteede, According to the lines expressed in the Pattent, And what they have purchased, shall injoy it wthout Mollestation from the Sachem or his People, Eyther of person or estate.

*8thly* That ye said Sachem shall live in peace with All ye Dutch & English wthin this Jurisdiction of the New-netherlands.

*9thly* The Governor doth promise for himselfe and All his people within the Jurisdiction to live in Peace wth the said Sachem and All his people, And the said Sachem and All his People shall keep According to the Aforesaid Articles wth the Governor and his People.

*10thly* That in case An Indian doe wrong a Christian Eyther in person or Estate, that yf Complaint be made to the Sachem, hee shall make full Sattisfaction : Likewise yf A Dutchman or an Englishman shall wrong an Indian, upon Complaint made to the Governor, the wrong doer shall make Sattisfaction According to Equity.

Heere under followeth the Names and Marks of the Indians that subscribed to the Aforesaid Articles of Agreement As I found them written in ye Coppy of the
Under written
Thomas Rushmur.

Waghtummoore  X  his marck.
Wigquatis  X  his marck
Uppahanuum  X  his marck
Tackapausha  X  his marck
Adam  X  his marck
Rumegie  X  his marck

Here doth follow the Names of the Witnesses that did Hear the Agreement as the Sachems confirmed these Articles.

John Sticklan
John Hicks
George Wolsey
Robert Jackson
Cornelis Vant Houen
Govert Loehermant
Gisbert Van Dicke

Fig. 9.1. Treaty between Tackapousha and the Dutch, March 12, 1656

# 9

# Wyandanch and Tackapousha: Alliance Sachems on the Long Island Frontier, 1655–1660

One of the patterns which emerged during the early post-contact period in North America was the development of alliances between local sachems and the European communities. We have seen the early stages of this pattern taking shape following the Pequot War as Miantonomi, Ninigret, Uncas, and Wyandanch emerged as prominent figures in New England and Long Island affairs. This pattern of alliances, which brought together two sharply contrasting cultural systems, is best expressed in the relationship between Lion Gardiner and Wyandanch. The sachems, unlike their European counterparts, governed by persuasion and had limited control over their followers. The Dutch and the English wanted a more predictable arena for their relations with the Algonquian communities.

The Europeans sought to achieve this goal by strengthening the power and influence of friendly sachems. This was accomplished with modest success by providing access to highly valued trade goods, alcohol, military supplies, and, in rare instances, limited military protection to the "alliance sachems" (White 1991:36-40). The Europeans expected the alliance sachems to control their own communities, to keep in close touch with their European ally, to prevent any of their people from harming the European settlers or their property, and to negotiate and enforce the terms of land sales (Metcalf 1974:652). The sachems, of course, had their own agendas which often created unexpected problems for their European allies.

### Wyandanch: "Chiefe Sachem of Long Island"

In the spring of 1655, Wyandanch was faced with a serious dispute between his people and the English in East Hampton. The conflicts over land use, described earlier in Chapters 7 and 8, had continued to escalate as more and more fences marked off large tracts of the ancient Algonquian hunting and planting grounds. Domestic livestock now competed successfully with game animals, driving them into shrinking habitats. Cattle frequently invaded Montaukett corn fields and destroyed winter food supplies. Wyandanch and two of his advisors, Sassakata and Pauquatoun, met with Gardiner, the Reverend Thomas James, and several representatives from East Hampton to discuss this issue. Both parties also wanted to clarify questions about the remaining unpurchased Montaukett lands and to define Wyandanch's role as an alliance sachem (MID: folder 3).

Requiring the English to build and maintain a fence which would protect the Montaukett fields resolved the conflict over grazing rights. The English also promised to pay for damages caused by any livestock that got through the fence during the late spring and summer when the crops were in the ground. In return, the Montauketts allowed English livestock to graze at will after the fall harvest until the time came for the spring planting. The English were also granted access to the salt hay near the wetlands. This settlement was much better for the Montauketts than the one the Sebonac Indians were able to get from the Southampton officials. Possibly Wyandanch's increasing power and influence, following his defeat of Ninigret at Block Island, made the difference.

The English, however, were still concerned about the threat which the Dutch posed to their exclusive purchase rights on Long Island. They attempted to resolve this concern by including a clause in the treaty which prohibited Wyandanch and his successors from selling their land to any party other than the proprietors of East Hampton and proclaimed Wyandanch to be the "chief sachem" of Long Island. This inflated title presumed to establish Wyandanch's authority over sachems west of Southampton who had never before accepted a tributary relationship under the Montauketts.

The East Hampton magistrates now began to establish a form of indirect rule over the Montauketts through Wyandanch. In order for the system to be effective, the English had to make sure that Wyandanch's authority over his people was continually reinforced. A good example of how the system worked both to enhance Wyandanch's power and, at the same time, serve the interests of the English was the imposition of limitations on the consumption of alcohol by the Montauketts.

There was a growing concern among the English about the damage done to persons and property by Indians under the influence of liquor. Obviously, there is an element of hypocrisy here because members of the English community were constantly using alcohol to manipulate the Indians. The magistrates issued a resolution prohibiting Indians from purchasing liquor without a "written ticket" from Wyandanch (RTEH, 1:81). This placed the responsibility for controlling alcohol consumption on the sachem and enhanced his authority in several ways. His people now had to come to him for the tickets, which gave him means to reward loyal supporters or to punish those who incurred his disfavor. The system also reminded the Montauketts that Wyandanch had the full authority of the English behind him and that he alone controlled access to English trade goods.

Wyandanch's authority over other sachems to the west of Shinnecock was another matter. The arbitrary nature of his new title was illustrated on April 14, 1655 when Warawakmy, a sachem from Setauket, sold a tract of land between present-day Stony Brook and the ponds which form the headwaters of the Peconic River, to John Scupper and a company of settlers (see Appendix C-8 map; RTBH, Hutchinson 1888:1–2; Tooker 1962:153, 159; Bayles 1882:1–2). There was no mention of the Montaukett sachem in the deed. Clearly, Wyandanch, in spite of his grand title, had no authority over Warawakmy at the time. That was soon to change.

Warawakmy and fourteen of his "next kindred" received for the land ten coats, twelve hoes, twelve hatchets, fifty muxes, one hundred needles, six kettles, ten fathom of wampum, seven chests of powder, one pair of children's stockings, ten pounds of lead, and one dozen knives. A familiar clause obligated both parties to give satisfaction for damages done by them to the persons or property of the other. Specific mention was made of damages by Indian dogs to English livestock, indicating once again the problems posed by the introduction of domestic animals into the ecosystem. In addition, Warawakmy agreed not to hold large powwows attended by "strange Indians, or others" near the English settlement and promised to inform the English of any plot against them by other Indians. The English, unfamiliar with the nature of the large seasonal powwows, feared that the gatherings would be used to plot against them and incite violence. Some were convinced that the dances and rituals were the work of the devil, who might foment violence against the Christian communities.

## Tackapousha: "Chiefe Sachem" over the Massapequas, Matinecocks, Secatogues, Merricks, Rockaways, and Canarsies

In the fall of 1655, the Dutch were having much more serious problems with their Indian neighbors. Hendrick Van Dyck, a former attorney general for the colony who had been recently dismissed by Stuyvesant for drinking on duty and taking bribes, killed an Indian woman when he caught her picking some peaches from his orchard. A war party of about eleven hundred Esophus, Hackingsacks, Mohegans, Tappans, and Tankitekes descended upon New Amsterdam looking for Van Dyck (Ruttenber, 1872:121). They shot him in the chest with an arrow and killed a Dutch soldier before the Dutch could organize a resistance (O'Callaghan 1966, 2:290–91). A brief skirmish followed in which three Indians were killed and the war party retreated from the town. The Indians crossed the Hudson, attacked the settlements of Hoboken and Pavonia, and then advanced on Staten Island, killing over fifty people and destroying twenty-eight farms.

Although no Mohawk warriors were involved, these attacks were the inspiration for an often repeated myth about the dominance of the Iroquois over the Indians of western Long Island. Two nineteenth-century historians, Gabriel Furman (1874:19–23) and Richard Bayles (1874), wrote that the war party which attacked New Amsterdam and Staten Island was led by the Mohawks. There is no mention, however, of Mohawk participation in any of the colonial documents. Furman went on to describe a campaign which he claimed had "undoubtedly" destroyed the Canarsie Indians. The Mohawk attacked, explained Furman, because the Canarsie refused to pay their regular tribute of wampum and dried clams. Frederick Van Wyck repeated Furman's account in his rambling, disorganized, seven-hundred-page tome, *Keskachauge or the First White Settlement on Long Island* (1924:643–47). The Mohawk story has unfortunately become a part of Long Island folklore. There is no documentation in the records that such an attack ever took place, nor is there any evidence that any of the Long Island Indian communities were paying tribute to the Mohawk. Neither of the nineteenth-century authors, Edmund Bailey O'Callaghan (1966, 2:290–93) and E. M Ruttenber (1872:121–24), nor modern historian Allen Trelease (1971: 138–41), mention the Mohawks or the alleged extermination of the Canarsies.

None of the western Long Island Indians joined the northern Indians in the attack on New Amsterdam. The local Dutch settlers, however, remained concerned. They complained to Stuyvesant that their English neighbors were carrying on normal relations with the Indians and repeated a rumor that the Indians planned to attack the Dutch and leave the English alone (Trelease 1971:141). It was true that the Hempstead officials had given two guns and some powder and lead to sachems Ruckquaheag, Ronnessoke, and eight other Indians for a tract of land on Rockaway Neck south of Hempstead just two days before the attack on Manhattan (DSBD, 2:161). Adam (Achitteronose), who may have served as an interpreter, also signed the deed. It was also true that Adam and Ronnessoke had demonstrated their loyalty to the English two years earlier when they reported Ninigret's attempt to recruit Long Island sachems to fight for the Dutch. There is no evidence, however, that the English were doing anything more than cultivating potential Indian allies in case the conflict should spread to Long Island.

Witaneywen, who had now taken the name Tackapousha, saw an opportunity to advance his own interests in this situation. On November 27, 1655, he sent Adam with a delegation to New Amsterdam (NYCD, 13:58). Adam, who was fluent in both Dutch and English, reminded Stuyvesant that his people had done no harm to the settlers since the end of the war in 1645. The sachem gave the Dutch a present of wampum as a token of his friendship and promised not to give any assistance to the Dutch enemies. In return, Tackapousha asked that he be included in any peace settlement and pressed Stuyvesant to build a fortified trading post on the north shore of Long Island (NYCD, 14:368-369; RTNSH, 1:44–45).

The Dutch were concerned about the security of the north shore, but they lacked the resources to construct a fort. In fact, they were hard pressed to prevent the English from encroaching over the boundary line established at Hartford in 1650. They had received word at the beginning of 1655 that a party of English, led by William Leverich, had established a settlement without Dutch permission on Martin Gerritsen's Bay (renaming it Oyster Bay). The Dutch issued a letter of protest to Leverich on April 2, 1655, stating that he had "settled within the limits of New Netherland, on land named Martin Gerrit's Bay, purchased from the natives, the right owners and proprietors, and paid for and long possessed by the Netherland nation" (RTOB, 1:671–72). Cornelis Van Tienhoven, speaking for the Dutch government ordered Leverich to leave the area within the next thirty days. The English, who had also purchased the land from the Indians (the

1653 deed signed by Asharoken), refused to leave. The Dutch, unwilling to provoke a military confrontation with England, took no further action (O'Callaghan 2:282).

Tackapousha must have been well aware of the tensions on the border between the two European powers when he sought to open negotiations with the Dutch. He formed an alliance with sachems Waghtummore, Wogquatis, Uppahanuum, Adam, and Rumegie, representing the villages of Secatogue, Maskinekaug (Matinecock), Merrick, Rockaway, and Canarsie, to represent them in negotiations with the Dutch. The negotiations were held in Hempstead on March 12, 1656 (Pelletreau 1903:85; Brodhead 1853–71, 1:519). The presence of the Secatogues in Tackapousha's sphere of influence must have disturbed the English because the Secatogue lands stretched along the south shore of Long Island from Babylon to Islip, well east of the Hartford Treaty line (Tooker 1962:234). In terms of geography and cultural affinity, however, the association with Tackapousha was to be expected. Although the Secatogue villages were located in the "gray" area of uncertain cultural affinity between the Munsee-speaking groups and the eastern villages who had closer ties with southern New England, they undoubtedly shared many cultural aspects and perhaps the Munsee language with the Massapequas.

The Dutch, of course, were undoubtedly pleased to have an alliance which included villages in an area that they had so reluctantly abandoned to the English. Many of Stuyvesant's critics in New Amsterdam, who viewed these concessions to be a temporary expedient, welcomed a foothold, however fragile, east of the treaty line. The Dutch, therefore, eagerly anointed Tackapousha as the "Chiefe Sachem" over the Indians of western Long Island and agreed to an alliance of peace (RTNSH, 1:43–44).

Both parties to the treaty agreed, "That all injuries formerly past . . . shall be forgiven and forgotten. . . . That Tackapousha being chosen Chiefe Sachem . . . doth ask the Governor of New Netherlands to [be] his and his peoples protector and in consideration of that do put under the said protection, all of their lands and territories upon Long Island, so far as the Dutch line doth run according to the agreement made in Hartford" (see fig. 9.1, p. 214 and Appendix B; DSBD, 2:129–31). They also agreed to consult each other on all negotiations with other Indian groups, and Tackapousha promised not to harbor any enemies of the Dutch (Trelease 1971:146; RTNSH, 1:43–45). Governor Stuyvesant promised to build a fortified trading post on the north shore within the next six months.

Later, in the fall of 1656, the settlers in Brooklyn, Midwout, and New Amersfoort complained to Governor Stuyvesant that some clothing had been stolen by Indians from Secatogue, who were under Tackapousha's authority. They told the governor that they had "very gloomy forebodings," and feared that the thefts might be followed by an attack (NYCD, 14:368). Tackapousha, realizing that his alliance with Stuyvesant was threatened, moved quickly to assert his authority over the Secatogues. He ordered them to return the goods, "else it might create disharmony and quarrels" and promised the settlers that whenever a theft was reported to him he would provide restitution (NYCD, 14:369). The sachem was rewarded with a present of gunpowder from the settlers.

Tackapousha and Wyandanch, supported by their European allies, soon became the two most powerful and influential sachems on Long Island. Both men became the primary liaisons between their people and the new immigrants to Long Island, as well as important players in the international struggle between the English and the Dutch for control over Long Island.

### Wyandanch Faces Challenges at Home and Abroad

When Wyandanch was threatened again by Ninigret in the fall of 1655, the English moved quickly to protect their loyal ally. The United Colony commissioners ordered John Youngs, an experienced sailor from Southold, to patrol the Sound and block any attempt by Ninigret to attack the Montauketts. The commissioners instructed Youngs to take, sink, or destroy Ninigret's canoes (RCNP, 10:151). The action successfully thwarted any plan the Niantic sachem may have had to retaliate for his defeat on Block Island.[1] He did not initiate any further action against the Montauketts until after Wyandanch's death in 1659. Youngs maintained the blockade for over a year and was paid £153 by the United Colonies. In contrast, the missionary John Eliot was paid a yearly salary of only £50 by the United Colonies for his "Indian work." Clearly, missionary work was far less important to the English than the protection of their alliance sachem. Few Long Island sachems would now openly challenge any leader who could draw on this level of English support.

The importance of a reliable Algonquian ally who had the power to influence the behavior of his fellow sachems was becoming more evident as the scramble for Indian lands continued. English settlers and speculators were purchasing Long Island real estate from any Algonquian sachem who appeared to have some authority over a given tract of land. This inevitably led to conflict because some Indians viewed the transactions as a lease which could be sold again to another buyer, and others purposely misled English buyers into purchasing land which did not belong to them.

On July 30, 1656, Asharoken, who, as we have seen in Chapter 7, had sold Eaton's Neck twice, sold a parcel of land to Jonas Wood of Huntington, which again included Eaton's Neck and a tract of land on the western bank of the Nissequogue belonging to Nassaconseke, the Nissequogue sachem (Appendix C-9; RTH, 1:6–7; Street 1882:9; Morice 1950a:229–30). The Huntington purchase was later voided on the grounds that Asharoken had no right to sell Nissequogue lands. The towns of Oyster Bay, Huntington, and Smithtown squabbled for years over their boundary lines as court costs and lawyers' fees mounted.[2] The English would soon turn to Wyandanch for help in such matters, but in the early spring of the following year an incident of far greater seriousness occurred in the town of Southampton.

Several Shinnecock men and an African American woman conspired to burn down several buildings in the settlement. One of the buildings was the home of Eleanor Howell, the widow of Edward Howell, who had helped to found the town in 1640. One or more of the conspirators may have been servants in the Howell household, possibly retaliating for an unpleasant incident involving the servants of the Howells years before. A young Indian servant woman named Hope had a child by another servant named George Wood. The town court found the couple guilty of "carnal filthiness" and sentenced them to be publicly whipped. The child was given to the Howells to serve as a domestic in their house until he reached the age of thirty (RTSH, 1:35). Unfortunately, there is no further mention of Hope or her child in the town records.

According to the sparse court records from the Particular Court of Connecticut, Wigwagub, a Shinnecock, testified that he had been hired to burn the Howell home by two other Shinnecocks named Awabag and Agagoneau (RPCC, 22:175–76). Awabag gave him a gun and Agagoneau paid him seven shillings, six pence. Another man, Auwegenum, was present when Wigwagub was hired, but his role in the affair was not mentioned. No motive was mentioned in the records, but it was not simply an act of revenge against the Howells, because several other buildings in the town were also burned. Possibly the attacks were also related to the conflicts over the invasion of Indian planting grounds by English livestock, a common problem during this period. The Shinnecocks had frequently complained to Wyandanch about the English horses that wandered into their corn fields and destroyed their crops (RCNP, 10:180).

The court records did not mention the African American woman, but Wyandanch later reported that the servant woman was "far deeper in that capital miscarriage than any or all of the Indians" (RCNP, 10:180). It is possible that Wyandanch was attempting to shift the blame away from the Indians, but even so, his account raises some fascinating questions about the relationship between the small population of African American servants and slaves and the Indians. Both groups certainly shared common frustrations in their relations with the dominant white settlers. The suggestion that a woman had taken a role of leadership in the small rebellion is also noteworthy.

When news of the house burnings reached Hartford, the colonial authorities raised a troop of nineteen men, armed them with twenty-five pounds of powder and fifty pounds of shot, and sent them to Southampton under the command of John Mason, the veteran who had commanded the troops at Mystic during the Pequot War (RPCC, 22:176). The mere presence of the man who ordered the massacre of the Pequots must have unsettled the Shinnecocks. Mason was ordered to consult with Wyandanch about the matter and to determine whether or not any of the Indians involved in the incident were under Wyandanch's authority.

Mason arrived in Southampton to find that the magistrates had issued gunpowder to the townsmen in preparation for a conflict. The town passed a resolution allowing only four representatives from Shinnecock to enter the English village. The magistrates appointed Wapeacom, Powcowwantuck, Suretrust, and James to carry on all relations between the two communities (RTSH, 1:114–15).

There is no record of Mason's activities in the town, but there is a reference in a later document to a Shinnecock man who killed himself to avoid "just execution" by the English (RCNP, 10:180). The man may have been Wigwagub, the only one who confessed to the arson. Mason, apparently not satisfied to leave the matter at that, imposed an exorbitant fine of £700 on the Shinnecock community. The Shinnecocks, well aware of Mason's role in the massacre of the Pequots, agreed to accept the fine, which was to be paid over a seven year period (RCNP, 10:180). The fine forced them into a debt servitude which could be used both as an instrument of social control by the English and as a means to press for the sale of land to pay the fine. For the Shinnecocks, who were not yet engaged in the European economic system, the sum was an impossible burden.

Wyandanch demonstrated that the role of the alliance chief could be more than that of a passive conduit for English governance when he sent a representative with a written petition to the United Colonies session in Boston the following September and appealed the Connecticut court's fine (RCNP, 10:180). The Montaukett sachem's decision to go over the head of the Connecticut court and the articulation of his arguments indicate a growing familiarity with English institutions.

When he submitted the petition, Wyandanch also sent seventy-eight fathoms of wampum to the United Colonies' treasurer in New Haven. The wampum was undoubtedly intended to influence the commissioners (RCNP, 10:194). The sachem began his presentation to the commissioners by reporting that the Shinnecocks had already sustained losses from English horses that destroyed their crops. He then argued that Mason had not been fully informed about the arson when he imposed the fine. He told the commissioners that the African American woman was primarily to blame for the arson and that the Shinnecock involved was dead. Given these circumstances, argued Wyandanch, the fine was excessive. The United Colonies' commissioners agreed with Wyandanch and asked the Connecticut court to reconsider the amount.

While the matter was pending before the Connecticut court, the town of Southampton paid the widow Howell twenty shillings to repair her losses. The damage was apparently not very severe. John Mason received £20 from the town for his role in the affair. The cost of repairing the damage and paying the troops certainly did not justify a fine of £700. When the Connecticut court reconsidered the matter, they reduced the amount to £500 over a six year period (RCC, 1:316–17). For the Shinnecocks, the reduction had little significance because the fine was still far beyond their means.

The Hartford court appointed a group of prominent Southampton men to collect the fine and distribute payment to those who had suffered damages. The committee was empowered to "take from them a certain company of ye Indian men," if the payments were not made (RTSH, 2:206–7). The brief reference does not explain what was to be done with the captives, but most likely it was intended that they would be sold as slaves in the West Indies to pay the debt. Although John Ogden, a member of the committee, apparently favored such action, the magistrates refused to take such a drastic measure, knowing full well that it might provoke a much more violent reaction among the local Indians. The Indians were well aware of the fate which befell those shipped out to the West Indies.

Fines of this kind were often used in New England as an effective means of social control. As long as an Algonquian community remained under the shadow of the debt, the English could intervene in their community affairs. The debt was also a strategy used to obtain Indian lands. According to historian Francis Jennings, a favorite strategy of the English was "the imposition of fines for a wide variety of offenses, the Indians' lands becoming forfeit if the fines were not paid by their due date" (Jennings 1976:144–45). As we shall see, the English on Long Island were to make equally effective use of this strategy.

## "Deed Diplomacy" on the Long Island Frontier

The purchase of Indian lands was a major focus of English policy, but it was proving to be chaotic and costly. The major cost, however, was not the price paid to the Indians; it was the loss in time and the cost of seemingly endless litigation over land title. In order to limit the cost of such litigation, the English and Dutch turned to alliance sachems for help. One of the problems was the absence of clearly defined boundaries between Algonquian village groups. The planting fields were well marked, but hunting territory was impossible to determine with the precision required in the European real estate market. As a result, there was usually controversy over boundary lines which often had to be settled years later in the courts as trespass cases.

These concerns prompted the Southampton magistrates to document the eastern boundary of the town shortly after the fine was imposed on the Shinnecocks. They may have anticipated a conflict with the town of East Hampton over the border. Wyandanch sent a Shinnecock sachem, probably Mandush and his wife, to meet with the magistrates and determine the eastern border of Shinnecock lands included in the 1640 deed. Their answer was characteristically vague. The couple said that their land "went to Georgica [Pond] or Wainscot at least, or thereabouts" (RTSH, 1:114). The two towns fought over the boundary for the next thirty years (Pelletreau 1882:18).

A short time after the troubles in Southampton, Wyandanch became involved in a negotiation which brought him into a potential conflict with Tackapousha and drew him into the Anglo-Dutch scramble for land. He was asked to endorse the sale of Secatogue lands on the Great South Bay in the present-day town of

Babylon. Jonas Wood of Huntington paid Wyandanch twelve coats, twenty hoes, twenty hatchets, twenty knives, ten pounds of powder, ten pounds of lead, one large kettle, and a coat a year for the next six years (Appendix C-10). These lands were located on the eastern side of the Hartford Treaty line and were still coveted by the Directors of New Netherland in Holland, who were sharply critical of Stuyvesant for signing the Hartford agreement in 1650. The directors had urged Stuyvesant on several occasions to take a more aggressive stand against what they viewed as English encroachments on Dutch lands (NYCD, 14:302, 322–23, 332–33; 1:359–61). As long as Tackapousha held influence over the Secatogue sachems, the Dutch claim to this land might someday be reasserted.

This was the homeland of Keeossechok, a Secatogue sachem, who apparently did not accept Tackapousha's authority over him, in spite of the assertion in the 1656 treaty with the Dutch. As we have noted, Algonquian sachems held power over their followers only by persuasion, much to the frustration of their European allies. Keeossechok may have decided to link his fortunes to the English, whose communities were growing up all around him, rather than with the Dutch whose future on Long Island seemed uncertain. It is possible, of course, that he or some of his close kinsmen were involved in the theft of goods, which Tackapousha demanded be returned. They may have resented Tackapousha's actions. It is also quite possible that the English pressed Keeossechok to formally accept an alliance with Wyandanch in order to block any attempt by the Dutch to compromise the Hartford Treaty line. In any event, Keeossechok went so far as to resign "all that right and interest," he had in the necks of land to Wyandanch (RTH, 1:10–11).

The clear implication here is that Wyandanch and the English were gaining ascendancy in areas that had formerly been a part of Tackapousha's sphere of influence. The Secatogue sachem apparently received nothing more than a gesture of English friendship, for the deed states that the goods were to go to Wyandanch. Tackapousha, apparently, was in no position to protest the defection of the Secatogue sachem, since there is no indication in the records that he took any action. The English must have been very pleased with the transaction because it placed Wyandanch in a position to supervise all of the unpurchased land east of the Hartford Treaty line. This would greatly facilitate future land sales and prevent the problems the English had with Asharoken .

A month later, on July 4, 1657, Wyandanch and Cockenoe, his advisor and interpreter who was now married to his sister, went to Hempstead to help negotiate a settlement between a delegation of Indians led by Tackapousha, Mangwobe the sachem from Rockaway, and Indians representing the Merrick villages, and the representatives from Hempstead led by John Hicks, Edward Spragg, John Carman, and Richard Gildersleeve. The meeting, which took place in Gildersleeve's home, was called by the Hempstead officials to confirm the deed Tackapousha had signed with John Carman and Robert Fordham in 1643 for the area that is now the town of Hempstead, and to purchase the land in present-day North Hempstead which was included in the Dutch patent of 1644 (see Chapter 7 above). The confirmation of the 1643 deed posed no problem for the sachems, but the question of the lands north of the 1643 deed line was another matter entirely.

Although the North Hempstead lands had not been purchased from the Matinecock owners, the English settlers had established farmsteads there soon after the patent was issued in 1644. The prevailing European attitude towards Indian sovereignty is reflected in the actions of the English settlers. Only the Dutch sovereignty was taken seriously. The question of Matinecock ownership was an annoying afterthought that was given consideration only to avoid a violent confrontation with the Indians. The "alliance sachems," it was hoped, would keep the peace.

The Hempstead men apparently assumed that Tackapousha, who had the support of the Matinecocks when he negotiated the treaty with the Dutch the previous year, could sell the Matinecock lands. This would certainly have facilitated Hempstead's purchase, but it soon became clear that the traditional Algonquian political structures could not be remolded to suit European interests simply by putting words into a treaty. As we have seen, the Secatogue sachem Keeossechok may have rejected Tackapousha's authority over him because he felt that an alliance with the English was in the best interest of his people. Tackapousha's influence over the western Long Island sachems, therefore, rested entirely on his ability to provide them with political or economic benefits. Apparently, neither the Secatogues nor the Matinecocks, who had endorsed Tackapousha's treaty with the Dutch, understood that they were turning over control of their lands to the Massapequa sachem. Twenty years later, Edward Spragg, one of the Hempstead men, testified that when Wyandanch had asked who spoke for the Matinecocks, Tackapousha answered that he did. (RTNSH, 1:312–13). The Matinecock sachems and Tackapousha vehemently denied this. Tackapousha maintained that he never negotiated the transfer of land.

The sachems who met at Gildersleeve's home in July were given some livestock, ammunition, wampum, guns, and trading cloth in exchange for their confirmation of the 1643 deed. The Hempstead men testified later that they understood the payments were for both the confirmation of the 1643 deed and the purchase of the northern half of the Dutch patent. Ignoring the fact that the authority of the sachems present in Gildersleeve's home to dispose of the northern half of the patent was clearly in doubt, the text of the agreement they wrote stated that Algonquian sachems had surrendered all right and title to "the whole tract of land concluded upon with the governor of Manhattans" (NYCD, 14:416). Tensions over this issue continued throughout the following fall and were soon to threaten the peace.

The meeting had other significance as well. Wyandanch played a key role as an intermediary between the two parties. The Montaukett sachem, with his English backing, was the dominant Indian leader in the negotiations. Even though Hempstead was in Dutch territory, Tackapousha was forced to take a subordinate role, perhaps reflecting the waning power of Tackapousha's Dutch allies over the English towns on western Long Island. Wyandanch had now pushed his sphere of influence across the Hartford Treaty line into New Netherland.

The Dutch now found that their alliance sachem had been eclipsed within their territorial border by the ally of the English. Again there is no indication in the records that Tackapousha objected to Wyandanch's second intrusion into his territory, but he undoubtedly felt some resentment. Ironically, Tackapousha's stature among the Matinecocks increased as he became more and more involved as a strong advocate of their land claims against Hempstead.

This confirmation process also demonstrates a common problem with land transactions between the Algonquians and the Europeans. As we have noted, the Algonquian sachems often viewed the sales as leases which would continue to pay dividends to them. When they learned that the purchasers were selling the land to other Englishmen at a substantial profit, they frequently demanded additional payments.

Peter Stuyvesant warned both the English and the Dutch settlers not to reveal the market value of the lands to the Indians lest it cause unrest among them (O'Callaghan 1966, 2:249). Stuyvesant's attitude typified the European view that the Algonquians had no legitimate land title to begin with. The arguments based on the "right of discovery" by "Christian princes" to lands which were not controlled by Christians had not lost their currency. In addition, Puritan scholars such as John Winthrop and Francis Higginson put forth the doctrine of *vacuum domicilium* which held that North America was a "vacant" land waiting for God's chosen people. It was their Christian duty, they argued, to "take a land which none useth, and to make use of it" (Salisbury 1984:176–77). The English and Dutch on Long Island agreed in principle with the Puritan spokesmen, that "heathen" peoples who did not develop the land with "modern" tools had no legitimate claim to "true" ownership.

The Algonquian peoples, therefore, were to be humored with gifts when necessary to keep them peaceable, but they were denied equal status in the European real estate market. In some cases, the Europeans delayed payments or paid only a portion of the agreed upon price until the Indians threatened to take violent action. In 1652, for example, the Indians threatened to burn the buildings in Flatbush because they had not been paid for the land (O'Callaghan 1966, 2:194–95). The incidents at Flatbush and Southampton may well have been on the minds of the Hempstead leaders when they called the meeting with Tackapousha, Wyandanch, and Cockenoe.

A few weeks after the meeting in Hempstead was concluded, Wyandanch was in Setauket to join with Wenecoheage, the local sachem, in the sale of two necks of land on the south shore (Appendix C-11), near present-day Mastic (RTBH, Hutchinson:2–3; Bayles 1882:3; Tooker 1962:280). Once again a local sachem had acknowledged Wyandanch's right to supervise the negotiations and to receive a share of the payment. The deed clearly indicated that the payment would go to both sachems. The goods given to the sachems included twenty coats, twenty hoes, twenty hatchets, forty needles, forty muxes, ten pounds of powder, ten pounds of lead, six pairs of stockings, six shirts, one well-made trooper's coat, twenty knives, and one gun.

Three days later, on July 23, 1657, Wyandanch was called to Huntington where he met again with Jonas Wood and Keeossechok to negotiate the sale of a small parcel of meadowland on a neck which bordered on the Massapequa lands (Appendix C-12; RTH, 1:12–13; Street 1882:10). This time, however, Wyandanch shared the trade goods which included a new gun, a pistol, and two pounds of powder, with Keeossechok. Once again, however, Wyandanch reinforced his authority over the Secatogues.

During the fall of 1657, tensions between the settlers of Hempstead and the Matinecocks finally led to raids on the English farmsteads. The Indians were careful, however, not to harm any of the settlers. Their protest was similar to the actions taken by the Indians in Flatbush; they killed large numbers of pigs and drove off cattle (Marshall 1962:29–30). Now that open warfare with the Europeans was no longer an option for the Indians, they resorted, in desperation, to guerrilla tactics. The acts of arson against the Southampton community the previous spring was another example of this pattern.

The Hempstead settlers sent an appeal with John Hicks, one of the founding fathers of Hempstead, to Governor Stuyvesant, complaining that the Indians "hold us in suspense by their delays and we cannot get them to show us the bounds of our lands" (quoted by Marshall 1962:29). More ominously, the settlers asked for powder, lead, and flint to arm and equip the town militia (NYCD, 14:411). They also asked for a troop of forty professional Dutch soldiers and an officer to come to the aid of their militiamen. Clearly, the Hempstead settlers were preparing to resolve the issue by force of arms.

When Stuyvesant did not comply with the request, the settlers, led by Hicks and Gildersleeve, again turned to Wyandanch for help in resolving the conflict. On March 28, 1658, the Montaukett sachem sent Cockenoe to bring together the magistrates and Tackapousha to go over the boundary lines once more and come to a resolution that both parties could accept (NHCP:91). Some progress was made. The sachems and the Hempstead representatives, Richard Gildersleeve, John Seaman, Edward Spragg, John Carman, and John Hicks, held another meeting on May 11, 1658. Although the only reference we have about the negotiations comes from the testimony of the Hempstead men twenty years later, it appears that an additional payment was made to the sachems at Wyandanch's request. Once again the Hempstead men argued that they understood that the payment was for the land in North Hempstead (NYCD, 14:416–17). Tackapousha, however, contended that the agreement was only for the use of grazing land in the north (NYCD, 14:474).

One of the striking features of this settlement was that the Indians were paid in pounds sterling and in cattle, as well as with trade goods. When the Hempstead men made their offer of £30, the sachems protested that it was not enough. Wyandanch, demonstrating that he retained some independence from the English, agreed with the sachems and demanded that Hempstead raise their offer. The offer was then raised to £42, still a bargain for the English, but a much better deal than the Indians got in most of the other transactions (RTNSH, 1:313). It is quite possible, of course, that the settler's account of this meeting is inaccurate. Indians were seldom paid in pounds sterling for their lands until much later. The unusually high amount which they claimed to have paid the sachem also raises questions about the testimony.

Wyandanch's role as a certifying agent for the deeds set an important precedent which the English hoped would bring some order to the process of land dispossession. The English settlers were now accepting the endorsement of the "chief sachem" as a requirement for the purchase of Algonquian land. Wyandanch signed several of these deeds with "stick figures" which apparently represented his close relationship with the English. He drew two small figures standing side by side, and, in one instance, the figures are even holding hands (see fig. 9.2).

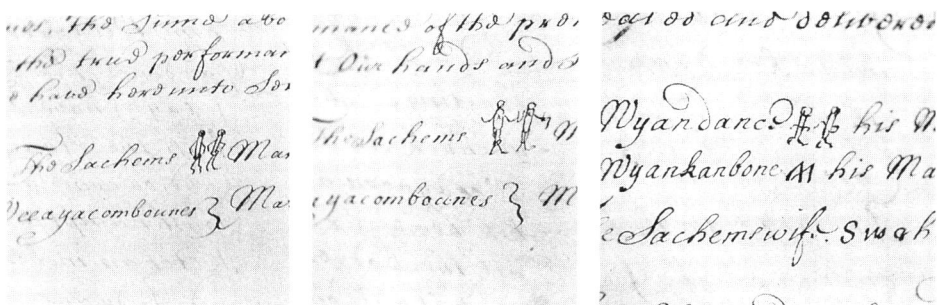

Fig. 9.2. Wyandanch "stick figure" signatures

Wyandanch's new capacity as an arbiter soon brought the claimants of the tract of land on Lloyd Neck to him. Samuel Andrews, a private entrepreneur from Oyster Bay, bought Samuel Mayo's title for £100. Asharoken, who had sold the land first to Richard Holbrook and the Huntington settlers and then to Samuel Mayo for trade goods worth only a small fraction of that amount, must have felt cheated, but we have no record of his reaction.

Andrews went immediately to seek out Wyandanch and get his endorsement on his deed. The Huntington magistrates, hearing of this, sent their representatives to Wyandanch as well. Andrews got to the Montaukett sachem first and received his endorsement. Wyandanch stated that he would "maintain the said title thereof forever unto Samuel Andrews, his heirs, administrators or assigns, as being the true repurchasers thereof from Samuel Mayo and company"

(RTH, 1:15; Street 1882:12–13). According to local legend, Andrews met the Huntington men on his way back and mocked them, waving his endorsement at them and telling them that they might as well go back home. After a long court battle, Andrews' claim was upheld, primarily because he had obtained Wyandanch's endorsement (RTH, 1:16). Lloyd Neck remained a part of the town of Oyster Bay until 1886 when it was transferred back to Huntington.

Two weeks after his endorsement of Andrews' title, Wyandanch turned his attention to the Shinnecock land west of Canoe Place where the Shinnecock Canal is located today. The Montaukett sachem had been given control over these lands after the Halsey murder and his authority over Shinnecock affairs had been reaffirmed following the arson incident. Wyandanch demonstrated his experience as a negotiator and his understanding of English institutions in these transactions. On May 29, 1658, he leased to Thomas Topping for ten years, a small tract of meadowland near the present-day village of Westhampton Beach (Appendix D-9). After that time, the land was "to be surrendered peaceably unto the said sachem, his heirs, or successors, to be disposed of, at his or their discretion" (DSBD, 2:152). For the first and, unfortunately, the last time, the Indian concept of limited use appears in the text of a land transaction. Wyandanch managed, for a brief moment, to bring the English to terms with the traditional Algonquian concept of land use.

Less than two weeks later, Wyandanch, along with his advisors, Cockenoe, Sassakata, Momoweta (Mawweehew) and his young son, Wyancombone, sold Lion Gardiner a large tract of beach land in the same area for an undisclosed sum of money and trade goods (Appendix D-10; RTSH, 1:170–71). Once again, however, Wyandanch insisted on a clause which would provide him and his family with a regular income. Gardiner agreed to pay the sachem and his heirs twenty-five shillings a year each October, forever. The whales which were cast up on the beach, a major source of wealth on the south shore of Long Island, remained Wyandanch's property. The Indians also retained the right to cut flag grass and bullrushes, which they used to make mats for their wigwams. These transactions with Topping and Gardiner were unique in that they guaranteed a continuing return of income rather than a final dispossession. Six months later, Gardiner granted the right to use a portion of the tract to a Southampton man named John Cooper, on the condition that he pay Wyandanch the yearly fee (RTSH, 1:171).

In August, Wyandanch, Cockenoe, and Sassakata were back in Huntington to sell three more necks of land on the south shore lying to the west of the land purchased by Jonas Wood the year before (Appendix C-3). Henry Whitney, who made the purchase for the town, paid Wyandanch twelve coats, twenty pounds of powder, twenty Dutch hatchets, twenty Dutch hoes, twenty Dutch knives, ten shirts, two hundred muxes, five pair of "handsome stockings," one good Dutch hat, and a looking glass. Cockenoe, who was paid a separate fee for marking out the boundaries, received one coat, four pounds of powder, six pounds of lead, one Dutch hatchet, and seventeen shillings worth of wampum. The specification of Dutch goods suggests that they were considered superior to those produced by the English.

This land, located near present-day Amityville, was clearly within the boundary of Tackapousha's Massapequa domain. He testified later that the sale "grieved his heart" but that he was unable to challenge Wyandanch's authority at the time (Paltsits 1910, 2:414; RTH, 2:18). The Montaukett sachem, supported by Lion Gardiner, gave Tackapousha a small share of the payment and sent him away. The English supported Wyandanch in this matter because they were eager to press their land claims as close to the Hartford Treaty line as they could. Wyandanch, of course, had done very nicely for himself as well. He had received a handsome payment and forced the submission of his powerful rival for all the sachems of Long Island to see.

In one instance, Wyandanch overreached his authority. He prohibited the Pequots from coming to Long Island for quahog shells which were used in the manufacture of wampum. The Pequots, realizing that the traditional means of resolving such grievances were no longer possible, brought their case to the United Colonies and asked that their ancient privileges be restored. The commissioners agreed with them and gave notice to Wyandanch that "the Pequots . . . bee permitted to freely fetch shells there . . . as formerly they had done" (RCNP, 10:199–200).

The English concern for keeping the control of wampum resources and production in their hands is easy to understand. They had established a monopoly over the wampum trade in the Connecticut Valley following their defeat of the Pequots in 1637 and, as a result, soon dominated the lucrative fur trade on the Connecticut River (McBride 1994:41). The English, who were collecting significant amounts of tribute wampum from the Pequots, did not want any limitation on their access to quahog shells.

This minor setback may have prompted Wyandanch to strengthen his alliance with Gardiner and the influential men in the East Hampton community whenever he could. The land titles were, of course, a primary concern of the English, but another important source of wealth on the eastern end of Long Island was whale oil. The Montauketts took the tails and fins of the whales for their ceremonial feasts (see Chapter 5) and cooked some of the flesh, but the English were primarily interested in the oil and bone because these commodities could be turned into hard currency on the European market (Strong 1989a:30). Drift whales, it could be said, were the first cash crop produced on Long Island.

The question of drift whales came up again in November 1658 when Wyandanch gave Lion Gardiner and the Reverend Thomas James of East Hampton one-half of the whales "or other great fish" which drifted onto the beach between Napeague and the far end of Montauk. This was an important grant because it gave the two men an exclusive right to all of the ocean beaches on Montaukett lands. The town of East Hampton owned the whale rights from

Napeague west to the Southampton border and held them in common trust. Wyandanch did require a small percentage of their profit, but left it to James and Gardiner to pay "what they shall judge meete and according as they find profit by them" (RTEH, 1:150).

Wyandanch's generosity to the two influential East Hampton men may have served him well two months later when he brought suit in the town courts against a young townsman named Jeremy Vaile for damages to his large canoe. The vessel, probably one used for trips across the Sound, may have been thirty or forty feet long. The suit is significant because it is one of the earliest recorded instances of an Indian plaintiff seeking damages from an Englishman in an English court.

Lion Gardiner testified for Wyandanch against Vaile, who was charged with negligence. Vaile and Anthony Waters, another East Hampton man, borrowed the canoe to carry some goods over to Gardiners Island and ran into some bad weather. They landed the canoe on the island, but failed to secure it properly. Gardiner ordered them to return and make sure it was safe, but by the time they got back, the canoe was damaged and full of water. The court ruled for the plaintiff and awarded Wyandanch ten shillings (RTSH, 1:152)

As Wyandanch's influence grew, proprietors from all over Long Island sought him out to bolster their land claims. The Southold magistrates, led by Barnabas Horton, met with Wyandanch, Cockenoe, and the Corchaug Indians in January 1659 to clear up some questions about who had the right to sell the land on the North Fork of eastern Long Island (Pelletreau 1882:9). Unfortunately, we have no record of the specific issues involved in the dispute, but later documents indicate that Plum Island was one of the areas in contention. Some questions had apparently been raised about the property on Plum Island, which had been purchased by Governor Eaton from Momoweta and Paummis in 1648. Southold officials, probably William Wells and Richard Woodhall, bought the island from Eaton for the use of the town, but no settlement had ever been established there. Later, John Youngs bought the land, but he never occupied it either (DSBD, 1:15). The Corchaugs, acting on their traditional view of ownership, apparently reasserted their control over the island by default. The Southold settlers called upon Wyandanch to resolve this matter and other questions about the rest of the North Fork as well.

Wyandanch asserted that the Corchaugs were not now, nor had they ever been, the owners of either the North Fork or Plum Island. These lands, said the Montaukett sachem, were inherited from his ancestors, and had been sold to Richard Woodhall and William Wells "diverse years since" (RTS, 1:194). The Corchaugs did not protest this claim by Wyandanch and "remained wholly silent not in the least contradicting what the sachem said." Their silence may have been a commentary on Wyandanch's growing power and influence rather than a sign of their agreement with his assertion of hegemony over their lands.

Tackapousha, however, was apparently not so intimidated. In March he and his younger brother, Chopeyconnaws, sold some meadowland near South Oyster Bay to the three Wright brothers (Anthony, Nicholas, and Peter), Daniel Whitehead, John Richbell, and Samuel Andrews. The property began on the western boundary of Oyster Bay (near present-day Seaford) and ran eastward to the Warraseketuck River, which marked the boundary with Huntington (the town of Huntington then included the present-day town of Babylon; they divided in the 1870s); see Appendix C-15 (RTOB, 1:347–49). Tackapousha received four large kettles, two guns, three coats, two gallons of "strong waters," two swords, four pairs of shoes and stockings, two "close" cloth coats, eight pounds of powder, and eight pounds of shot.

A month later, Tackapousha sold to John Richbell of Oyster Bay, the rights to all of the drift whales cast up on what is today the western portion of Jones Beach, from the Huntington border to Jones Inlet (DSBD, 2:67-68). Richbell agreed to pay Tackapousha wampum valued at £6 sterling for each whole whale carcass and a lesser sum for damaged or partial carcasses. Indians who carried the news of any beached whales would receive a shirt or some wampum.

The Huntington officials were alarmed about these agreements between their rivals in Oyster Bay and the Massapequa sachem. Fearing that Andrews and Richbell might again encroach on their town boundaries, and following Andrews' own example, Huntington called upon Wyandanch to review the deed and make certain that the existing town boundaries were clearly defined and guaranteed. Wyandanch confirmed the boundaries and assured Huntington that "if there appear any part thereof sold or confirmed by me to ye inhabitants of Huntington I will see the said Tackapousha and Chipyconnaw (Chopeyconnaws) shall abate what is reason. . . . And for confirmation of the premises I oblige myself and successors forever" (RTOB, 1:349). Wyandanch did not challenge Tackapousha's right to sell the land, but he again asserted his authority over the Massapequa sachem by acting as a guarantor of the deed boundaries.

Wyandanch's authority over the Corchaug lands on the North Fork of eastern Long Island, however, was not challenged by the local sachems. A year after he asserted his ownership of their lands, he sold Plum Island to Samuel Willys of Hartford (DSBD, 1:15). The question of rightful ownership concerned Willys who did not want to find himself in a lengthy dispute over his title. Willys met with Youngs and Wyandanch on Gardiners Island to draw up a deed which could survive any challenges in court.

Curiously, Gardiner did not witness the deed. Willys was careful to make sure that Wyandanch clearly stated that he was the true owner at the time of Willys' purchase and that he had not sold the island to anyone else in the past. Wyandanch swore that he was the "rightful owner of the said island and that I never before sold it to anyone nor received anything for it." This statement satisfied Willys, who then paid the sachem a barrel of biscuits, a coat, one hundred muxes, and some fish hooks for the island.

A memorandum was added to the bottom of the deed stating that John Youngs had sold all of his rights to the island to Willys. There was no mention of the price paid to Youngs, but it is safe to assume that it far exceeded the value of the goods given to Wyandanch. For the English, the transaction between Youngs and Willys was the "real" deed. They saw the settlement with Wyandanch as little more than a "nuisance" cost of dealing with Algonquian "presumptions" of sovereignty.

A few weeks later on May 12, 1659, Wyandanch and his young son, Wyancombone, gave to John Ogden a large tract of land from what is now the Shinnecock Canal to the village of Westhampton Beach, as a partial payment on the fine for arson in 1657 (Appendix D-11; RTSH, 2:354). Ogden had apparently purchased the debt from the Southampton officials who were unsuccessful in forcing payment from the Shinnecocks. The boundaries included some meadowland which had previously been leased to Thomas Halsey, probably under the same terms as Wyandanch had negotiated with Topping for meadowland on the western border of this deed. When Halsey's lease ran out, the land went to Ogden, but the small parcel of meadow along the south beach, which Gardiner had leased from Wyandanch in 1658 and turned over to John Cooper, was excluded from Ogden's deed. Wyandanch was careful to include a clause which protected the Indians' rights to fishing, hunting, and the gathering of wild plants in the area. The deed was witnessed by Lion Gardiner and his son David.

That same day Wyandanch, Gardiner, and their sons confirmed the purchase of a half neck of land by Jonas Wood in 1657 (RTH, 1:21–22). Apparently, Tackapousha and the Massapequa sachems challenged that purchase of Secatogue land from Keeossechok (RTH, 1:21n). Once again Wyandanch had asserted his authority over a major rival and, at the same time, served the English interests by helping to avoid another expensive and disruptive legal battle in the colonial courts.

The following month, Gardiner leased the whale rights to a section of the Atlantic beach running west from the boundary of the area he had purchased from Wyandanch the year before, to a place called "Kitchaminchoke" on Moriches Bay (DSBD, 2:85–86). The lease was to run for twenty-one years, and Wyandanch was to receive £5 sterling, or an equivalent amount of goods, for each whale carcass. The sachem reserved the tails and fins for himself. Gardiner then turned over the whale rights to John Cooper, who was beginning to develop a whaling enterprise which would soon become a major industry on the south shore of eastern Long Island.

On July 14, 1659, Wyandanch and his wife and son, signed a document which is, in effect, a last will and testament.

> Be it known unto all men, both English and Indians, especially those on Long Island, that I Wyandanch, sachem of Pamanack, with my wife and son, Wyancombone, my only son and heir, having deliberately considered how this past twenty-four years we have . . .

received much kindness of him [Lion Gardiner] and from him, not only by counsel and advice in our prosperity, but in our great extremity, when we were almost swallowed up of our enemies, then we say he appeared to us not only as a friend, but as a father, in giving us his money and goods, whereby we defended ourselves, and ransomed my daughter and friends, and we say and know that by his means we had great comfort and relief from the most honorable English nation heare about us; so seeing that we yet live, and both of us being now old, and not that wee at any time have given him any thing to gratify his fatherly love, care, and charge, we having nothing left that is worth his acceptance but a small tract of land which we desire him to accept of for his himself, his heirs, executors and assignes forever (DSBD, 2:118–19).

The land granted to Gardiner was no small tract. It included 30,000 acres of prime land between Huntington and Setauket which dramatically increased in value over the years (Wunderlich 1989:9; Tooker 1962:20–21; Smith, 1882:2–3). The tract included most of the present-day town of Smithtown (Appendix C-16; RTSM, 1:16–17).[3] Soon after Wyandanch's death, Gardiner sold a portion of the tract to Richard Smith of Smithtown, who had signed as a witness to the will.

Sometime during these last months of Wyandanch's life, he sold two small parcels of land north of the village of Setauket on the north shore (Appendix C-17; RTBH, Hutchinson:16; Tooker 1980:185). Unfortunately, neither of these deeds are dated, but they were very likely negotiated in the spring or summer of that year when he was so actively involved in land transactions. The inhabitants paid the sachem six coats, six kettles, one brass gun, one trooper's coat, ten knives, one pair of shoes, two pounds of powder, two pounds of lead, twenty muxes, and forty needles for the land.

The last document signed by the aging sachem was another lease of whale rights to Lion Gardiner. This twenty-one year lease was for the beach extending west from the former boundary at Kitchaminchoke to Enaughquamuck, which Tooker believed to be Moriches Inlet (RTSH, 2:34–35). Wyandanch and his heirs were to receive £5 for each whole carcass, but the money would not be paid until two years after the oil and bone had been processed and sold. If there were not at least four or five whales beached during the twenty-one year period, Gardiner would receive the next five whales no matter how long it took. The sachem, of course, reserved the fins and tails of the beached whales for himself and his people. This beach land extended westward into the territory of the Unkechaugs, so the agreement had to be acknowledged by sachems Tobacus and Wenakceaskam. They both testified that the whale rights on the beach belonged to Wyandanch and his heirs and "not ours nor our heirs."

Some time after this, according to Lion Gardiner, Wyandanch was poisoned. Unfortunately, Gardiner gives no further details nor is the incident mentioned in any of the surviving colonial documents. There were many rival sachems including Tobacus, Tackapousha, and the Corchaug sachems who may have wished him ill because of his role in selling their lands. Death by poisoning was not uncommon in the power struggles among Algonquian sachems. Uncas, Ninigret, and Wyandanch himself were all rumored, at one time or another, to have plotted with sachems to poison a rival. It is also quite possible that an Englishman might have used this method to throw suspicion on an Indian.

Wyandanch's passing was one of the events which marked the end of an era in Indian-white relations on Long Island—an era characterized by the scramble of imperial powers at one level, and aggressive individual entrepreneurs at another, to establish and defend claims to as much land as possible. The other important events were the death of Lion Gardiner in 1663, the English conquest of New Netherland in 1664, and the great plague which, according to Lion Gardiner, took the lives of an estimated two-thirds of the Algonquian population in 1660 and 1661 (L. Gardiner 1980:146).

There was no longer a need for a "Grand Sachem" of Long Island.[4] The growth of the English settlements and the declining Indian population shifted the demographics heavily in favor of the whites. The English were now in a position to dominate the Algonquian people. The need for a single Indian leader who could arbitrate disputes and control local sachems, however, was now over. In 1665, Richard Nicolls, the first governor of the newly established colony of New York, officially declared that there was no longer any "grand sachem" of Long Island. "Every sachem," said the governor, "shall keep his particular property over his people as formerly" (DSBD, 2:127). The English, who had created the position of grand sachem, had now abolished it.

## "Melted down by this disease": The Smallpox Epidemics of 1659–1664 on Long Island

European diseases, such as smallpox, measles, and several other unidentified viruses, took a frightful toll of Native American lives during the seventeenth century (Dobyns 1983). These virulent pestilences had been active in Europe for centuries and continued to take thousands of lives there in spite of a natural immunity which had developed over the centuries of exposure. London, for example, averaged more than 5,000 deaths per year from smallpox from 1681 to 1690. Although the disease flourished in the crowded urban slums, no one was entirely safe, not even royalty. Queen Mary contracted the disease and died from it in 1694. The Indians, however, who had no immunity at all to the European germs, died in far greater numbers. When smallpox was first introduced to the New World by Cortez's troops in 1520, over three million Indians died within two years (Shurkin 1979:104).

The psychological impact of the epidemics added to the suffering. The silent killers respected no one. Women, children, the elderly, the weak, and the strong were struck down in the same relentless manner. The Algonquian shamans were helpless to relieve the fears or the agony of the victims. The traditional healing rituals and practices actually aided in the rapid spread of the highly infectious diseases. When relatives came to take part in the group ceremonies (see Chapter 5 above), they crowded around the patient to give support and comfort. The close interaction enabled the virus to infect most of the well-intended visitors, and in a very short time the whole village was often wiped out (Stearn and Stearn 1945:27).

The first great epidemic to be documented spread through southern New England from 1616 to 1619, destroying an estimated seventy percent of the Algonquian population (Cook 1973:499; Thomas 1979:53–55). The disease responsible has not been determined to everyone's satisfaction, but it was probably either a virulent hepatitis (Spiess and Spiess 1987:79) or a form of the bubonic plague (Cook 1973:489). There is no record of this epidemic on Long Island, but the close kinship connections linking the communities on both shores of the Sound would have facilitated its spread to the eastern villages.

The first documented smallpox outbreak struck in the winter of 1633 and spread throughout the Great Lakes region, Canada, and New England. The outbreak was followed by a string of epidemics which lasted for eight more years (Cook 1973:492). The epidemic may have spread to Long Island, because Adriaen van der Donck was told by an Algonquian informant that before the smallpox broke out, the Indians "were ten times as numerous and that their population had been melted down by this disease, whereof nine-tenths of them have died" (quoted in Jennings 1976:25). The disease took such a swift and complete toll in the villages that the traditional burial ceremonies were abandoned. William Bradford reported that "many did rot above the ground for want of burial" (1981:302).

The outbreak in 1659 reported by Lion Gardiner is not described in any other documents from that time, but the East Hampton records indicate that the Montauketts were still suffering from the ravages of smallpox five years later. Early in 1664, the town passed a resolution isolating Indians from any contact with whites. "It is ordered that no Indian shall come to town . . . upon penalty of paying 5 s[hillings] or be whiped untill they be free of the small poxe" (RTEH, 1:201). Montauketts who wished to trade their corn with the whites had to stop outside the village limits and call to the townspeople to come out to meet them.

Another brief mention of the epidemic comes several years later from Daniel Denton, who said that in the area around the Hempstead settlement "where there were six towns, they are reduced to two small villages" (1968:7). Unfortunately, we have no documented census figures for the Algonquian peoples of Long Island, either before or after the epidemic. Although the total population was drastically reduced, there were Indian communities scattered all across Long Island. Fifty years later Azariah Horton, the energetic missionary preacher, addressed groups of Indians from Brooklyn to Montauk, and today, over three hundred years later, there are four surviving Indian communities—two reservations and two groupings of enclaves. Denton is wrong, however, when he attributes warfare between Indians as another cause of population decline. Intertribal conflicts seldom took a heavy toll of life, as Denton himself noted later in the same 1670 account (1968:9). Wars waged by the Dutch and English, in contrast, took a heavy toll of Indian men, women, and children. It should also be noted that many of those conflicts between Indians which occurred in the seventeenth century were provoked or directed by Europeans.

It is difficult for the modern reader to understand or appreciate the suffering that the more virulent forms of smallpox inflicted on their victims. The virus is carried through the air in moist droplets, which enter the victim's respiratory system and spread throughout the body. During the first stage of the illness the victim suffered chills alternating with fever, headache, nausea, vomiting, severe backache, and dizziness. Generally, on the third or fourth day, the "eruptive" stage began. Sores filled with pus broke out all over the body, including the mouth and nasal passages, making it difficult to swallow and breathe. The stench from the sores was unbearable. The virus soon attacked the heart, liver, and lungs. Sometimes the blood vessels burst, causing the victim to bleed from the mouth.[5]

William Bradford wrote the following description of the suffering experienced by Indians living along the Connecticut River in 1634:

> This spring, also, those Indians . . . there fell sick of ye small poxe, and died most miserably: for a sorer disease can not befall them: they fear it more that ye plague: for usually they . . . fall into a lamentable condition as they lye on their hard mats: ye pox breaking the mattering, and running into one another, their skin cleaving . . . to the mats . . . when they turn them a whole side will flea off at once and they will be all of a gore blood, most fearful to behold; and they being very sore . . . they die like rotten sheep.

The suffering was compounded, said Bradford, because whole households and villages were stricken at once leaving no one in condition to aid the others, no one to make a fire, bring water, or to bury the dead. "Some would crawl out on all fours to get a little water, and sometimes die by ye way, not able to get up againe" (1981:302).

The devastating loss of population weakened the Algonquian people and undermined their capacity to resist the steadily increasing European intervention into their community affairs. An era had ended. The Algonquian people were now forced to adopt new strategies to ensure their survival in the midst of the rapidly expanding English communities. These strategies included merger with other Indian communities, intermarriage with African Americans, and geographic relocation (Axtell 1992:103-21).

## Summary

The English and Dutch wanted to establish a stable relationship with the Algonquian sachems which would enable them to negotiate the transfer of land and resolve conflicts without violence. The English formed an alliance with

Wyandanch for this purpose and proclaimed him to be the "grand sachem" of Long Island. A short time later, the Dutch formed a similar relationship with Tackapousha.

The two sachems, who saw these alliances as an opportunity to increase their power and influence, cooperated with the Europeans and facilitated the transfer of land titles. They were both well aware that they had few options left now that the Europeans had established military superiority over them. On occasion, however, both Wyandanch and Tackapousha used their influence and their knowledge of European political institutions to defend themselves and their people from exploitation.

As the English settlements expanded, town officials and independent entrepreneurs increased their efforts to obtain titles to adjacent tracts of land. The negotiations with local sachems to purchase these lands continued to be complicated by the vast cultural differences between the Algonquian peoples and the English discussed earlier in Chapters 7 and 8. The English and Dutch did not view the Algonquian land claims as legitimate equivalents to European property ownership. Many Algonquian sachems, in spite of the precise language in the deeds, viewed the sales as a lease rather than as the permanent transfer of absolute control over the land.

Wyandanch was proclaimed "Grand Sachem" of Long Island by the English and sent to supervise most major land sales from 1657 until his death two years later. His involvement in these affairs undoubtedly made him some enemies in both English and Algonquian communities. According to a brief comment by Lion Gardiner, Wyandanch was poisoned by persons unknown. His passing, along with the English conquest of New Netherland in 1664 and the smallpox epidemic of 1659–1664, marked the end of an era characterized by the scramble of imperial powers and aggressive entrepreneurs to establish and defend claims to as much land as they could.

The smallpox epidemic, according to Lion Gardiner, took the lives of two-thirds of the Algonquian people on Long Island. Daniel Denton, writing in 1670 reported that six Algonquian settlements near Hempstead had been reduced to two by the epidemic. Although we do not know what the population base was before the disease struck, it was not, as some writers have suggested, the first stage in the "final extinction" of the Long Island Indians.

# 10

# Dispossession and Survival, 1660–1703

During the latter half of the seventeenth century, the English population overwhelmed the Algonquian peoples, pushing them into small enclaves scattered across Long Island. As more and more of their ancient hunting grounds were cleared for agricultural production, and their dependency on manufactured tools and other trade goods increased, the Indians were drawn into the European economic system. Once the fur and wampum trade waned, the only things of value to the Europeans were the Indians' land and their labor. By the beginning of the eighteenth century, all of the land, except for a few small parcels, was gone and most native peoples were working as domestics, unskilled laborers, guides, and seamen (Strong 1995a:13–15). Sachems such as Tackapousha (Massapequa), and his brother, Chopeyconnaws, Suscaneman (Matinecock), Tobacus (Unkechaug), Poniute (Montaukett), Quashawam (Sunksquaw of the Montaukett), and Pongumo (Shinnecock), saw their power and influence gradually decline following the defeat of King Philip (Metacomet) in 1675.

### Tackapousha and the Dutch, 1660–1664

After the death of Wyandanch, Tackapousha emerged as the most influential sachem on Long Island. He proved to be a skillful diplomat, adept at manipulating both his adversaries and his allies. Tackapousha took full advantage of the tensions between the Dutch authorities in New Amsterdam and the English settlers at Hempstead. He also learned, as had Uncas, Ninigret, and Wyandanch, how to adapt the political skills and powers of persuasion required of an Algonquian sachem to the European political system.

Tackapousha immediately assumed Wyandanch's role in the land transactions with the English towns on western Long Island. On January 21, 1660, Tackapousha confirmed his previous sale of meadowland to Oyster Bay and received a coat, two kettles, two swords, shoes and stockings, and four yards of linen from John Richbell, one of the Oyster Bay pur-

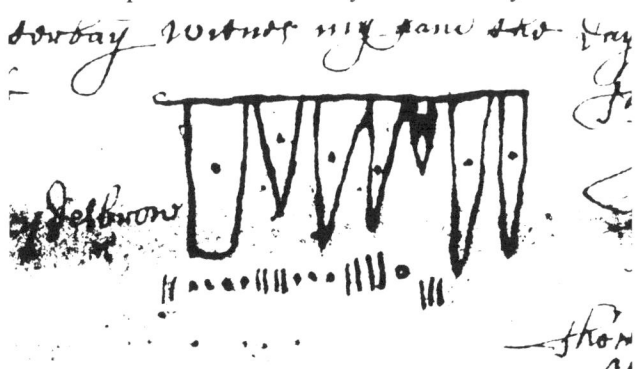

Fig. 10.1. Drawing on January 21, 1660 deed

chasers. Cockenoe signed as a witness and may have served as an interpreter (RTOB, 1:350).[1]

The Massapequa sachem kept in close touch with the Dutch on all matters relating to Algonquian affairs. The most pressing area of concern for the Dutch in the early spring of 1660 was the threat of a major conflict with the Esopus Indians in the mid-Hudson Valley (see Appendix B map). The previous fall, Dutch soldiers had opened fire on a small group of Esopus men who had been drinking heavily near the settlement. They killed one man and took another prisoner (O'Callaghan 1966, 2:396; Trelease 1971:152). The Indians retaliated in a series of attacks and laid siege to the Dutch settlement. When Stuyvesant sent out an appeal to the towns on Long Island for volunteers to march against the Esopus, twenty-six Massapequas, probably with Tackapousha's encouragement, joined the expedition. The troops sailed up the Hudson to the Esopus territory, but the Esopus abandoned the siege and retreated, refusing to engage the Dutch in open combat. In frustration, Stuyvesant left some supplies and a few men at the settlement and returned to New Amsterdam.

The Dutch, fearing that the Esopus would seek alliances with the Hackensacks, the Wiechquaesgecks, and the Long Island Indians, invited these groups to come to New Amsterdam for a peace conference. As Stuyvesant promised in the treaty of 1656, Tackapousha was included in this peace settlement as a partner to the Dutch. The treaty, signed on March 6, 1660, guaranteed that the Dutch would protect the Massapequas from their enemies, and it successfully isolated the Esopus from their potential allies in the southern Hudson valley (NYCD, 13:147–49; Trelease 1971:156–57).

Tackapousha was soon to make use of the leverage the Massapequas had earned with the Dutch. A month after the treaty was signed, he complained to Stuyvesant that the Hempstead settlers were trespassing on Matinecock lands, building fences and threatening to burn their wigwams if they did not move from their land within eight days time (NYCD, 14:460; Marshall 1962:50). Stuyvesant interceded, ordering Hempstead not to take the threatened action against the Matinecocks. He further ordered both parties to come to New Amsterdam to present their arguments.

John Hicks presented the Hempstead case to Stuyvesant, claiming the land in question had been purchased and that the Indians simply refused to move. They also complained that the dogs from the Matinecock villages were a constant threat to English livestock. Stuyvesant, however, had also received complaints from Indians who had begun to experiment with domesticated animals that their hogs and cattle were often stolen by settlers who slaughtered them and sold the meat (NYDH, 1:422). Tackapousha brushed aside the complaint about the dogs and repeated the arguments he had made two years before, stating that he had only sold grazing rights to the settlers. He told Stuyvesant that his people had already planted their crops and could not abandon the fields now. They needed the food in order to survive the winter (NYCD, 14:474).

Stuyvesant, who had rejected an appeal from Hicks and the Hempstead settlers for troops to attack the Matinecocks in 1658, again ruled against the settlers. He ordered that the Matinecocks did not have to move until after their harvest, but he made no mention about what was to happen after that. On the question of the dogs, Stuyvesant ruled against Tackapousha. He ordered that the Matinecocks would have to kill their "great dogs." The damages to livestock by Indian dogs, as noted above, had been a source of contention from the time of the first European settlements and continued as such into the next century. The Matinecocks, as did most other Algonquian committees, resisted all efforts to reduce their dog population because the dogs were an integral part of village life (see Chapter 2). It is unlikely that the Matinecocks did much more than make a token gesture to please the settlers.

Stuyvesant also addressed the Indians' complaints about the theft of their livestock by whites. Taking note that there were confirmed reports of such thefts "by Christians, or by men who go by the name of Christians," he ordered that no animals could be slaughtered without notifying the local magistrate and obtaining a permit (NYDH, 1:423). Stuyvesant's intervention had prevented an outbreak of violence, but the bad feelings between Tackapousha and the Hempstead settlers continued.

Stuyvesant's attention was turned again to the Esopus who had renewed their raids in late March. By the end of the summer of 1660, however, the Dutch negotiated a settlement ending the hostilities. Although a treaty was signed, Stuyvesant angered the Esopus by deporting eleven of his prisoners to the West Indies and told the Esopus sachems that they must now regard the captives "as dead" (O'Callaghan 1966, 2:419–20). Although the eleven captives were later returned to New Netherland, the Esopus, a fiercely independent people, deeply resented Stuyvesant's actions and the Esopus sachems never forgave him.

The Dutch again invited Tackapousha to take part in the peace agreement and again gave him assurance that they would provide assistance if an enemy threatened the Massapequas. In September, Tackapousha sent an envoy to New Amsterdam with a gift of wampum to "renew" the peace treaty and reported that Ninigret had again raided the Algonquian villages on the east end. He reminded the Dutch of their promise of aid and requested a supply of powder and shot from the Dutch. Tackapousha was probably much more concerned about the settlers at Hempstead than he was about the remote possibility of an attack by Ninigret. He knew, however, that the Dutch would never grant him ammunition to use against the whites. His attempt to manipulate the Dutch failed. Stuyvesant, who had refused to send military aid to Hempstead, also rejected Tackapousha's request.

In 1661, the controversy over the Matinecock lands became even more complicated when the town of Oyster Bay contested Hempstead's claim to the lands lying to the east of Hempstead Harbor. The land was within the Hempstead patent but, as Tackapousha also argued, it was not included in the Indian deed.

Oyster Bay demanded that the Hempstead settlers stop cutting grass on this land. The towns were still at an impasse in 1663, when Hempstead announced that it was subdividing all of the land between Hempstead Harbor and Oyster Bay and opening it up to settlement. The dispute between the towns, however, prevented the subdivision from taking place (Marshall 1962:130–33). No mention was made by either side about Tackapousha's claim that the land still belonged to the Matinecocks.

A new outbreak of fighting between the Esopus, who lived in the area around present-day Kingston, New York, and the Dutch interrupted the land controversy. The uneasy peace with the Esopus ended in 1663, when the Dutch attempted to found a new settlement in their territory. The Esopus attacked both settlements and Stuyvesant turned once again to the towns around New Amsterdam for military recruits (Trelease 1971:160–62). Stuyvesant promised that every soldier who joined the Dutch force could keep any captives he took as his own property.

In spite of this incentive, the English settlers, who were not enthusiastic about helping the Dutch, sent only five or six men to Stuyvesant. Tackapousha, sensing an opportunity to win Dutch gratitude and gain some political advantage in his conflict with Hempstead, sent a troop of forty-six men under the command of his younger brother, Chopeyconnaws. The Long Island Indians served under Martin Crieger, who had fought in the campaigns against the Indians on the Delaware (Ruttenber, 1872:149). After a frustrating campaign in which they destroyed deserted villages and burned corn fields, but did not manage to engage the Esopus in a single battle, the Matinecocks told Crieger that they were going back home (Trelease 1971:162–64). Crieger offered them payments of wampum if they would stay, but they refused (NYCD, 14:286).

After the Matinecocks left, Crieger finally located a fortified village and attacked before the Esopus could escape. His troops killed over thirty people, burned the village, and destroyed most of their corn supply. Finally, in the spring of 1664, after a winter of near starvation, the Esopus negotiated a peace settlement with the Dutch.

The peace settlement may have encouraged the expansion of the towns on western Long Island. Small groups of English investors purchased, from the Algonquian owners, tracts of land near Gravesend (DSBD, 3:1–2), Flatbush (Stiles 1867, 1:77–78), and Jamaica (DSBD, 2:163, 235). The increase in the English towns under Dutch control undoubtedly played a role in the collapse of the New Netherland colony in the early summer of 1664. Ironically, only two months after the Dutch victory over the Esopus, the English invaded and conquered New Netherland.

## Governor Nicolls and the Long Island Sachems

When Richard Nicolls, the commander of the victorious English troops, became governor, he called for representatives from the Long Island towns to come to a convention in Hempstead and pressed them to accept a code of laws which he had drafted and aptly labeled the "Duke's Laws" (Lincoln 1894:7–83). With considerable reluctance, the elected officials accepted these laws in spite of the fact that their request for an elected colonial assembly had been rejected. Although no Algonquian sachems participated, the English assumed jurisdiction over them as the self-evident right of Christians to govern "barbarians" within their boundaries.

The number of Algonquian people living on Long Island at the time is not known. The population estimate, set at one thousand by some historians, is probably too low, but the demographics had certainly shifted strongly in favor of the colonists, who numbered about ten thousand (Trelease 1971:178). Nevertheless, the Indians were a significant constituency in the Duke of York's newly established colony and required the governor's careful attention.

Once the Duke's Laws were in place, the dispossession of Indian land continued. In April 1665, the towns of Gravesend and Amersfoort purchased tracts of land from local sachems (DSBD, 3:3, 33). Later that spring, the Gravesend settlers bought another tract of land on the south shore from sachem Tanganawamans (DSBD, 3:5–6).

Nicolls wanted the process of dispossession to continue as peacefully as possible. He met for three days with the Long Island sachems in the following fall to discuss issues of mutual concern (DSBD, 2:123–27; Strong and Karabag 1991:197–98). On the first day, he ruled that the title of "Chiefe Sachem" was no longer valid and that local sachems alone had control over their lands. He met the next day with Wyandanch's daughter, Quashawam, the Montaukett sunksquaw and the East Hampton magistrates to resolve several long standing disputes.[2] Most of the issues were related to the provisions of the treaty Wyandanch had negotiated with East Hampton ten years before. They were very similar to those raised by Hempstead and nearly every other Long Island town at one time or another during the seventeenth century—damage done by English livestock to Indian planting grounds, damage done to English livestock by Indians and their dogs, the use of Indian planting fields after the harvest and before spring planting by the English for grazing, controversies over boundary lines, and English objections to the seasonal burning of the planting grounds and the lands around the villages.

Quashawam reached an agreement with East Hampton, marking her western border with East Hampton at Fort Pond where the present-day village of Montauk is located. She also confirmed the eastern and western boundaries of the Shinnecock lands. Such boundary designations were becoming increasingly important as the process of dispossession progressed. The town of Southampton, for example, tied its boundaries to the land which the Shinnecocks "owned" before the whites arrived. The boundary between Southampton and Southold was finally settled in court by testimony from Indian witnesses who convinced a jury that the land in question had belonged to the Shinnecocks.

Quashawam and East Hampton also reached an accommodation on some of the other issues. The English wanted the Montauketts to stop their seasonal burning of the planting grounds so that they could graze their livestock there from October through March. In return, East Hampton agreed to pay compensation for any damage done to Montaukett crops by their cattle. Quashawam, perhaps aware of the complaints by Tackapousha and other Algonquian sachems about whites who "reinterpreted" grazing rights to mean absolute possession, had a memorandum added to the agreement stating that the permission to graze cattle on Montauk did not compromise her title to the land.

The meeting with the sachems convinced Nicolls that the process of dispossession was going to be a long struggle. He realized that he would frequently be called upon to serve in the difficult role as arbiter between contending interests. In an attempt to keep in touch with these problems in the far reaches of eastern Long Island, he appointed a commission "to determine differences between Christians and Indians" (DSBD, 2:49–50). Nicolls charged the commissioners to make sure that all parties honored the settlement involving Quashawam, East Hampton, and Southampton. Unfortunately, the commissioners generally supported the interests of the local whites and soon lost their credibility with the Indians.

The Duke's Laws set forth the general framework for Governor Nicolls' Indian policy. The laws were organized into categories, such as "assaults," "Indians," "summons," and so forth, all in alphabetical order. The provisions relating to Indians provide important insights into the developments which were taking place within the Algonquian communities during the latter half of the seventeenth century.

The first entry under the "Indian" category addressed the governor's most pressing concern—the orderly and peaceful acquisition of Algonquian land. The provisions in the code read as follows:

> No purchase of lands from Indians after the first day of March, 1665, shall be esteemed a good title without leave first had and obtained from the Governor and after leave so obtained, the purchasers shall bring the sachem and right owner of the lands before the Governor to acknowledge satisfaction and payment for the said lands whereupon they shall have a grant from the governor and the purchase so made and prosecuted is to be entered upon record in the office and from that time to be valid to all intents and purposes (Lincoln 1894:40–42).

The governor was putting the towns and the individual entrepreneurs on notice that he was going to supervise all land purchases in an attempt to bring some order to the chaotic scramble for Indian land. Quarrels continually erupted between individual entrepreneurs and town officials, between towns over boundary lines, and between Indians and settlers over interpretations of deeds (Marshall 1962:125–48; Street 1882:12–13, 17–18; Smith 1882:6–8). It was a mess. The courts were full of trespass suits, leading one historian to comment that the seventeenth century was the "golden age" of lawyers on Long Island. In fact, the legal squabbles lasted well beyond the seventeenth century, in spite of the best efforts of Nicolls and his successors. Nicolls was also worried that the rush to obtain title to Indian land might push the Indians to rebellion and disrupt the progress of economic development.

The new procedures established in the Duke's Laws did not mean that the English view of Indian sovereignty had changed. The law was designed primarily as a practical matter to keep the peace. The governor knew that if the Indians were cheated, they might react violently or cause some other disturbance. His primary concern was the peaceful economic development of the colony. The English viewed the Indian land claims as annoying impediments in the inevitable growth of their towns.

The difficulties inherent in the relations between Nicolls' English and Indian constituencies very quickly became apparent. The October 1666 meeting of the Court of Assizes, a body created under the Duke's Laws consisting of the governor, his councilors, and the justices of the peace from each administrative subdivision of the colony, was confronted with complaints from Indians living on both ends of the island, as well as from two rival groups of English in Southampton who had purchased the same land from two different Shinnecock groups. The Matinecocks petitioned the governor about the Hempstead settlers who were encroaching on their lands (RTOB, 2:669), and the Shinnecocks complained that they were "too much straightened by ye inhabitants" of Southampton (NYCD, 14:589). The Shinnecocks were concerned about damages to their crops by English livestock and wanted proper fencing to be constructed. The governor ordered the town of Southampton to share the costs of the fence construction with the Shinnecocks.

The conflicting land claims in Southampton also required the governor's intervention. Nicolls called the parties into New York to settle a dispute, to present their arguments about their claims to land lying west of the town of Southampton. The land included the tract which Wyandanch had given to John Ogden to pay off a part of the fine imposed on the Shinnecocks for the arson incident in 1657. The property passed through two owners and was finally purchased by the town of Southampton.

In 1662, the same land, which had not been occupied by the town, was sold to Thomas Topping, an independent entrepreneur, by a Shinnecock sunksquaw named Weany (see Appendix D-12 map; Strong and Karabag 1991:200). A long and bitter controversy between Topping and the town forced Nicolls' intervention (Pelletreau 1882:8–9). Nicolls called all of the parties to come to a hearing and present their evidence. After listening to them, he ruled that the property belonged to the town of Southampton. Rather than attempting to determine the validity of the two deeds, he simply required the town to pay Topping £5 sterling and made certain that the two Shinnecock groups were satisfied with their payments. The relative legitimacy of the two aboriginal titles was of little concern to Nicolls.

The Matinecocks' complaint posed a more difficult problem. Nicolls appointed John Underhill, who had commanded troops in two brutal massacres of Indian villages, to represent the Matinecocks in the court hearing (RTOB, 2:668). Underhill, now a citizen of Oyster Bay, had his own interest to protect. He wanted the governor to invalidate the Hempstead title because he was negotiating to purchase some of the Matinecock lands himself. In fact, he was one of the first of the English settlers on the Matinecock lands. Underhill, whose wife and son were Quakers, had other reasons to dislike the Hempstead officials. These officials had let it be known that if their claims to the Matinecock lands were upheld, they would not allow Quakers to reside there.

Nicolls listened to the arguments presented by Underhill and the Hempstead officials, but rather than resolve the question of ownership he attempted to press a settlement on the Indians by offering them some blankets and planting rights on the land if they would sign "a firm and absolute deed of conveyance of the said land to the inhabitants of Hempstead" (RTOB, 2:669). The Matinecocks agreed not to molest the families who had established farmsteads on Matinecock land, but they refused to sell any of the land to Hempstead. The governor also failed to reconcile the rival claims of Oyster Bay and Hempstead to the Matinecock land. The troublesome refusal of the Matinecocks to transfer their lands to the English remained unresolved.

On eastern Long Island, however, the pace of dispossession was proceeding in a manner which must have pleased Nicolls. On June 10, 1664, shortly before Nicolls arrived with his conquering army, three deeds were negotiated between the settlers in what is now the town of Brookhaven and the Algonquian peoples from Setauket and Unkechaug (Bayles 1882:3). One of these, negotiated with the Unkechaug sachem, Tobacus, was a tract of land between present-day Bellport and the Carmans River, running from the middle of the island to the south shore (Appendix C-18; Tooker 1962:4–5, 295–96; RTBH, Hutchinson:10–11). The second small tract was purchased from a sunksquaw, who, unfortunately, is not named, and a sachem named Massetewse. The land appears to be located somewhere near Mount Sinai (RTBH, Hutchinson:12–13; Gramley and Gwynne 1982:186). A third sachem, Mayhew, sold a small tract of land in the same area on the same day (RTBH, Hutchinson:13).

Conflicts over boundary lines prompted some of the towns to negotiate confirmation agreements for land purchased earlier. The town of Southold, for example, confirmed the previous deeds to the North Fork in 1665. The southern border of the tract was in dispute between the towns of Southampton and Southold for several years.

The central question in the dispute was whether the Shinnecocks or the Corchaugs owned the land prior to the English purchases. Southold maintained that they had purchased from the Corchaugs in 1649, the land south of the Peconic

River to Red Creek, a small stream flowing into Peconic Bay about two miles south of present-day Riverhead (see Chapter 7). Southampton claimed that the land had belonged to the Shinnecocks and therefore the Corchaugs had no right to sell it to Southold (Pelletreau 1882:12–13).

The problem, of course, was that the arguments were based upon European concepts of political organization and property which they arbitrarily imposed on Algonquian realities. The towns had no patience with such complexities as kinship ties, vaguely defined hunting territories, or symbolic gestures of temporary land use rights. They simply wanted testimony which provided a "European" rationale acceptable in the colonial courts.

In the spring of 1667, the two towns held a meeting in the Southampton schoolhouse to discuss the issue (NYCD, 14:600–2). Several Corchaug and Shinnecock men were brought in to testify about the "ancient boundaries." The Algonquian men told the town officials that it was their custom to recognize hunting territory by giving symbolic gifts to the sachem who held the rights to use the land in question. Any outsider who came on the land was required to honor the territorial rights of the "owner" by sending gifts such as young eaglets found in nests or the skins of deer or bear that drowned. One of the Shinnecocks testified that at one time a bear had been drowned in the territory south of the Peconic. The skin and grease were carried to the Shinnecocks to honor and recognize their authority over the hunting area.

After the meeting, the Southampton officials collected more testimony to bolster their case. They sent to Montauk for two elderly Montaukett women, who had lived on the south bank of the Peconic as children. The women had probably married Montaukett men and left their home village to live with their husbands.

One of the women testified that the Shinnecocks had won control over the land south of the Peconic in a war many years before, and that this was affirmed when her people killed a bear in that area and took the skin to the Shinnecock sunksquaw. She knew this to be true, she said, pointing to her teeth, because she had eaten meat from that same bear. She also identified the sunksquaw as the "old Montaukett" sachem's sister and wife of a Shinnecock man named Ackkonmi.

The woman's account suggests that these groups may have had a patrilocal residence pattern and a matrilineal or bilineal system of property rights inheritance, but the data base is far too small to demonstrate a consistent pattern (Grumet 1990:19–23). It does clearly indicate, however, that women played an important role in village affairs. The skin was sent to the sunksquaw, not to her husband, indicating that she was the primary authority at Shinnecock for such matters.

It should be noted that the English clerk did not record the names of any of the women involved, yet he carefully took down the names of all the Algonquian men. This reflects the prevailing English view of female status and distorts our understanding of the role played by women in Algonquian society. There were undoubtedly many other women who played important roles in village affairs whose names and actions were ignored by the English observers (see Strong 1996b).

The two towns argued bitterly over the land case throughout the following summer. Southampton finally brought suit in the colonial court and won its case (NYCD, 14:602). The jury awarded the land to Southampton, and Southold immediately appealed the ruling. The appeals court recommended that the towns meet again and work out their differences, but the verdict was not revoked. Finally, the colonial authorities in New York intervened, sending two representatives to mediate the dispute. They managed to work out a compromise which gave most of the land to Southampton.

### "They take our land away every day, a little and a little"

Governor Francis Lovelace, Nicolls' successor who arrived in the spring of 1667, continued the campaign to free the land for development. He soon learned that, in spite of Nicolls' efforts to establish orderly procedures, the situation had not improved very much. The previous October, Governor Nicolls had managed to get the town of Hempstead to disclaim its title to the lands lying to the east of Matinecock and acknowledge that the property belonged to Oyster Bay (Paltsits 1910, 2:569–70). The Hempstead men remained adamant, however, that the Matinecock lands belonged to them.

There was probably little else that Nicolls could have done anyway because the scramble for land, driven by the greed of the English entrepreneurs and complicated by cultural misunderstandings, was inherently unstable. This became evident a few months after Lovelace arrived, when a group of Matinecocks led by Asharoken (spelled "Aseton" here,[3] the sachem who had negotiated one of the earliest deeds with the English twenty years before), Arumpas, and Sehar defied Hempstead and met with a small group of men from Oyster Bay at John Underhill's home and negotiated the sale of seven parcels of land ranging in size from four to sixty acres (Cocks 1961:2–4; RTOB, 1:80-81, 89–90, 629, 682–84).

Asharoken and one of the purchasers, Robert Williams, had a relationship that dated back to 1648 when Asharoken witnessed a deed between Williams and Pugnipan, another Matinecock sachem (RTOB, 1:625). Both men were well aware of the cultural differences regarding property ownership, but it seems clear that Asharoken now understood the English market system somewhat better and was attempting to get a better deal for him and his people by restricting land sales to small tracts rather than selling off huge parcels of thousands of acres at one time for a small payment. In this manner, he could guarantee a steady income for an extended period of time.

The following February, John Underhill purchased one hundred and fifty acres from the sachems (RTOB, 1:681-82). The deeds, understandably, were quite similar. They described the property, identified Asharoken and the others as the owners, and stated that the Matinecocks had "received full satisfaction" for the land, but did not cite the actual payment. The tracts were about the right size for a modest family farmstead (Hawke 1988:32–39). We can get some idea of the market value of the property because Simson sold his forty acre tract seven years later for £70 sterling (RTOB, 1:90). The Matinecocks had taken over more control of the deed process, and they improved their bargaining position, but they certainly did not receive anything close to the market price in the English economy.

These sales apparently prompted the Hempstead magistrates to again challenge the Matinecocks' right to sell this land. Tackapousha became involved with the case because he had signed the deeds in 1657 and 1658 as a representative of the Matinecocks, but he denied that he ever had the authority to sell Matinecock land. In March 1668, after nearly two years at an impasse, Tackapousha sent an angry testimonial to Governor Francis Lovelace, denouncing the Hempstead men as liars and maintaining once again that the Matinecocks still owned the lands which ran from Hempstead Harbor eastward to Oyster Bay. His statement was endorsed by four other sachems, Pamelaci, Nimhi, Wompatan, and Shoskcock, who stated that the Hempstead men were liars (RTOB, 1:677–78). This document included a map of the Matinecock lands drawn under Tackapousha's direction (see fig. 10.2). Tackapousha's statement was taken at

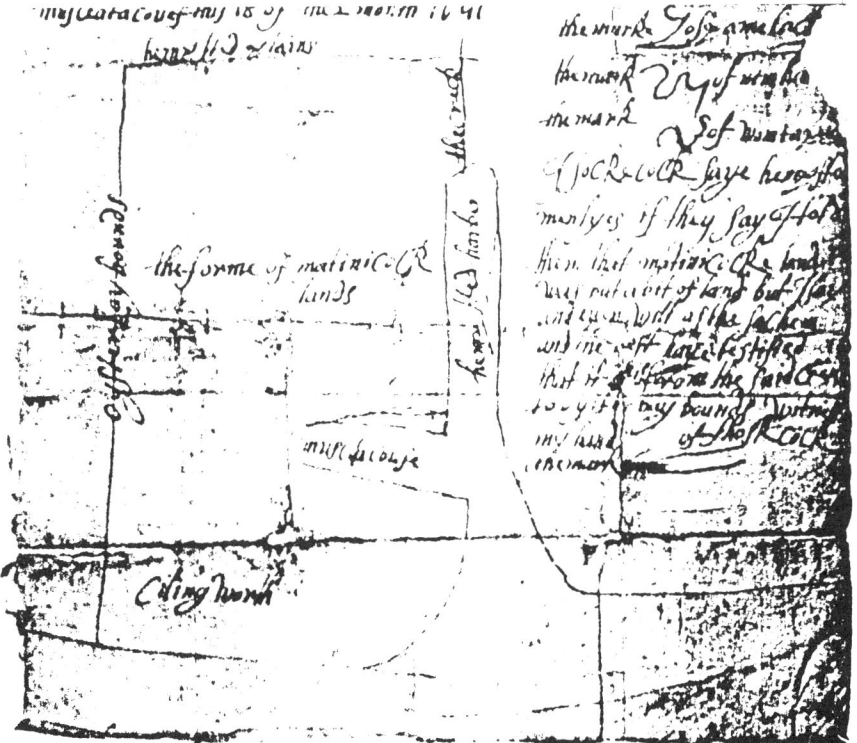

Fig. 10.2. Tackapousha's map of the Matinecock lands looking south, 1668

Killingworth, the name Underhill had given to his home in honor of his ancestral home in England (Cocks 1961:1–11). Underhill's home had apparently become an informal headquarters for the Oyster Bay men. John Underhill, Henry Redock, and two of the new property owners, William Simson and John Dyer were there to witness the testimony.

On May 24, 1668, Ronnessoke, who had taken the name "Suscaneman," sold small parcels of land on both sides of Musketa Cove (Glen Cove) to Joseph Carpenter (RTOB, 1:629; NYCD, 14:606). Suscaneman, who was now taking a leading role in relations between the English and the Matinecocks, has been rescued from the obscurity which shrouds most of the Algonquian sachems of the seventeenth century by the exhaustive research of anthropologist, Robert Grumet (1996). Suscaneman eventually took Asharoken's place as the most influential Matinecock sachem. Suscaneman was probably the sachem identified as "Shoskock" who spoke in defense of Tackapousha in the Hempstead land dispute (Grumet 1996:118)

Later that year, Asharoken, Arumpas, and Sehar sold two more tracts of land to Oyster Bay men. The deeds were nearly identical in form to the others (RTOB, 1:682–83, 685). Suscaneman's name appears on the bottom of the row of signatories, perhaps indicating that he was becoming recognized as a person of

---

> Killing Worth this 22 of march 1667 [1668] upon the day and date aforesaid I tackapouchie Sechem of massepeage doe acknolege and declare that hemsted men lyes that [say] mattiniCocke landes comes no furder West then musCetaCofe. I all wayes oWned the Said Cove to be matiniCock land and that my land never Went furder [w]est than the Creeck that Runneth into the head of hemsted harber and all to the east of the Creck to Oysterbaye bounds I owne and ever Will it to be matiniCock and Will prove it by many more Indians then hear have testified Who knowe if then these that are not good Witnesses. this testimony aforemenshoned I doe oWne to be the truth under my hand and mark in presents of us hose names are heare unto subscribed
> 
> John Underhill the mark X of tacpouchs
> Henry Redocke Wee saye and know this to
> William Simson be treu the shachem have
> John dier under Written and
> Wee testefie the Same the marke X of pamelaci
> the marke X of nimhai
> the marke X of Womtapan
> I SoskeCock say hemsted men lyes if they sayd I told them that matiniCocke land Was but a bit of land but I say and ever Will as the Sachem and the rest have testified that it is from the said Creeck to oysterbay bounds
> Wittnes my
> the mark X of ShoskCock
> a tru Coppi of an atestation by taCapouCha Sachem by me Joseph Carpenter

Fig. 10.3. Transcription of Tackapousha's 1668 testimony

status within the Matinecock community. This status, of course, was undoubtedly related to his connections with the English. The following May, Asharoken, Arumpas, Sehar, Nothe, Soometamok, Shoskene (Suscaneman), and Matares sold a tract of land to James Coke. A month after that, in June of 1669, the governor called upon Hempstead to provide proof that they held title to Matinecock (RTOB, 2:671). The renewed controversy apparently was a primary factor in blocking any further Matinecock land sales for a decade.

During these years, Tackapousha continued to use his skills of persuasion and diplomacy in his relations with the English. He realized that however many disagreements he might have with the governor, it was important to cultivate him as a potential ally against Hempstead. The Massapequa sachem made yearly trips to see the governor, accompanied by other Algonquian leaders, bearing wampum or some other gift (DSBD, 3:39, 40, 41). In March 1667, for example, he brought Nicolls a string of wampum as a symbol of his friendship and loyalty. Nicolls responded with gifts of powder and lead and a "small gun" for Tackapousha's son, Tapaweh (DSBD, 3:38). This pattern was probably an ancient ritual followed by sachems who were in a tributary relationship with a more powerful tribe.

The following May, Tackapousha came with three sachems who spoke for the Secatogues, Merricks, and Rockaways to pay their respects to the new governor, Francis Lovelace. The delegation brought two strings of wampum this time. Lovelace greeted them warmly and pledged that if Tackapousha continued his loyal support and remained quiet and peaceful, his people would be "ye happiest Indians of any of their neighbors" (DSBD, 3:39).

In the late spring of 1670, Tackapousha came on his yearly visit to the governor with the customary wampum gift. He was accompanied by sachems from Secatogue, Merrick, and Rockaway. The sachems took the opportunity to complain that their lands were being taken away "every day a little and a little" (DSBD, 3:40). They charged that a man from Hempstead built his house on their lands without paying them and that Richard Smith of Nissequogue had leased some land from them and now claimed it for his own. Lovelace said that he would investigate and make sure that the payments were made, but there is no record of such action.

Later that year, Lovelace's attention was turned from Tackapousha and Hempstead to a conflict over the purchase of a large tract of Montaukett land. He was soon involved in a most delicate issue. The Commission for Indian Affairs, appointed initially by Governor Nicolls, had levied a fine of 400 bushels of corn on the Montauketts in 1668 for refusing to pay the court costs for a man who had been convicted of molesting an English woman from East Hampton (Strong 1994a:575–77). When the Montauketts refused to pay the fine, the commission pressed them to sell a tract of their land on Montauk.

In response to these pressures, some of the Montauketts again sought assistance from Ninigret. This rebellion against the Montaukett leadership, unlike the attempted coup against Wyandanch in 1653 (see Chapter 7), is well documented. A Montaukett delegation, led by Manecopungun and Akomias, went to Rhode Island to negotiate an alliance with the Niantic sachem. Ninigret's ambitions for establishing tributaries on Long Island had not waned. Three years earlier, one of his rivals, a Pokanoket sachem named Metacomet, known to the English as King Philip, had warned the English that Ninigret was again plotting to form an alliance with Indians there (Leach 1966:24; CSP, 380). This time, however, it appears that the Montauketts sought out Ninigret and offered to accept a tributary status under him. Manecopungun and Akomias brought the Niantic sachem some gifts, including a gun that had belonged to Wyandanch (RCRI, 2:270–71). The gun probably symbolized the transfer of power to Ninigret. When the East Hampton officials learned of this action, they immediately sent a troop of armed men to Montauk and seized all of the weapons from the Ninigret faction.

The accommodationist faction among the Montauketts was quickly restored to a position of dominance. In 1669, the Montauketts, led by Poniute (who later identified himself as Wyandanch's grandson and took his grandfather's name), swore allegiance to Governor Lovelace and acknowledged the governor as their "Chiefest sachem" (NYCD, 14:627). They further added that they did "utterly disclayme any such vassalage" to Ninigret. John Mulford, not surprisingly, was one of the witnesses to the testimony.

On December 1, 1670, Poniute and his associates signed over one hundred and eighty acres of land to John Mulford and two associates (Appendix D-13; Smith 1926:32–34). Once again, as we saw with the Shinnecocks in 1657, a fine was imposed to coerce the sale of Indian land. This time there was a blatant conflict of interest because John Mulford, one of the commissioners, was the primary purchaser. After negotiating the deed with the Montauketts, Mulford and his company notified the governor, as specified in the Duke's Laws, and asked for his approval. By this time the provisions requiring the purchaser of any Indian land to appear with the sachem to testify before the governor had been abandoned as impractical.

Mulford's purchase was immediately challenged by the town proprietors of East Hampton, not because it was unfair to the Montauketts, but because they feared Mulford would close off access to some of the best grazing land on Montauk. The proprietors argued that their patent from the former Governor Nicolls granted them, as a corporate body, the exclusive right to purchase Montaukett land. Lovelace held up his approval until the proprietors reached a settlement with Mulford in which he turned the property over to the proprietors and was given, in exchange, another parcel of land in the town.

By 1670, the English in Southampton and East Hampton had begun to take a more direct role in the internal affairs of the Shinnecocks and Montauketts. Both towns now required the Indians to elect a sachem and a "constable," who was charged with keeping order among his people. These officials undoubtedly also needed to have the support of the town magistrates. The Shinnecocks elected Quaquashaug, a staunch ally of the English, as sachem, and Cawbutt, a more independent-minded man, to be their constable (NYCD, 14:647). Governor Lovelace endorsed both men and issued a similar commission to East Hampton. Lovelace did not know the name of the Montaukett officials, so he simply sent his endorsement to East Hampton with blanks for the officials to fill in whatever name they wished. The sachem was probably Poniute, the leader of the accommodationist faction, who signed over the tract of land to John Mulford and his associates (Strong 1994a:580).

The sham of self-government was exposed less than three years later when Cawbutt was stripped of his office and accused, along with other Shinnecocks, of breaking windows in town and other mischievous acts. Such pranks undoubtedly reflected a continuing undercurrent of resentment against the settlers. The town officials threatened to have the Shinnecocks sent to New York in chains unless they reformed (RTSH, 2:202).

Soon after the East Hampton purchase was confirmed, Lovelace turned again to the Matinecock controversy. He was frustrated by what he characterized as an unreasonable and stubborn "hindrance to the planting and improvement of those parts which otherwise had been ere this settled for ye good and benefit of these his Royal Highness his territoryes" (RTOB, 2:677). The governor increased the pressure on the Matinecock sachems by calling them, once again, to New Amsterdam for a hearing about the question of ownership. The Hempstead officials came with their lawyers to recite the same arguments that they had repeated over and over since 1658. Robert Williams of Oyster Bay, who wanted to invalidate the Hempstead claim and open up the Matinecock lands to purchasers from Oyster Bay, represented Tackapousha and the Matinecocks.

In hopes of breaking the impasse, the governor proposed to buy the land for Hempstead, but the Indians asked for more time to consider the issue and returned home. Certainly they were encouraged to reject the offer by Williams and Underhill. Again no settlement could be reached. The Matinecocks apparently held such deep and long standing grievances with Hempstead that they simply did not want to see their land go to them under any circumstances (Marshall 1962:133).

The process of dispossession was briefly interrupted in 1673 when the Dutch recaptured New York. When the English returned in the following year, the Duke of York replaced Lovelace with Edmund Andros, a professional soldier, who governed the colony until 1683. Soon after Andros' arrival, the process of dispossession resumed. In the fall of 1674, the town of Brookhaven negotiated a deed with Tobacus for the land between the Connetquot River on the west and the Mastic River on the east (Appendix C-19; RTBH, Hutchinson:32–33). The rest of Brookhaven, with the exception of some small parcels along the south shore, was purchased in a series of four transactions from 1675 to 1690.[4]

## The Impact of King Philip's War on Long Island, 1675–1678

When King Philip launched his desperate rebellion which swept across New England in 1675, the English on Long Island were alarmed. By the end of 1675, Philip's troops had destroyed several towns and threatened English control over New England. The English leaders on Long Island moved quickly to disarm the local Indians, even though there was no indication at all that any of these Indians were interested in supporting Philip (Trelease 1971:191).

Governor Andros ordered that no liquor, guns, or ammunition be sold to Indians and that all canoes on the north shore be secured by the local town officials (RTOB, 1:664–65). He also ordered that the Indians be disarmed "during ye present troubles" (NYCD, 14:711). The East Hampton magistrates, concerned about the anti-English faction who had allied themselves with Ninigret, were eager to comply. They seized all of the Montauketts' weapons and reinforced their control over internal Montaukett affairs.

In the fall of 1675, rumors spread that Tackapousha was plotting to join King Philip and bring the war to Long Island. Andros again confiscated Indian weapons, and ordered all Indians to remain "quarantined" in their home villages, and prohibited any travel without permission from the English authorities. Some exemptions were given to Indian whalers who were needed for the fall season.

The rumors about Tackapousha may have come from Hempstead in hopes that a military campaign against him and the Matinecocks might be used as a pretense to seize their lands. If so, the tactic failed because Tackapousha, rather than being intimidated, again complained about Hempstead, this time to Governor Andros. He now accused Hempstead of settling on land along the south shore at Merrick, for which they had never paid. The Hempstead officials argued that they had paid, but they had no record of the payment and could not remember the exact amount (RTOB, 2:680–81). There is no record of any action taken by the governor. The animosity between Tackapousha and Hempstead continued unabated.

On eastern Long Island, the process of dispossession continued throughout the war. The pressures on local sachems to sell their lands increased. As we have noted, the boundaries of the territory under the control of these sachems was vaguely defined. English purchasers, eager to close deals before one of their rivals could establish a claim, often negotiated secretly and in haste with any sachem who had the slightest claim to a given tract of land. This often led to lengthy court battles involving rival purchasers and rival sachems who both claimed the same tract of land. On November 19, 1675, for example, Massetewse and Gy (Gie), another sachem from Setauket, sold several tracts of land between present-day Stony Brook and Wading River to the Setauket proprietors without the knowledge or consent of Tobacus and Mayhew, both of whom claimed authority over some of this area (Appendix C-20; RTBH, Book A:41–42; Bayles 1882:4). The transaction also included a gift of some meadowland to Richard Woodhall, who negotiated the sale for the proprietors. The sale was later challenged by Tobacus and Mayhew who took their complaint to Governor Edmund Andros in 1677. The governor warned against such secret negotiations and ordered that all land transactions with Indians must be made in public and approved by the governor or his court. Andros ruled that he "would have no land to bee disposed of but publickely and acknowledged before a Court or the Gov." (NYCD, 14:734). Woodhall agreed to "give satisfaction" to Tobacus and Mayhew, but there is no record of that settlement.

A month after the Setauket purchase in 1675, Governor Andros again took action in response to the settlers' fears of Algonquian attacks. The English on the south shore reported with alarm, that the Indians from Rockaway to the Unkechaug lands near the western border of Southampton, were planning to have a *kintecoy* (powwow) at Secatogue. There is no indication in the records that the powwow was anything more than the annual mid-winter religious observance (see Chapter 5 above). Andros, however, sent a small squad of armed men to the gathering with orders to disarm the participants and send them back to their villages with a warning not to plan any more such celebrations (NYCD, 14:709).

By the late summer of 1676, King Philip had been defeated, ending any threat of large scale military action by Indians in New England and Long Island. Philip was killed and his wife and son were sold into slavery in the West Indies (Vaughan 1965:319). The Indians in New England and on Long Island were now faced with no choice but to make the best accommodation they could with the English who no longer had any fear of an uprising. Decimated by disease and surrounded by a growing English population of farmers who continually pushed them into smaller and smaller areas, the Indians struggled just to survive.

As a result of Philip's defeat, the English were now less concerned with alienating or angering Indians who resisted the expansion and development of the English settlements. The final military defeat of the eastern coastal Indians may well have been one of the reasons which emboldened the Hempstead officials to reassert their old claim to the Matinecock lands. In June of 1677, Richard Gildersleeve, one of Hempstead's founders, now seventy-six years old, testified before the governor's council that the town paid Tackapousha great and small cattle, wampum, stockings, hatchets, knives, trading cloth and some powder and lead. He thought "they went away . . . very well satisfied for all the land that Hempstead men bought of the said sachums and Indians" (RTOB, 2:681).

Although the council remained skeptical and took no action on Hempstead's behalf, the pressure on the Matinecocks to sell their land increased. A few months later, Governor Andros gave Thomas Townsend of Oyster Bay a license to purchase the Matinecock lands and the process of dispossession began again. The Matinecocks were either finally worn down or, perhaps, they were convinced by the other changes around them that they no longer had any choice but to sell their last remaining lands.

## Struggling to Survive: Suscaneman Plays the Deed Game

Suscaneman emerged as the dominant Matinecock sachem in 1677 and remained in that position for more than two decades before passing the mantle of leadership to his son, Surrukunga (Grumet 1996:122). Suscaneman's family had enhanced their power and influence by establishing a close kinship connection with Tackapousha's family. This was accomplished when Suscaneman's sister married Tackapousha's brother, Chopeyconnaws, thereby uniting prominent Matinecock and Massapequa families (Grumet 1996:121–22). Another important source of Suscaneman's power and influence was his success in negotiating and confirming land sales to such influential Englishmen as John Underhill and Robert Williams.

A deed signed on November 16, 1677, bears only Suscaneman's signature, indicating that he had achieved sufficient status within the Matinecock community to negotiate land sales. This deed, similar in form to the previous ones signed by Asharoken and the other sachems, gave ten acres of land to William Frost for an unspecified payment (RTOB, 1:148–49). Suscaneman was convinced that he could protect his people's interests by taking advantage of conflicting interests and jurisdictions within the English colonial system (Grumet 1996:30). This approach was, in fact, a variation on the strategies used by Wyandanch, Uncas, Ninigret, and Tackapousha.

Suscaneman, however, had a much greater challenge because his political base was weakening as more and more of his people left their villages and sought both residence and employment in the English settlements. A similar pattern has been documented in most coastal Algonquian communities from New England to Virginia (Rountree 1990:128; Kraft 1986:225; Richmond 1994:106–7). Helen Rountree describes this as a process of "spinning off" from a core settlement area to a cultural "middle ground" near the English settlements. The gradual exodus was, in part, a result of the gradual erosion of hunting and planting grounds.

Suscaneman's approach to the deed process is best demonstrated on July 5, 1681, when he and Werah met with a small group of Englishmen led by Thomas Townsend of Oyster Bay and sold four parcels of land to four different purchasers (RTOB, 1:135–37). Townsend, who had received permission to purchase Matinecock land by Governor Andros in 1677, witnessed all of the transactions. The amount of acreage in one of the deeds is not listed, but the other three were all ten acre lots. The amount paid to the Matinecocks was not mentioned.

This procedure was repeated the following October when Suscaneman, Sehar, and Werah sold three more ten acre parcels, and no payment was listed. Once again, Thomas Townsend, who did not purchase any of the land himself, witnessed the transactions. On April 26, 1682, three more parcels were sold, but this time two of the tracts were fifty acres and the third was a bit larger. Another difference was that one of the purchasers, Isaac Horner, paid the Matinecocks £15 sterling in three installments over the next year (RTOB, 1:146–48). This transaction is one of the earliest indications that the Indians were becoming involved in the English cash economy.

In a series of eight transactions, which took place two months later, the size of the parcels grew to range from fifteen to sixty acres (RTOB, 1:151–56). Unfortunately, no payments were noted for any of them. It appears that the cash payment in April was a preliminary development in a very gradual social change.

Suscaneman was learning how to work within the English system to his advantage, but he had much to learn from the wise old Massapequa sachem. At the October session of the Court of Assizes, Tackapousha demonstrated, once again, his political skill and his knowledge of English institutions. The Hempstead proprietors, having conceded the land on the north shore between Hempstead Harbor and Oyster Bay to the town of Oyster Bay, now renewed their legal struggle to validate their claim to the land west of Hempstead Harbor. Hempstead sued Tackapousha, indicating that the Massapequa sachem now had control of some Matinecock land, a power he denied having in 1657. They had taken their case to the court of session at Jamaica the previous June, repeating their claim that the town had purchased this land in 1657, and charging that Cow Neck, on the peninsula between Hempstead Harbor and Manhasset Bay (where Port Washington is now located), belonged to them. Hempstead won the case, but Tackapousha immediately appealed to the higher court which met every October in New York City (NYHS, 1913:32–33).

The governor appointed John West, a clerk of the court, to plead Tackapousha's case. Tackapousha testified that he had never sold the tract and had never received any payment. After reviewing the arguments of both parties, the court held that Hempstead had no right to the land and was obligated to pay the court costs. Tackapousha understood both the formal procedures at court and the importance of political influence. Sometime before the trial, he had given Governor Andros half of the land on Cow Neck as a personal gift (NYHS, 1913:33). On March 28, 1683, he gave a tract for a nominal fee of six shillings to John West for winning the case.[5]

Tackapousha refused to sell any land to the town of Hempstead, and Suscaneman, who continued to sell off small parcels, began to require hard cash as payment. Apparently, the Indians were becoming more aware of the relative value of the goods they had often received in the past exchange for the land. The Indians living at Secatogue, led by Tackapousha's nephews Will Cheppie and Qurapin, also demanded currency in exchange for land (RTH, 2:54–55). Even so, they were still only paid about half the market value of the property.[6] The money was apparently distributed among the Indians in the same fashion as the trade goods had been. Suscaneman signed a memorandum on January 8, 1684, stating that his people had empowered him to sell Matinecock land, but had required him to give Tackapousha and "every Indian or squaw concerned" a share (RTOB, 1:182). This agreement suggests that the Matinecocks had, by this time, granted Tackapousha authority over all of their land transactions. Suscaneman

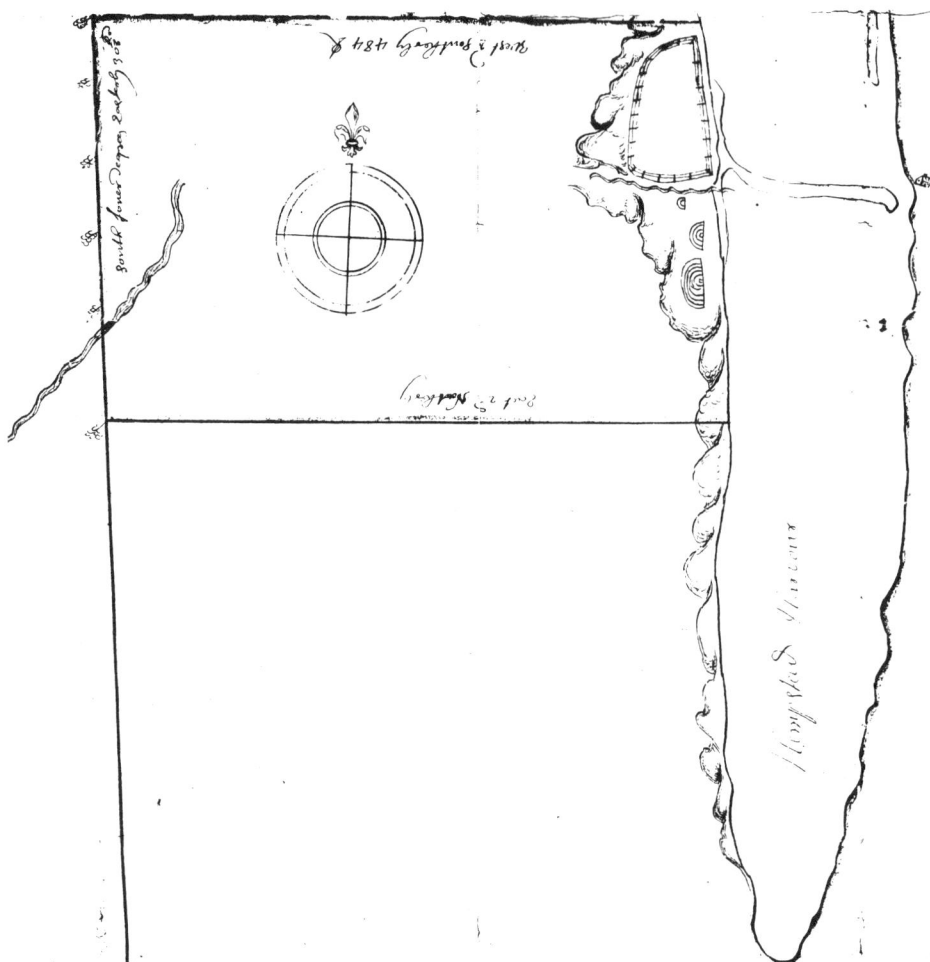

Fig. 10.4. Map of John West property with longhouse and wigwams

signed thirteen more deeds in 1685 and 1686, receiving small payments in pounds sterling.

On February 19, 1684, a most unusual transaction took place between Suscaneman, Werah, and an Oyster Bay settler named Henry Bell. The Englishman had married a Narragansett woman who had taken the English name "Jane" (RTOB, 1:313–14). The Matinecock sachem gave the Bells a gift of fifty acres of land because Jane was "one of our own nation." We have no way of knowing what was in Suscaneman's mind; perhaps he was impressed that Bell had married Jane rather than fathering her child and then abandoning her as was done by other whites who had sexual relations with Indian women.

Most of these Englishmen were like Joseph Jennings of Hempstead, who abandoned an Indian woman named Mogrub and their son, Kewewaquna, forcing her to petition the town court for relief in 1665. There were, according to Hempstead historian Bernice Marshall, many such petitions in the Hempstead parish records (Marshall 1962:50). The close proximity of African, white, and Indian people inevitably led to a blending of the races. Indian and African female servants were particularly vulnerable to white employers. Unfortunately, we can only guess at Suscaneman's motives, although, undoubtedly, the Indians must have harbored resentment about the exploitation of their women.

The exploitation of servant women was of no great concern to most Englishmen, but the plight of an Indian minority without land did begin to trouble some of the colonial leaders. There may have been fears that impoverished and homeless Algonquian peoples would some day become a burden on the growing English towns. The slowly disappearing Matinecock lands may have become a concern to Governor Thomas Dongan, who had replaced Andros in 1682 (Grumet 1996).

## "To Have and to Hold": The Matinecock Reservations

In June of 1687, Governor Thomas Dongan gave the Matinecocks two small reservations, one on each side of Hempstead Bay. The first, on the west side, was a one hundred fifty acre plot granted to Tackapousha (see fig. 10.5 and Appendix C-21), and the other, on the east side, was a two hundred acre tract of land granted to Suscaneman (Appendix C-22; Grumet 1995; NYSA, Letters Patent, Book 6:240–41; RTOB, 1:519). These reservations were to be permanent residences for the Indians and their descendants "to have and to hold" forever. The terms in the grants included a very important stipulation protecting the Indians' title to the reservations. A clause in Tackapousha's grant, which bordered on the plot of land he had sold to John West in 1683, stated that "it shall not be in the power of the said Indians or their heirs to grant or convey the said land and premises to any person or persons whatsoever" (NYSA, Land Patents, Book 6:241). In the second grant, the governor, by the authority of his office and King James II gave Suscaneman (Runisuck) a two hundred acre parcel of land (RTOB, 1:519; see fig. 10.6). The governor entered a clause similar to one in his grant to Tackapousha which guaranteed that the land could not be sold.

John Cox, the Oyster Bay historian who edited the town records in 1916, inserted a note under the document suggesting that Dongan was using the reservation grants to block purchase rights to the tract as a tactic to pressure Oyster Bay into accepting a change in their patent which would raise the tax rate on their lands. This explanation is certainly consistent with the assessment of Dongan's administration by historians (Ritchie 1977:180–97), but it is also quite possible that Dongan was simply following a pattern established in New England to concentrate the Indians on a small piece of land where they could be more easily controlled. Similar grants of land were made to local Indians by the towns of East Hampton in 1686 (see below), Brookhaven in 1700 (Gonzales 1986:119), and Southold in 1685 (NYHSL, Southold Indian Papers). The reservation would also provide a last place of refuge for the Indians and prevent them from becoming indigents dependent on the local towns for food and lodging. If this

> **Recorded for Tackapousha and company**
>
> Thomas Dongan, Captain General Governor in Chief and Vice Admiral in and over the Province of New York and territories depending there on in America under his most sacred majesty James the Second by the grace of God, King of England, Scotland France, and Ireland, defender of the Faith and to all to whom these presents shall come, sendth greeting whereas there is a certain piece or parcel of land on the east side of Cow Neck between Mr. John West and Mr. Richard Cornwell, containing the quantity of one hundred and fifty acres, which said land is situate and lying in Queens County on Long Island. Know yee that by virtue of the commission and authority unto me received, and power in me residing, I have given granted ratify release and confirmed and by these presents do give ratify release and confirm unto Tackapancha Sachem for himselfe and the rest of the Indians of the said place all the before scribed piece or parcel of land with all and singular its rights pasture feedings meadows marshes woods [two words illegible] brooks ponds and appurtenances whatsoever belonging or in any wise appertaining to have and to hold the said piece or parcel of land and premises with their and every of their appurtenances unto the said Tackapancha and the rest of the said Indians aforesaid and their heirs to their only proper use benefit and behoove of them the said Indians and their heirs forever yielding rendering and paying therefore yearly and every year forever unto his sacred Majesty, his heirs and successors or to such officer or officers as shall by him or them be appointed to receive the same one shilling currant Money at the City of New York provided always that it shall not be in the power of the Indians or their heirs to grant or convey the said land and premises to any person and persons whatsoever any thing in this patent to the contrary in any wise not with standing in testimony where of I have caused these presents to be hereunto affixed this far and twentieth day of June, one thousand 600 eighty seven and in the thrd year of his Majesty's reign.
>
> By command of his Excellency
> Swinton
>
> Thomas Dongan

Fig. 10.5. Tackapousha's 1687 Matinecock reservation patent from Governor Dongan (see Appendix C-22 map)

was Dongan's plan, it failed and was soon forgotten. Later that year, Dongan was replaced by Edmund Andros who returned as governor of New York and of King James' newly formulated administrative structure called the Dominion of New England.

There is no record of any attempt by the Matinecocks to settle on the lands and to establish a tribal home base there. The pace of the land sales declined as the Matinecock land base continued to shrink. There is also no record of what happened to the first grant, but six years later a document purportedly signed by Suscaneman, Sehar, and Werah, gave their reservation to James Townsend as a free gift in direct violation of the Dongan grant (RTOB, 2:116–17). Governor Dongan clearly stated in his grant that the Matinecocks could not sell or give away their land even if they wanted.

It is quite possible, however, that the Townsend deed is a fraud anyway. "The scent of chicanery," concludes Robert Grumet, pervades the document, because Suscaneman, apparently unaware of the "gift," appeared before the colonial

Dispossession and Survival, 1660-1703

council in 1694 to protest that Hempstead settlers were cutting timber on his reservation land without his consent (1996:131–32). The New York Council was also unaware of the previous sale because it ordered a new survey of the reservation and stipulated that the new survey should not compromise the original Dongan grant.

There are other reasons to be suspicious of the deed. That same day Suscaneman gave land which bordered on the reservation to Moses Mudge "for his many kindnesses," and gave Moses and his son Gervis permission to build a house on the reservation (RTOB, 1:527–29). This is most curious. If Suscaneman had given the reservation to Townsend that same day, why is he giving Mudge permission to build on land he no longer owns? In another deed, dated February 4, 1696, Suscaneman and Sehar make a reference to their two hundred acre reservation in defining the boundaries of adjoining land (RTOB, 1:529–30). The wording here certainly

> Day & Date above Written David Underhill acknowledged before me one of their ma$^{ties}$ Justices of ye peace that this above written is his reall & voluntary act & Deed
> Nathaneill Coles:
> This Assignm$^t$ is of a Deed from Anthony Wright to David Underhill & it is entred in this Booke in page 357:
>
> ——THOMAS DONGAN Cap$^t$ General Governour in Chiefe & Vice Admiral in & over ye Prvince of New Yorke & Teritorys Depending thereon in America, Ud$^r$ his Ma$^{tie}$ James ye Second by the Grace of God of England, Scotland, ffrance & Ireland Defend$^r$ of ye ffaith &c TO all whome these p$^r$sents Shall come SENDETH GREETING; WHEREAS there is a Certain peece or parcel of Land on ye East Side of Hempsteed Harbour between Sd Harbor & ye Cartway Leading from Musketo Cove to Hempsteed Containing the quantity of Two hundred Acres w$^{ch}$ Said Land is Scituate & Lying in Queens County on Long Island KNOW YEE that by vertue of ye Comission & Authority to me Derived and power in me Residing I have Given, Granted, Rattified, Released & Confirmed; and by these p$^r$sents Do Give, Grant, Rattifie & Confirme unto Runisuck of Matenicock for & on ye behalf of himself & ye Rest of ye Indians of ye Sd place All ye before Receited peece or parcel of Land w$^{th}$ all & Singular its Rights, pastures, ffeedings, Meadows, Marshes, Woods, Underwoods, Lakes, Brookes ponds & Appurtenances w$^t$soever belonging or in any wise Apprtaining TO HAVE & TO HOLD the Sd peece or parcel of Land & p$^r$mises w$^{th}$ their & every of their Appurtenances unto ye Sd Runasuck & ye rest of ye Sd Indians aforesaid & their Heires, to their only proper use, Benefit & behoofe of ye Sd Indeans & their Heires forever Yeilding Rendring & paying therefore yearly & every Year forever unto his Most Sacred Ma$^{tie}$ his Heires & Suckessors or to Such Officer or Officers as Shall by him or them be Appoynted to receive ye Same one Shilling Cur$^{tt}$ Money at ye City of New Yorke PROVIDED alwaies that it Shall not be in ye power of ye Sd Indeans or their Heires to Grant or Convey ye Sd Land & p$^r$mises to any person or persons whatsoever Anything in this pattent to ye Contrary in any wise not withstanding IN TESTIMONY whereof I have caused these p$^r$sents to be Recorded in ye Secretary office And ye Seal of the Province to be Hereunto affixed this 27th Day of June X 1687 and in ye Third year of his Ma$^{ties}$ Reigne
> Examined June 27: 1687          Tho Dongan
> W nicolls

Fig. 10.6. Suscaneman's 1687 Matinecock reservation patent from Governor Dongan granting two hundred acre parcel of land (see Appendix C-23 map)

indicates that Suscaneman still considered the reservation his land. Clearly, the Townsend deed was not recognized by either the council or by the Matinecocks.

In 1711, Thomas Townsend, who apparently inherited the land from James, gave a tract of land, which appears to include the two hundred acre reservation, to his sons-in-law Thomas Jones and Abraham Underhill. By that time, the remaining Matinecocks had been dispersed to small enclaves near English towns and were unable to protest. In 1702 and again in 1707, petitions were sent to the governor requesting the right to purchase tracts which appear to include the western Matinecock reservation (Grumet, February 2, 1995: pers. com.). Unfortunately, there is no record of the governor's response or of a subsequent purchase. It is possible that the tract is now a part of Hempstead Harbor Beach County Park.

Tackapousha, his sons, and Suscaneman continued to sell small tracts of land during the last decade of the century.[7] They also gave away eight tracts of land to Oyster Bay settlers in return for "many favors and kindnesses." Although this may have been viewed by the Indians as a form of potlatch in which gifts were expected to bring a return of more favors and kindness in the future, there is no indication that the settlers felt that any such obligation was implied by these gifts.

### Holding on to the Land: The Unkechaugs, Montauketts, and Shinnecocks on Eastern Long Island

By the end of the seventeenth century, the only large parcels of land left were the Shinnecock and Montaukett lands on the South Fork of eastern Long Island.[8] In 1687, the East Hampton proprietors purchased all of the remaining Montaukett lands (Appendix D-14) for £100 sterling which, according to the deed, was already "in hand"(RTEH, 2:213-14). Poniute, who now had taken the name of his grandfather, Wyandanch, led the negotiations for the Montauketts and later testified that the money had, in fact, not been in hand at the time.

The next day an agreement was reached which underscores, once again, the problems inherent in the relations between Indian and English on Long Island. Now that the English owned all the Montaukett land, where were the Montauketts to go? In the English system when land was sold, the former owners left, and the new owners simply took over the vacated area. East Hampton realized that they could not proceed in such a manner without provoking considerable suffering, and, perhaps, a violent response by some of the Montauketts, so they introduced a mechanism to avoid these problems. East Hampton granted the Montauketts residence rights on Montauk for themselves and their descendants "forever on the land as purchased of them by us" (Smith 1926:48–49). It later became clear that East Hampton anticipated "forever" to really mean until the Montauketts died out or left Montauk. The town took action in the eighteenth and nineteenth centuries designed to hasten those events (Strong 1992; Strong 1993).

In 1700, William Smith set aside a reservation of 175 acres at Poospatuck (Appendix C-24) for the remaining Unkechaugs and their heirs, forever (Gonzales 1986:119). "Forever" turned out to be about thirty years. The Smith family took back one hundred acres in 1730 and a series of questionable transactions over the years has reduced the reservation to about fifty acres. This land is located on the Forge River near the village of Mastic in the town of Brookhaven.

Soon after Smith had made his grant to the Unkechaugs, the Montauketts voiced their disillusionment about the 1687 agreement. They complained that they had not received the money as promised and raised a number of other complaints as well. A committee appointed by the town heard the complaints, which, unfortunately, were not recorded, and dismissed them, declaring that the Montauketts were "obstinate and adverse to agreement" (RTEH, 3:7, 35–36). The tensions continued, but the Montauketts had no recourse until the fall of 1702 when Rip Van Dam, a wealthy New York merchant and close friend of the governor, Lord Cornbury, provided them with an opportunity to strike back at East Hampton.

Van Dam, with the governor's approval, took advantage of the fact that East Hampton had never paid the full price promised in the 1687 deed and purchased the land himself. Governor Cornbury, a nephew of Queen Anne and one of the most corrupt and venal administrators in the colonial period, had no qualms about overriding the patents issued by his predecessors to please his close associate (Hawke 1966:328, 477). Wyandanch and his elderly advisor, Sassakata, traveled to Jamaica in September where they met with Van Dam and signed a deed transferring all of the Montaukett land to him in exchange for a £200 bond, which would provide the Montauketts with a guaranteed yearly income and residence rights on Montauk forever.

East Hampton immediately challenged the deed, but not on the basis of their 1687 purchase, which they apparently believed was vulnerable to a challenge. Instead, they protested that Van Dam had violated their exclusive patent rights to purchase all Montaukett lands and added that he had used alcohol to "befuddle" the Montaukett sachems (Jameson 1883:236). This charge by East Hampton is both hypocritical and self-serving. Rip Van Dam, who gave the Montauketts a much better deal than they had ever received from East Hampton, certainly did not need to ply the Montauketts with alcohol to win their approval. The charge was probably made because the use of alcohol to manipulate and control Indians was so frequent in the seventeenth century. Deeds usually had a memorandum added stipulating that witnesses confirm that the Indian signatories were sober and understood the terms of the contract.[9]

The use of alcohol was pervasive among the English during the colonial period. It was not uncommon to drink before breakfast and to take several nips throughout the day. Lion Gardiner's son, David, was reported to have consumed a bottle of rum a day (JTEH, 2:59). Most business deals were not considered properly consummated until the participants sealed them with a drink (Rorabaugh 1979:18). The English soon learned, however, that Indians, unaccustomed to drinking as part of a social interaction, consumed the alcohol quickly when business was being discussed and became vulnerable to manipulation.

The Europeans had several thousand years of experience with alcohol. Although, like smallpox, it still took a toll on their physical and mental health, it had been tamed by social mores into a less destructive force in their everyday lives. For the Indians, however, alcohol consumption and its effects were a relatively new experience for which there were no social rules of behavior. As their way of life and their land became increasingly constricted, many turned to alcohol in their despair, making them even more vulnerable.

Although the Duke's Laws prohibited all liquor sales to Indians unless the merchant or innkeeper was licensed and had paid a security to cover damages committed by intoxicated Indians, these laws were very difficult to enforce. It should also be noted that they were primarily designed to protect English lives and property from harm rather than to save the Indians from the ravages of alcohol (Lincoln 1894:41).

A month after the Montauketts signed Rip Van Dam's deed, they formally denounced it, stating that they were drawn into and signed "what we knew not" (Pelletreau 1903, 2:372–73). Unfortunately, we do not know what means were used by East Hampton to force this action by Wyandanch and Sassakata. Our only clue is the testimony of Benjamin and Stephen Pharaoh given to the New York State Assembly in 1800, long after the event:

> The agreement of 1703 is the one they are now oppressing us with every line of which is tinged with evidence of fraud . . . The East Hampton people have ever made it one rule when ever they want to make a bargain with us to attack us upon the weak side that is to say they always begin treating of us till they get us pretty well smoked with white faced rum before they divulge their business they always carry their points as they are often boasting of only get them in a right trim and we can do with them as we please (Gonzales 1993:71).

The Pharaohs, of course, were not eyewitnesses, but they were repeating what was probably an oral folk history of the event. Their account is quite plausible, given the historical context.

Wyandanch and his advisors negotiated four agreements with East Hampton on March 3, 1703. They confirmed the 1687 deed to the Montaukett lands and agreed to accept a yearly interest payment of forty shillings for as long as the £100 remained in the hands of the town (MID 1974:15, folder 4; Smith 1926:53–54). The Montauketts were forced to accept a bond of £2,000 sterling for their "good behavior" as a guarantee that they would never again act as they had with Rip Van Dam. They received, in return, a guarantee of residence rights to Montauk for themselves and their posterity (Appendix D-15). Thirty-two Montaukett males signed the agreements in the presence of two of the justices of the peace for East Riding (present-day Suffolk County). The justices affirmed that they, "being sober and thoroughly to understand the whole purport," came before us today (Smith 1926:52–56).

The rights granted in the agreement, however, were severely restricted. The Montauketts were responsible for fencing in their crops to protect them from English livestock which were allowed to graze freely over all unfenced areas of the peninsula. The Indians were allowed a quota of two hundred and fifty pigs and fifty head of horses and cows combined. They were not permitted to keep livestock for anyone who was not a member of their tribe. These restrictions on economic growth ensured that the Montaukett community would remain stagnant. In contrast to the Matinecocks, the Montauketts settled on their small reservation and struggled to survive as a community until they were finally pushed off the land at the end of the nineteenth century (Ales 1993:51–52; Strong 1993:85–87).

When Southampton learned of Rip Van Dam's activities in East Hampton, it moved to protect its title to their town. On Friday, August 13, 1703, Southampton began negotiations with the Shinnecock sachems and elders. Shinnecock sachems were courted with gifts of money. Sachem Pongumo was given £2 and fifteen shillings and Chice, another Shinnecock sachem, received £2 (Appendix D-16; RTSH, 2:358–59). Pongumo's gift was roughly equivalent to three weeks wages for an English laborer on Long Island at the end of the seventeenth century (RTEH, 2:220; RTSH, 5:5).

Later generations of Shinnecocks repeated an accusation about the use of alcohol at the negotiations which was very similar to the one told by the Pharaohs to the New York State Assembly. In 1888, when Alice Fletchner, the scholar who had been commissioned to do an intensive study of Indian education, presented her report to Congress, she included a reference to the 1703 deed. She was told by the Shinnecocks that the sachems had "in a drunken moment conveyed all of their land to the whites" (Fletchner 1888:567).

The Southampton records do indicate that a very generous supply of liquor was purchased for the town by Thomas Herrick "for the Indians and entertaining the trustees" (RTSH, 2:358–59). Herrick was reimbursed £1, enough to purchase about five gallons of rum or two barrels of hard cider (RTSH, 5: appendix no. 6). That amount of liquor for the negotiations does give credibility to the Shinnecock folk tradition.

Three separate documents were signed on the following Monday. The first transferred all of the remaining Shinnecock lands to the Southampton proprietors for £20 sterling, a price well below the market value of the land at the time. The money was paid to sachems Pongumo, Chice, and Mahanum. Pongumo, apparently the highest ranking leader, received £10 to distribute to his followers. Chice and Mahanum were each given £5. There is no record of the distribution to the rest of the Shinnecocks, but there were thirteen men who signed the deed along with the three sachems and twenty-one more who endorsed the deed a week later

(RTSH, 2:178). If the sachems divided up the money evenly among the signatories, each of the men would have received about twelve shillings.

If the money was distributed to all of the male Shinnecocks, the shares would have been much smaller. The census taken by the town five years earlier had indicated that there were between one hundred and fifty and two hundred Indians living at Shinnecock (Howell 1887:42–43). Howell recorded the names of fifty-two men and reported that he was told that there were about fifty women and fifty children, as well. The accuracy of the account is questionable because Howell did not make a serious effort to locate and record the total population. "The heathens," he said, "are so scattered to and Fro," that he could not get a more accurate count. Nineteen of the men who signed the deed in 1703 were not listed in the 1698 census. No matter how the shares were divided, it is certain that the money soon came back into the hands of the Southampton merchants.

A second deed was negotiated with Sachem Wiangonhut (Giangonhut) and his sister, sunksquaw Sumono, for the Unkechaug lands within the western border of Southampton. The brother and sister were paid £5 for their interest in the property. Sumono was married to Pongumo, linking the neighboring communities of Unkechaug and Shinnecock and demonstrating, once again, that women who left their home village to live with their husbands still retained their property rights, probably from their mothers (RTSH, 2:179–80).

The immediate concern following the closing of the deed was what to do with the Shinnecocks now that the land had all been sold. It was the same dilemma faced by the East Hampton officials, but Southampton came up with a different solution. The elected town trustees leased land back to the Shinnecocks for a thousand years (RTSH, 2:372–73). This tract included the present-day reservation and all of the land from the western border of the English settlement to Canoe Place where the Shinnecock Canal is located today.

The "thousand year" lease was abrogated in 1859 when the Southampton proprietors wanted to develop the area west of the village known as Shinnecock Hills (Appendix D-17). The proprietors pressed the Shinnecocks to trade the lease for a deed in fee simple to a reservation of about eight hundred acres on Shinnecock Neck lying west of the Southampton village boundary. An additional fifty acre tract west of the Shinnecock Canal known as "Westwoods" was later added to the reservation (Stone 1983:308–10). The New York State legislature approved the arrangement, but it was never submitted to the United States Congress under the terms of the 1790 Non-Intercourse Act which requires that all subsequent acquisitions of Indian land be brought before Congress for a review.

The 1703 transactions at Montauk and Shinnecock mark the end of an era in Indian-English relations on Long Island. The Indians were either concentrated on the reserved lands at Shinnecock, Montauk, and Poospatuck or were scattered in tiny enclaves across the Island. They continued the process of a gradual adaptation to the European economy which had actually begun soon after the Dutch arrived at the beginning of the century.

The Shinnecocks and Montauketts had negotiated deeds under highly suspicious circumstances in 1703 which were later denounced by both tribes. The Montauketts were promised residence rights in perpetuity, only to have them abrogated two hundred years later. The Shinnecocks were promised that the area called the Shinnecock Hills, lying between the village of Southampton and Canoe Place (where the canal is located today), would be theirs for a thousand years. The thousand year lease was abrogated in 1859 when the Southampton proprietors wanted to develop the hills and run the railroad through (see Strong 1983a).

## Summary

During the latter half of the seventeenth century, the Indian lands were taken over by the European settlers, leaving only two undisputed tracts, one at Shinnecock and the other at Poospatuck. Cultural misunderstandings, deceit, patent violations, manipulation, the calculated use of alcohol, and payments made at roughly half of the market value characterized most of this tragic process of dispossession.

King Philip's War briefly interrupted the process of dispossession. The English on Long Island feared that Tackapousha and some of the other local sachems might join Philip in his resistance against English control. Governor Andros ordered that all Indians were to remain in their villages unless they were engaged in the whaling enterprise. As it turned out, there is no evidence that any of the Long Island Indians went to aid Philip in New England.

Another characteristic of the scramble for Indian land was the constant bickering among the English over land titles and town boundary lines. Hempstead and Oyster Bay fought over their claims to land on the north shore; Southampton and Southold both claimed title to the land south of the Peconic River; Huntington and Oyster Bay contested the rights to Lloyd Neck; and Richard Smith of Smithtown sued the town of Huntington over disputed land on the west bank of the Nissequogue. All of these legal battles involved the original purchases from the Indian owners.

Tackapousha and Suscaneman managed to buy some time against the demographic shift which overwhelmed their people. The sachems carefully parceled out their legacy, staving off the engulfing tide of English settlement, but they eventually ran out of land to sell. By the time Tackapousha died (sometime around 1697), few tracts were left. Even the two Matinecock Reservations which Governor Dongan had granted to the Matinecocks in the 1687 patents had been taken away. In spite of Dongan's clear stipulation that the tracts could not be sold off by the Matinecocks, no public official raised a hand in protest when the land was taken.

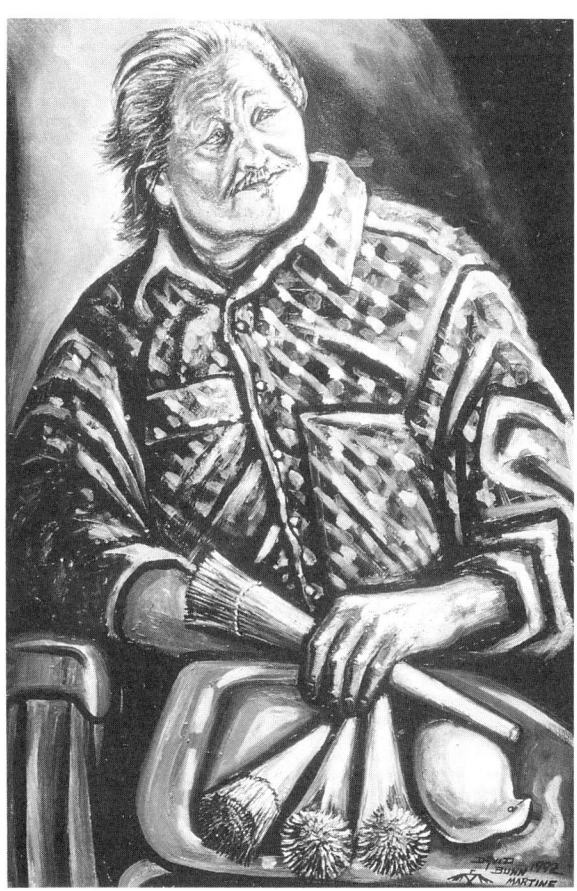

James Kellis with scrub brushes he made

# 11

# Algonquian Labor Patterns in the Seventeenth Century

The first three decades of interaction between European and Algonquian cultures were marked by a gradually increasing demand for European goods, which forced many Indians to seek employment with the whites. The aboriginal subsistence economy did not produce items which could be traded to the whites for such highly valued goods as guns, copper kettles, blankets, shoes, coats, and liquor. The request for corn in the 1640 treaty with Southampton suggests that the Shinnecocks did not produce an agricultural surplus which could be used for trade. Once the demand for wampum waned, the Indians had only two things of value to the whites: their land and their labor.

As their land base eroded away, the Indians were left with only one marketable commodity. Many entered the colonial labor market as whalers, free laborers, indentured servants, and slaves. Although there were constant pressures on the Indians to abandon their ancient ways altogether, they resisted to a remarkable degree. The Algonquian people continued to fish, hunt, and forage for food to such an extent that they were frequently in conflict with the white settlers over the right to have access to land the English now claimed as their exclusive property.

Some of the Algonquian traditional skills and activities could be turned to commercial enterprises. Hunting, fishing, and handicraft skills brought them some revenue. The English frequently purchased shellfish, fish, venison, and other game from Algonquian hunters. Feathers from wild fowl were in constant demand for bedding. Indians were often hired to hunt wolves until the animals were finally exterminated on Long Island. Helen Rountree, in her research on the Powhatans of Virginia, found that Indian crafts such as mats, wooden bowls, trays, and tanned deer hides were often reported in colonial household inventories (1990:132). Algonquian women on Long Island continued to sell their handmade baskets and scrub brushes to the English into the early decades of the twentieth century.

Shinnecock artisans produced many craft items which were sold to local white households. Shinnecock scrub brushes are still used today in some households to scour pans. The brushes are made by carefully splitting the end of a small oak stave and binding the split ends. Many other craft materials produced for sale to the English during the seventeenth century were still being produced in the twentieth century. Among the Shinnecock artisans in the first half of the twentieth century who loaded up their wagons with baskets, caned chairs, beaded

Fig. 11.1. Alice Osceola Bunn Martinez holding a basket she made as a young woman

moccasins, embroidered table linens, eel traps, corn and herb mortars, duck decoys, wooden ladles, and scrub brushes and peddled them in the nearby white communities were Frances and Daniel Bunn, Eugene Cuffee, Alice Bunn Martinez, Harriett Crippen Anderson, Anthony Beaman, Eliza Beaman, and three generations of the Kellis family (Stone and Smith 1983:291–93; Stone and Cuffee 1983:303). James Kellis, a skilled carver, was producing scrub brushes until his death in 1993.

Fig. 11.2. Charles Bunn with his duck decoy display at the National Sportsman Show, c. 1920. (Bunn is seated in the center.)

Eugene Cuffee (1866–1941) and Charles Sumner Bunn (1865–1952), the great-grandfather of artist David Martine, were highly skilled carvers of duck decoys (Gerard, Jr. 1983:297–98). Charles Bunn's decoys of such indigenous species as blackduck, broadtail, pintail, canvasback, and brant, were sold regularly at the annual Sportsman's Show at Madison Square Garden in New York City. In addition to his skills as a carver, Eugene Cuffee established a reputation for training hunting dogs. Both men also served as guides for sportsmen who came out from New York to hunt and fish.

The most dramatic example of a traditional skill which brought in revenue to the Indian community was their expertise as whalers. Other ancient skills and knowledge were also in demand. The Algonquians were familiar with the medicinal and nutritional qualities of plants and, in at least one instance, a shaman was hired to restore the health of an English settler. Ralph Cardwell, who lived in Gravesend in 1652, was reported to be in "some Indian doctor's . . . cure" (RTG, Book 1, Box 144:103). Unfortunately, the record provides no details of the sickness or of the remedy, but we do know that Cardwell regained his health.

Helen Rountree (1990) found very similar patterns in Virginia during this same time period. She distinguishes between the "core" people who remained aloof from the white communities and the "fringe" people who gravitated to the margins of the English towns in search of work and trade goods. She also noted that there was an important gender difference in the process of acculturation. The women who entered the colonial economy as domestics did not have to learn many new skills and their work was on an equal status with the work of the English women. Men, with the exception of whalers, were required to learn new skills and do work which had the lowest status for males in the English community.

Another pattern which emerged during the latter decades of the seventeenth century, both in Virginia and on Long Island, was an increasing social relationship, including marriage, between African Americans and Indians. This relationship was inevitable, in part, because both groups frequently worked together as laborers and domestics. There were cultural similarities as well. Both communities placed great emphasis on lineages and kinship systems, and they shared a belief system which viewed the natural world as a sacred place. They also shared a place at the bottom of the colonial class system. For a brief time, however, the Indians on eastern Long Island who were skilled whalemen earned a relatively good income and were in great demand.

## "Ye Whale Designe"

In October, as the arctic freeze reduces its food supply, the northern right whale *(Eubalena glacialis)* migrates south along the Atlantic coast to spawn in the warmer waters off the coast of the Carolinas and Georgia (Kraus, et al. 1986:139–44; Reeves and Mitchell 1986:206). The whales remain in these waters until March when they return north. The right whales are vulnerable to hunters because they feed on the surface and swim close to the shore. Long before the arrival of the whites, Native Americans on Long Island and in southern New England had harvested beached whales and hunted sea mammals that came into the shallow coastal waters (Strong 1983:32–34).

The English settlers on eastern Long Island immediately recognized the economic potential in the beached whale carcasses. There was a virtually inexhaustible demand in London for whale oil and baleen. Whale oil was used in lamps and as a lubricant for leather working, and the baleen, the thin, horny strips in the whale's mouth which filter the food, was in demand for corset stays, shoe horns, and anything that required flexible support. Profits from the oil and baleen were a major source of eastern Long Island's capital during the seventeenth century. Private debts, as well as the salaries of ministers and school teachers, were frequently paid in whale oil.

Individuals and towns vied for control of the rights to the carcasses. The towns of East Hampton and Southampton, of course, assumed the rights to whales on the beaches in their boundaries, but conflicts with individual entrepreneurs, who purchased whale rights from local Indian sachems, were fought out in court for several decades. These entrepreneurs also fought each other in court. The desire for the profits from the carcasses even turned brother against brother as John Cooper sued his brother Thomas for taking a whale from his beach (RTSH, 2:27–28).

The potential profits from the sales of whale oil and baleen to London merchants soon prompted local entrepreneurs to begin hunting live whales rather than waiting for the creatures to beach themselves. They formed companies which combined Indian whaling skills with English technology. Beginning around 1650, whaling companies were formed by settlers who hired Indian whalers and provided them with twenty-eight to thirty-foot cedar boats with oak ribs, iron harpoons, and other tools necessary for hunting the whales and processing the oil from the blubber (Edwards and Rattray 1956:55–63). During the next two decades, the owners paid the Indians with such trade goods as coats, cloth, boots, stockings, powder, shot, and alcohol. The bargaining power of the Indians and the importance of the whaling industry are underscored by the willingness of the colonial authorities to exempt whaling company owners from the laws prohibiting the sale of ammunition and alcohol to the Indians (NYCD, 14:608–9).

Most companies sent out two boats, each containing six men, a harpooner, a steersman, and four oarsmen (Wooley 1968:38–39). The average adult right whale is about fifty feet long and weighs one hundred tons, a formidable challenge to the Indians in their small boats. The attack on the whale involved considerable skill and courage. Boats had to be steered within fifteen feet of the whale to give the harpooners a chance to drive their weapons deep enough into the whale's body. The harpooner had to cast his shaft into a moving target as the steersman and crew struggled to keep the boat close to the prey. Standing in the

*Algonquian Labor Patterns in the Seventeenth Century* 271

Fig. 11.3. Indian whalers

prow of the boat, with one leg braced into a notch carved for this purpose, the harpooner had to gauge the pitching motion of the sea and throw his shaft, with line attached, into the undulating body of his quarry. Once the first harpoon, with its razor sharp point and multiple barbs, was set, and the lines to the boat secured, several narrow pointed harpoons were plunged into the whale. The hunt could be over in an hour or so if the lances hit a vital spot, but it was not unusual for the struggle to take half a day.

After the kill, the long, exhaustive process of towing the whale to shore began (Strong 1989a:31). A nineteenth-century account of this process describes the struggle of a crew bringing in a whale killed about ten miles offshore (Edwards and Rattray 1956:53–54). It took them about an hour of strenuous rowing to tow the carcass one mile. After six hours of back-breaking rowing, family and friends came out in small boats with food and water for the crew. Another six hours of rowing were required to finally bring the whale to shore.

The whales were usually towed in at high tide, tail first, and pulled up on the beach as far as possible. An anchor was then attached to the lip to keep the carcass from moving with the pull of the falling tide. Once the carcass was exposed on the tidal flats, the Indian crews began the process of butchering. They severed the head with axes and boat spades. The boat spade resembled a shovel with a razor sharp blade. The baleen was then removed from the mouth and the workers then turned to the messy business of removing the blubber.

Using the boat spades, the men cut the blubber into strips and pulled them off with a hawser and tackle. As soon as the strips were pulled free, they were loaded into carts and taken to the tryworks, where they were cut into chunks and boiled or "tryed" in huge, 250 gallon kettles on a stone furnace. As the oil melted out of the blubber, it was skimmed off and poured into cooling vats. The scraps of whale flesh were fished out and used to fuel the fire. When the oil cooled down, it was then transferred to barrels and stored for shipment to London, New York, or Boston. It was a dirty, smelly business. The odor was so pungent that a Southampton town ordinance forbade the location of a trying station near the village. The boat crews worked in shifts around the clock for as long as a week on one whale carcass.

The English were dependent on the Indians, who had the skill and the courage to go out after the whales from November through March when the freezing waters meant death to those thrown from the small whale boats. The demand for skilled Indian whalers increased as the number of whaling companies grew. Company owners began to offer the Indian crews a half share of the blubber and baleen (identified as "bone" in the seventeenth century documents) and made liberal use of alcohol and other gifts in the negotiating process. Rival owners lured away whalers who had made commitments to other companies. In what appears to have been a response to this, the companies in Southampton, East Hampton, and Brookhaven drew up written contracts and recorded them with the town clerks. These contracts provided many important insights into the developing relationship between Indians and whites in the decades after the establishment of the English settlements.

About one hundred whaling contracts were recorded in the town records of East Hampton, Southampton, and Brookhaven between 1670 and 1685. The contracts, however, failed to bring order or predictability to the whaling enterprise, in part because of the cultural differences between the whalers and the owners. The Indians were accustomed to "gift exchanges" of goods or services rather than narrowly prescribed, written contractual arrangements set in specific time frames. Whalers who received "gifts" in the spring for a promise to go whaling the next fall might approach the owner in mid-summer asking for more gifts. If they were rebuffed, they saw no reason not to establish a new relationship with another owner. The English, of course, were both angered and frustrated with this behavior, which appeared to them to be deceitful and "immoral."

Their exasperation was expressed by John Topping, a whaling company owner from Southampton, in a petition to Governor Andros in 1680. Topping complained that the owners were "much disappointed and damnified in their business of whaling by the deceits and unfaithfulness of the Indians," who had been signed to a contract the previous spring by one owner, received some goods for signing and then, later in the summer, signed again with another owner (NYCD, 14:756–57). The Indians, continued Topping, "having received goods of one man in the spring upon account of whaling and now again of another to fit them for sea, leave their masters to quarrel." Topping asked that the town constables and officials intervene and stop the abuses, but there is no record of any action taken by either the governor or the local officials. It may well have

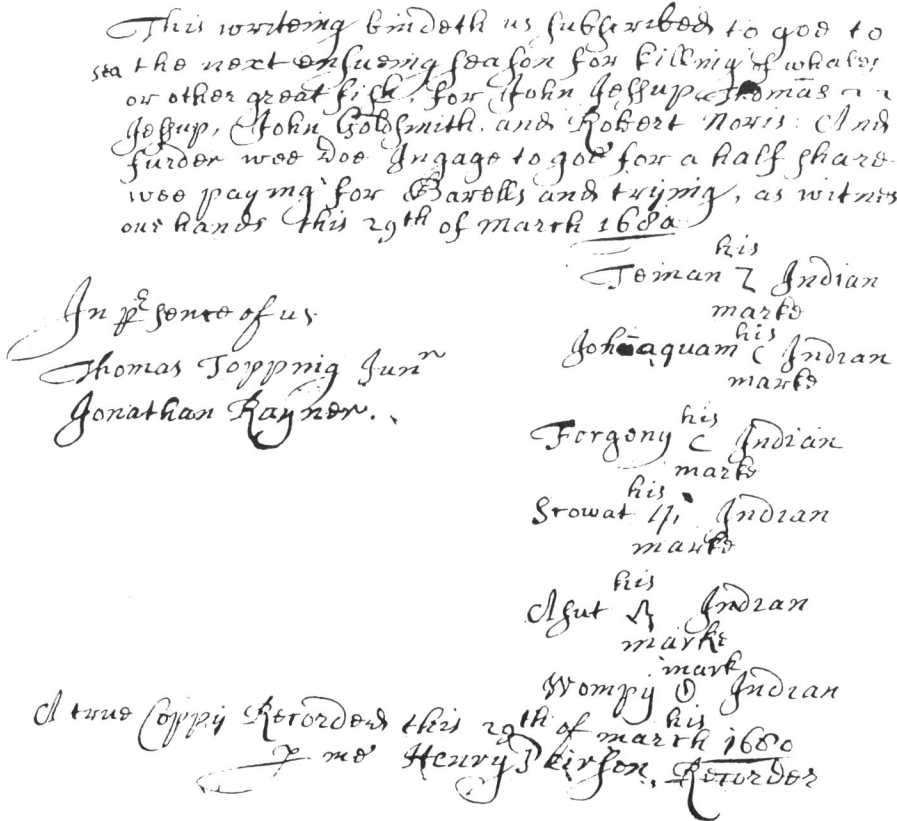

Fig. 11.4. Whaling contract, March 29, 1680

been that the officials had little sympathy for the owners, because they were not honest with each other. The owners were guilty of tampering with their rivals' Indian crews whenever it suited their advantage. The practice of recording whaling contracts in the town books was abandoned after 1685,[1] perhaps because the owners found another means of controlling the Indian whalers. The owners gradually drew the whalers into a system of debt peonage, described below, by giving them goods on credit at the end of the season rather than as initial payments.

In 1687, the seven whaling companies operating out of Southampton and East Hampton produced 3,604 barrels of oil valued at from £1.5 to £2 sterling per barrel (Reeves and Mitchell 1986:203; Edwards and Rattray 1956:201). Standards of measurement set by the colonial authorities required each barrel to contain 31.5 gallons. Although precise records were never kept by the companies, it has been estimated that an average of from twenty-five to thirty whales were taken off eastern Long Island each year during the latter half of the seventeenth century (Reeves and Mitchell 1986:204). The average yield of oil per whale was about thirty-six barrels. At that rate, the whaling enterprise was producing over £2,000 sterling a year for the eastern Long Island communities. In order to appreciate the purchasing power of this income in the late seventeenth century, consider the following prices: farm land cost from £1 to £3 per acre (Kross 1983:150–51; RTBH, Book B:44); a herd of sixteen cows cost £64 (RTSH, 2:10); a horse cost £10, and the entire estate of John Stretton Sr., one of the wealthiest men in East Hampton, was valued at £291 (RTEH, 2:441).

It is difficult to know how much of this profit found its way into the Indian communities. The whalers had a competitive advantage over the owners because they were in great demand. Few Englishmen cared to risk their lives in small boats on the open water in mid-winter. The English soon found ways, however, to limit the impact of this advantage. Whaling company owners complained about the bargaining power of the Indians and appealed to the colonial government to place a cap on the wages paid to the Indian whalers. In 1672, Governor Lovelace complied by setting a limit of one-half share of the season's hunt to be divided among the crew, and a cloth coat for each whaler for every whale killed (NYCD, 14:675). The Indians' share, however, was not paid to them in cash; it was "laid by" in the owner's hands as a credit line.

The share or "lay" system of payment was very similar to the sharecropping system in the South during the late nineteenth and early twentieth centuries (Strong 1990:19ff). Historian Daniel Vickers, who studied a similar lay system for Indian whalers on Nantucket, concluded that it was a form of debt peonage little different in principle from slavery (1983:583). Whaling contracts were usually negotiated at the end of the season in March or April for the next year. The whaler would then be able to purchase goods from the company owner on credit against the next season's share.

The owner would enter the value of the goods he gave each whaler in his account book. When the season ended, the total value of the whale oil and baleen from the whales killed by the Indian crew would be determined by the company owner. The value of the goods taken on credit was also set by the owner, who would then calculate the cash value of the individual share for each crew member and deduct the amount owed him. This system enabled the owners to have the total income from the season's hunt less only the cost of the goods which they sold, at a profit, to the Indians.

Two contracts negotiated in 1682 indicate that some of the Indian whalers suspected that the owners were inflating the prices of the goods extended in credit and reducing the cash value of the blubber in the Indians' share. Awonsis, Lenard, and Obadiah signed with James Hildreth with the stipulation that Hildreth charge them for the goods "at the same price as they can buy from others" (SHTA, Book D2:87–88). Another crew, led by Wompy, Owanamako, Patumbum, and Panalsam, required owner, Samuel Barnes, to pay them "as much as any other man will" for their share of the blubber (SHTA, Book D2:107–8).

The whaling account book of William "Tangier" Smith, whose company operated out of Brookhaven from 1696 until 1721, provides detailed information about the nature of the lay system (Strong 1990:17–28). None of the thirty-two Indian whalers who worked for Smith during those years ever got out of debt (Strong 1990:22-23, table 6). A whaler named Abraham, who worked for eleven seasons, ended up £10 in debt to Smith. Another Indian named Sacutacca, who worked for ten seasons from 1697 to 1707, still owed Smith £6, six shillings, and eight pence.

Many whalers found themselves so deeply in debt that they were forced to sign indentures for indefinite periods of time. One Shinnecock whaler named Artor, who had served several Southampton whaling companies between 1671 and 1679, owed so much money that "not knowing how to make satisfaction for the said debt," he agreed to indenture himself to John Fordham until the debt was paid (SHTA, Liber A:133). Artor's case was not unique. Many of the whaling contracts signed between 1677 and 1685 included a clause obligating the Indians to continue working from season to season until their debts were paid off (RTEH, 1:407–9, 2:78–79, 86-87, 152–53; SHTA, Book D2:72, 87-88, 93, 99, 107–8, 112, 117–18, 127, 168, 172, 187).

The debt peonage system established in these contracts differs from the indentured servant system in one crucial aspect—it does not set a term limit on the labor commitment. The whaler lost his freedom to sell his labor on the open market for an undetermined length of time. When a Montaukett whaler named Witness, who was in debt to Samuel Mulford of East Hampton, signed a contract to whale for John Wheeler, Mulford immediately protested that Witness was in debt to him and could not whale for anyone else until the debt was paid. Mulford entered his official protest into the record along with his own company contract which included Witness and three other Indian whalers (RTEH, 2:98-100).

Although the system was exploitive, the credit line with the company owners gave the whalers access to such highly valued European goods as powder, shot, cloth, coats, shoes, and alcohol. Undoubtedly, they were accorded fairly high status in their own communities. Their own people probably saw them as great hunters in a traditional context rather than as exploited servants of the English. Six of the whalers were identified as sachems in their contracts: Wennahum of Shelter Island; Chice, Pongumo, and Mahmanum of Shinnecock; and Mousup and Wampanacomps of Montauk (RTSH, 2:68; SHTA, Liber A:99, Book D2:75, 168; RTEH, 1:407–9). Even though the whalers were often charged inflated prices for the goods they purchased on the lay system, they were a conduit for the flow of considerable amounts of European trade goods into their communities. During the last half of the seventeenth century, they may have brought in more trade goods than their people had received from the sales of their lands (Strong 1995b).

## Indentured Servitude

The indenture system served several important functions in the colonial labor market. Although it is best known as a mechanism providing poor immigrants with a means of paying their passage to the colonies, the system provided a basic structure for the unskilled labor market. This market included Indians, African Americans, and poor whites who were born in the colonies. Town officials used the system to place paupers, orphans, and abandoned children with families who could afford to keep them as servants (Lott 1964:125; Galenson 1981:6-8; Jernegan 1931:106; Seybolt 1917:90). Occasionally, parents in poor families would negotiate indentures for their children, which called for a cash payment upon signing the contract and a guarantee that the child would be properly fed and clothed, taught to read and write, and given training in a skilled trade.

Provisions for literacy and skills, however, were seldom included in the indentures for Indians and African Americans (Seybolt 1917:89-90). One interesting exception to this pattern is an indenture negotiated between an Indian named Toby and Arthur Futhy, a carpenter in Brookhaven in 1684.[2] Toby agreed to work for a term of three years, during which he would serve his master by day and night and never leave his residence without permission.

The contract also listed, in rather demeaning terms, all the things that Toby should not do (RTBH, Book B:191-92). He was not to steal from his master, nor to damage his goods, nor to allow them to be stolen or damaged by anyone else. Toby was admonished to keep his master's secrets and to behave in such a way that he himself would have nothing at all to hide. He was not to frequent taverns or ale houses nor to "play cards or dice or any unlawful game." The terms also included two very intrusive personal prohibitions. Toby was told that "matrimony he shall not contract, fornication he shall not commit." These prohibitions are commonly found in seventeenth-century and eighteenth-century indentures, suggesting that the servants actually had a very lively social life which their masters sought, in vain, to curtail (HTHA: indenture file; Seybolt 1917:88).

In exchange for Toby's service, disciplined behavior, and silence, Arthur Futhy agreed to teach Toby the "art and mystery of a house carpenter soe far as he shall be capable to learn." Arthur also promised to provide room, board, and clothing. At the end of Toby's three-year term, Arthur would give him two new suits of apparel "from head to foot," one for working days and the other for holy days, one broad ax, one hand saw, one square, a pair of compasses, a broad and a narrow chisel, a gouge, an auger, and forty shillings.

Toby's indenture was not at all typical for an Indian laborer. Few Indians ever got such an opportunity to learn a skilled trade. A year earlier, for example, an Indian named Humphrey, alias Mahcarack, signed an indenture with Andrew Gibb of Brookhaven for a two-year term which included the same restrictions. Gibb paid off Humphery's £11 debt to Richard Woodhall, but the Indian received no money and no training. He was provided with room and board and promised a coat at the end of his indenture (RTBH, Book B:172-73).

The earliest English reference to an Indian servant on Long Island in the Long Island colonial records provides some important social insights. In 1644, only a few years after the settlement of Southampton was established, an Indian servant woman named Hope was charged by the court in Southampton with adultery (see above, Chapter 9). Hope was a servant in the home of Edward Howell, a prominent Southampton settler. It seems likely that Hope came with the Howells from Massachusetts in 1640. She may have been one of the Pequot women taken prisoner in the devastating Pequot War. The child was assigned to Edward Howell to be his indentured servant until the "basely begotton" child reached the age of thirty.

Hope is one of the few Indian servant women mentioned in the colonial records.

> This Indenture made betwene Thomas James Mynister of Easthampton And Tom : Indyan late servant to Roger Smith as ffolloweth :
>
> That the aforesaid Tom Indyan doth bind himselfe : Apprentice to the aforesaid Thomas James his heires or assignes for the full tearme of three yeares & a halfe, to doe him true & ffaithfull service & to be obedient to all his Lawfull Commands by Day or night, for which service the said Tho. James doth bind himselfe his heires or assignes to allow the said Tom meate drinke & Clothing sufficient for him, & a coate a yeare which shalbe at his owne Dispose of trucking Cloth, & when his three yeares And a halfe is out to leave him as well Clothed as I find him & Two coates of Trucking Cloth In Confirmation of the premises we mutually set to our hands & Seales. This agreement made with Consent of Abel his brother : this 15 ffebruarie : 1677-78.
>
>                 TOM T INDIAN
>                    his marke
>                 THO. JAMES.
>
> Abel        his
> marke
> Subscribed & Sealed
> in presense of us
>                   Arther Cresse
>                   John Mulford.

Fig. 11.5. Indian indenture, February 15, 1678

She is mentioned, of course, because of the scandal, but most of the entries refer to men. Several of the indentures in the East Hampton town records involve Indian whalers and their families. One of the earliest of these contracts, signed in 1678, bound an Indian named Tom to the Reverend Thomas James for the term of three and one half years. The contract was witnessed by Tom's brother, Abel, who went to sea for James' whaling company in 1677 (RTEH, 2:407–9).

Tom was obligated to serve the clergyman for three and one-half years and to do him "faithful service and to be obedient to all his lawful commands by day or night," in return for which James promised to "allow the said Tom meate drinke and clothing sufficient for him, and a coate a year . . . and when his three years and a half is out to leave him as well clothed as I find him and two coates of trucking cloth" (see fig. 11.5; RTEH, 1:411). Tom had been indentured to another settler named Roger Smith prior to his contract with James. Tom's indenture, which is typical of the Indian indentures, stands in sharp contrast to

Toby's contract. Tom got two coats, no other clothes, no training, and no tools for the same term of service.

The specific terms of the indentures varied widely. John Indian, a Montaukett, bound himself out to Richard Stretton of East Hampton for a two-year term in 1683. John was to receive £12 at the end of the term. If he went out on a whaling expedition, however, he was to receive his half share in addition to the £12 payment (RTEH, 2:132-33). John Mahue, also a Montaukett, indentured himself to Philip Leake of East Hampton for only three months and was paid £3, six shillings—about twice the monthly rate paid to John Indian. Jeffrey, another Montaukett, bound himself out to Richard Shaw for a term of seven years for a payment of £20—less than £3 a year— and room and board (RTEH, 2:212).

In some instances, parents who negotiated indentures for their young children received a few shillings when the contract was signed. Two such contracts were negotiated by a veteran Montaukett whaler named Papasequin for his son and daughter. Papasequin's name appears on eight whaling contracts between 1675 and 1683 (RTEH, 2:78-79, 86-87, 95-96, 373-74; SHTA, Liber A:90; SHTA, Book D 2:74, 85, 117-18). In 1685, Papasequin and his wife bound out their seven-year-old son, Quansurh, to Jacob Schellinger for a ten-year term beginning in 1688 (RTEH, 2:173). Papasequin, who had gone to sea for Schellinger in 1679, may have wanted his son to become a whaler. Schellinger paid Papasequin twenty shillings when the child was delivered to him in 1688 and £10 to Quansurh at the end of his term.

Six years later, Papasequin and his wife bound out their daughter, Marget, to Daniel Osborn for a seven-year term (EHPLC, 10 WB:126). Osborn paid the parents £3 and gave their daughter room and board and £3 when she finished her term. Both children undoubtedly experienced a rather dramatic immersion in English culture and values, but there was no provision for teaching them to read or write English or preparing them for a trade.

Jerred, an Indian servant to John Youngs of Southold, bequeathed his six-year-old son, Young Jerred, to his master in 1678 (RTS, 1:154). Jerred, who was dying of consumption, indentured his son to Youngs for nineteen years. There was no mention in the agreement of any payment to either Jerred or to his son when the term was completed. Not all children had parents who could represent them in negotiating their indenture. A one-year-old Montaukett orphan named Hopewell was indentured by his Indian guardians to John Fixthand, an East Hampton man, for a twenty-five-year term. When the child was six, Fixthand sold the remaining nineteen years of the indenture to the Reverend Thomas James for £15 sterling (EHTC, Leather Bound Book:34). James agreed to pay Hopewell £10 at the end of his nineteen year term and to give him a suit of clothes. Fixthand made more on the transaction than Hopewell made for his long years of labor.

Hopewell's experience raises another unpleasant aspect of the indenture system. Servants, like slaves, could be bought and sold without their consent.

They could also be leased or "rented out" by their masters. An Indian named Adso, for example, who had signed a contract with John Miller, Jr. of East Hampton for two whaling seasons beginning in 1684, was sent by Miller to whale for Richard Shaw on December 11, 1684 (RTEH, 2:152-53).

In contrast to the Indian indentures, the bonds for whites were more likely to include a clause requiring the children to be taught a trade and basic reading and writing skills (Seybolt 1917:91). In 1683, for example, Renock Garrison bound out his six-year-old son Samuel to Isaack and Elizabeth Mills until he reached his twenty-first birthday (RTEH, 2:133–34). The boy was to be trained as a carpenter and taught to read and write. The Garrisons also bound out two other children, John aged twelve and Anna aged three, to be apprenticed to a weaver. These children were also to receive reading and writing instruction. The difference is significant because it clearly indicates that the Indians were viewed as a permanent underclass who would provide domestic and unskilled labor for the English.

## Indian Slavery

Some Indians were slaves who served for life and were chattel in the eyes of the law. Unfortunately, the data relating to Indian slavery in colonial America is very sparse (Lauber 1913:105–17). The primary sources of Indian slaves in southern New England and on Long Island were the captives from the Pequot War (1637) and King Philip's War (1675–76). A small number of Indian slaves were also imported from the Carolinas and from the Spanish colonies. Indian captives were usually sold into slavery in some distant port, because they could easily escape to a friendly refuge if they remained near their own people.

Some Indians were enslaved by court order as a penalty for a crime, but these were usually shipped to the West Indies or Bermuda (Lauber 1913:201). Nangenutch, a Montaukett found guilty of attempted rape, was sentenced to be whipped and sold into slavery in the West Indies in 1668 (Strong 1994a). However, he broke out of jail in New York City where he was awaiting deportation and was not recaptured.

One of the Indian slaves who came to Long Island in the slave trade was a young girl named Beck. In 1677, James Loper purchased Beck from Samuel Rogers, who lived in New England. Beck, who is identified in the town records as a "captive," was probably captured by English troops during King Philip's War. She was purchased, said Loper, to help his wife with her household chores. According to the bill of sale, Loper was "to hould possess and enjoy as his . . . proper estate during her natural life" (see fig. 11.6; RTEH, 1:412–13).

Indian slavery was abolished by the colonial government in 1679, when it ordered that all Indians were to be set free except for those who had been imported into the colony and sold here (NYCD, 13:537–38). These "foreign" Indian slaves brought into the colony had to be exported within six months or they would be freed. The six month period was apparently granted to allow a slave trader to sell

> Theise presents witneseth yt I Samuell Rodgers of New London in his Maties Collony of Conectticut in New England for a valuable Consideration by me allready in hand received of Mr. James Loper of Easthampton on Long Island have Sould allianated & past over and by these presents for me my heires Executors administrators Doe sell alianate & pass over In Open Market unto ye sd James Loper his heires Executors or assignes one Indian Captive girle about Thirteene or foorteene yeeres of age Comonlie Called or knowne by ye name of Beck for him ye sd James Loper his heires or assignes or Either of them for to have hould posses and enjoy as his or their proper estate duringe her naturall life and doe by theise presents Declare my selfe to bee the true & Right Owner of the said girle and therefore have good & Lawfull power soe to doe. In Witnes whereof I the said Samuell Rodgers have hereunto Sett my hand & seale the Eighteenth Day of March 1677-8.
>
> SAMUELL RODGERS. [L.S.]
>
> Signed sealed & Deliverd
> In presents of
> > Issaack Molyne
> > J. Wheeller.

Fig. 11.6. Sale of Beck, an Indian slave girl

the Indian slaves to a buyer who would take the Indians out of New York. The law was not enforced because there are many references to Indian slaves both in New York and on Long Island until all slavery was ended in 1827. Complaints were made to Governor Clinton as late as 1750, that Indian children born in New York were being sold as slaves (Lauber 1913:200).

In 1687, Thomas Hawarden of New York sold an Indian slave named Will to Christopher Dene in Hempstead. The boy was to belong to Dene "forever." Hawarden said that he was "legally seized of the said Indian boy as his own proper slave and hath full power and legal authority to sell and dispose of the same to the said Christopher Dene" (RTNSH, 2:60). Hawarden had apparently purchased Will in New York from a slave dealer. There is no indication in the records that Dene's purchase was ever challenged by the colonial authorities. Shortly thereafter, Dene sold the boy to Nathaniel Prime (Moss 1993:11).

In Newtown (Elmhurst), three Indian slaves were listed in the estate records. In 1691, Jonathan Strickland, a resident of Newtown, listed an Indian slave boy in his estate and valued him at £10 sterling. Four decades later, William Parcell left an Indian woman and a young boy to his daughter in his will (Kross, 1983:92). William Smith, patriarch of St. George's Manor in Brookhaven, bequeathed Negro and Indian slaves to his children in 1704. In 1724, Arent Schuyler of New York left two Indian slave women to his daughters (Lauber 1913:114).

Private citizens ignored the law, and public officials cooperated in the return of Indian slaves who tried to escape illegal captivity. Advertisements were run in the Manhattan newspapers identifying runaway Indian slaves. In July 1733, the *New York Gazette* advertised for the return of a runaway Indian slave from

Flushing. In the February 6–13, 1739 edition of the *Gazette*, Moses Gombauld, a merchant, asked for the return of an eighteen-year-old Indian slave boy who spoke French, English, and Spanish. Later that same year, William Sims announced that his slave, a twenty-five-year-old Indian, had run away. The Indian had previously been owned by Obediah Smith of Smithtown. (McKee 1935:115). Similar advertisements were run in the *New York Weekly Mercury* in 1740 and 1756 for Indian slaves from New York and Long Island (Lauber 1913:115).

In one case, however, a courageous Indian slave named Sarah, "the daughter of Dorkas, an Indian woman," did raise a challenge in her own behalf. Sarah had been sold to John Parker of Southampton by James Parshall for £16 when she was only eight years old (Adams 1918:120). According to the entry in the town record, Sarah became Parker's property "during her natural life." In 1712, when she was 23, Parker sold her and an Indian boy named Abel, to John Wick of Bridgehampton for £21, twelve shillings. Wick sold Sarah to Captain Robert Walters of New York, who took her to the island of Madeira to be sold in the slave market there.

Sarah, with a surprising display of resourcefulness given her circumstances, petitioned the English consul on the island and claimed that she was born of free Indian parents. She further charged that neither Parker nor Wick held a valid title of ownership and asked that they be challenged to produce proof of their claims. The consul granted her request and arranged for her return to Long Island where she petitioned the governor for her freedom (Rabito-Wyppensenwah 1993:430).

Sarah's claim that she was born of free Indian parents raised an important legal issue because the colony had enacted a law in 1707, which stated that "all and every Negro, Indian, Mulatto and Mestee Bastard child and children who are and shall be born of any Negro, Indian, Mulatto or Mestee shall follow ye state and condition of the mother and he be esteemed reputed taken and adjudged a slave to all intents and purposes whatsoever" (Lincoln 1894:598). The children of free Indian men and African American slave mothers, therefore, became slaves because of their mother's status. Sarah probably had this statute in mind when she testified that her mother, Dorkas, had been free.

The increasing number of references to "mustees" and "mulattos" in the early eighteenth-century records probably refer to these children. Although many of these "mustees" were as much Indian as they were African American, the whites categorized them into a lower socio-economic status, denying them their "Indianness." This arbitrary racial classification was romanticized by the whites who "lamented the vanishing Indians."

The relationship between Indian and African American slaves and servants is not surprising. They suffered much the same exploitation, and they shared the same servants' quarters in the English households. In a few instances, they joined together in violent revolt against their masters. The house burning incident which took place in Southampton in 1657, apparently was a result of such a conspiracy (see Chapter 9). Unfortunately, no other records of this intriguing event have survived, so we can not corroborate Wyandanch's testimony. If the sachem's account is true, it would certainly be interesting to hear what the woman's grievance was and how she managed to have such influence over her Shinnecock co-conspirators.

The threat of conspiracies involving African and Indian slaves became a growing concern among the whites. Although we have no record of slave revolts until the beginning of the eighteenth century, a colonial ordinance passed in 1682 clearly indicated that some disturbances had taken place. According to the Court of Assizes, "Great evils and inconveniences have . . . [been] committed and done by Negroes and Indian slaves." The problem was attributed to large gatherings of Indians and African Americans on Sundays "and at other unseasonable times" when they engaged in "several rude and unlawful sports and pastimes to the dishonor of God, profanation of his holy day, breach and disturbance of the peace and quiet." Local town officials were even more dismayed to find that many of their own people were attracted to these gatherings. These whites, they lamented, "are likewise drawed aside and misled to be spectators of such evil practices and thereby diverted from the more suitable and pious duty and service" (NYHS 1912:37-38).

The court ordered, therefore, that no Negro or Indian slaves could leave their masters' plantations or homes on the Sabbath or on any other "unseasonable" time without a written pass, signed and dated by their owners. Slaves caught without such authorization were to be arrested and "forthwith severely whipped." Their owners were fined to pay the court costs. Apparently, these gatherings of Indians and Africans frightened the whites as much as the powwows had in the past. Large numbers of slaves and servants coming together without white control and supervision was most unsettling to the local officials. Unfortunately, we know very little about the social activities which took place at these meetings, but they were probably lively and colorful mixtures of African and Native American traditions. In spite of all efforts to curb these gatherings, they were still being held in the nineteenth century and are probably related to the spring celebration called "June Meeting" which is still honored at Shinnecock and Poospatuck today (see Epilogue and Strong, 1996a).

In 1750, Governor Clinton ordered that all Indian children born of free parents who were still held as slaves be returned to their parents. In spite of the governor's order, there were still isolated instances of Indian slavery on Long Island for several years (Lauber 1913:201). All of the Indian slaves, including those who were imported in the slave trade, were finally freed along with the African American slaves in 1827.

## Indian Free Labor

Not all Indians entered the English economic system as slaves or indentured servants. Free laborers were hired for the day or for a specific job and were paid upon completion of the task in money or in goods. Many Indians worked on a part-time basis for English farmers, merchants, and artisans. Some of these jobs, such as fence watching, tending livestock, rescuing livestock from wetland swamps, carrying flour from the mill to the homes, and doing chores around the farm, did not require much skill, but a few tasks, such as the construction of rail fences, guiding hunters and fishermen, and the trying of whale oil were skilled crafts. Indians also produced some goods such as baskets, scrub brushes, meat from game animals, fish and shellfish, tanned hides, and feathers, which they sold or traded for English manufactured goods. By the beginning of the eighteenth century many Montauketts were raising livestock of their own. They recorded the earmarks of their cattle, swine, and horses in the town records along with the English farmers' marks (RTEH, 3:134, 170, 186–87, 271, 317, 423; 24:9, 124). Most of the food from these animals, however, was consumed by the owners rather than sold for a profit.

Many Indians were attracted to the English towns where they could find odd jobs. Nangenutch, the young Montaukett who was accused of molesting three different English women in East Hampton, had been hired to carry sacks of flour from the mill to the kitchens where the alleged molestations occurred (Strong 1994a). Nangenutch had previously been employed as a servant to Richard Shaw of East Hampton. The incidents of sexual contact, however, were much more likely to involve English masters and Indian servant women. John Lyon Gardiner, the seventh lord of the manor on Gardiners Island, recorded in his farm ledger in 1792 that his grandfather, John Gardiner the third, was the father of a Montaukett woman named Betty Fowler. George Pharaoh, an elderly Montaukett, told John Lyon Gardiner that his grandfather, "Old Mr. John," spoke Algonquian and "came to their wigwams to eat fresh fish and he liked the young squaws of the old sachem [Wyandanch] breed" (Gardiner n.d.:157–58). Gardiner also reported that the Montauketts had been promised, perhaps by "Old Mr. John," that they could have improvement rights to land on Gardiners Island. The Montauketts asked Gardiner why they did not have that right anymore. He did not record his answer.

Betty Fowler's daughter, Mary, married Samson Occom and their descendants have been traced by genealogists Rudi and Will Ottery, to families on Long Island and in Brotherton, Wisconsin, where many Montauketts migrated in the eighteenth century. None of these people, however, has ever been accepted by the Gardiners as family members, nor were they ever given any share in the Gardiner wealth (Ottery 1993:315–26).

Some of the Indian women who interested "Old Mr. John" were employed on Gardiners Island to tend the corn fields. "Squaws in those days," wrote John Lyon Gardiner in his Farm Book, "were supposed to be the best hands for raising maize" (Gardiner n.d.:142). The employment of women in the corn fields is striking because such field work was considered to be in the male domain by the

English. Unfortunately, we do not have much information about this practice on Long Island.

There were undoubtedly many Indians who did odd jobs in the colonial settlements throughout Long Island. We know of Nangenutch's work because of the sensational trial, but most of the information about unskilled labor is limited to brief references in public and private account books. An entry in the *East Hampton Trustees Journal,* for example, authorized the payment of nine pence to Montauketts who brought them information about livestock mired in the swamps or about dead animals whose skin was still salvageable. If the Indians rescued an animal they would be paid eighteen pence (EHTJ, 1:137).

In the spring of 1698, the town of East Hampton paid two Montauketts, Ben and Pharaoh, seven shillings, six pence for repairing and maintaining the fence around the grazing fields at Montauk for the summer (RTEH, 2:392). The average daily pay for unskilled labor in the latter half of the seventeenth and early eighteenth centuries was three shillings (RTEH, 2:220, RTSH, 5:5; Kross 1983:134). Even if we assume that Ben and Pharaoh were not on duty every day all summer, the pay is well below the daily rate for an English worker.

That same spring, Weomp, a veteran Montauk whaler who had gone to sea as a young man for three different East Hampton whaling companies (1675–1681),[3] was given £1 sterling, "as part pay for Ginning" (RTEH, 2:392). "Gin," derived from the pre-industrial word for "engine," meaning a device of some sort, was used in the eighteenth century to describe a trap or enclosure for livestock. The animals were driven into the gin before they were moved from the summer grazing areas to the winter fields so that they could be counted. The ear marks on each animal identified the owners who were then charged for the grazing rights. Weomp was paid much more than Ben and Pharaoh, perhaps because the ginning required more skill and responsibility.[4]

Some of these labor contracts included a clause setting a bond obligation guaranteeing completion of the assigned tasks. When Hanable, an Indian from Shelter Island, signed an agreement on March 5, 1698, to search the woods and wetlands for Nathaniel Sylvester's cattle over a six week period, he agreed to pay his employer £10 sterling if he failed to find all of the livestock. Hanable was to be paid £2 sterling in advance and £2 more at the end of his term.[5] He would earn about three shillings a day, but he also ran the risk of assuming a debt that was more than twice his salary for six weeks labor.

Few of the other domestic servants and unskilled day workers appear in the colonial documents unless they are mentioned in written contracts. One such contract was negotiated in December 1679, between Thomas Biggs, Jr. of Brookhaven and Gie (Gy), a sachem from Setauket. Gie agreed to clear five acres of land for Biggs, cutting down all of the little trees, "that is about as big as ones leg" (RTBH, Book B:28). In return, Biggs was to pay the sachem £4, ten shillings if the work was completed in time for the spring planting in May. If the work was not finished until the fall, Gie would be paid £4 in trading cloth at ten shillings per yard. Gie was given one coat when the contract was signed and a second coat when the task was finished.

Another of the unskilled jobs which was important enough to the English to require written contracts, was fence minding on Montauk. An agreement between the Montauketts and East Hampton, signed in 1655, allowed the settlers to graze their livestock in the Indians' planting grounds after the fall harvest until the spring planting in late April or early May. The settlers agreed to construct fences that would keep their animals from the Indians' crops during the summer growing season.

Fences needed constant watching; even those built "pig tight, horse high, and bull strong" were often weakened by the weather and the constant probing of the livestock. The town of East Hampton hired Indians from Montauk to monitor the fences, day and night, from April to October. The Indians were asked to set up their wigwams just inside the fences and to live there for the season. The timing was perfect for whalers, because their season was finished by April. The Indians were paid by a barter system rather than in cash.

In April 1683, for example, Quaquehide (Harry) was hired to watch the Montauk fence and in return the town would arrange to have an acre of land plowed near his wigwam and give him ten bushels of corn (RTEH, 2:125–26). The town paid ten shillings to have the acre plowed and four shillings a bushel for the corn (RTEH, 2:393; 3:143). The total value of the goods and services, therefore, was £2, ten shillings. Quaquehide would be finished with his fence duties in time to go to whaling in November. The following year, another whaler,

Fig. 11.7. Indian men constructing a post-and-rail fence

named Jeffrey, and his wife, were hired under a similar arrangement, except that the couple received a coat in addition to the plowing and the corn (RTEH, 2:145–46).

Fences, of course, play a vital role in any agricultural system. There were serious legal consequences for any farmer who did not keep his fences in good repair. If his livestock got out because his fences were allowed to fall into disrepair, he would be liable for any damage they caused. Fence construction, therefore, was a highly valued skill. Indians, who were accustomed to working with the wood from local trees, were often recruited and trained in the use of iron woodworking tools.

In November 1681, Gie, the Setauket sachem who had cleared the land for Thomas Biggs, was hired by John Roe to construct a post-and-rail fence, five rails high at eighteen pence a rail (RTBH, Book B:509). The fence had to be completed for the spring planting in April. Gie was to be assisted by an Indian named Gudger, who also worked as a whaler (RTBH, Book B:105). This New England-style fence, unlike the postless split rail "zig-zag" fences in the southern colonies, required considerable skill. The six-foot long posts were cut from foot-thick chestnut or cedar trees and split in half. A hole was then chiseled every four to six inches in the upper portion of the post. Eleven-foot long rails were cut from oak or ash trees and fitted into the holes in the posts (Hawke 1988:35).

Two Indians, Arastottle and Cellis (Kellis), signed a similar fence contract with John Tooker, Jr. of Brookhaven, in May of 1683 (RTBH, Book B:148–49). Arastottle was to cut two hundred eleven-foot rails and seven five-hole posts and have them ready in three weeks. Kellis agreed to cut sixty more five-hole posts in one month's time. The contract does not mention the payment for the two men. It is possible that Arastottle and Kellis were working to pay off a previous debt. This was the case in another fence contract in 1685 between Jeremy and Bumbrest and Arthur Futhy who had signed a relatively enlightened indenture with Toby the year before. The two Indians agreed to cut six hundred split rails and to have them ready for carting in six weeks (RTBH, Book B:242–43). In return, Futhy was to pay Adam Smith £1, thirteen shillings, and John Thomas six shillings. Apparently, these were debts owed by the Indians to the Englishmen. Jeremy and Bumbrest did receive six shillings when they signed the contract. Jeremy, like Gudger and several other Indians, had a second job. He had gone whaling for Andrew Gibb of Brookhaven in 1682 (RTBH, Book B:105).

If the Indian workers did not meet the deadlines set in the contracts, they could be hauled into court and sued by their employer. When Bumbrest was unable to deliver the rails on time, Futhy took Bumbrest to court and forced him to cut an extra one hundred rails as a penalty (RTBH, Book, B:254). The Indian also had to give Futhy six days of labor and pay the court costs. That same day in court, John Tooker, Jr. also sued Bumbrest along with Kellis, who had worked for Tooker in 1683. The court ruled that the Indians "having made an agreement with John Tooker for a certain parcel of fencing akording to the writing between them and they not doing of it akording to time, therefore they both of them agree to give the above said John Tooker twenty shillings and pay court charges" (RTBH, Book B:254). The two Indians were thereby forced out of the free labor market and trapped in a cycle of debt peonage. Another important task requiring specific skills was the processing (trying) of the whale oil described above. Although most whaling companies expected the whaling crews to process the blubber into marketable oil, some owners negotiated individual contracts with Indians to carry out this arduous task.

In 1680, Jonathan Hildreth and John Carwithy hired Sequanah, who was probably from Shinnecock, to try the blubber from the season's hunt. Hildreth and Carwithy provided the pots and the wood for the fire. Sequannah was to be paid two shillings, six pence per barrel, "or that which is equivalent." The last clause suggests that he might be paid in goods or credit rather than in cash (RTSH, 2:80). The following year, Weeis and Masagandsag negotiated a better rate—three shillings, six pence—from Thomas Cooper and Samuel Barnes, but they had to agree to pay for any oil that was lost because of their negligence (SHTA, Book D2:71).

Apparently, the rate of two shillings, six pence was generally accepted because two other contracts, one in 1682 and a second in 1683, were set at that rate (SHTA, Book D2:84, 131). Gie, the Setauket sachem, and an Indian named Towaring, were hired by Andrew Gibb at that rate as well, but Gibb added a bonus of two bushels of corn (RTBH, Book B:109).

## Summary

As the land base was slowly nibbled away the Indians became increasingly dependent on the English market system. The desire for English manufactured goods gradually entrapped more and more Indians in a web of debt. Some of the Indians on the eastern end of Long Island were recruited as whalers, provided with boats and iron harpoons, and sent out to kill the whales which spawned each year in the waters along the south shore. Others engaged in less skilled work as indentured servants, slaves and free laborers. The Indians and the Africans were viewed by the English as part of a permanent underclass. The employers seldom made any effort to teach the non-white servant children to read or write. Although the Indians became dependent on the outside economy and were given little chance to advance in status because of local prejudices, they did maintain a separate cultural tradition which continues to distinguish them from other ethnic groups.

Fig. 12.1. Powwow at Shinnecock, 1954 with Native Americans from different tribes

# Epilogue

## Continuity and Reaffirmation

The Algonquian peoples of Long Island have struggled quietly since the beginning of the eighteenth century to maintain their culture and their Indian identity as the rapidly growing non-Indian population overwhelmed them. A brief account of this struggle and a description of their current status can be found in *"We Are Still Here!" The Algonquian Peoples of Long Island Today* (Strong 1996a).

The four surviving communities have devoted much of their time and energy in a continuing fight to protect or regain their lands. The Shinnecocks and the Unkechaugs have had to fight desperately against attempts to nibble away at the boundaries of their reservations. The Poospatuck Reservation, as noted earlier, was reduced from the original grant of 175 acres to about fifty. In 1859 the Shinnecocks were forced to relinquish their rights to the Shinnecock Hills, a large parcel of land west of the village of Southampton. In 1955, however, the Shinnecocks successfully blocked an attempt by a developer to establish a title to nine acres on the northern border of the reservation (Gumbs 1983:118-29). The Montauketts and the Matinecocks are currently reviewing strategies to reclaim parcels of their lands in areas which have not yet been developed.

The Indians have continued to participate in seasonal gatherings such as June Meeting, the fall Powwow, and the Mid-Winter Feast. These communal celebrations reunite tribal members and reaffirm traditional culture. Funerals are also

Fig. 12.2. Flag of Unkechaug Nation

Fig. 12.3. Shinnecock Community Center

an occasion for the communities to come together to help in the preparation of food for the close relatives and friends of the deceased during the period of mourning. During the 1960s, the younger generation of Indians at Shinnecock began to revive the sweat lodge and tobacco rituals practiced by their ancestors.

One of the more dramatic developments in the reaffirmation of Indian identity which has taken place since World War II is the strengthening of community programs on the Shinnecock Reservation. In all societies community bonds are reinforced by age-set associations, which unite members around common needs, and by voluntary associations which focus on specific shared interests. The youth, the women, and the elders have formed their own groups which serve their particular interests within the context of the larger tribal society. All of these programs are directed and staffed by the Shinnecocks themselves. The tribe has established the Shinnecock Nation Cultural Center and Museum. At this cultural learning center visitors can participate in a half-day program which includes a nature trail with a guided introduction to nutritional and medicinal plants, a storytelling session, a visit to the traditional Native American garden project, and a traditional meal of succotash and sassafras tea. Another important development at Shinnecock is the increased role of the Shinnecock women in tribal affairs. Women now vote in all tribal elections and several serve on the Tribal Council

Fig. 12.4. Chief Thunder Bird (Henry Bess) and his daughter, Chee Chee, 1974. Chief Thunder Bird was Shinnecock ceremonial sachem from 1939–1989 and revived the powwow at Shinnecock.

The Shinnecock youth formed a group dedicated to the study and preservation of their culture. They study traditional songs, chants, dances, and arts, and perform at their annual powwow. They also travel widely to participate in powwows on other reservations. A "Title V" Indian Education grant now provides daily tutoring for the elementary and secondary students on the reservation. The senior citizens have taken advantage of government programs for the elderly and organized hot lunch programs, transportation, and medical care services on the reservation. A Family Preservation Center will soon be constructed at Shinnecock, which will serve the needs of all the generations.

The Shinnecock Indian Health Service, established in 1993, has now expanded from a small two-room building to a much larger facility. A physician and professional nurse are on duty on a regular schedule to provide free medical care to all of the Shinnecocks. The health service center is open five days a week for annual check-ups and preventive care. The family support services include programs for substance abuse referrals, prenatal care, and AIDs awareness. The facility has a resource library and a cardiac rehabilitation area.

There has also been a rapid growth of economic activity on the Shinnecock and Poospatuck Reservations in the 1990s. In 1995 the Shinnecock Tribal council established an Economic Development Committee to study the potential for tribal enterprises and to make recommendations for investments. With the exception of the Shinnecock Powwow, however, most of the economic activity on the two reservations has been family-owned operations. There are two trading posts, a cigarette shop, a bakery, and an organic coffee company at Shinnecock and three trading posts at Poospatuck. The shops all benefit from the sale of tax-free cigarettes. The two Shinnecock trading posts also sell Indian arts and crafts and feature items made by Shinnecock artists.

The Unkechaugs have also experienced many positive changes in the recent past. Chief Harry Wallace has focused on the reaffirmation of traditional culture, a campaign to reclaim tribal lands, and the improvement of reservation facilities. His wife, Margo Thunder Bird, a Shinnecock, has established an educational program for Unkechaug children and a research project on Unkechaug history and language. The students meet in the Poospatuck community center for tutoring in their school subjects and for classes in Indian arts, crafts, songs, and dances.

The Montaukett and Matinecock people have had a much more difficult time holding onto their culture and their communal ties because they have no land base. In the nineteenth century, scattered groups formed or joined congregations of the African Methodist Episcopal (A.M.E.) Zion Church. In 1840, the Montauketts helped to found a parish of the A.M.E. Zion Church in Sag Harbor and eight years before, a Matinecock group had joined with local African Americans to form the A.M.E. Zion Church in Manhasset. Both groups also have their own informal tribal gatherings in their homes and frequently participate in communal

Fig. 12.5. St. David's A.M.E. Zion Church, Sag Harbor

*Continuity and Reaffirmation*                                                                                              293

celebrations at Shinnecock and Poospatuck. Chief Osceola Townsend of the Matinecocks and Chief Robert Pharaoh of the Montauketts are each involved at present in organizing campaigns to reclaim some of their ancient lands and to obtain official recognition as a tribe. They are working with legal consultants and tribal members to collect the necessary documentation.

The current mood among most of the Algonquian groups on Long Island today is one of enthusiasm for their current endeavors and optimism for the future. They have survived military defeats, cultural repression, racial prejudice, discrimination, and the loss of most of their land. Surviving all these assaults with their culture and their identity intact, however, is a victory which gives them great pride and satisfaction. This is best expressed in a phrase heard often by outsiders who ask them about their long struggle to survive. They say with great feeling, *"We are still here!"*

**Shinnecock Nation Museum Seal**

Fig. 12.6. The seal has drawings of whales which were important sources of food and a major power in spiritual belief. The wampum belt signifies a great art of traditional Shinnecock culture. The wigwam, thunderbird, and man with traditional pipe symbolize traditional cultural practice.

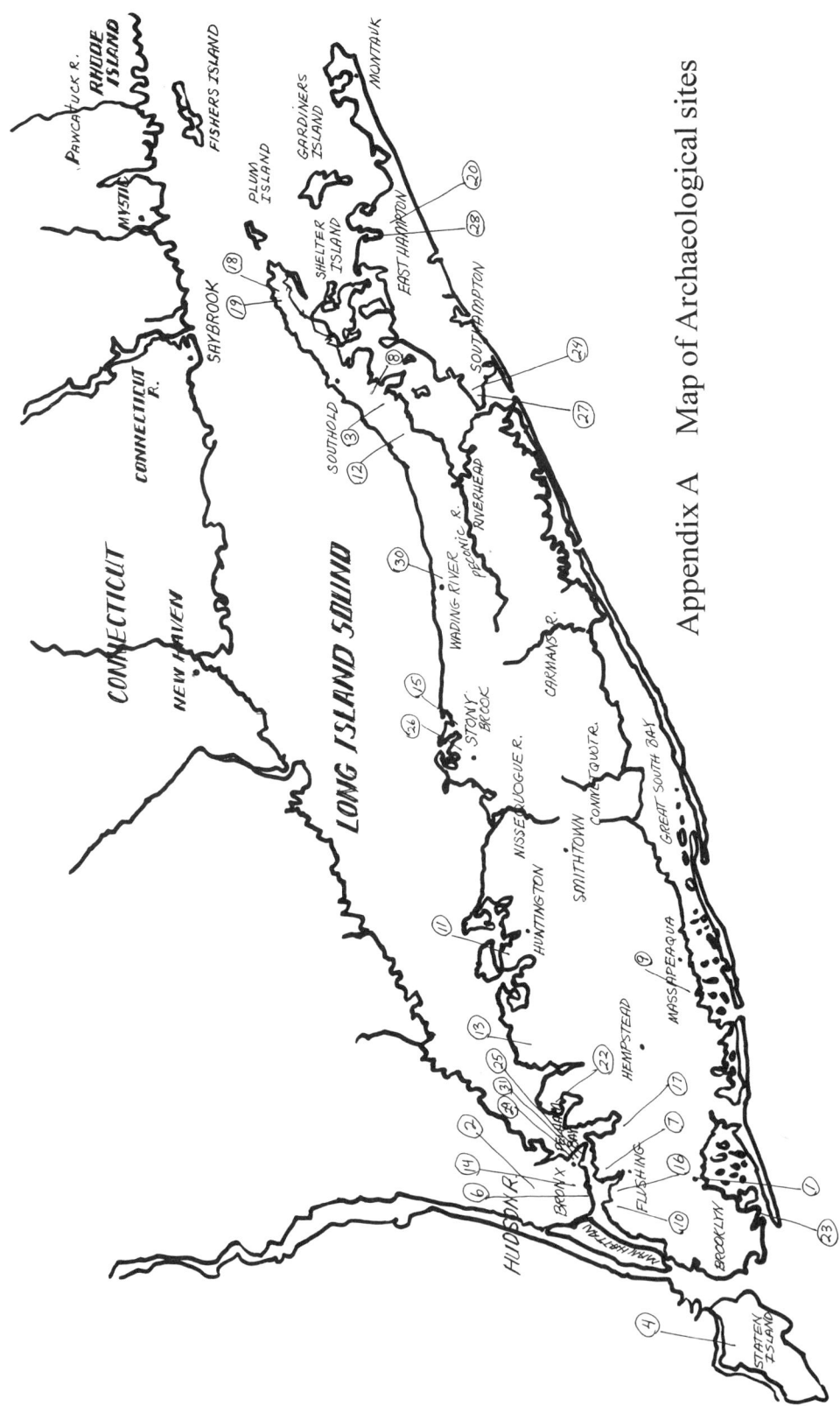

Appendix A  Map of Archaeological sites

# Key to Appendix A Map
# Archaeological Sites

| No. | Name of Site | Archaeological Report |
|---|---|---|
| 1 | Aqueduct | Smith 1982:230 |
| 2 | Archery Range | Kaeser 1978d:20-22 |
| 3 | Baxter | W. Ritchie 1969:165-70; Salwen 1982:39-43 |
| 4 | Bowmans Brrook | Bolton 1922 |
| 5 | Burial Ridge | Jacobson 1980 |
| 6 | Clasons Point | Skinner 1919:49-126 |
| 7 | Clearview | C. Smith 1950:134-35 |
| 8 | Fort Corchaug | Solecki 1950:3-40 |
| 9 | Fort Massapeag | Solecki and Grumet 1994:18-28 |
| 10 | Grantville | C. Smith 1950:173-76 |
| 11 | Henry Lloyd Manor | Silver 1991 |
| 12 | Jamesport | Latham 1940 |
| 13 | Matinecock Point | Orchard 1977:66-69; C. Smith 1950:135 |
| 14 | Morris Estate Club | Kaeser 1978c:35-45 |
| 15 | Mount Sinai | Gwynne 1982; Bernstein 1990; 1990a; Gramley 1982 |
| 16 | North Beach | C. Smith 1950:135-37 |
| 17 | Oakland Lake | Kaeser 1978:263-68; Venuto 1982:126-33 |
| 18 | Orient 1 | Latham 1935 |
| 19 | Orient 2 | Latham 1935a |
| 20 | Pantigo | Sayville 1977:12-29 |
| 21 | Pelham Boulder | Lopez 1982a:249-57 |
| 22 | Port Washington | Harrington 1982:88-89 |
| 23 | Ryders Pond | Lopez and Wisniewski 1978:207-27; 1978a:233-47 |
| 24 | Sebonac | Harrington 1977a:30-64 |
| 25 | Schurz | Lopez 1982c:102-19 |
| 26 | Stony Brook | Ritchie 1965:10-49 |
| 27 | Sugar Loaf Hill | Ritchie 1965:62-74; Latham 1936 |
| 28 | Three Mile Harbour | Latham 1978a |
| 29 | Throgs Neck | Lopez 1982c; Skinner 1919 |
| 30 | Wading River | Ritchie 1965:78-88; Wyatt 1982:70-82 |
| 31 | Weir Creek | Skinner 1919:49-126 |

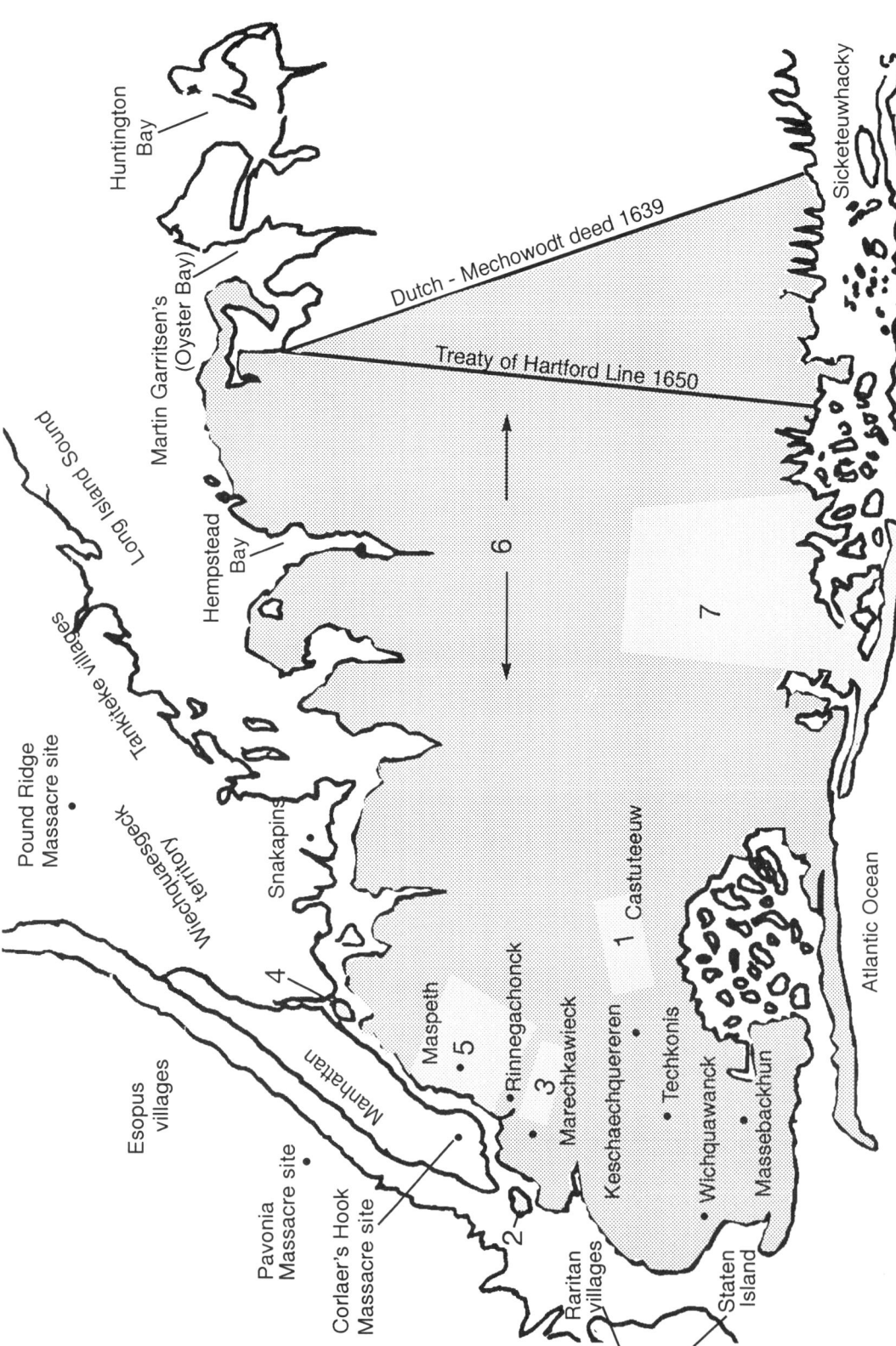

Appendix B. Map of New Netherland - Deeds, Treaties, and Algonquian Place Names, 1636-1650

## Key to Appendix B Map
## New Netherland Deeds and Place Names, 1636–1650

| No. | Parties to Deeds | Date | Source |
|---|---|---|---|
| 1 | Penhawis-New Netherland | 1636 | NYCD 14:2-4 |
| 2 | Penhawis-New Netherland | 1637 | NYCD 14:4 |
| 3 | Penhawis-New Netherland | 1637 | NYCD 14:4 |
| 4 | Seyseys-New Netherland | 1637 | NYCD 14:5 |
| 5 | Cakapeteyno-New Netherland | 1638 | NYCD 14:14 |
| 6 | Mechowodt-New Netherland | 1639 | NYCD 14:15 |
| 7 | Tackapousha-Hempstead | 1643 | NYCD 14:530 |

Note: The eastern boundary for the Mechowodt deed is uncertain. It may have extended to Huntington Bay on the north shore and to the Carmans River on the south shore.

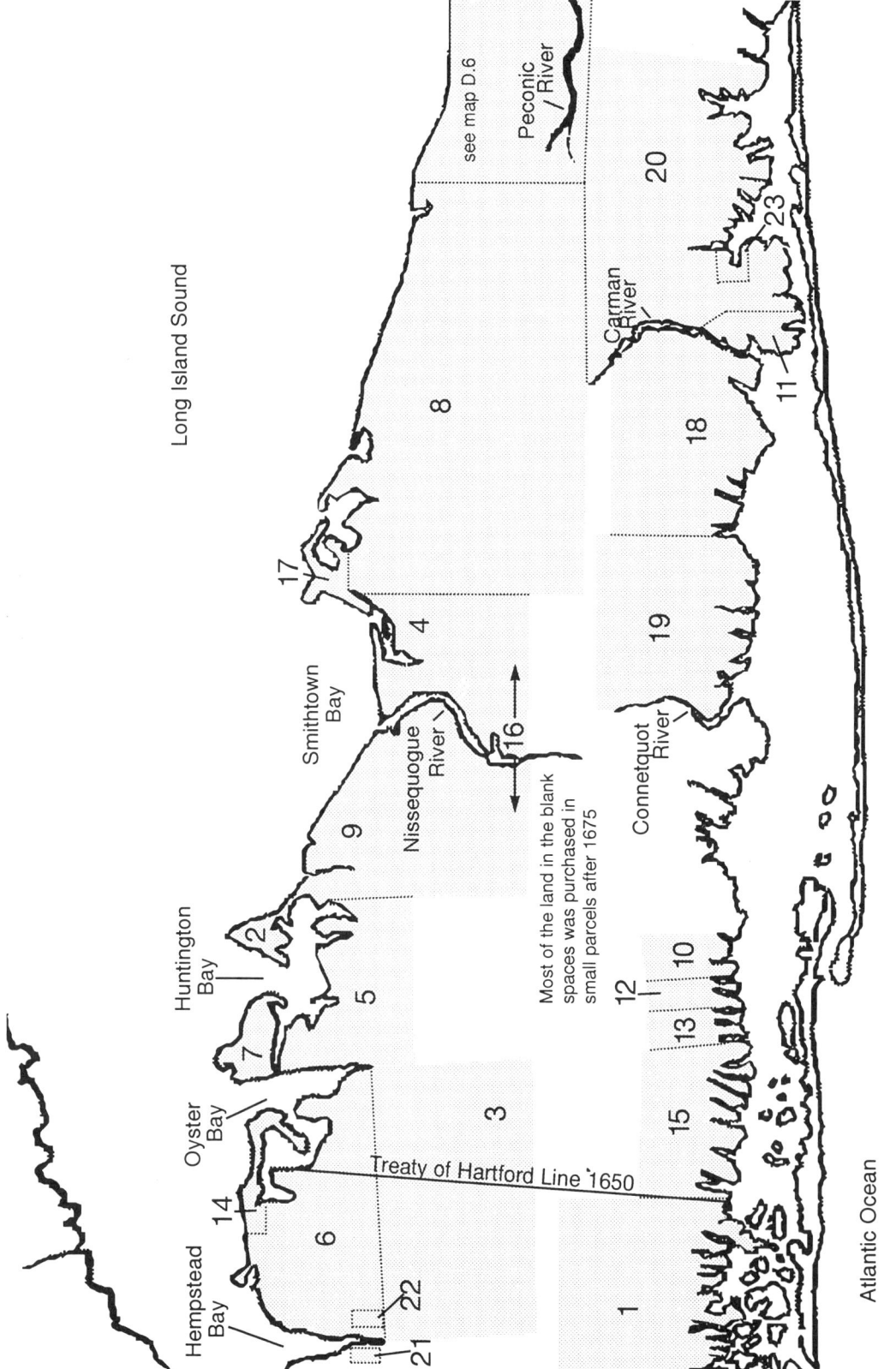

Appendix C. Map of Approximate Locations of Algonquian - English Deeds, 1643-1675

*Appendix*

# Key to Appendix C Map
# Approximate Locations of Indian-English Deeds, 1643-1675

| No. | Parties to Deeds | Date | Source |
|---|---|---|---|
| 1 | Tackapousha-Hempstead | 1643 | NYCD 14:530 |
| 2 | Asharoken-Eaton | 1646 | Street 1882:9-10 |
| 3 | Pugnipan-Williams | 1648 | RTOB 1:625-26 |
| 4 | Nassaconseke-J. Wood | 1650 | RTSM 1:24 |
| 5 | Asharoken-Holbrook | 1653 | RTH 1:1-3 |
| 6 | Asharoken-P. Wright | 1653 | RTOB 1:334, 355-56 |
| 7 | Asharoken-Mayo | 1654 | RTH 1:4-5 |
| 8 | Warawakmy-Scupper | 1655 | RTBH, Hutchinson:2-3 |
| 9 | Asharoken-J. Wood | 1656 | RTH 1:6-7 |
| 10 | Wyandanch-J. Wood (Keeossechok) | 1657 | RTH 1:10-11 |
| 11 | Wyandanch-Woodhull (Wenecoheage) | 1657 | RTBH, Hutchinson: 2-3 |
| 12 | Wyandanch-J. Wood (Keeossechok) | 1657 | RTH 1:2-13, 21-22 |
| 13 | Wyandanch-Whitney | 1658 | RTH 1:16-18 |
| 14 | Josias Indian-Whitehead | 1658 | RTOB 1:354 |
| 15 | Tackapousha/Chopeyconnaws-A. Wright | 1659 | RTOB 1:347-49 |
| 16 | Wyandanch-Gardiner | 1659 | DSBD 2:118-19 |
| 17 | Wyandanch-Setauket | 1659 | RTBH, Hutchinson:16 |
| 18 | Tobacus-Brookhaven | 1664 | RTBH, Hutchinson: 10-11 |
| 19 | Ambuscow-Southold | 1665 | RTS 1:249-51 |
| 20 | Tobacus-Setauket | 1674 | RTBH, Hutchinson: 32-33 |
| 21 | Gy-Brookhaven | 1675 | Bayles 1882:4 |
| 22 | Dongan-Tackapousha | 1687 | NYSA Land Patents, Book 6:241 |
| 23 | Dongan-Suscaneman | 1687 | RTOB 1:516 |
| 24 | Smith-Unkechaug | 1700 | Gonzales 1986:119 |

Note: Asharoken sold Eaton's Neck (C-2) to Eaton in 1646. In 1653 he sold a tract of land which included Eaton's Neck and Horse Neck (C-7) to Richard Holbrook (C-5). In 1654 he sold Horse Neck to Samuel Mayo. In 1656 Asharoken sold a tract of land which again included Eaton's Neck (C-9). In 1659 Wyandanch gave what is now Smithtown to Lion Gardiner.

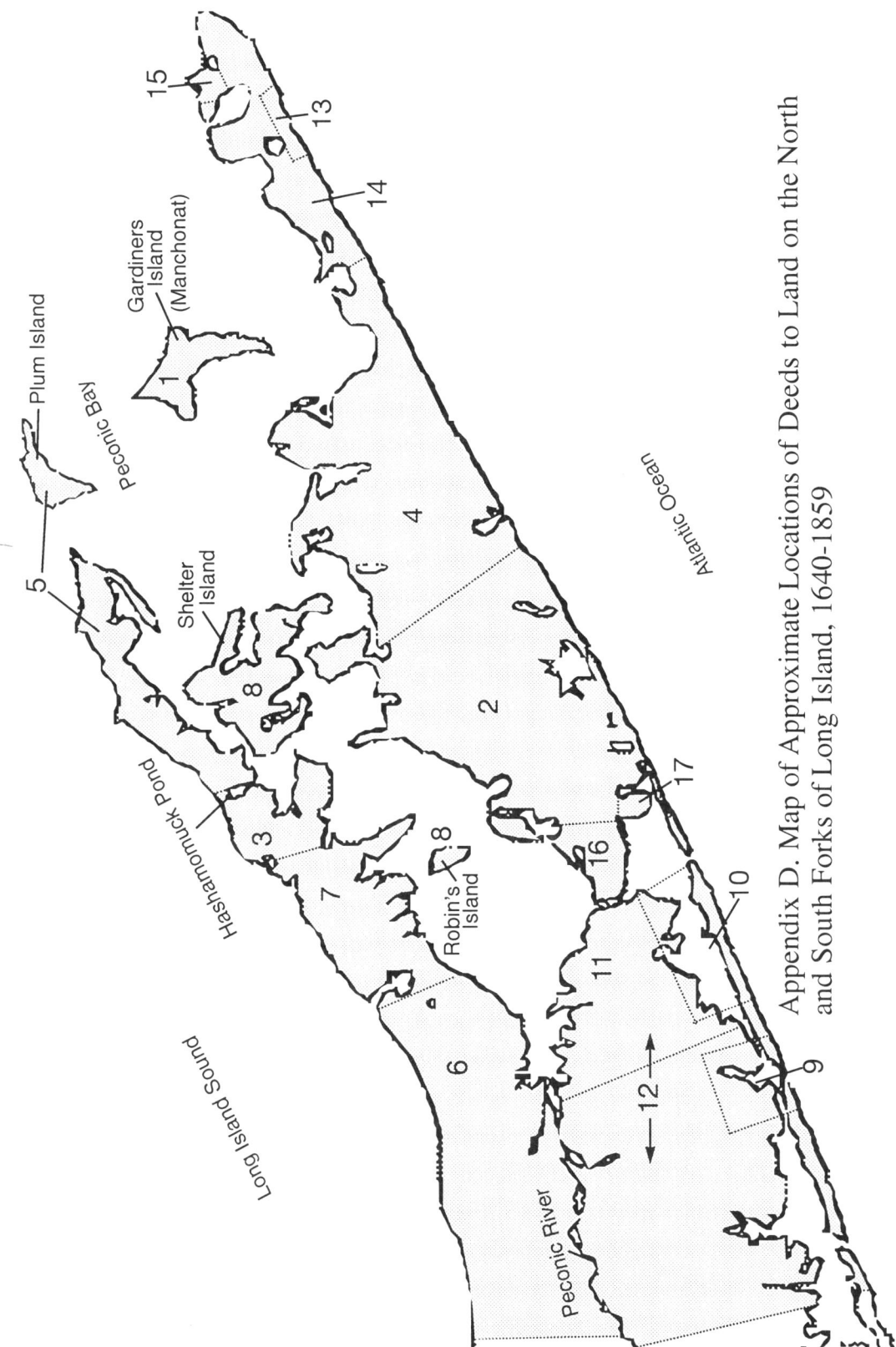

Appendix D. Map of Approximate Locations of Deeds to Land on the North and South Forks of Long Island, 1640-1859

## Key to Appendix D Map
## English-Algonquian Deeds on the North and South Forks of Long Island, 1640-1859

| No. | Parties to Deeds | Year | Source |
|---|---|---|---|
| 1 | Yovawan-Gardiner | 1639 | C. Gardiner 1890:599 |
| 2 | Mandush-Southampton | 1640 | RTSH 1:11 |
| 3 | ?-Southold | 1640 | Deed has not survived |
| 4 | Wyandanch-Eaton | 1648 | RTEH 1:2-4 |
| 5 | Momoweta-Eaton | 1648 | DSBD 2:214 |
| 6 | OccomboomaquusEaton | 1649 | DSBD 2:210-11 |
| 7 | Paummis-Eaton | 1649 | Craven 1906:14-15 |
| 8 | Yovawam (Youghoo)-Goodyear | 1651 | RTEH 1:96-97 |
| 9 | Wyandanch-Topping | 1658 | DSBD 2:152 |
| 10 | Wyandanch-Gardiner | 1658 | RTSH 1:170-71 |
| 11 | Wyandanch-Ogden | 1659 | RTSH 2:354 |
| 12 | Weany-Topping (includes land in D-9, 10, 11) | 1662 | RTSH 2:167-68 |
| 13 | Poniute-Mulford | 1670 | Smith 1926:32-34 |
| 14 | Poniute-East Hampton | 1686 | RTEH 2:213-14 |
| 15 | Wyandanch (Poniute)-East Hampton | 1703 | Smith 1926:52-56 |
| 16 | Pongumo-Southampton | 1703 | RTSH 2:178 |
| 17 | Shinnecock Trustees-Southampton | 1859 | Stone 1983:308-310 |

Note: The Topping Purchase (D-12) included land sold by Wyandanch to Gardiner (D-10) and Ogden (D-11) and the meadowlands leased from Wyandanch by Topping (D-9).

# Notes

## Chapter 1

1. The term "Algonquian" (Algonkian), referring to a linguistic root, is often confused with the name "Algonkin" (Algonquin) referring to a specific Native American community in Canada.

2. There are several orthographic variations of "Montaukett" in the early records from 1648 to 1818: Mentacut (1648), Meantauk (1649), Mohansick (1650), Montaukut, Montuckett, and Mantuckett (1655), Montacult (1657), Montaquet (1657), Meantaquit (1660), Muntacut and Muntaucit (1662), Meantauk, Meantauket, and Mantauket (1687), Muntoket (1719), Montauk (1745), Meantauk, Meantock (1754), Montauk (1800 and 1818). The descendents today refer to themselves as Montauketts. Similarly, there are variations in spelling of other Algonquian words. Even in English, spelling was often phonetic and not standardized in the colonial period. In this book, variant spellings are shown in parenthesis following the Algonquian word.

3. In the fall of 1995, the Matinecock Council of Elders was formed; Cheryl Brady is the chairperson of this body.

## Chapter 2

1. There are several variations of this myth which have been preserved by missionaries (see Kraft 1986:2-7). Kraft notes that many Native Americans today turn to these myths as evidence that their ancestors were always here, rejecting the theories based on archaeological and anthropological research. Kraft and some other anthropologists, such as Alice Kehoe, view these beliefs as a legitimate assertion of cultural uniqueness similar to creation myths in the Christian Bible (Kehoe 1992:2).

2. In a controlled scientific excavation, the artifacts (objects modified by human action) and features (patterns or stains in the soil indicating the use of an area for such things as a fireplace or a wigwam) are carefully recorded and located in reference to a datum point set on a grid map of the site. This point serves as a reference for all measurements in the excavation and enables investigators to relate each of the artifacts and features in the context of the site.

Excavation units are plotted in the grid and the slow process of removing the soil layer by layer begins. The layers or "strata" are carefully marked in order to record the depth and association of the artifacts and features. Although there are some exceptions, the general rule is that the older artifacts will be found in lower strata. Many archeological sites are "multicomponent," i.e. they were occupied over a long period of time by people who went through several significant cultural changes or by migratory groups passing through. The lower strata of an excavation, for example, might have been occupied by people who had no pottery whereas the higher strata would likely contain extensive amounts of pottery sherds (fragments). The association of artifacts and features in a given stratum is also very important because it establishes a relationship which helps the archaeologist to understand the lifeways of the people who used them. This is why archaeologists are so frustrated when well-meaning people simply dig up artifacts and destroy the stratigraphic context. Projectile points in cigar boxes or mounted on mats in floral leaf designs over the fireplace have lost most of their meaning. As one archaeologist put it, "it's as if you were working on a jigsaw puzzle and someone came along and grabbed a handful of pieces and walked away."

3. Unfortunately, the Sugar Loaf Hill site was destroyed by a real estate developer who bulldozed the top of the hill for his house (*Southampton Press*, December 8, 1988).

4. An interesting pattern in these features was the placement of a celt about a foot above each individual cache. None of the celts had been ceremonially "killed." Another common feature was the presence of iron pyrites in all of the caches. Ritchie believed that these were used with quartz "strikers" to start fires (1965:59-60). He noted that John Brereton, who had accompanied Bartholomew Gosnold on his voyage along the Atlantic coast in 1602, had seen the native people on Martha's Vineyard lighting fires by striking sparks from "mineral stones" that they carried in small leather pouches. It is certainly possible that the close association of pyrite and quartz indicates the existence of a "fire making kit," but the deteriorated condition of the pyrite in the caches raises questions about any interpretation. The pyrite was in the form of a limonite sand which left a rusty red color on the objects. Although Latham and Ritchie concluded that the original pyrite had decomposed into sand, their conclusion must be taken with a grain of that sand.

5. One of the three large red ocher deposits, located in the center of the Orient Two pit, had a quartz blade and four steatite vessel fragments embedded in the ocher mass. There were several tools lying around the edges of the deposit which appeared to be in direct association with the feature. Latham concluded that the ocher had been placed here in a basket; the steatite and the blade were then pushed down into the ocher and the tools leaned against the container. The basket decayed completely away leaving the artifacts as Latham found them.

The second of the three large ocher deposits, near the center of the Sugar Loaf Hill pit, contained no artifacts, but there were projectile points around the edge and a scattering of mixed charcoal and cremated bone fragments surrounding the feature. The third such deposit, found in the northern section of the Jamesport pit, contained a large "six gallon" steatite vessel broken into three parts, but there were no tools or charcoal and bone scattering surrounding the ocher. There was a large deposit of such material forty inches to the west and a second broken steatite vessel in the fill above the ocher.

## Chapter 3

1. Anna Shepard's research (1968), has helped anthropologists understand this industry. She provides detailed explanations for each stage of the manufacture. The clay was gathered in baskets, carried to the workshop stations (which were probably located near the clay deposits), and washed. If the clay contained pebbles and twigs or was lumpy, it would be dried, pounded into a powder, and sifted. Water was then kneaded into the refined clay to form a soft putty. After the grit temper was added, the wetted clay was repeatedly lifted and thrown with some force down onto a flat stone. The clay was again kneaded as more water was added (59-60).

Once the base was shaped, the potter would then either coil strips of clay in a spiral or lay rings of clay strips on top of each other to set the walls. The walls would then be blended and smoothed with a wooden paddle wrapped in a cord. The paddle was pressed against one side of the wall while another tool, serving as an anvil, supported the other side (Shepard, 1968:57-60). This process left the characteristic cord markings on the interior and exterior of the vessel.

The pots were left to dry for several days before the final and most difficult stage began. A fire was kindled in a shallow pit protected from the wind and burned down to a bed of coals (Shepard, 1968:75-77). The pot was filled with thin strips of wood or bark and inverted over the coals. More strips of wood were then piled around the vessel. As the strips burned off, new ones were added until the pot glowed a dull red. At this point the cooling began, but it had to be done slowly to prevent cracking. Ashes were poured over the vessel as it cooled to avoid a sudden drop in temperature. The new pots were then placed in the wigwams and storage areas alongside the baskets, wooden bowls, and bark containers.

2. Lucianne Lavin has put forth an interesting hypothesis about the transition from Early Woodland to Middle Woodland on Long Island and in Southern New England. She suggests that peoples from coastal Virginia migrated into this area sometime after the year 300 bringing with them their pottery technology and their long experience with harvesting food resources from the tidal marshes and wetland environment. Lavin noted that the warming climate which produced a richer wetland ecosystem on Long Island had begun much earlier in Virginia. The increase in available food sources soon led to an increase in population and prompted some to migrate north into areas which were still sparsely populated.

The major changes which are associated with the shift from Early Woodland to Middle Woodland—shell tempered pottery, increased forest efficiency, larger and more permanent settlement patterns—may have been introduced from the south by new immigrants. Lavin acknowledged that much more research has to be done on this hypothesis and she encouraged her colleagues to pursue some of these themes (1995).

3. Similar strategies were used in the tidewater areas of Virginia (Rountree 1989:40; Ewan and Ewan 1970:385).

4. Although no mica ornaments or carvings have been found on Long Island on scientific excavations, a curious mica tablet was found in a ploughed field in Brookhaven in 1849. The triangular-shaped tablet is approximately 7.75 inches long by 6.25 inches at its widest, and 2.5 inches at the narrow end (Lisa Anderson, May 23, 1996: pers. com.). The images are very difficult to make out, but there appears to be a serpentine or whale-like effigy with several horns on its head in the center of the tablet. Around the edges, there appear to be images of whale tail fins (see illustration in Matthiessen 1986:316). The image may be a variation of the horned serpent beings found in Iroquois, Cherokee, and Mississippian belief systems (Hudson 1976: 145-46, Strong 1989). The tablet was given to the New York State Museum in Albany by Dr. Nathaniel Miller (Lisa Anderson, May 1996: pers. com.).

## Chapter 4

1. The general consensus among archaeologists is that the smaller, unstemmed, triangular projectile points were used for arrows rather than for spears (Griffin 1978:254). The bow may have been in use in parts of the Northeast as early as the Middle Archaic Period (Rountree, April 1995: pers. com.).

2. Kevin McBride, who has done extensive archaeological research in southern New England, believes that the household or homestead unit played a much larger economic role than had been acknowledged in previous interpretations by Salwen and Snow (McBride 1984).

3. Canonicus, a Narragansett sachem from Rhode Island, held court in a large circular structure about fifty feet in diameter. The building was framed with saplings and covered with woven mats (Johnson 1910:162). Daniel Gookin reported seeing some buildings from sixty to one hundred feet long and thirty feet wide (Gookin 1972:10). The house where the Wampanoag sachem, Nanepashemet, held court was built on a platform six feet above the ground and was described as "largely built," but no dimensions were given (Mourt 1841:226).

4. The French explorer Samuel de Champlain, who sailed along the north Atlantic coast in 1604, reported seeing a village of two hundred at what is now Gloucester, Massachusetts, and as many as six hundred in a village on Cape Cod (Russell 1980:24). The Pequot villages which were raided and burned by John Endicott during the Pequot War each had about thirty wigwams. In 1761, George Wawkeets, a Niantic, and Ben Uncas, a Mohegan, told Ezra Stiles, the president of Yale College and one of America's pioneer ethnographers, that seven people could sleep comfortably in a wigwam ten to thirteen feet in diameter (Russell 1980:52; Stiles 1916:131; Sturtevant 1975:440). Roger Williams reported that two families could live in a little round house "of some fourteen or sixteen foot over" (1973:118). Unfortunately, Williams does not tell us how many people he thought there were in a "typical" family. If we use Stiles' data on the relationship between space and numbers of inhabitants, it is likely that Williams considered a nuclear family unit to have five or six members. The best we can do with this uncertain data is to guess that there may have been about three hundred people in each of the Pequot villages attacked by Endicott.

The fortified Pequot village near what is now Mystic, Connecticut, which was destroyed by English troops in 1637, enclosed sixty to seventy wigwams. John Underhill, one of the English officers who led the massacre of the village, reported that the Pequots told him that there were about four hundred people in the village, but John Mason, one of Underhill's fellow officers, said that six or seven hundred were killed and that only seven inhabitants escaped (Underhill 1638:80-81; McBride 1990:102-3; Mason 1897:31). Mason's larger estimate is supported by the data from Stiles and Williams. When the Dutch troops under John Underhill massacred over five hundred Wiechquaesgeck people who lived in a settlement near what is now Bedford, New York, in a surprise attack during the winter of 1644, they found the wigwams set in three rows about two hundred forty feet long (JNN 1909:282-83; Grumet 1981:60-61). If seven to ten people lived in each wigwam, there must have been between sixty and seventy wigwams with twenty to twenty-three in each row. Robert Grumet suggests that the Wiechquaesgeck village may have been the one named "Nanichiestawack" on Van der Donck's 1656 map of New Netherland (facing p. 294 in Jameson, 1909). The Wiechquaesgeck were Munsee speakers, closely related to the people living on western Long Island. These estimates require a cautionary note. They are based on the admittedly speculative assumption that ten by thirteen feet was an "average size" wigwam. The two wigwams excavated by Mark Harrington at the Sebonac site were a bit larger (Harrington 1977a:36-37). The estimates based on seven per wigwam, therefore, may be conservative.

5. Lynn Ceci was reluctant to use the term "village" to describe settlements on Long Island. She called them "multicomponent central base camps" (1990:1-3). Ceci also rejected the interpretation (traditional paradigm, she called it) endorsed by Ritchie, Salwen, and others, which holds that sedentism increased after 1,000 B.P. as a result of

the introduction of horticulture. Her new paradigm holds that sedentary village life developed after European contact, sometime after 1524. Ceci re-examined data from five village sites: Tottenville (Staten Island), Bowmans Brook (Staten Island), Pelham Bay, Port Washington, and Sebonac (near Southampton). Ceci ran some new carbon 14 dating tests and concluded that the native peoples of Long Island shifted from free wandering camping stations to multicomponent central base camps during the transition from Middle to Late Woodland Periods before the introduction of horticulture or European contact (1990:21). Ceci concluded that none of these sites satisfied the standard anthropological criteria for a "village," i.e. more than one acre in area, evidence of occupation by one hundred to five hundred people, food remains consistent with year-round occupation, and evidence of ceremonialism in hearths, storage pits, and burials. Ceci's conclusions are rejected by archaeologists such as Silver (1979, 1980), Gwynne (1982), Salwen (1978), and Lightfoot (1987) who have done extensive work on Long Island. The issue is difficult to resolve because of the sparse data for the Long Island area. When placed in the larger context of data for the Atlantic coast, however, there is considerable support for Ceci's critics. Ceci's most important contribution is her evidence that sedentism began before the introduction of horticulture.

6. Many of the woodcut drawings were used to illustrate maps of the "New World" (Allen 1991:45-62; Kraft 1986:121). One of the earliest was Willem Janzoon Bleau's map printed in 1635. Bleau's map was probably based on John White's 1585 drawings of Roanoke. These images were often repeated by seventeenth-century mapmakers.

7. Roger Williams also noted that the Indians frequently moved their wigwams around in the village area . In the spring they moved closer to their fields and in mid-summer they often moved to a new house to get rid of the lice and fleas (1973:127-28).

8. Brief descriptions of wigwam construction and furnishings in the New England area can be found in Wood 1968:94-95; Gookin 1972:9-10; Mourt 1841:144-45; Williams 1973:117-29; Morton 1967:135; and Josselyn 1988:91.

9. Harrington refers to the material used in the mats as "blue vent" grass, but Larry Penny, member of the East Hampton Town Natural Resources Department, knows of no grass by that name. He believes that Harrington may have picked up a local colloquial term from his informants.

10. The degree of reliance on cultigens by the Native Americans of Long Island has been hotly debated over the past two decades. In 1975 Lynn Ceci challenged the conventional interpretations of Late Woodland culture, arguing that the Indians did not fertilize their corn fields with fish, nor did they plant much corn at all until after the contacts with the whites began (1975:26-30). She also argued that the coastal Algonquian peoples did not settle in year-round villages until the whites arrived (1977; 1990). Questions about the use of fish fertilizer had been raised by ethnologist Regina Flannery (1939) and geographer Erhard Rostlund (1957), but it was Ceci's 1975 article in *Science* which provoked a widespread debate among her contemporaries. Stephen Mrozowski excavated a seventeenth-century Indian garden site on Cape Cod and found fish bones in the corn hills, but unfortunately he was unable to get a radiocarbon date earlier than 1630 (1994).

11. For general information about the origins of plant domestication in the Midwest see Ford (1985), Keegan (1987), B. Smith (1985). Evidence of corn has been found in only three Late Woodland sites on Long Island (Ceci 1977:94-95; 1982a:9-11). The few

pollen studies which have been done on Long Island have produced no evidence of other cultigens such as beans, squash, chenopodium, amaranth, or even sunflowers (Ceci 1982a:12-13).

12. See Isaack de Rasieres (1909:107), JNN (1909:271), David De Vries (1909:218), Robert Juet (1909:21), Nicolaes van Wassenaer (1909:71), and Adriaen van der Donck (1968:75). Lynn Ceci has raised questions about these reports in her dissertation (1977:119-34). She argues that although the reports establish that corn was grown here, they provide very little information on the process of cultivation or the degree of Native American dependence on cultigens. It would be a great mistake, however, to dismiss this data. Rather the reports should be treated as are the archaeological artifacts and be carefully examined in the broader context of an ever-growing data base about the Late Woodland Period. It should also be noted that Isaack de Rasieres (1909:107) did describe the cultivation strategy for corn and beans in some detail.

13. There are a number of theories about the origins of agriculture. See Cohen (1977), chapter 1 "The Problem of Agricultural Origins" and chapter 2 "Population Pressure and the Origins of Agriculture." See also B. Smith 1985:51-56; Keegan 1987; Ford 1979, 1981, 1985. Bruce Smith argues that the process of clearing space for wigwams and the regular burning away of undergrowth to clear the way for hunting, inadvertently opened up an ecological niche for chenopodium, sunflower, sumpweed, maygrass, and knotweed by destroying their competitors. When the women who gathered wild plants recognized the nutritional value of these seed-bearing plants, they began to harvest them. These plants gradually adopted human settlements and were then integrated into the Native American lifeway (Smith 1985:54; Ford 1979:316).

14. There were several subspecies identified in the English accounts. John Winthrop, Jr. described white, yellow, blue, and red corn, but noted that the majority were yellow and white (Winthrop 1937:125).

15. The interpretation of these data was the focus of a debate between Lynn Ceci and Annette Silver. Ceci argued that Native Americans on Long Island lived in small, shifting encampments and did not cultivate much corn until after the Europeans arrived (1977, 1979, 1982a, 1990). Silver rejects these conclusions and argues that the native peoples here lived in permanent village sites as early as the Archaic Period and that they began experimenting with corn soon after 1,000 B.P. (Silver 1979, 1980).

16. Accounts of crop cultivation, harvesting and storage on Long Island are found in the following sources: Juet 1909:18-20; De Vries 1909:206-7, 218-20, 230-31; Wooley 1968:36; Danckaerts 1969:54-55; De Rasieres 1909:107-8; Van Wassenaer 1909:69, 72; Van der Donck 1968:75, 77. The best source on horticulture in southern New England is Eva Butler's monograph "Algonkin Culture and the Use of Maize in Southern New England" (1948).

17. The importance of horticulture in coastal Algonquian society is underscored in the language. There are three words for "hoe": a generic term, *anaskhig;* a term for the implement used in the heavy work of breaking up the soil, *Anaskhomwautowwin;* and *Monaskunnummautowwin*, a hoe used for general weeding and lighter work (Butler 1948:14). Wolley reports that the Lenape word for hoe was *tom-a-hea-kan* (Wolley 1968:36). The similarity to the word for ax, *tomahawk*, suggests that the tool was used for the heavy work of breaking up the fields prior to planting.

18. John Winthrop, Jr. says that the corn hills were five to six feet apart (1937). Winthrop may have been measuring from the center of each corn hill whereas De Rasieres measured from the outer circumference.

19. "Maize" is a West Indian word for corn which was brought to Europe by the Spanish. In seventeenth-century England, the word "corn" was used as a generic reference to all grains. In the English colonies "maize" or "Indian corn" was used to distinguish the plant from other grains. Gradually, in English-speaking North America, the word "corn" has become widely understood to mean the native maize. The Algonquian language has several words for the plant which distinguish a variety of forms and uses:

Narragansett (Williams 1973)

| | |
|---|---|
| *Scannemeneash* | seed corn |
| *Wompiscannemeneash* | white seed corn |
| *Nasaump* | unparched corn meal |
| *Aupummineanash* | parched corn |
| *Nokechick* | parched corn cakes |
| *Waweekanash* | sweet corn "in the milk" |

Massachusett (Winthrop 1937:125)

| | |
|---|---|
| *Weachim* | generic for all corn |

Montauk (J. Gardiner 1980)

| | |
|---|---|
| *Wewauchum* | generic word for corn |
| *Wedamus* | roast (parched) corn |
| *cut-daus* | boiled corn |
| *seaump* | pounded corn |
| *yeokeheag* | roast pounded corn |

Unkechaug (Jefferson 1980)

| | |
|---|---|
| *samp* | boiled corn |
| *sowahaemen* | generic for corn |

20. John Winthrop, Jr.'s treatise on corn, presented to the Royal Society of London, was published in abbreviated form by the society in *Philosophical Transactions of the Royal Society,* 1678 (142, vol. 12:1,065-68). The full treatise was edited by Fuller Mood and published in the *New England Quarterly* 10 (1937):121-33.

21. The name "tobacco" comes from a Spanish interpretation of an Arawak word, but each linguistic group had its own name for the plant. The Powhatans in Virginia, for example called it *uppowoc.*

22. One observer, Captain Martin Pring (1603), reported that he saw tobacco growing all mixed together with corn, beans, pumpkins, and squash in gardens on the New England coast (Russell 1980:162). Buffalo Bird woman, the Hidatsa who served as primary informant to anthropologist Gilbert L. Wilson in 1916, said that the men loosened the earth and then drew rows about eighteen inches apart in the soil with digging sticks. The tobacco was planted in the small furrows and covered over. When the plants came up they had to be thinned and then hilled (Wilson 1979). (The Hidatsa lived in small villages on the Knife River in North Dakota.)

23. Modern experiments with storage pits have demonstrated the effectiveness of these structures. In the late fall of 1991, Othmar Dickbauer, a student in the author's seminar on the Native Americans of Long Island at the Southampton campus of Long Island University, constructed a storage pit as a class project. Students in the same class

had cultivated a Native American garden and harvested the crops for a class meal, which they prepared with the help of Josephine Smith, a member of the Shinnecock tribe. Dickbauer took the surplus corn and squash for his experimental storage pit. He dug a pit about four feet deep and three feet wide, lined it with bark, placed several handfuls of small twigs on the bottom, and substituted a jute bag from a local nursery for the bluestem grass mats. He filled the bag with corn and squash, which he had dried on a rack made from saplings, and packed it into the pit. Next he covered the bag with a thick layer of seaweed (eelgrass, *Zostera marina*) collected from the bay near the Shinnecock Reservation. He closed the pit with a layer of wood slats and covered them with a layer of earth.

The winter of 1991-1992 was very wet. We expected that the heavy rains during November and December would cause a considerable amount of mold damage and decay by the time we opened the pit in late December at the end of the fall semester. We did find that the eelgrass layer was very wet at the top, but when we got down to the bag with the corn and squash, a small cloud of dry dust floated up. Although there was some mold on a few squash slices, everything else was well preserved. Dickbauer took out samples of the corn and squash and gave them to the students who were working on a Native American cooking project. The rest of the food was reburied and excavated in April. Once again we found only a minimum of mold and decay, and the plants were used successfully in the cooking project. Many of the students, particularly those who began the projects with considerable skepticism, were surprised at the effectiveness of the storage pits.

Christopher Turnbow, the associate director of the Sunwatch Village Archaeological Park in Dayton, Ohio, constructed several storage pits for the corn, beans, and squash grown in their gardens in the summers of 1991 and 1992. According to Turnbow (August 1991, May 1992: pers. com.) there was very little spoilage over the winter. The pits at Sunwatch were lined with grass following the design of pits described in the ethnographic reports on the Ojibwa people in the Great Lakes area.

## Chapter 5

1. Iris and Alonzo Gibbs make a strong case for this interpretation. They reject William Wallace Tooker's conclusion that Manetto simply meant "a hill surpassing others in the vicinity" (Tooker 1962:99-100).

2. Cautantowwit is spelled differently by each of the observers who recorded responses from Algonquians about their religion. *Kautantowwit* (Williams 1973:190), *Kiethan* (Winslow 1841:355), *Kickeron* (Danckaerts 1969:268), *Ketanitowet* (Harrington 1921:19), *Cauhluntoowut* (Occom 1993:151-54); see also Levine 1980a:211, and Gehring and Grumet 1987:118-19. Of much more significance is the fact that a similar powerful deity is found in the ethnographic records from both the Lenape and the Mohegan Pequot culture areas.

3. According to Nicolaes van Wassenaer, a seventeenth-century Dutch observer, the Lenape called their holy men *kitzinackas* (1909:68).

4. The Dutch observer Jasper Danckaerts (1969) reported that all of the Lenape religious ceremonies were simply called *kintekayen*. Kintekayen may be a form of *kintika* which means "dance" (Harrington 1921:116). There was, of course, dancing at nearly every ceremony. Unfortunately Danckaerts did not press for a more precise identification of the Lenape powwows.

5. Daniel Denton mentions in his 1670 account that hunters are sent out for a supply of venison when a powwow is to be held (Denton 1968:8). Although he does not mention the Big House ceremony by name, the context clearly indicates that this is what he is describing.

6. The term *rites of passage* was introduced by anthropologist Arnold van Gennep in 1909. These rites mark a three-stage process in which an individual abandons one social role (separation), remains in limbo during a brief period of initiation (transition), and is finally introduced to the community as a new person with a new status (incorporation); see Aceves and King 1979:367-68, 443-47; Barnouw 1982:224-25.

7. Elise Brenner argues in her Ph.D. dissertation, that these simple pit burials do characterize the Late Woodland cultures and that there is no need to look elsewhere for more complex burial sites located some distance from the villages (1984:188). She concludes that the village pit burials "may indicate little need for concern for reaffirmation of the living groups' collective identity. If the Late Woodland bands were characterized by personal mobility, fluctuation, and the ephemeral nature of group membership, there was, therefore, no stable group whose corporate, collective identity had to be reaffirmed during crises, such as the death of one of its members." Brenner's conclusion is certainly plausible, but the limited numbers of adult males in the data base (on Long Island) raise questions which are not addressed in her analysis. Herbert Kraft excavated Late Woodland burials in the Delaware Valley which were lined with bark and contained grave goods, but found no evidence of palisades or such wooden structures in association with the graves (1986:188).

8. In the Great Lakes Algonquian communities, the relationship between the herbalist and the *powwaw* differed from village to village and was likely determined by personal attributes. The Ojibwas, an Algonquian community living near the Great Lakes, distinguished between the *Mashki-kike-winini* (herbalist), and the *Midewiwin* (shaman). Often the two roles were performed by the same person, generally a woman. This belief is reflected in the considerable number of medicinal herbs used by the Indians which were purgatives or diaphoretics designed to cleanse the body and drive out the evil spirit causing the illness (Vogel 1973:19-20, 161-66).

9. The author interviewed Wati (James Waters) and three Shinnecocks—Lamont Smith, Jonathan Smith, Lanette Cooke—who participate in sweat lodge rituals. A two hour round-table discussion with Jonathan Smith and Lanette Cooke was videotaped (January 1993) and is available for viewing at the Social Science office, Southampton Campus of Long Island University, Southampton, NY 11968, (516) 287-8204.

10. The Lenapes living on the lower Delaware have a similar belief, but they tell a different origin story. They say that the doll beings came to them when some children carved faces on sticks while they were playing. The children were surprised to find that the stick dolls talked to them. They delighted in their new playmates and told their parents about them. The parents became concerned and ordered the children to throw the dolls away. The children obeyed, but were very sad and grieved the loss for a long time. One girl began to have dreams about the dolls. In one dream a doll said, "Find me and keep me always, and you and your family will ever enjoy good health." Then the doll instructed the girl to give it new clothing and hold a dance for it every spring (Harrington 1921:162-63).

When her parents noticed how upset she was they asked her what was troubling her. She told them about her dream and said she wanted the doll to come back and talk to her. The parents now realized that they had made a mistake so they told her to find the doll and dress it as she had been told in her dream. The family then killed a deer, prepared a feast and held a dance to honor their doll being (ibid.).

11. The engraved mica tablet reportedly found in Brookhaven also has a serpentine motif (see note 4 in Chapter 3).

12. Unfortunately, both of the boulders were moved from their original locations when a housing complex called the "Hunt Club" was constructed on the site in the 1980s. No record was made of their relocation. In November 1995, Joseph Markowski and the author were given permission to search for the stones by Barbara Bird, the managing agent, and the Total Community Management Corporation board of directors which supervises the Hunt Club. Larry Dill, the Hunt Club superintendent, graciously took time from his busy schedule to help us search for the stones. The grid coordinates recorded by Lenik indicated that the original site was now under a parking lot. Dill suggested that perhaps the stones may have been used in one of the many embankments around the gardens and lawns in the complex. We were not able to locate them at the time, but a few days later Dill called me to say that he had found a stone with a glyph consisting of a bow and arrow and a triangle, very similar to the one on the smaller of the two stones. I examined and photographed the boulder, which was now located at the entrance to the complex, and concluded that it was, in fact, the original glyph (see fig. 5.12).

13. There has been some speculation about the use of tobacco in the vision quest. Alexander von Gernet, a Canadian anthropologist who has made an extensive study of tobacco use among the Iroquois, concluded that the native species of tobacco in North America, *Nicotiana rustica,* was powerful enough to induce an altered state of consciousness (1992:176-79). There is evidence that *rustica* has a much higher percent of nicotine than other species of tobacco and that a relatively small amount does make one a bit giddy (Underhill 1965:163-64, 185-86). While it is certainly plausible that the Indians used tobacco as a part of the vision quest rituals, there is no documentation to support the thesis (Von Gernet 1992:168).

14. For readers who wish to learn more about Native American belief systems, there are many excellent sources. One of the best anthropological studies of religion is Anthony Wallace's *Religion: An Anthropological View* (1966). Two very informative anthologies are Arthur C. Lehmann and James E. Myers, eds. *Magic, Witchcraft, and Religion: An Anthropological Study of the Supernatural* (1993), and William A. Lessa and Evan Z. Vogt, eds., *Reader in Comparative Religion: An Anthropological Approach* (1979). Most introductory anthropology textbooks will have a chapter on religion which provides a context for understanding Native American belief systems. A very accessible, comprehensive study of Native American religion in North America is Ruth Underhill's *Red Man's Religion* (1965). An excellent collection of Native American sacred texts, *Native North American Spirituality of the Eastern Woodlands*, has been edited by Elizabeth Tooker (1979). There are, unfortunately, a growing number of "new age" cult books on the market which distort and demean Native American belief systems for commercial gain. The reader should be very suspicious of any book which does not have footnotes and an extensive bibliography.

## Chapter 6

1. Heckewelder was told that the incident made such a deep impact on the Indians that they called the place "Mannahattanink" meaning "island or place of general intoxication." Most scholars reject this interpretation. Tooker (1962:93-94) argues that Manhattan is derived from "Manah" meaning "island" and "atin" meaning "hill." Ruttenber (1971:14) and Beauchamp (1907:129) agree with the first part of Tooker's translation, suggesting that the word meant "small island" or "cluster of islands" (see Grumet 1981:23-24).

2. The descriptions of these "sachemdoms" and "confederacies" by such early European observers as John Smith, Verrazano, Wood, Josselyn, Gookin, Williams, and Champlain have often misled historians into concluding that these were static traditional systems which had been in place for many generations (see Brenner 1984:31-35 and Salwen 1978:168).

3. The Late Woodland burials, with the exception of the dog ceremonials, were relatively unpretentious. The mortuary customs and grave goods do not indicate the existence of a social hierarchy or significant material wealth. The seventeenth-century mortuary customs are much richer in both ceremonialism and material content. Daniel Denton observed, "When any Indian dies amongst them, they bury him upright, sitting upon a seat, with his gun, money, and such goods as he hath with him" (1968:9). Adriaen van der Donck (1968:87) described a similar burial procedure and elaborated further on the mortuary customs associated with the inhumation, "the nearest relatives extend the limbs and close the eyes of the dead; and after the body has been watched and wept over several days they bring it to the grave." Van der Donck also described the grave: "Then they place as much wood around the body as will keep the earth from it. Above the grave they place a pile of wood, stone, or earth, and around and above the same they place palisades resembling a small dwelling. All their burial places are secluded and preserved with religious veneration and care, and they consider it wicked and infamous to disturb or injure their burial places." David De Vries, a Dutch merchant, who lived in New Amsterdam for several years and published his journal about the same time as Van der Donck, reported a more elaborate grave structure: "They make a large grave, and line it inside with boughs of trees, in which they lay the corpse, so that no earth can touch it. They then cover this with clay, and form the grave, seven or eight feet high, in the shape of a sugar loaf, and place palisades around it" (1909:223).

Samson Occom, writing a century later, also described an elaborate mortuary custom, which was reported to him by the Montauketts (1993:151-54). The Montaukett mortuary ceremony began with the washing of the body. After the ritual cleansing, sacred colors and, perhaps, symbols were painted on the body. The female relations painted their own faces black and kept them that way until the mourning period was over, a year later. The Indians carried the deceased to the grave in a funeral procession which included most of the village community. The women, said Occom, "make a doleful and very mournful and loud lamentation, all the way to the grave." The mourners place the body into the grave along with many goods belonging to the deceased.

The people then pulled down the wigwam of the deceased and gave away the remainder of his or her goods. The women, who were in mourning, did not wear fine clothes or ornaments, nor did they dance or sing. When the mourning period was over, the women removed their black paint and modest attire and a great dance was held which lasted all night. A funerary specialist may have supervised these procedures rather than a *powwaw*. Among the Narragansetts, according to Roger Williams, a respected elder, called a *Mockuttasuit*, supervised the ceremony.

Although no burials such as those described above have been excavated on Long Island, archaeologists have found several sites in southern New England (Brenner 1984:188-211). These burials took place during the late sixteenth and early seventeenth centuries just before the Europeans established settlements in New England and on Long Island. The graves were located in cemeteries rather than in village sites and included a significant number of European manufactured grave goods.

4. William Wallace Tooker translated *Nahican* as "the people of the point." Tooker believed that the map label might have been an error by Block, who confused Nahican with the "Anglicized" name of the Narragansetts who lived across the Sound in Rhode Island (Tooker 1962:150). This speculation seems a bit strained. If Tooker's translation is correct, it would seem to be quite appropriate for people living near Montauk Point. If Nahican does actually refer to a southern New England group, it is much closer to "Mahican" than to Narragansett. A different name for the people of western Long Island was reported by Johannes de Laet, a director of the Dutch West India Company, who compiled a geography entitled *New World* in 1625. De Laet referred to "a nation of savages ... called Matouwax" who lived on Long Island (Jameson 1909:44). De Laet's book may have influenced the Dutch map maker, Willem Blaeu, who produced a map of southern New England and Long Island in 1635. Blaeu moved the label "Nahican" to the Narragansett lands in Rhode Island and placed "Matouwacs" on Long Island. Tooker believed that Matouwacs was a variation of the Massachusetts Algonquian word *Meht-anaw-ack* meaning "land of the periwinkle" or "country of the ear shell," and listed the following variants he found in the historical documents, Matoouacks, Meilowacks, Metoac, Meitowacks, Matowcas, Mattanwake, and Matowa (1962:124-25). Tooker's comparison with the Massachusetts' dialect is rather arbitrary because De Laet is more likely to have heard the word from the Munsee speakers who lived around New Netherland.

Although the origin of "Matouwacs" is obscure, we do know that the Native Americans living on western Long Island told the Dutch in 1636, that Long Island was "by them called Sewanhacky" (NYCD, vol. 14:2-3; Tooker 1962:232-34). Tooker once again demonstrated his resourcefulness in coming up with imaginative solutions to a difficult linguistic problem. "Sewan," he said, was closely related to the Narragansett word *Seawhoog*, which had been translated by Roger Williams to mean "they are scattered." The last half of the word, continued Tooker, comes from the Delaware-Munsee word *hacky* meaning "land" or "country." Putting together two words from entirely different dialects and assuming that what was scattered must have been shells even though *anaw*, the word he had said meant shell, was not present, Tooker concluded that Sewanhacky meant "land of shells." The only consistency in these translations is Tooker's assertion that both terms were references to shells. Tooker's interpretations are plausible, but, if he is correct, it is a conclusion based on speculation not linguistic analysis (Bassett 1967:9).

Although the sachems repeatedly referred to Long Island as "Sewanhacky," the map makers apparently only paid attention to the "mother maps," which continued to be used as references for new maps (Allen 1991:47). The name "Matouack" appears on three subsequent Dutch maps in 1635, 1656, and 1662, and on two English maps as late as 1755 and 1779 (Levine and Bonvillain 1980:165-67; Allen 1991:47-60). "Matouack" was placed on the 1656 Jansson-Visscher map twice; first in large print as the name for Long Island, and the second in a smaller size font on the far eastern end of the island in what appears to be a "tribal" designation for the Montauketts (Allen 1991:50). In the 1664 patent from Charles II to his brother, the Duke of York, "Meitowax" is again given as the "Indian" name for Long Island (Tooker 1962:124-25). On the English maps, "Matouaks" (Matouacks) appears as a tribal name for the people living along the south shore from Hempstead to Southampton. The 1779 map indicates that this was the location of the "ancient settlements of the Matouacks Indians." Curiously, neither of the English maps locate the "Matouacks" on the eastern tip of Long Island where the Montauk lived.

Certainly the Dutch were well aware that the Native Americans were divided into many separate groups. Johannes de Laet noted that "the barbarians, being divided into many nations and peoples, differ much from one another in language though not in custom" (Jameson 1909:57). De Laet identified the "Sankikans" who lived in what is now northern New Jersey, the "Siwanois" on the mainland north of Hellgate, the "Manattans, a bad race of savages," and the mysterious "Matouwacs" of Long Island; but he did not mention any other names for the Native American communities on Long Island.

The term "tribe" was first used by Nicolaes van Wassenear, a Dutch scholar and physician who used it interchangeably with "nation" in a 1628 report (Jameson 1909:67-68). Van Wassenaer did not report the names of any Long Island Indians, but he did locate the "Manhates" and the "Esopes" near the mouth of the Hudson. With the exception of the confusing references to "Nahican" and "Matouacks," the first mention of a Long Island Native American group by name, curiously, is the Shinnecock. None of the western Long Island groups who were close neighbors of the Dutch are named prior to 1639.

5. There are three modern accounts of the Pequot Wars: Salisbury (1984), Jennings (1976), and Vaughan (1965). Jennings and Vaughan have sharply contrasting interpretations of the conflict. Jennings holds the English responsible, whereas Vaughan concludes that the English should not be faulted for the "inevitable collapse" of Native American society in New England. Salisbury argues that Vaughan's assumption of inevitability is a restatement of a theme which can be traced back to the early Puritan historians, who viewed the Indian defeat as a part of God's plan. Incorporating the work of archaeologists, anthropologists, and linguists, Salisbury provides a broader and deeper context for his analysis. He noted that trappers, traders, and explorers often lived in harmony with Indians until the settlers arrived and demanded control over the land.

6. The firsthand accounts by Mason and Underhill and two accounts by contemporaries, Lion Gardiner and Philip Vincent can be found in Charles Orr's *The History of the Pequot War* (1897).

7. Several prominent sunksquaws have been mentioned in the historical literature. Some of them led military campaigns against their enemies. Quaiapan, a Narragansett sunksquaw, commanded an army of three hundred men in an attack on a tributary band who had defied her authority (Grumet 1980:52). Two sunksquaws, Weetamoo, a Pocasset, and Awashonks, a Sakonnet, allied their people with King Philip and led their troops against the English. The role of other sunksquaws on Long Island, Quashawam, Wuchikitaubit, and Askickotantup, of the Montaukett, and Weany (Old Woman) of Shinnecock, is described in later chapters and in Strong 1996b.

8. Stoughton had captured 120 Pequots in June 1637, but, in his zealousness to send a message to the other Indians about the consequences of resisting English authority, he took most of the men out in a ship and threw them overboard to be drowned (Hubbard 1677:128; De Forest 1852:142; Jennings 1976:226). Stoughton took a young Pequot woman, "the fairest among them," he later told John Winthrop, as his own "servant," and gave several of his officers their choice of the other female captives (Lauber 1913:310; Bourne 1990:76). The remainder of the women and children were later apportioned out to the Narragansett and Mohegan sachems.

9. In his study of the relations between the French and Algonquian alliance chiefs, Richard White argues that mediation was a means of affirming French dominance on the "middle ground" (White 1991:33-34). The English in New England were using their roles as mediators in the same fashion.

10. The practice of changing names to mark a transition in life or in response to a dream causes considerable confusion for historians. Ninigret, for example, was known in his youth as Aonemo (Janemo, Jannemo, Einemo). Fortunately the English and Dutch frequently noted "aliases" in their documents which enable historians to confirm a particular name change. In the absence of such "confirming" documents, scholars must make an educated guess based on the context of the documents. (For a discussion of these problems, see Grumet 1989:1-2.) The confirming document for Aonemo-Ninigret is in 1647 identifying one of the sachems as "Jannemo alias Nenegelett" (RCNP, 9:45) Another problem, of course, is posed by the idiosycratic spelling of the same Indian name by different white clerks. Ninigret's name, for example, has been spelled at least five different ways: Nenekunat, Nenegratt, Ninicraft, Niniglud, and Nenegelett. The kinship relations linking schamens during the seventeenth century are poorly understood. Ninigret, for example was either a cousin to Miantonomi (Drake 1857:67), his uncle (Potter 1835:173), or his nephew. Ninigret's relations with Miantonomi's brother, Pessacus, is also unclear, but the two Narragansett sachems may have been his uncles (Sehr 1977). Ninigret married the sister of Cashawashett, who was later called Harmon Garrett (Drake 1857:67). Cashawashett was either Ninigret's uncle or his nephew. His sister, Quaiapen (the Old Queen), along with Pessacus, went to war on the side of King Philip.

## Chapter 7

1. In fact, the company did intervene the next year and invalidated the Corlaer and the Van Twiller deeds after learning that Corlaer had transferred his plot to Von Twiller. The company held that Von Twiller had taken advantage of his position to gain title to the plots (Bailey 1949:34).

2. *Pomanocc*, which has been spelled some fourteen different ways in the records, was first translated by Tooker to mean "land where there is travel by water." This seems quite appropriate for the area around Peconic Bay where Yovawan lived. Tooker based his translation on the similarity of Pomanocc to *pomma' hum*, a Munsee word meaning "travel by water." Tooker later changed his mind, saying only that further "investigation compelled me to reject it" (1962:183). He now believed that Pomanocc was closer to the Narragansett words *pauman* or *pummen'um*, meaning "he offers," and *up-paupau-men-uk*, meaning "he habitually offers it," hence "land of tribute," a reference to the whole of Long Island. One can easily see here the arbitrary nature of Tooker's translations and the meager data base he worked with. According to research

by modern scholars, the best reference for the languages of the eastern Long Island bands is Mohegan-Pequot or Quiripi rather than the Munsee or Narragansett dialects of Algonquian (Goddard 1978:70-77).

3. Unfortunately both the deed and the English translation were apparently among those documents destroyed by fire in 1911. The English translation by Adrian van der Kemp, the eighteenth-century Dutch scholar who was hired by Governor De Witt Clinton to translate the New Netherland records, was cited by two historians, John Brodhead (1853-71, 1:297) and Edmund B. O'Callaghan (1966, 1:215). Neither of the two historians, however, reproduced the full text of the deed. A contemporary reference to the deed in the colonial documents (NYCD, 14:28) confirms its existence.

4. This document in the Calendar of State Papers (Colonial Series, America and the West Indies) is dismissed by James Truslow Adams as an example of English prejudice against the Dutch. It was written, says Adams, twenty-three years after the fact by an overzealous Englishman who wanted to malign the Dutch. Adams, however, offers no evidence to support his contention that the account is an example of how history may be "muddied by nationality" (Adams 1918:49).

Mention of "staking out" as a form of torture was made by Lion Gardiner in his 1660 account of the Pequot War. He urged the colonies to be more alert against an Indian attack for he wanted to die a peaceful death rather than to have "a sharp stake set in the ground, and thrust into my fundament" (L. Gardiner 1980:140).

5. The exploitation of Indian women became such a common practice that it apparently offended some of the influential Dutch families. The governor's council, perhaps as a rebuke to Van Tienhoven, passed a law in 1638 prohibiting sexual intercourse between Indian and Dutch. There is no evidence, however, that the law was ever enforced.

6. There are two copies of this deed extant, one in the *New York Colonial Documents* (NYCD, 14:530) dated November 13, 1643, and the other in the Albany Book of Deeds dated December 13, 1643 (reprinted in *Long Island Forum,* 1978, 41:44; and in Marshall 1962:11; see also Naylor 1994:14, 174; Smits 1994:17; Luke 1994:81-83). The copy in the *Colonial Documents* came from the Carman family papers and the copy in the Book of Deeds was entered into the records by John Hicks on February 14, 1666/1667. There are two other differences in the deeds. The November deed describes the land as running south from Hempstead "with a straight square line to the south side." In the December deed, the word "side" is replaced by 'Sea," making it clear that the deed included all the land to the Atlantic Ocean. Another difference is found in the Indian signatures. The last Indian name on the November deed is "Yarafus," but on the December deed that name is replaced with "Gerasco."

7. The only source for the campaign is the "Journal of New Netherland," an anonymous account located by John Brodhead in the Royal Library of the Hague (NYCD, 1:179-88). J. Franklin Jameson concluded that the account was written by one of Kieft's supporters because of its general tone and the citation of documents from Kieft's copybook (1909:267-68). This document is in sharp contrast to the many attacks on Kieft in most of the surviving records from the period. Kieft and his papers are believed to have been lost at sea in transit to Holland after he was removed from office.

Another intriguing account of the battle comes from a letter by Samuel Jones, published in the New-York Historical Society *Collections* in 1821. Jones, who wrote the letter in 1810, says he heard the following story of the battle in his youth, about 1752.

> After the battle at Fort Neck, the weather being very cold, and the wind northwest, Captain Underhill and his men collected the bodies of the Indians, and threw them in a heap on the brow of the hill and then sat down on the leeward side to eat their breakfast.
>
> When this part of the country came to be settled, the highway across the neck passed directly over the spot where it was said the heap of Indians lay, and the earth in the spot was remarkably different from the ground around it, being strongly tinged with a reddish cast, which the old people said was occasioned by the blood of the Indians (3:322-23).

8. In 1935, the *Nassau Daily Review* reported that two local amateur archaeologists had excavated the remains of twenty-four people, who appeared to have been buried in a shallow trench, from a site south of Merrick Road in Massapequa. The two men excavated an area seven feet by ten feet and found six hundred pieces of pottery, twelve projectile points, and other artifacts which, unfortunately, were not described in the newspaper article. They also described a most intriguing feature which may have been part of a funerary ritual. They found the remains of twenty to thirty burned snail shells under the chin of each skull in the grave. George Combes, the Hempstead Town Historian at the time, speculated that the remains may have been Indian victims of the Dutch campaign in 1644 (May 7 and 10, 1935; see Grumet 1995:26-27). N. C. Nelson, curator of the American Museum of Natural History, visited the site and removed one of the skulls for further study (see Chapter 4).

9. In a curious incident about three years later, Maria, Lord Stirling's widow, sent a Scotsman named Andrew Forrester to New Amsterdam with a document claiming that the Stirling family still held a valid patent to western Long Island. Forrester claimed that he had been appointed governor of Long Island by Maria Stirling and wanted to meet with Stuyvesant (NYCD, 14:80). One can imagine the immediate response of the volatile Dutch Governor to such a claim. Forrester was arrested at a local tavern the day after he arrived and deported (O'Callaghan 1966, 2:46-47). The English governors of New Haven and Connecticut, of course, wanted to hear no more from the Stirling claims either. Governor Eaton wrote to Stuyvesant assuring him that they were not going to challenge his deportation of Forrester (RCNH, 2:516).

10. William Wallace Tooker was convinced that these were the same four sachems who had negotiated the tributary agreement with the English at Hartford the previous spring. He argued that Rochkouw, Weyinteynich, Mamawichtouw, and Witaneywen were Dutch spellings for Youghco, Wyandanch, Moughmaitow (Momoweta), and Weenagaminin. Unfortunately, there is no corroboration of this in the colonial records.

It is most unlikely that a Shinnecock sachem could speak for the villages as far west as Rockaway. John Morice was one of the first to suggest that Witaneywen might have been the young Tackapousha, but he had no documentation to support his conjecture (1949:116). Robert Grumet, who has studied these documents for several years, also concluded that Witaneywen was Tackapousha. He cites a 1655 document that identifies Tackapousha as the former "Meautinnemin" and argues that this is an orthographic variant of Witaneywen (1994:84-85). The fact that Witaneywen claims to speak for the western Long Island Indian communities supports Grumet's conclusion.

## Chapter 8

1. In Gardiner's account of the incident, he says that there were four men captured, but the records of the United Colonies indicate that only three men were taken to Hartford (RCNP, 10:98). Local folklore identifies the woman as Phoebe Halsey, but her Christian name does not appear in the colonial documents. In fact, the Southampton town records do not even mention the murder until several years later.

2. An Indian village site in this tract, located on Ryder's Pond near Sheepshead Bay, was excavated by amateurs around 1900. Some of the artifacts were given to Roy Latham who placed them in the Southold Indian Museum, where they are currently on display. Several burials were discovered near the site when Avenue U was constructed, but no record was made of their provenance or associated grave goods. The artifacts were examined by Julius Lopez and Stanley Wisniewski in 1971-1972 (1978:207-27; 1978a:233-47).

3. The English were alarmed about the prospect of Ninigret obtaining flintlock muskets. Contrary to the stereotyped image of childlike Indians easily duped by shining beads and trinkets, they were very knowledgeable consumers. The Indians soon realized that the matchlock muskets introduced by the sixteenth and early seventeenth-century traders were ill-suited to the Indian style of warfare. These muskets weighed about twenty pounds and had to be fired with the barrel resting on a forked stick. They were not very accurate beyond fifty yards, required some forty separate motions to load, fire and reload, and were useless in damp weather (Malone 1971:76). Although they worked well enough in European massed formations on open battlefields, the Indians were used to fighting in the forests, using the elements of stealth and surprise in hit-and-run engagements.

    The Indians wanted flintlocks, a much more expensive gun which could be loaded more easily, quickly, and safely than the cumbersome matchlocks. They could be used more effectively against moving targets. The English and Dutch also realized the advantages of the flintlock and they gradually adopted them in spite of the increased expense (Malone 1971:92). They were particularly concerned about having these new muskets fall into the hands of the Indians.

4. Stanton, who favored more direct action against Ninigret, may have intercepted the wampum from Wyandanch to provoke a conflict.

5. Verne Dyson (*Heather Flower and Other Indian Tales of Long Island*, 1967), Forest Monroe (*Maid of Montauk*, 1902), and Nathan J. Cuffee and Lydia Joycelyn (*Lords of the Soil,* 1905) all used the kidnapping and wedding theme. Nathan J. Cuffee, a Shinnecock, and Lydia Joyceln, the daughter of a missionary to the Sioux in South Dakota, introduced an interesting twist, perhaps based on Cuffee's knowledge of oral traditions. In *Lords of the Soil*, Gardiner is portrayed as a villain rather than as the generous benefactor who paid the ransom for the Montaukett captives (Strong and Karabag 1991:192). In the novel, he conspires with Ninigret to kidnap Wyandanch's daughter so that Gardiner can buy their freedom and put Wyandanch in his debt. He then pressed the Montauketts to return the favor by giving him thirty thousand acres of land in what is now Smithtown (Wunderlich 1989:8). Cuffee had been involved with Montaukett land claims for many years. He testified before a U.S. Senate committee in 1900 about the loss of Shinnecock and Montaukett land and was an active participant in the 1909 suit to reclaim Montaukett land.

6. Roger Williams, however, in a letter to the commissioners, said that thirty men were killed, including the son of Ninigret's brother, a sachem named Wepiteammocks (RCNP, 10:442).

## Chapter 9

1. Ninigret, prevented from using traditional means to expand his influence, turned to the very English institutions which protected Wyandanch. In an effort to undermine the Montaukett sachem's alliance with the English, he sent his agent, Newcom, to the United Colonies' meeting in 1656 with several carefully selected charges which he believed would impress them (RCNP, 10:169). Newcom began by accusing Wyandanch of hiring a man named Wampeage, who was living at Montauk, to murder an Englishman named Drake in what must have been an unsolved crime several years in the past. He next charged that Wyandanch had broken the peace treaty by attacking Ninigret on Block Island after the settlement, which had resulted in the release of the Montaukett prisoners. This charge was discussed in Chapter 8.

The third charge concerned witchcraft which both cultures took very seriously. This charge may be related to the one Uncas brought against Wyandanch in 1650. Uncas charged that Wyandanch had killed some of his men and "bewitched diverse others and himself also" (RCNP, 9:167). The commissioners asked John Mason, Edward Howell, and John Gosmer (the representatives from Southampton), and Thomas Benedict (representing Southold), to investigate. Unfortunately, there is no record of their report. The matter was probably dropped because Wyandanch was such a staunch ally of the English. This time, however, the commissioners ordered Wyandanch to appear and respond to Ninigret's accusations.

Wyandanch came and denied the charges, and John Youngs told the commissioners that the English and Indians on Long Island believed Wyandanch. Although one Indian witness testified that he had heard Wampeague confess to the murder, the commissioners ignored his testimony and ruled that Wyandanch "stood free from this foul charge" (RCNP, 9:170).

Ninigret's attempt at using the English institution did not work for him in this instance, but the incident provides an insight into the developing patterns of accommodation which were taking place on the frontier. Alliance sachems were becoming more adept at using European institutions to advance their own political agendas. Newcom showed a great deal of ingenuity and understanding of English court procedures in his use of witnesses and in his presentation of the charges.

2. Eaton's Neck was sold by Eaton and passed down through several hands. The owners fought off three successive suits by the town of Huntington and finally won a clear title from Governor Nicolls in 1666 (Morice 1950a:239). A similar, bitter court struggle ensued over the title to Lloyd Neck (Street 1882:12-13; NYCD, 14:570-72). The town of Huntington and John Richbill of Oyster Bay had both purchased Lloyd Neck from Asharoken. The Huntington officials won in the Court of Assizes in 1665, but lost on appeal to Richbill. In 1691, the colonial legislature ruled that Lloyd Neck was a part of Oyster Bay (Street 1882:13). Huntington, however, finally ended up with jurisdiction over the disputed neck of land in 1886.

Huntington's purchase of land on the western bank of the Nissequogue from Asharoken in 1656 was disputed in three separate trials by Richard Smith. Smith lost the first two, but he finally won in his third suit in 1675 (J. Smith 1882:6-7; NYCD,

14:640-43). Smith also successfully contested a 1650 deed between Jonas Wood and Nasseconseke for land on the east side of the Nissequogue.

3. This land was within the boundaries of a controversial purchase made by Jonas Wood and his company from Asharoken in 1656. Asharoken's claim to this land had been challenged by Nasseconseke and the Nissequogue, who were determined to have court which overturned the Huntington claim in see preceding note above). Wood apparently assaconseke. According to John Lawrence Smith, ;onseke gave the land on the west side of the for a small parcel which he reserved for himself

pt by some of the English landowners to keep the :ombone, endorsed Samuel Andrews' deed (May oung man claimed that "both English and Indians "Chief Sachem" in his father's place (RTH, 1:20). old enough to assume his father's role, was under ich's widow, whose name does not appear in the auketts. It was customary among the Algonquian ʲ as female sachem when there was no male heir 1980). The matter was further complicated when : claimed to be Wyancombone's guardian in an naining Montaukett lands (Strong 1993:79-80). )ners of the United Colonies that Gardiner would , 10:249-50).

Ogden was right. Gardiner and the East Hampton officials did take advantage of the tribe, weakened by the recent loss of their sachem to the ravages of smallpox, and by a renewal of Ninigret's raids. Although Gardiner's attempt to purchase all of the Montaukett lands was blocked by Ogden's protest, he did manage to persuade Wyandanch's widow and son to give the East Hampton settlers a large parcel of land extending East Hampton's boundary eastward from Napeague to Fort Pond, where the village of Montauk is located today. The land was given to East Hampton, said Wyancombone, as an outright gift in gratitude for protecting the Montauketts from Ninigret's raids (R. Smith 1926:25-29).

Although the sunksquaw and her son confirm several more of Wyandanch's transactions (DSBD, 2:156-57; RTNSH, 1:46-47), the title of grand sachem had lost all credibility by 1662 when Wyancombone died. His mother passed away the following year; both probably died from smallpox.

5. The most severe form of smallpox is *Purport variolosa* or fulminating smallpox, which usually resulted in death a few days after the eruptions began to spread over the body. The patient suffered severe pain as well as psychological depression (Dixon 1962:5-14). The description by Bradford quoted in the text, clearly indicates that those Indians were afflicted with fulminating smallpox. A slightly less virulent form called "malignant confluent" was nearly as devastating. The survival rate was slightly higher (20 to 30 percent), but the suffering could last for two weeks as the disease ran its course. A third form, "malignant semi-confluent" smallpox, had a 70 to 80 percent survival rate, but the patient was usually badly scarred (Dixon 1962:20).

## Chapter 10

1. The copy of the deed in the Oyster Bay town archives (Liber B) bears the enigmatic drawing shown in fig. 10.1. The only other drawing on the Long Island deeds of this period are the small stick figures on many of Wyandanch's documents, which apparently symbolize the agreement between the two parties (DSBD, 2:82-86, 103, 118-19, 152). Unlike the stick figures (see fig. 9.2), however, this design was clearly not intended to be a signature. Its meaning remains a mystery.

The Indians and the non-literate whites always made some sign on the documents to signify their names, but most were in the form of simple letters or circles. Occasionally an individual would use the same symbol every time he or she signed a document, but most were random marks placed beside their names after they were entered by the clerk.

2. After the death of Wyandanch's widow and son, Wyancombone, the sole remaining heir who was acceptable to both the English and the Montauketts was Wyandanch's daughter, Quashawam. (For a brief biography of Quashawam see Strong and Karabag 1991:189-204.) She is probably the daughter that Ninigret kidnapped in 1652. Her name first appears on a most unusual document in 1664 which officially proclaimed her to be "the great sunksquaw" over the Shinnecocks and the Montauketts, and "true heir" of Wyandanch (RTSH, 2:36-37). She was called upon to endorse some of her father's transactions, but she disappears from the records after 1666.

3. Robert Grumet (1996) has demonstrated that Asharoken, Asiapum, Aseton, Ratiocan, Rasaocume, Raseoken and Rashaokan are all orthographic variations of the same name. He also believes that Shoskene, one of the signatories of the 1667 deed, was Suscaneman, who later took over the leadership of the Matinecocks after Asharoken.

4. In 1676, a Setauket sachem named Gy (Gie) and six of his kinsmen, including Massetewse and Mayhew, confirmed the purchase of all the land on the north shore of Brookhaven from Stony Brook to Wading River. Most of this tract was within the boundaries of the 1655 deed between Warawakmy and the Setauket settlers (see Chapter 8). The remaining lands in Brookhaven were purchased in three more transactions. In 1681, Mayhew, now known as John Mahue, sold Richard Woodhull a neck of land on the south shore near Seatuck Creek. Four years later, Winecroscum and a group of Unkechaug men sold a large tract of land along the south beach, east of Moriches Inlet to Brookhaven. The land included the tract sold to Gardiner by Wyandanch in 1658 and granted to the town of Southampton by Governor Nicolls in 1666. The Unkechaugs said that Wyandanch had no right to sell the land because it had always belonged to them. The disputed tract, however, remained in the bounds of Southampton. In 1688, a sachem named Wopehege sold a parcel of land to Samuel Terril, which overlaps the land Tobacus sold to Brookhaven in 1664. In 1690, Tobacus sold Richard Woodhull highway rights and confirmed the previous deeds to the southern part of Brookhaven. The last transaction was not negotiated until 1755, when eleven Unkechaugs, led by Rubin, Sunney and Solomon, sold the remaining land on the south bay to Brookhaven (RTBH, Hutchinson:44-45, 50-51, 69-71, 75-76, 177-78).

5. A copy of this deed was given to the author by Osceola Townsend. The original is in the New York City Register for Queens County (Liber 59:431). A map of the tract, dated April 9, 1683, is located in the New York State Archives, Office of the Secretary of State, and is listed by David E. E. Mix (1859:138, Land Papers 2:12). Although West was charged a nominal fee of six shillings by Tackapousha, outright gifts of land were often made by Indians to both towns and individuals throughout the seventeenth century.

The Montauketts, for example, gave a "gift deed" to the town of East Hampton in 1661 for sheltering them from Ninigret's raids (Cooper 1993:183-86). In 1688, sachem Wopehege from Setauket gave a small tract of land to Samuel Terril, perhaps for personal favors (RTBH, Hutchinson:70-71). Another such gift was recorded for Tobacus, another sachem from Setauket, on December 8, 1690, to Richard Woodhull of Brookhaven (RTBH, Hutchinson:75-76). Chippy (Chopeyconnaws), Tackapousha's brother, gave eight acres to William Buckler for "his many favors and kindnesses," and sold him twelve acres for £3 sterling in 1690 (RTOB, 2:66-67). In 1693, Suscaneman gave Thomas Townsend the Matinecock reservation "in consideration of his many favors and kindnesses . . ." (RTOB, 2:116-17). This document, as indicated earlier in the text, may be fraudulent. On April 30, 1694, Chippy (Chopeyconnaws) gave William Frost a tract of land, again for "his many kindnesses and favors" (RTOB, 2:23-24). That same day, Chippy and Suscaneman gave more land to Frost and a tract to John Cock of Oyster Bay (RTOB, 2:25-26). On August 20, 1696, Will Chippy gave land to Thomas Townsend "in ye consideration for manifold favors and kindnesses from time to time" (RTOB, 2:281-82).

6. It is difficult to determine the precise cost of the land in the deeds. Under Governor Andros, property was valued at an arbitrary £1 sterling an acre for tax purposes (Munsell 1882:58) The actual market prices were probably higher. As we have seen, William Simson sold his forty acres for £70 sterling. The problem here is that land obviously varied in quality and the deeds are often not very specific. As a general rule, most land probably ranged from £1 to £2 an acre, unless it was swamp or wetland. Suscaneman sold two parcels in 1684 for silver. The first one, sold in August, brought him only £10 for fifty acres. Unfortunately, the land is not described (RTOB, 5:126). In the December 15, 1684 sale, Suscaneman received £20 for forty acres of land with a source of fresh water, meadows and some timber (RTOB, 1:502-3). Suscaneman sold John Applefield a sixty acre tract for £12 and his heir sold it for £29 two years later (RTOB, 1:509-10). Suscaneman received £19, ten shillings for eighty acres on March 26, 1685 (RTOB, 1:359). In 1690, Chippy (Chopeyconnaws) received £3 for twelve acres (RTOB, 2:66-67). Clearly the sachems were not receiving a fair market price.

7. On one occasion, Tackapousha, his son Sames (Samos), and his brother Chopeyconnaws took action against another one of his sons, Opesum, for selling land without family permission. Opesum, also known as "Captain Opassum," was one of six sons whom Robert Grumet has identified as the children of Tackapousha (Grumet, February 2, 1995: pers. com.). Unfortunately, there is no explanation in the documents about the origin of his military title.

The family testified before the Oyster Bay officials that they had recently been informed that "Opesum an Indian son of Tackapousha did formerly in his life sell and dispose of certain lands at ye south . . . unto several Englishmen of Oyster Bay and elsewhere. . . . Now we ye said Indians and proprietors . . . declare that ye said Opesum Indian never had any power nor authority neither in himself nor from any other to sell or dispose of any of ours the abovesaid Indians' land" (RTOB, 1:520-21). Tackapousha may have wanted to establish some order in his family as both he and his brother, Chopeyconnaws, neared death. Tackapousha, who must have been nearly eighty years old in 1693, disappears from the records after 1697. His younger brother, Chopeyconnaws, died sometime between 1693 and 1696, and was succeeded by his son, Will Chippy. Tackapousha's family was connected to Suscaneman's family through the marriage of Chopeyconnaws to Suscaneman's sister. These two family groups dominated Indian affairs on western Long Island during the latter half of the seventeenth century (Grumet, February 1, 1995: pers. com.).

Three years later, in 1696, Thomas Townsend officially rejected his title to a neck of land in the south bay, which he had purchased from Opesum (RTOB, 1:521). Townsend apparently felt that a minor, temporary loss to himself was a small price to pay for keeping on good terms with the Tackapousha and Suscaneman families. He was undoubtedly influenced in the matter by a gift of land on Fort Neck from Will Chippy, the previous August (RTOB, 2:281-82).

8. For a detailed discussion of the process of land alienation on eastern Long Island, see Strong 1983a and 1993.

9. When Mahanarok, an Unkechaug man, sold some land to Andrew Gibbs of Brookhaven in 1690, a memorandum was attached to the deed stating that the deed, "was faithfully interpreted unto ye said Indian, he being sober and nowise overtaken in drink" (Southampton Town Archives). Simon Seren received compensation "for wine to ye Indians 14 shillings, 8 pence," and Henry Persall was paid five shillings for providing a bottle of drams for a sagamore (RTNSH, 1:66). On April 15, 1662, the Jamaica proprietors gave eight bottles of liquor to Waumitumpacke and his associates "to confirm deed to land" (RTJ, 1:99, 114). In 1671, the whites who were going to negotiate a purchase of Indian land in Brookhaven were instructed to "take some likers with them to the Indians" and charge the town for the expense (Ross 1902:991).

## Chapter 11

1. The owners, of course, kept their own account books, but few have survived. Fortunately, William "Tangier" Smith's "Pigskin Book," which includes his whaling accounts from 1696 to 1721 (Strong 1990), did survive. The contracts list the names of nearly three hundred Indians, and some identify the individuals by geographic location.

2. This may have been the same Toby who went to sea for Benjamin Conkling in 1681 (RTEH, 2:95-96), and is listed in the 1698 census for the town of Southampton (Strong 1983a:102-3). It is possible, of course, that there was more than one Indian named Toby on eastern Long Island.

3. Although the spellings differ slightly on the whaling contracts (Weomp, Wehomp, Weaump, Weeump, Wemup), they are undoubtedly the same person. Weomp went to sea for Thomas James in 1675 (RTEH, 1:382), John Wheeler in 1680 (RTEH, 2:86-87), and Benjamin Conkling in 1681(RTEH, 2:95-96). Weomp also signed the 1703 treaty which endorsed the 1687 land sale to East Hampton and gave the Montauketts residence rights to Montauk "forever" (MID, folders 12 and 13).

4. The following year, Weomp was again paid £1 for "Jinning" (RTEH, 2:396). Two other Montauketts, Will and Wittoness, were listed in the same document for "Mending and maintaining" the Montauk fence. Will was paid £1, two shillings, and six pence in 1700, and Wittonees was paid three shillings in 1696.

5. This document is located in the Harry B. Sleight Collection (S.14) in the John Jermain Library, Sag Harbor, New York. The monetary term used in the document is "rials," a gold coin introduced by Edward IV of England in 1465, which was still in use in the early eighteenth century. A rial was originally worth about ten shillings. This currency, rarely mentioned in seventeenth-century Long Island documents, may have

had a different value in 1698, but it is unlikely that Hanable would have been paid more that three shillings per day.

# Credits and Sources for Illustrations

## Credits

Christina Grupico: Appendix Maps B, C, D
Eastville Community Historical Society, courtesy of Kathy Tucker: Fig. 12.5
Fred Kossen: Figs. 2.4; 3.3; 3.8; 4.11; 5.1
David Bunn Martine: Figs. 1.1; 2.1-2.3; 2.5-2.8; 3.2; 3.4-3.7; 4.2-4.10; 5.3-5.9; 6.1; 7.1; 8.1; 11.3, 11.8; pp. 1, 16, 92, 94, 266 (unnumbered drawings); Appendix Map A; figs. 11.1-11.2 and 12.1 are from his photograph collection
Joseph d'Oronzio: Fig. 5.10
Edward Lenik: Fig. 5.11
Long Island Studies Institute: Map, p. 10, Paltsits 1910, 2:xii; Fig. 10.2
New York State Archives: Fig. 9.2; 10.1; 10.4-10.5
Red Thunder Cloud: Fig. 3.1
Shinnecock Nation Museum Cultural Center Complex: Fig. 12.6
Shinnecock Powwow Program, 1974, courtesy of Chee Chee: Fig. 12.4
Southold Indian Museum: Fig. 5.2
John Strong: Photographs, p. 12; Fig. 1.3; 5.2; 5.12; 12.2-3
Toba Tucker: Fig. 1.2

## Sources

Fig. 2.8. Based on Ritchie 1955:131
Fig. 3.1. Stone 1993:588
Fig. 3.2 Based on Kaeser 1978a:69
Fig. 4.1. Library of Congress
Fig. 4.3. Based on C. Smith:1954
Fig. 4.11. Based on Kaeser 1978a:73
Fig. 5.1. Based on Harrington 1921:83-84, 130; Skinner 1909:229
Fig. 5.4. Based on Harrington 1977a:56
Fig. 5.6. Based on Gramley and Gwynne 1982:172; Gwynne 1982a
Fig. 5.7. Based on Brinton 1980:304
Fig. 5.8. Based on Levine and Bonvillain 1980:307
Fig. 5.9. Based on C. Smith 1980:311
Fig. 5.10. Tablets in East Hampton Public Library
Fig. 5.11. Lenik, 1978:350-52.
Fig. 9.2. DSDB 2:82, 86, 119
Fig. 10.1. Liber 1:350, Oyster Bay Town Clerk's Archives
Fig. 10.2. Paltsits 1910, 2: facing p. 569
Fig. 10.3. RTOB: 677-78
Fig. 10.4. NYSA, series AO272, Land Papers series I, book 2, p. 12
Fig. 10.5. NYSA, Letters of Patent, Book 6:240-41
Fig. 10.6. RTOB 1:519
Fig. 11.3. Based on painting at Kendall Whaling Museum, Sharon, MA
Fig. 11.4. SHTA, liber A, no. 2:126
Fig. 11.5. RTEH: 1:411
Fig. 11.6. RTEH, 1:412-13

# References

Individuals who have provided information and are cited in the text as "pers. com." (personal communication) are identified at the end of the references.

In addition to the references cited in the text, some additional entries are included which should be of interest to those who wish to pursue the subject further. For the contemporary situation, consult also the Bibliography and the Reading and Resource sections in John A. Strong's companion volume, *"We Are Still Here!"* (1996:89-97).

Abbott, Charles Conrad. 1876. "The Stone Age in New Jersey." In *Annual Report of the Smithsonian Institution for 1875,* 246–380. Washington DC: Government Printing Office.

Aceves, Joseph and H. Gill King. 1979. *Introduction to Anthropology.* Morristown, NJ: Silver Burdett Company.

Adams, James Truslow. 1918. *A History of the Town of Southampton.* Reprint, Port Washington: Ira J. Friedman, 1962.

Ales, Marian Fisher. 1993. "A History of the Indians on Montauk, Long Island." In *The History and Archaeology of the Montauk,* edited by Gaynell Stone, 4–66. 2d ed. Stony Brook: Suffolk County Archeological Association (hereafter SCAA). Originally M.A. thesis, New York University, "A History of the Indians on Montauk, Long Island," 1950 by Marian Elizabeth Fisher.

Allen, David. 1991. "Dutch and English Mapping of Seventeenth-Century Long Island." *Long Island Historical Journal* 4 (1): 45–63.

Angier, Bradford. 1978. *Field Guide to Medicinal Plants.* Harrisburg, PA: Stackpole Books.

\_\_\_. 1974. *Field Guide to Edible Wild Plants.* Harrisburg, PA: Stackpole Books.

Asch, David, L. and Nancy B. Asch. 1985. "Prehistoric Plant Cultivation in West-Central Illinois." In *Prehistoric Food Production,* edited by Richard I. Ford, 149–203. Ann Arbor: University of Michigan, Museum of Anthropology.

Axtell, James. 1981. *The European and the Indian; Essays in the Ethnohistory of Colonial North America.* New York: Oxford University Press.

\_\_\_. 1985. *The Invasion Within: The Contest of Colonial Cultures in Colonial North America.* New York: Oxford University Press.

\_\_\_. 1992. *Beyond 1492: Encounters in Colonial North America.* New York. Oxford University Press.

Bailey, Paul, ed. 1949. *Long Island: A History of Two Great Counties, Nassau and Suffolk.* 2 vols. New York: Lewis Historical Publishing Company.

\_\_\_. 1956. "Decline and Fall of Tribal Life." *Long Island Forum* 19 (9): 165-66, 175–77.

\_\_\_. 1959. *The Thirteen Tribes of Long Island.* Reprint, Syosset, NY: Friends for Long Island's Heritage, 1982.

Barbour, Philip. 1986. *The Complete Works of Captain John Smith.* 3 vols. Chapel Hill: University of North Carolina Press.

Barkham, Selma Huxley. 1984. "The Basque Whaling Establishments in Labrador 1536–1632—A Summary." *Arctic* 37 (4): 515–19.

Barnes, Viola Florence. 1966. "Land Tenure in the English Colonial Charters of the Seventeenth Century." In *Essays in Colonial History Presented to Charles McLean Andrews,* 1931, 4–40. Freeport NY: Books for Library Press.

Barnouw, Victor. 1982. *Ethnology.* Homewood, IL: Dorsey Press.

Bassett, Preston R. 1967 "History of Long Island Maps." *Journal of Long Island History* 7: 1–24.

Bayles, Richard. 1874. *Historical and Descriptive Sketches of Suffolk County . . . With a Historical Outline of Long Island, From its First Settlement by Europeans.* Port Jefferson, NY: William Overton.

___. 1882. "History of Suffolk County" and "The Town of Brookhaven." In *The History of Suffolk County, New York,* edited by W. W. Munsell, 49–82 and 1–101. (The book is not paginated sequentially; each town history is paginated independently.) New York: W. W. Munsell.

Beale, Carleton. 1972. "An Overview of the Phenomenon of Mixed Race Isolates in the United States." *American Anthropologist* 74: 704–10.

Beardsley, Gretchen. 1940. "The Ground Nut as Used by the Indians of Eastern North America." *Papers of the Michigan Academy of Science* 25: 507–15.

Beauchamp, William, M. 1901. "Wampum and Shell Articles." *Bulletin of the New York State Museum* 8 (41): 321–480.

___. 1907. "Aboriginal Place Names of New York." New York Museum, *Bulletin* 108.

Becker, Marshall J. 1988. "A Summary of Lenape Socio-Political Organization and Settlement Pattern At The Time of European Contact: The Evidence for Collecting Bands." *Journal of Middle Atlantic Archaeology* 4: 79–83.

Berkeley, Edmund and Dorothy Smith Berkeley, eds. 1965. *The Reverend John Clayton: A Parson with a Scientific Mind.* Charlottesville, VA: University of Virginia Press.

Berkhofer, Robert F., Jr. 1979. *The White Man's Indian.* New York: Vintage Books.

Bernstein, David. 1990. "Trends in Prehistoric Subsistence on the Southern New England Coast: The View From Narragansett Bay." *North American Archaeologist* 11 (4): 321–52.

___. 1990a. "Prehistoric Seasonality Studies in Coastal Southern New England." *American Anthropologist* 92: 96–115.

___. 1995. "Prehistoric Inland Adaptations on Long Island." Paper presented at the Eastern States Archaeological Federation Annual Meeting, Wilmington, DE, October 26–29.

Berry, Brewton. 1963. *Almost White.* New York: Macmillan.

Binford, Lewis and Sally Binford, eds. 1986. *New Perspectives in Archaeology.* New York: Academic Press.

Bittman, Mark. 1993. "Leafy Green and Yellow Bodyguards." *New York Times Magazine,* April 25: 67.

Bolton, Reginald Pelham. 1922. "Indian Paths in the Great Metropolis." *Contributions From the Museum,* 23. New York: Museum of the American Indian, Heye Foundation.

___. 1934. *Indian Life of Long Ago in the City of New York.* New York: Harmony House. (Expanded edition published in 1972 by Ira J. Friedman.)

___. 1975. "New York in Indian Possession," 1920. *Indian Notes and Monographs* 2 (7). 2d ed. New York: Museum of the American Indian, Heye Foundation.

Booth, Nathaniel. 1982. "The Archaeology of Long Island," 1949. In *The Second Coastal Archaeology Reader,* edited by James E. Truex, 54–60. Stony Brook: SCAA.

Bourne, Russell. 1990. *The Red King's Rebellion.* New York: Oxford University Press.

Boyd, Glenda F. 1982. "The Transitional Phase on Long Island," 1962. In *The Second Coastal Archaeology Reader: 1900 to the Present,* edited by James E. Truex, 64–78. Stony Brook: SCAA.

Bradford, William. 1981. *Of Plymouth Plantation 1620-1647.* New York: McGraw-Hill.

Bragdon, Kathleen. 1996. *Native Peoples of Southern New England 1560–1650.* Norman: University of Oklahoma Press.

Brasser, T. J. 1978. "Early Indian-European Contacts." In *Handbook of the North American Indians,* vol.15, *The Northeast,* edited by Bruce Trigger, 78–88. Washington DC: Smithsonian Institution Press.

Brenner, Elise M. 1984. "Strategies for Autonomy: An Analysis of Ethnic Mobilization in Seventeenth Century Southern New England." Ph.D. diss., University of Massachusetts.

___1988. "The Sociopolitical Implications of Mortuary Ritual Remains in 17th-Century Native Southern New England." In *The Recovery of Meaning, Historical Archaeology in the Eastern United States,* edited by Mark Leone and Parker Potter, 147–81. Washington: Smithsonian Institution Press.

Brinton, Daniel. 1868. *Myths of the Americas; Symbolism and Mythology of the Indians of the Americas.* Reprint, Blauvelt, NY: Rudolph Steiner Publications, 1976.

___. 1884. *The Lenape and their Legends; With the Complete Text and Symbols of the Walam-Olum.* Reprint, St. Clair Shores, MI: Scholarly Press, 1976.

___. 1980. "On an 'Inscribed Tablet' From Long Island," 1893. In *Languages and Lore of the Long Island Indians,* edited by Gaynell Stone Levine and Nancy Bonvillain, 304-6. Stony Brook: SCAA.

Brodeur, Paul. 1985. *Restitution: The Land Claims of the Mashpee, Passamaquoddy, and Penobscot Indians of New England.* Boston: Northeastern University Press.

Brodhead, John Romeyn. 1853–71. *History of the State of New York.* 2 vols. New York: Harper Brothers.

Browning-Hoffman, Kathryn. 1982. "Indian Textiles as Reconstructed from Impressions Left on Long Island," 1974. In *The Second Coastal Archaeology Reader: 1900 to the Present,* edited by James E. Truex, 276–80. Stony Brook, NY: SCAA.

___. 1982a. "Can Incised Pottery Give Clues to Prehistoric Basketry?" 1979. In *The Second Coastal Archaeology Reader: 1900 to the Present,* edited by James E. Truex, 268–75. Stony Brook, NY: SCAA.

Bullock, Frances Collins. 1969. "Poospatuck June Meetings." *Long Island Forum* 32: 210.

Bunce, James E. and Richard P. Harmond, eds. 1977. *Long Island as America: A Documentary History to 1896.* Port Washington, NY: Kennikat Press.

Burggraf, James. 1982. "Some Notes on the Manufacture of Wampum," 1938. In *The Second Coastal Reader Archaeology Reader, 1900 to the Present,* edited by James E. Truex, 285–89. Stony Brook: SCAA.

Burton, John W. 1976. "Hellish Fiends and Brutish Men: Amerindian-European Interaction in Southern New England, an Interdisciplinary Analysis, 1600–1750." Ph.D. diss., Kent State University.

Butler, Eva. 1945. "Sweat-Houses in the Southern New England Area." Massachusetts Archaeological Society, *Bulletin* 7 (1): 11–15.

___. 1948. "Algonkian Culture and the Use of Maize in Southern New England." Archaeological Society of Connecticut, *Bulletin* 22: 2–39.

___. n.d. "Northeast Indians: Tobacco Pipes and Smoking Customs." Butler Notebook, "Tobacco." In The Indian and Colonial Research Center, Old Mystic, CT.

Butler, Jon. 1979. "Magic, Astrology, and the Early American Religious Heritage." *American Historical Review* 84 (2): 317–46.

Calder, Isabel. 1966. "The Earl of Stirling and the Colonization of Long Island." In *Essays in Colonial History Presented to Charles McLean Andrews,* 1931, 74–95. Freeport, NY: Books for Libraries Press.

Caldwell, Joseph R. 1958. "Trend and Tradition in the Prehistory of the Eastern United States." *Illinois State Museum Papers.* Number 10. Memoir Number 88. Springfield, IL: American Anthropological Association.

___. 1970. "Interaction Spheres in History." *Hopewellian Studies.* Illinois State Museum, Scientific Papers, 12: 133–43.

Callahan, Errett. 1981. "Pamunkey Housebuilding: An Experimental Study of Late Woodland Construction in the Powhatan Confederacy." Ph.D. diss., Catholic University of America.

Carr, J. D. and Carlos Westez. 1980. "Surviving Folktales and Herbal Lore among Shinnecock Indians of Long Island." In *Languages and Lore of the Long Island Indians,* edited by Gaynell Stone Levine and Nancy Bonvillain, 278–83. Stony Brook: SCAA.

Cassedy, Daniel F. 1993. "New Data on Maize Horticulture and Subsistence in Southwestern Connecticut." Paper presented at the Northeastern Anthropological Association Annual Meeting, Danbury, CT.

___. 1995. "Prehistoric Clambakes on the Coast of Connecticut." Paper presented at the Eastern States Archaeological Federation Annual Meeting, Wilmington, DE, October 26–29.

Ceci, Lynn. 1975. "Fish Fertilizer: A Native American Practice?" *Science* 188: 26–30.

___. 1977. "The Effect of European Contact and Trade on the Settlement Pattern of Indians in Coastal New York, 1524–1664." Ph.D. diss., City University of New York. (Published by Garland Publishing Company in 1990.)

___. 1978. "Watchers of the Pleiades: Ethnoastronomy Among Native Cultivators in Northeastern North America." *Ethnohistory* 25 (4): 301–17.

___. 1979. "Maize Cultivation in Coastal New York: The Archaeological, Agronomical, and Documentary Evidence." *North American Archaeologist* 1: 45–74.

___. 1982. "The First Fiscal Crisis in New York," 1980. In *The Second Coastal Archaeology Reader: 1900 to the Present,* edited by James E. Truex, 306–12. Stony Brook: SCAA.

___. 1982a "Method and Theory in Coastal New York Archaeology: Paradigms of Settlement Patterns." *North American Archaeologist* 3 (1): 5–36.

___. 1990. "Radiocarbon Dating 'Village' Sites in Coastal New York: Settlement Pattern Change in the Middle to Late Woodland." *Man in the Northeast,* no. 39,

1–28. Ceci had submitted the manuscript just before her death. Because Dr. Ceci never saw the referee's comments, their notes were added by the editor.

___. 1990a. "Native Wampum as a Peripheral Resource in the Seventeenth Centure." In *The Pequots in Southern New England: The Fall and Rise of an American Indian Nation,* edited by Laurence M. Hauptman and James D. Wherry, 48–68. Norman, OK: University of Oklahoma Press.

Clifton, James. 1984. *The Pokagons. 1683–1983: Catholic Potawatomi Indians of St. Joseph River Valley.* Lanham, MD: University Press of America.

Cocks, George. 1961. "Old Matinecock." *Nassau County Historical Journal,* 22:1–11.

Cohen, Mark, N. 1977. *The Food Crisis in Prehistory: Overpopulation and the Origins of Agriculture.* New Haven: Yale University Press.

Coles, Robert. 1954. *The Long Island Indian.* Glen Cove, NY: Little Museum.

Cook, Sherburne, F. 1973. "The Significance of Disease in the Extinction of the New England Indians." *Human Biology* 45 (3): 485–508.

Cooper, James B. 1882. "The Town of Babylon." In *The History of Suffolk County, New York,* edited by W. W. Munsell, 1–34. (The book is not paginated sequentially; each town history is paginated independently.) New York: W. W. Munsell.

Cooper, Thomas, ed. 1993. *The Records of the Court of Session of Suffolk County in the Province of New York, 1670–1688.* Bowie, MD: Heritage Books.

Cowan, C. Wesley. 1985. "Understanding the Evolution of Plant Husbandry in Eastern North America: Lessons From Botany, Ethnography and Archaeology." In *Prehistoric Food Production,* edited by Richard Ford, 205–43. Ann Arbor: University of Michigan, Museum of Anthropology, no. 77.

Craven, Charles. 1906. *The History of Mattituck.* Mattituck, NY: Published by the author.

Cronon, William. 1983. *Changes in the Land.* New York: Hill and Wang.

Cronon, William and Richard White. 1978. "Ecological Changes and Indian-White Relations." In *Handbook of the North American Indians,* vol. 15, *The Northeast,* edited by Bruce Trigger, 417–29. Washington, DC: Smithsonian Press.

Crosby, Constance A. 1988. "From Myth to History, or Why King Philip's Ghost Walks Abroad." In *The Recovery of Meaning, Historical Archaeology in the Eastern United States,* edited by Mark Leone and Parker B. Potter, Jr., 183–209. Washington: Smithsonian Institution Press.

Cross, Dorothy. 1956. *Archaeology of New Jersey.* 2 vols. Trenton: Archaeological Society of New Jersey.

___. 1986. "Canoes of the Lenni Lenape." *Bulletin of the Archaeological Society of New Jersey* 40: 25.

CSP. 1661–1668. *Calender of State Papers Colonial Series America and the West Indies.* London: Great Britain Public Record Office.

Cuffee, Eugene and Gaynell Stone. 1983. "Shinnecock Families." In *The Shinnecock Indians: A Culture History,* edited by Gaynell Stone, 311–29. Stony Brook: SCAA.

Danckaerts, Jasper. 1969. *Journal of Jasper Danckaerts, 1679–1680,* 1913, edited by Bartlett Burleigh James and J. Franklin Jameson. New York: Barnes and Noble.

De Champlain, Samuel. 1922. *Voyages and Explorations, 1604–1618,* edited by Edward Gaylord Bourne. New York: Allerton Book Company.

De Forest, John. 1852. *History of the Indians of Connecticut From Earliest Known Period to 1850.* Hartford, CT: W. J. Hammersley.

De Laet, Johannes. 1909. "New World, or Description of West-India," 1625. In *Narratives of New Netherland,* edited by J. Franklin Jameson, 31–60. New York: Charles Scribner.

Densmore, Christopher, ed. 1992. "Indian Religious Beliefs on Long Island: A Quaker's Account." *New York History* 73: 431–42.

Denton, Daniel. 1968. "A Brief Description of New York," 1670. In *Historical Chronicles of New Amsterdam, Colonial New York, and Early Long Island,* edited by Sidney Pomerantz, 1–22. Port Washington: Empire State Historical Publications. Extensive excerpts from Denton's account are in *Roots and Heritage of Hempstead Town,* edited by Natalie A. Naylor, 193–96. Interlaken, NY: Heart of the Lakes Publishing, 1994.

De Rasieres, Isaack. 1909. "Letter to Samuel Blommaert, 1628." In *Narratives of New Netherland, 1609–1664,* edited by J. Franklin Jameson, 102–15. New York: Charles Scribner's Sons.

De Vries, David. 1909. "Short Historical Journal Notes, 1633–43." In *Narratives of New Netherland,* edited by J. Franklin Jameson, 183–234. New York: Charles Scribner's Sons.

Dincauze, Dena F. 1968. "Cremation Cemetaries in Eastern Massachusetts." *Papers of the Peabody Museum of Archaeology and Ethnology, Harvard University* 59 (1): 3–103.

———. 1973. "Prehistoric Occupation of the Charles River Estuary." *Bulletin of the Archaeological Society of Connecticut,* no. 38: 25–39.

———. 1975. "The Late Archaic Period in Southern New England." *Arctic Anthropology* 12 (2): 23–34.

Dixon, C. W. 1962. *Smallpox.* New York: Little, Brown, and Company.

Dobyns, H. F. 1983. *Their Numbers Became Thinned: Native American Population Dynamics in Eastern North America.* Knoxville: University of Tennessee Press.

Drake, Samuel G. 1857. *The Book of Indians; or Biography and History of the Indians of North America, From its First Discovery to the Year 1841.* 8th ed. Reprint, Detroit, MI: Gale Research, 1970.

Driver, Harold, E. 1969. *Indians of North America.* Chicago: University of Chicago Press.

DRNN. 1924. *Documents Relating to New Netherland, 1624–1626,* edited by A. J. F. Van Laer. San Marino, CA: Henry Huntington Library.

DSBD. Department of State Book of Deeds. Unpublished Documents. Office of the Secretary of State, Albany, NY. (New York State Archives Series 453 vols. 1–9.)

Duke, James. 1986. *Handbook of Northeastern Indian Medicinal Plants.* Lincoln, MA: Quarterman Publications.

Edwards, Everett, and Jeanette Rattray. 1956. *Whale-off: The Story of American Shore Whaling,* 1932. Reprint, New York: Coward and McCann.

Eells, Earnest Edward. 1993. "Indian Missions on Long Island," 1939. In *The History and Archaeology of the Montauk,* edited by Gaynell Stone, 155–90. 2d ed. Stony Brook: SCAA.

EHPLC. East Hampton Public Library, Long Island Collection, East Hampton, NY.

EHTC. East Hampton Town Clerk's Office, East Hampton, NY.

EHTJ. 1926. *East Hampton Trustees Journal,* 7 vols. East Hampton Trustees.

Ewan, Joseph and Nesta Ewan, eds. 1970. *John Banister and His Natural History of Virginia, 1678–1692.* Chicago: University of Ilinois Press.

Fawcett, Melissa. 1994. "How the Mohegan Tribe Won Federal Recognition." Paper presented at International Congress of Americanists, Stockholm, Sweden (copy on file with author).

Flannery, Regina. 1939. *An Analysis of Coastal Algonkin Culture.* Washington, DC: Catholic University Press.

Fletchner, Alice. 1888. *Indian Education and Civilization.* Washington DC: Government Printing Office.

Flint, Martha. 1967. *Long Island Before the Revolution* (original title, *Early Long Island*, 1896). Reprint, Port Washington: Ira J. Friedman.

Fogelson, Ray. 1989. "History of the Study of Native Americans." In *Native American Religions: North America,* edited by Lawrence Sullivan, 147-54. New York: Macmillan.

Forbes, Allyn B., ed. 1929–47. *Winthrop Papers.* 5 vols. Boston: Massachusetts Historical Society.

Ford, Richard. 1979. "Paleoethnobotany in American Archaeology" In *Advances in Archaeological Method and Theory,* edited by M. Schiffer, 285–336. New York: Academic Press.

___. 1981. "Gardening and Farming before A.D. 1,000: Patterns of Prehistoric Cultivation in North America." *Journal of Ethnobiology* 1: 6-27.

___. ed. 1985. *Prehistoric Food Production.* Ann Arbor: University of Michigan, Museum of Anthropology, no. 77.

Foster, Steven and James Duke. 1990. *Medicinal Plants.* Peterson Guide Series. Boston: Houghton Mifflin.

Fowler, William, S. 1966. "Cache of Engraved Pebbles from New Brunswick." *Bulletin of the Massachusetts Archaeological Society* 28 (1): 15–16.

___. 1968. "Stone Bowl Making at the Westfield Quarry." *Bulletin of the Massachusetts Archaeological Society* 30 (1): 6–16.

___. 1975. "The Diagnostic Stone Bowl Industry." *Bulletin of the Massachusetts Archaeological Society* 36 (3–4): 1-10.

Fried, Morton. 1975. *The Notion of Tribe.* Menlo Park: Cummings Publishing Company.

Furman, Gabriel. 1874. *Antiquities of Long Island.* Reprint, Port Washington, NY: I. J. Friedman, 1968.

Galenson, David W. 1981. *White Servitude in Colonial America: An Economic Analysis.* London: Cambridge University Press.

Galinat, Walton, C. 1985. "Domestication and Diffusion of Maize." In *Prehistoric Food Production,* edited by Richard Ford, 245–78. Ann Arbor: University of Michigan, Museum of Anthropology.

Gardiner, Curtis. 1890. *Lion Gardiner and his Descendants.* St. Louis: A. Whipple. (Available in East Hampton Library, Long Island Collection.)

Gardiner, David. 1871. *Chronicles of the Town of East Hampton.* Reprint, Sag Harbor, NY: Isabel Gardiner Mairs, 1973.

Gardiner, John Lyon. 1980. "Montauk Vocabulary, recorded from George Pharoah . . . March 25, 1798." In *Languages and Lore of the Long Island Indians,* edited by Gaynell Stone Levine and Nancy Bonvillain, 15–16. Stony Brook: SCAA.

___. n.d. The Journal and Farm Book of John Lyon Gardiner. East Hampton Public Library, Long Island Collection, East Hampton, NY.

Gardiner, Lion. 1980. "Relation of the Pequot Wars," 1897. In *The History of the Pequot War,* edited by Charles Orr, 112–49. Reprint, New York: AMS Press.

Gardiner, Sarah. 1947. *Early Memories of Gardiner's Island.* East Hampton, NY: East Hampton Star.

Gehring, Charles. 1980. *New York Historical Manuscripts: Dutch, Volumes GG, HH, and II, Land Papers.* Baltimore: Genealogical Publishing Co.

Gehring, Charles and Robert Grumet. 1987. "Observations of the Indians From Jasper Danckaerts Journal, 1697-1680." *William and Mary Quarterly* 44, 3d series, no. 1: 104–20.

Gentry, Howard Scott. 1969. "Origin of the Common Bean." *Phaseolus vulgaris. Economic Botany* 22: 55–69.

George, David R. 1995. "Variation in Late Prehistoric Plant Use in Southern New England." Paper presented at the Eastern States Archaeological Federation, Annual Meeting, Wilmington, DE, October 26–29.

Gerard, Robert, Jr. 1983. "Shinnecock Indian Duck Decoys." In *The Shinnecock Indians: A Culture History,* edited by Gaynell Stone, 297–99, Stony Brook, NY: SCAA.

Gibbs, Iris and Alonzo Gibbs. 1981. "Mannetto: Deity or Hill?" *Long Island Forum* 44: 10–11.

Gill, Sam D. 1982. *Native American Religions.* Belmont, CA: Wadsworth Publishing Company.

Goddard, Charles. 1936. "Notes on the Sugar Loaf Hill Site." Unpublished 18–page report on file in the Southold Indian Museum Archives, Southold, NY (also in New York State Archaeologist office records, Albany, NY).

Goddard, Ives. 1978. "Eastern Algonquian Languages." In *Handbook of the North American Indians,* vol. 15, *Northeast,* edited by Bruce Trigger, 70–77. Washington, DC: Smithsonian Institution Press.

___. 1978a. "Delaware." In *Handbook of the North American Indians,* vol. 15, *Northeast,* edited by Bruce Trigger, 213–39. Washington, DC: Smithsonian Institution Press.

Gonzales, Ellice. 1984. "From Unkechaug to Poospatuck." Monograph prepared for the National Park Service, Fire Island National Seashore, Patchogue, NY. (Chapters paginated independently.) Available in National Park Service Library, Patchogue, NY.

___. 1986. "Tri-racial Isolates in a Bi-racial Society: Poospatuck Ambiguity and Conflict." In *Strategies for Survival: American Indians in the Eastern United States,* edited by Frank W. Porter, 113–37. New York: Greenwood Press.

___. 1993. "Montauk Ethnohistorical Sources." In *The History and Archaeology of the Montauk,* edited by Gaynell Stone, 67–77. 2d ed. Stony Brook, NY: SCAA.

Gookin, Daniel. 1972. *Historical Collections of the Indians in New England,* 1674. Reprint, New York: Arno Press.

Gramley, Richard Michael. 1982. "Archaeological Investigations at Pipestave Hollow, Mt Sinai Harbor, Long Island: A Preliminary Report," 1977. In *The Second Coastal Archaeological Reader: 1900 to the Present,* edited by James E. Truex, 161–72. Stony Brook: SCAA.

Gramley, Richard Michael, and Gretchen Gwynne. 1982. "Two Late Woodland Sites on Long Island Sound," 1979. In *The Second Coastal Archaeology Reader: 1900 to the Present*, edited by James Truex, 173–89. Stony Brook: SCAA.

Griffin, James. 1978. "The Midlands and Northeastern United States." In *Ancient Native Americans*, edited by Jessie Jennings, 221–79. San Francisco: W. H. Freedman.

Grim, John, A. 1987. *The Shaman*. Norman, OK: Oklahoma University Press.

Grumet, Robert Steven. 1979. "We Are Not Such Great Fools: Changes in Upper Delawarean Socio-Political Life, 1630–1758." Ph.D. diss., Rutgers University.

———. 1980. "Sunksquaws, Shamans, and Tradeswomen: Middle Atlantic Coastal Algonquian Women During the 17th and 18th Centuries." In *Women and Colonization: Anthropological Perspectives*, edited by Mona Etienne and Eleanor Leacock, 43–62. New York: Praeger.

———. 1981. *Native American Place Names in New York City*. New York: Museum of the City of New York.

———. 1989. *The Lenapes*. New York: Chelsea House.

———. 1989a. "The Selling of Lenapehoking." *Bulletin of the Archaeological Society of New Jersey* 44: 1–6.

———. 1990. "That Their Issue be not Spurious: An Inquiry Into Munsee Matriliny." *Bulletin of the Archaeological Society of New Jersey* 45: 19–24.

———. 1994. "New Information From an Old Source: Notes on Adam the Indian's Testimony in the New Plymouth Colony Records." *Bulletin of the Archeological Society of New Jersey* 49: 83–87.

———. 1995. "The Indians of Massapeag." *The Long Island Historical Journal* 8 (1): 26–38.

———. 1996. "Suscaneman and the Matinecock Lands." In *Northeastern Indian Lives*, edited by Robert S. Grumet, 116–39. Amherst, MA: University of Massachusetts Press.

Gumbs, Harriet Crippen Brown. 1983. "The Land Defended: The Cove Realty Case." In *The Shinnecock Indians; A Culture History*, edited by Gaynell Stone, 118–29. Stony Brook, NY: SCAA.

Gwynne, Gretchen. 1982. "The Late Archaic Archaeology of Mount Sinai Harbor, New York: Human Ecology, Economy and Residence Patterns on the Southern New England Coast." Ph.D diss., SUNY Stony Brook. (Ann Arbor: University Microfilms, no. 8218079.)

———. 1982a. "Pipestave Hollow Ideography." *Expedition* 24 (3): 14–19.

Hagan, William. 1992. "Full Blood, Mixed Blood, Generic, and Ersatz: The Problem of Mixed Identity." In *The American Indian*, edited by Roger L. Nicols, 278–88. New York: McGraw Hill.

Hagerty, Gilbert W. 1985. *Wampum, War and Trade Goods West of the Hudson*. Interlaken, NY: Heart of the Lakes Publishing.

Hall, Robert. 1976. "Ghosts, Water Barriers, Corn, and Sacred Enclosures in the Eastern Woodlands." *American Antiquity* 41 (3): 360–64.

Hariot, Thomas. 1972. *A Briefe and True Report of the New Foundland of Virginia*, 1590. Reprint, New York: Dover.

Harner, Michael. 1982. *The Way of the Shaman*. New York: Bantam Books.

Harrington, Mark. 1921. *Religion and Ceremonies of the Lenape*. Reprint, New York: AMS Press, 1984.

———. 1977. "Ancient Shellheaps Near New York City," 1909. In *Early Papers in Long Island Archaeology*, edited by Gaynell S. Levine, 1–15. Stony Brook: SCAA.

___. 1977a. "Ancient Village Site of the Shinnecock Indians," 1924. In *Early Papers in Long Island Archaeology*, edited by Gaynell S. Levine, 30–64. Stony Brook: SCAA.

___. 1982. "Exploration of an Ancient Burial Ground and Village Site near Port Washington, Long Island," 1900. In *The Second Coastal Archaeology Reader*, edited by James E. Truex, 83–89. Stony Brook: SCAA.

Harris, Marvin. 1993. *Culture, People, Nature.* 6th ed. New York: Harper Collins.

Hawk, William. 1984. "The Revitalization of the Matinnecock Indian Tribe of New York." Ph.D. diss., University of Wisconsin, Madison.

Hawke, David Freeman. 1966. *The Colonial Experience.* New York: Bobbs-Merrill.

___. 1988. *Everyday Life in Early America.* New York: Harper and Row.

Hayes, Rose Oldfield. 1976. "An Ethnographic and Demographic Study of the Pres'qile" (Shinnecock). Ph.D. diss., State University of New York at Buffalo.

___. 1983. "A Case of Cultural Continuity: The Shinnecock Kinship System," 1975. In *The Shinnecock Indians: A Culture History*, edited by Gaynell Stone, 336–43. Stony Brook: SCAA.

___. 1983a. "Shinnecock Land Ownership System and Use: Prehistoric and Colonial Influences on Modern Adaptive Modes," 1976. In *The Shinnecock Indians: A Culture History*, edited by Gaynell Stone, 331–35. Stony Brook: SCAA.

Heckewelder, John. 1876. *History, Manners and Customs of the Indian Nations Who Once Inhabited Pennsylvania and the Neighboring States.* Philadelphia: Historical Society of Pennsylvania.

Hicks, David and Margaret Gwynne. 1994. *Cultural Anthropology.* New York: HarperCollins.

Hill, George. 1971. "Delaware Ethnobotany." *Newsletter of the Oklahoma Anthropological Society* 19 (3): 3–18.

Hoebel, E. Adamson. 1960. *The Cheyennes: Indians of the Great Plains.* New York: Holt, Rinehart and Winston.

Hoffman, Walter, J. 1885–1886. "The Mide'win or Grand Medicine Society." *Seventh Annual Report of the Bureau of American Ethnology*, 149–300. Washington, DC: Government Printing Office.

Horton, Azariah. 1993. "The Journal of Azariah Horton, 1741–44." In *The History and Archaeology of the Montauk*, edited by Gaynell Stone, 195–220. 2d ed. Stony Brook: SCAA.

Hosmer, James Kendall, ed. 1946. *Winthrop's Journal, History of New England*, 1690. 2 vols. New York: Barnes and Noble.

Hostek, Albert. 1976. *Native and Near Native.* Ronkonkoma, NY: Environmental Centers of Setauket-Smithtown.

Howard, Michael. 1989. *Contemporary Cultural Anthropology.* New York: Scott, Foresman and Company.

Howell, George Rogers. 1887. *The Early History of Southampton.* Albany: Weed Parsons.

Howes, William J. 1954. "Aboriginal New England Pottery." Massachusetts Archaeological Society, *Bulletin* 4: 81–86.

HTHA. Huntington Town Historical Archives. Huntington Town Historian's Office, Huntington, NY.

Hubbard, William. 1677. *A Narrative of the Troubles with the Indians in New England.* Boston: John Foster.

___. 1848. *A General History of New England,* 1682. Reprint, Boston: Charles Little and James Brown.

Huddleston, Lee Eldridge. 1967. *Origins of the American Indians: European Concepts, 1492–1729.* Austin: University of Texas Press.

Hudson, Charles. 1976. *The Southeastern Indians.* Knoxville: University of Tennessee Press.

Hultkrantz, Ake. 1980. *The Religions of the American Indians,* translated by Monica Setterwall. Berkeley: University of California Press.

Hunt, David. 1992. *Native Indian Wild Game, Fish and Wild Foods Cookbook.* Lancaster, PA: Fox Chapel Publishing.

Jacobson, Jerome. 1980. "Burial Ridge, Tottenville, Staten Island, NY: Archaeology at New York City's Largest Prehistoric Cemetery." Monograph published by the Staten Island Institute of Arts and Sciences.

Jameson, J. Franklin. 1883. "Montauk and the Commonlands of Easthampton." *Magazine of American History* 9 (4): 225–39.

___, ed. 1909. *Narratives of New Netherland.* New York: Barnes and Noble.

Janiver, Thomas A. 1967. *The Dutch Founding of New York,* 1903. Reprint, Port Washington, NY: Ira J. Friedman.

Jaray, Cornell, ed. 1968. *Historical Chronicles of New Amsterdam, Colonial New York and Early Long Island.* Port Washington, NY: Ira J. Friedman.

Jefferson, Thomas. 1980. "Vocabulary of Unquachog or Puspatuck," 1791 and 1817. In *Languages and Lore of the Long Island Indians,* edited by Gaynell Stone Levine and Nancy Bonvillain, 17–20. Stony Brook: SCAA.

Jennings, Francis. 1976. *The Invasion of America: Indians, Colonialism, and the Cant of Conquest.* New York: W. W. Norton.

___. 1990. *The Ambiguous Empire: The Covenant Chain Confederation of Indian Tribes with English Colonies from its Beginnings to the Lancaster Treaty of 1744,* 1984. New York: W. W. Norton and Company.

Jernegan, Marcus Wilson. 1931. *Laboring and Dependent Classes in Colonial America.* New York: Frederick Ungar.

JNN. 1909. "Journal of New Netherland, 1647." In *Narratives of New Netherland 1609–1664,* edited by J. Franklin Jameson, 267–84. New York: Charles Scribner's.

Johannemann, Edward. 1993. "Indian Fields Site, Montauk, Suffolk County, Long Island New York, Part I." In *The History and Archaeology of the Montauk,* edited by Gaynell Stone, 645–54. 2d ed. Stony Brook: SCAA.

Johnson, Edward. 1910. *Wonder Working Providence of Zion's Saviors in New England,* 1654, edited by J. Franklin Jameson. New York: Barnes and Noble.

Johnson, Eric. 1996. "Uncas and The Politics of Contact." In *Northeastern Indian Lives,* edited by Robert S. Grumet, 63–94. Amherst, MA: University of Massachusetts Press.

Johnson, Frederick, et al. 1942. "The Boylston Street Fishweir." In *Papers of the R. S. Peabody Foundation for Archaeology.* Vol. 2. Andover, MA: Peabody Foundation.

Jones, Samuel. 1821. "Notes on the Pamphlet Entitled 'A Discourse Delivered Before the New-York Historical Society.'" *Collections of the New-York Historical Society for the Year 1821,* 3: 322–28.

Jones, William. 1905. "The Algonkin Manitou." *Journal of American Folklore* 18: 183–90.

Josselyn, John. 1972. *New England Rarities Discovered,* 1672. Reprint, Boston: Massachusetts Historical Society.

———. 1988. "An Account of Two Voyages to New England, 1675." In *John Josselyn, Colonial Traveler,* edited by Paul Lindholt. Hanover, NH: University Press of New England.

Juet, Robert. 1909. "The Third Voyage of Henry Hudson, 1610." In *Narratives of New Netherland,* edited by J. Franklin Jameson. New York: Barnes and Noble.

Kaeser, Edward J. 1978. "The Oakland Lake Site (Har-13-4)," 1974. In *The Coastal Archaeology Reader,* edited by Gaynell S. Levine, 263–90. Stony Brook: SCAA.

———. 1978a. "A Primer for Pottery Classification, Metropolitan Coastal New York," 1964. In *The Coastal Archaeology Reader,* edited by Gaynell S. Levine, 68–75. Stony Brook, NY: SCAA.

———. 1978b. "The Middle Woodland Placement of Steubenville-Like Projectile Points in Coastal New York's Abbott Complex," 1968. In *The Coastal Archaeology Reader,* edited by Gaynell S. Levine, 124–42. Stony Brook: SCAA.

———. 1978c. "The Morris Estate Club Site," 1963. In *The Coastal Archaeology Reader,* edited by Gaynell S. Levine, 38–45. Stony Brook: SCAA.

———. 1978d. "The Archery Range Site," 1962. In *The Coastal Archaeology Reader,* edited by Gaynell S. Levine, 20–22. Stony Brook: SCAA.

Kammen, Michael. 1975. *Colonial New York: A History.* New York: Charles Scribner's Sons.

Karklins, Karlis. 1993. "The Beads of the Pantigo Site, A Montauk Cemetery on Eastern Long Island, N. Y." In *The History and Archaeology of the Montauk,* edited by Gaynell Stone, 629–41, 2nd ed. Stony Brook, NY: SCAA.

Kavasch, Barrie. 1979. *Native Harvests Recipes and Botanicals of the American Indians.* New York: Vintage Books.

———. 1994. "Native Foods of New England." In *Enduring Traditions: The Native Peoples of New England,* edited by Laurie Weinstein, 5–30. Westport, CT: Bergin and Garvey.

Keegan, William, F. 1987. *Emergent Horticultural Economies of the Eastern Woodlands.* Occasional Paper no. 7. Carbondale, IL: Southern Illinois University Center for Archaeological Investigations.

Kehoe, Alice Beck. 1989. *The Ghost Dance: Ethnohistory and Revitalization.* New York: Holt, Rinehart, and Winston.

———. 1992. *North American Indians: A Comprehensive Account.* Englewood Cliffs, NJ: Prentice Hall.

Kessler, Henry and Edward Rachlis. 1959. *Peter Stuyvesant and his New York.* New York: Random House.

Kevitt, Chester. 1968. "Aboriginal Dugout Discovered at Weymouth." *Bulletin of the Massachusetts Archaeological Society* 30 (1): 1–5.

Kiev, A. 1964. *Magic, Faith, and Healing.* New York: Free Press of Glencoe.

King, Frances. 1985. "Early Cultivated Curcurbits in Eastern North America." In *Prehistoric Food Production,* edited by Richard Ford, 73–97. Ann Arbor: University of Michigan, Museum of Anthropology.

Klein, Michael J. 1995. "The Transition From Soapstone Bowls to Marcey Creek Ceramics in the Middle Atlantic Region: A Consideration of Vessel Technology, Ethnographic Data, and Regional Exchange." Paper presented at the Eastern States Archaeological Federation Annual Meeting, Wilmington, DE, October 26–29.

Kraft, Herbert, C. 1970. "Prehistoric House Patterns in New Jersey." *Bulletin of the Archaeological Society of New Jersey* 26: 1–11.

___. 1975. "Petroglyphs on Small Artifacts." *Bulletin of the Archaeological Society of New Jersey* 32: 14.

___. 1978. "The Miller Field Site in New Jersey and its Influence Upon the Terminal Archaic and Transitional Stages in New York State and Long Island," 1970. In *The Coastal Archaeology Reader 1954–1977*, edited by Gaynell S. Levine, 152-64. Stony Brook: SCAA.

___. 1986. *The Lenape: Archaeology, History and Ethnography.* Newark: New Jersey Historical Society.

___. 1991. "An Effigy Face From Lake Hopatcong." *Bulletin of the Archaeological Society of New Jersey* 46: 1–12.

Kraus, Scott D., et al. 1986. "Migration and Calving of Right Whales *(Eubalaena glacialis)* in the Western North Atlantic." In *Right Whales: Past and Present Status,* edited by Robert I. Brownell, Peter B. Best, and John H. Prescott, 201–20. Cambridge, MA: International Whaling Commission, Special Issue no. 10.

Kross, Jessica. 1983. *The Evolution of an American Town: Newtown New York, 1642–1775.* Philadelphia: Temple University Press.

Lamb, Trudi. 1981. "Squaw Sachems: Women Who Rule." *Artifacts* 9 (Winter): 1–3.

Latham, Roy. 1935. "The Orient Focus of Eastern Long Island, New York: Site One of the Orient Focus." Unpublished 7–page report on file in the Southold (NY) Indian Museum archives, Southold, NY.

___. 1935a. "Site Two of the Orient Focus Burials on Eastern Long Island." Unpublished 12–page report on file in the Southold (NY) Indian Museum archives, Southold, NY.

___. 1936. "The Third Component of the Orient Focus Burials: Sugar Loaf, Shinnecock Hills." Unpublished 6-page report on file in the Southold (NY) Indian Museum archives.

___. 1940. "The Fourth Component of the Orient Focus Graves: Manor Hill, Jamesport." Unpublished 5–page report, Southold (NY) Indian Museum archives

___. 1941? (undated). "Comments and Notes on the Orient Focus." Unpublished 8–page report on file in the Southold (NY) Indian Museum archives, Southold, NY.

___. 1978. "Seventeenth-Century Graves at Montauk, Long Island," 1957. In *The Coastal Archaeology Reader,* edited by Gaynell S. Levine, 6. Stony Brook: SCAA.

___. 1978a. "Three Mile Harbor Sites, East Hampton, Long Island, New York," 1961. In *The Coastal Archaeology Reader,* edited by Gaynell S. Levine, 18–19. Stony Brook: SCAA.

___. 1978b. "More Notes on the Stone Utensils in the Orient Burials," 1964. In *The Coastal Archaeology Reader,* edited by Gaynell S. Levine, 65–67. Stony Brook: SCAA.

___. 1978c. "A Review of the Noyac Site," 1960. In *The Coastal Archaeology Reader,* edited by Gaynell S. Levine, 15–18. Stony Brook: SCAA.

___. 1982. "Notes on the Orient Focus of Eastern Long Island." In *The Second Coastal Archaeology Reader, 1900 to the Present,* edited by James E. Truex, 61–63. Stony Brook: SCAA.

Lauber, Almon Wheeler. 1913. *Indian Slavery in Colonial Times Within the Present Limits of the United States.* New York: Columbia University Press.

Laudin, Harvey. 1983. "The Shinnecock Powwow," 1972. In *The Shinnecock Indians: A Culture History,* edited by Gaynell Stone, 345–66. Stony Brook: SCAA.

Laufer, Berthold. 1917. "Origin of the Word Shaman." *American Anthropologist* 19: 361–71.

Lavin, Lucianne. 1987. "The Windsor Ceramic Tradition in Southern New England." *North American Archaeologist* 8 (1): 23–40.

___. 1995. "Pottery Production and Social Process Along Long Island Sound." Paper presented at the Eastern States Archaeological Federation Annual Meeting, Wilmington, DE, October 26-29.

Leach, Douglas Edward. 1966. *Flintlock and Tomahawk, New England in King Philip's War,* 1958. New York: W. W. Norton and Company.

Leechman, Douglas. 1969. *Vegetable Dyes From North American Plants.* Toronto: Southern Ontario Unit of the Herb Society of America.

Lehmann, Arthur C. and James E. Myers, eds. 1993. *Magic, Witchcraft, and Religion; An Anthropological Study of the Supernatural.* 3d ed. Mountain View, CA: Mayfield Publishing Company.

Lenik, Edward. 1978. "The Jericho, N.Y. Petroglyph," 1976. In *The Coastal Archaeology Reader,* edited by Gaynell S. Levine, 349–53. Stony Brook: SCAA.

Leonardi, Michael J. and David Bernstein. 1995. "Eagles Nest: A Multi-Component Site on the North Shore of Long Island." Paper presented at the Eastern States Archaeological Federation Annual Meeting, Wilmington, DE, October 26–29.

Lerch, Patricia. 1988. "Articulatory Relationships: The Waccamaw Struggle Against Assimilation." In *Sea and Land, Cultural and Biological Adaptations on the Southern Coastal Plain,* edited by James Peacock, 76–91. Athens: The University of Georgia Press.

___. 1992. "Pageantry, Parade, and Indian Dancing: The Staging of Identity Among the Waccamaw Sioux." *Museum Anthropology* 16 (2): 27–34.

___. 1993. "Powwows, Parades and Social Drama Among the Waccamaw Sioux." In *Celebrations of Identity, Multiple Voices in American Ritual Performance,* edited by Pamela R. Frese, 75–92. Westport, CT: Greenwood Publishing Group, Bergin and Garvey.

Lessa, William A. and Evon Z. Vogt, eds. 1979. *Reader in Comparative Religion: An Anthropological Approach.* New York: Harper and Row.

Leveille, Alan. 1993. "Eastern Woodland Burial Practices as Reflected in Canine Burial Features at the Lambert Farm Site, Warwick, Rhode Island." *Bulletin of the Massachusetts Archaeological Society* 54 (1): 19–24.

Levine, Gaynell Stone, 1980. "Rites and Customs: Visual Expressions of Beliefs." In *Languages and Lore of the Long Island Indians,* edited by Gaynell Stone Levine and Nancy Bonvillain, 301–3. Stony Brook: SCAA.

___. 1980a. "Ideology and Cosmology: Beliefs." In *Languages and Lore of the Long Island Indians,* edited by Gaynell Stone Levine and Nancy Bonvillain, 210–11.

Levine, Gaynell Stone and Nancy Bonvillain, eds. 1980. *Languages and Lore of the Long Island Indians.* Stony Brook: SCAA.

Levi-Strauss, Claude. 1966. *The Savage Mind.* Chicago: University of Chicago Press.

Lightfoot, Kent, et al. 1987. *Prehistoric Hunter-Gatherers of Shelter Island, New York: An Archaeological Study of the Mashomack Reserve.* Contributions of the University of California Archaeological Research Faculty 46, Berkeley.

Lightfoot, Kent G., and Robert M. Cerrato. 1988. "Prehistoric Shellfish Exploitation in Coastal New York." *Journal of Field Archaeology* 15 (2): 141–50.

Lincoln, Charles Z. 1894. *The Colonial Laws of New York from 1664 to the Revolution.* Albany, NY: James B. Lyton.

Linton, Ralph. 1924. "Use of Tobacco Among North American Indians." Chicago Field Museum of Natural History, *Anthropology Leaflet* no. 15.

Little, Elizabeth and J. Clinton Andrews. 1982. "Drift Whales at Nantucket: The Kindness of Moshup." *Man in the Northeast* 23: 17–38.

Lloyd Papers. 1926. *Papers of the Lloyd Family.* 2 vols. New York: New-York Historical Society.

Lopez, Julius. 1982. "Some Notes on Interior Cord-Marked Pottery From Coastal New York," 1957. In *The Second Coastal Archaeology Reader: 1900 to the Present,* edited by James E. Truex, 240-48. Stony Brook: SCAA.

___. 1982a. "Curvilinear Design Elements in the New York Coastal Area," 1958. In *The Second Coastal Archaeology Reader: 1900 to the Present,* edited by James E. Truex, 249–57. Stony Brook: SCAA.

___. 1982b. "The Areal Distribution and Complexities of 'Abbott' Ceramics," 1961. In *The Second Coastal Archaeology Reader: 1900 to the Present,* edited by James E. Truex, 263–67. Stony Brook: SCAA.

___. 1982c. "Preliminary Report on the Schurz Site: Throg's Neck Bridge, Bronx County, NY," 1955. In *The Second Coastal Archaeology Reader: 1900 to the Present,* edited by James E. Truex, 102–19. Stony Brook: SCAA.

Lopez, Julius and Roy Latham. 1982. "Faces on Sebonac Pottery From Eastern Long Island," 1960. In *The Second Coastal Archaeology Reader: 1900 to the Present,* edited by James E. Truex, 258–62. Stony Brook: SCAA.

Lopez, Julius and Stanley Wisniewski. 1978. "The Ryders Pond Site, Kings County, New York," 1971. In *The Coastal Archaeology Reader,* edited by Gaynell S. Levine, 207–27. Stony Brook: SCAA.

___. 1978a. "The Ryders Pond Site II," 1972. In *The Coastal Archaeology Reader,* edited by Gaynell S. Levine, 233–47. Stony Brook: SCAA.

Lott, Roy. 1964. "Indentured Servants in Huntington." *Long Island Forum* 22 (6): 125–26.

Luke, Myron H. 1994. "Vignettes of Hempstead Town, 1643–1800." In *The Roots and Heritage of Hempstead Town,* edited by Natalie A. Naylor, 79–126. Interlaken, NY: Heart of the Lakes Publishing.

Lurie, Nancy. 1971. "The Contemporary American Indian Scene." In *North American Indians in Historical Perspective,* edited by Eleanor Burke Leacock and Nancy Ostereich Lurie. New York: Random House.

MacCleod, William Christie, ed. 1941. "The Indians of Brooklyn in the Days of the Dutch." U.S. Work Projects Administration, Historical Records Survey. Manuscript on file in the library, Brooklyn Historical Society, Brooklyn, NY.

Malone, Patrick. 1971. "Indian and English Military Systems in New England in the Seventeenth Century." Ph.D. diss., Brown University.

___. 1973. "Changing Military Technology Among the Indians of Southern New England, 1600–1677." *American Quarterly* 25 (1): 48–63.

Mannello, George. 1984. *Our Long Island,* 1964. Reprint, Malabar, FL: R. E. Krieger.

Marshall, Bernice. 1962. *Colonial Hempstead,* 1937. Reprint, Port Washington, NY: Ira J. Friedman. (Originally published under the name Bernice Schultz.)

Martin, Morgan. 1981. "Native American Medicine: Thoughts for Post-traditional Healers." *Journal of the American Medical Association* 245 (2): 141–43.

Mason, John. 1897. "A Brief History of the Pequot War." In *History of the Pequot War,* edited by Charles Orr, 1–46. Reprint, New York: AMS Press, 1976.

Mathews, Zena. 1976. "Huron Pipes and Iroquois Shamanism." *Man in the Northeast* 12: 15–31.

Matthiessen, Peter. 1986. *Men's Lives: The Surfmen and Baymen of the South Fork.* New York: Random House.

McBride, Kevin. 1984. "The Prehistory of the Lower Connecticut River Valley." Ph.D. diss., University of Connecticut.

___. 1990. "The Historical Archaeology of the Mashantucket Pequots, 1637-1900." In *The Pequots in Southern New England: The Fall and Rise of an American Indian Nation,* edited by Lawrence Hauptman and James D. Wherry, 96–116. Norman: University of Oklahoma Press.

___. 1994. "The Source and Mother of the Fur Trade: Native-Dutch Relations in Eastern New Netherlands." In *Enduring Traditions,* edited by Laurie Weinstein, 31–51. Westport, CT: Greenwood Press, Bergin and Garvey.

McBride, Kevin and Robert Dewar. 1987. "Agriculture and Cultural Evolution: Causes and Effects in the Lower Connecticut River Valley." In *Emergent Horticultural Economies of the Eastern Woodlands,* edited by William F. Keegan, 305–28. Southern Illinois University at Carbondale, Center for Archaeological Investigations, Occasional Paper No. 7.

McCartlin, Glenn and James Rementer. 1986. "Some Additional Lenape Indian Medicines." *Bulletin of the Archaeological Society of New Jersey* 40: 15–20.

McKee, Samuel. 1935. *Labor in Colonial New York, 1664–1776.* Reprint, Port Washington, NY: Ira J. Friedman, 1965.

McNickle, D'Arcy. 1971. "Americans Called Indians." In *North American Indians in Historical Perspective,* edited by Eleanor Burke Leacock and Nancy Lurie, 29–63. New York: Random House.

Mellgrin, Guy. 1959. "Red Paint Cremations at Cemetery Point." *Bulletin of the Massachusetts Archaeological Society* 20 (3): 47.

Metcalf, P. Richard. 1974. "Who Shall Rule at Home? Native American Politics and Indian-White Relations." *Journal of American History* 61: 651–65.

MHSC. Massachussetts Historical Society Collections. Boston: Massachusetts Historical Society.

MID. Montauk Indian Deeds. Collections no. 1974: 15. Brooklyn Historical Society Library Archives, Brooklyn, NY. (Copies available in the East Hampton Library, Long Island collection.)

Miller, Robert. 1990. "Stage II Archaeological Investigation of the Bayberry Hills Site, Shinnecock Hills, Town of Southampton." Prepared by Clover Associates for the Town of Southampton. Report on file in Rogers Memorial Library, Southampton, NY.

___. 1990a. "Stage II Archaeological Investigation of Timber Ridge at the Plains Parcel, Greenlawn, Town of Huntington." Prepared by Clover Archaeological Services for the Huntington Town Planning Board. (Copy on file in Social Science Division, Southampton College, Southampton, NY.)

Mills, William, C. 1922. "Explorations of the Mound City Group." *Ohio Archaeological and Historical Quarterly* 31: 423–584.

Mitchell, Joseph. 1978. "The American Indian: A Fire Ecologist." *American Indian Culture and Research Journal* 1 (2): 26–31.

Mix, David E. E. 1859. *Catalogue of Maps and Surveys in the Office of Secretary of State, State Engineer, Surveyor, and Comptroller, the New York State Library.* Albany: Charles van Benthuysen.

Moerman, Daniel E. 1986. *Medicinal Plants of Native America.* 2 vols. Ann Arbor: University of Michigan, Museum of Anthropology.

Morice, John. 1943. "Still More About Island's Indians." *Long Island Forum* 6 (7): 135–37.

___. 1949. "The Indians of Long Island." In *Long Island: A History of Two Great Counties,* edited by Paul Bailey, 1: 107–46. New York: Lewis Historical Publishing.

___. 1950. "Indian Deeds of Oyster Bay Town." *Long Island Forum* 13 (1): 3–6, 17.

___. 1950a. "Huntingtown Indian Deeds." *Long Island Forum* 13 (12): 229–30, 239.

Morison, Samuel Eliot. 1971. *The European Discovery of America: The Northern Voyages.* New York: Oxford University Press.

Morton, Thomas. 1967. *New England Canaan, book one,* 1637, edited by Charles Francis Adams, Jr., 1883. Reprint, New York: Burt Franklin.

Moss, Richard Shannon. 1993. *Slavery on Long Island: A Study in Local Institutional and Early American Life.* New York: Garland Publishing.

Mourt, G. 1841. "Bradford and Winslow's Journal, Mourt's Relation, 1622." In *Chronicles of the Pilgrim Fathers,* edited by Alexander Young, 109–230. Boston: Little and Brown.

Mrozowski, Stephen. 1994. "The Discovery of a Native American Cornfield on Cape Cod." *Archaeology of Eastern North America* 22: 47–62.

Muller, John. 1978. "The Southeast." In *Ancient Native Americas,* edited by Jessie Jennings, 281–325. San Francisco: W. H. Freeman and Company.

Munsell, W. W. 1882. *History of Suffolk County.* New York: Munsell.

Murphy, Robert Cushman. 1991. *Fish-Shape Paumanok: Nature and Man on Long Island,* 1964. Reprint, Great Falls, VA: Waterline Books.

Myers, Albert Cook, ed. 1912. *Narratives of Early Pennsylvania, West New Jersey and Delaware, 1630–1707.* New York: Charles Scribner's Sons.

Naylor, Natalie A., ed. 1994. *The Roots and Heritage of Hempstead Town.* Interlaken, NY: Heart of the Lakes Publishing under the auspices of Hofstra University.

NHCHS. New Haven Colony Historical Society Collections. New Haven, CT. (Southold Indian deed, May 16, 1648; MSS 28, item no. 28 misc. oversize documents.)

NHCP. North Hempstead Court Proceedings, 1657–1660. On file in the Town Clerk's office, Manhasset, NY.

NYCD. 1856–87. *Documents Relative to the Colonial History of the State of New York,* edited by Edmund Bailey O'Callaghan and Berthold Fernow. 15 vols. Albany: Weed, Parsons.

NYDH. 1849–1851. *Documentary History of the State of New York,* edited by Edmund Bailey O'Callaghan. 4 vols. Albany: Weed Parsons.

NYHS. 1912. New-York Historical Society. "Proceedings of the General Court of Assizes, 1680–1682," 3-38. In *Collections, 1912.* New York: New-York Historical Society.

NYHSL. New-York Historical Society Library, New York City.

NYSCA. New York Supreme Court Archives, Historical Documents Room, Riverhead, NY.

NYSA. New York State Archives, Albany, NY.

O'Callaghan, Edmund Bailey. 1966. *History of New Netherland,* 1845–1848. 2 vols. Spartanburg, NC: The Reprint Company.

Occom, Samson. 1993. "An Account of the Montauk Indians on Long Island," 1804. In *The History and Archaeology of the Montauk,* edited by Gaynell Stone, 151–53. 2d ed. Stony Brook: SCAA.

Orchard, F. P. 1977. "A Matinecoc Site on Long Island," 1928. In *Early Papers in Long Island Archaeology,* edited by Gaynell S. Levine, 66–69. Stony Brook: SCAA.

Ostrander, Stephen M. 1894. *A History of the City of Brooklyn and Kings County.* Brooklyn. Published by subscription.

Ottery, Rudi and Will Ottery. 1993. "Where Did All The Montauks Go?" In *The History and Archaeology of the Montauk,* edited by Gaynell Stone, 315–26. Stony Brook, NY: SCAA.

Overton, Jacqueline. 1969. *Indian Life on Long Island.* 1938. Reprint, Port Washington, NY: Ira J. Friedman.

Paltsits, Victor Hugo, ed. 1910. *Minutes of the Executive Council of the Province of New York: Administration of Francis Lovelace.* 2 vols. Albany: State of New York.

Papageorge, Toby T. 1983. "Records of the Shinnecock Trustees, 1792–1983." In *The Shinnecock Indians: A Culture History,* edited by Gaynell Stone, 141–225. Stony Brook: SCAA.

Paredes, J. Anthony. 1974. "The Emergence of Contemporary Eastern Creek Identity." In *Social and Cultural Identity: Problems of Persistence and Change,* edited by T. K. Fitzgerald, 63–80. Athens: University of Georgia Press.

Parker, Arthur. 1910. *Iroquois Uses of Maize and Other Food Plants.* Reprint, Ohsweken, Ontario, Canada: Iroqrafts, 1983.

———. 1927. *The Indian How Book.* Reprint, New York: Dover Publications, 1975.

Pastorius, Francis, Daniel. 1910. "Circumstantial Geographical Description of Pennsylvania, 1700." In *Narratives of Early Pennsylvania, West New Jersey and Delaware 1630–1707,* edited by Albert Cook Meyers, 360-448. New York: Charles Scribner's Sons.

Penn, William. 1970. *Account of the Lenni Lenape or Delaware Indians,* edited by Albert Cook Myers, 1683. Somerset, NJ: Middle Atlantic Press.

Pelletreau, William. 1882. "The Town of Southampton." In *The History of Suffolk County,* edited by W. W. Munsell, 1–54. (The book is not paginated sequentially; each town history is paginated independently.) New York: W. W Munsell.

———. 1903. *The History of Long Island,* vol. 2. New York: Lewis Publishing Company. Note: the first volume was edited by Peter Ross and is listed separately under his name.

Porter, Frank. 1986. "Nonrecognized American Indian Tribes in the Eastern United States." In *Strategies for Survival: American Indians in the Eastern United States,* edited by Frank Porter, 1–42. New York: Greenwood Press.

Potter, Elisha R., Jr. 1835. *The Early History of Narragansett.* In *Collections of the Rhode Island Historical Society,* 3: 1–315.

Prime, Nathaniel. 1845. *A History of Long Island, From its First Settlement by Europeans to the Year 1845, With Special References to Ecclesiastical Concerns.* New York: Robert Carter.

Rabito-Wyppensenwah, Philip. 1993. "Native American Slavery on Eastern Long Island." In *The History and Archaeology of the Montauk,* edited by Gaynell Stone, 429–31. Stony Brook, NY: SCAA.

Rabito-Wyppensenwah and Robert Abiuso. 1993. "The Montauk Use of Herbs: A Review of the Recorded Material." In *The History and Archaeology of the Montauk,* edited by Gaynell Stone, 585–87. Stony Brook: SCAA.

Rainey, Froelich G. 1936. "A Compilation of the Theoretical Data Contributing to the Ethnography of Connecticut and Southern New England." *Bulletin of the Archaeological Society of Connecticut* no. 3: 1–89.

RCC. 1968. *The Public Records of the Colony of Connecticut,* 1859, edited by J. Hammond Trumbull. 1859. 15 vols. Reprint, New York: AMS Press.

RCNH. 1857. *Records of the Colony and Plantation of New Haven From 1638–1649,* edited by Charles J. Hoadly. 2 vols. Hartford: Case Tiffany.

RCNP. 1968. *Records of the Colony of New Plymouth,* 1859, edited by David Pulsifer. 10 vols. Reprint, New York: AMS Press. (Vols. 9 and 10 contain Acts of the United Colonies 1643–1679.)

RCRI. 1968. *Records of the Colony of Rhode Island and Providence Plantations in New England, 1850–65,* edited by John R. Bartlett. 10 vols. Reprint, New York: AMS Press.

Reeves, Randall, and Edward Mitchell. 1986. "The Long Island, New York, Right Whale Fishery: 1650–1924." In *Right Whales: Past and Present Status,* edited by Robert I. Brownell, Peter B. Best, and John H. Prescott, 201–20. Cambridge, MA: International Whaling Commision.

Richmond, Trudi Lamb. 1994. "A Native Perspective of History: The Schaghticoke Nation, Resistance and Survival." In *Enduring Traditions: The Native Peoples of New England,* edited by Laurie Weinstein, 103–12. Westport, CT: Greenwood Press, Bergin and Garvey.

Ritchie, Robert C. 1977. *The Duke's Province: A Study of New York Politics and Society, 1664–1691.* Chapel Hill: University of North Carolina Press.

Ritchie, William A.. 1955. "Recent Discoveries Suggesting an Early Woodland Burial Cult in the Northeast." New York State Museum and Science Service, *Circular* no. 40.

———. 1965. *The Stony Brook Site and its Relation to Archaic and Transitional Cultures on Long Island,* 1959. New York State Museum Science Service, Bulletin 367.

———. 1969. *The Archaeology of New York State,* 1959. Reprint, Garden City, NY: Natural History Press.

———. 1969a. *The Archaeology of Martha's Vineyard.* Garden City, NY: Natural History Press.

Ritchie, William and Robert Funk. 1973. "Aboriginal Settlement Patterns in the Northeast." New York State Museum Science Service, *Memoir* 20.

Robbins, Maurice. 1956. "Some Evidence of the Use of Red Ochre into Historic Times." *Bulletin of the Massachusetts Archaeological Society* 17 (2): 18–22.

___. 1959. *Wapanucket #6: An Archaic Village in Middleboro, Massachusetts.* Attleboro: Massachusetts Archaeological Society.

___. 1963. "Secondary Cremation Burial Number 2, The Hawes Site." *Bulletin of the Massachusetts Archaeological Society* 24 (2): 30–33.

Roessel, Faith. 1989. "Federal Recognition: A Historical Twist of Fate." *Native American Rights Fund Legal Review* 14: 3–5.

Rorabaugh, W. J. 1979. *The Alcoholic Republic: An American Tradition.* New York: Oxford University Press.

Rosier, James. 1907. "Report on Weymouth's Voyage to New England, 1605." In *Early English and French Voyages,* edited by Harry Burrage, 355–94. New York: Scribner.

Ross, Peter. 1902. *A History of Long Island.* Vol. 1. New York: The Lewis Publishing Company. Note: vol. 2 was written by William S. Pelletreau and is listed under his name.

Rostlund, Erhard. 1957. "The Evidence for the use of Fish as Fertilizer in Aboriginal North America." *The Journal of Geography* 56: 222–28.

Rountree, Helen. 1989. *The Powhatan Indians of Virginia: Their Traditional Culture.* Norman, OK: Oklahoma University Press.

___. 1990. *Pocahantas's People: The Powhatan Indians of Virginia Through Four Centuries.* Norman: University of Oklahoma Press.

___. 1993. *Powhatan Foreign Relations: 1500–1722.* Charlottesville: University Press of Virginia.

RPCC. 1928. *Records of the Particular Court of Connecticut, 1639–1663.* Connecticut Historical Society Collection, vol. 22.

RTBH, Book II. 1924. *Records of The Town of Brookhaven, Book II: 1662–1679,* edited by Archibald Weeks. New York: Tobias Wright.

RTBH, Book A. 1930. *Records of the Town of Brookhaven Book A,* edited by Osborn Shaw. New York: Derrydale Press.

RTBH, Book B. 1932. *Records of the Town of Brookhaven, Book B: 1679–1756,* edited by Osborne Shaw. New York: Derrydale Press.

RTBH, Hutchinson. 1888. *Records of the Town of Brookhaven, up to 1800,* edited by Henry P. Hutchinson. Patchogue, NY: Advance.

RTEH. 1887. *Records of the Town of East Hampton,* edited by Joseph Osborne. 5 vols. Sag Harbor, NY: Hunt.

RTG. Records of the Town of Gravesend. Municipal Archives of the City of New York, 31 Chambers Street.

RTH. 1887–1889. *Huntington Town Records,* edited by Charles R. Street. 3 vols. Huntington, NY: Town of Huntington.

RTJ. 1914. *Records of the Town of Jamaica, Long Island, New York 1656–1751,* edited by Josephine Smith. 3 vols. New York: Long Island Historical Society.

RTNSH. 1896–1904. *Records of the Towns of North and South Hempstead,* edited by Benjamin Hicks. 8 vols. Jamaica NY: Long Island Farmer Print.

RTOB. 1916–1931. *Oyster Bay Town Records,* edited by John Cox. 8 vols. New York: Tobias Wright.

RTS. 1882. *Southold Town Records,* edited by J. Wickham Case. 3 vols. Southold: S. W. Green.

RTSH. 1874–1877 *Records of the Town of Southampton,* edited by William Pelletreau. 8 vols. Sag Harbor: Hunt.

RTSM. 1898–1931. *Town Records of Smithtown,* edited by William Pelletreau. 3 vols. Huntington: Long Islander Print.

Russell, Howard. 1980. *Indian New England Before the Mayflower.* Hanover, NH: University Press of New England.

Rutsch, Edward S. 1978. "An Analysis of the Lithic Materials Used in the Manufacture of Projectile Points in Coastal New York," 1970. In *The Coastal Archaeology Reader,* edited by Gaynell S. Levine, 182–93, Stony Brook: SCAA.

Ruttenber, Edward Manning. 1906. "Indian Geographical Names of the Valley of the Hudson's River." *New York State Historical Association,* 6.

———. 1971. *History of the Indian Tribes of the Hudson's River,* 1872. Reprint, Port Washington, NY: Kennikat Press.

Sainsbury, John. 1971. "Miantonomo's Death and New England Politics 1630-1645." *Rhode Island History* 30 (4): 111–23.

Salisbury, Neal. 1984. *Manitou and Providence, Indians, Europeans, and the Making of New England, 1500–1643.* New York: Oxford University Press.

Salwen, Bert. 1978. "Indians of Southern New England and Long Island." In *Handbook of the North American Indians,* vol. 15, *The Northeast,* edited by Bruce Trigger, 160–89. Washington DC: Smithsonian Institution Press.

———. 1982. "Sea Levels and Archaeology in the Long Island Sound Area," 1962. In *The Second Coastal Archaeology Reader: 1900 to the Present,* edited by James E. Truex, 35–43. Stony Brook: SCAA.

Sautter, Richard. 1966. "Cremation Cult of the Dead at Swan Hold." *Bulletin of the Massachusetts Archaeological Society* 28 (2): 17–24.

Saville, Foster. 1977. "A Montauk Cemetery at East Hampton, Long Island," 1920. In *Early Papers on Long Island Archaeology,* edited by Gaynell S. Levine, 16–29. Stony Brook: SCAA.

Saxon, Walter. 1978. "The Paleo-Indian on Long Island," 1973. In *The Coastal Archaeology Reader,* edited by Gaynell S. Levine, 251–61. Stony Brook: SCAA.

SCAA. Suffolk County Archaeological Association. *Readings in Long Island Archaeology and Ethnohistory* series, 1977-. Articles cited are listed under author.

Schmidt, Frederick P. 1972. "Controversy at Cantiague Woods." *Long Island Forum* 35: 124–27.

Schultes, Richard. 1976. *Hallucinogenic Plants.* New York: The Gold Press.

Schur, Robert. 1942. "The Long Island Indians." *Long Island Forum* 5: 105–8.

Scott, Kenneth. 1961. "The New York Slave Insurrection of 1712." In *New-York Historical Society Quarterly* 54: 43–74.

Sears, William, H. 1956. "Settlement Patterns in Eastern United States." In *Prehistoric Settlement Patterns in the New World,* edited by Gordon Wiley, 45–51. New York: Wenner-Gren Foundation, Viking Fund Publication in Anthropology, 23.

Seeman, Mark. 1979. "Hopewell Interaction Sphere: The Evidence for Interregional Trade and Structural Complexity." *Prehistory Research Series* 5: 237–438. Indianapolis: Indiana Historical Society.

Sehr, Timothy J. 1977. "Ninigret's Tactics of Accommodation: Indian Diplomacy in New England 1737–1675." *Rhode Island History* 36 (2): 42–53.

Sesso, Gloria, and Regina White. 1990. *The Long Island Story.* Austin, TX: Steck-Vaughn.

Seybolt, Robert Francis. 1917. *Apprenticeship Education in Colonial New England and New York.* New York: Columbia University Press.

Shattuck, Martha Dickinson. 1994. "*Heemstede:* An English Town Under Dutch Rule." In *The Roots and Heritage of Hempstead Town,* edited by Natalie A. Naylor, 47–78. Interlaken, NY: Heart of the Lakes Publishing.

Shepard, Anna, O. 1968. *Ceramics for the Archaeologist.* Washington, DC: Carnegie Institution of Washington, no. 609.

Shinnecock Trustees. 1983. "The Shinnecock Tribal Oyster Project." In *The Shinnecock Indians: A Culture History,* edited by Gaynell Stone, 400–44. Stony Brook: SCAA.

SHTA. Southampton Town Archives, Town Hall, Southampton, NY.

Shurkin, Joel. 1979. *The Invisible Fire: The Story of Mankind's Victory Over the Ancient Scourge of Smallpox.* New York: G. P. Putnam.

Silver, Annette. 1979. "A Critique of 'The Effect of European Contact and Trade on The Settlement Patterns of Indians in Coastal New York, 1524–1665: The Archaeological and Documentary Evidence' by Lynn Ceci." M.A. thesis, New York University.

———. 1980. "Comment on Maize Cultivation in Coastal New York." *North American Archaeologist* 2 (2): 117–30.

———. 1991. "The Abbott Interaction Sphere: A Consideration of the Middle Woodland Period in Coastal New York and A Proposal For a Middle Woodland Exchange." Ph.D. diss., New York University.

Simmons, William. 1975. "Southern New England Shamanism: An Ethnographic Reconstruction." *Papers of the Seventh Algonquian Conference,* edited by William Cowan, 218–56. Ottawa: Carleton University.

———. 1986. *Spirit of the New England Tribes: Indian History and Folklore: 1620–1984.* Hanover, NH: University Press of New England.

Skinner, Alanson. 1909. *Archaeology of the New York Coastal Algonquian.* New York: American Museum of Natural History, Anthropological Papers, 3: 213–35.

———. 1914. "The Algonkin and the Thunderbird." *The American Museum* [of Natural History] *Journal* 14: 71–72.

———. 1919. Exploration of Aboriginal Sites at Throgs Neck and Clasons Point, New York City." *Contributions,* Museum of the American Indian, Heye Foundation, 5 (4): 49–126.

Sleight, Harry D., "Historical Long Island, June 6 Meeting," *Long Island Railroad Information Bulletin.* In clipping file "Indians, Shinnecock," Queens Public Library, Jamaica, NY.

Smith, Bruce D. 1985. "The Role of Chenopodium as a Domesticate in Pre-Maize Garden Systems of the Eastern United States." *Southeastern Archaeology* 4 (1): 51–72.

———. 1987. "The Independent Domestication of Indigenous Seed-Bearing Plants in Eastern North America." In *Emergent Horticultural Economies of the Eastern Woodlands,* edited by William F. Keegan, 3–47. Carbondale: Southern Illinois University Center for Archaeological Investigations, Occasional Paper no. 7.

———. 1994/95. "Origins of Agriculture in the Americas." *Evolutionary Anthropology* 3 (5): 174–84.

———. 1995. *The Emergence of Agriculture.* New York: Scientific American Library.

Smith, Carlyle. 1950. "The Archaeology of Coastal New York." *Anthropological Papers of the American Museum of Natural History* 43, part 2.

___. 1954. "A Note on Fort Massapeag." *American Antiquity* 1: 67-68.

___. 1980. "A Stone Effigy From Long Island," 1946. In *Languages and Lore of the Long Island Indians,* edited by Gaynell Stone Levine and Nancy Bonvillain, 311. Stony Brook: SCAA.

___. 1982. "Clues to the Chronology of Coastal New York," 1944. In *The Second Coastal Archaeology Reader: 1900 to the Present,* edited by James E. Truex, 227-37. Stony Brook: SCAA.

___. 1982a. "Revised Chronology for Coastal New York," 1955. In *The Second Coastal Archaeology Reader: 1900 to the Present,* edited by James E. Truex, 238-39. Stony Brook: SCAA.

Smith, John Lawrence. 1882. "The Town of Smithtown." In *The History of Suffolk County,* edited by W. W. Munsell, 1–42. (The book is not paginated sequentially; each town history is paginated independently.) New York: W. W. Munsell.

Smith, Raymond, ed. 1926. *In Re Montauk.* East Hampton, NY: East Hampton Town Trustees.

Smits, Edward J. 1994. "News from *Lange Eylandt:* The 1640s and 1650s." In *The Roots and Heritage of Hempstead Town,* edited by Natalie A. Naylor, 15–26. Interlaken, NY: Heart of the Lakes Publishing.

Snipp, C. Matthew. 1991. *American Indians: The First of This Land.* New York: Russell Sage Foundation.

Snow, Dean. 1980. *The Archaeology of New England.* New York: Academic Press.

Snyderman, George S. 1951. "Concepts of Land Ownership Among the Iroquois and Their Neighbors." *Bulletin of the Bureau of American Ethnology* 149 (2): 15–38.

Solecki, Ralph. 1950. "The Archaeological Position of Historic Fort Corchaug, L. I., and its Relation to Contemporary Forts." *Bulletin of the Archaeological Society of Connecticut,* no. 24: 3–40.

___. 1982. "An Indian Burial at Acqueduct, Long Island." In *The Second Coastal Archaeology Reader,* edited by James E. Truex, 91–95. Stony Brook: SCAA.

Solecki, Ralph S. and Robert Steven Grumet. 1994. "The Fort Massapeag Archaeological Site National Historic Landmark." *The Bulletin,* Journal of the New York State Archaeological Association 108: 18–28.

Speck, Frank. 1919. "The Functions of Wampum Among the Eastern Algonkian." *Memoirs of the American Anthropological Association,* no. 6.

___. 1931. *A Study of the Delaware Indian Big House Ceremony.* Harrisburg, PA: Pennsylvania Historical Commission.

Spiess, Arthur and Bruce Spiess. 1987. "New England Pandemic of 1612–1622: Cause and Archaeological Implication." *Man in the Northeast* 34: 71–83.

Stearn, Wagner E. and Allen E. Stearn. 1945. *The Effect of Smallpox on the Destiny of the Amerindian.* Boston: Bruce Humphries.

Stewart, R. Michael. 1994. "Late Archaic Through Late Woodland Exchange in the Middle Atlantic Region." In *Prehistoric Exchange Systems in North America,* edited by Timothy Baugh and Jonathan Ericson, 73–98. New York: Plenum Press.

Stiles, Ezra. 1916. *Extracts From the Itineraries and Other Miscellanies of Ezra Stiles, D.D., LL.D 1755–1794,* edited by F. B. Dexter. New Haven, CT: Yale University Press.

Stiles, Henry Reed. 1867. *A History of the City of Brooklyn.* 3 vols. Brooklyn, NY: Published by Subscription.

Stokes, Isaac Newton Phelps. 1967. *The Iconography of Manhattan Island*, 1895–1928. 6 vols. Reprint, New York: Arno.

Stone, Gaynell. 1983. "Shinnecock Demography." In *The Shinnecock Indians: A Culture History*, edited by Gaynell Stone, 308-310. Stony Brook: SCAA.

___, ed. 1983a. *The Shinnecock Indians: A Culture History*. Stony Brook: SCAA.

___ 1989. "Long Island as America: A New Look at the First Inhabitants." *Long Island Historical Journal* 1 (1): 159–69.

___. 1991. *The Montauk: Native Americans of Eastern Long Island*. Exhibit leaflet, 8 pp.

___, ed. 1993. *The History and Archaeology of the Montauk*. 2d ed. Stony Brook: SCAA.

Stone, Gaynell and Eugene Cuffee. 1983. "Economic Activities." In *The Shinnecock Indians: A Culture History*, edited by Gaynell Stone, 303-7, Stony Brook, NY: SCAA.

Stone, Gaynell and Josephine Smith, with Alice Martinez, Harriett Gumbs, and Alice Phillips. 1983. "Material Culture," 291–95. In *The Shinnecock Indians: A Culture History*, edited by Gaynell Stone, 291-96. Stony Brook: SCAA.

Street, Charles R. 1882. "The Town of Huntington." In *The History of Suffolk County*, edited by W. W. Munsell, 1–90. (The book is not paginated sequentially; each town history is paginated independently.) New York: W. W. Munsell.

Strong, John A. 1983. "The Evolution of Shinnecock Culture." In *The Shinnecock Indians: A Culture History*, edited by Gaynell Stone, 7–51. Stony Brook: SCAA.

___. 1983a. "A Documentary History of the Shinnecock Peoples: How the Land was Lost." In *The Shinnecock Indians: A Culture History*, edited by Gaynell Stone, 53–117. Stony Brook, NY: SCAA.

___. 1985. "Late Woodland Dog Ceremonialism on Long Island in Comparative and Temporal Perspective." *The Bulletin*, Journal of the New York State Archaeological Association, no. 91: 32–38.

___. 1987. "The Shinnecock People: An Introduction." In *A Shinnecock Portrait*, by Toba Tucker. East Hampton, NY: Guild Hall.

___. 1989. "The Mississippian Bird-Man Theme in Cross Cultural Perspective." In *The Southeastern Ceremonial Complex: Artifacts and Analysis*, edited by Patricia Galloway, 211–37. Lincoln: University of Nebraska Press.

___. 1989a. "Shinnecock and Montauk Whalemen." *The Long Island Historical Journal* 2 (1): 29–40.

___. 1990. "The Pigskin Book: Records of Native American Whalemen." *The Long Island Historical Journal* 3 (1): 17–29.

___. 1991. "The Long Island Frontier." *The Long Island Historical Journal* 3 (2): 253–59.

___. 1992. "Who Says the Montauk Tribe is Extinct? Judge Abel Blackmar's Decision in the Case of Wyandank Pharaoh v. Benson." *American Indian Culture and Research Journal* 16 (1): 1–22.

___. 1992a. "The Thirteen Tribes of Long Island: The History of a Myth." *Hudson Valley Regional Review* 9 (2): 39–73.

___. 1993. "How the Montauk Lost Their Land." In *The History and Archaeology of the Montauk*, edited by Gaynell Stone, 77–146. 2d ed. Stony Brook, NY: SCAA.

___. 1993a. "The Ancestors: Montauk Prehistory." In *The History and Archaeology of the Montauk*, edited by Gaynell Stone, 601–11. Stony Brook, NY: SCAA.

___. 1994. "The Reaffirmation of Tradition Among the Native Americans of Eastern Long Island." *The Long Island Historical Journal* 7 (1): 42–67.

___. 1994a. "The Imposition of Colonial Jurisdiction Over the Montauk Indians of Long Island." *Ethnohistory* 41(4): 561–90.

___. 1995. "Algonquian Women as Sunksquaws and Caretakers of the Soil: The Documentary Evidence in the Seventeenth Century Records." Paper presented to the American Indian Workshop, Fernando Pessoa University, Oporto, Portugal, April 1995.

___. 1995a. "Indian Labor During the Post-Contact Period on Long Island." In *To Know the Place,* edited by Joann P. Krieg and Natalie A. Naylor, 13–39. 2d. ed. Interlaken, NY: Heart of the Lakes Publishing under the auspices of Hofstra University.

___. 1995b. "Native American Whalers: The New Elites in Seventeenth Century Algonquian Society on Long Island." Paper presented at the Mystic Seaport Conference on Race, Ethnicity, and Power in Maritime America, September 14.

___. 1996. "Wyandanch, Sachem of the Montaukett." In *Northeastern Indian Lives,* edited by Robert Grumet, 48–73. Amherst, MA: University of Massachusetts Press.

___. 1996a. *"We Are Still Here!" The Algonquian Peoples of Long Island Today.* Interlaken, NY: Heart of the Lakes Publishing.

___. 1996b. "The Role of Algonquian Women in Land Transactions on Long Island." Paper presented at Conference on Long Island Women, Hofstra University, March 23.

Strong, Lara M. and Selcuk Karabag. 1991. "Quashawam: Sunksquaw of the Montauk." *Long Island Historical Journal* 3 (2): 189-204.

Strong, Lisa M. and Frank F. Holmberg II. 1983. "The Shinnecock Trustee System, 1792–1983." In *The Shinnecock Indians: A Culture History,* edited by Gaynell Stone, 226–30. Stony Brook: SCAA.

Struever, Stuart and Gail L. Houart. 1972. "An Analysis of the Hopewell Interaction Sphere." In *Social Exchange and Interaction,* edited by Edwin Wilmsen, 47–77. *Anthropological Papers*, no. 46. Ann Arbor: University of Michigan, Museum of Anthropology.

Sturtevant, William. 1975. "Two Wigwams at Niantic, Connecticut." *American Antiquity* 40 (4): 437–44.

___. 1983. "Tribe and State in the Sixteenth and Twentieth Centuries." In *The Development of Political Organization in Native North America,* edited by Elisabeth Tooker, 3–16. Washington DC: The American Ethnological Society.

Sturtevant, William, and Samuel Stanley. 1968. "Indian Communities in the Eastern United States." *The Indian Historian* 1: 15–19.

Tantaquidgeon, Gladys. 1977. *Folk Medicine of the Delaware and Related Algonkian Indians.* Harrisburg, PA: Pennsylvania Historical and Museum Commission, Anthropological Series no. 3.

Thomas, Peter. 1976. "Contrastive Subsistence Strategies and Land Use as a Factors for Understanding Indian-White Relations in New England." *Ethnohistory* 26 (1): 1–18.

___. 1979. "In the Maelstrom of Change: The Indian Trade and Cultural Process in the Middle Connecticut River Valleys, 1638–1665." Ph.D. diss., Department of Anthropology, University of Massachusetts.

Thompson, Benjamin. 1918. *History of Long Island from its Discovery and Settlement to the Present Time.* 3rd ed., rev. and enl. by Charles Warner. New York: Robert H. Dodd. Reprint, Port Washington, NY: I. J. Friedman, 1962.

Thulman, Melburn. 1978. "The 'Hopewell' Influence at Abbott Farm: A Demurrer." *Archaeology of Eastern North America* 6: 72–78.

Tooker, Elisabeth, ed. 1979. *Native North American Spirtuality of the Eastern Woodlands.* Mawah, NJ: Paulist Press.

Tooker, William Wallace. 1962. *Indian Place Names on Long Island,* 1911. Reprint, Port Washington, NY: Ira J. Friedman.

___. 1980 "Cockenoe-De-Long Island," 1896. In *Languages and Lore of the Long Island Indians,* edited by Gaynell Stone Levine and Nancy Bonvillain, 176-89. Stony Brook: SCAA.

Trelease, Allen W. 1971. *Indian Affairs in Colonial New York: The Seventeenth Century,* 1960. Reprint, Kennikat Press.

Trigger, Bruce. 1991. "Early Native North American Responses to European Contact: Romantic versus Rationalistic Interpretations." *Journal of American History* 77 (4):1195–1215.

Tuck, James. n.d. [1975]. "Archaic Burial Ceremonialism in the Far Northeast." In *Essays in Northeastern Anthropology in Memory of Marian E. White,* edited by William E. Engelbright and Donald Grayson, 67–77. Occasional Publications in Northeastern Anthropology Number 5.

Tuck, James and Robert Grenier. 1981. "16th Century Basque Whaling Stations on Labrador." *Scientific American,* November, 180–90.

Tupahache, Asiba. 1991. "June Meeting." *The Spirit of January* 13: 1.

___. 1994. "The Holy One." *The Spirit of January* 26: 1, 12.

Turano, Frank and Randolph Donahue. 1988. An Archaeological Evaluation of the Prehistoric Cultural Resources at the Bridgewater Estate Townhouse at Riverhead, N.Y. Unpublished report on file at the Institute for Long Island Archaeology, State University of New York at Stony Brook, NY.

Underhill, John. 1638. "News From America, 1638." In *A History of the Pequot War,* 1897, edited by Charles Orr, 47–92. Reprint, New York: AMS Press.

Underhill, Ruth. 1965. *Red Man's Religion.* Chicago: University of Chicago Press.

van der Donck, Adriaen. 1968. *Description of The New Netherlands,* 1655, edited by Thomas F. O'Donnell. Syracuse, NY: Syracuse University Press.

van Gastel, Ada. 1990. "Van der Donck's Description of the Indians: Additions and Corrections." *William and Mary Quarterly* 47 (3): 411–21.

van Lear, A. J. F. 1924. *Documents Relating to New Netherland, 1624–1626.* San Marino, CA: The Henry E. Huntington Library.

van Wassenaer, Nicolaes. 1909. "Historical Account, 1624–30." In *Narratives of New Netherland,* edited by J. Franklin Jameson, 61–96. New York: Charles Scribner.

van Wyck, Frederick. 1924. *Keskachauge or the First White Settlement on Long Island.* New York: G. Putnam's Sons.

Vaughan, Alden. T. 1965. *New England Frontier: Puritans and Indians, 1620–1675.* Boston: Little and Company.

Venuto, P. B. 1982. "The Oakland Lake Site, Bayside, N.Y. I. Site Description," 1967. In *The Second Coastal Archaeology Reader: 1900 to the Present,* edited by James E. Truex, 126–33. Stony Brook: SCAA.

___. 1982a. "The Oakland Lake Site, Bayside, N.Y. II Physiochemical Analysis and Possible Source of Argillite Artifacts." In *The Second Coastal Archaeology Reader: 1900 to the Present,* edited by James E. Truex, 134–142. Stony Brook: SCAA.

Vickers, Daniel. 1983. "The First Whalemen of Nantucket." *William and Mary Quarterly* 40: 560–83.

Vogel, Virgil. 1973. *American Indian Medicine,* 1970. Reprint, New York: Ballantine Books.

von Gernet, Alexander D. 1992. "Hallucinogens and the Origins of the Iroquoian Pipe/Tobacco/Smoking Complex." In *Proceedings of the 1989 Smoking Pipe Conference,* edited by Charles F. Hayes III, 171–85. Rochester, NY: Rochester Museum and Science Center.

Wallace, Anthony. 1966. *Religion: An Anthropological View.* New York: Random House.

___. 1972. *The Death and Rebirth of the Seneca.* New York: Vintage Books.

Ward, Harry. 1961. *The United Colonies of New England 1643–1690.* New York: Vantage Press.

Weatherhead, L. R. 1980. "What is an Indian Tribe? The Question of Tribal Existence." *American Indian Law Review* 8: 1–47.

Weeks, George. 1965. *Isle of Shells.* Islip, NY: Buys Brothers.

Werner, Ben, Jr. 1982. "The Strong's Neck Site," c.1968. In *The Second Coastal Archaeology Reader: 1900 to the Present,* edited by James E. Truex, 202–13. Stony Brook: SCAA.

Weslager, C.A. 1973. *Magic Medicines of the Indians.* Somerset NJ: Middle Atlantic Press.

Whitaker, Thomas and Hugh Cutler. 1965. "Curcurbits and Cultures in the Americas." *Economic Botany* 19: 344–49.

White, Richard. 1991. *The Middle Ground: Indians, Empires, and Republics in the Great Lakes Region, 1650–1815.* New York: Cambridge University Press.

Wiegand, Ernest A. 1995. "The Indian Field Site, Greenwich, Connecticut." Paper presented to the Eastern States Archaeological Federation Annual Meeting, Wilmington, DE, October 26–29.

Wilbur, C. Keith. 1978. *The New England Indians.* Chester, CT: Globe Pequot Press.

___. 1990. *Indian Handcrafts.* Chester, CT: Globe Pequot Press.

Wilcox, U. Vincent. 1982. "The Manufacture and Use of Wampum in the Northeast," 1976. In *The Second Coastal Archaeology Reader 1900 to the Present*, edited by James Truex, 295–305, Stony Brook: SCAA.

Williams, James Homer. 1995. "Great Doggs and Mischievous Cattle: Domesticated Animals and Indian-European Relations in New Netherland and New York." *New York State History* 76 (3):245–64.

Williams, Lorraine. 1972. "Fort Shantok and Fort Corchaug: A Comparative Study of the Seventeenth Century Culture Contact in the Long Island Sound Area." Ph.D. diss., New York University.

Williams, Roger. 1973. *A Key into the Language of America,* 1643, with notes by John J. Teunissen and Evelyn J. Hinz. Detroit: Wayne State University Press.

Willoughby, Charles. 1906. "Houses and Gardens of the New England Indians." *American Anthropologist*, New Series, 8: 115–25.

Wilson, Gilbert. 1979. *Agriculture of the Hidatsa Indians: An Indian Interpretation,* 1917. Reprint, New York: AMS Press.

Winslow, Edward. 1841. "Of the Manners, Customs, Religious Opinions, and Ceremonies of the Indians," 1623. In *Chronicles of the Pilgrim Fathers,* edited by Alexander Young, 354–59. Boston: Charles C. Little and James Brown.

Winthrop, John, Jr. 1937. "The Culture and Use of Maize," 1678, edited by Fuller Mood. *New England Quarterly* 10: 121–33.

Wolley (Wooley), Charles. 1968. "A Two Years Journal in New York," 1678–80. In *Historic Chronicles of New Amsterdam, Colonial New York and Early Long Island,* edited by Cornell Jaray, 1–97. Port Washington: Ira J. Friedman.

Wood, Silas. 1826. *A Sketch of the First Settlement of the Several Towns on Long Island,* 1824. Rev. ed. Brooklyn: Alden Spooner.

Wood, William. 1968. *New England's Prospect,* 1634. New York: De Capo Press.

Wooley, Charles, 1968. See Charles Wolley.

WP. 1865. *Winthrop Papers.* Collections of the Massachusetts Historical Society, vol. 7, 4th series.

Wyatt, Ronald. 1982. "The Archaic on Long Island," 1977. In *The Second Coastal Archaeology Reader: 1900 to the Present,* edited by James E. Truex, 70–78. Stony Brook: SCAA.

Wunderlich, Roger. 1989. "An Island of Mine Own: The Life and Times of Lion Gardiner, 1599–1663." *Long Island Historical Journal* 2 (1): 3–14.

Yarnell, Richard. 1964. *Aboriginal Relationships Between Culture and Plant Life in the Upper Great Lakes Region.* Ann Arbor: University of Michigan, Museum of Anthropology, Anthropological Paper 23.

Young, Alexander. 1841. *Chronicles of the Pilgrim Fathers.* Boston: Charles Little and James Brown.

## Identification of Individuals Cited in Text as Sources of Information

Anderson, Lisa. Curator, New York State Museum, Albany.

Barber, Linda. Department of Anthropology, Suffolk Community College.

Barcel, Ellen. Curator, Southold Indian Museum.

Bernstein, David. Director of Long Island Regional Archaeological Research Center, State University of New York at Stony Brook.

Blakey-Smith, Sherry. Director of Title V Education Program at Shinnecock; Cree-Ojibway.

Chee Chee (Elizabeth Haile). Tribal storyteller, Shinnecock Tribal Council, Museum Board; Shinnecock.

Christoph, Peter. Editor, *New York Historical Manuscripts.*

Collins, Donna. Thunderbird Coffee Shop; Shinnecock.

Cooke, Lanette. Shinnecock tutoring program; Shinnecock.

Cooper, Robert. Police Department East Hampton (retired); member of East Hampton Town Board, 1991–1995; Montaukett.

Folts, James. Archivist, New York State Archives, Albany.

Franklin, Sherry. Secretary, Southampton College of Long Island University; Shinnecock.

Goree, Lisa. Community health worker; Shinnecock.

Grumet, Robert. National Park Service, Philadelphia, PA.

Gumbs, Harriett Crippen. Shinnecock elder, historian, founder of Shinnecock Outpost; Shinnecock.

Haile, Elizabeth. See Chee Chee.

Johanneman, Edward. Archaeologist (retired); former president of the Suffolk County Archaeological Association.
Johnson, Michelle. Director of Shinnecock Senior Citizens' Nutrition Program; Shinnecock.
Kraft, Herbert. Anthropology Department, Seton Hall University; author of *The Lenape* (1986).
Krause, Maureen. Department of Marine Biology, Southampton College of Long Island University.
Mades, Kenneth. Bayman, Hampton Bays, NY.
Marshall, June. Secretary, Southampton College of Long Island University; Shinnecock.
McBride, Kevin. Anthropology Department, University of Connecticut.
Miller, Robert. Archaeologist, Northport, NY.
Pharaoh, Robert. Chief of the Montaukett, Sag Harbor, NY.
Randall-Williams, Lauryn. Shinnecock.
Rountree, Helen. Department of Anthropology, Old Dominion University, Norfolk, VA.
Shumway, Sandra. Department of Marine Biology, Southampton College of Long Island University.
Smith, Gerrod. Director, Shinnecock Nation Museum and Learning Center Project; Shinnecock.
Smith, Jonathan. Manager, Shinnecock Smoke Shop; Shinnecock.
Smith, Josephine. Native American food specialist; Shinnecock.
Smith, Lamont. Native American crop specialist; Shinnecock.
Smith, Maguerite. Lawyer; Shinnecock.
Thunder Bird, Margo. Director, Native American Culture and Language Workshop, Poospatuck Reservation; daughter of Henry Bess, former ceremonial chief, Shinnecock Reservation.
Townsend, Osceola. Chief of Matinecock tribe; Kew Gardens, Queens.
Treadwell, Donald (Lone Otter), deceased. Herbalist, healer, former Poospatuck tribal historian, author, *My People, The Unkechaug: The Story of a Long Island Indian Tribe* (The Netherlands: De Kiva Publishers, 1992).
Wati Wampatoques (James Waters). Computer consultant; Matinecock-Shinnecock-Montaukett.

# Index

References to illustrations and maps are printed in **boldface** type; to documents and tables, in *italics*.

## A

Abbott Farm site, 71-76
Abbott interaction sphere, 58, 73, 76
Abbott-style zoned pottery, **58**, 71, 73-74, 76
Adam, 191-92, 205-6, 216-17
Adena, 59
African American, 17-18, 31, 282, 292
  mixed races, 19, 29, 33, 235, 257, 269
  servitude, 219-20, 276, 281-82, 287
agriculture, 42, 59, 237, 267, 286, 308n.13. *See also* horticulture
Akomias, 250
alcohol, 146, 261-62
  impact of, 143, 147, 161, 176, 262
  manipulation with, 150, 214, 261-263, 265, 272
  trade in, 213, 270, 275
  usage of, 214, 270
Alexander, William. *See* Stirling, Earl of
Algonquian language, 26-27, 31, 43, 95, 116, 154, 217
  Europeans, fluent in, 172, 192
  Goddard, Ives, 23, 27, 77
  recovery projects, 32, 292
  relationships in, 18, 23, 149
Allard, Carolus, map, **10**
alliance sachems, 213, 218, 221, 223-33, 235-36, 320n.1
American Indian Archaeological Institute, 86
American Museum of Natural History, 56, 88, 133, 318n.8
Amersfoort, New, 217, 241
Amityville, 24, 228
Anderson, Harriet Crippen, 268
Andrews, Samuel, 226-27, 230, 321n.4
Andriaensen, Maryn, 177-79
Andros, Edmund, 25, 251-58, 272, 323n.6
Anne, Queen, 261
Antinome. *See* Tackapousha
Aqueduct site, 124-25, *295*
Archaic Period, 35, 38-53, 95, 109, 132
  baskets, 46-47, 68
  cooking, 40, 47-49, 52
  hunting and fishing, 38-41, 53
  pre-ceramic sites, 38-40, 48-49
  social organization of, 38-53
  steatite bowls, 47-48
  tools, 40, 43-48, **44, 45**, 53
  transition from, 51, 55, 77
Archery Range site, 74, *295*
Argall, Capt. Samuel, 151
argillite
  implements, 59, 76, 113
  projectile points, 58-59
arson, 220, 225, 227, 231, 243
Arumpas, 246, 248-49
Asharoken (Aseton/Raseoken), 217, 222, 226, 254, 322n.3
  land dealings, 191, 195, 204-5, 216-18, 246-49, *299*, 320-21nn.2-3
Athapascan language, 18
atlatl, 43, **45**, 47, 53, 79
Aunt Amy's Creek, 40

## B

Babylon, 217, 222, 230
bands, 21-22, 36, 39-40, 53, 154, 158, 162
Basque fisherman, 145-46, 161
Baxter site, 41, *295*
Bay Ridge, 204
Beaman, Anthony, **54**, 268
Beaman, Eliza Fowler, **54**, 65, 268
Beothunks, 144-45
Berkhofer, Robert F. Jr., 17-18, 29
Big House ceremony, 115, 120-21, 140
Block, Adriaen, 151, 314n.4
Block Island, 174-75, 209-11, 214, 218, 320n.1
Block Island site, 62, 83
bloodroot, 65, 68
bow and arrow, 45, 79, 105, 134, 137-38, 312n.12
Bowmans Brook site, 93, 102, *295*, 306-7n.5
Bownas, Samuel, 110-12
Bradford, William, 97, 192, 234-35
Bradstreet, Simon, 207-8
Brookhaven, 26, 165, 244, 251, 257, 261, 272, 275-76, 280, 284, 286, *299*, 305n.4, 312n.11, 322-24nn.4,5,9

*Index*

Brooklyn, 37, 77, 80, 85, 152, 163-65, 178, 217, 234, **294**
Bunn, Ada, 65
Bunn, Charles Sumner, **268**, 269
Bunn, Daniel, 268
Bunn, Frances, 268
Bunn, Ralph, 24
Bureau of American Ethnography (BAE), 26
Bureau of Indian Affairs, 24
Burial Ridge site, 74-75, *295*
Bushwick, 165

## C

Cabot, John, 144
Cakapeteyno, 163-65, 179, *297*
Caldwell, Joseph, 59, 76
Canarsie, 19, 25-27, 168-69, 179, 184
canoes, 42-43
Carman, John, 182, 222, 225
Carmans River, 165, 244, **294**, **298**
carvings, sacred, 47, **112**, 113, **114**, 120, 132-39
Castuteeuw, 164, **296**
Catawbas, 57
*Cautantowwit*, 95, 111-12, 117-18, 122-23, 130, 132, 134, 283, 310n.2
*Cauwonnuntoh*, 95
Cawbutt, 251
Ceci, Lynn, 22, 39, 93, 97-98, 306-8nn.5,10,12,15
celt (axe), 48
ceremonies, **16**, 23, 31-33, 38, 42, 47, 59, 76, 79, 99, 107, 109, 139
Champlain, Samuel de, 81-83, **82**, 146
Charles I, 163, 182
Charles II, 315n.4
charter, 152, 163, 188
chenopodium. *See* lambs quarters
Cherokees, 52
chert, 37, 45, 105
Chice, Sachem, 23, 263, 275
chiefdom, 21-22
Chippy (Cheppie), Will, 255, 323-24nn.5,7
Chopeyconnaws, 230, 237, 240, 254, *299*, 322-24nn.5-7
circles, sacred, 49-52, 73, 75, 109, 125
clan, 24-25, 42, 146-47, 173, 197
 affiliation, 21-22, 25, 32
 exogamy, 42, 121
Clasons Point site, 73, *295*
Clearview site, 58, 73, *295*
Clinton, De Witt, 280, 282, 317n.3
Clovis, 36, **37**. *See also* projectile points

Cockenoe, 211, 227, 229, 238
 Hempstead-Indian settlement 1657, 222-25
 United Colonies representative 1652, 202-3
 Wyandanch, advisor to, 193-94, 199
Cold Spring Harbor, 204
College Point, 38, 55
Columbus, Christopher, 17
Comanches, 72
*Conconchus*, 91, 95, 111
Connetquot River, 251, **294**, **298**
Cooke, Lanette, 311n.9
cooking, 40, 47-49, 52, 56-57, 61, 64, 88, 100-107, 228, 310n.23
Cooper, Robert, 24
Corchaugs, 19, 26-27, 154, 184, 187, 192, 229-30, 233, 244-45
Corlaer's Hook, 176-80, **296**
corn, 69, 81, **82,** 91-99, **91, 92, 96**, 107, 166, 249, 268, 283
 commodity, 149, 155, 158, 160, 170, 182, 194, 234, 267, 285-87
 festivals, 118, 120, 140
 food, 102-106
 processing and storage, 88, 100, **101**, 103
 threats to, 99, 105, 171, 178, 202, 213, 219, 240
Cornbury, Lord, 261
Cortiaensen, Hendrik, 151, 153
Court of Assizes, 195, 243, 255, 282, 320n.2
creation story, **34**, 35
Creeks, 72
cremations, 49-51, 71
Cross, Dorothy, 58, 74
Cuffee, Eugene, 268-69
Cuffee, Rev. Paul, 32
Cuffee, Wickham, 30, 32
curing rituals, 72, 125-31, 133, 140, 234

## D

dances (*canticas*), **114**, 115
Danckaerts, Jasper, 35, 80, 86-89, 92, 100
Dean, Nora Thomas, 126
de Champlain, Samuel. *See* Champlain
deer hunting, 39, 60-61, 72, 121
de Laet, Johannes, 314n.4
Denton, Daniel, 29, 60-62, 65, 114-15, 123, 234-36, 311n.5, 313n.3
Denton, Rev. Richard, 182
de Rasieres, Isaack, 97, 103, 123, 152-53

devil. *See* evil spirit force
De Vries, David, 28, 60, 95, 98, 103, 106, 128-29, 172, 177-82, 313n.3
Dincauze, Dena F., 52
dogs, 38, 53, 90, 98, 171, 215, 238-39, 241, 269
Dongan, Thomas, 257-58, *258, 259, 299*
Dosoris tablet, **134**, 135, 138
Downs Creek, 41
duffel cloth, 153, 165, 195
Duke of York, 241, 251
Duke's Laws, 240-43, 250-252, 262
Dutch Treaty 1645, 188-89, 191-92
Dutch West India Company, 151-52, 163-64, 187-88, 233
dyes, 66-69, *68*, 74, 92

## E

Early and Middle Woodland Periods, 55-77
 archaeological sites, 58, 69-71, 73
 ceramic technology, 55, 57
 food, storage of, 55-56
 forest efficiency, 55, 59-69
 mica, 73-75
 plants, 59-68, **59,** *63*
 pottery, 55-59, **58**
 trading networks, 76-77
 tubular pipes, **72**
East Hampton, 24, 26, 63, 102, 135, 170, 194, 196, 201-2, 205, 208-9, 213-14, 221, 228-29, 234, 241-42, 249-52, 257, 260-64, 270, 272-75, 277-79, 283-85, 307n.9, 321n.4, 323n.5, 324n.3
East Hampton area site, 55, 76
East Hampton Library, 135
East River, 58, 73, 152, 165, 178-79
Eaton, Theophilus, 164, 170, 185, 191-96, 204, 210, 218, 229, *299, 301,* 318n.9
Eatons Neck, 191, 193, 195, 204, 218, 320n.2
Eliot, Rev. John, 17, 119, 193-94, 218
Endicott, Governor, 206-8
epidemics, 29, 147, 167, 233-36, 262
Esopus, 238-40, **296**
ethnic group, 19, 31-32, 92, 287
evil spirit force, 72, 111-12, 116-17, 119, 126, 128, 140, 174, 215, 311n.8
exogamous marriages, 38, 42, 154, 181
extinction, myth of, 19, 28-29, 31, 33, 216, 236

## F

Farrett, James, 167-70, 185, 202
federal recognition of tribes, 24, 31, 292
fences
 construction of, 199-200, 283-84, **285**, 286
 contracts for, 286-87
 effects of, 171, 197-200, 213, 238, 243
 rules about, 214, 171, 199, 263, 285-86
 watching of, 283, 285
fines for punishment, 155, 220-21, 231, 243, 249-50
fish
 catching of, 38-43, 53, 62, 80, 84, 103, 131, 143-45, 148, 161, 166, 179-80, 194, 210, 228, 231, 267, 269
 fertilizer, use of, 97-98
 food, use of, 63-64, 91, 100, 103-7, 118
Flushing, 24, 280-81
Flushing Bay, 38, 55
Fordham, Robert, 182, 186, 222, 275
forest efficiency, 55, 59-69
Fort Corchaug, 81, 83-84, *295*
Fort Hill, 83
Fort Massapeag, 81, **83,** *295*
Fort Neck, 80, 183
Fort Saybrook, 155-56, 169, 198
Fort Shantok, 81, 83
Fox Creek site, 58
Fried, Morton, 22
Frobisher, Martin, 144
fur trade, 145, 150-54, 158, 161-63, 192, 228, 237

## G

Gardiner, Lion, 19, 23, 116, 155-56, 160-61, 174-77, 197-98, 205, 208-10, 213, 234, 236, 261, 283, *299*
 Island bought from Yovawam, 166-67, 184
 whaling rights of, 227-33
Gardiners Island, 36-37, 166-67, 229-30, 283, **294**, **300**
genetic classification, 28, 31, 33
Gildersleeve, Richard, 222-23, 225, 253
Glen Cove, 55, 135, 138, 248
Goddard, Ives, 23, 27, 77
Goodyear, Stephen, 185, 194-96, 202
goosefoot. *See* lambs quarters
Governors Island, 164
Grantville site, 38, *295*
Gravesend, 181-82, 191, 201-2, 240-41, 269
Great Neck tablet, **135**
Grumet, Robert, 22, 258

*Index* 359

Guawarowe, 184, 186-87
Gy (Gie), 252-53, 284-87, *299*, 322n.4

# H

Hackingsacks, 176-77, 180, 215, 238
Halsey, Mrs. Thomas, 197, 210, 227, 319n.1
Halsey, Thomas, 231
Hands Creek Site, 55, 76
Harrington, Mark, 56-57, 71, 88-89, 102, 120, 124, 135
Hartford, 154, 184-85, 193, 195, 198, 200-201, 207, 216-19, 221, 318n.10, 319n.1
Hartford Treaty Line, 217, 222, 224, 228, **296**, *297*, **298**
Hashamomuck Pond, 194, **300**
Hawk, William, 23
Hayes, Rose Oldfield, 32
Haynes, John, 174, 207
hearths, 40, 49-50, 57, 87-88, 102-6, 115, 120, 122, 124, 307n.5
Heckewelder, John, 126, 129-31, 142-44, 149-50
hemp, 66, 101, 103
Hempstead, 27, 29, 186, 201, 205, *212*, 216-17, 237-38, 255-57, 280, **294**
  confirmation of purchase 1657, 222-26
  Convention 1664, 241, 243
  Massapequa land, sought by, 192, 252
  Matinecock animal problems with, 239, 241
  Matinecock land disputes, 243-44, 246, **247**, *248*, 249, 251, 255, 265
  Nicolls made Duke's Laws at, 243
  Oyster Bay, 239-40, 248, 265
  purchase of, 1643, 182, *183*, 223, *299*
  Stuyvesant arbitration, 201, 239-40
  Suscaneman, 248-49
  Townsend grant and deed, 253, 258-59
Hempstead Harbor Bay, 165, 239-40, 247, 255, 257, **296**
Hempstead Harbor Beach County Park, 260
Hempstead plains, 23
Henry VII, 144
Henry Lloyd Manor site, 74, 76, *295*
herbs
  medicinal, 65-66, *66*, 72, 92, 125, 131, 140-41
  other uses, 67, 88, 106, 118, 128
herbalists, **54**, 126
Hicks, John, 222, 225, 238-39, 307n.6
Hicksville, 195
*Hobbamock.* *See* evil spirit force

Hopewell culture, Ohio, 59, 74
Hopewell interaction sphere, 73-74, 76
Hopkins, Edward, 170, 185, 193
horticulture, 21, 98, 105, 107-8
  agriculture, contrast to, 59
  planting techniques, 92-93
  sedentism, 22, 84
Howe, Daniel, 167-70, 175-76, 197
Howell, Edward, 167, 170, 197, 219, 277, 319n.1
Howell, Eleanor, 219-20
Hubbard, William, 175-76, 197
Hudson, Henry, 80, 85, 143-44, 148, 161
Hudson River, 62, 80, 143, 154, 176, 180, 206, 215, 238, **294**
Huntington, 191, 204, 218, 222, 225-27, 230, 232, 265, **294**
Huntington Bay, 165, 191, **298**
Huntington site, 85

# I

idols, 132-34
Islip, 187, 217

# J

Jackson, Rev. Sharon, 24
James, Rev. Thomas, 209, 213, 228-29, 277-78, 324n.3
James II, 257-58
Jamesport site, 48-51, *295*, 304n.5
Jericho, 135-38, 195
Jericho glyphs, **136, 137**
Jones, William, 110, 120, 129
Juet, Robert, 148-50
June Meeting, 32, 106, 119, 282, 289

# K

Kaeser, Edward, 58, 71, 73-74, 103
Kavasch, Barrie, 64
Keeossechok, 222-23, 225, *299*
Kehoe, Alice, 119, 303n.1
Kellis, James, **266**, 268
Kellis, Mary Rebecca, 30
Keshaechquereren, 25, 151, 164-65, **296**
*Kickeron*, 35
Kieft, William, 166, 168-69, 184, 192, 203
  inquiry and removal, 186-88
  wars with Indians, 33, 80, 171-74, 176-81
Kievet's Hook, 169
King Philip, 119, 250

King Philip's War, 118, 237, 252-53, 265, 279
kinship systems, 21-23, 31-32, 38, 42, 79, 121, 146, 149, 151, 154, 156, 181, 234, 245, 254, 269. *See also* clan; ethnic group
*Kintecoy. See* powwow
*Kinte Kaeye (kintekayen)*, 186, 310n.4
Kraft, Herbert, 57, 84, 86, 88
Kroeber, Alfred, 22

## L

labor, 237, 263, 267, 269, 276, 282, 287
 indentured, 267, 275-79, *277*, 282, 286-87
 slavery, 267, 274, 278-82, *280*, 287
Lady Moody, 181-82
Lake Montauk, 125
Lake Muskalonge, 51
lambs quarters, 36, 42, *60*, 64-65, 67, 92-93
Lamoka Lake site, 40
LaMontagne, Johannes, 183
land ownership, 169, 196, 223, 240, 244, 246, 281
 Charters and Patents, 163, 169, 188
 conflicting concepts of, 144, 153, 165-68, 194-95, 204, 236
 deeds and disagreements, 223, 229-30, 246
 dispossession of, 237-265
Late Woodland Period, 79-108
 food processing and storage, 100-102
 gardens, 95-100
 hearths, 102-7
 plant domestication, origins of, 91-95
 village settlements, 79-84
Latham, Roy, 48-51, 125, 135, **138**, 304nn.4-5, 319n.2
Leechman, Douglas, 67
Lenapes, 16-17, 64, 68, **115,** 118-32, 148-54, 161
 alcohol, uses of, 105, 143-44
 tribes on Long Island, 23, 77, 111, 124, 129
Levanna point **37**
Little Neck Bay, 58, 65, 71, 73, 166-68
liquor. *See* alcohol
Lloyd Neck, 81, 204, 226-27, 265
Lockermans, Govert, 172, 177, 193, 201-2, 206
longhouses, 24, 33, 40, 77, 78, 80-89, **82, 85**, 103, 107, 113, 116, 118, 120, 140, **256**
Lovelace, Francis, 246-51, 274

Ludlow, Roger, 158-60, 175-77

## M

"Manatus," map, of w. Long Island, **78**
Mandush, 23, 170, 221
Mangwobe, 222
Manhanset, 26, 154, 158, 202
Manhasset, 19, 24, 292
Manhasset Bay, 165, 255
Manhattan, 80-81, 150-51, 153, 161, 176, 188, 199, 216, 223, 280, **294, 296,** 303n.1
*manitos*, 111-17, 121, 126, 130-32, 140, 143
*Manitou*, 110-12, 120-21, 125, 129, 135, 139-40
maps, **10, 78, 247, 256, 294, 296, 298, 300**
Marechkawieck, 152, 163, 177-78, 184, **296**
Marechkawiecks, 25, 27, 164
marriage, 38, 109, 121-23, 154, 158, 181, 196, 235, 269, 324n.7
Marshall, Bernice, 183, 256
Martin Garritsen's Bay, 165-66, **296**
Martine, David Bunn, 11, **12**, 13, 16
Martinez, Alice Osceola Bunn, **268**
Mary, Queen, 233
Mashomuck, 83
Mason, John, 155-56, 158, 160, 207, 219
Maspeth, 25, 80, 183, **296**
Maspeths, 27-28
Massapequa, 80-81, **83**, 165, 183-84, 318n.8
Massapequas, 19, 192, 206, 215-17, 223, 228-31, 237-39, 249, 254-55
Massebackhun, 202, **296**
Massetewse, 244, 252-53, 322n.4
Mastic, 187, 224, 261
Mastic River, 251
Matinecock Point site, 55, 71, 93, *295*
Matinecocks, 18-19, 23-24, 26, **30**, 32-33, 168, 265
 land, 222-26, 237-40, 243-44, 246-49, 251-57, 289-93
 maps, **247, 256**
 reservations, 257-60, *258, 259*
 sachems, 184, 191, 195, 204, 215-18
Matouacks, 10, 314-15n.4
Matsepe, 80, 183
Mayhew, 244, 252-53, 322n.4
McBride, Kevin, 62, 83, 93, 305n.2
Mechowodt, 165-66, 168, **296,** *297,* **298**
Merrick, 25, 217, 222, 252

Merricks, 19, 27-28, 215, 249
*Mesingw,* **112,** 113, **114**, 115, 120-21, 132, 135, 140
Metacomet, 119, 250
Miantonomi, 156-62, 173-76, 202, 208, 213
mica, 57, 73-76
Minuit, Peter, 153, 173
miscegenation, 19, 29, 31, 33
Mohawks, 158, 203, 174-77, 187-88, 215-16
Momoweta, 184, 187, 192-94, 196-97, 227, 229
Montauk, 23, 25, 33, 83, 101, 154-55, 170, 174, 184, 187, 200, 205-8, 228, 234, 241-42, 245, 249-50, 260-64, 275, 284, 285, 320n.1, 321n.4, 322nn.3-4
Montauk Point, 36
Montauk Tablets, **136**
Montauketts, 32-33, **54**, 65, 95-98, 111, 116-17, 122, 132, 156, 303n.2, 303n.3, 304n.4, 305n.7. *See also* fences; labor; whaling
  land, 170, 194-96, 199, 210, 225-29, **226**, 241-49
  neighbor relations, 205, 213-14, 218, 234, 242, 249-50, 263, 283
  reclamation, 18, 23-24, 289-92
  reservation, 260, 263, 265
  sachem, 19, 156, 160-62, 175, 196-201, 208-10, 214, 220, 223, 237, 250-51, 320-21nn.1,4, 322n.5
  tribute, 159-60, 174, 205-10, 249-50
Montauks. *See* Montauketts
Moriches Bay and Inlet, 231-32
Morris Estate Club site, 71, 73, 76, *295*
Moughmaitow. *See* Momoweta
Mount Sinai site, 39-41, 95, 132, 244, *295*
Mousup, 275
Mulford, John, 250-51, *301*
murder, 155, 176, 178-79, 182, 198, 207
  Indian view of, 153, 173, 197
  Halsey murder, 197, 210, 227
Musketa Cove, 248
Mystic, 81, 83, 155-56, 174, 183-84, 219, **294**, 306n.4

# N

*nanitis,* 132-34
Napeague Harbor, 83, 228-29
Narragansett Bay, 144-45, 156
Narragansetts, 147, 203, 256
  conspiracy against English, 173-76
  Pequot War and aftermath, 156-59
Nassaconseke, 218, *299*
nations, 26, 65, 106, 256, 289-90, 293, 314n.4
Navasinks, 148-150
Naumeags, 160
Nayack, 25, 80, 86, 100
Nayacks, 27-28
Netherlands, 210
New Amsterdam, 151-53, 161, 168-69, 171-73, 178-82, 184, 186, 188, 191, 201, 203, 205, 215-17, 237-40, 251
New Haven, 175, 182, 203, 206-10, 220, 318n.9
New Netherland, 35, 43, 60, 67, 118, 149, 151, 168, 172, 176-78, 182, 188, 193, 201, 203, 206, 208, 216-17, 224, 234
  Council of, 163, 187-88
  directors of, 222-23
  Dutch West India Company 1621, 151-52, 188
  English conquest 1664, 233, 236, 240
Newcom, 208-9, 320n.1
Newfoundland, 144-45, 148, 161
Newtown, 182
Nickommos, 118-19
Nicolls, Richard, 233, 240-44, 246, 249
Ninigret, 119, 160, 162, 176, 200-201, 205, 209-11, 214, 233
  Dutch alliance, 203-5, 213, 216
  Long Island, raids on, 159-60, 162, 165, 175, 206-7, 218, 239
  Montauketts alliance with, 249-50, 252
  political skill, 208, 237, 254
Nissequogue River, 23-24, 187, 218, 265, **294**, **298**, 320-21nn.2-3
Nissequogues, 19, 25, 218, 321n.3
"Noble savage," 17, 29
North Beach site, 55, **56**, 58, 71, 73, 77, *295*
North Hempstead, 223, 225
Nowedonah, 193
Numers, 164, 177, 179
*Nunnowa,* fall celebration, 33

# O

Oakland Lake site, **58**, 59, 73, 76, *295*
Occom, Samson, 111-12, 117-18, 122, 283, 313n.3
Occomboomaquus, 196
ocher, red, 49-53, 67, 71, 109
Ogden, John, 197, 221, 231, 243, *301*, 321n.4
Old Field site, 93

orache, 67
Oratamin, 180
Orient One site, 48-49, *295*
Orient Point sites, 52, 69, 48
Orient Tablet, **133**, 138
Orient Two site, **37,** *295*, 304
   burial cult, 49, 51, 69-71, 74, 124
   red ocher, 49-51, 53, 67, 71, 109
Oyster Bay, 93, 165-66, 195, 201, 204-5, 216, 218, 226-27, 230, 237, 239-40, 244, 246-48, 251, 253-57, 260, 265, **298**

## P

Pachem, 180-81, 184
Paleo-Indian Period, 35-38, 53
   chert and tools, 37, 43
   creation story, **34**, 35
   hunting, 35-38
   projectile points, 36-38, **37**
Pantigo site, *295*
Parker, Arthur, 56-57, 68, 102, 106
Patchogue, 19, 26-28
Paucump, 194
Paummis, 196, 229
Pauquatoun, 213-14
Pavonia, 176-80, 187, 215, **296**
Peconic Bay, 41, 166-67, 195, 198, 245, **300**, 316n.2
Peconic River, 214, 244-45, 265, **298**
Pelham Bay Park, 71
Pelham Boulder site, 55, 71, *295*
Penhawis, 163-65, 168-69, 171, 174, 178-84, 187-88, 194, *297*
Pequot fort, 81-83
Pequot War, 154-62
Pequot War aftermath, 164, 167, 170, 174-75, 183-84, 194, 198, 205, 277-79
  Mason, John, 160, 207, 213, 219-20
  Wyandanch and Gardiner, 156, 160-61, 228-33
Pequots, 18, 23, 69, 103, 151
Pharaoh, Benjamin, 262-63
Pharaoh, Carolyn, 24, 65
Pharaoh, Chief Robert, 24, 293
Pharaoh, George, 283
Pharaoh, Maria, 65
Pharaoh, Olive, **24**, 65
Pharaoh, Peggy, 24
Pharaoh, Steven, 30, 262-63
Pharaoh, Wyandank, 33
Pipestave Hollow site, 39
plants, 92, 95, 103-5, 131, 231, 290, 307-10nn.13-23

   ceremonies, seasonal, 118-22
   cultivation of, 77, 91-94, 98-99
   dyes from, 67, *68*
   edible, 36, 39, **59,** 59-64, **61**
   herbal, 72, 100, 131, 140
   lunar planting calendar, **132**
   medicinal, 65, *66*, 126, 129, 269
   mythic origins of, 95, 99, 115
   nutrients in, *60*, *63*
Pleasant Hill site, 93
Plumb (Plum) Island, 194, 229-30, **300**
Pongumo, 23, 237, 263-64, 275
Poniute, 237, 250-51, 260, *301*
Poospatuck Reservation, 261, 264-65, 282, 289, 292-93
Poospatucks, 23-24, 31, 33. *See also* Unkechaugs
Port Washington site, 124, 255, *295*, 307n.5
post molds, 40
pottery, 46-47, 55-58, 79, 88, **112**, 113, **115**, 304-5nn.1-2
   sherds, 40, 71, 88, 106, 303n.2
   styles, 55, **56, 58**, 73, 76-77, **102**, 103, 107
Pound Ridge, 187, **296**
Powhatans, 43, 62, 80, 91, 97, 267
*powwaws*, 99, 116-19, 121-22, 125-30, 132-33, 140, 143
powwow, 63, 116-21, 140, 215, 253, 282, **288**, 289, 291-92, 311n.5
projectile points, **58**, 76, 107, 124
   assemblage, 45-46, 48-49, 58, 75
   Clovis, 36, **37**
   locations, 39-40, 50-51, 55, 58, 75-77, 79, 105
   Paleo-Indian, 36, **37**, 53
Pugnipan, 179, 195, 205, 246, *299*

## Q

Quashawam, 237, 241-42, 315n.7, 322n.2

## R

Raritans, 171-73, 177, 193, **296**
religion, 18, 31, 79, 109-41. *See also* ceremonies
   *Conconchus*, 91, 95, 111
   corn, mythic origins, 95, 99, 115
   creation story, **34**, 35
   curing rituals, 72, 125-31, 133, 140, 234
   dogs, sacrifices of, 124-25, 313n.3
   Early Woodland burials, 69-71, 124
   Late Archaic practices, 49-53

*Index* 363

Middle Woodland rituals, 69-75
mortuary rituals, 48-53, 59, 69, 71, 74-76, 234, 313n.3
rites of passage, 122-24, 131
seasonal celebrations, 72-73, 99-100, 115-27, 132, 140, 146, 228
star gazing, 132-33
Richbell, John, 230, 237
Rinnegachonck, 164, **296**
Ritchie, William, 35, 38-40, 50-52, 304n.4, 306n.5
Riverhead, 37, 195, 245
Roanoke, 57, 81, 146
Robins Island, 36, 185, **300**
Rockaway, 25, 28, 106, 165, 187, 216-17, 318n.10
Rockaways, 19, 26-27, 184, 215, 249, 253
Ronkonkoma Moraine and Lake, 36
Ronnessoke. *See* Suscaneman
Rountree, Helen, 157, 254, 267, 269
Ryders Pond site, *295*, 319n.2

## S

Sag Harbor, 24, 125, 135, 292, 324n.5
Sassacus, 155-58, 175
Sassakata, 213-14, 227, 261-62
Schouts Bay, 165, 183
Schurz site, 58, 71, 73, 75-76, *295*
seasonal round, model of, 39
Sebonac Creek, 88, 198
Sebonac site, 56, 76, 83, 93, 112, 115, 124, *295*, 306-7nn.4,5
Sebonac thunderbird, **115**
Sebonacs, 198-99, 214
Secatogue, 25, 118, 217, 221, 231, 253, 255
Secatogues, 19, 26, 215, 217, 222-23, 225, 249
Sehar, 246, 248-49, 254, 258-59
Sequassen, 207
Setauket, 106, 187, 224, 232, 252-53, *299*
Setaukets, 19, 26, 214, 244, 284, 286-87, 322-23nn.4-5
Seyseys, 164-65, 179, 191, 204, *297*
shaman, 99, **114**, 116, 120, 164, 174, 203, 311n.8
shamanic rituals, 72, 135, 139, 233, 269
shellfish, women preparing, **61**
Shelter Island, 26, 36, 41, 83, 154, 158, 167, 185, 187, 193-94, 202, 211, 275, 284
Shinnecock Canal, 170, 227, 231, 264
Shinnecock Hills, 199, 265, 289

Shinnecock Neck, 264
Shinnecock Reservation, 18, 48, 93, 170, 264, 289-93, 309-10n.23
Shinnecocks, 16, 19, 24, **54**, 63-65, 83, 86, 89, 96, 100, 102, 106, 119, 124, 130, 139-40, 153, 175, 197, 219-21, 251, 267, 282, 287, 311n.9, 315nn.4,7, 318n.10, 319n.5, 322n.2. *See also* fines; labor; whaling
baskets, **46**, 67
land sales, 170, 193-94, 198-99, 202-3, 210-11, 221-22, 225-31, 238, 241, 243-45, 250, 260, 263-65, 275
Nation Museum, 106, 290, 293
political sovereignty, 184-85
pottery manufacture, 56, **115**
reaffirmation, 289-92
sachem, 23, 197, 210, 214, 237
tribal council, 290, 292
tribe, 27-33, 198, 290, 315n.4
tribute, 154, 174, 318n.10
village site, old, 56, 88, 115. *See also* Sebonac site
Shoreham, 55, 93
Silver, Annette, 71, 76, 307n.5, 308n.15
smallpox, 29, 147, 233-36, 262, 321nn.4-5
Smith, Carlyle, 38, 55-56, 58, 71, 83, 183
Smith, Gerrod, 86, 106
Smith, John, observations of
Algonquian ways, 43, 46, 62, 146
housing, 80, 86, 89-90
planting, 97, 99
Smith, Jonathan, 311n.9
Smith, Josephine, 64, 309-10n.23
Smith, Lamont, 63, 100, 139
Smith, William, 261, 280
Smithtown, 218, 232, 265, 281
Smithtown Bay, 40
Southampton, 23, 169, 196. *See also* labor; whaling
archaeological sites, 40, 48, 76, 88, 98
dispossession of Indian lands, 241-44
Dutch-Indian-English relations in, 188, 192, 201
Hartford Treaty 1644, 185, 197-98
Indian sovereignty, loss of, 63, 185, 231, 250-51, 253
settlement, 1640 of, 170-71, 188, 194, 267
trespass disputes in, 63, 197, 199, 201-2, 210, 214, 243
Southampton land disputes, 208, 213
East Hampton, 193, 221
Mandush, 170, 221

Sebonac planting fields, 198-99, 214
Southold, 195, 244-47
Shinnecock, 170, 198-99, 241, 243
Southold, 29, 93, 113, 170, 201, 203, 257
  Eaton purchases, 194-95
  land disputes in, 195, 229, 241, 244-46, 265
Squanto, 97
St. David's A.M.E. Zion Church, **292**
St. Lawrence River, 145
Stanton, Thomas, 193, 199, 209, 319n.4
Staten Island, 74-75, 93, 171-72, 179-80, 215, **294, 296**, 307n.5
Stirling, Earl of, 167, 188
Stirling Patent, 163, 185, 192-93
Stony Brook (SUNY), 35, 37, 165
Stony Brook site, 40-41, 51, **294**, *295*
Stony Brook village, 214, 252
Stoughton, Israel, 156-58, 167
Strongs Neck, 106
Stuyvesant, Peter, 187, 206, 215, 224-25, 240
  Ninigret relations, 201, 203
  Tackapousha relations, 191-92, 216-17, 238-39
  treaties signed by, 201, 222, 238
Sugar Loaf Hill site, 48-51, 83, *295*, 304nn.3,4
sunksquaw, 156-58, 237, 241, 243-45, 264, 315n.7, 321n.4, 322n.2
Suscaneman, 23, 205-6, 237, 248-49, 254-60, *259*, 265, *299*, 322-24nn.3-7
sweat lodge, 32, **128**, 128-30, 140

## T

Tackapousha, 252-56
  dispossession, **237, 247, 248,** 237-65
  Dongan patent 1687, 257, *258,* 265
  Dutch dealings, 188, *212*, 216, 218, 236, 237-40
  English dealings, 182, 221-225, 228, 236-38, 240-66
  land deals, 237, 247-49, 253-58, **256,** *297, 299*
  names for, other, 23, 179, 191
  Rockaway alliance, 187, 215, 217
  Stuyvesant relations, 191-92, 216-17, 238-39
  tribal dealings, 213, 215-17, 223
  Wyandanch dealings, 221-24, 228, 230-33, 237
Tankiteke, 180, 215, **296**
Tantaquidgeon, Gladys, 60, 65, 67
Techkonis, 25, **296**

Three Mile Harbor site, 55, *295*
Throgs Neck site, 71, 75, 93, *295*
Thunder Bird, Margo, 292
tobacco, 72, 88, 92-95, 100, 107, 113, 130-31, 148-49, 195, 290
Tobacus, 232-33, 237, 244, 251-53, *299*, 322-23nn.4-5
Tooker, William Wallace, 20, 26-27, 83, 184-85, 193, 232, 310n.1
Topping, John, 272
Topping, Thomas, 227, 231, 243
Topping Purchase, *301*
Townsend, Chief Osceola, 24, 33, 293, 322n.5
Townsend, James, 258-60
Townsend, Thomas, 253-54, 260, 323n.5, 324n.7
Townsend deed, 253-54, 258-60
Treaty of Hartford 1650, 195, 224
Tupahache, Asiba, 24

## U

Uncas, 154-56, 159-60, 162, 200, 203, 206-7, 209, 213, 233, 237, 254, 320n.1
Underhill, John, 155, 183-84, 186-87, 244, 246, 248, 251, 254, 306n.4, 315n.6, 318n.7
Unkechaugs, 19, 21, 23, 27-28, 119, 187, 237, 253, 289, 292
  land, 232, 244, 261, 264, *299*, 322n.4, 324n.9
  language, 31-32, 92, 98, 309n.19
United Colonies, 159, 182-85, 200-203, 206-9, 218-20, 228, 319n.1, 320n.1, 321n.4
Uxroupasson, 196

## V

van der Donck, Adriaen, 43, 67-68, 103-5, 118, 128, 131, 234
Van Dyck, Hendrick, 173, 215
Van Tienhoven, Cornelis, 169, 172-73, 177-78, 186-87, 192, 201, 216, 307n.5
Van Twiller, Wouter, 163-64, 166, 316n.1
Van Wassenaer, Nicolaes, 95, 117-18, 126, 131, 310n.3, 314n.4
Verrazano, Giovanni da, 95, 144
Vespucci, Amerigo, 18
Vingboons, Johannes, 78, 81

## W

Wading River site, 39-41, *295*
Wallace, Chief Harry, 292
wampum, **16,** 69, **70,** 121, 123, 133, 151-61, 165, 172, 174, 176, 181, 191, 194-96, 202-6, 209, 215-16, 220, 223, 228, 230, 237-40, 247, 253, 267
Warawakmy, 214-15, *299*, 322n.4
Waters, Oney, 30
Waters, Susan, 30
Waymouth, Captain George, 105, 145, 161
Weenagaminin, 184, 193
Weir Creek site, 73, 75, *295*
Wenecoheage, 224
Weomp, 284, 324nn.3-4
Werah, 254, 256, 258
West, John, 255-57
West Islip, 165-66
whaling
   capture methods, 41, 62, 104-5, 145, 194, 252, 265, 267, 269-70, **271**
   contracts for, *273*, 274-75
   early Europeans and, 145, 161
   religion and, 88, 105, 116
   rights for, 228, 230-32, 270, 272, *273*, 277, 279, 283, 285
White, John, 57, 81, 105, 307n.6
Whitehead, Daniel, 204, 230
Wiangonhut, 264
Wichquawank, 25, 149, **296**
Wiechquaesgecks, 153, 171-73, 176-77, 180, 184, 238, **296**, 306n.4
wigwams, 40, 53, 64, 67, 73, 80-90, **82, 87, 90**, 98, 100, 103, 107, 116, 119, 122-23, 127-28, 130, 134, 139, 156, 159-60, 175, 179, 184, 199, 227, 238, **256,** 283, 285
Williams, Roger, writing about
   allies and enemies, 159, 174, 178, 182, 206-7, 209
   feasting, 118-19
   names for Indians, 17, 20
   observations, 69, 91, 95, 97, 99-100, 119, 130, 200, 207
   planting, 95, 97, 99
   wigwams and longhouses, 85, 89, 91
Willys, Samuel, 230-31
Winthrop, John, 43, 97-98, 153-54, 156, 159, 167-70, 176, 209, 224
Winthrop, John, Jr., 99, 103, 155
Witaneywen. *See* Tackapousha
Wood, William, 84, 98, 117, 127, 313n.2
Woodhall, Richard, 229, 252-53, 276
Wolley, Rev. Charles, 25-26, 129, 308n.17
Wyancombone, 231, 227, 321n.4, 322n.2
Wyandanch, 19, 23, 155, 184, 198, 214, 220, 233
   daughter, ransom of, 208-10
   drift whale rights, 228-31
   Dutch Peace, 187, 192
   English, alliance with, 158, 160-62, 174, 196-98, 211-13, 254
   land sales, 167, 193, 223-25, **226**, 227-30, *299*
   last will of, 231-32
   leadership challenged, 205-6, 250
   Miantonomi plot, 174-75, 177
   Ninigret, conflicts with, 159-60, 200-201, 207-10
   Pequot War, 155-56, 160-61
   Southampton arson jurisdiction, 219-21, 243
   Uncas, 203, 209

## Y

Youghco, 158, 184, 187, 192-93, 202-3
Youngs, John, 218, 278

# About the Author

John A. Strong is professor of history and director of the Social Science Division at the Southampton College of Long Island University. He has written extensively on Long Island Indians. His articles have appeared in *Ethnohistory*, *Long Island Historical Journal, Papers of the Algonquian Conference,* and *The American Indian Culture and Research Journal.* Dr. Strong has also contributed two articles to *The Encyclopedia of American Indian Biography.* His companion volume, *"We Are Still Here!" The Algonquian Peoples of Long Island Today,* was published under the auspices of Hofstra University's Long Island Studies Institute in 1996.

John A. Strong in his office at Southampton College. Professor Strong is holding a Shinnecock scrub brush made by James Kellis. (Photograph by Mark McQueen.)

# The Long Island Studies Institute

The Long Island Studies Institute is a cooperative endeavor of Hofstra University and Nassau County. This major center for the study of local and regional history was established in 1985 to foster the study of Long Island history and heritage. Two major research collections on the study of Nassau County, Long Island, and New York State are located in the Special Collections Department on the University's West Campus, 619 Fulton Avenue, Hempstead. These collections—the Nassau County Museum collection and Hofstra University's James N. MacLean American Legion Memorial collection—are available to historians, librarians, teachers, and the general public, as well as to Hofstra students and faculty. Together, they offer a rich repository of books, photographs, newspapers, maps, census records, genealogies, government documents, manuscripts, and audiovisual materials.

The Long Island Studies Institute is open Monday-Friday (except major holidays), 9-5 (Fridays to 4 in the summer). For further information, contact the Institute, 516-463-6411. The Institute also houses the historical research offices of the Nassau County Historian and Division of Museum Services (516-463-6418).

The Institute collections and reading room are on the second floor of the Library Service Center on Hofstra's West Campus

In addition to its research collections, the Institute sponsors publications, meetings, and conferences pertaining to Long Island and its heritage. Through its programs, the Institute complements various Long Island Studies courses offered by the University through the History Department, New College, and University College for Continuing Education.

## Long Island Studies Institute Publications

### Heart of the Lakes Publishing:
*The Aerospace Heritage of Long Island*, by Joshua Stoff (1989).
*The Algonquian Peoples of Long Island from Earliest Times to 1700*, by John A. Strong (1997), Empire State Books imprint.
*The Blessed Isle: Hal B. Fullerton and His Image of Long Island, 1897-1927*, by Charles L. Sachs (1991).
*Evoking a Sense of Place*, edited by Joann P. Krieg (1988).
*From Airship to Spaceship: Long Island in Aviation and Spaceflight*, by Joshua Stoff (1991), Empire State Books imprint (for younger readers).
*From Canoes to Cruisers: The Maritime Heritage of Long Island*, by Joshua Stoff (1994), Empire State Books imprint (for younger readers).
*Long Island and Literature*, by Joann P. Krieg (1989).
*Long Island Architecture*, edited by Joann P. Krieg (1991).
*Long Island: The Suburban Experience*, edited by Barbara M. Kelly (1990).
*Making a Way to Freedom: A History of African Americans on Long Island*, by Lynda R. Day (1997).
*Robert Moses: Single-Minded Genius*, edited by Joann P. Krieg (1989).
*Roots and Heritage of Hempstead Town*, edited by Natalie A. Naylor (1994).
*Theodore Roosevelt: Many-Sided American*, edited by Natalie A. Naylor, Douglas Brinkley, and John Allen Gable (1992).
*To Know the Place: Exploring Local History*, edited by Joann P. Krieg and Natalie A. Naylor (rev. ed., 1995).
*"We Are Still Here!" The Algonquian Peoples of Long Island Today*, by John A. Strong (1996), Empire State Books imprint.

### Long Island Studies Institute:
*The Calderone Theatres on Long Island: An Introductory Essay and Description of the Calderone Theatre Collection at Hofstra University*, by Miriam Tulin (1991).
*Cumulative Index, Nassau County Historical Society Journal, 1958-1988*, by Jeanne M. Burke (1989).
*Exploring African-American History*, edited by Natalie A. Naylor (1992, 1995).
*To Know the Place: Teaching Local History*, edited by Joann P. Krieg (1986).
*Vignettes of Hempstead Town, 1643-1800*, by Myron H. Luke (1993).

### Greenwood Press:
*Contested Terrain: Power, Politics, and Participation in Suburbia*, edited by Marc L. Silver and Martin Melkonian (1995).
*Suburbia Re-examined*, edited by Barbara M. Kelly (1989).

NOV 14 1997
40.00

SOUTH HUNTINGTON PUBLIC LIBRARY
3 0652 00015 5509

970.44721
STRONG, JOHN A.
THE ALGONQUIAN PEOPLES OF LONG
 ISLAND FROM EARLIEST TIMES
 TO 1700

98  08
85  03
    Local History

**South Huntington Public Library**
Huntington Station, New York
11746-7699

GAYLORD M